AKADEMIEKONFERENZEN

Band 17

Gift Giving and the 'Embedded' Economy in the Ancient World

Edited by

FILIPPO CARLÀ
MAJA GORI

im Auftrag der Heidelberger Akademie der Wissenschaften, Akademie der Wissenschaften des Landes Baden-Württemberg

Universitätsverlag
WINTER
Heidelberg

Bibliografische Information der Deutschen Nationalbibliothek

Die Deutsche Nationalbibliothek verzeichnet diese Publikation
in der Deutschen Nationalbibliografie;
detaillierte bibliografische Daten sind im Internet
über *http://dnb.d-nb.de* abrufbar.

UMSCHLAGBILD

Part of a procession of women
bringing gifts from the Mycenean palace in Thebes, Boeotia.
Reconstruction by H. Reusch, modified by M. Gori.

ISBN 978-3-8253-6331-4

Imprimé en Allemagne · Printed in Germany
Druck: Memminger MedienCentrum, 87700 Memmingen

Gedruckt auf umweltfreundlichem, chlorfrei gebleichtem
und alterungsbeständigem Papier

Den Verlag erreichen Sie im Internet unter:
www.winter-verlag.de

Table of Contents

Section 3. Gift and Religion

Section 4. The Object Gift

Filippo Carlà – Maja Gori

Introduction

1. Sex, gift and commerce in classical Athens: an introductory case

In the last one of his surviving comedies, *Ploutos*, represented in the version known to us for the first time in 388 BCE, Aristophanes presents us with a discussion between the slave Cario, his master Chremylus and the god of wealth Plutus, concerning the difference between 'bad' and 'good' young boys:

> "Chremylus: Most assuredly. Whatever is dazzling, beautiful or charming in the eyes of mankind, comes from you [Plutus]. Does not everything depend on wealth?
> Cario: I myself was bought for a few coins; if I'm a slave, it's only because I was not rich
> Ch.: And what of the Corinthian whores? If a poor man offers them proposals, they do not listen; but if it be a rich one, instantly they turn their arses to him
> Ca.: It's the same with the lads; they care not for love, to them money means everything
> Ch.: You speak of male whores; yet some of them are honest, and it's not money they ask of their patrons
> Ca.: What then?
> Ch.: A fine horse, a pack of hounds
> Ca.: Yes, they would blush to ask for money and cleverly disguise their shame".[1]

This passage shows, in an extremely lucid way, the 'contrast' and the overlay between gift and commercial exchange. Leaving aside the aspect of sexual connotation – which has been analyzed e.g. by J. N. Davidson[2] – it is immediately evident that a direct exchange of a service (in this case a sexual one) for money, which is explicitly given only to get the service, is characterized as 'commerce', and is therefore in this case morally disputable. On the contrary, receiving a horse or hounds is connoted as a 'gift', implying therefore not a payment for the service but the recognition of a personal relationship, with an accent posed on the persons rather than on the 'objects' which are exchanged – and this cannot be qualified as prostitution. But the border between the two aspects is all but clear, as Cario's last sarcastic joke makes evident, and the categories of 'gift' and 'commerce' *in se*, as the presumed 'ontological' dif-

[1] Aristoph., *Plout.* 143-159; transl. E. O'Neill.
[2] Davidson 1997, pp. 132-150.

ference between money (which for its very nature of a neutral instrument to measure value is not apt to be a 'gift')[3] and 'objects', become blurred and allow a huge space for contradiction, superposition and short-circuit.[4]

The sexual sphere indeed allows seeing in a perfect way how the acquisition of material goods could be placed at a complicated crossing between commerce and gift, and how this changed the nature of the capital connected to the goods themselves and thus caused a never ending tension with moral issues and social status.[5] Xenophon presents us e.g. with the figure of Theodote, a beautiful woman "who was ready to keep company with anyone who pleased her". Asked by Socrates about the source of her apparently conspicuous incomes, Theodote admits living "on the generosity of any friend I pick up", thus presenting her high life standard as the consequence of gifts bestowed on her by friends. But these friends are, as Socrates further formulates, searched for, and the entire Socratic discourse plays exactly on the thin border between the acceptance of the language of gift and the underlying idea that Theodote in the end sells her body:

> "you must ask such favours of your suitors as they will grant without a moment's hesitation; and next you must repay their favours in the same coins; for in this way they will prove most sincerely your friends"; "you must prompt them by behaving as a model of propriety, by a show of reluctance to yield, and by holding back until they are as keen as can be; for then the same gifts are much more to the recipient than when they are offered before they are desired".[6]

The tension between 'gift' and 'payment' in love relationship goes on constituting important chapters of ancient literature, and becomes, for instance, central in the literary construction of the Latin elegiac *puella* and of her attitude to her lover(s), as Coffee has very recently well shown in particular in reference to Ovid's *Amores*.[7]

As it is well known, this complicated superposition and short circuit between gift and commercial exchange had relevant consequences also in the public sphere: famously, Aeschines reacted to an accusation presented against him by Timarchus in 346 BCE with a counter-accusation which aimed at demonstrating that Timarchus had been a prostitute in youth and had therefore, according to

[3] On money as a gift, see *infra*.

[4] On the importance of the superposition between the concepts of gift, commerce and debt and the sexual sphere, see now Graeber 2011, pp. 173-183, claiming – in not completely acceptable terms – that exactly to this superposition should be traced back the origin of patriarchate.

[5] See also, for a relevant example from Terentius' *Eunuchus*, Konstan 2013, in particular pp. 100-104.

[6] Xen., *Mem.* 3.11; transl. O. J. Todd.

[7] Coffee 2013, pp. 81-89.

Athenian law, lost his civil rights – and therefore also the right to accuse other persons. Since

> "the law as written opened up a large gray area because it applied not merely to professional prostitutes registered as such for tax purposes but to amateurs",[8]

Aeschines must concentrate in his (in the end successful) oration *Against Timarchus* exactly on the ambiguous statue of gifts given to a lover and propose that their amount, as Timarchus' generally suspicious behavior, lets them rather be understood as 'payments' for sexual services, and astutely uses to his advantage once again the 'embeddedness' and the lack of clear borders between gift and commerce.

These aspects of the relationship and 'tensions' between gift-giving and commerce, two forms of exchange which cannot at all be conceived as chronologically successive to each other – as it will be shown – but are present in every society and are deeply intermingled with each other, constituted the topic underlying the organization of a conference which was held in Heidelberg at the local Akademie der Wissenschaften in February 2012. This volume consists almost entirely of the proceedings of that meeting.

2. Gift-giving, 'gift economy', 'market economy'

It is certainly superfluous to underline the importance of such a topic in understanding ancient civilizations, their economies as well as their social and cultural structures. Gift and its mechanisms have been in the very center of scholarly attention not only since the epoch-making *Essai sur le don* of Marcel Mauss (originally published 1923-1924 in the journal *L'Année Sociologique*),[9] but already in previously and less widely known contributions about ancient societies and ancient economies – e.g. in the works of Karl Bücher, as it will be shown in this volume by Beate Wagner-Hasel.[10]

The aim of this publication is not to re-open the general question about gift-giving and its rules in the ancient world, but rather to concentrate exactly on the interaction of wealth, performance and status in the mechanisms connected to gift-giving and gift-exchange, starting from the mentioned 'tension' existing between gift and commerce and with a particular awareness, therefore, for the

[8] Skinner 2005, p. 113.

[9] Mauss 1923-1924. For a biography of Marcel Mauss, see Fournier 1994.

[10] For a presentation of Mauss' work in the context of contemporary European research, see also Geary 2003, pp. 136-140; for a clear presentation of the 'roots' of his theory of the gift, Wagner-Hasel 2003.

interactions between different forms of exchange and their repercussions on social capital and social visibility.

The idea that gift-exchange should represent a 'primitive' form of exchange, which pre-existed commerce and was in the end replaced by it in the long run must be finally rejected, exactly as it has been also demonstrated that barter does not constitute an exchange form preceding commerce – eventually placed between 'gift economy' and 'commercial exchange' – and teleologically evolving into it,[11] since its existence in an idealtypical and exclusive form (i.e. not in coexistence with other forms of exchange, independently from the fact that barter could be the major one), which would imply a complete lack of trust among the actors,[12] appears extremely difficult to realize from a theoretical perspective,[13] and was indeed never demonstrated in anthropological research.[14]

In the same way, the idea, of Aristotelic origin, and adopted in many traditional ethnographic texts, of a primitive 'gift economy', in which gift should have taken place and was later overtaken by barter and finally by trade[15] (since these are recognized to be the three basic form of transaction),[16] and therefore the central function of allowing a circulation of wares, must be radically rejected – together with the very concept of 'gift economy' itself, as shown here by Hénaff – by realizing that these forms of exchange always presuppose the existence of an economy, and that "Trobriand islanders cannot live on gifts only any more than we do".[17] Mirowski has in particular developed from the economic perspective arguments which, opposing the dominating neoclassical model – too often reflected also in anthropological studies and cause of endless contradictions –, reveal that there are "no gifts without payment systems", and that gift is "a function of a money-based value schema":

[11] Anderlini – Sabourian 1992, p. 90; Graeber 2001, p. 36; Graeber 2011, pp. 41-42.

[12] Anderlini – Sabourian 1992, p. 100; it can be noticed how this contradicts ancient and modern 'romanticized' visions of barter, on which more will be said later, claiming that such a form of exchange was more 'personal' and 'ethical'. See also Humphrey – Hugh-Jones 1992, pp. 8-9; Graeber 2011, pp. 27-45.

[13] Anderlini – Sabourian 1992, pp. 77-81. See also Humphrey – Hugh-Jones 1992, p. 6: "there are few if any whole economies on any sizeable scale which are known to have operated by barter alone. […] So barter should be seen as one mode of exchange amongst others, not as the single means of running an economy".

[14] Graeber 2011, pp. 34-35.

[15] The construction of a polar opposition between gift and commercial exchange has indeed led often to neglect barter and redistribution: see Humphrey – Hugh-Jones 1992, p. 7

[16] Rössler 2007, pp. 4-7.

[17] Hénaff 2013, pp. 17-18. See also Frow 1997, pp. 124-126, even if Frow still uses the concept of "gift economy".

> "one should not confuse the synchronic quarantine of money from gifts with some diachronic precedence of gifts over money. Gifts are an attempt to transcend the system of value; but that system transcendence already presupposes some form of monetary structure".[18]

In Grahame Clark's pioneering works on prehistoric economies it is argued that commerce – intended as "peaceful and systematic exchange of goods" – existed in a recognizable form already in the most basic types of hunter-gatherers societies.[19] Comparing the social formations of prehistoric Europe with ethnographic societies from Melanesia, Australia and New Zealand, Clark showed that gift-giving and reciprocity have to be regarded as components of prehistoric economies, and not as the exclusive type of transactions in use. The concept of a 'gift economy' that pre-existed commerce is thus completely absent from Clark's work, which specifically focuses on those 'primitive societies' for which the very concept of 'gift-economy' was constructed.[20] Following Clark's theories, it can be observed how the concept of 'gift economy' – and the related theoretical debate – has gradually disappeared from archaeological literature dealing with pre-state economies, while remaining present mainly in anthropological and ethnological literature.[21]

In the same way, it is necessary to reject over-simplifying dichotomies which, while neatly dividing gift and commerce along not only chronological, but also social, economic or political lines, fail to recognize the complete interactions and the constant 'embeddedness' that we showed through the

[18] Mirowski 2001, pp. 452-456. It is important to underline that this should imply a thorough discussion of the concept of value itself, as proposed by Graeber 2001, in particular pp. 1-22; gift does not transcend the concept of value if it is assumed e.g., following Graeber (p. 49) that one should "create a theory of value starting from the assumption that what is ultimately being evaluated are not things, but actions". On the different forms of value and capital, see *infra*.

[19] Clark 1965, p. 97. Clark can be regarded as one of the founders of the New Archaeology as some of its constituting principles stressing on economic and social issues' importance in the archaeological agenda were already present in his writings decades ago.

[20] Clark 1965, pp. 97-130.

[21] E.g. confront Rowlands' position expressed in 1973, pp. 589-590, and twenty years later, in 1994, p. 1. Recently, Kerig – Zimmermann 2010, pp. 114-149, discussed the reception of Clark's works in the German-speaking archaeological milieu pointing out that direct references to Clark's ideas were often absent because of his holistic and materialistic approach to prehistoric economy. Archaeology in Germany was noticeably influenced by political circumstances, and after the Second World War German archaeologists were not ready to embrace Clark's view of inequality as an important motor of history, a perspective which can be considered close to an overturned version of Marx's class struggle.

concrete example of classical Athenian sexuality. An example of such an overtly simplifying approach can be found e.g. in the rather mechanical application to ancient societies of the Kipp-Schortman model. The latter, developed by Rita Kipp and Edward Schortman in 1989 and largely based on the Frankenstein-Rowlands model as on the works of Patrice Brun, was aimed at delineating the mechanisms leading to the birth of State formations.[22]

According to this model, which was e.g. recently applied to Etruria by Theodore Peña,[23] when traders from already existing state societies develop exchange relations with chiefdoms and a context of trade diaspora (i.e. the migration of groups of traders to establish trade settlements) develops, these relations assume firstly the form of a gift exchange among members of the elites. These acquire so-called 'exotic' objects, which may be either kept as prestige markers or passed further, either to other elite members or to persons of lower rank. In both cases the property or the passage of property of these goods marks and strengthens the social position of the elites. In a further moment, the traders tend to establish new and independent exchange relations; these take the form of market exchange, which, following Polanyi's model,[24]

> "operates largely through impersonal considerations of value based on supply and demand, as well as on the presumption of profit/value maximization between parties",[25]

and end up destabilizing the political structure of the chiefdom:

> "trade introduces the requirement that leaders minimize the likelihood that others will get rich enough to compete with them for power".[26]

For the European Iron Age, Rowlands talks thus of a

> "loss of control of status holders over the increased circulation of wealth [...]. In an era when everyone could be a chief it would be necessary to transform the nature of wealth in order to retain control over people".[27]

The response of the elite to this situation is then the establishment of a connection between status and wealth: the elite members must now reassert themselves on the market level, demonstrating not only that they – and only they – can afford such goods, but also institutionalizing forms of control of trade and

[22] Kipp – Schortman 1989, in particular pp. 373-376.
[23] Peña 2011.
[24] Polanyi 1957b.
[25] Kipp – Schortman 1989, p. 372.
[26] Kipp – Schortman 1989, p. 375.
[27] Rowlands 1994, p. 2.

> "Domestic economy centralized home manufacture; wage-work is dispersed commercial customer work; handicraft is commercial customer production; publishing is decentralized and factory centralized commercial production of goods".[26]

Economists integrated the terms developed in this article into their own typology. For Max Weber, Bücher's terminology formed e.g. the argumentative base for the rejection of the term 'factory' as a designation for ancient production facilities.[27] Also, Bücher's distinction between "traffic-less economy", "economy of direct exchange", "economy with the circulation of goods" as well as "home manufacture", "customer production" and "production of commodities",[28] have been accepted by national economists like Werner Sombart.[29]

This commitment to creating new terms can also be seen in the way he treated the main topic of the national economist: exchange. Bücher was affiliated to the theoretical tradition of the Historical School of national economy, which tried to deconstruct the universal applicability of Adam Smith's liberal theory. In his essay *Die Entstehung der Volkswirtschaft*, as well as in his work *Die Wirtschaft der Naturvölker* (1899),[30] Bücher dissociated himself from the idea of the originality of exchange, which he rejected as a "rationalistic construct" of liberal classical theory.[31] This refers to a profit-oriented, self-interested form of exchange. According to the economic historian Werner Plumpe, this concept originated in the sixteenth century. Plumpe interprets it as a "result of the disintegration of the cosmological ethics of Europe".[32] In his essay on *Gift, Loan and Boon-Work* (1918), Bücher contrasted this self-interested exchange with reciprocal giving, a form recognized by legal historians as 'primitive'.[33] For the beginning of history, he assumed the "unpaid transfer of goods" to be the earliest way of "how goods and services were transferred from one economy to the other".[34] Next to loan and boon-work, Bücher counted giving among the unpaid forms, which then developed into taxes, tolls, tributes and compulsory labour

[26] Bücher 1892, pp. 922-950. The article was reversed and extended twice. See vol. 4 in the edition of 1898, pp. 360-393 and vol. 5 in the edition of 1909, pp. 847-880.

[27] Deininger 2006, p. 12 and 40 argues that Max Weber's view of ancient economy was strongly influenced by this article.

[28] Bücher 1892, p. 945.

[29] Sombart 1916^2, p. 94 and p. 137.

[30] Bücher 1899.

[31] Bücher 1918, p. 3.

[32] Plumpe 2007, p. 320.

[33] Bücher 1918, p. 12. See also Bücher 1899, p. 75, n. 2. For discussion see Wagner-Hasel 2000, pp. 34-35.

[34] Bücher 1899, p. 92: "The obligation to give always and everywhere as well as the custom to regard food almost as free goods leave little room for self-interest"; 1918, p. 4.

over time. Although he characterized these forms of unpaid transfer as "altruistic", he assumed "egoistic motives", especially in the beginning. In general, Bücher emphasized the necessity of service in return.[35] In contrast to exchange, no exact balancing of value took place.

> "In all these cases, the objective is not to acquire without return, but to give with the purpose of obtaining something else, the value of which could, to a certain degree, be determined by oneself".[36]

Especially with lending, Bücher saw the entitlement for reciprocity. Here, he refers to ancient sources, for example Hesiod.[37] Yet according to Bücher, other forms of unpaid transfer like hospitality and wedding gifts also required returns, resulting from the acceptance of these presents.

> "Refusing the gifts would have been a severe insult to the donor; the acceptance obliged the recipient unequivocally. The giving was only completed when the donor declared his satisfaction with the return gift. Until then, the initial gift remained revocable".[38]

Here, Bücher pre-formulated the obligatory character of giving, a fact Marcel Mauss did not tire to emphasize.

Bücher's essay on *Gift, Loan and Boon-Work* (1918) presents an important transmission point from the national economical critique on egoistic exchange to the ethnologic theory of gift exchange. Although Bücher also used the terms "gift-exchange" or "gift-traffic",[39] he did not develop them. It was Germanist legal historians working on pre-modern forms of gift-giving who, for the first time, introduced the concept of 'gift-exchange' (*Gabentausch*, *Geschenktausch*). Jacob Grimm's (1785-1863) etymologically oriented study *Über Schenken und Geben* from 1848 stands at the beginning of this research.[40] In the 1880s and 1890s a series of further works followed. Among these Karl von Amira's two-volume study *Das Nordgermanische Obligationenrecht*, published between 1882 and 1885, stands out. Amira conceptually distinguished between gifts in the Old-Swedish and West-Nordic Middle Ages and modern gifts. In the former there was no transfer of assets: Pre-modern giving represented, for Amira, "marks of favour", which invited gratitude and thus were rewarded with counter-gifts.[41]

[35] Bücher 1918, p. 6.
[36] Bücher 1918, p. 6.
[37] Bücher 1918, p. 12.
[38] Bücher 1899, p. 76; 1918, pp. 6-7.
[39] Bücher 1918, p. 5 and p. 22.
[40] Grimm 1848.
[41] Von Amira 1882, I, p. 506: "It follows from the fact that gifts [are] not conceptually the

> "Favour for favour! The receiver must pay for the gift ... A gift demands a counter-gift ... [This is] a legal tenet which has been definitively confirmed ... One gives either because one expects a gift in return, or because the gift itself is supposed to demonstrate the giver's gratitude for favours received or promised".[42]

This invention of typology shows the attempt to denote a third position between altruistic giving and egoistic exchange. The modern definition of gift-giving, stated in the BGB (German Civil Code) in 1899, assumes that making a gift is not aimed at receiving a gift in return. Giving enriches the receiver, not the donor. As early as the 1880s, Rudolph von Jhering, in reference to Roman law, had juxtaposed the altruism connected to giving and the egoism associated with exchange with another category: mutualism. He argued that the reciprocal giving of gifts was neither acting in self-interest nor in self-denial.[43]

This process of standardizing the concept of gift-giving in modern law and reducing it to the economic dimension of the unpaid transfer of assets – which also occurred in a similar way in other countries – made manifest the distance to past European practices as well as to forms of interaction observed in the colonies of European Empires. It created awareness that it was necessary to rethink those forms of human interaction which could neither be classified as market exchange nor as gift-giving in the sense of the German Civil Code. It is thus no accident that the concept of 'gift exchange' appeared for the first time in the legal-historical literature of the 1880s and 1890s, although descriptions of the phenomena are clearly older. With this new concept, a third category was created in addition to paid surrender (barter, purchase) and the unpaid surrender ('pure' gifting): a category which combined the elements of both — mutuality and morality.[44]

In his elaborations, Bücher could rely on numerous economic and legal ethnological studies, which he had partly reviewed in the *Zeitschrift für die gesamte Staatswissenschaft*. He had been the journal's publisher from 1903 to 1922.[45] Due to his stage-model, Bücher also took the non-European world into account, although his economic-historical research was focussed on Antiquity and the Middle Ages. He, nonetheless, did not neglect the contemporary period. Next to the then existing ethnological literature, he attempted to produce his own source material by using questionnaires like the ones he had developed for his

allocation of assets that their aim is not directed conceptually towards the enrichment of the receiver. Their conceptual aim is rather mark of favour. As a mark of favour, they call for gratitude".

[42] Von Amira 1882, I, pp. 507-509. See also Meyer 1898.

[43] von Jhering 1904-1905[4]. See also von Dargun 1885, whose arguments are based on von Jhering. Cf. Wagner-Hasel 2000, pp. 36-37.

[44] For references see Wagner-Hasel 2000, pp. 32-37.

[45] For references see Wagner-Hasel 2011, pp. 169-172 and pp. 218-221.

socio-empirical work. In Basel, Bücher had already designed questionnaires enquiring about the route of raw materials from producers to consumers. He sent these – most likely via the Basel Missionary Society – all around the world. In Bücher's estate, there is a filled-in copy by a missionary, who gives precise information on the conditions in Leh in the present Indian federal state of Ladakh, West Tibet. Bücher inquires about the scale of production for subsistence as well as the extent of purchases and sales of goods. The missionary's answers illustrate the importance of subsistence economy for most households in Ladakh, insofar as only wool was purchased. Questionnaires, which he also gave to his numerous non-European students, confirmed his thesis of the unity of production and consumption at an early stage of economic development.[46]

Bücher also took over this comparative perspective in his study *Arbeit & Rhythmus (Work and Rhythm)*, a collection of work songs from all over the world, which introduced an additional argument to the challenge of a primitive egoistic exchange. In Bücher's opinion, work songs helped to rhythmically organize the work as well as to regulate an economic use of strength. For Bücher, work is primarily collective work; singing is used to coordinate the cooperation. In addition, he emphasizes the aesthetic and sensual qualities, as the

> "rhythm arouses pleasurable sensations; it not only makes the work easier, but is also one of the sources of aesthetic pleasures and the one element of art which evokes an intrinsic sentiment in all people without distinction".[47]

The emphasis on the sensual side of work was a starting point for Bücher's colleagues from the Historical School of national economy to question the neoclassics' concept of the originality of egoistic exchange as the drive for economic actions.[48] The aspect of work lust elicited broad resonance, especially in ethnology. In his studies on the tillage of the inhabitants of the Trobriand Islands in the 1930s, Bronislaw Malinowski, for example, had been inspired by Bücher's insights and turned his attention to the ritualistic aspects of the work progress.[49]

There are theoretical and methodological reasons which may explain Bücher's contribution to a theory of gift-giving. His affiliation to the theoretical tradition of the Historical School of national economy evoked his interest in deconstructing the universal applicability of the liberal theory of Adam Smith by developing new categories to distinguish between different types of economy and a new perspective on economic behaviour. It was this new understanding of the motifs of work in combination with his use of the ethnologic-comparative

[46] See Wagner-Hasel 2011, pp. 72-74.
[47] Bücher 1896, pp. 358-359.
[48] See Barth 1897, pp. 321-322; Normano 1931, p. 655.
[49] Spittler 2008, pp. 221-242.

method which enabled Bücher to reach the early sociologists and ethnologists: Marcel Mauss, Bronislaw Malinowski, Richard Thurnwald and Karl Polanyi. I would like to further delineate, in conclusion, this hidden research genealogy.

5. Successors

In part, Bücher was in direct contact with his successors. This is particularly true in the case of Richard Thurnwald (1869-1954), who coined the term 'reciprocity' for the exchange of gifts,[50] which in turn was used by Karl Polanyi. Bronislaw Malinowski (1884-1942), the founder of ethnologic fieldwork, most likely met Bücher in person as well.[51] He was the son of a slavist and had studied science and philosophy in Kraków. He wrote a philosophical dissertation on empirio-criticism, an extreme type of Positivism. After his dissertation in 1908, he studied three semesters under the experimental and ethno-psychologist Wilhelm Wundt in Leipzig. Malinowski subsequently used a fellowship from his home university in Kraków to study at the London School of Economics, where he eventually switched to ethnology. In his study on the famous ring exchange of the inhabitants of the Trobriand Islands from 1922, which he named *Argonauts of the Pacific* after the ancient Argonauts myth, Malinowski acknowledged Bücher's pioneer work in the area of economic ethnology:

> "The best analysis of the problem of the economy of primitives can be found in Karl Bücher's *Die Entstehung der Volkswirtschaft*, 1893, despite many abbreviations".[52]

However, Malinowski dissociated himself from Bücher's assessment of trade.[53] Unlike Bücher, he assumed the universality of trade, yet he relativized the profit-orientation as a general feature.

Both Bücher and Thurnwald shaped the work of the Hungarian-American economic historian Karl Polanyi (1886-1964). Polanyi's differentiation of exchange forms between reciprocity, redistribution and market exchange influenced the following ethnological and ancient historical research the most.[54] Until the 1940s, people referred to Bücher's article on giving when needing verification for the reciprocal nature of giving in antiquity.[55] Nowadays,

[50] Thurnwald 1936. Cf. Wagner-Hasel 2011, pp. 251-261 and pp. 289-295.

[51] For the influence of Bücher on Malinowski see Köcke 1979, p. 153, who calls him a student of Bücher. For Malinowski's career see Stagl 1991, pp. 91-105.

[52] Malinowski 1922, pp. 129-130.

[53] Malinowski 1922, p. 118, n. 1.

[54] von Reden 1995; Möller 2004.

[55] See e.g. Laum 1924; Bolkestein 1939, p. 157; Köstler 1950, p. 23.

however, Polanyi's work is the decisive reference literature.[56] The reception of Bücher's position by Karl Polanyi has contributed more to the transfer of the anti-modernistic view of ancient economy in the Anglo-Saxon world than the present nearly unknown English translation of *Die Entstehung der Volkswirtschaft* with its confusing title *Industrial Evolution.*

Polanyi had read Bücher's works on the matter extensively. There is a detailed excerpt of Bücher's *Die Entstehung der Volkswirtschaft* in his estate.[57] Polanyi is also the author of an article on Karl Bücher in the *International Encyclopaedia of Social Sciences*.[58] His teacher Felix Somló had most likely imparted this knowledge of Bücher's notions. Polanyi had studied Law and Philosophy in Budapest,[59] and had obtained his doctorate from the jurist Felix (Bódog) Somló (1873-1920) in Kolozsvár/Klausenburg (today: Cluj-Napoca).[60] In 1909, Somló had submitted a study on goods traffic in primitive society, which presented a modification of Bücher's concept of the independent household economy. Somló argued that already at the lowest stage of development one has to assume that a composite, not a closed and self-sufficient economic unit, existed. Somló emphasized the role of giving in early goods traffic even more than Bücher, which was not only positively noted by his reviewer in the *Jahrbücher für Nationalökonomie und Statistik*, but also by Marcel Mauss. Mauss owed, in his own words, valuable insights to Somló.[61]

After his graduation, Polanyi concentrated on issues of economic policy. Among other things, he published an article on Socialist accounting in the *Archiv für Sozialwissenschaft und Sozialpolitik*, published by Max Weber and Werner Sombart.[62] Only after his emigration to the United States did he turn to economic historical topics. From 1947 to 1953, he taught economic history as a visiting professor of economics at Columbia University, New York. His great work on the social and economical transformation phase of the nineteenth and twentieth century was published in 1944 as *The Great Transformation*. Polanyi held with Bücher's opinion that ancient societies did not meet the needs for everyday goods on the market, but rather on the level of reciprocal personal relationships.[63] He did not deny the importance of the market in antiquity, but disputed

[56] von Reden 1995; Gill – Postlewaith – Seaford 1998; Möller 2004.

[57] Maucourant 2000, p. 34, n. 118. For the influence of Bücher on Polanyi see Köcke 1979, p. 121; Nafissi 2005, p. 127.

[58] Polanyi 1968, vol. 1/2, pp. 163-165.

[59] For the scientific career see Humphreys 1969; Polanyi-Levitt 1990, pp. 18-29 and pp. 78-84.

[60] Stolleis 2001, p. 590.

[61] Somló 1909, p. 177. For the influence of Somló on Mauss see Wagner-Hasel 2000, pp. 30; 39.

[62] Polanyi 1922.

[63] Polanyi 1944, p. 76.

the existence of a system of self-regulating markets.[64] 'Embeddedness' is a key term of his theory, which takes the experiences of the crisis years after World War I into account. For Polanyi, the liberalisation of the economy from the previously existing social and political restrictions was the real cause for the depression of the late 1920s. He considered the structural embeddedness of economy into politics to be the crucial difference between ancient and modern economy.

6. Conclusion

Why has Karl Bücher fallen into oblivion? It seems to me that one decisive factor lies in the demise of stage-theories. Around the turn of the twentieth century, the faith in progress had already begun to waver and had been replaced by culturally pessimistic movements. These movements took effect in politics and science particularly in the 1920s.[65] The age of stage-theory was over; models of cultural relativism had replaced evolutionist concepts, which had influenced Bücher's reasoning. Most national economists had already rejected the stage-theory while Bücher's disciple Johannes Plenge was still arguing about the authorship of the stage-theory of closed household economy to a town and national economy with his teacher in 1916.[66] It was Max Weber who perceived Bücher's economy stages as ideal-types,[67] which did not describe reality, but interpreted it.[68] Otto von Zwiedineck, Weber's follower at Munich, therefore emphasized the ideal-typical character of Bücher's model in his obituary.[69] In his appraisal of the ancient-historical research in the 1920s, the economic historian

[64] In his thesis on the lack of a system of self-regulating markets, Polanyi cites from Bücher's *Die Entstehung der Volkswirtschaft*: "Weder in der Antike noch im frühen Mittelalter – und dies muß besonders betont werden – wurden die Güter des täglichen Lebens regelmäßig gekauft und verkauft (Neither in Antiquity nor the Early Middle Ages – and this has to be emphasized – have everyday goods been bought or sold on a regular basis)": Polanyi 1944, p. 247.

[65] See Beßlich 2000.

[66] Cf. Wagner-Hasel 2011, pp. 261-264.

[67] Weber 1909[3], p. 55.

[68] See the arguments of Hartmann 1896.

[69] von Zwiedineck-Südenhorst 1931. See also Normano 1931, p. 656: "Bücher himself emphasized continually that his scheme did not correspond chronologically to the usual division of human history into three ages. He regarded the stages merely as ideal types in the sense of Max Weber, as a methodological apparatus. It is also clear that Bücher did not 'invent' or 'discover' the scheme, for the principle of his stages can be found even in the writings of Bruno Hildebrand; Rodbertus first gave the description of the natural stages (οἶκος economy), and Gustav von Schönberg of the city stage; but Bücher incorporated economic evolution into a system, at once scientific, clear, and fascinating".

Edgar Salin characterized all stage-teachings as “useful as a means of knowledge, yet never as reflections of reality”.[70]

This paradigmatic change does explain why the contribution of Karl Bücher to the development of ideal-types is currently forgotten. His followers did not combine them with historical epochs. But there are other reasons for the disregard of his contribution to the theory of gift-giving. In my opinion, it was the surplus of criticism of modernity in the theory of gifts. With their alternative models to “egoistic exchange”, national economists and legal historians established the basis for the development of influential counter-models to modern economy. These counter-models have been operating under the heading of ‘gift-exchange’ or ‘reciprocity’ (*Gegenseitigkeit*) since the 1920s.[71] While Bücher still stuck to progressive thinking, this conviction diminished over time. Especially the concept of gift-exchange developed by Marcel Mauss, now widely read in classical studies, presents a reverse image of modern capitalism. Mauss ended his *Essai sur le don* from 1925 with a critique of the principles of modern ‘rationalism’ and ‘mercantilism’. Their victory, he wrote,

> “was needed before the notions of profit and the individual were given currency and raised to the level of principle”.[72]

The focus on profit orientation as a decisive feature to distinguish between modern and archaic economy based on gift exchange was due to Werner Sombart’s study on capitalism from 1902, where we find profit orientation as the main characteristic element of modern capitalism. The economic historian Reinhold Reith speaks of a new antithesis between *Nahrungsprinzip* (principle of food) and *Gewinnstreben* (profit orientation).[73] The idealisation of gift giving as a kind of non-profit-oriented exchange has its roots in this concept of modern economy. It was Marcel Mauss who argued that the main aim of gift-giving was to create social bonds. We find this concept of gift-giving as a social act without economic purposes in many studies about gift-giving in antiquity.[74] With this concept Mauss offered an influential grounding myth to the new discipline of sociology.

[70] Salin 1930, p. 355.
[71] Wagner-Hasel 2000, pp. 31-68. For Bücher‘s influence on the early ethnologists see Spittler 2008, pp. 94-96.
[72] Mauss 1923-1924, p. 76 (translation modified).
[73] Reith 2004, p 49. For further references see Wagner-Hasel 2011, pp. 280-289 and pp. 332-336.
[74] See e.g. Finley 1965, p. 66: “Behind the market lies the profit motive, and if there was one thing that was taboo in Homeric exchanges it was gain in the exchange”, and p. 131: “There were delicate distinctions here, between honorable acquisition and trading gain”.

This reverse image is taken up by recent sociological as well as ethnological studies. For Helmuth Berking, sociologist and author of a study on *Giving: On the Anthropology of the Gift* (1996), gift-exchange offers an "opposing image to an excessively utilitarian morality", for such exchange represents a "form of praxis" in which "the symbolic order and the moral vocabulary of archaic sociability are crucially grounded".[75] In his book *L'énigme du don* (1996), the French ethnologist Maurice Godelier made a similar argument. The crises in the fabric of contemporary society – the dependence of the individuals' social existence on the economy, the weakening of the social fabric (*tissu social*) through unemployment and cutbacks in the welfare system – motivated him to a renewed investigation of the practices of gift-exchange. For him even the most secularised societies require religious objects such as gifts to guarantee social cohesion.[76] The philosopher Marcel Hénaff followed his foot-steps. His book, *Le prix de la verité. Le don, l'argent, la philosophie* (2002), contains the 'utopic' message that gifts in modern societies offer mainly one benefit: social respect of the other.[77]

On the one hand, gift-exchange functions as a counter image to modern economy; on the other hand, the concept of gift-exchange finds its way into new theories of market economy. The ethnologists Maurice Bloch and Jonathan Parry have argued that gift-giving and commodity exchange coexist even in archaic societies and gifts can change into commodities and vice versa.[78] Whereas the strong differences between gifts and commodities seem to disappear in ethnological research, modern economists create new distinctions. In the current economical debates, the figure of the *homo reciprocans* is recognized as the counter-type to the *homo oeconomicus,* who maximises the benefits. This *homo reciprocans* is no longer considered as an archaic type. Rather, he is invoked as the addressee of the global economy of charitable contribution, who rates fairness above self-interest.[79] The early concept of gift-giving as a reciprocal act demanding a counter-gift is forgotten. The economists do not know their history. Concluding, I would therefore like to propose the 'heretical' thesis that such theories are more telling of the society that developed them than the society they supposedly describe.[80] To understand ancient gift-giving practices we should forget all these ideas of a fixed kind of giving with common features and become aware of the plurality of gift giving in former societies.[81]

[75] Berking 1996, p. 11.
[76] Godelier 1996, p. 16.
[77] Hénaff 2002, p. 402.
[78] Bloch – Parry 1989.
[79] Plumpe 2007, p. 320.
[80] Wagner-Hasel 2000, pp. 41-52.
[81] See Weiner 1980, who proposed to replace 'reciprocity' by 'reproduction'. Otherwise we won't become aware of the relationship and cohesion between different acts of giving

Bibliography

Andreau, Jean: *Vingt ans après L'économie antique de M. I. Finley*, in: *AnnHSS* 50 (1995), pp. 947-960.

Barth, Paul: *Review of K. Bücher, Arbeit & Rhythmus*, in: *Archiv für soziale Gesetzgebung und Statistik* 10 (1897), pp. 321-324.

Berking, Helmuth: *Schenken. Zur Anthropologie des Gebens*, Frankfurt – New York 1996.

Beßlich, Barbara: *Wege in den ‚Kulturkrieg'. Zivilisationskritik in Deutschland 1890-1914*, Darmstadt 2000.

Bloch, Marc: *Karl Bücher*, in: *AnnHES* 4 (1932), pp. 65-66.

Bloch, Maurice – Jonathan Parry: *Introduction: Money and the Morality of Exchange*, in: *Money and the Morality of Exchange*, ed. by Maurice Bloch – Jonathan Parry, Cambridge 1989, pp. 1-32.

Bolkestein, Hendrik: *Wohltätigkeit und Armenpflege im vorchristlichen Altertum*, Utrecht 1939.

Bruhns, Hinnerk: *De Werner Sombart à Max Weber et Moses I. Finley: La typologie de la ville antique et la question de la ville de consommation*, in: *L'origine des richesses dépensées dans la ville antique*, ed. by Philippe Leveau, Aix-en-Provence 1985, pp. 255-269.

Bruhns, Hinnerk – Wilfried Nippel (ed. by): *Max Weber und die Stadt im Kulturvergleich,* Göttingen 2000.

Bücher, Karl: *Die Wohnungs-Enquete in der Stadt Basel vom 1.-19. Februar 1889*, in: *Auftrage des Regierungsrates bearbeitet*, Basel 1891.

Bücher, Karl: *Gewerbe*, in: *Handwörterbuch für Staatswissenschaften*, vol. 3, Jena 1892, pp. 922-950.

Bücher, Karl: *Die Entstehung der Volkswirtschaft. Sechs Vorträge*, vol. 1, Tübingen 1893; Engl. Transl: *Industrial Evolution*, New York 1901.

Bücher, Karl: *Arbeit & Rhythmus*, Leipzig 1896.

Bücher, Karl: *Die Wirtschaft der Naturvölker*, in: *Jahrbuch der Gehe-Stiftung* 3 (1899) pp. 51-119.

Bücher, Karl: *Die Großstädte in Gegenwart und Vergangenheit*, in: *Jahrbuch der Gehe-Stiftung zu Dresden* 9 (1903), pp. 1-31.

Bücher, Karl: *Die Entstehung der Volkswirtschaft. Vorträge und Versuche. 2. Sammlung*, Tübingen 1918.

Bücher, Karl: *Lebenserinnerungen. Erster Band 1847-1890*, Tübingen 1919.

Daston, Lorraine: *Die wissenschaftliche Persona. Arbeit und Berufung*, in: *Zwischen Vorderbühne und Hinterbühne. Beiträge zum Wandel der Geschlechterbeziehungen in der Wissenschaft vom 17. Jahrhundert bis zur Gegenwart*, ed. by Theresa Wobbe, Bielefeld 2003, pp. 109-136.

Deininger, Jürgen: *Einleitung*, in: Max Weber, *Zur Sozial- und Wirtschaftsgeschichte des Altertums. Schriften und Reden 1893-1908*, ed. by Jürgen Deininger, Tübingen 2006, pp. 1-69.

Durkheim, Émile: *Textes. Éléments d'une théorie sociale*, vol.1, Paris 1975.

within a given society.

Ehmer, Josef: *„Historische Bevölkerungsstatistik", Demographie und Geschichtswissenschaft*, in: *Herausforderung Bevölkerung. Zur Entwicklung des modernen Denkens über die Bevölkerung vor, im und nach dem „Dritten Reich"*, ed. by Josef Ehmer – Ursula Ferdinand – Jürgen Reulecke, Wiesbaden 2007, pp. 17-30.

Eich, Armin: *Die politische Ökonomie des antiken Griechenland*, Köln 2006.

Finley, Moses I.: *The World of Odysseus*, New York 1954; Revised ed. 1965.

Giddens, Anthony: *Die klassische Gesellschaftstheorie und der Ursprung der modernen Soziologie*, in: *Geschichte der Soziologie. Studien zur kognitiven, sozialen und historischen Identität einer Disziplin*, ed. by Wolf Lepenies, Frankfurt 1981, vol. 1, pp. 96-136.

Gill, Christopher – Norman Postlewaith – Richard Seaford (ed. by): *Reciprocity in Ancient Greece*, Oxford 1998.

Godelier, Maurice: *L'énigme du don*, Paris 1996.

Grimm, Jacob: *Über schenken und geben*, in: *Abhandlungen der königlichen preußischen Akademie der Wissenschaften zu Berlin aus dem Jahre 1848*, pp. 121-151 = Id.: *Kleinere Schriften 2: Abhandlungen zur Mythologie und Sittengeschichte*, Berlin 1865, pp. 173-210.

Hartmann, Ludo Moritz: *Rezension von Eduard Meyer, Die wirthschaftliche Entwicklung des Alterthums*, in: *Zeitschrift für Social- und Wirthschaftsgeschichte* 4 (1896), pp. 153-157.

Hasebroek, Johannes: *Staat und Handel im Alten Griechenland. Untersuchungen zur antiken Wirtschaftsgeschichte*, Tübingen 1928; Repr. Hildesheim 1966.

Hénaff, Marcel: *Le prix de la verité. Le don, l'argent, la philosophie*, Paris 2002; German Transl.: *Der Preis der Wahrheit. Gabe, Geld und Philosophie*, Frankfurt 2009.

Hübinger, Gangolf: *Gelehrte, Politik und Öffentlichkeit. Eine Intellektuellengeschichte*, Göttingen 2006.

Humphreys, Sally C.: *History, Economics and Anthropology: The Work of Karl Polanyi*, in: *History and Theory* 8 (1969), pp. 165-212.

Köcke, Jasper: *Some Early German Contributions to Economic Anthropology*, in: *Research in Economic Anthropology* 2 (1979), pp. 119-167.

Köstler, Rudolf: *Homerisches Recht*, Wien 1950.

Krause, Konrad: *Alma mater Lipsiensis. Geschichte der Universität Leipzig – von der Gründung 1409 bis zur Gegenwart*, Leipzig 2003.

Laum, Bernhard: *Heiliges Geld. Eine historische Untersuchung über den sakralen Ursprung des Geldes*, Tübingen 1924.

Liverani, Mario: *Immaginare Babele. Due secoli di studi sulla città orientale antica*, Roma – Bari 2013.

Malinowski, Bronislaw: *Argonauts of the Western Pacific. An Account of Native Enterprise and Adventure in the Archipelagoes of Melanesian New Guinea*, London 1922; Germ. Transl.: *Argonauten des westlichen Pazifik. Ein Bericht über Unternehmungen und Abenteuer in den Inselwelten von Melanesisch-Neuguinea*, Frankfurt 1979.

Maucourant, Jérôme: *Échange, commerce et monnaie dans les économies non modernes. Un réexamen de l'approche de Karl Polanyi*, in: *Transeuphratène* 20 (2000), pp. 9-43.

Mauss, Marcel: *Essai sur le don. Forme et raison de l'échange dans les sociétés archaïques*, in: *L'Année sociologique* n.s. 1 (1923-1924), pp. 30-186; Engl. Transl.: *The Gift: The Form and Reason for Exchange in Archaic Societies*, foreword by Mary

Douglas, New York 1990.

Mazza, Mario: *Meyer vs Bücher: il dibattito sull'economia antica nella storiografia tedesca tra Otto e Novecento*, in: *Società e storia* 29 (1985), pp. 507-546.

Meyer, Richard M.: *Geschichte des Schenkens*, in: *Zeitschrift für Kulturgeschichte* 5 (1898), pp. 18-29.

Möller, Astrid: *Zur Aktualität der Wirtschaftsanthropologie Karl Polanyis*, in: *Commerce and Monetary Systems in the Ancient World: Means of Transmission and Cultural Interaction*, ed. by Robert Rollinger – Christoph Ulf, Stuttgart 2004, pp. 218-232.

Morley, Neville: *Trade in Classical Antiquity*, Cambridge 2007.

Nafissi, Mohammed: *Ancient Athens and Modern Ideology. Value, Theory and Evidence in Historical Sciences: Max Weber, Karl Polanyi and Moses I. Finley*, London 2005.

Nippel, Wilfried: *Max Weber's "The City" revisited*, in: *City States in Classical Antiquity and Medieval Italy*, ed. by Anthony Molho – Kurt Raaflaub – Julia Emlen, Stuttgart 1991, pp. 19-30.

Nippel, Wilfried: *Nachwort*, in Max Weber, *Wirtschaft und Gesellschaft. Die Wirtschaft und die gesellschaftlichen Ordnungen und Mächte. Nachlaß. Teilband 5: Die Stadt*, ed. by Wilfried Nippel, Tübingen 1999, pp. 103-122.

Normano, João Frederico: *Karl Bücher. An Isolated Economist*, in: *Journal of Political Economy* 34 (1931), pp. 655-657.

Ostwald, Wilhelm: *Lebenslinien. Eine Selbstbiographie. Zweiter Teil: Leipzig 1887-1905*, Berlin 1927.

Plumpe, Werner: *Die Geburt des „Homo oeconomicus". Historische Überlegungen zur Entstehung und Bedeutung des Handlungsmodells der modernen Wirtschaft*, in: *Menschen und Märkte. Studien zur historischen Wirtschaftsanthropologie*, ed. by Wolfgang Reinhard – Justin Stagl, Wien – Köln – Weimar 2007, pp. 319-352.

Polanyi, Karl: *Sozialistische Rechnungslegung*, in: *Archiv für Sozialwissenschaft und Sozialpolitik* 49 (1922), pp. 377-420.

Polanyi, Karl: *The Great Transformation*, London 1944.

Polanyi, Karl: *Karl Bücher*, in: *International Encyclopedia of the Social Sciences*, vol. 1/2, New York 1968, pp. 163-165.

Polanyi-Levitt, Kari (ed. by.), *The Life and Work of Karl Polanyi. A Celebration*, Montréal – New York 1990.

Reith, Reinhold: *Abschied vom „Prinzip der Nahrung"?*, in: *Nahrung, Markt und Gemeinnutz. Werner Sombart und das vorindustrielle Handwerk*, ed. by Robert Brandt – Thomas Buchner, Bielefeld 2004, pp. 37-66.

Salin, Edgar: *Staat und Handel in Hellas in archaischer und klassischer Zeit*, in: *Zeitschrift für die Gesamte Staatswissenschaft* 89 (1930), pp. 353-361.

Schöttler, Peter: *Das ‚Annales Paradigma' und die deutsche Historiographie im Umbruch*, in: *Nationale Grenzen und internationaler Austausch. Studien zum Kultur- und Wissenstransfer in Europa*, ed. by Lothar Jordan – Bernd Kortländer, Tübingen 1995, pp. 205-217.

Schneider, Helmuth: *Die Bücher-Meyer Kontroverse*, in: *Eduard Meyer. Leben und Leistung eines Universalhistorikers*, ed. by William M. Calder III – Alexander Demandt, Leiden 1990, pp. 417-445.

Simiand, François: *Review of Karl Bücher, Die Entstehung der Volkswirtschaft, Tübingen 1898*[2], in: *L'Année sociologique* 2 (1897-1898), pp. 440-448.

Sombart, Werner: *Der moderne Kapitalismus. Band 1: Einleitung, die vorkapitalistische*

Wirtschaft, die historischen Grundlagen des modernen Kapitalismus, München 1916[2].
Somló, Felix: *Der Güterverkehr in der Urgesellschaft*, Brüssel – Leipzig 1909.
Spahn, Peter: *Die Anfänge der antiken Ökonomik*, in: *Chiron* 14 (1984), pp. 301-323.
Spahn, Peter: *Max Weber et la typologie des modes d'activités industrielles de Karl Bücher*, in: *Sociologie économique et économie de l'antiquité. À propos de Max Weber*, ed. by Hinnerk Bruhns – Jean Andreau, Paris 2004, pp. 115-142.
Spittler, Gerd: *Founders of the Anthropology of Work. German Social Scientists of the 19th and Early 20th Centuries and the First Ethnographers*, Berlin 2008.
Stagl, Justin: *Malinowskis Paradigma*, in: *Geschichte und Gegenwart* 2 (1991), pp. 91-105.
Stolleis, Michael, (ed. by): *Juristen – Ein biographisches Lexikon von den Anfängen bis zum 20. Jahrhundert*, München 2001[2].
Thurnwald, Richard: *Gegenseitigkeit im Aufbau und Funktionieren der Gesellungen und deren Institutionen*, in: *Reine und angewandte Soziologie. Eine Festgabe für Ferdinand Tönnies zu seinem achtzigsten Geburtstag*, Leipzig 1936, pp. 275-297.
von Amira, Karl: *Nordgermanisches Obligationenrecht*, Leipzig 1882-1885.
von Dargun, Lothar: *Soziologische Studien I: Egoismus und Altruismus in der Nationalökonomie*, Leipzig 1885.
von Jhering, Rudolf: *Der Zweck im Recht*, 2 voll., Leipzig 1904-1905[4].
von Reden, Sitta: *Exchange in Ancient Greece*, London 1995.
von Zwiedineck-Südenhorst, Otto: *Gedenkworte. Zum Gedächtnis von Karl Bücher. Gestorben den 12. November 1930*, in: Gerhard Kessler – Otto von Zwiedineck-Südenhorst, *Zum Gedächtnis von Karl Bücher. Gestorben den 12. November 1930*, Leipzig 1931, pp. 5-11.
Wagner-Hasel, Beate: *Der Stoff der Gaben. Kultur und Politik des Schenkens und Tauschens*, Frankfurt – New York 2000.
Wagner-Hasel, Beate: *Le regard de Karl Bücher sur l'économie antique et le débat sur théorie économique et histoire*, in: *L'histoire et l'économie politique en Allemagne autour de 1900*, ed. by Hinnerk Bruhns, Paris 2004, pp. 159-183.
Wagner-Hasel, Beate: *Hundert Jahre Gelehrtenstreit über die antike Wirtschaft: Zur Aktualität von Karl Büchers Wirtschaftsanthropologie*, in: *Historische Anthropologie* 17 (2009), pp. 178-201.
Wagner-Hasel, Beate: *Die Arbeit des Gelehrten. Der Nationalökonom Karl Bücher (1847-1930)*, Frankfurt – New York 2011.
Weber, Max: *Agrarverhältnisse*, in: *Handwörterbuch der Staatswissenschaften*. vol.1, Jena 1909[3], pp. 53-188 = Id.: *Zur Sozial- und Wirtschaftsgeschichte des Altertums. Schriften und Reden 1893-1908*, ed. by Jürgen Deininger, Tübingen 2006, pp. 300-747.
Weiner, Annette B.: *"Reproduction": A Replacement for Reciprocity*, in: *American Ethnologist* 7 (1980), pp. 71-85.
Will, Eduard: *Trois quarts de siècle de recherches sur l'économie grecque antique*, in: *AnnESC* 9 (1954), pp. 7-22.

MARCEL HÉNAFF

Is There Such a Thing as a Gift Economy?

1. Introduction

The term 'gift economy' has been used fairly frequently by scholars, and this use has generally not been challenged. Yet it is impossible to use to the term without some sense of irony, since the association of its two constituents verges on the oxymoronic: it is accepted that rational economy, as we know it, is based on self-interest and cannot be based on gift-giving understood as an unconditional generous gesture. Conversely, such gift-giving necessarily constitutes a break with the rational economy. At most it can be a marginal aspect of this economy.

The term 'gift economy' has been used, however, in relation to three theoretical directions that can be summarized as follows:

- Either the term is meant to designate the economic model assumed to prevail in so-called archaic societies, where gift exchange plays such an important role that it appears to constitute the main form of the circulation of goods. This presupposition explains the recourse to such terms as 'gift-exchange societies', which are assumed to precede 'barter societies', based on trade.
- Or the term designates a certain number of practices of distribution and redistribution in our modern societies, whose purpose is to ensure mutual aid, assistance to the most underprivileged (through charities), or the funding of various non-profit projects (philanthropic foundations). These are activities of compensation or promotion whose purpose is not to transform the market economy, but to mitigate it by sharing the surplus generated by profitable activities.
- Some go even further, calling 'gift economy' a complete reconstruction of the economy intended to break with the market economy and whose primary purpose is assumed to be social solidarity. We know this is Mauss's intent in the conclusion of *The Gift*, where he used (and perhaps coined) the term. He then presents a few directions for this gift economy based on solidarity, referring to the practices of ritual gift exchange analyzed in his book (an association that I consider highly debatable, as we will see).

In this paper I propose to present two main arguments:

1. In no way do gift exchanges in traditional societies constitute a gift economy, because these exchanges do not have an economic character; their aim is not profit; even less do they constitute an alternative to trade. Furthermore, I will argue that the purpose of these exchanges is not only to exchange precious goods in a spirit of civility, not even as an expression of generosity, but to

achieve reciprocal public recognition and establish lasting alliances through these goods.

2. It is possible – if one insists on it – to speak as Mauss does of a 'gift economy' with respect to practices based on solidarity, but, contrary to what he believed and so many scholars still believe (whether because of his influence or independent of him), these institutions of solidarity have nothing to do with ritual gift exchanges.

A consideration of these two points will lead us to recognize the heterogeneity of the different types of giving and rethink the reason for being of ceremonial exchanges.

2. Ritual gift exchanges do not have an economic character

Three remarks should be sufficient to establish this:

- First, my focus is only the ritual gift exchanges that can be observed in traditional societies and are practiced among groups, not the gracious, unilateral, and private form of giving, or even philanthropic or mutual aid giving. My own presupposition is that there are several different forms of giving, relatively heterogeneous and to which the same criteria cannot be applied. I will return later to these necessary distinctions.
- Second, in most anthropological textbooks and introductory literature, as well as in encyclopedias, ritual gift exchanges are discussed in chapters on economic exchanges. This choice already amounts to a theory – and an erroneous one. Either these books present gift exchanges as a primitive form of trade, or they contrast true trade (rational and aiming at profit) with what they describe as a more generous, festive, and almost irresponsible form of exchange of goods.
- Third, historians of the economy generally have a similar theoretical attitude with respect to gift exchange. They view it as a minor phenomenon, and a rather irrational one because of the useless expense it involves. There is nothing surprising about such judgments on the part of supporters of the standard theory, according to which every genuine economic activity is the expression of a rational choice motivated by self-interest. This lack of understanding is more surprising, however, on the part of economic historians renowned for their open-mindedness and their ability to grasp the logic inherent in gift exchanges in societies very different from ours. Two authors embody this paradox: Max Weber and Karl Polanyi. They are both well aware of the specificity of traditional economies, whose aim is the balancing of accounts and the settling of debts, but also solidarity within society. Yet it is difficult for them to understand gift exchanges, precisely because they attempt to integrate them as components of this traditional economy.

3. Ceremonial gift exchange as a pact of recognition

If the gifts exchanged during ceremonies (such as in the *kula* ring or on the occasion of weddings) are not mere physical goods useful in everyday life, then what are they? The answer is obvious: they are symbols. But what do they symbolize? According to Malinowski – and to Mauss after him – they carry prestige and express reciprocal esteem, thus reinforcing the bond between the parties. These interpretations are unquestionable. But, we could ask, why does the offer consist in precious goods rather than praise and mutual services alone, which also constitute important aspects of these rituals? There is a deeper reason: these gift exchanges amount to a gesture of reciprocal recognition specific to human groups. I will attempt to demonstrate this fundamental thesis in a few words to better justify my critique of the notion of gift economy.

To understand what is at stake in ceremonial gift exchange, the best approach is an analysis of the first encounters among traditional groups. These encounters are essentially characterized by gift exchanges called opening gifts. This has been observed in every traditional society. It can be said that through the mediation of the goods they give each other, these groups recognize and accept each other and establish an alliance. To understand the importance of this procedure – its ontological dimension – it may be useful to examine encounters and associations among nonhumans, mammals for example. Depending on the species, these encounters involve messages conveyed through smells, sounds, gestures, and postures that follow precisely-coded sequences. In some bird and reptile species objects or foods can intervene, but they do so according to an immutable programming. The procedure in which a precious object stands as a token and substitute of the giver is kept as witness to the reciprocal recognition, and generates a reciprocating action, is never observed in nonhumans, not even in apes. This is a gesture specific to human groups, and it expresses the recognition of their very humanness. The following anecdote should shed light on this. It was reported by the British anthropologist Andrew Strathern, who in his investigation of the high valleys of New Guinea's Mt Hagen during the 1970s used an informer who in his youth during the 1920s had witnessed the arrival of the first white men in his village. According to local legends the dead became, for a while, pale cannibalistic ghosts. One day the villagers saw a strangely dressed white-skinned character walk toward their village. They were very afraid. Was he going to devour them? They decided to put his humanness to the test and presented him with pigs. The character – in fact an Australian civil servant apprised of the local traditions – took from his bag precious shells used in various local ceremonies. "Then, the informer said, we understood that he was a human being like ourselves".[6]

[6] Strathern 1971, p. xii.

I believe that this simple story contains the entire enigma and reveals the true meaning of ceremonial gift exchange as the procedure by which humans recognize each other, in the three senses of the word:

1. They identify one another as humans (vs. nonhumans);
2. They accept one another, and therefore establish a state of peace (rather than confrontation);
3. They honor one another through the precious objects they exchange.

This act or procedure of recognition is at the same time a challenge and a chosen alliance. It is a challenge in the sense that each party incurs significant risk. The gesture of giving requires a reply from the other party, according to the fundamental principle of reactivity that rules the relationships among living beings: a blow for a blow, or a gift for a gift. This rule of reciprocity is observed everywhere. The ceremonial gift-exchange relationship is therefore agonistic: it is not a bland consensus or a neutral contract.

Ceremonial gift exchange is a decision of alliance primarily in the sense that it amounts to a convention accepted by both parties. In this the gifts offered are symbols in the literal sense: *sym-bola*, that is, things shared as witness to the agreement. This is also why the main form of alliance is the matrimonial alliance: a wife is the ultimate form of the gift, as Lévi-Strauss stated in his description of the elementary structures of kinship.[7] The wife is an essential part of the giver group; through her, life will be passed down. Marriage expresses the strongest possible commitment between the parties involved in gift exchange. The prohibition of incest is not primarily a sexual taboo, but the obligation to establish a reciprocal relationship with other groups is what makes us specifically human: they must find a wife in another group and accept to reciprocate by letting their daughters or sisters marry outside their own group. All groups are exogamic, that is, based on reciprocity; hence the special status of women as living embodiments of otherness and alliance.

If we understand this relationship of challenge and agonistic reciprocity and this commitment in the alliance, then we also understand that a purely economic or economistic interpretation is null and void. But we must go further in our effort at clarifying the nature of ceremonial gift exchange. We must be careful not to confuse it with two other forms of gift: such confusion indirectly opens the way to economistic reductionism. I propose a distinction among three clearly heterogeneous forms of gift:

– The specifically ceremonial gift that we have just discussed. This gift is and must be reciprocal. A pact entails the existence of two parties equally committed to the procedure. Let us note that, contrary to a common prejudice, reciprocity in this case refers to the requirement to reply, and not to a wish

[7] Lévi-Strauss 1949.

that what was given should be returned, as some sociologists (such as Bourdieu),[8] or philosophers (such as Derrida),[9] believe.

- The specifically gracious gift, which is and must be unilateral. Its aim is to please the recipient, in a generous way and without self-interest. This particular notion of the gift dominates our concept of giving, and we tend to view it as its model. Based on this model of unilateral giving (believed to be pure) ritual gift exchange is deemed impure, because it is reciprocal – an irrelevant criticism, as we have shown.
- The gift out of solidarity. Its aim is to help people in need, such as victims of a catastrophe or an economic crisis. A clear criterion is that the goods given are primarily useful and functional, whereas in the two other cases they are primarily precious and symbolic goods.

This typology allows us to understand that each type of gift is legitimate within its own order, and that it is inappropriate to pass judgment on one type based on criteria applicable to another (this kind of false judgment, however, is constantly observed as part of reflections on giving).

4. Returning to the question of the gift economy: additional clarifications

Based on these distinctions we can now return to our discussion of the notion of 'gift economy'. Some authors use the term in reference to the gifts given out of solidarity. This notion does not stand up. Although this form of mutual assistance and charitable support to those in need (whether individual or institutional) presupposes the existence of an economy, in no way does it constitute an economy. Such an action can correct a situation, whether accidental (a catastrophe or crisis) or generated by a chronic injustice (economic inequality or exploitation).

It is legitimate, however, to speak of an economy based on solidarity, with a higher degree of social justice, a more intense associative life, and genuine mutual assistance. Such an economy, however, does not substitute the gift for the market. It restrains and corrects the market, and it ensures redistribution. This is in fact the type of economy Mauss has in mind at the end of his *The Gift*. Such a project certainly deserves our support. It can even be called a 'gift economy', if one insists on it, in the sense that it involves non-profitable exchanges. But this has nothing to do with ceremonial gift exchange. Ritual gift exchanges are primarily commitments through precious goods that serve as symbols, whereas economic activity involves commercial goods that are primarily useful. These are two different orders and modes of exchange. To use the term 'gift economy'

[8] Bourdieu 1972.

[9] Derrida 1991 developed this misguided interpretation of Mauss. See my criticism in Hénaff 2009, pp. 215-34.

entails the risk of reiterating the old confusions. It would be more appropriate to speak of a 'solidarity-based economy'.

As for ceremonial gift exchange, does it take on a new form in our modern world? If it is in fact a procedure of public recognition among groups in societies without a central state (in which the formal conditions of this recognition are recreated by each exchange), then it can be said that in modern state-based societies this public recognition is ensured by the law and the whole of the legal and economic institutions. This, rather than some hypothetical gift economy, is the heritage of ceremonial gift exchange.

At this point we must clear away a significant source of misunderstandings associated with the difference between the different fields under consideration by anthropologists and historians. For anthropologists, ritual gift exchanges cannot be simply defined as noncommercial exchanges, because this view presupposes that what matters is the exchange of goods, not the exchange of symbols. Anthropologists primarily discuss nonurban societies, without a state or writing, and with low degrees of techno-economic development. Because historians and philologists work based on written documents, they deal most often with urban societies with a state, writing, and significant economic exchanges using currencies. In such societies the procedures of gift exchange no longer have the foundational function they have in more traditional societies. This discrepancy is even greater with modern societies such as ours, in which the ancient gift exchanges have almost completely disappeared. There is a risk that the two disciplines will focus on two different kinds of objects, which could occasion a misunderstanding between historians and anthropologists. Therefore we must now clarify the specificity of the mercantile exchange and its forms.

5. The trade form of exchange and the model of the contract

Mercantile exchange aims at reducing the risk of personal involvement by doing away with the primary requirement of reciprocal recognition in the movement of goods – a requirement implied by gift-giving relationships; even if the partner is granted some esteem, this is not the purpose of the transaction, which aims at acquiring or selling these goods as objects of material appreciation and evaluation; if there is a deception it will concern these goods, regardless of any friendly or deferent attitude on the part of the seller.

When the purpose is to acquire or provide goods rather than recognize a partner, money makes it possible to set fair equivalences. Such exchanges presuppose precise and efficient procedures of reciprocal commitment. Such is the contract, which, in its forms and implications, is the exact opposite of the reciprocal ceremonial gift. This is precisely why it provides a guarantee of fairness and independence. Before attempting to describe its characteristics, we may note that Mauss made a surprising use of this term in the context of exchanges of ceremonial presents.

In *The Gift*, the term "contract" is often used to describe commitments made between partners ("exchanges and contracts take place in the form of presents"; "we shall describe the phenomena of exchange and contract in these societies…"; "There is total service in the sense that it is indeed the whole clan that contracts on behalf of all..."; "this system of contractual gifts in Samoa...").[10] Sacrifice is also viewed as a relationship of this type with the gods ("we can begin at this point a theory and history of the sacrifice as contract…").[11] The choice of the concept of contract is clearly inappropriate in the case of the ceremonial gift; but we must first understand why Mauss uses this term. At least two reasons may be considered. One is general: Mauss broadly resorts to this notion to designate any type of mutual commitment between partners; he might as well have used the term pact, which he sometimes does.

But there is another, more crucial reason: in gift-exchange practices the obvious element of constraint can be compared only to the constraint implied by a contract. In fact, Mauss's interest in the question of the gift started with his work on the origins of the contract and certain archaic legal forms (Roman, Scandinavian or Hindu). At the same time, another sociologist and student of Mauss, Georges Davy, was working on these questions and published, in 1922, a book on this topic, *La foi jurée*,[12] which focuses primarily on the Kwakiutl, Tlingit and Haida potlatch of the northwest coast of America. From the outset, the ceremonial gift is situated or rather pre-interpreted within a legal framework stemming from European culture. At first, Mauss seems to adopt this approach, because using the paradigm of the contract to interpret the ritual gift enabled him to recognize the two central characteristics of any 'social fact' according to Durkheim: that is, being coercive and being immediately collective. Several reticent references made by Mauss to Davy (in *The Gift* or elsewhere), however, make his discomfort obvious. Besides Davy's situating of the potlatch within an evolution that would lead to the modern contract, what made Mauss most uncomfortable was that the agonistic character of the potlatch makes it incompatible with the very concept of contract. Or, rather, for Mauss the contract is related to only the compulsory aspect of the gift, which is neither a variant nor the ancestor of the contract, but a specific fact – it is even a "total social fact", as previously mentioned. A passage from *The Gift* clearly outlines the different status of the contract with respect to the games or gambling phenomenon,

> "which, even today, is not considered contractual, but rather a comprised of situations in which honour is engaged and where property is surrendered even

[10] Mauss 1923-1924, pp. 3; 4; 6; 8.
[11] Mauss 1923-1924, p. 15.
[12] Davy 1922.

> when it is not absolutely necessary. Gambling is a form of potlatch and a part of the gift system".[13]

In short, even when Mauss continues to use the term contract, he precisely does not want to consider the ceremonial gift in terms of legal criteria, as does Davy, following an evolutionist model; Mauss's purpose is to help us understand one of the crucial characteristics of the ceremonial gift: obligation. His whole essay clearly aims to bring forth the irreducible originality of reciprocal gift exchange.

We can now try the reverse approach, briefly pointing to the main characteristics specific to the model of the contract and distinguishing it from the model of the traditional gift. Since our purpose is to underline the contrast with the ceremonial exchange, we shall restrict our consideration to the contract of sale and purchase:

1. Such a contract presupposes a negotiation between partners in view of obtaining the greatest mutual advantage; this negotiation may be either easy or harsh, and even hostile, with each partner attempting to defend his interest.
2. Even if the contract is made between individuals (two in general, whether actual persons or institutions; but there are also contracts of association – called partnership contracts – which may involve several partners), it does not have a personal nature; the partners are not involved as particular persons, but as legal subjects; the contract thus has an impersonal form; if something is bought or sold between friends, their friendship may be recorded but cannot as such be part of the grounds of the contract (one cannot commit oneself by contract to remain friends, nor define love relationships).
3. In a contractual exchange the goods exchanged are defined and described exhaustively; the transaction concerns these goods, and not others; the object of the contract is thus strictly limited.
4. By hypothesis the goods involved in a contractual procedure of sale are alienable (persons, honors or public functions, for instance, cannot be sold by contract without the sale being immoral and illegal).
5. The obligation contracted by the partners is public and legally defined; breaches of commitments are subject to legal sanctions (fines, physical constraint, loss of rights).
6. Finally – and this is a crucial point – the specificity of the contract consists in its limitation with respect to time; it is in force over a defined duration, beyond which it becomes null and void.

We can see that each of these points contradicts profoundly the logic of the gift. The contract of sale is a procedure whose aim is not to request recognition by the partner, but to perform a clear, efficient, and measurable exchange. This is

[13] Mauss 1923-1924, p. 101, n.119. The notion of rhythm also developed by Mauss is very helpful in order to understand the very source of the drive to play. "Man is a rhythmic animal," he writes in Mauss 1947, p. 85.

why the monetary instrument is so suitable to the contract. It is also why it is important to distinguish it from the gift relationship. The Protestant ethics established this distinction by instituting a radical separation between the universe of the gift – the realm of grace, reserved to God – and business – the realm of men and the object of the 'inner-world';[14] conversely one can show, as did B. Clavero,[15] how the Catholic ethics allowed a contamination between these two logics. But beyond these religious references there is a deeper ethical aim shared by all kinds of social activities: trust.

6. Trust, rational action, and the calculation of risk in standard economic theory

Modern economic theory is based on the hypothesis that the system of production and the realm of the marketplace have become autonomous. For over three centuries economic theory has been constructing the figure of *homo œconomicus*, now called rational economic agent. While reducing traditional gift relationships to mere archaic mercantile exchanges it has also proposed to do away with such practices. Economic activity claims to be a clear and efficient mode of operation, the very mode defined by contractual relationships. Every economic theory was developed against the background of this strict rationality, whose most accomplished figure is probably the calculating agent outlined by game theory. This agent makes choices based solely on his/her own interest. This theory presupposes as an unquestionable truth that the selfish aim is natural and thus legitimate. Individual self-interest is taken to be the ultimate horizon of any rational behavior. This is also why game theory has been able to provide the various interactional models of society with powerful conceptual tools. These models make it possible to coordinate the total sum of rationally-directed individual choices within a social organization, itself understood as the total sum of the interactions. The agent's every action is thus a strategic relational choice.

One soon came to suspect, however, that this rational actor, constantly busy working out his 'moves', might be nothing more than a fictional figure that one would be hard-pressed to find in ordinary social experience. Granted, this is a model, and as such it is entitled to be an abstraction; it still remains that the model must be operational. Yet it is far from being so when we take into account the particular character of interactions. Interactions do not amount to mere moves within a neutral space. We have come to better understand that rational choice theory (especially with respect to the famous prisoner dilemma) presupposes the central question of trust. What does this mean? It is not enough to demonstrate, based on game theory, that in the final analysis agents have everything to gain by cooperating, and even by being altruistic, in short by granting trust to their

[14] Weber 1920.
[15] Clavero 1991. See my comment on this essay in Hénaff 2002, pp. 268-90.

partner. Trust understood in such a way remains purely strategic, a mere element in the computation of interests (as shown, for instance, by O. Williamson, or M. Hollis).[16] The question of trust, by contrast, is at the core of reciprocal gift relationships, not as a useful dimension, but as the foundation of a current or future alliance and as inseparable from a sense of honor and a generous attitude.

We must then understand where this specific form of trust, crucial to the logic of rational choices, originates; either it is generated by these very choices and remains, in the end, a parameter in the calculation of interests; or it precedes them and makes them possible, in which case it is important to identify its origin and manifestations. When confronting the problem of trust within interactions the oversimplifications (and sometimes dead ends) of game theory come from a failure to realize the following: trust can only appear at the local level in a particular 'move', because it is not a mere parameter that may or may not come into play, but a foundational element of any relationship among individuals. A shortcoming of social analysis (with respect to the concrete conditions of trust) combines at this point with an epistemological shortcoming (with respect to the diversity of parameters). Yet the question of trust must be articulated at two different levels of social depth. On the first level, trust must be situated within the entirety of the collective mediations that make it operational within a given society; in traditional societies such mediations are closely tied to ethnicity, rituals, ways of living, and religious beliefs; in modern societies these mediations may be legal, ethical or associated with reputation (which does not exclude the powerful continued influence of ethnic or religious elements). In short, the granting or denial of trust cannot be separated from what constitutes a community: its rules, values, and traditions. Economic agents always make their decisions within such situations. In other words, even if in any given case agents may theoretically decide of their own attitude and calculate their own interest, it remains that what determines their choices and incites their trust empirically is an entire set of parameters tied to representations shared within their community.

This, in any case, is the objection most frequently raised against the interactional model based on game theory. It signals a kind of return to Durkheim's position on society as a totality; or at least it proposes to correct the individualistic aim through a holistic interpretation. This correction seems necessary because it makes it possible to integrate a fuller and more complex set of parameters. It aims at accounting for a socially, emotionally, and culturally defined agent, rather than a pure model of interaction. In traditional societies ceremonial gift exchange exemplifies the type of relationship foundational to all forms of social interaction, including mercantile ones.

[16] Williamson 1993; Hollis 1998.

6. Conclusion: Market economy and total social fact

Hence my final remark: Polanyi rightly notes that in a society such as the Trobriand's *kula*, ritual exchanges dominate the entire social life, and that all other activities, including the economy, are "embedded" within these exchanges. As I mentioned above, this is the meaning of Mauss's term "total social fact". I also said that a total social fact is a fact that not only integrates all others, but also gives them meaning. Such a fact defines the reason for being of a group, its mode of being together, and the enjoyment it experiences in living (as did public life in Athens, or Christian faith in Medieval Europe). Yet today we observe that the economy has come to be the activity that claims to integrate all others and decide their fate. Everything is subjected to marketing and processed by finance. Everything is "embedded" in the market economy. But did this economy become a total social fact? It certainly has not – or if it has, it has in the mode of an imposture: the economy pretends to explain everything, but it gives meaning to nothing. It is not a total social fact, but a domineering and even tyrannical social fact. The market economy cannot give meaning to societies and human beings. By definition, the realm of freedom, truth, and dignity escapes commercial equivalences. Of these values and norms the economy has nothing to say. This is why it leaves them to religion and the media. This is also why in the West these two activities have often tended to become meaning-generating machines whose product is provided for consumption in the global market of metaphysical scarcity.

Translated from French by J.-L. Morhange

Bibliography

Bourdieu, Pierre: *Esquisse d'une théorie de la pratique*, Paris 1972; Engl. Transl.: *Outline of a Theory of Practice*, Cambridge 1977.

Clavero Salvador, Bartolomé: *Antidora. Antropología católica de la economía moderna*, Milano 1991.

Davy, Georges: *La foi jurée. Étude sociologique du problème du contrat: la formation du lien contractuel*, Paris 1922; Repr. New York 1975.

Derrida, Jacques: *Donner le temps 1. La fausse monnaie*, Paris 1991; Engl. Transl.: *Given Time: I. Counterfeit Money*, Chicago 1992.

Hénaff, Marcel: *Le prix de la vérité. Le don, l'argent, la philosophie*, Paris 2002; Engl. Transl.: *The Price of Truth: Gift, Money, Philosophy*, Stanford 2010.

Hénaff, Marcel: *The Aporia of Pure Giving and the Aim of Reciprocity: On Derrida's Given Time*, in: *Derrida and the Time of the Political*, ed. by Pheng Cheah – Suzanne Guerlac, Durham – London 2009, pp. 215-234.

Hollis, Martin: *Trust within Reason*, Cambridge 1998.

Lévi-Strauss, Claude: *Les structures élémentaires de la parenté*, Paris 1949; Engl. Transl.: *The Elementary Structures of Kinship*, Boston 1969.

Mauss, Marcel: *Essai sur le don. Forme et raison de l'échange dans les sociétés archaïques*, in: *L'Année sociologique* n.s. 1 (1923-1924), pp. 30-186. Engl. Transl.: *The Gift: The Form and Reason for Exchange in Archaic Societies*, foreword by Mary Douglas, New York 1990.

Mauss, Marcel: *Manuel d'ethnographie*, Paris 1947.

Polanyi, Karl: *The Great Transformation*, New York 1944; Repr. Boston 1957.

Strathern, Andrew: *The Rope of Moka*: *Big-Men and Ceremonial Exchange in Mount Hagen, New Guinea*, Cambridge 1971.

Weber, Max: *Die protestantische Ethik und der Geist des Kapitalismus*, Tübingen 1920; Engl. Transl.: *The Protestant Ethic and the Spirit of Capitalism,* New York 1958.

Weber, Max: *Wirtschaftsgeschichte. Abriss der universalen Sozial- und Wirtschaftsgeschichte*, München 1923; Engl. Transl.: *General Economic History*, New Brunswick 1981.

Williamson, Oliver E.: *Calculativeness, Trust and Economic Organization*, in: *Journal of Law and Economics* 36 (1993), pp. 453-486.

David Reinstein

The Economics of the Gift

1. Introduction

This essay broadly considers gifts, giving, and gift economies, modern and pre-modern, from a mainstream (and behavioral) economics perspective. I present a selective survey of the literature focusing on six key points:

1. Commercial transactions sustained by reputation are not easily distinguishable from gift exchange economies;
2. Gift-giving allows the recipient and the giver to accumulate goods that cannot be purchased commercially;
3. When the giver retains some use, experience, or control over the gift, she shares in the consumption of it;
4. Considering behavioral issues such as regret aversion, gift-giving may offer overlooked *efficiencies* that may balance out the deadweight losses from 'inadequate gifts';
5. Aggregate (anonymous) giving can be an important signal of overall group identity and character;
6. Historical modes of 'giving under pressure' offer insights for modern public policy and philanthropy.

Van de Ven presents a wide-ranging survey of several economic approaches to gift-giving in modern economies.[1] He focuses on two main empirical features. The first is *inadequacy*: gifts are often given in some form that are not optimal for the receiver, given the expense incurred. From the standard economic perspective, the recipient should always prefer a cash gift, as this allows her maximal freedom of choice, hence she can optimize her utility. Yet cash gifts are often taboo. The second feature is *non-reciprocity*: gifts are often given without the expectation of a gift or reward in return. He classifies six several competing classes of models of gift-giving, considering how well they can explain these two features.[2]

Beginning with a key example, the first model he mentions is altruism, *à la* Becker, where "my state of happiness is dependent on that of the other".[3] Al-

[1] Van de Ven 2000.

[2] These are: 1. "Altruism – making other people happy", 2. "Egoism I – exchange", 3. "Egoism II – warm glow, social approval", 4. "Strategical – signaling, building trust", 5. "Fairness – norms, reducing inequity" and 6. "Survival – selection" (Van de Ven 2000, p. 4). See also the introduction to this volume.

[3] Becker 1974.

though it can explain non-reciprocal giving,[4] this model struggles with inadequate giving; the altruist, seeking to maximize the utility of another, would presumably give her a cash gift. Note that an extreme interpretation of Andreoni's "warm glow" model,[5] where the donor gains utility over the amount she sacrifices without caring where it goes, would neither imply nor rule out inadequate giving. While the warm glow model offers some convenient theoretical results, it is essentially a black box, raising more questions than it answers.

In the following sections I incorporate three more of Van de Ven's classifications: altruism, a gift economy with symbolic utility, reputation, social approval, and signaling; I leave out the models of fairness and the evolutionary models ('survival') for space concerns.

2. Personal exchanges, market exchanges, and gift economies

Exchange is useful when two parties have different relative costs in producing one or another good, and/or they have different preferences over goods. If I value my last apple at two oranges, and you value your last orange at two apples, then if I give you an apple in exchange for your orange we are both better off. But, for a given amount of goods produced, the chain of exchanges that achieves efficiency may be long and complicated. Classical economists have labored to specify precise formal models and conditions under which free exchange can achieve this *Pareto efficiency*, where no one can be made better off without making someone else worse off. Even where these conditions hold, the efficient outcome may not be one that we would consider equitable.

In modern systems these exchanges occur through a *numeraire* good – money. With large and functioning markets and a generally accepted currency, each person can buy and sell without having to find a precise *coincidence of wants*. If I have apples and want oranges, I do not have to look around and find someone has oranges and wants apples (i.e., barter); we can both go to the general marketplace to buy and sell. With the *idealized* efficient marketplace, we can do no better by making individual trades – just go to the market and you will get (or receive) the best price.

However, this takes a lot for granted. Who is providing and monitoring the validity of this generally accepted currency? Who is setting up the marketplace and determining the prices at which the markets clear? Who is guaranteeing that the oranges I buy will be of the type and quality promised? Who ensures that my

[4] Although Van de Ven doesn't mention it, this model struggles to explain *reciprocal* giving, i.e., why two individuals would give each other gifts – only the 'net gift' should matter for this model.

[5] Andreoni 1990.

apples are not stolen as I bring them to the market, and that I am accurately informed of the prevailing price and paid for my apples? The canonical general equilibrium model involves a market in which no one has market power but all are *price-takers* and, crucially, the true quality of every item is common knowledge. There are no individual interactions but only a 'Walrasian auction-neer' who finds the price at which demand equals supply in all markets.[6] No one believes this is how even the largest, most standard, and most efficient markets actually work. The argument is that with greater numbers of buyers and sellers the outcomes will converge to those predicted by this model.

Economic history has often been characterized, most prominently by Adam Smith, as a progression from self-sufficiency (within the family or close group) to barter to centralized, institutionalized, and globalized markets, with complicated chains of contracts and ownership rights enforced by central governments and international institutions.[7]

In institutionalized markets, with greater distance between buyer and seller, there is less opportunity to develop a relationship that may permit trust. In the game theoretical sense, with a single interaction both parties will act in their own best interests. If we cannot immediately observe fruit quality, I will give you a rotten apple, and you give me a rotten orange. The idealized markets cannot easily deal with this problem of *asymmetric information* and there will be inefficiency – mutually beneficial trades will not take place.[8]

However in indefinitely repeated games, cooperation can be (but need not be) sustained in equilibrium.[9] If we are patient enough, each party may sacrifice her immediate interest in favor of a continued relationship. I will give you the good apple and you will give me the good orange because we have the mutual *common knowledge* understanding that if either of us gives rotten fruit, in any future interaction we will never give fresh fruit again. Note that this refers to a specific relationship between two individuals, and not a general system of laws or customs.

In models where some agents have reciprocal or other-regarding preferences, substantiated in much experimental work, there is an even stronger incentive to 'play nice'. Here, even if we both know that our interaction is coming to an end, we also know that some people want to reward good behavior and punish bad behavior, even if it does not directly increase their own wealth. Thus, even if we

[6] For an intermediate textbook explanation of Walrasian equilibrium, see, e.g., Nicholson – Snyder 2011[11], pp. 457-497. The original theory was formulated by Walras 1926[4]. The term 'Walrasian auctioneer' may have originated with Leijonhufvud 1967.

[7] Smith 1776. Although this progression seems logical, there is some argument over the historical accuracy of this. As discussed throughout this volume there is debate over the extent to which gift exchanges, with or without an explicit *quid pro quo,* served as a bridge, consisted an economy in itself, or coexisted with other forms of exchange

[8] Akerlof 1970.

[9] Fudenberg – Maskin 1986.

are selfish, we may give the good fruit just in case our partner turns out to be one of these reciprocators. And we also will want to convince the other fellow that we ourselves will reciprocate.[10]

This repeated relationship, where I give you a quality product in exchange for your quality product (or monetary payment), is in one sense very much like a gift exchange. In fact, in these models such cooperation need not result from an explicit *quid pro quo*, nor a reckoning after each period, as long as we are patient and we have a mutual understanding that good behavior will be reciprocated down the road. We do not need a formal agreement that I will give you an apple every Monday, and you will give me an orange every Friday; this can take the form of one gift following another, *ad infinitum*.[11]

To sum up, a repeated 'commercial' exchange sustained by reputation and reciprocation concerns may not be terribly distinct from a repeated 'gift exchange'. Here I refer to a 'gift economy' mainly driven by self-interest, essentially constituting an alternate form of exchange (but as noted above, perhaps strengthened by other-regarding preferences). One might alternately imagine a gift economy, or gift-giving relationship, where altruism plays the dominant role; for example, within an immediate family. Other cases may be intermediate, as within a small tribe or between friendship groups.[12]

Van de Ven's second category (which he calls "egoism I") begins with a gifts economy as in Kranton.[13] He extends this (especially in Van de Klundert and Van de Ven) to consider the benefits of gift exchange in a social context[14] – my discussion below largely falls into this category. Even where a gift exchange appears to provide less 'substantive utility' than a comparable market exchange, the seeming inadequacy may disappear when we also add in 'symbolic utility'. While a strict exchange-based approach does not allow for non-reciprocal giving, the symbolic benefits to the giver (and other benefits discussed below) may justify this.

[10] An initial gift can serve as a signal that one is averse to cheating, as in Camerer – Weigelt 1988; we return to this later. Gift giving in the Roman world (as shown in this book by K. Verboven) may have served this role in the absence of formal enforcement institutions.

[11] Kranton 1996 offers a formal model of this sort of gift economy. Arrow 1973 (among others) has argued that this sense of 'social responsibility' is vital to economic efficiency. Recent work, e.g., Guiso – Sapienza – Zingales 2006, argues that a common knowledge of trust and trustworthiness, perhaps *social capital*, is important to modern economic development. Akerlof 1982 argues that labor contracts and *efficiency wages* can be seen in terms of a gift exchange.

[12] A gift giving relationship might evolve into an explicitly recognized *quid pro quo*, which might evolve into an institutional market; this relationship is considered in a Roman context by Verboven in this volume.

[13] Kranton 1996.

[14] Van de Klundert – Van de Ven 1999.

3. Reputation and other rewards

The standard economic model considers a single maximization decision for each individual. Individuals do not separately maximize in distinct spheres, such as health, goods consumption, and reputation, but always consider the trade-offs both within and between these categories.[15] However, we typically model diminishing returns to consumption of each good, and some goods are seen as *necessities* – as the consumption of a necessity, say water, approaches zero, the individual would be willing to give up nearly anything else to get a small glass of water.

For the 'markets are efficient' predictions to come to bear, we require that every good (more broadly 'everything we care about') can be privately owned, priced, and traded, and one person's consumption comes at the expense of another's. But some things are difficult or impossible to buy or sell directly. Other goods are taboo to trade.[16] In particular, one cannot go to a store to purchase a good reputation.

In ancient and modern times prestige and reputation are seen as valuable in themselves (in addition to their instrumental value in influencing others and getting better treatment in a variety of spheres, including commercial transactions). In a sense we can directly 'eat our reputation'. Gifts and donations may be an indirect way of buying reputation. In signaling models, if some get more direct pleasure from giving then others, these 'good types' can separate themselves from the selfish types through their giving. A pair of individuals engaged in a repeated series of high-stakes gift exchange can also signal to one another, and to outsiders, their mutual trust and trustworthiness. Everyone can see that either party could 'quit while she is ahead', yet they do not, demonstrating their trustworthiness. Their trustworthiness may be driven by regard for one another specifically or as fellow humans, regard for principle, religious or moral values, and their patience and confidence in the long-term relationship. Some combination of these admirable traits – each of which suggests future trustworthiness – is being publicly signaled. This is exemplified by Bertelli's paper in the present volume: through gift exchange two men can sustain and increase the public perception of their esteem (τιμή).

The more well-regulated and rule-based the transactions are, the less they allow people to demonstrate their trustworthiness. In a formal market each transaction is carefully monitored by a government regulation or a private authority. Where there is no scope to cheat there is no scope to prove ones

[15] Although in a particular instance we may limit ourselves to a narrow choice set and use simple heuristics.

[16] Roth 2007 calls these "repugnant transactions". This is relevant to the transfer of relics (see Carlà's contribution in this volume), and the teaching of philosophy (see Blank's article).

honesty. Gift exchanges as well as less regulated transactions may offer such benefits.[17]

This discussion relates to Van de Ven's third category: "social approval". His depiction has the flavor of a zero-sum game, here social status is only gained at the expense of another. However, this is one of numerous models where giving conveys status or reputation (see, e.g., Harbaugh in the philanthropy context).[18] In his game-theoretic equilibrium the less-wealthy player can be driven out of this 'giving game' leading to non-reciprocal giving; inadequate gifts can also be explained under given assumptions.[19]

4. Gifts and shared consumption

Fireworks are often considered a 'public good', being largely non-excludable (people who do not purchase them see them anyways) and non-rival (my seeing the fireworks does not reduce your ability to see them). However, every year millions of people purchase and light fireworks on holidays such as New Years, American Independence Day, and Guy Fawkes Night; abundant public displays are followed by families setting off their own small rockets. Presumably there is a particular enjoyment from 'ownership' – specifying exactly where and when they are set off, and knowing that you are the cause of the flash and bang. Dur and Glazer model the relevance of this 'desire for impact' in the work environment,[20] citing a range of psychologists and social scientists; McCleland in particular.[21]

Gift-giving may have a similar nature. Even though the receiver may be wearing the sweater, the giver has chosen its color and brand, may enjoy seeing it worn, and may enjoy the sense of impact. The giver may also specify the way it is to be used, retaining some control, i.e., 'ownership'.[22] In this way the consumption or the use value may be shared through a gift exchange, bringing costs and benefits not offered by a market exchange.

[17] Bowles 1998 makes a related point. Van de Klundert – Van de Ven 1999 model an equilibrium where some goods are exchanged via a gift economy and others through a market economy; however, the distinction may not always be so clear.

[18] Harbaugh 1998b.

[19] The story: making my gift less beneficial to you makes you less well-off, giving you a higher utility of own-consumption, making it relatively more expensive to give, improving my position in the giving game.

[20] Dur – Glazer 2008.

[21] McCleland 1988.

[22] The *peculium* offers an interesting example; see Fleckner in the present volume.

5. The deadweight loss/gain of Christmas and bounded rationality

Some economists are puzzled by the ubiquity of gift-giving. Waldfogel has prominently noted and tried to estimate the "deadweight loss of Christmas", extrapolating from a survey on a select group of students.[23] The essential argument is that, at best, the giver will choose the object that the receiver would have chosen with the money, and more likely, if the giver does not perfectly understand the preferences of the recipient, the gift will be mismatched. In the terminology of Van de Ven,[24] the gift will be "inadequate", offering less pleasure to the recipient then she could have obtained herself with the same expenditure.

Others have questioned Walfogel's empirical findings,[25] instead finding a gain in value over the cost of the gifts. The standard explanation for this is that gifts gain a sentimental or symbolic value. Other gains may accrue to the giver, such as the shared consumption benefits and signaling benefits considered above, or the ability to signal one's understanding of the receiver's tastes and needs.[26]

A further benefit to the receiver arises in the context of bounded rationality, in particular considering 'regret aversion'.[27] Choosing to consume a luxurious good may lead both to feelings of guilt and regret. Indeed, for many people simply the act of handing over money is painful. It forces the consumer to consider what she is sacrificing (her 'opportunity cost') in making this choice. And she may have built-in feelings of guilt in spending (this may be a mechanism to counter myopia and even a survival mechanism).[28]

If she is given a cash gift, this may go immediately into the 'general account'. And then if and when it is spent on a luxurious good, the joy of enjoying this good (e.g., drinking the $100 bottle of champagne) may be mitigated by the accompanying guilt in spending, and perhaps regret afterwards. On the other hand, if a person is given a fine wine as a gift, there is little choice but to consume it (at some point) – selling it would be both gauche and a considerable effort (and probably involve a financial loss relative to the retail price). Hence the recipient can enjoy the wine without the accompanying feeling of guilt, nor regret – she did not choose to purchase the wine herself. Similarly, if she gets a gift certificate to Victoria's Secret, she can purchase fripperies without worrying about whether this was the 'best' use of her money.

[23] Waldfogel 1993.

[24] Van de Ven 2000.

[25] Solnick – Hemenway 1996; List – Shogren 1998.

[26] Ed Glaeser made this final point in a New York Times Op-Ed., *In Defense of Holiday Gift-Giving* (29 Dec. 2009). This is echoed in the discussion of the "exchange of culturally appropriate and valued ... greeting gifts" in Bronze Age Cyprus: see Steel 2013, p. 7.

[27] Samuelson – Zeckhauser 1988.

[28] Suvorov – Van de Ven 2008.

This argument is undermined if the individual can direct the gifts she will receive (she could have asked for simple socks and underwear and not lingerie) or she experiences equivalent regret over the giver's decision ("he wasted his hard-earned money"). But directed gift-giving is often discouraged and many individuals express a preference for being surprised – further distancing themselves from the decision. It seems likely that, concerning regret, the recipient is at least somewhat distanced from the giver, so she feels less difficulty receiving the lingerie than purchasing it herself. She can persuade herself that the giver "enjoyed the act of giving". In fact, the institutionalized giving itself distances givers and recipients from the decision – "it's Christmas, I had to give something" is a convenient justification for extravagance. This argument also helps explain the popularity of credit cards that give 'hotel points' or frequent flyer miles, instead of just cash back. It is a 'sneaky' way to fool myself into putting something aside that I can only spend luxuriously, and it feels less like I am making a conscious decision to put money aside for frivolities. Note that the limited nature of holidays and birthdays, and the distancing aspect of gift-giving allows alleviation of the potential excesses of guilt and goal-setting without a complete abandonment of these rules and feelings which may be, on the whole, beneficial for survival and long term welfare.

I illustrate this point with a very basic model and example. Consider a 'psychological' utility function U(x,y) with two arguments (two goods), that is constructed from another 'material' utility function v(x,y).

$$U(x,y) = v(x,y) - \beta v(x',y')$$

where:

$$(x',y') \equiv argmax_{\tilde{x},\tilde{y}}\, v(\tilde{x} \neq x, \tilde{y} \neq y)\ s.t. \text{ standard constraints}$$

Essentially, the psychological utility U(x,y) represents the material utility from the choice made (x,y), subtracting a fraction of the utility of the next-best choice. This represents the utility of someone who feels a personal loss when considering what she sacrificed when making her choice.

Example: $x \in \{0,1\}$, $y \in \{0,1\}$, $v(1,0) = 2$, $v(0,1) = 1$, with income $I = 1$ and no other constraints, unit prices, budget constraint: $x + y \leq 1$.

Optimization of U(x,y) here leads to consumption $(x^*, y^*) = (1,0)$, second choice $(x',y') = (0,1)$ and resulting utility $U(1,0) = v(x,y) - \beta\, v(x',y') = 2 - \beta$. In comparison, with the additional constraint y=0 (or constraint x=1) we get the same consumption but utility $U(1,0) = v(1,y) - \beta v(0,0) = 2$. This example illustrates that the 'gift certificate' that constrains choice may increase utility.

6. Public (or anonymous) giving to signal values and support

Van de Ven's fourth approach, "gifts as signaling device", following, e.g., Camerer,[29] involves a gift as a preamble to a later interaction requiring mutual investments. This assumes individuals have different 'types', and 'honest types' prefer to cooperate when others do, while 'cheaters' always prefer not to cooperate. Here the gift serves as a way for the honest to make themselves better off by separating themselves from the cheaters. For this 'separation' to work we require that an honest player gains more from convincing others she is honest than a cheater would gain from falsely convincing them of this. This approach permits reciprocal or non-reciprocal giving: either in an individual interaction (when the honest type wastes her signal on a cheater) or regularly (if one group is seen as trustworthy enough *ex ante* so as not to need to signal). It can also explain inadequacy: mutual exchange of valuable gifts may not be a truly costly signal.

The above approach fails to explain anonymous giving. Hugh-Jones and Reinstein consider the benefit of taking a costly action, here called a "ritual", that is observed only in its aggregate:

> "Suppose … that conditional cooperators gain more from inducing others' future cooperation. Then, performing the ritual may send a signal that 'there is one additional cooperator in the group', and only conditional cooperators may perform the ritual, justifying this belief".[30]

Making an anonymous gift to charity, doing a random act of kindness, or taking care of a public resource may let other conditional cooperators know that they are not alone.[31] This may improve future cooperation, particularly where it cannot be easily enforced. In particular, they envision:

> "…difficult or propitious periods, in which the present benefits of selfishness may outweigh the future costs of a breakdown of cooperation… poor harvests… bankruptcy… a prolonged strike, and… frontline combat".[32]

The authors argue that earlier anonymous contributions are more informative than public ones. While selfish types may feel compelled to give when giving is public – to preserve their reputation and avoid being excluded, when giving is

[29] Camerer 1988.

[30] Hugh-Jones – Reinstein 2010.

[31] Religious gifts to the gods in Ancient Greece, often of substantial value, publicly recorded, and typically presented without a name or text, may have served this function – see I. Berti in this volume. Also see M. Gori's article on Late Bronze Age bronze hoards and M. Satlow's contribution on tithing in Roman Palestine, although the latter seems to have conferred a variety of potential benefits.

[32] Hugh-Jones – Reinstein 2013.

anonymous only the intrinsically motivated, conditional cooperators (or altruists) will give. Thus, when giving is anonymous, the aggregate rate of giving will be a more accurate signal that may allow better future coordination. However, this holds under the specified conditions where greater knowledge of others' types (preferences) helps on average; in alternative cases ignorance is preferable.

7. Gifts of public goods and taxation

In the standard model, individuals contribute to a *Pure Public Good*, which has two defining characteristics. (1) It is *non-rival* – everyone derives a benefit from the aggregate provision and one person's use does not reduce another's benefit; (2) It is *non-excludable*: no one can be shut out from using it. If the welfare of the poor is a general concern, services (or direct transfers) for the needy may also fall into this category. However, many goods provided by government, such as health care and education, arguably do not. This definition is strict; even the strongest examples – such as a radio broadcast or public defense – may not exactly meet these definitions. But even *impure* public goods, with some *congestion* and/or some ability to exclude, are thought to be under-provided by the market in general.

This is often labeled the 'free-rider' problem: if the contributor does not derive the full benefit of her contribution, the aggregate contribution will fall short of the efficient provision. Depending on relative preferences and the slope of the benefit functions, contributions, even from the selfish, may be non-zero. For example, I may put a streetlight in front of my house because my private benefit exceeds the cost, even if I ignore the benefit for the rest of the town. However, this will be, in general, suboptimal.[33] If all members of society could be compelled to give somewhat more, all would be better off. But, at equilibrium – where the good is underprovided – no individual will have an incentive to unilaterally contribute any more.

Enforced taxation is seen as a response to the aforementioned free-riding problem. If individual benefits of each type of public good can be measured (this is itself a difficult *mechanism design information aggregation* problem), these can be sponsored by the government and paid for through general tax revenue. Thus, in theory, *allocative* efficiency – the right mix of private and public goods – can be achieved. However, the information aggregation problem remains, as do difficult issues of public choice. The political environment might not be trusted to make the right decisions, nor the policymakers to implement these efficiently. Furthermore, in order to redistribute to the poor, taxes (or benefits) basically

[33] In addition, there may be coordination problems: I might be better off buying one streetlamp if my neighbor does not, but I may prefer to wait to see if she will buy it first. Here the equilibrium predicts one of us will buy the streetlamp, but the coordination may not be easily resolved.

must depend on individual choices; e.g., my income tax bill depends on my income which in turn depends in part on my hours worked. Thus the tax system may cause distortions. I might farm for only 30 hours per week if there is a 25% tax, even though I would be willing to farm for an additional ten hours if I were allowed to keep all of the additional produce.

Where does this leave charitable giving and philanthropy? Is it something the government should encourage? Such gifts have been interpreted as driven by the desire to attain private benefits from supplementing a public good.[34] However, this interpretation is problematic, particularly in explaining large individual voluntary contributions to causes with diffuse benefits.[35] Essentially, in contrast to a reasonable interpretation of the public goods model, some individuals give far too much, give to too wide a selection of charities,[36] and donations seem to be not substantially 'crowded out' by other contributions. Furthermore, there is strong experimental and observational evidence that giving is driven by other motivations. These include reputation-seeking,[37] reciprocity,[38] personal social pressure,[39] and empathy.[40] There is also some evidence made that people donate to improve their self-image ('self-signaling')[41] and apply self-serving justifications to avoid donating.[42]

Should we exert strong pressure and offer incentives to encourage charitable giving, or should we rely on the modern welfare state? If public aid 'crowds out' or substitutes for private giving, or if strongly encouraging private giving leads to a smaller government, this is an important concern, motivating several further questions. Is private provision more or less efficient then government provision? Which leads to greater individual satisfaction, on the part of the donors or taxpayers? (There is some debate, however, over whether this "warm glow" should be included in policy considerations).[43] Which has a less distorting effect on other decisions, particularly the labor-leisure choice?

Recent work considers the incentive effects of 'taxation' or enforced contributions – on real effort and on additional contributions – in laboratory settings and small scale field settings.[44] The USA's Negative Income Tax experiments

[34] Becker 1974.
[35] Sugden 1982; Andreoni 1990; Duncan 2004; Atkinson 2009.
[36] Reinstein 2011.
[37] Harbaugh 1998a.
[38] Falk 2007.
[39] DellaVigna – List – Malmendier 2012.
[40] Andreoni – Rao 2010.
[41] Gneezy – Gneezy – Riener – Nelson 2012.
[42] Fong – Oberholzer-Gee 2011.
[43] Andreoni 2006.
[44] McKenzie 2008; Kossmeier – Ariely – Bracha 2009; Hall 2010; Blumkin – Ruffle – Ganun 2012; He 2012; Tonin – Vlassopoulos 2012.

found strong income and substitution effects of taxation.[45] However, none of these offered a direct comparison or examined the response of effort to knowing you would be asked,[46] nor compared this effect to that of enforced contributions.

David Cameron's "Big Society" speech[47] mentions both "the harm that means-tested benefits do to work incentives" and the desire to "create a new social norm around volunteering or charitable giving". An implicit assumption here is that encouraging charitable giving will not also impact incentives and the labor/leisure tradeoff. Such an effect would arise naturally from the models and evidence of recent authors,[48] where being the target of fundraising may reduce my welfare, although it induces me to donate. Other experiments have elicited a positive price that subjects are willing to pay avoid making a decision in a dictator game.[49] This disincentive is likely to play a greater role in a society that relies less on a tax-funded welfare state and relies more on aggressive fundraising, family, community, and religious pressure to induce giving and sharing. In pre-Welfare State societies, there were often strong expectations and obligations on patrons, landowners, and the heads of large family groups. Informal insurance arrangements in present-day low-income agrarian economies may also affect incentives.[50]

There is a longstanding debate over the incentives, efficiency, and virtues of relying on taxation versus encouraging voluntary contributions to fund public services and poor relief.[51] Another argument concerns the merits of personalized and connected giving versus institutionalized giving (e.g., giving locally to individuals and small charities versus giving to UNICEF). Historically, there has been a third category, sometimes called 'liturgy'. Wealthy and prominent citizens in the Greek world were essentially required to provide public goods, but they were able to claim these as their gifts, and claim some ownership and control over them.

Here I consider three dimensions of the personal benefit of giving, and how different institutions can satisfy this better or worse. The first aspect is the

[45] Robins 1985.

[46] Tonin – Vlassopoulos 2012 field experiment does examine the response to a variety of private incentives, automatic contributions, and commitments to contribute at a certain rate. However (i) they do not consider the anticipation of being asked ex-post, (ii) they use between-subject variation, vulnerable to demand and contrast effects, (iii) they do not directly compare a tax and donation regime that raises the same amount and (iv) their field experiment does not offer methodological guidance for future lab work.

[47] http://www.conservatives.com/News/Speeches/2009/11/David_Cameron_The_Big_Society.aspx [last access 13th Aug. 2013].

[48] Della Vigna – List – Malmendier 2009; von Kotzebue – Wigger 2008; Tonin – Vlassopoulos 2010.

[49] Broberg – Ellingsen –Johannesson 2007.

[50] Coate – Ravallion 1993.

[51] Vickrey 1962; Hall 2010.

voluntary nature, the idea that I can choose whether or not to make the donation; this may motivate giving in various models, including 'self signaling'. A second aspect is the public recognition. A third aspect is the personal connectedness to the gift; this includes whether one can claim it as their own gift, whether one can make decisions over its character and use, and whether one sees its direct impact on others in incremental sense. In the table below I note how these aspects are differently bundled in various modern and ancient institutions.

	Patronage	Liturgy	"Local" or individual donation	"UNICEF"	Taxation
Voluntary choice	Yes/Maybe	No	Yes	Yes	No
Public recognition	Yes	Yes	Maybe	Little	No
Personal connection	Yes	Yes	Yes	No	No

The voluntary choice aspect is clearly removed through taxation, but it may also arguably be removed through great social pressure. If one is compelled to give, they may no longer derive some of the self-satisfaction of having chosen to give. The voluntary aspect is also removed in the Greek institution of liturgy.[52] There is neurological evidence that the hedonic benefits of giving stem, in part, from the *voluntary* nature of the contribution.[53]

Private and personal giving – evolving away from euergetism (see Colpaert in the present volume, who claims this is removed from the modern economy), and away from patronage, has largely been institutionalized in modern times. The church played some role in doing this, when private giving was channeled through the power of bishops. 'Giving' through taxation is clearly institutionnalized. Larger organizations like UNICEF have also depersonalized giving, removing the connection between giving, empathy, and a feeling of ownership. The liturgy institution may have preserved this while taking away the voluntary aspect. There is evidence that visible impact, a personal connection,[54] and the ability to make choices are important drivers of giving,[55] and that these are crucial to the emotional benefits of giving.[56]

[52] See here L. Cecchet.

[53] Harbaugh – Mayr – Burghart 2007.

[54] Jenni – Loewenstein 1997.

[55] Anecdotally, we can observe the success of organizations like "DonorsChoose.org", which allows specifically targeted gifts to US school classrooms, and claims to have raised over $175 million http://www.donorschoose.org/about/impact.html [last access 13th Apr. 2013]. Kiva.org offers the opportunity to choose to lend to a small entrepreneur, underwent some controversy when it was discovered that the loans had already been

Public recognition is absent from most tax regimes, and to an extent absent from large charitable gifts, and lessened through institutions that encourage anonymous giving. Here liturgy is interesting, as it may preserve the public recognition and personal connection aspects, while removing the voluntary aspect, alleviating free-riding problems.

Bibliography

Akerlof, George A.: *The Market for "Lemons": Quality Uncertainty and the Market Mechanism*, in: *The Quarterly Journal of Economics* 84 (1970), pp. 488-500.

Akerlof, George A.: *Labor Contracts as Partial Gift Exchange*, in: *The Quarterly Journal of Economics* 97 (1982), pp. 543-569.

Aknin, Lara B. – Elizabeth W. Dunn – Ashley V. Whillans – Adam M. Grant – Michael I. Norton: *Making a Difference Matters: Impact Unlocks the Emotional Benefits of Prosocial Spending*, in: *Journal of Economic Behavior & Organization* 88 (2013), pp. 90-95.

Andreoni, James: *Impure Altruism and Donations to Public Goods: A Theory of Warm-Glow Giving*, in: *The Economic Journal* 100 (1990), pp. 464-477.

Andreoni, James: *Philanthropy. Handbook of Giving, Reciprocity and Altruism*, Amsterdam 2006.

Andreoni, James – Justin M. Rao: *The Power of Asking: How Communication Affects Selfishness, Empathy, and Altruism*, in: *Journal of Public Economics* 95 (2010), pp. 513-520.

Arrow, Kenneth J.: *Social Responsibility and Economic Efficiency*, in: *Public Policy* 21 (1973), pp. 303-317.

Atkinson, Anthony B.: *Giving Overseas and Public Policy*, in: *Journal of Public Economics* 93 (2009), pp. 647-653.

Becker, Gary S.: *A Theory of Social Interactions*, in: *The Journal of Political Economy* 82 (1974), pp. 1063-1093.

Blumkin, Tomer – Bradley J. Ruffle – Yosef Ganun: *Are Income and Consumption Taxes Ever Really Equivalent? Evidence from a Real-Effort Experiment with Real Goods*, in: *European Economic Review* 56 (2012), pp. 1200-1219.

Bowles, Samuel: *Endogenous Preferences: The Cultural Consequences of Markets and Other Economic Institutions*, in: *Journal of Economic Literature* 36 (1998), pp. 75-111.

Broberg, Tomas – Tore Ellingsen – Magnus Johannesson: *Is generosity involuntary?*, in: *Economics Letters* 94 (2007), pp. 32-37.

arranged in advance and the lender's choice did not affect this. There was a similar controversy in the late 1990s when "several child sponsorship organizations amended their disclosures after a series of articles in The Chicago Tribune revealed that while they were soliciting money to sponsor a specific needy child, that child was not necessarily receiving the money directly": Stephanie Strom, *Confusion on Where Money Lent via Kiva Goes*, *The New York Times*, November 9, 2009.

[56] Aknin – Dunn – Whillans – Grant – Norton 2013.

Camerer, Colin: *Gifts as Economic Signals and Social Symbols*, in: *American Journal of Sociology* 94 (1988), *Supplement: Organizations and Institutions: Sociological and Economic Approaches to the Analysis of Social Structure*, pp. S180-S214.

Camerer, Colin – Keith Weigelt: *Experimental Tests of a Sequential Equilibrium Reputation Model*, in: *Econometrica* 56 (1988), pp. 1-36.

Coate, Stephen – Martin Ravallion: *Reciprocity without Commitment: Characterization and Performance of Informal Insurance Arrangements*, in: *Journal of Development Economics* 40 (1993), pp. 1-24.

DellaVigna, Stefano – John A. List – Ulrike Malmendier: Testing for Altruism and Social Pressure in Charitable Giving, *NBER Working Paper 15629* (2009) [http://www.nber.org /papers/w15629; last access 19th Aug. 2013].

Della Vigna, Stefano – John A. List – Ulrike Malmendier: *Testing for Altruism and Social Pressure in Charitable Giving*, in: *The Quarterly Journal of Economics* 127 (2012), pp. 1-56.

Duncan, Brian: *A Theory of Impact Philanthropy*, in: *Journal of Public Economics* 88 (2004), pp. 2159-2180.

Dur, Robert A. J. – Amihai Glazer: *The Desire for Impact*, in: *Journal of Economic Psychology* 29 (2008), pp. 285-300.

Falk, Armin: *Gift Exchange in the Field*, in: *Econometrica* 75 (2007), pp. 1501-1511.

Fong, Christina – Felix Oberholzer-Gee: *Truth in Giving: Experimental Evidence on the Welfare Effects of Informed Giving to the Poor*, in: *Journal of Public Economics* 95 (2011), pp. 436-444.

Fudenberg, Drew – Eric Maskin: *The Folk Theorem in Repeated Games with Discounting or with Incomplete Information*, in: *Econometrica* 54 (1986), pp. 533-554.

Gneezy, Ayelet – Uri Gneezy – Gerhard Riener – Leif D. Nelson: *Pay-What-You-Want, Identity, and Self-Signaling in Markets*, in: *Proceedings of the National Academy of Sciences of the United States of America* 109 (2012), pp. 7236-7240.

Guiso, Luigi – Paola Sapienza – Luigi Zingales: *Does Culture Affect Economic Outcomes?*, in: *The Journal of Economic Perspectives* 20 (2006), pp. 23-48.

Hall, Daniel T.: *The Efficiency-Equality Tradeoff in Public Sector Charity Provision*, in: *Research in Experimental Economics* 13 (2010), pp. 77-111.

Harbaugh, William T.: *The Prestige Motive for Making Charitable Transfers*, in: *American Economic Review* 88 (1998a), pp. 277-282.

Harbaugh, William T.: *What do Donations Buy? A Model of Philanthropy Based on Prestige and Warm Glow*, in: *Journal of Public Economics* 67 (1998b), pp. 269-84.

Harbaugh, William T. – Ulrich Mayr – Daniel R. Burghart: *Neural Responses to Taxation and Voluntary Giving Reveal Motives for Charitable Donations*, in: *Science* 316 (2007), pp. 1622-1625.

He, Tai-Sen: *Tax or Transfer? The Framing Effect of Redistribution Policy: Experimental Evidence, Job Market Paper* (2012) [http://www.econ.brown.edu/students/Tai-Sen_he/jmp.pdf; last access 19th Aug. 2013].

Hugh-Jones, David – David A. Reinstein: *The Benefit of Anonymity in Public Goods Games, Working Paper. University of Essex, Department of Economics, Discussion Papers 689* (2010) [http://davidreinstein.files.wordpress.com/2011/05/secret_santa_experiment_may.pdf; last access 19th Aug. 2013].

Hugh-Jones, David – David A. Reinstein: *Targeted Exclusion Can Reduce Cooperation in Public Goods Games*, in: *Mimeo* (2013) [http://www.webmeets.com/files/papers/res/

2013/13/Anonymity%20in%20PG%20Games%20Hugh-Jones%20and%20Reinstein%20%20Feb%202013%20update.pdf; last access 19th Aug. 2013].

Jenni, Karen – George Loewenstein: *Explaining the Identifiable Victim Effect*, in: *Journal of Risk and Uncertainty* 14 (1997), pp. 235-257.

Kossmeier, Stephan – Dan Ariely – Anat Bracha: *Doing Good or Doing Well? Image Motivation and Monetary Incentives in Behaving Prosocially*, in: *American Economic Review* 99 (2009), pp. 544-555.

Kranton, Rachel E.: *Reciprocal Exchange: A Self-Sustaining System*, in: *American Economic Review* 86 (1996), pp. 830-851.

Leijonhufvud, Axel: *Keynes and the Keynesians: A suggested interpretation*, in: *American Economic Review* 57 (1967), pp. 401-410.

List, John A. – Jason F. Shogren: *The Deadweight Loss of Christmas: Comment*, in: *American Economic Review* 88 (1998), pp. 1350-1355.

McClelland, David C.: *Human motivations*, Cambridge 1988.

McKenzie, *Tom: Tax or Beg? Mandatory Payments to Charity and their Effects on Donor Behavior, NCVO/VSSN Researching the Voluntary Sector 2009* (2008) [http://www.ncvo-vol.org.uk/sites/default/files/UploadedFiles/Research_Events/McKenzie.pdf, last access 19th Aug. 2013].

Nicholson, Walter – Christopher M, Snyder: *Microeconomic Theory: Basic Principles and Extensions*, Stamford 2011[11].

Reinstein, David A.: *Does One Charitable Contribution Come at the Expense of Another?*, in: *The BE Journal of Economic Analysis and Policy* 11 (2011), pp. 1-54.

Robins, Philip K.: *A Comparison of the Labor Supply Findings from the Four Negative Income Tax Experiments*, in: *Journal of Human Resources* 20 (1985), pp. 567-582.

Roth, Alvin E.: *Repugnance as a Constraint on Markets*, in: *Journal of Economic Perspectives* 21 (2007), pp. 37-58.

Samuelson, William – Richard Zeckhauser: *Status Quo Bias in Decision Making*, in: *Journal of risk and uncertainty* 1 (1988), pp. 7-59.

Smith, Adam: *An Inquiry into the Nature and Causes of the Wealth of Nations*, London 1776.

Solnick, Sara J. – David Hemenway: *The Deadweight Loss of Christmas: Comment*, in: *American Economic Review* 86 (1996), pp. 1299-1305.

Steel, Louise: *Materiality and Consumption in the Bronze Age Mediterranean*, New York – London 2013.

Sugden, Robert: *On the Economics of Philanthropy*, in: *Economic Journal* 92 (1982), pp. 341-350.

Suvorov, Anton – Jeroen Van de Ven: *Goal Setting as a Self-Regulation Mechanism, Working Paper* (2008) [http://papers.ssrn.com/sol3/papers.cfm?abstract_id=1286029; last access 19th Aug. 2013].

Tonin, Mirco – Michael Vlassopoulos: *An Experimental Investigation of Intrinsic Motivations for Giving, Discussion Papers in Economics and Econometrics 1008* (2010) [http://eprints.soton.ac.uk/154439/; last access 19th Aug. 2013].

Tonin, Mirco – Michael Vlassopoulos: *Social Incentives Matter: Evidence from an Online Real Effort Experiment, IZA Discussion Paper 6716* (2012) [http://ftp.iza.org/dp6716.Pdf; last access 19th Aug. 2013].

van de Klundert, Theo – Jeroen van de Ven: *On the Viability of Gift Exchange in a Market Environment, CentER Discussion Paper* 1999-113, pp. 1-28; available at http://arno.uvt.nl/show.cgi?fid=3993 [last access 17th Feb 2014].

van de Ven, Jeroen: *The Economics of the Gift, Discussion Paper from Tilburg University, Center for Economic Research*; available at http://arno.uvt.nl/show.cgi? fid=4105 [last access 17th Feb 2014].

Vickrey, William: *One Economist's View of Philanthropy*, in: *Philanthropy and Public Policy*, ed. by Frank G. Dickinson, New York 1962, pp. 31-56.

Von Kotzebue, Alexander – Berthold U. Wigger: *Charitable Giving and Fundraising: When Beneficiaries Bother Benefactors, Working Paper* (2008) [http://www.uni-graz.at/socialpolitik/papers/von%20Kotzebue.pdf; last access 25th Feb. 2014].

Waldfogel, Joel: *The Deadweight Loss of Christmas*, in: *American Economic Review* 83 (1993), pp. 1328-1336.

Walras, Léon: *Eléments d'economie politique pure ou théorie de la richesse sociale*, Paris 1926^4; Engl. Transl. *Elements of Pure Economics or the Theory of Social Wealth*, London 1954.

LUCIO BERTELLI

The Ratio of Gift-Giving in the Homeric Poems

1. Introduction

For whomever works on Homeric institutions – marriage, social relations, and so forth – it is unavoidable to face, in A. Snodgrass' words, "the sorely vexed question [that] cannot be shirked":[1] do these institutions refer to a specific historical context, and if they do, what age is this?

Scholars are divided between those that believe that Homeric society is

> "an artificial cultural amalgam of elements derived from many different stages of the developing oral tradition"[2]

and therefore completely or partially lacking historical reliability,[3] and those that hold that Homeric society is a coherent and historical society. These, however, disagree as for the chronological setting of this society: some indicate the tenth-ninth century BCE (e.g. Finley),[4] while others prefer a dating a low as the early seventh century BCE.[5]

But even if we accept that the Homeric poems depict a historical and coherent society, the medium of its depiction – the Homeric poems themselves – is the product of a long tradition of oral poetry which took shape over at least three centuries (eleventh-eighth c. BCE). According to a reasonable hypothesis, based on the typical features of an oral tradition, the 'saga' – i.e. the contents of the poems (the ten-years war, the heroes, Odysseus and his voyage etc.) – dates

[1] Snodgrass 1971, p. 389. I wish to extend a special thank to my former student dr. Mirko Canevaro, now Chancellor's Fellow in Classics at the University of Edinburgh, for his generous collaboration in the translation of the text and for the many bibliographical suggestions that gave me.

[2] Kirk 1962, p. 181; see also p. 123; Snodgrass 1971, p. 389. See also Long 1970, pp. 122 and p. 137, n. 57; Cartledge 1996, pp. 687-689.

[3] See Cartledge 1996, p. 688: although for Cartledge the so-called "Homeric world" is an "universo fittizio", he admits that "ciò naturalmente non significa che qualsiasi dettaglio dei *Realien* in Omero sia frutto di una pura invenzione o debba essere di necessità falso o distorto".

[4] Finley 1954, p. 55.

[5] Late 9th-8th century BCE: Raaflaub 1991, p. 251; 1997, pp. 624-648; 1998, pp. 169-193; Quiller (1981); 2nd half of the 8th century: Janko 1982, pp. 228-231; Morris 1986a, pp. 81-138; 1997, pp. 535-559; ca. 700 BCE: Crielaard 1995; 2002; Osborne 2004.

all the way back to the age when the Homeric epos first took shape, and was transmitted generation after generation until its form was fixed in the eighth century. On the other hand the 'fiction' – the culture and the society (or at least some of their features – in which the action is set) "is created directly out of immediate experience and visible environment" of the poet that gave final shape to this oral tradition.[6] This distinction between traditional 'saga' and 'fiction', which is contemporary to the poet, has been generally accepted in Homeric scholarship. One of its most recent variants has been elaborated by I. Morris on the basis of the studies by M. Parry and A. Lord on oral tradition:

> "The institutions, attitudes, and conditions of action that we find in the *Iliad* and *Odyssey* must of necessity be derived in some way from those of the functioning societies that Homer himself knew".[7]

Thus, the widespread importance of gift-giving in Homeric society is generally recognized even by those that deny any historical reliability to Homer.[8] M. Finley is responsible for recognizing the importance of this custom: in *The World of Odysseus* [9] he demonstrated that

> "gift-giving in the Homeric poems is consistent, I might even say absolutely consistent, with the analysis made by Mauss (who, curiously, ignored the ancient Greeks in his study)".[10]

To the objection that Homer did not describe any actual historical society, but nothing more than a 'heroic ideal', Finley countered the following paradox:

> "by a most remarkable intuition, Homer was a predecessor of Marcel Mauss, except that he (or his tradition) *invented* an institution which nearly three thousand years later Mauss *discovered* to be a social reality"[11].

He therefore concluded that gift-exchange,

[6] Carpenter 1946, p. 32.
[7] Morris 1986a, p. 90.
[8] See in particular Quiller 1981; Donlan 1982; 1989b; Morris 1986b; Beidelman 1989; Seaford 1994; von Reden 1995.
[9] In particular Finley 1954, pp. 70-75; 101-113; 140-143.
[10] Finley 1974, p. 16; Mauss 1923-1924, p. 139, n. 2, actually apologized for not taking into account gift-exchange among the Greeks because of his insufficient knowledge of Greek law.
[11] Finley 1974, p. 16.

> "if it is integral to the account and reasonably consistent in the portrayal, must – I choose my words carefully – must be accepted by us as part of a social reality. It cannot be the product of poetic imagination or invention".[12]

And, of course, the most convincing parallel to the Homeric institution was found by Finley among the 'primitive' peoples studied by Mauss and other anthropologists.[13] Yet it was not necessary to look so far afield, and to populations so different from those of the Homeric poems. Looking back only a few centuries, and dealing with the practice of gift-giving in the Mycenaean Age, one can not only find the word *doron* with the very same meaning as in Homeric (and later) Greek time periods,[14] but also contexts of gift-exchange analogous to the Homeric ones: offers of gifts to gods and men.[15] And moreover, gift-exchange was a wide-spread practice also in contemporary Near-East societies.[16] The objection that the chronological break between Mycenaean and Homeric society does not allow such comparisons is weak: gift-exchange is a long-standing institution. It survived the archaism and is fully attested in the *poleis* of classical times.[17] There is therefore no reason to believe that it could not survive the transition between the end of the Mycenaean Age and the 'Dark Age'. Snodgrass objects that if Finley's description of Homeric society is correct, it lacked such a "high material standard of living"[18] to support the abundant gift-exchange described by Homer. Yet the archaeological finds in this respect are very unhelpful,[19] and it is important to keep in mind that the Homeric epics do not provide us with a precise picture of a specific society,[20] but rather with an ideologically charged depiction of society from an "aristocratic vantage point",[21]

[12] Finley 1974, p. 16.
[13] Finley 1954, p. 73; see also Finley 1974, p.16.
[14] *Do-so-mo* = *dosmós* ("gift made to a deity"): PY Un 718 (Ventris – Chadwick 1959, pp. 282-283; Chadwick – Baumbach 1963, p. 185); *do-ra* ("offerings given to deities"): PY Kn 02 (Tn 316; see Ventris – Chadwick 1959, pp. 286-289); see also PY Ta 711 (Ventris – Chadwick 1959, pp. 335-336) perhaps an inventory of gifts given when a *da-mo-ko-ro* ("official of *da-mo*") was appointed (so Webster 1964^2, p. 13) or, as Palmer 1957, p. 86, supposed, "a tolerably complete household equipment deposited in the tomb" of Si(?)kewa Damoklos.
[15] Webster 1964^2, pp. 12-13.
[16] Webster 1964^2, pp. 12-13.
[17] Snodgrass 1980, p. 132: "Yet this element in it, the phenomenon of gift-exchange and hospitality, particularly with foreigners, remained entirely familiar in the Greek world long after Homer". See also Morris 1986b.
[18] Snodgrass 1974, p. 124.
[19] See Morris 1986b, p. 9.
[20] Seaford 1994, p. 5; see also Morris 1986b, p. 120.
[21] Morris 1986b, p. 124.

in a period in which the aristocratic model was entering a crisis.[22] Therefore, gift-exchange, which is not an invention of the Dark Ages, had to be accommodated in its material contents to the ideal standard of wealth and generosity of the *aristoi* that practised it.

Since Finley's *World of Odysseus*, scholarship about gift-giving in Homer has generally attempted to match the Homeric evidence to the categories used to describe the same phenomenon in the so-called 'primitive' societies studied by anthropologists.[23] This assimilation of Homeric society with 'primitive' societies[24] has been justified with the remark that Homeric society is still mostly pre-political.[25] We shall not deal here with the complex issue of whether comparisons are legitimate between societies that are very different in terms of social structure and culture.[26] We shall instead take into account two fundamental features of Homeric society that are key for the understanding of gift-exchange in Homer. The Homeric king – whether he is called with the authoritative title of *anax* or with the term *basileus* – has no longer anything to do with the *wanaks* of the Pylos or Knossos tablets.[27] The Homeric *basileus*, according to a hypothesis that is supported by the continuity of the term, stems from the official named in the tablets *qasireu* (> *basileus*), in charge of a local community, possibly with the help of a council of elders, (myc. *Kerosija* = *geronsia* > *gerousia*).[28] After

[22] Morris 1986b, pp. 124-125; see also Raaflaub 1991, pp. 213-215; Donlan 1998, p. 54; Crielaard 2002.

[23] See in particular Donlan 1982; Herman 1987; Seaford 1994; von Reden 1995; Morris 1986b.

[24] On the use of anthropological categories connected with Sahlins' "tribal societies" (see in particular Sahlins 1965 and Service 1971^2). See also Donlan 1982, pp. 172-173.

[25] See Posner 1979; Runciman 1982; see also Thomas 1966a; Morris 1986a, pp. 104-105; Donlan 1989b; Raaflaub 1991, pp. 239-247.

[26] But see Schofield 1986 for some reservation about the "primitivist step" of the social representation provided by Finley in *The World of Odysseus*.

[27] Homeric kingship and its relationship with the Mycenaean past has been extensively studied in Homeric scholarship: see e.g. Leumann 1950, pp. 42-44; Finley 1954, pp. 85-124; Finley 1957, pp. 140-144; Thomas 1966b; Andreev 1979; Quiller 1981; Gschnitzer 1991; Raaflaub 1991, pp. 230-238; 1997, pp. 633-645; Hammer 1997. On the Mycenean *wanax* see in particular Thomas 1976 (with extensive bibliography). On the different uses and meanings of *anax* and *basileus* in the Homeric poems, see Yamagata 1997; see also the two fundamental entries Grimm (*anax*) and Schmidt (*basileus*) in the *Lexikon des frühgriechischen Epos*.

[28] *Qasireu* in the Pylos tablets: PY Jn 431; Jo 438; 601; 845, always with a proper noun; it is likely to indicate a local magistrate with authority over the distribution of bronze and gold; the connection with the *kerosija* (*gerousia*) is clear from PY An 22, where it appears together with a name mentioned elsewhere as *quasireu*. On the fuctions of the *qasireu* see Page 1959, pp. 186-188; Ventris – Chadwick 1959, pp. 121-122; Lejeune 1961, p. 422;

the fall of the Mycenaean state structures, centered on the palace of the *wanax*, the local *basileus*, throughout the period of territorial dispersion of village communities in the Dark Age,[29] becomes a 'paramount chief'. This is due to his military ability, to the prestige of his ancestry and, most importantly, to his wealth that allows him to secure a substantial following of *hetairoi* and supporters.[30] The foundation of his power was the ability to attract followers through alliances and through his generosity: hence the fundamental role of gift-giving to secure their loyalty. This key figure in Homeric society, who has no absolute authority according to the Mycenaean ideal, but is rather no more than a "highborn leader" along his peers (this is the minimalist definition provided by Drews),[31] has often been interpreted within the anthropological framework of the 'big man', typical of the tribal societies of Melanesia, which shows features consistent with the Homeric picture of the *basileus*. These features are: personal power founded on military prowess, leadership acquired through generous distributions of gifts to the followers, precarious status due to the strong competition.[32] The applicability of this analogy to the definition of the functions of the Homeric *basileus* is however limited. The *basileus*, in fact, unlike the 'big man', acts within a social context lacking "large corporate groups" at a higher level than the *oikos*.[33] *Phylai* and *phratriai*, which are scantily attested in Homer,[34] were not, as already noted by Bourriot and Roussel,[35] "kinship groups" of a genetic or tribal nature. They were rather "loosely organized political/ military associations"[36] founded on geographical vicinity and subjected to a *basileus*.[37] The core around which the Homeric society revolves, and which constitutes the power-basis of the *basileis*, is the *oikos*. This has been recognized by Finley, and supported by much scholarship ever since:

Pugliese Carratelli 1962, pp. 178-180; Thomas 1976, pp. 106-107.
29 Snodgrass 1971, pp. 360-378.
30 See Finley 1957, pp. 139-202; Page 1959, pp. 186-188; Pugliese Carratelli 1962; Maddoli 1970, pp. 51-57; Donlan 1985; 1989b; 2007.
31 Drews 1983, p. 129.
32 For the use of this anthropological model see in particular Quiller 1981; Donlan 1982; 1985; 1989b; 2007.
33 Donlan 1985, p. 302: Donlan uses often the category of the "big man" also elsewhere, and highlights the fact the in the Homeric society there are no "nested corporate groups" (2007, p. 35); see also Donlan 1985, p. 302; 1989b, p. 8. He also recognizes the derivation of the "local leader, a 'big man' type" from the Mycenaean *qasireu* (Donlan 1989b, p. 20).
34 *Il.* 2. 362-363; 668; 9.63-64.
35 See Bourriot 1976; Roussel 1976.
36 Donlan 1985, p. 298; see also Roussel 1976, pp. 39-50; 95-97; 109-122.
37 See Donlan 2007, p. 32.

> "The authoritarian household, the *oikos*, was the centre around which life was organized, from which flowed not only the satisfaction of material needs, including security, but ethical norms and values, duties, obligations, and responsibilities, social relationship, and relations with the gods. The *oikos* was not merely the family, it was all the people of the household and its goods..."[38]

And the centre of the *oikos* is the *thalamos*, the warehouse where the riches (*keimelia*) gathered through gift-exchange were kept, ready to be used again for further offers to guests and gods.[39] The acquisition of precious objects is tangible evidence that the *oikos* was the centre from which the network of relationships with the outside world spread, whether these relationships were pacific ones (marriage, guest-friendship) or aggressive ones (sacking, plundering).[40] The riches of the *oikos*,[41] derived from the property of the *basileus* (cattle, land),[42] which served the purpose of supporting the family, the other permanent members of the *oikos* (slaves, *therapontes*, i.e. retainers) and the foreign guests; and from the proceedings of war, sacking and plundering (mostly cattle and slaves). But the other main venue of accumulation of riches in the economy of the *oikos*, in particular as far as precious metals and objects (items of clothing, cloaks, carpets, weapons etc.) were concerned, has its origin in gift-giving and exchange which took place during the travels of the Homeric heroes.[43] These goods (*keimelia*) were kept in the 'warehouse' of the household and were a reserve available for gift-giving in any circumstance. The gifts exchanged or donated were fundamental in the economy of the *oikos* and for its prestige, and they ritually sanctioned all social relationships in the Homeric world, from marriage, through reparation for an offence, to ransom of dead and living.[44]

[38] See Finley 1954, p. 66; see also Quiller 1981, pp. 117-124; Donlan 1989, pp. 7-13; Raaflaub 1997, pp.630-633.
[39] *Il.* 6.288-295; *Od.* 2.337-343. See Finley 1954, pp. 70-72.
[40] This is the "negative reciprocity" effected through violence that is discussed by Sahlins 1965, pp.148-149. This phenomenon has been described in the Homeric poems by Donlan 1982, pp. 141-143.
[41] Of course, speaking of *oikos* in Homer, one refers to the *oikoi* of the *aristoi* or *basileis*, not of the *demos*: as a model of small farmer one could point to Laertes, the father of Odysseus, who lives away from the city, in a small farm with only a few servants, and who farms by himself his "well-kept field" (*Od.* 24.203-12).
[42] See e.g. the list of Odysseus' riches by Eumeus at *Od.* 14.96-104; Odysseus is also the owner of a *temenos* in Ithaca (*Od.* 17.299), which Telemachus inherited in the absence of his father, as we learn from *Od.* 11.185; for the private property of the *basileus* (*temenos*) cf. *Il.* 6.194; 9.574; 12.313; 18.550; 20.184; *Od.* 6.293; 17.299; cf. Finley 1957, pp. 149-156; Link 1994, pp. 241-245.
[43] See *Od.* 4.125-132; 14.191-354; 17.425; 19.172-202; 24.266-79.
[44] See Finley 1954, p. 75.

Claiming, therefore, that in Homer

> "gift-giving remains little more than a polite custom and never takes on [...] institutional aspects"[45]

equates to denying the structural role of gift-exchange in Homeric society. It also means ignoring that this practice is described through a remarkably specialized language, which cannot be the invention of the *aoidos* that gave the poems their final form, since this language must have formed throughout the oral tradition of the poems, and must have been recognizable by their audience.

2. The vocabulary of the gift in Homer.

The most generic term, which is suitable for most contexts, is δῶρον/(plur.) δῶρα. This has its own formulaic use:[46] it is used to refer to gifts in compensation for an offence, as ransom,[47] as rewards for services,[48] or in connection with guest-relationships,[49] and marriage.[50] Yet in order to refer to gifts given to a guest, Homeric Greek also uses specialized terms such as ξείνια/ξεινήϊα, stemming from ξεῖνος (foreigner/guest), which are part of an extensive lexical family.[51] The act of giving a gift is often expressed through the *nomes actionis*

[45] Hooker 1989, p. 90: Hooker of course does not believe in a 'Homeric society' with a historical foundation according to the model of Snodgrass (p. 87). For criticism of Hooker's method see Seaford 1994, pp. 14-15, n. 59.

[46] ἀγλαὰ δῶρα (at the end of the verse): *Il.* 1.213; 11.124; 16.381; 867; 18.84; 19.18; 24.278; 475; 536; *Od.* 4.589; 7.132; 9.201; 16.230; 19.413, alternative to κάλλιμα δῶρα (*Od.* 4.130; 8.439; 15.206).

[47] *Il.* 1.213; 9.121; 261; 263; 378; 602; 604; 679; 699; 18.449; 19.172; 190; 248; 24.447; *Od.* 9.201.

[48] *Il.* 4.97; 9.576; 598; 10.401; 17.225; 23.297 (to avoid providing a service); 24.434; *Od.* 2.186; 15.537 – 17.164 – 19.310.

[49] This is the most wide-spread use in the *Odyssey*: *Il.* 9.121; 23.745; *Od.* 1.311; 4.130; 589; 8.397; 417; 420; 439; 545; 11.339; 357; 13.41; 135; 15.51; 75; 206; 16.230; 327; 17.76; 21.13; 24.273; 285; 314; gifts from a grandfather (Autolicus) to his grandson (Odysseus): *Od.* 19.413; 460; 24.335.

[50] *Od.* 15.18 (in endyadis with ἔεδνα); 18.279; 282; 286; 291; 301; 303; 20.342.

[51] ξείνια ("gifts of a host"): *Il.* 11.779; 18.387; *Od.* 5.91; 9.229; 356; 365; 517; 14.404; 15.188; 514; 19.185; 20.296; formulaic expression ἵνα τοι πὰρ ξείνια θείω (*Il.* 18.387 = *Od.* 5.91; 9.517); ξεινήϊα: *Il.* 6.218; 10.269; 11.20; 18.408; *Od.* 3.490; 4.33; 8.389; 9.267; 370; 22.290; 24.273; ξενίη ("hospitality", abstract): *Od.* 24.286; 314; ξείνιος/ξένιος (epithet of Zeus protector of guests): *Il.* 13.625; *Od.* 9.271; 14.389; the oath formula in the *Odyssey* is noteworthy: ξενίη τε τράπεζα ("hosting table"): *Od.* 14.158; 17.155; 20.230;

δόσις (*Il.* 10.213; *Od.* 4.651; 18.287), with the formula δόσις δ' ὀλίγη τε φίλη τε ("small gift, yet dear": *Od.* 6. 208 = 14. 58) when the gift goes to guests in need (ξεῖνοί τε πτωχοί τε).[52] Another term within the semantic range of gift is δωτίνη (*Od.* 9.268; 11.352), which can however also have the meaning of payment owed by the subjects to a king in recognition of his *timé* (honour) (*Il.* 9.155 = 297)[53]. The same semantic range is covered by the *liparai*; θέμιστες in the very context of *Il.* 9.156 (= 298). These can be interpreted as "prerogatives",[54] or as "dues" or "customs" owed to the chief.[55]

The most specific term to refer to nuptial gifts, normally offered by the suitor to the father of the bride,[56] is ἕδνα/ἔεδνα (metrical variants). These are obviously more widely attested to in the *Odyssey*,[57] because of the centrality of the theme of Penelope's marriage in that context. Yet we find occurrences in the *Iliad*.[58] A particular kind of gift is the offer from the community; this is linked to the partition of a booty or a prize, or to the recognition of a privileged status: in this case the generic δῶρον is replaced by the technical term γέρας which marks

> "une avantage en nature, conféré par l'ensemble des membres d'un groupe social en vertu d'un partage, lors d'une prise de dépouilles... au moyen d'une mise préalable en commun de tout ce boutin sur lequel précisément est prélevé ce *géras*, part du chef".[59]

ξεινοδόκος ("the host"): *Il.* 3.354; *Od.* 8.210; 15.55; 70; ξεινίζειν ("being a host"): *Il.* 3.232; 6.174; *Od.* 3.355; 7.90; 24.288.

52 For the meaning of δόσις and its use in Homeric context see in particular Benveniste 1969, vol. 1, pp. 67-68.

53 For the meaning of this complex term see in particular Benveniste 1969, vol. 2, p.51: "Il s'agit de la part de la part d'honneur et d'avantages matériels que les hommes accordent à un personnage, en vertue de sa dignité, de sa condition". See also Adkins 1960; Pötscher 1960, pp. 35-38; Riedinger 1976; Filkenberg 1998.

54 See Benveniste 1969, vol. 1, p. 68; the interpretation of Hirzel 1907, pp. 39 and 414-415 ("gewinnbringenden Ermahnungen"), is not persuasive.

55 In fact Aristonicus in *Schol. Vet. D ad Il.* 9.156.a3 meant λιπαρὰς θέμιστας as λαμπροὺς φόρους ("rich tributes"). Shipp 1972^2, p. 267, and Hainsworth 1993, p. 79, also intend them in this sense.

56 See Seaford 1994, p. 16, but for the variety of cases see below.

57 *Od.* 1.277 = 2.196; 6.159; 8.318; 11.117; 282; 13.378 (= 11.117); 15.18; 16.391; 19.529; 21.161.

58 *Il.* 16.178; 190 = 22.472.

59 Benveniste 1969, vol. 2, p. 69; Benveniste (vol. 2, pp. 48-49) dismisses the relation between γέρας and γέρων ("elder")/γῆρας ("old age"), which has been traditionally postulated (e.g. by Frisk 1960, pp. 299; 304-5); for a possible derivation from Myc. *Kera* see Ventris – Chadwick 1959, p. 396.

From this sense, which is linked in particular to the partition of the booty in the *Iliad* and to the *querelle* between Achilles and Agamemnon,[60] the term evolves to acquire the general meaning of "privilege", as the distinctive mark of the *basileus*, in the *Odyssey*.[61] With this meaning it is then extended to some specific categories: gods, elders, the dead.[62]

In procedures of reparation of an offence, or in payments for blood crimes, the Homeric vocabulary uses the words ἄποινα/ποινή, which indicate the offer of redress through gifts.[63] But even if these terms are connected to the concept of 'paying in exchange' for something, they are specialized in two different directions: ἄποινα is used to mean the ransom of prisoners, of those that have been defeated in battle, or of the corpse of a warrior – in this sense we naturally find it only in the *Iliad*[64] – whereas ποινή is linked to the meaning of "vengeance" and "punishment" for an offence (*Il.* 3. 290) or for a blood crime (*Wergeld*) (*Il.* 18. 498).[65]

The very range of the lexicon connected to gift-giving is evidence of how widespread and pervasive this institution was. It was not, as Hooker claims,[66] limited to gift-exchange among hosts and guests. It was rather a key element of all kinds of relations in the context of the Homeric society.

3. *Xenie* and its rituals

The relationship of guest-friendship, or *xenie*,[67] is, without a doubt, central among those that have been defined as "balanced reciprocities".[68] Yet, as normal

[60] *Il.* 1.118; 123; 133; 135; 138; 161; 167; 185; 276; 356 = 507 = 2.240; 9.111; 367; 433; 16.54; 56; 18.444; 19.89; 20.182; *Od.* 11.534; 20.287 (ironic); about the procedures of partition of the booty in Homer see in particular Borecký 1965.

[61] *Od.* 7.10; 150; 11.176; 184; 15.522.

[62] *Il.* 4.49 = 24.70; 4.323; 9.422; 16.457 = 675 = 23.9; *Od.* 4.197; 24.190 = 296.

[63] The two words are connected: ἄποινα is nothing more than the substantive for ἀπόποινος (Frisk 1960, p. 123); both words stem from the theme $k^{w}ei$- from which also τίνω (to pay) and τίσις (punishment, revenge) derives; see Frisk 1970, pp. 573-574; Benveniste 1969, vol. 2, p. 50; the relationship with τίω/τιμή ("to honour"/ "honour") is controversial; according to Frisk 1960, p. 574, they stem from a common theme, according to Benveniste 1969, vol. 2, p. 55, from two different forms of the same theme, carrying different meanings.

[64] *Il.* 1.13; 23; 95; 111; 372; 377; 2.230; 6.46; 427; 9.120; 10.380; 11.131; 134; 19.131; 134; 19.138; 21.99; 22.349; 24.137; 139; 276; 502; 555; 579; 594; 686.

[65] See also *Il.* 9.632; 13.659; 14.483; 16.398; 17.207; *Od.* 23.312; ransom for a kidnapping (Ganimedes): *Il.* 5.66.

[66] Hooker 1989, p. 80.

[67] It is clear that *xenie* – "guest-friendship" – is from Homer on a 'ritualized' relationship,

in the epic style, Homer is not contented with describing the episodes of *xenie* involving the heroes of the *epos*, but

> "is prompted to repeat for the record a great deal of ritual prescription and procedure (and belief) which equally form part of the tribal encyclopaedia".[69]

First of all, the offer of hospitality is represented as an obligation, along the behaviours established by *themis* – however we understand the term[70] – and sanctioned by Zeus *Xenios*, in his role as "protector of the guests and the suppliants". Odysseus, when he introduces himself as a suppliant before the Cyclop, asks for hospitality with these words:

> "But now in turn we come to you and are suppliants at your knees, if you might give us a guest present or otherwise some gift of grace, O best of men. We are your suppliants, and Zeus the guest god, who stands behind all strangers with honours due them, avenges any wrong toward strangers and suppliants".[71]

Themis also requires the offer of gifts by the host, and the obligation of future reciprocity by the guest.[72]

The scenes of hospitality, in particular in the *Odyssey*,[73] follow (almost) a fixed scheme, with variations which are justified by the diversity of situations

with its own behavioural code. See Herman 1987, pp. 10-72.

[68] See Donlan 1982, p. 148; for the concept of "balanced reciprocity", following Sahlins 1965, pp. 47-49, see Donlan 1982, pp. 143-148.

[69] Havelock 1963, p. 70.

[70] Finley 1954, p. 90: "*Themis* is untranslatable [...] sometimes it means right custom, proper procedure, social order, and sometimes merely the will of the gods..."; see Bonner – Smith 1930, p. 9 ("what was right and proper"); Dodds 1951, p. 31 ("established usage of mankind"); Benveniste 1969, vol. 2, p. 103 ("Dans l'épopée, on entend par *thémis* la prescription qui fixe les droits et les devoirs de chacun sous l'autorité du chef du *génos*"); Lloyd-Jones 1971, p. 116, n. 23 ("declaration of a divine command or of a command advised by a god"); see also the classic treatment of Hirzel 1907, pp. 1-56 ("Guter Rath") and de Vos 1956; see now Pelloso 2012.

[71] *Od.* 9.266-71: ἡμεῖς δ' αὖτε κιχανόμενοι τὰ σὰ γοῦνα / ἱκόμεθ', εἴ τι πόροις ξεινήϊον ἠὲ καὶ ἄλλως / δοίης δωτίνην, ἥ τε ξείνων θέμις ἐστίν. / ἀλλ' αἰδεῖο, φέριστε, θεούς· ἱκέται δέ τοί εἰμεν. / Ζεὺς δ' ἐπιτιμήτωρ ἱκετάων τε ξείνων τε, / ξείνιος, ὃς ξείνοισιν ἅμ' αἰδοίοισιν ὀπηδεῖ; transl. R. Lattimore. About Zeus protector of aliens and guests see also *Il.* 13.624-625; *Od.* 6.208; 14.56-58; 158; 389; 17.155.

[72] Offer: *Il.* 11.779; *Od.* 1.312; 24.273; reciprocation (*amoibé*): *Od.* 1.317-318; 24.285-286; 314. About the ritual of *xenie* in Homer see Donlan 1982, pp. 148-149.

[73] In the *Iliad* we do not find occasions for hospitality, with the exception of the reception of the Achaean embassy in Achilles' tent (*Il.* 9). The context is not however very hospital; the encounter between Priam and Achilles at *Il.* 24 on the other hand is due to the request

involving the *xeinos* requiring hospitality.[74] The unknown *xeinos* appearing on the threshold of the host *oikos* first of all is transformed from 'stranger' to 'guest', welcome through the invitation to take part in the eating and drinking. Athena, disguised as the stranger Mentes, is invited by Telemachus to enter and take in part in the meal. Only afterwards will she be asked for the reason of her arrival.[75] The stranger is asked about his identity (and his ancestry, origin, the aim of his journey, and whether there is any pre-existing guest-friendship)[76] only after he has been 'integrated' into the *oikos* through the sharing of a meal.[77] After the meal it is not deemed offensive to interrogate him with questions such as:

> "Strangers, who are you? From where do you came sailing over the watery ways? Is it on some business , or are you recklessly roving as pirates do, when they sail on the salt sea and venture their lives as they wander, bringing evil to alien people?".[78]

to ransom Hector's body and is rather a *hiketeia* (supplication) scene. Achilles in fact invited Priam to sleep *outside* his tent, not *inside* (*Il.* 24.650). On *hiketeia* see Herman 1987, pp. 54-58; Giordano 1999; Naiden 2006.

[74] For the hospitality scenes in the Odyssey it would be excessive to talk about 'typical scenes' according to the criteria provided by Arend 1933 and Fenik 1968: we can however talk of a recurring 'ritual'.

[75] *Od.* 1.123-124: in the salutation χαῖρε, ξεῖνε it is clear that *xeinos* means "stranger" and not yet "guest".

[76] See *Od.* 1.169-177; cf. *Od.* 3.69-74: Telemachus reveals to Nestor immediately his identity and the reasons for his visit to a friend of his father; Telemachus' identity in Sparta is revealed gradually through a kind of recognition scene of the traits of Odysseus in his son by Helen and Menelaus (*Od.* 4.138-154).

[77] Cf. *Od.* 3.69-70 (Pylos); 4.31-36 (Sparta): Menelaus' welcome in Sparta is particularly interesting: when the *therapon* (retainer) Eteoneus announces that there are two 'strangers' at the door, Menelaus reproaches him reminding him of the hospitality he has received from other strangers; Donlan 1982, p. 149, talks of "orbit of kinship relations", and Herman 1987, p. 16, also considers the relationship of 'guest-friendship' "in some respects" akin to that of kinship.

[78] *Od.* 3.71-74: ὦ ξεῖνοι, τίνες ἐστέ; πόθεν πλεῖθ' ὑγρὰ κέλευθα; / ἤ τι κατὰ πρῆξιν ἦ μαψιδίως ἀλάλησθε / οἷά τε ληϊστῆρες ὑπεὶρ ἅλα, τοί τ' ἀλόωνται / ψυχὰς παρθέμενοι, κακὸν ἀλλοδαποῖσι φέροντες; transl. R. Lattimore. The same question is asked to Odysseus and his companions by the Cyclop (*Od.* 9.252-255). The difference is that the question asked by the Cyclop, given his savage nature which does not respect the rules of hospitality (*Od.* 273-8), lacks any preemptive gesture of hospitality, unlike Nestor's question to Telemachus; see Rose 1969, p. 389. On the meaning of πρῆξις, generically "activity" (*Il.* 24.524), "good result" (*Od.* 10.202; 568), or "business" connected to trade (*Od.* 3.72-74 = 9.253-255), see Bravo 1977, pp. 33-36; Mele 1979, pp. 58-64.

In the episode of the Phaeacians, Odysseus waits to declare his identity, and is persuaded to do so only after two requests by his hosts. First, he is asked by Aretes (*Od.* 7.237-239), to whom Odysseus does not reveal yet his identity; he replies instead recalling his journey from Ogygia to the island of Scheria. He is asked again by Alcinous (*Od.* 8.548-556), following Odysseus' reaction to the song of Demodochus about the Trojan Horse. Only at the beginning of *Od.* 9 does Odysseus eventually reveal his name and his ancestry, hoping to establish for the future a relationship of guest-friendship with the Phaeacians (*Od.* 9.16-19). The hospitality scene with the Phaeacians is in fact peculiar under many respects, including the departing from the rule of the return in gift-exchange between guests.

In the island of the Phaeacians Odysseus goes through all the steps of hospitality:[79] first of all, when he meets Nausikaa (6.149-315), Odysseus is a supplicant who needs food, drink and clothes; then, he is an anonymous supplicant by the fireplace in Alcinous' court (7.140-309); finally, he is a guest recognized for his value through the stories of his adventures in Troy and his vicissitudes on his way home. The generosity of Alcinous and the Phaeacians changes according to the revealing of the guest's heroic *arete* and identity as Odysseus, king of Ithaca: from the simple promise to give him the means to go back home (*pompé*, 7. 191-194), to the offer of rich gifts of hospitality to satisfy Odysseus' request not to let him go back home empty-handed (11. 354-361). In all these manifestations of generosity there is no reference to a possible future return: the only justification is that of memory, alleged by Alcinous (8.430-431) when he is offering a precious cup, or when he compares the guest to a brother (8.546). The lack of mention of a return in the relation of hospitality between Odysseus and the Phaeacians probably depends on the peculiar 'history' of these people: although they are willing to give a 'lift' by boat to everybody who arrives at Scheria, indeed, the Phaeacians usually do not have relationships with the external world, even if they respect the duty to protect ξεῖνοί τε πτωχοί τε according to divine sanctions (6.208).[80] To sum up, the Phaeacians confirm the duty of hospitality – and, in the end, they are *philoxenoi* –, but their hospitality is unilateral, without expectation of a future link or a future return because of their peculiar condition.

The final scene in the episodes of hospitality is the gift-giving as part of the farewell: Telemachus offers Mentes a gift which Mentes promises to reciprocate in the future (*Od.* 1.311-318). In Sparta the ritual of handing gifts to the departing guest Telemachus is more solemn and complex. Menelaus offers three horses, a chariot and a beautiful cup for libations to the gods, so that Telemachus

[79] See Rose 1969, pp. 389-390.
[80] Rose 1969.

may remember his host. Telemachus refuses the horses, because they are not appropriate for Ithaca's environment, but he accepts the other gifts (*Od.* 4.600; 15.130-132).[81] In fact, the farewell by Menelaus is also a chance for him to rehearse a quick summary of the correct practices of hospitality: the *xeinodokos* must neither make haste to the guest to leave, nor must he keep him against his will (*Od.* 15.68-74).[82] In the case of Odysseus' stay among the Phaeacians, the obligation of gift-giving evolves together with progressive recognition of the *arete* of the guest: up until *Od.* 8.386 Alcinous simply promises to provide the *pompé* requested by the unknown guest, but after he shows his valor in the athletic games, and his wisdom, Alcinous – and Arete – start talking about *xeneia* by envisioning ever growing gifts, until finally they encourage the Phaeacians chiefs not to be restrained in their gift-giving (*Od.* 11. 336-341).

A feature that is clear in the relations of hospitality is the wish to accumulate goods and improve one's wealth and prestige: Menelaus admits that during his travels in Cyprus, Phoenicia, Egypt and Lybia he amassed plenty of wealth (*Od.* 4.90). In one of the stories Odysseus recounts in Ithaca while disguised as a beggar, he tells Penelope that 'Odysseus' after collecting already plenty of gifts from the Phaeacians, decided to delay his return because

> "in his mind he thought it more profitable (*kerdion*) to go about and visit much country, collecting possessions. For Odysseus knew profitable ways (*kerdea*) beyond all other men who are mortal, no other man could rival him at it".[83]

And according to the king of the Thesprotians, Odysseus accumulated goods (*ktemata*) which "would feed a succession of heirs to the tenth generation" (*Od.* 19.294).[84] There is here clearly plenty of epic exaggeration – such amounts of wealth could not be transported on a ship – but these *keimelia* are at any rate clear evidence of a search for *kerdos* (profit) in relations of hospitality.

[81] Menelaus adds to his gifts a *krater* received in turn from Faedimus of Sidon (*Od* 4.613 619 = 15.114-119). This is a clear example of the circulation of the *keimelia* in the practice of gift-giving. On the 'history' of gifts in the Homeric poems see Grethlein 2008.

[82] The only exception is the lack of farewell by Telemachus in Pylos, because the son of Odysseus is in hurry to go back to Ithaca and fears that Nestor will try to keep him longer (*Od.* 15.195-201); the son of Nestor, Peisistratus, who led him to Pylos from Sparta, points out that his father will be angered by this (*Od.* 15.209-214).

[83] *Od.* 19.283-286: ἀλλ' ἄρα οἱ τό γε κέρδιον εἴσατο θυμῷ, / χρήματ' ἀγυρτάζειν πολλὴν ἐπὶ γαῖαν ἰόντι· / ὣς περὶ κέρδεα πολλὰ καταθνητῶν ἀνθρώπων / οἶδ' Ὀδυσεύς, οὐδ' ἄν τις ἐρίσσειε βροτὸς ἄλλος; transl. R. Lattimore.

[84] The adventure among the Thesprotians and the gathering of remarkable gifts was already part of the 'false' story told by Odysseus to Eumaeus at *Od.* 14.316-330.

And in fact, Odysseus, replying to Alcinous promise of returning him to his home with rich gifts, asserts that he would be willing to stay with him even one year,

> "because it would be more convenient (*kerdion*) [to him] go back to his fatherland with full hands, because he would be more highly respected (*aidoioteros*) and loved by everyone".[85]

Yet these *kerdea* (profits, advantages) – compatible with hospitality to an *aristos*, are completely different from the *kerdea harpalea* of the man "who plies his ways in his vessel, master over mariners who also are men of business (*prekteres*), a man who, careful of his cargo and grasping for profits, goes carefully on his way" (*Od.* 8. 161-64; transl. R.Lattimore). The *prekter* evoked in the insult thrown at Odysseus by Eurialus during the athletic games of the Phaeacians is a man who pursues profit (*kerdos*) through legitimate and illegitimate means.[86] The *kerdos* is to him the only means to support himself, whereas to the *aristos* it is no more than an occasional 'ruse' to increase his own prestige, beside other means, such as military endevours.[87] One can therefore agree with Donlan that "along with war-spoil and marriage prestations the guest-gift is a major means of material enrichment and prestige".[88]

The rule of *xenie* is not, however, valid only for the *aristoi*, who are already protected by their ancestry and by hereditary guest-friendship relationships with the *oikos* that hosts them. It is extended throughout the social ladder, all the way down to the beggars (*ptochoi*), who are also protected by Zeus *Xenios*.[89] The formula of gift-giving to them is that pronounced by Nausicaa in front of the shipwrecked Odysseus, and also by Eumaeus when he welcomes his master disguised as a beggar: δόσις δ' ὀλίγη τε φίλη τε ("small gift, yet dear", *Od.* 6.208 = 14.58).

A gift-exchange outside the context of the *oikos* is that between Glaucus and Diomedes (*Il.* 6.119-236). This strange episode happens on the battlefield. Glaucus and Diomedes meet each other on the battlefield, but before starting the

[85] *Od.* 11.358-361: καί κεν πολὺ κέρδιον εἴη / πλειοτέρῃ σὺν χειρὶ φίλην ἐς πατρίδ' ἱκέσθαι, / καί κ' αἰδοιότερος καὶ φίλτερος ἀνδράσιν εἴην / πᾶσιν; transl. R. Lattimore.

[86] About the Homeric πρηκτήρ see Bravo 1977, p.34; Mele 1979, p. 59: there is no doubt that the *prekteres* of *Od.* 8 are "gens vils", as argued by Bravo: the text however does not allow to categorize them as "esclaves ou libres" who travel on behalf of the aristocrats, as suggested by Bravo. The typical merchants – usually dishonest – in the *Odyssey* are the Phoenicians (*Od.* 14.288; 15.415; 419); in *Il.* 23.741-745 however they are just normal merchants; on the Phoenicians in Homer see Mele 1979, pp. 87-91.

[87] See Cozzo 1988, pp. 20-28; von Reden 1995, pp. 58-74.

[88] Donlan 1982, p. 151.

[89] *Od.* 6.270-278; 14.56-59.

duel the Achaean hero asks his opponent to declare his identity. Glaucus tells the story of his lineage from Bellerophon to Hippolochus, his father. Due to that story Diomedes recognizes Glaucus as an "old family's guest" (*xeinos patroios palaios*) because of the ancient links of hospitality between Oeneus, Diomedes' grandfather, and Bellerophon, Glaucus' grandfather, who exchanged guests' gifts. For that reason Diomedes is a "guest friend" (*xeinos philos*) in Lycia, country home of Glaucus, and Glaucus is Diomedes' guest friend at Argos. When Diomedes recognizes these links, he decides to suspend the duel and to refresh the relation of *xenie* through an exchange of arms – Glaucus' gold arms in exchange for Diomedes' bronze arms –, because he wants that all the soldiers – Achaeans and Trojans – recognize the reciprocal condition of guests, which they are proud of. Until this point all hang together according to the usual model of rules of *xenie*, more evident because of the peculiarity of the occasion, a missed duel on the battlefield. What is strange is the poet's commentary, judged as a "nearly burlesque ending" by Leaf:[90]

> "But Zeus the son of Kronos stole away the wits of Glaucos who exchanged with Diomedes the son of Tydeus armor of gold for bronze, for nine oxen's worth the worth of a hundred".[91]

This commentary shows a 'trading' spirit incongruous with the ethic of generosity of the Homeric heroes and has become a headache for the scholars, who have looked for the reason of this unequal exchange between Glaucus and Diomedes. The explanations are very different: some scholars think that Glaucus is recognizing his inferiority in front of Diomedes,[92] while according to others, he is stating his superiority through the offer of a gift of bigger value.[93] Kirk dismisses any "*literal* and *realistic* understanding of the exchange":[94] here the poet

> "withdraws for a moment from his regular narrative mode and proposes a typical folktale-type transaction",[95]

alien to the 'normal epic genre'. The poet puts this episode – which must have been traditional – in particular relief. Such an episode presumably required a different conclusion, not the normal exchange of weapons between the duelists,

[90] Leaf 1886, p. 212.
[91] *Il.* 6.234-236: ἔνθ'αὖτε Γλαύκῳ Κρονίδης φρένας ἐξέλετο Ζεύς, / ὃς πρὸς Τυδεΐδην Διομήδεα τεύχε'ἄμειβε / χρύσεα χαλκείων, ἑκατόμβοι'ἐννεαβοίων; transl. R. Lattimore.
[92] Craig 1967; Calder 1984; Traill 1989.
[93] Donlan 1989a.
[94] Kirk 1990, pp. 190-191.
[95] Kirk 1990, p. 191.

as happens elsewhere.[96] The poet, in order to highlight the extraordinary status of the episode, would have "risked a rare virtuoso conclusion to it".[97]

4. *Hedna* or 'wedding gifts'.

If the gift-exchange between guests normally ratifies the decision to create an alliance between *oikoi* to increase the glory of both parts, thus an analogous relation is implicit in another occurrence of gift-exchange which is widespread in the poems: marital alliances. If the links of *xenie* can be – or better, have to be – extended to the beggars,

> "marriage was... a major occasion, and particularly so in the upper social circles in which the Homeric heroes moved... in fact, marriage and guest-friendship were the two fundamental devices for the establishment of alliances among the nobles and chieftains".[98]

The normal procedure – or, at least, the most widespread in the Homeric poems – is the offer of 'wedding gifts' (*hedna*)[99] by the potential bridegroom to the bride's kin.[100] In several cases however it appears that the gifts – *hedna* or

[96] See *Il.* 7.287-310: the exchange of weapons between Hector and at the end of a duel stopped because of the even skills and bravery of the two warriors; here the exchange is not due to the discovery of ancient links of *xenie* – like in the case of Glaucus and Diomedes – but by a "temporary pact of *philotes*" (Donlan 1982, p. 145), which will not prevent future fights (e.g. *Il.* 13.824-832). On this episode see also Herman 1987, p. 60, n. 56.

[97] Kirk 1990, p. 191.

[98] Finley 1955, p. 179. In fact, apart from the allusion of Eumaeus to the possibility that Odysseus could give him a woman 'wanted by many' (πολυμνήστην γυναῖκα) (*Od.* 14.64), the marriages in *Iliad* and the *Odyssey* are all among *aristoi*.

[99] I prefer this translation (see *LSL*) of ἕδνα/ἔεδνα because the alternatives "bride-price" or "bridewealth" used by Donlan 1982, pp. 146-147; Morris 1986a, pp. 105-13; von Reden 1995, pp. 49-51, which employ the standard for of the anthropological concept (e.g. Murdock 1949, in particular pp. 19-22; Radcliffe-Brown 1950, in particular pp. 43-72; Goody 1969; 1973; Strathern 1984), are not entirely suitable to the Homeric system of exchange of marital gifts; see Finley 1955, pp. 178-187; Lacey 1966, p. 56; von Reden 1995, p. 50 ("Unfortunately the epics do not describe any single system of marriage transfer consistent with ethnographical data").

[100] One can speak of a 'normal' procedure on the basis of the words of Penelope to the Suitors at *Od.* 18.275-279: μνηστήρων οὐχ ἥδε δίκη τὸ πάροιθε τέτυκτο, / οἵ τ' ἀγαθήν τε γυναῖκα καὶ ἀφνειοῖο θύγατρα /μνηστεύειν ἐθέλωσι καὶ ἀλλήλοισ' ἐρίσωσιν· / αὐτοὶ τοί γ' ἀπάγουσι βόας καὶ ἴφια μῆλα / κούρης δαῖτα φίλοισι, καὶ ἀγλαὰ δῶρα διδοῦσιν· ("the behavior of these suitors is not as it was in time past, when suitors desired to pay their

dora – change hands in the opposite direction: from the father of the bride or from the bride herself to the betrothed. We can start from the most uncertain case: both Andromache and Penelope are referred to with the epithet πολύδωρος (*Il.* 6.394; 22. 88; *Od.* 24.294), which can be understood both as "she who brings many gifts" to the husband, and also as "she who had received many gifts". Half of the *scholia* to these verses endorse the first meaning and half the second,[101] and modern scholars do not agree on the matter.[102]

court to a noble woman and the daughter of a rich man, and rival each other. Such men themselves bring in their own cattle and fat sheep, to feast the family of the bride, and offer glorious presents"; transl. R. Lattimore). In this case Penelope speaks of δῶρα, not of ἕδνα, and according to Lacey 1966, pp. 57-58 (see also Köstler 1950, p. 59, n. 42) the two terms are not synonyms (the *dora* are additional gifts given by the bridegroom to the father of the bride to induce her to agree to the marriage; the *hedna* on the other hand are the gifts promised for the wedding). Finley 1954, p. 182, n. 46 believes instead that the two are the same thing, also on the basis of *Od.* 15.16-18. A confirmation of the 'normal' custom evoked by Penelope comes from the words of Odysseus and Nausicaa at *Od.* 6.158-159. As for the occurrence of this procedure in the Homeric poems, out of 28 cases of marriages, without taking into account the formula ἄλοχος πολύδωρος, about which see below, the exceptional cases of Otrioneus, Achilles, Bellerophon, Nausicaa betrothed to Odysseus by Alcinous, about which see below, and the two texts already considered, we can find this procedure with certainty in 13 cases (with δῶρα: *Od.* 15.18; 20.335; with ἕδνα/ἔεδνα: *Il.* 16.175-178; 189-190; 22.471-472; *Od.* 8.318; 11.117; 282; 13.378; 15.18; 16.390-392; 19.528-529; 21.160-161.

101 See *Schol. Vet. D ad Il.* 6.394 ("who took many other gifts from the husband"); *Schol. Vet. ad Il.* 22.88a (Aristonicus): (ὅτι ἕδνα ἐδίδοσαν οἱ παλαιοὶ ταῖς θυγατράσι· καὶ πολύδωρον λέγει τὴν πολύεδνον; "the ancients gave wedding gifts to the daughters; thus *poludoron* means *poluednon*": clearly the *hedna* here are intended as from the father of the bride to the bridegroom), but *Schol. Genev.* understands on the contrary that the *hedna* were given to the bride, with reference to *Il.* 22.472. Here we read in fact that Hector "gave infinite gifts" (*hedna*) in order to marry Andromache; *Schol. Vet. ad Od.* 24.294 (Penelope): ἡ πολλοῖς δώροις εἰς γάμον ἐλθοῦσα. Q. ("who has gone to marriage with many gifts", with no direction explicit); ἡ πολλοῖς δώροις γαμηθεῖσα. V. ("married with many gifts", in this case received); Hesych. Lex., *s.v.* πολύδωρος glosses πολλὰ λαβοῦσα δῶρα. πολύφερνος. πολύεδνος, where *dora* and *hedna* are the same, yet the provenance of the 'gifts' of the bride is not clear.

102 Finley 1954, p. 181, n. 44: "bringing many gifts to the husband"; Snodgrass 1974, p. 117, recognizes the ambiguity of the term, but believes (wrongly) that the meaning "richly dowered" is prevalent; Lacey 1966, p. 58, in accordance with the distinction he draws between *dora* and *hedna*, believes that these are the many 'additional' gifts given by the father of the bride to show that he agrees to the wedding; Morris 1986a, pp. 107-108, adopts Lacey's hypothesis, and accepts the meaning "bringing many gifts", yet in both directions. He rejects the reading "well dowered" by Snodgrass; von Reden 1995, p. 50, declares the question unsolvable.

The key case for the interpretation of both kinds of 'wedding gifts' – by the suitors to the bride, and by the relatives of the bride to the betrothed – is the uncertain status of Penelope's wedding. In most contexts dealing with her future wedding – were she to make a decision and stay in Odysseus' house – the offer of gifts (*hedna* and *dora*) – a veritable contest to donate more[103] – is by the suitors to the bride.[104] In other cases however the possibility is contemplated that Penelope, either of her own accord or ordered by Telemachus,[105] may go back to her father Icarius' *oikos*. In that case it will be his responsibility to provide the *hedna* for his daughter' wedding.[106] Both Finley and Snodgrass interpret *hedna*, in this case, as 'dowry'.[107] Yet the difference between the two systems – *hedna* and *dora* either by the suitor to the bride or her relatives, or by her relatives to the suitor – leads them to opposite conclusions. According to Snodgrass, if we compare the Homeric customs with the anthropological data we must conclude that the two systems are inconsistent in the same social typology. Thus, "Homer is describing a mixture of practises, derived from a diversity of historical sources",[108] and therefore he does not portray a "unitary and historical" society.[109] Snodgrass' application of anthropological categorizations to the Homeric context – in particular of J. Goody's distinction between "diverging

[103] See *Od.* 18.276-277; see also 16.391; 20.335; 21.161; in 18.291-303 the list of gifts (*dora*) offered by the suitors; see Finley 1955, p. 178; Lacey 1966, p. 56.
[104] See *Od.* 11.117; 282 (Cloris and Neleus); 13.378; 15.18; 16.390-392; 19.528-529; 20.335; 21.160-161.
[105] Of her own accord: *Od.* 1.275-276; ordered by Telemachus: *Od.* 2.195-197; the matter is complicated by the uncertainty regarding the identity of Penelope's *kyrios*: her father Icarius or Telemachus; *Od.* 2.195-197 and 20.335-344 suggest that it was Telemachus, as long as Penelope remains in Odysseus' house, of which Telemachus is the head; in fact at *Od.* 20.335-344, advised by Agelaus to invite the mother to "marry the most illustrious suitor who offers most gifts", Telemachus replies that he does indeed invite his mother to remarry, and offers "infinite gifts" (ἄσπετα δῶρα) for the purpose; see on this Lacey 1966, pp. 61-62.
[106] Cf. *Od.* 1.275-278 (but the text according to West 1981, pp. 229-231, is confused and incoherent); the verses are repeated at 2.195-197 and ascribed to Eurimachus; see also *Od.* 2.53, where it is stated that Icarius "should provide the *hedna* for the daughter" (ἐεδνώσαιτο): the verb ἐεδνόω occurs only here in Homer and the *Schol. Vet. ad Il.* understand it as "give a dowry", but also observe that the usage is incorrect because the *hedna* were properly given by the bridegroom to the bride; see also von Wilamowitz-Moellendorf 1927, p. 102; Finley 1955, p. 182, n. 49 (both meanings are possible); West 1981, p. 259.
[107] Finley 1955, pp. 181-182; Snodgrass 1974, p. 115.
[108] Snodgrass 1974, p. 118.
[109] Snodgrass 1974, p. 121. For criticism of the use of anthropological data by Snodgrass, see Morris 1986a, pp.111-112.

devolution" and "homogenous devolution", with the relative marital customs[110] – is too rigid.[111] It is clear, in fact, as argued by Finley and those who agree with his interpretation, that what matters in Homer when a marriage alliance is concluded is the gift exchange between the two parties. This can move in either directions, and this ought not to mark a confusion or mix of customs of different times and societies.[112] And moreover, in addition to these two customs, we also find in Homer exceptional cases when these customs are suspended, or are represented by the poet as suspended. The most remarkable case is without a doubt that of the offer from Agamemnon to Achilles, in reparation for the offence to his *timé* (*Il.* 9.144-8 = 286-90): Agamemnon, in addition to the "infinite reparatory gifts" (*apereisi'apoina*) listed at *Il.* 9.120-40, offers to Achilles one of his daughters in marriage ἀναέδνος, without requiring the usual *hedna*. He also adds the mysterious μείλια ("hespiatory" or "reparatory gifts"?),[113] in all likelihood the seven cities listed below. A similar situation is envisaged in the story of Bellerophon recounted by his descendant Glaucus at *Il.* 6.191-5: Bellerophon, in return for the display of his valor, received from the Lycians the daughter of the king of Lycia in marriage, together with "half the royal honour" and a *temenos* (a plot of land). This is similar to what Alcinous offers to Odysseus, if he could be persuaded to stay (*Od.* 7.311-14). An *anaednos* bride (Cassandra) is also promised by Priam to Otrioneus in exchange for his contribution to the defence of Troy (*Il.* 13.360-9).[114] And we even find in Homer a case of divorce, unique in the poems, in which the restitution of the *hedna* given to the father of the bride – Zeus – is required by the cuckold husband – Ephaestus (*Od.* 8.318-20).[115]

[110] See Goody 1969.

[111] In fact, Goody does not take into account cases when the circulation of gifts goes in both directions, as the example of a tribe in the Belgian Congo, reported by Radcliffe-Brown 1950, p. 47.

[112] Finley 1955, p. 186: "ξεινήϊα and ἕδνα, I suggest, were precisely comparable; the one meant gifts accompanying guest-friendship, the other the gifts accompanying marriage, and the same word could be used regardless of the direction in which the gifts travelled"; see Lacey 1966, p. 60; Morris 1986a, pp. 112-113.

[113] *Schol. Vet. ad Il.* 9.147.a1 (Aristarchus): ἐπιφέρνια ("dowry"); see Hainsworth 1993, p. 77: "propitiatory gifts"; see also Frisk 1970, p.194 (*Sühngaben*).

[114] Finley 1955, pp. 186-187; Lacey 1966, p. 59; Donlan 1982, p. 146; Morris 1986a, pp. 107-108 on all these cases, which confirm, because exceptional, the practice of the *hedna*.

[115] Finley 1955, p. 193, n. 87 stresses how exceptional this case is, which confirms once again the practice of the *hedna* offered by the suitor to the relatives of the bride. The solution of the problem of Penelope's second marriage, reached through the archery context, is atypical and inconsistent with the normal wedding procedures (*Od.* 19.572-576, and all the Book 21). The archery context in the *Odyssey* is surely typical of folk tales (West 1981, pp.74-75; Krischer 1992; Crissy 1997), and integrates the 'contest for

To conclude, rather than postulating contradictions, layers and mixing of customs from different ages, the Homeric evidence about marriage alliances and the relevant gift-exchanges witnesses a flexibility due both to the particular circumstances of the parties,[116] and to the status of the future bride and bridegroom.[117]

However, the common ground that characterizes all cases is the reality of gift-exchange – whether these are *hedna* or *dora*. There is evidence that the object of the exchange in arranging a wedding is not the woman but the gifts that come with her.[118] These are the tangible sign (even when they are given in the form of services) that the two families (*oikoi*) are committed to a relation of kinship and alliance.

5. Reparatory gifts (*apoina, poiné*)

Among the various forms of "balanced reciprocity" Sahlins included also the exchange of gifts aimed at composing disputes, at giving compensation for offences, and at providing redress for blood crimes ("*Wergeld* payments").[119] We find in the *Iliad* plenty of scenes in which gifts are offered as ransom for a captive or a defeated warrior in exchange for his life. In fact, the entire action of the poem originates from the offer of "infinite ransom gifts" (ἀπερείσι' ἄποινα) offered by Crises, the priest of Apollo, in exchange for his daughter – these are rejected by Agamemnon.[120] The poem finds eventually its conclusions with the offer of likewise "infinite gifts" to Achilles from Priam to ransom the body of his son Hector.[121] The offer is usually presented as a supplication,[122] which the *supplicandus* can either accept or refuse. This is normal in the case of defeated

the hand of the princess' with the martial contest with the bow. Because this is Iphitus' bow, inherited by him from his father Euritus and given as a gift to young Odysseus (*Od.* 21.11-41), it is possible that the 'story' of the bow, that had already been instrumental to a contest for the hand of Ioles, the daughter of Euritus (Apollod. 2.6.1-2), is mirrored by the contest in the *Odyssey*.

[116] The generosity of Agamemnon e.g. is explained by his will to repair the offence against Achilles with offers that a 'normal' hero could not reject.

[117] Donlan 1982, p. 147.

[118] Finley 1955, p. 186 favours this interpretation, endorsed enthusiastically by von Reden 1995, p. 51.

[119] Sahlins 1965, p. 176; see also Donlan 1982, pp. 143-144; von Reden 1995, p.19; Cairns 2011a; 2011b.

[120] *Il.* 1.13; 20; 23; 95; 111; 372; 377.

[121] *Il.* 24.137; 139; 276; 502; 555; 579; 594.

[122] For the importance of supplication in these contexts see Gould 1973; on the episode of Achilles and Priam, Zanker 1998.

warriors who promise gifts in exchange for their life.[123] The same mechanism is at work in the offers of compensation for an offence to someone's honour (*timé*). In these cases the supplication is replaced by providing justifications for one's mistake. This is particularly clear in the episode of the dispute between Agamemnon and Achilles: after admitting to the *ate* ("madness")[124] that caused the mistake and brought about the offence to Achilles' honour,[125] Agamemnon wants to give Achilles satisfaction (ἀρέσαι) by offering him "infinite gifts" (*Il.* 9.115-120).

With the recognition of Agamemnon's mistake, the episode turns into a series of offers and refusals between the *anax andron* and Achilles, which will end at *Il.* 19, with Achilles' late acceptance after Patroclus' death.[126] The reason of Achilles' initial refusal is the fact that, even if Agamemnon was offering him "infinite gifts", he did not renounce the claim to be acknowledged by him as superior because of his condition of "more king than the others" (*basileuteros*, *Il.* 9.157-161). Achilles' final acceptance of the gifts depends on the desire to avenge Patroclus' and other Achaeans' deaths, and not on an eventual submission to Agamemnon, who in the palinody of *Il.* 19 completely 'forgot' the claim to be recognized as a superior.

The concept of *poiné* is linked with that of *apoina*, but has a narrower meaning of repayment/revenge against a violent or unjust act. It can refer to the blood price (*Wergeld*) for a homicide. Within a system based on 'self-help', as the Homeric society is,[127] the *poiné* is first and foremost[128] the blood price the killer has to pay.[129] The alternative is either the revenge of the relatives, a life

[123] *Il.* 6.46-49; 10.380; 11.131-134; 21.99; 22.349; the exception is Andromaches' mother, ransomed in exchange for *apereisi'apoina* (*Il.* 6.427).

[124] So translated by E. Myers, but see Cairns 2012, p. 9: "delusion".

[125] See also the great palinody of Agamemnon in *Il.* 19.78-144, with the classic reading offered by Dodds 1951, pp. 2-18; on the concept of ἄτη see Wyatt 1982; Cairns 2012.

[126] *Il.* 19.147-148: the acceptance of Agamemnon's gifts by Achilles has plenty of qualification: even though Achilles is willing to forget the offence and put an end to his anger (*Il.* 19.65-68), he does not feel however any obligation as a result of the offer of gifts (*Il.* 19.146-148). The real reason of his return to the battlefield is the desire to avenge Patroclus and the co-fighters killed by Hector (*Il.* 19.199-214). He even refuses to take part in the reconciliatory banquet proposed by Odysseus (*Il.* 19.179-180); see Donlan 1989a, pp. 5-6; von Reden 1995, pp. 18-26.

[127] See Bonner – Smith 1930, pp. 11-21; MacDowell 1978, p. 19; Gagarin 2005.

[128] About punishment/revenge for the breach of an oath cf. *Il.* 3.290 (with Benveniste 1969, vol. 2, p. 55); about the ransom for Ganimedes' kidnapping: *Il.* 5.266; reciprocation: *Il.* 17.207; sacrifice of the young Trojans as redress/revenge for Patroclus' death: *Il.* 21.28; punishment of the Cyclop: *Od.* 23.312.

[129] *Poiné* for a killing: *Il.* 9.632-639; 13.659; 14.483; 16.398; 18.498.

against another life, or the exile of the killer.[130] In order to avoid a series of killings,

> "a killed man's family might accept an amount of gold or other property as recompense for the killing, after which the affair was closed".[131]

The famous scene from the description of the Shield of Achilles (*Il.* 18.497-508) abundantly clarifies the procedure: the dispute (νεῖκος) in the public place between two litigants concerns the *poiné* of the victim of a homicide. The killer declares before the people that he has paid the entire *poiné*, whereas the other party – the relative of the victim – denies that he has received anything.[132] In order to resolve the dispute, the litigants submit themselves to the judgment of an assembly of elders (γέροντες), which shows that the dispute could be composed through an agreement consisting in paying a satisfactory *poiné* to the relatives of the victim.

In a more positive sense – not as reparation for an offence, but as a prize for a service provided – the logic of "balanced reciprocity" is also applied to plenty of examples of services 'paid' with gifts: Pandarus will obtain "beautiful gifts" from Paris if he hits Menelaus with his arrow (*Il.* 4.94-99); Dolon wishes to obtain gifts for his night mission (*Il.* 10.401); Hector "wears out" the Trojans to offer gifts and food to the allies (*Il.* 17.225). In the short parainetic *epos* told by Phoenix to Achilles (*Il.* 9.527-59), the old Aetolians pray Meleager to return to fight and promise him some gifts and, among them, a beautiful plot of land (*temenos*). However, in another circumstance, Echepolos of Sycion gives a gift to avoid a service: he grants two horses to Agamemnon not to take part to the Trojan war (*Il.* 23.296-7). In the *Odyssey* this payment through gifts is reserved to people who give vaticinations or bring good news about the return of Odysseus to Ithaca[133]. But when it comes to rewards for manual work, or at any rate in a sphere outside the remit of the aristocratic values, the term is μισθός (wage),[134] which does not imply any "long-term relationship", but is rather connected with the "satisfaction of immediate needs":[135] it is not a case that the

[130] *Il.* 23.85-90; 24.480; *Od.* 13.259; 15.272-278.

[131] MacDowell 1978, p. 19.

[132] Among the many readings of this trial see Bonner – Smith 1930, pp. 30-33; Wolff 1946, pp. 34-49; Köstler 1950, pp. 65-77; Cantarella 1979, pp. 251-257; Gagarin 1986, pp. 19-50; Westbrook 1992; Thür 2007. Benveniste 1969, vol. 2, pp. 240-242, reads εὔχετο and ἀναίνετο (*Il.* 18.499-500) with different meanings.

[133] *Od.* 2.186; 15.537 = 17.164 = 19.310.

[134] von Reden 1995, p. 90: "payment to an inferior person"; cf. *Il.* 12.435 (wool-spinner); *Od.* 4.524-525 (the sentry Aegistus sent to check whether Agamemnon is returning); 10.84 (the pay of the shepherd); 18.358 (pay for farmers: food, clothes, sandals).

[135] Gottesman 2010, p. 290.

waged work to which Poseidon and Apollo are submitted by Laomedon for a year contemplates a μισθοῖο τέλος, "the time for payment" (*Il.* 21.450).[136] It may sound contradictory to use the same term for the night enterprise of *Il.* 10.303-331, where Hector promises a "great gift" (δῶρον μεγάλος, 10.304) to whomever will go spy the enemy camp. This gift is called in the same verse "sufficient payment" (ἄρκιος μισθός), the same expression used in the *Odyssey* (18.358) by Eurimachus with Odysseus, disguised as a beggar, when he offers him a pay "sufficient" for his work in the fields. In fact, as noted by Sitta von Reden,[137] the use of this term highlights the non-heroic character of the enterprise, undertaken only by Dolon among all Trojans, and of the character of Dolon himself, ugly and moved by desire for profit. The *misthos* is therefore in the aristocratic ideology of the Homeric poems a reward for more or less honourable services, yet it falls outside the remit of the aristocratic values.

6. The privileges of kingship (*geras, dotine, themistes*)

When addressed by Eurimachus with the malicious wish that he may not become king of Ithaka (despite his birth right), Telemachus frankly, and perhaps naively, answers:

> "Do you think that is the worst thing (*scil. basileuein*) that could happen to anyone? It is not bad to be king. Speedly the king's house grow prosperous, and he himself has rank beyond others".[138]

The key words of this view of kingships are wealth (ἀφνειός) and honour (τιμηέστερος). The most explicit description of the privileges of kingship – which are understood in Telemachus' reply – is in Sarpedon's words when he encourages Glaucus to fight:

> "Glaucus, wherefore is it that we twain are held in honour above all with seats, and messes, and full cups in Lycia, and all men gaze upon us as on gods? Aey, and we possess a great demesne by the banks of Xanthus, a fair tract of orchard and of wheat-bearing plough-land. Therefore now it behoveth us to take our stand amid the foremost Lycians, and confront the blazing battle, that many a one of the mail-clad Lycians may say 'Verily no inglorious men be these that rule in Lycia,

[136] Ambrose 1965, p. 54; for the mythical episode evoked by Poseidon see *Il.* 21.444-451; see also Richardson 1993, p. 91.
[137] von Reden 1995, p. 90.
[138] *Od.* 1.391-393: ἦ φῂς τοῦτο κάκιστον ἐν ἀνθρώποισι τετύχθαι; /οὐ μὲν γάρ τι κακὸν βασιλευέμεν· αἶψά τέ οἱ δῶ /ἀφνειὸν πέλεται καὶ τιμηέστερος αὐτός; transl. R. Lattimore.

> even our kings, they that eat fat sheep and drink choice wine, honey-sweet: nay, but their might too is goodly, seeing they fight amid the foremost Lycians'".[139]

These words express in the clearest fashion the relationship of exchange which is the foundation of the honour (*timé*) of chiefdom: the privileges are granted to the chief in exchange for the firm and vigorous protection the chief must offer his subordinates. Among these privileges, beside food, the mention of a *temenos* wide and well tilled stands out: the word, of Mycenaean origin,[140] indicates the portion of land 'cut out' and offered by the community as an appreciation of the chief's *timé* and his service.[141] There are other examples of a *temenos* offered or promised in exchange for a display of prowess: the *temenos* given by the Lycians to Bellerophon (to which Sarpedon refers) (*Il.* 6. 194-95) – and the Lycians themselves, not Iobates, their king, give Bellerophon this *temenos*. Another example is the *temenos* promised by the Aetolian elders to Meleager in exchange for his defence of the city (*Il.* 9. 577-80). During the duel between Achilles and Aeneas the Achaean hero wonders whether the Trojan is fighting in the front line because of the promise of a good *temenos* of land which can be farmed with grain or with fruit trees. (*Il.* 184-5). Odysseus also owns his own *temenos* (*Od.* 11.185; 17.299), as Alcinous (*Od.* 6. 293) does, but it is not clear as to how they came in possession of them – Odysseus probably by inheritance; Alcinous following the partition of the land of Scheria by his father Nausitous (*Od.* 6. 10).[142] Even when the topic is not a *temenos* but rather cities and lands, as with the land promised by Agamemnon to Achilles, Achilles still

[139] *Il.* 12.310-21: Γλαῦκε τί ἦ δὴ νῶϊ τετιμήμεσθα μάλιστα / ἕδρῃ τε κρέασίν τε ἰδὲ πλείοις δεπάεσσιν /ἐν Λυκίῃ, πάντες δὲ θεοὺς ὣς εἰσορόωσι, / καὶ τέμενος νεμόμεσθα μέγα Ξάνθοιο παρ'ὄχθας /καλὸν φυταλιῆς καὶ ἀρούρης πυροφόροιο; /τὼ νῦν χρὴ Λυκίοισι μέτα πρώτοισιν ἐόντας / ἑστάμεν ἠδὲ μάχης καυστείρης ἀντιβολῆσαι, /ὄφρά τις ὧδ'εἴπῃ Λυκίων πύκα θωρηκτάων· / οὐ μὰν ἀκλεέες Λυκίην κάτα κοιρανέουσιν /ἡμέτεροι βασιλῆες, ἔδουσί τε πίονα μῆλα / οἶνόν τ' ἔξαιτον μελιηδέα· ἀλλ'ἄρα καὶ ἶς / ἐσθλή, ἐπεὶ Λυκίοισι μέτα πρώτοισι μάχονται; transl. A. T. Murray.
[140] PY Er 312: *temeno* of the king (*wanakatero*) and of *lawagetas* (chief of the army); see Ventris – Chadwick 1959, p. 266; Finley 1957, p. 140.
[141] Finley 1954, pp. 109-110: "While the king reigned he also had the use of a separate estate, called a *temenos*, which the community placed at his disposal". But Finley 1957, pp. 148-151, retracts his previous interpretation, and reads *temenos* simply as "royal land". He accepts only in four cases (those of Bellerophon, of Meleager, of Aeneas and of Sarpedon and Glaucus) that the plot has been given as a gift to the owner. See also Donlan 1997, pp. 660-661: "The *temenos* is unambiguously described as the gift of the whole people [...]. The gift of a *temenos* is a good example of the finely tuned reciprocity that exists between the community and its leaders in Homeric society".
[142] See also the *temenos basileion* on the "Shield of Achilles" at *Il.* 18.550-560.

will receive "donations" (*dotinai*) for his *timé* and "rich tributes" (*themistes*: *Il.* 9.155-6)[143].

From the interpretative standpoint of the 'big man', Quiller highlighted that the key role of the king is that of a "redistributor":[144] in fact the Homeric king, whether a *primus inter pares* as Alcinous (*Od.* 8. 390-1) or the most powerful of kings like Agamemnon (*Il.* 1.277-81), is at the same time *receiver* and *redistributor* of privileges. The term used in Homer to indicate the extra-portion due to a king when goods are distributed in a community is *geras*:

> "an extra, or choice, portion (*geras*) is usually given, by the group, to the leader or to an outstanding warrior, as his due... In Homeric society... chiefly due is that something extra which accrues to the leader, *qua* leader, usually perceived as a reward due for his services to the group".[145]

The *geras* can be a special gift given by the community in recognition of kingly status, as in the case of the slave given by the people to Alcinous as a gift (*Od.* 7.10), or the part of a booty due to the chief during its partition (*Od.* 9.549-51). It can also have the abstract meaning of privilege, prerogative of the kingly status, like in Odysseus' wish to Alcinous (*Od.* 7.150), or in the allusions to the *geras* of Odysseus (*Od.* 11.175-84), where the meaning is clearly "royal prerogative".[146]

It is, however, chiefly in the partition of the booty that we can see tensions between the right to *geras*, measured by assessing each *aristos*' claim to *timé*, and the authority of the man who presides to the partition because he is superior in power – Agamemnon in the *Ilias*.[147] The conflict between Agamemnon and

[143] On the meaning of these two terms see above nn. 53 and 54 and the corresponding text.

[144] Quiller 1981, p. 114; see also Donlan 1982, pp. 154-159.

[145] Donlan 1982, pp. 158-159.

[146] Eurimachus aspires to marry Penelope, but also to obtain the *geras* – royal prerogatives – of Odysseus (*Od.* 15.522); *geras* is found with the abstract meaning of "someone's privilege" also to indicate what is due to particular categories, such as gods (*Il.*4.49), elders (*Il.* 4.323), the dead (*Il.* 16.457; *Od.* 4.197).

[147] In the majority of cases *geras* is given by the community of warriors – the Achaeans – (*Il.* 1.122-126; 133-138; 161; 185; 276; 16.54-56; 18.444). Yet, as is clear from Achilles' accusation against Agamemnon at *Il.* 9.333-334 that he "keeps many gifts and gives few", and from the few mention of the partition performed by the chief (*Il.* 9.330-334; 367; 11.687-705), one can argue that the collective division is supervised by the leading *basileus*. Achilles himself admits that the spoils of war are administered by Agamemnon (*Il.* 9.330-332). Donlan 1982, p. 158, postulates two different systems of social organization, represented by the partition operated by the group and that operated by the chief. The first is non-centralized, associated with the "social organization of tribes". The

Achilles originates from the claims to recognition of their respective *timai* as they are made explicit in the allocation of *geras*: Agamemnon cannot accept, after giving Criseides back to her father, to be left the only one among the Achaeans "without *geras*" (*agerastos*) (*Il.* 1.118). He is not satisfied by Achilles' reply that he should wait the next partition of the spoils of Troy, when the Achaeans will abundantly make up for his loss, because there are no common spoils (*xuneia*) to gather and divide anew (*Il.* 1.122-29). He will proceed instead to forcibly take away another *basileus*' *geras*, and Achilles is the victim. The old Nestor clearly understands this conflict: Agamemnon is wrong to take away from Achilles the gift that the Achaeans gave him. This dishonours the hero.[148] Achilles, on the other hand, should not challenge Agamemnon superior *timé* (*Il.* 1.275-281). And Agamemnon himself, in his final palinody (*Il.* 19.87-9), states that madness suggested him to take away Achilles' *geras*. To Achilles, Agamemnon's actions are all the more serious because, while he will take back to his fatherland the goods that he received, he has forcibly stolen the *geras* that he had himself given to Achilles (*Il.* 9.365-8). One of the accusations Achilles addresses to Agamemnon is that he is "greedy of riches" (*philokteanos*) (*Il.* 1.122) and "devourer of the people" (*demoboros*) (*Il.* 1.231).[149] In other terms, he violates the rule of generosity which is *noblesse oblige* for the chief that wants to keep his subjects loyal.[150]

7. Conclusions.

Hooker advanced three objections to Finley's theory about Homeric gift-giving:[151] 1) gift exchange is not an 'institution', but rather a "polite custom",[152]

latter on the other hand is a "ranked distribution, characteristic of the centralized economies of chiefdoms". This seeming contradiction is due to the application of anthropological concepts alien to the Homeric society, and not to the nature of the material. In Homeric society the *laos* is nothing more than an amalgam of units connected to their respective *basileis* (as Donlan 2007 admits), and there is no "centralized economy" subordinated to an alleged "chiefdom". There are only relationships regulated by the prerogatives, by the *timé*, of each social actor. On the partition of the spoils see Borecký 1965, which is still useful at least as a collection of the Homeric material, yet marred by the excessive use of the concept of "primitive communism" (see the review of Adkins 1968) and Detienne 1965; on Homeric *laos* see now Haubold 2000.

[148] *Il.* 9.111; see also 1.356; 507; 2.240.

[149] This insult reminds of Hesiod: Hes., *Erg.* 260-264; see Kirk 1985, p. 77.

[150] Sahlins 1965, p. 159; Donlan 1982, pp. 157 and 162.

[151] Hooker 1989, p. 80.

[152] Hooker 1989, p. 90: Hooker does not explain what he means with "custom" and in what sense this would differ from "institution". He probably means a literary motif

invented by the poem for literary reasons; 2) Reciprocity is not the rule in all gift transactions, as in the Homeric poems we find several cases when gifts are not reciprocated or are refused; 3) The society represented in the poems cannot be associated with a precise historical period, but is "a conflation of features drawn from various regions and various epochs".[153] The last objection is no more than an endorsement to Snodgrass' views. It is easy, on the basis of the picture of gift-giving provided in this essay, to answer to these objections.

1. If gift-exchange – in all its forms – is not perceived in the poems as an 'institution', how can we account for the fact that poet, in inventing it,[154] also invented a complex vocabulary which expresses in the poems the various forms that gift-giving assumes in different circumstances? In fact, these forms are perfectly coherent with the social system represented by the poems, centered on the *oikoi*, and in which the only form of social compact alternative to war is gift-exchange. This works also in the extreme scenario of the offer of gifts on the battlefield in exchange for one's life. And moreover, Hooker could not possibly explain the workings of *geras* – something he did not take into account in his analysis – as a "polite custom" without institutional importance.[155]
2. As for the rule of reciprocity, Hooker is correct when he points out that in some cases (such as Menelaus and the Phaeacians) the gift-giver does not expect future reciprocation. But the gift is nevertheless a duty of the host (*themis*), and establishes moreover a relationship of "friendship" (*philotes*) founded on the memory of the generosity of the gift-giver,[156] or strengthens any existing such relationship between the *oikoi*.

The structural function of gift-giving consists chiefly of two factors:

1. in the *oikos* economy, typical of the Homeric society, the gift-exchange constitutes an important strategy to increase wealth, together with the revenues which come from the property of the household and from raids, plunder and warfare. This wealth, amassed into the *oikos* 'treasure' in the form of *keimelia*,[157] is not used, but represents, as objects and goods of

invented for the occasion.

[153] Hooker 1989, p. 87.

[154] Hooker 1989, p. 87, speaks of "free invention of the bards".

[155] *Geras* with the meaning of 'privilege' is still found in Classical age: it is enough to look at Herodotus to see this (e.g. Hdt. 3.85.7; 4.143.1; 7.3.10; 134.5; 154.1; 9.27.5).

[156] Hooker 1989, p. 84, misunderstands the meaning of *Od.* 13.15 (ἀργαλέον γὰρ ἕνα προικὸς χαρίσασθαι): the matter is not the 'gratuity' of the gift, which does not require reciprocation. Alcinous is only saying that he will not be able to provide all the gifts by himself, but some of them will need to be gathered by the *demos*.

[157] On the "tresure economy" in Homer, see Donlan 1997, pp. 663-665.

prestige, the 'reserve' of the *oikos* and shows the power, wealth and fame of the family through its circulation in new future gift-exchange situations;

2. in a world such as the Homeric one, centered on the *oikos* and in which "the whole of what we call foreign relations and diplomacy ... was conducted by gift-exchange",[158] gift-giving – it does not matter if we are dealing with gifts of hospitality or a marital alliance or the creation of (temporary) links of *philotes* – represents the only form of social compact alternative to war, even though these social compacts do not involve the community but only two *aristoi* and their *oikoi*.

Bibliography

Adkins, Arthur W. H.: *'Honour' and 'Punishment' in the Homeric Poems*, in: *BICS* 7 (1960), pp. 23-32.

Adkins, Arthur W. H.: *Sharing in Greek Tribal Society*, in: *CR* 18 (1968), pp. 321-322.

Ambrose, Z. Philip: *The Homeric Telos*, in: *Glotta* 43 (1965), pp. 38-62.

Andreev, Juri V.: *Könige und Königsherrschaft in den Epen Homers*, in: *Klio* 61 (1979), pp. 361-384.

Arend, Walter: *Die typischen Szenen bei Homer*, Berlin 1933.

Beidelman, Thomas O.: *Agonistic Exchange: Homeric Reciprocity and the Heritage of Simmel and Mauss*, in: *Cultural Anthropology* 4 (1989), pp. 227-259.

Benveniste, Émile: *Le vocabulaire des institutions indo-européennes*, 2 vols., Paris 1969.

Bonner Robert J. – Gertrude Smith: *The Administration of Justice from Homer to Aristotle*, vol. 1, Chicago 1930.

Borecký, Bořivoj: *Survivals of Some Tribal Ideas in Classical Greek*, Prague 1965.

Bourriot, Félix: *Recherches sur la nature du genos. Études d'histoire sociale Athénienne*, Paris 1976.

Bravo, Benedetto: *Remarques sur les assises sociales, les formes d'organisation et la terminologie du commerce maritime à l'époque archaïque*, in: *DHA* 3 (1977), pp. 1-59.

Cairns, Douglas: *Ransom and Revenge in the Iliad*, in: *Sociable Man. Essays on Ancient Greek Social Behaviour in Honour of Nick Fisher*, ed. by Stephen D. Lambert, Swansea 2011a, pp. 87-116.

Cairns, Douglas: *Poiné and Apoina in the Iliad*, in: *"Böser Krieg". Exzessive Gewalt in der antiken Kriegsführung und Strategien zu deren Vermeidung*, ed. by Margit Linder – Sabine Tausend, Graz 2011b, pp. 35-50.

Cairns, Douglas: *Atê in the Homeric Poems*, in: *Papers of the Langford Latin Seminar. Fifteenth Volume*, Oxford 2012, ed. by Francis Cairns, pp. 1-52.

Calder, William M.: *Gold for Bronze: Iliad 6.232-36*, in: *Studies Presented to Sterling Dow*, ed. by Alan L. Boegehold, Durham 1984, pp. 31-35.

Cantarella, Eva: *Norma e sanzione in Omero. Contributo alla protostoria del diritto greco*, Milano 1979.

[158] Finley 1954, p. 76.

Carpenter, Rhys: *Folk Tale, Fiction and Saga in the Homeric Epics*, Berkeley – Los Angeles 1946.

Cartledge, Paul: *La nascita degli opliti e l'organizzazione militare*, in: *I Greci 2/1*, ed. by Salvatore Settis, Torino 1996, pp. 681-714.

Chadwick, John – Lydia Baumbach: *The Mycenaean Greek Vocabulary*, in: *Glotta* 41 (1963), pp. 157-271.

Cozzo, Andrea: *Kerdos. Semantica, ideologie e società nella Grecia antica*, Roma 1988.

Craig, J. D.: ΧΡΥΣΕΑ ΧΑΛΚΕΙΩΝ, in: *CR* 17 (1967), pp. 243-245.

Crielaard, Jan Paul: *Homer, History and Archaeology: Some Remarks on the Date of the Homeric World*, in: *Homeric Questions. Essays in Philology, Ancient History and Archaeology*, ed. by Jan Paul Crielaard, Amsterdam 1995, pp. 201-288.

Crielaard, Jan Paul: *Past or Present? Epic Poetry, Aristocratic Self-Representation and the Concept of Time in the Eighth and Seventh Centuries BC*, in: *Omero tremila anni dopo*, ed. by Franco Montanari – Paola Ascheri, Roma 2002, pp. 239-95

Crissy, Katherine: *Herakles, Odysseus, and the Bow: "Odyssey" 21.11-41*, in: *CJ* 93 (1997), pp. 41-53.

Detienne, Marcel: *En Grèce archaïque: géometrie, politique et société*, in: *AnnESC* 20 (1965), pp. 425-441.

de Vos, Harmen: *Themis*, Assen 1956.

Dodds, Eric R.: *The Greeks and the Irrational*, Berkeley – Los Angeles 1951.

Donlan, Walter: *Reciprocities in Homer*, in: *CW* 75 (1982), pp. 137-175.

Donlan, Walter: *The Social Groups of Dark Age Greece*, in: *CP* 80 (1985), pp. 293-308.

Donlan, Walter: *The Unequal Exchange between Glaucus and Diomedes in Light of the Homeric Gift-Economy*, in: *Phoenix* 43 (1989a), pp. 1-15.

Donlan, Walter: *The Pre-State Community in Greece*, in: *SO* 64 (1989b), pp. 2-29.

Donlan, Walter: *The Homeric Economy*, in: *A New Companion to Homer*, ed. by Ian Morris – Barry Powell, Leiden – New York – Köln 1997, pp. 649-667.

Donlan, Walter: *Political Reciprocity in Dark Age Greece: Odysseus and His Hetairoi*, in: *Reciprocity in Ancient Greece*, ed. by Christopher Gill – Norman Postlewaith – Richard Seaford, Oxford 1998, pp. 51-71.

Donlan, Walter: *Kin-Groups in the Homeric Epics*, in: *CW* 101 (2007), pp. 29-39.

Drews, Robert: *Basileus. The Evidence for Kingship in Geometric Greece*, New Haven – London 1983.

Fenik, Bernard: *Typical Battle Scenes in the Iliad*, Wiesbaden 1968.

Filkenberg, Margalit: *Timé and Areté in Homer*, in: *CQ* 48 (1998), pp. 14-28.

Finley, Moses I.: *The World of Odysseus*, New York 1954; Repr. Harmondsworth 1962.

Finley, Moses I.: *Marriage, Sale and Gift in the Homeric World*, in: *RIDA*, s. 3, 2 (1955), pp. 167-194.

Finley, Moses I.: *Homer and Mycenae: Property and Tenure*, in: *Historia* 6 (1957), pp. 133-159.

Finley, Moses I.: *The World of Odysseus Revisited*, in: *PCA* 71 (1974), pp. 13-31.

Frisk, Hjalmar: *Griechisches Etymologisches Wörterbuch, 1: A-Ko*, Heidelberg 1960.

Frisk, Hjalmar: *Griechisches Etymologisches Wörterbuch, 2: Kr-Ō*, Heidelberg 1970.

Gagarin, Michael: *Early Greek Law*, Berkeley 1986.

Gagarin, Michael: *Early Greek Law*, in: *The Cambridge Companion to Ancient Greek Law*, ed. by Michael Gagarin – David Cohen, Cambridge 2005, pp. 82-94.

Gernet, Louis: *Anthropologie de la Grèce antique*, Paris 1968.

Giordano, Manuela: *La supplica. Rituale, istituzione sociale e tema epico in Omero*, Napoli 1999.
Goody, Jack: *Inheritance, Property, and Marriage in Africa and Eurasia*, in: *Sociology* 3 (1969), pp. 55-76.
Goody, Jack: *Bridewealth and Dowry in Africa and Eurasia*, in: Jack Goody – Stanley J. Tambiah, *Bridewealth and Dowry*, Cambridge 1973, pp. 1-58.
Gottesman, Alex: *The Beggar and the Clod: The Mythic Notion of Property in Ancient Greece*, in: *TAPhA* 140 (2010), pp. 287-322.
Gould, John: *Hiketeia*, in: *JHS* 93 (1973), pp. 74-103.
Grethlein, Jonas: *Memory and Material Objects in the Iliad and the Odyssey*, in: *JHS* 128 (2008), pp. 27-51.
Gschnitzer, Fritz: *Zur homerischen Staats- und Gesellschaftsordnung: Grundcharakter und geschichtliche Stellung*, in: *Zweihundert Jahre Homer-Forschung: Rückblick und Ausblick*, ed. by Joachim Latacz, Stuttgart – Leipzig 1991, pp. 182-204.
Hainsworth, Bryan: *The Iliad: a Commentary, vol. 3: Books 9-12*, Cambridge 1993.
Hammer, Dean C.: *"Who Shall Readily Obey?": Authority and Politics in the "Iliad"*, in: *Phoenix* 51 (1997), pp. 1-24.
Haubold, Johannes: *Homer's People. Epic Poetry and Social Formation*, Cambridge 2000.
Havelock, Eric A.: *Preface to Plato*, Cambridge – London 1963.
Herman, Gabriel: *Ritualised Friendship and the Greek City*, Cambridge 1987.
Hirzel, Rudolf: *Themis, Dike und Verwandtes*, Leipzig 1907.
Hooker, James T.: *Gifts in Homer*, in: *BICS* 36 (1989), pp. 79-90.
Janko, Richard: *Homer, Hesiod and the Hymns*, Cambridge 1982.
Kirk, Geoffrey S.: *The Songs of Homer*, Cambridge 1962.
Kirk, Geoffrey S.: *The Iliad: A Commentary, vol. 1: Books 1-4*, Cambridge 1985.
Kirk, Geoffrey S.: *The Iliad: A Commentary, vol. 2: Books 5-8*, Cambridge 1990.
Köstler, Rudolf: *Homerisches Recht*, Wien 1950.
Krischer, Tilman: *Die Bogenprobe*, in: *Hermes* 120 (1992), pp. 19-25.
Lacey, Walter K.: *Homeric ΕΔΝΑ and Penelope's ΚΥΡΙΟΣ*, in: *JHS* 86 (1966), pp. 55-68.
Leaf Walter (ed. by): *The Iliad 1: Books 1-12*, London 1886.
Lejeune, Michel: *Les forgerons de Pylos*, in: *Historia* 10 (1961), pp. 409-434.
Leumann, Manu: *Homerische Wörter*, Basel 1950.
Link, Stefan: *"Temenos" und "ager publicus" bei Homer?*, in: *Historia* 43 (1994), pp. 241-245.
Lloyd-Jones, Hugh: *The Justice of Zeus*, Berkeley – Los Angeles 1971.
Long, Anthony A.: *Morals and Values in Homer*, in: *JHS* 90 (1970), pp. 121-139.
MacDowell, Douglas M.: *The Law in Classical Athens*, London 1978.
Maddoli, Gianfranco: *Δαμος e Βασιληες. Contributo allo studio delle origini della polis*, in: *SMEA* 12 (1970), pp. 7-57.
Mauss, Marcel: *Essai sur le don. Forme et raison de l'échange dans les sociétés archaïques*, in: *L'Année sociologique* n.s. 1 (1923-1924), pp. 30-186.
Mele, Alfonso: *Il commercio greco arcaico. Prexis ed emporie*, Napoli 1979.
Morris, Ian: *The Use and Abuse of Homer*, in: *ClAnt* 5 (1986a), pp. 81-138.
Morris, Ian: *Gift and Commodity in Archaic Greece*, in: *Man* 21 (1986b), pp. 1-17.

Morris, Ian: *Homer and the Iron Age*, in: *A New Companion to Homer*, ed. by Ian Morris – Barry Powell, Leiden – New York – Köln 1997, pp. 535-559.
Murdock, George P.: *Social Structure*, New York – London 1949.
Naiden, Fred S.: *Ancient Supplication*, Oxford 2006.
Osborne, Robin: *Homer's Society*, in: *The Cambridge Companion to Homer*, ed. by Robert Fowler, Cambridge 2004, pp. 206-219.
Page, Denys L.: *History and the Homeric Iliad*, Berkeley – Los Angeles 1959; Repr. Berkeley 1963.
Palmer, Leonard R.: *A Mycenaean Tomb Inventory*, in: *Minos* 5 (1957), pp. 58-92.
Pelloso, Carlo: *Themis e Dike in Omero. Ai primordi del diritto dei Greci*, Alessandria 2012.
Posner, Richard A.: *The Homeric Version of the Minimal State*, in: *Ethics* 90 (1979), pp. 27-46.
Pötscher, Walter: *Moira, Themis und τιμή im homerischen Denken*, in: *WS* 83 (1960), pp. 5-39.
Pugliese Carratelli, Giovanni: *Dal regno miceneo alla polis*, in: *Dalla tribù allo stato. Atti del convegno internazionale*, Roma 1962, pp. 175-189.
Quiller, Bjørn: *The Dynamics of the Homeric Society*, in: *SO* 56 (1981), pp. 109-155.
Raaflaub, Kurt A.: *Homer und die Geschichte des 8.Jh.v.Chr.*, in: *Zweihundert Jahre Homer-Forschung: Rückblick und Ausblick*, ed. by Joachim Latacz, Stuttgart – Leipzig 1991, pp. 205-256.
Raaflaub, Kurt A.: *Homeric Society*, in: *A New Companion to Homer*, ed. by Ian Morris – Barry Powell, Leiden – New York – Köln 1997, pp. 624-648.
Raaflaub, Kurt A.: *A Historian's Headache: How to Read 'Homeric Society'?*, in: *Archaic Greece: New Approaches and New Evidence*, ed. by Nick Fisher – Hans van Wees, London 1998, pp. 169-193.
Radcliffe-Brown, Alfred R.: *Introduction*, in: *African Systems of Kinship and Marriage*, ed. by Alfred R. Radcliffe-Brown – Cyrill D. Forde, Oxford 1950, pp. 1-85.
Richardson, Nicholas: *The Iliad: A Commentary, vol. 6: Books 21-24*, Cambridge 1993.
Riedinger, Jean-Claude: *Remarques sur la τιμή chez Homère*, in: *REG* 89 (1976), pp. 244-264.
Rose, Gilbert P.: *The Unfriendly Phaeacians*, in: *TAPhA* 100 (1969), pp. 387-406.
Roussel, Denis: *Tribu et cité. Études sur les groupes sociaux dans les cités grecques aux époques archaïque et classique*, Paris 1976.
Runciman, Walter Garry: *Origins of States: The Case of Archaic Greece*, in: *CSSH* 24 (1982), pp. 351-377.
Sahlins, Marshall D.: *On the Sociology of Primitive Exchange*, in: *The Relevance of Models for Social Anthropology*, London 1965, pp. 139-238.
Schofield, Malcolm: *Euboulia in the Iliad*, in: *CQ* 36 (1986), pp. 6-31.
Seaford, Richard: *Reciprocity and Ritual*, Oxford 1994.
Service, Elmar R.: *Primitive Social Organization: An Evolutionary Perspective*, New York 1971^2.
Shipp, George P.: *Studies in the language of Homer*, Cambridge 1972^2.
Snodgrass, Anthony M.: *The Dark Age of Greece: An Archaeological Survey of the Eleventh to Eighth Century BC*, Edinburgh 1971.
Snodgrass, Anthony M.: *An Historical Homeric Society?*, in: *JHS* 94 (1974), pp. 114-125.
Snodgrass, Anthony M.: *Archaic Greece. The Age of Experiment*, London 1980.

Strathern, Marilyn: *Marriages Exchanges: A Melanesian Comment*, in: *Annual Review of Anthropology* 13 (1984), pp. 41-73.

Thomas, Carol G.: *Homer and the Polis*, in: *PdP* 21 (1966a), pp. 5-14.

Thomas, Carol G.: *The roots of Homeric kingship*, in: *Historia* 16 (1966b), pp. 387-407.

Thomas, Carol G.: *The Nature of Mycenaean Kingship*, in: *SMEA* 17 (1976), pp. 93-116.

Thür, Gerhard: *Der Reinigungseid im archaischen griechischen Rechsstreit und seine Parallelen im alten Orient*, in: *Rechtsgeschichte und Interkulturalität: zum Verhältnis des östlichen Mittelmeerraums und 'Europas' im Altertum*, ed. by Robert Rollinger – Heinz Barta – Martin Lang, Wiesbaden 2007, pp. 179-195.

Traill, David A.: *Gold Armor for Bronze and Homer's Use of Compensatory τιμή*, in: *CPh* 84 (1989), pp. 301-305.

Ventris, Michael – John Chadwick: *Documents in Mycenaean Greek*, Cambridge 1959.

von Reden, Sitta: *Exchange in Ancient Greece*, London 1995.

von Wilamowitz-Moellendorf, Ulrich: *Die Heimkehr der Odysseus*, Berlin 1927.

Webster, Thomas B. L.: *From Mycenae to Homer*, London 1964^2.

West, Stephanie: *Omero. Odissea, vol. 1 (libri I-IV)*, Milano 1981.

Westbrook, Raymond: *The Trial Scene in the Iliad*, in: *HSCPh* 94 (1992), pp. 53-76.

Wolff, Hans Julius: *The Origin of Judicial Litigation among the Greeks*, in: *Traditio* 4 (1946), pp. 31-87

Wyatt, William F.: *Homeric ἌΤΗ*, in: *AJPh* 103 (1982), pp. 247-276.

Yamagata, Naoko: *Anax and Basileus in Homer*, in: *CQ* 47 (1997), pp. 1-14.

Zanker, Graham: *Beyond Reciprocity: The Akhilleus-Priam Scene in Iliad 24*, in: *Reciprocity in Ancient Greece*, ed. by Christopher Gill – Norman Postlewaith – Richard Seaford, Oxford 1998, pp. 73-92.

KOENRAAD VERBOVEN

'Like bait on a hook'. Ethics, Etics and Emics of Gift-Exchange in the Roman World

Since Finley's *World of Ulysses*, gift-exchange has been widely used by classicists to explain social relations and interactions in Greco-Roman society. It has been interpreted as the underlying rationale of Greek *philia* and Roman *amicitia*, of ritualized guest-friendship, patronage, inter-state relations, political alliances, credit and sureties, and so forth.[1]

In this paper, I argue that the explanatory force of the concept has been overstretched. Although gift-exchange was important both morally and practically, it was not the only or even the dominant principle of interpersonal relations in Greco-Roman society. In many cases it was no more than a symbolic frame of reference actively used to justify social claims and actions that had little to do with gift-exchange as such.

1. Anthropology – cultural diversity

a. Gift-exchange – reciprocal altruism

The principles of gift-exchange occur in widely different cultures throughout history. They are genetically rooted in the propensity for 'reciprocal altruism' – the tendency to spend or forego resources on behalf of genetically unrelated others in the expectation that the recipients will return the benefits at a future occasion. Reciprocal altruism is observed by socio-biologists in all social animals (including primates and hominids) endowed with sufficient cognitive capacities to recognize and remember individual actions.[2] As socially programmed behavior, however – i.e. as a social institution – gift-exchange is articulated in many different ways depending on how culturally evolved institutions integrate or reject the genetic propensity to 'reciprocal altruism'.

Mediterranean cultures generally emphasized gift-exchange as a central principle in social interaction. It occurs in Greek literature since Homer; in the

[1] I sincerely wish to thank the editors and anonymous reviewers for their very helpful comments. Of course all remaining errors are mine only.

[2] Gouldner 1977; Trivers 2006; Silk – Boyd 2010. Note, however, that the evidence for reciprocal altruism in non-hominid species is limited, contrary to the abundant evidence of tit-for-tat interactions and biological markets.

earliest Latin literature of the third century BCE and runs on through the ages down to twentieth century Italian, Greek, Spanish, Berber, Arab and Turkish culture.[3]

b. Civic institutions – strong reciprocity / true altruism

But gift-exchange was never the only important principle governing social exchange in the Mediterranean area. Jewish prophets for instance stressed submission to God and divine law to impose charity alongside norms of fairness and of cooperation. Christianity and Islam adopted the same idea – and like Judaism allowed ample room for gift-exchange in practice.[4] The ideology and organization of Greek *poleis*, the *populus Romanus* and Roman cities, as well, cannot be explained by gift-exchange. Contrary to the particularistic reciprocity of gift-exchange, the rights and obligations of citizens invoked a general reciprocity of the kind that 'all should do their part and receive their share in return'. Citizens were entitled to support in matters of personal security, enforcement of property rights, voting rights, and much more. In return they had to invest time and resources in the city's functioning and survival, up to the point that it could cost them their life. Roman legends are filled with heroes like Marcus Curtius who sacrificed himself to preserve his city,[5] or Lucius Brutus who ordered the execution of his own sons for their involvement in a conspiracy to reinstall the tyrant King Tarquinius Superbus.[6]

Civic culture relied on cooperation based on the willingness of individuals to spend or forego resources for the community without clear prospects of personal benefits other than the moral respect of their fellow citizens or in extreme cases merely the satisfaction of 'doing the right thing'. The central principle underlying this behavior is not "reciprocal altruism", but another "human universal" defined as "strong reciprocity": the tendency

> "to cooperate with others and punish non-cooperators, even when this behavior cannot be justified in terms of extended kinship or reciprocal altruism".[7]

[3] See e.g. Benveniste 1948-1949; Michel 1962, pp. 449-601; Finley 1977², pp. 64-66 and 120-123; Saller 1982, pp. 8-39 and 143; Herman 1987, pp. 73-82 (and *passim*); Gallant 1991, pp. 143-153; Millett 1991, pp. 27-44 (and *passim*); Dixon 1993; Lendon 1997, pp. 63-69; Tandy 1997, pp. 94-101; Gill – Postlewait – Seaford 1998; Bourdieu 2000², pp. 31-35 and 337-341; Herman 2006; Schwartz 2010, pp. 1-20.

[4] Schwartz 2010; on gifts in Jewish culture see also Satlow elsewhere in this volume.

[5] Liv. 7.6.

[6] Liv. 2.3-4.

[7] Gintis 2000; Gintis – Bowles – Boyd – Fehr 2005; Gintis – Henrich – Bowles – Boyd – Fehr 2008; Fehr – Fischbacher 2003 for a review. Note the confusing terminology:

Strong reciprocity implies true altruism, in some cases to the point of self-destruction. It is a crucial factor in human history. Both laboratory experiments and ethnographic evidence show that reciprocal altruism fails to explain cooperation even in small-scale societies such as forager bands, nomadic herding groups, horticulturalists or small-scale agriculturalists.[8]

Socio-biologists disagree on the genetic foundations for true altruism between genetically unrelated individuals.[9] Traditionally, biologists have argued that true altruism and impersonal morality are (fortunate) maladaptations of the human mind, grown out of reciprocal altruism.[10] Recently, however, a number of socio-biologists have shown that altruism can provide an evolutionary stable strategy provided that it includes an altruistic willingness to punish free-riders and non-cooperators and provided that effective mechanisms are available to detect these and inflict punishment. When these conditions are met, 'strong reciprocity' results in a significant increase of the general fitness of a population. Gene pools with alleles programming for strong reciprocity will fare better than gene pools without.[11]

The differences between societies, however, are profound. They hinge upon the costs of altruistic punishment and on the institutions available to enforce cooperative norms. Altruistic punishers are vulnerable to anti-social retaliatory punishment from close kin and associates of non-cooperators and free-riders. Impersonal cooperative norms fail when societies lack sufficiently strong institutions to suppress such antisocial punishment. When this is the case, kin-based cooperation and conditional reciprocity take over. Social norms and beliefs play a crucial part. They determine when pro-social punishment is legitimate and will therefore be backed up by formal and informal norms.[12]

In other words, the morality and practice of altruism have a universal genetic basis. But the conditions under which it is possible for these genetic traits to become manifest depend not only on cognitive capacity but as much and more on socially learned (cultural) behavior signaling intentions and allowing social

"reciprocal altruism" is true reciprocity but only apparent altruism; "strong reciprocity" is reciprocity only in the sense that the altruistic individual enjoys the social support of his community. Contrary to simple "true altruism" the concept of "strong reciprocity" denotes altruistic rewards and punishments for norm abiding or violating behavior. For a critique, see Trivers 2006.

[8] For ethnographic examples see Bowles – Gintis 2011, pp. 93-147; Mathew – Boyd 2011. For a combined approach of cross-cultural experiments with ethnographic data from 15 small-scale societies see Henrich – Boyd – Bowles Camerer – Fehr – Gintis 2004.

[9] For a discussion see Gintis – Henrich – Bowles – Boyd – Fehr 2008.

[10] Price 2008; in the same vein Trivers 2006.

[11] Bowles – Gintis 2011 and see above n. 6. Alleles are variants of genes that (may) produce differences in organisms.

[12] Gintis – Henrich – Bowles – Boyd – Fehr 2008; Bowles – Gintis 2011, pp. 26-29.

agents to build reputations that reliably predict future actions.[13] Hence true altruism takes on many different shapes in different cultures.

We should not make the mistake of thinking that the altruism supported by strong reciprocity is universally good. The willingness to cooperate and punish non-cooperators, even against one's own interests, manifests itself most strongly in warfare.[14] Although strong reciprocity lies at the root of all great cultures, including Greco-Roman civic culture, the institutions it generates profoundly shape self-interested behavior. The institutional fabric of complex societies can make instincts for strong reciprocity of large segments of the population subservient to the interests of small privileged elites. The willingness to sacrifice or forego resources on behalf of others or of the community that one feels a part of can support a status quo that is favorable only to a small privileged minority.

c. Interaction between gift exchange and civic institutions?

As we noted above, gift-exchange (reciprocal altruism) flourishes when institutions upholding 'strong reciprocity' are weak. However, the relation between gift-exchange, self-interest and institutions based on strong reciprocity is not straightforward. Gift-exchange acquires a significantly larger potential if transgressors are actively punished by disinterested third party intervention and when the socially learned norms governing it are ascribed a universal transcendent value. Left on its own, gift-exchange relies on the consideration of the agents that if they violate the terms of their relation they stand to lose future benefits because they acquire a reputation of unreliability. When, however, the exchange is embedded in an institutionalized setting reflecting norms of fairness backed up by strong reciprocity, the cost for default is much higher, particularly if the norms in question have been formalized into laws and contracts that trigger public enforcement mechanisms.

Roman society provides many examples of this. For instance, a commission to buy something for a friend in Rome was not just an *officium* within *amicitia*; it was also a formless contract of *mandatum* that created enforceable obligations

[13] On gene-culture evolution as a condition see Gintis 2003; Bowles – Gintis 2011, *passim*.

[14] Mathew – Boyd 2011; Bowles – Gintis 2011, pp. 102-106 and 133-147. Warfare may have contributed to spread the gene for 'strong reciprocity' among Pleistocene forager bands. Under roughly similar conditions regarding group size and weapon technology, populations where the allele was less manifest would have had lower levels of altruistic cooperation. Hence they were massacred or forced to abandon resource rich environments (Bowles – Gintis 2011, *loc. cit.*).

both ways.[15] Partnerships (*societates*) were nearly always based on kin or gift-exchange relations, but also entailed legally enforceable obligations.[16]

Conversely, 'strong reciprocity' imposes limits on gift-exchange. Cicero asserts that in friendship nothing shameful (*turpis*) should be asked nor done.[17] Seneca warns not to accept favors from 'unworthy' persons.[18] When his brother, as governor of Asia, intervened illegally to favor a friend, Cicero admonished him: "sometimes, the law doesn't allow *gratia*".[19]

d. Market exchange

Civic institutions rooted in strong reciprocity, however, are not the only alternative to gift-exchange in shaping social exchange. *Quid pro quo* exchanges occur in all human populations and market-like interactions – in which exchange rates are determined by supply, demand and a desire to maximize personal utility – have been described even for other social animals.[20] The market as an instituted process however (that is as learned behavior, as opposed to the abstract market of neo-classical economics) is a social construct that reflects the specific cultural settings in which it develops.[21]

For most of human history, institutionalized markets remained marginal phenomena. Although hunter-gatherer cultures show great diversity in social arrangements, none left much room for market exchange in their internal institutional setup. Barter of course occurs in all human populations, but mainly as an aside to social relations to fulfill reciprocal needs of the partners in the exchange. Supply and demand is not a driving force because the exchange partners share long-term (although not necessarily very deep) relations of mutual cooperation and dependency. Hence supply and demand at a single moment in time are largely irrelevant in determining the exchange rate, and neither is there a fixed price that would affect supply and demand rates. Instead exchange rates directly reflect the needs and desires of the exchanging parties.[22]

[15] Verboven 2002, pp. 227-274.
[16] Verboven 2002, pp. 275-286.
[17] Cic., *Amic.* 40.
[18] Sen., *Ben.* 2.18.5.
[19] Cic., *Ad Quint. fr.* 1.2.10: *uis iuris eius modi est quibusdam in rebus ut nihil sit loci gratiae*. See also Cotton 1986 on the role of *existimatio*.
[20] See Barret – Henzi 2006; Noë 2006.
[21] Polanyi 1957; for a recent neo-institutionalist view of how culture drives the development of institutions that are necessary for markets see North 2005 (esp. pp. 87-102); North – Wallis – Weingast 2009.
[22] Humphrey – Hugh-Jones 1992.

Outside close knit groups, however, barter glides into institutionalized market exchange. In these, objects are accorded an exchange-value that is independent from the needs of the specific partners in the exchange. For many thousands of years, institutionalized market exchange occurred primarily between strangers as an alternative to violence and was conducted mostly in highly ritualized settings.[23] During the Neolithic in some parts of the world (such as the Near and Middle East) institutionalized markets began to expand in tandem with growing population levels that created large organized sedentary groups within walking distance of each other and increased the number of (and the occasion for) interactions between unrelated self-interested individuals. Gradually, market exchange became more and more acceptable also for in-group exchanges. Exchange ratios no longer reflected the individual needs of the exchanging partners, but referred to an impersonal 'value' invested in the objects. This process took thousands of years. Part of the reason why this was so is that neither instincts for reciprocal altruism nor for strong reciprocity are in themselves able fully to control intense interactions between unrelated self-interested individuals. People will readily cheat when they do not feel institutionally constrained, bound either by formal enforceable rules or by informal norms. In economic terms, market exchange is limited by prohibitive transaction costs if it is not supported by institutions that lay down and enforce the 'rules of the (market) game'.[24]

The development of institutionalized markets hinges upon the development of means to express the impersonal value of resources and services. Common measures of value have to be developed and intermediate resources have to be available that store easily and can be trusted to maintain their desirability. Significantly, money itself relies on a social institution: the socially learned belief that goods and services have an exchange value expressible in symbolic terms, and that they should be exchanged in return for tokens symbolizing this exchange value.[25] Money in the form of commodities or bullion was institutionalized long before the invention of coinage. Since at least the third millennium BCE, city states in Mesopotamia used weighed silver, copper, and grain as equivalencies to express the value of items stored, distributed, donated or traded.[26]

[23] Sahlins 1972; Gowdy 1999; Graeber 2011, pp. 29-32

[24] Information costs: the time/effort/resources needed to acquire all relevant information (for instance is something I need available for sale or not? is someone else offering the same commodity cheaper? is it worthwhile to wait a little longer? is its quality good enough? etc.); bargaining costs: the time/efforts/resources needed to arrive at an acceptable agreement. Enforcement costs: the time/effort/resources needed to make sure the agreement is properly executed.

[25] On money as a social institution see Ingham 1996.

[26] Le Rider 2001; Schaps 2004. See also Peyronel's paper in this volume.

The importance of markets for in-group exchanges, however, increased significantly since the sixth century BCE when coinage linked monetary symbolism with civic institutions.[27] By the fourth century BCE monetization in the Greek *poleis* had reached even small day-to-day transactions. Aristotle sketched the natural evolution of the τέχνη κτητική into barter and hence into monetized market exchanges.[28] His origins' theory is historically incorrect, but testifies to the centrality of monetized exchange to the Greek mind. The Roman jurists took over the same idea. They sharply distinguished between money as a measure of value (*pretium*) and commodities (*merx*) subject of barter or sale.[29] In the Hellenistic and Roman period, markets and market exchanges were everywhere and society was inconceivable without them. They had become a central part of their institutional makeup subject to social and legal norms.[30]

e. Interplay gift-exchange – civic institutions – markets

Institutionalized markets and civic institutions provide two examples of how Greco-Roman social institutions tapped into the universals of human behavior. The list could be expanded. Reputation and prestige (*dignitas*), for instance, were tremendously important in Roman society. They too are a universal feature of human populations that occurs in vastly different cultural forms but is only loosely related to reciprocal altruism and strong reciprocity.[31] Although prestige can be signaled and reinforced through gift-exchange, it cannot be reduced to it. Family ties, previous accomplishments, religious roles, education and many more criteria determine who is endowed with it. In the institutional fabric of societies, prestige and reputation building is intertwined with self-interest, reciprocal altruism and strong reciprocity, generating constraints and possibilities for human behavior.

So, although gift-exchange was a much emphasized form of social interaction, the institutional fabric of Greek and Roman society had many more roots and was much more complex than forager bands, tribes or the chiefdoms that

[27] Coinage itself was a Lydian/Ionian invention from the 7th century BCE but its emphatic link with civic institutions and diffusion over the entire Greek world was a 6th century phenomenon. See Kim 2001; Kim 2002; Schaps 2004.
[28] Arist., *Pol.* 1.1257a; see also Plat., *Rep.* 371b
[29] Paulus in *D* 18.1.1. The distinction emphasized by Roman jurists of the Proculian school between *merx* and *pretium* is prefigured by Plato (*Rep.* 371b) and Aristotle (*EN* 1133a, 17-20) when they discuss convention rather than metal content as the basis for the value of money. See also Verboven 2007.
[30] Ioh. Chrys., *In princ. act.* 4.3; on money and the Greek mind see also Seaford 2004; and see Verboven 2009 on 'deep monetisation'.
[31] Plourde 2010.

characterized most parts of the Mediterranean during the Late Bronze and Early Iron Age.[32] If we want to understand the role of gift-exchange in Roman society, the challenge is not to study it as an institution in itself but to look at how it related to other institutions such as markets, money, family, law, political assemblies and so forth. In doing so it is useful to distinguish between gift-exchange as a social practice and the significance and meaning attached to it by social agents.

2. Etics and emics

The distinction between 'etic' and 'emic' in cultural anthropology denotes the difference between an analysis based on the outsider perspective (etic) in terms that are not culture-dependent, and an analysis based on the insider perspective (emic) in terms that are meaningful to the social agents of a particular culture.

An emic perspective includes ideology and value judgments, but is not limited to these. It focuses on interpretations and meanings attached by social agents in a particular culture to social actions. It looks at mental maps agents use to orient their behavior and to identify the motives of others. It also allows us to analyze the discrepancies between behavior and ideals as observed by social agents and to identify when and why the discourse of gift-exchange is used in connection with institutions that are not based on gift-exchange practices.

Sydel Silverman used the distinction to describe the role of patronage ideology in the relations between local elites (mostly landowners) and their *mezzadria* tenants in a middle Italian village. She noted that gift-exchange between presumed patrons and clients was infrequent and of little value, but the rhetorical importance of patronage was extensive.[33] Richard Saller applied the concept to argue that Roman conceptions and presentations of patronage should be distinguished from the actual importance of patron-clients relations in terms of asymmetrical exchange relations based on trust and reciprocity.[34] I myself used it to distinguish Roman patronage as an idiosyncratic cultural phenomenon from patronage as a sociological concept.[35]

[32] Cf. Ferguson 1991; Gilman 1991.

[33] Silverman 1977.

[34] Saller 1982.

[35] Verboven 2002, pp. 60-62.

a. The 'ethics' of gift-exchange

The ideology of gift-exchange in Roman culture is easy to trace and has often been discussed. Gifts and favors were acts of kindness (*beneficia*) that signified good-will on the part of the giver. Ideologically they came with no strings attached.

> "Whoever gives *beneficia* imitates the gods, whoever asks for a return (imitates) usurers".[36]

However, they created an obligation of *gratia* on the part of the receiver. Not to return a *beneficium* was disgraceful.[37] Notwithstanding this moral obligation to reciprocate, the return gift itself was voluntary and therefore also constituted an act of kindness:

> "There are two kinds of generosity, one that consists in giving a *beneficium*, the other of returning one".[38]

Because the obligation to return was non-specific and all *beneficia* signaled dispositions of goodwill, the obligation of *gratia* bound both parties in a relationship of instrumental friendship – they became *beneficiis devincti.*[39] Ideally this relation was enduring because a debt of *gratia* never expired. The exchange of gifts and favors should never stop. "For I owe (still) when I have returned, start again, but friendship stays".[40]

Underlying the relation was *fides*: trust and loyalty. *Fides* was crucial to social life. There was a *communis fides* owed to all, and specifically to fellow citizens. *Fides* guaranteed international treaties and commercial contracts. It expressed a debtor's solvency and his credibility.[41] It guaranteed that social obligations would be upheld and was manifest in the upholding of obligations derived from *gratia.*[42] It was the cement of personal relations and the core of friendship.[43] Cicero describes it as the "prop of stability and constancy" (*firma-*

[36] Sen., *Ben.* 3.15.4: *Qui dat beneficia deos imitatur, qui repetit, faeneratores.* See also *Ben.* 1.2.3; 6.1; Cic., *Amic.* 31; Michel 1962, pp. 526-527; Hands 1968, pp. 44-45.
[37] Cic., *Off.* 1.48: *non reddere viro non licet.*
[38] Cic., *Off.* 1.48.
[39] Cf. e.g. Cic., *Ad fam.* 10.8.3; *Off.* 2.65; 69; Sen., *Dial.* 7.24.2.
[40] Sen., *Ben.* 2.18.5; cf. Cic., *Off.* 1.69.
[41] Cf. Freyburger 1986, pp. 115-166; for *fides* in commercial contracts see Imbert 1959; cf. Gell. 20.1.41; Cic., *Off.* 2.40.
[42] Cf. Cic., *Ad fam.* 3.9.1; *Marc.* 14; Plaut., *Trin.* 1128.
[43] Cf. e.g. Claudius Caecus, *Sententiae* 249 (ed. Ribbeck): *amicitiae unica est fides coagulum.* See also Brunt 1965, p. 355.

mentum stabilitatis constantiaeque) of *amicitia.*[44] As a city without a port cannot be a safe haven to ships, so a soul with no *fides* cannot be steadfast for friends.[45]

These moral principles were guaranteed by reputation (*existimatio*). Honor and prestige depended on a person's ability to live up to social obligations.[46] Stinginess, ingratitude, or disloyalty destroyed a person's reputation.[47] No one desired *amicitia* with someone who was reputedly *ingratus*, and *infidus*.[48]

This ideology of the gift was obviously an important factor in how Romans gave meaning to what they and others did, and deserves attention in any emic approach. But the meanings attached to gifts and favors were not all inspired by this ideology. Appreciations of gifts and favors often vary considerably from what the ethics prescribe; 'emics' are more than 'ethics'. For a good understanding of how the emics of gift-exchange worked, however, we first need to look at the 'etics' of gift-exchange.

b. The 'etics' of Roman gift exchange

From an 'etic' point of view, gift-exchange is characterized by (1) reciprocity, (2) a time lag between gift and counter-gift, and (3) personal but (4) non-specific obligations. By far most attested gifts and favors in Roman society were of low value. They served as tokens of goodwill and pledges of support. Martial presents an extensive list: earthenware he gave to his protector Arruntius Stella,[49] nuts given by clients to their patrons at New Year,[50] olives from Picenum, preserved figs, Lucanian sausages, Faliscan entrails, cheap Syrian wine, etc.[51]

The form and value of gifts had to reflect the status of the giver. Notables were under pressure to be generous. Martial ridicules his 'great friends' who gave him only worthless gifts, like Lupus who gave him a piece of land smaller than a flower pot.[52] Postumianus generously started with four pounds of silver,

[44] Cic., *Off.* 1.65.
[45] Cic., *Inv.* 1.47: *Nam ut locus sine portu nauibus esse non potest tutus, sic animus sine fide stabilis amicis non potest esse*; cf. also Plaut., *Merc.* 839.
[46] Cf. Publ. Syr., *Sent.* D4 (ed. Meyer): *Dixeris male dicta cuncta, cum ingratum hominem dixeris.*
[47] Worse than death according to Cic., *Quinct.* 49; 98; *Pro Q. Rosc.* 16.
[48] Michel 1962, pp. 589-590.
[49] Mart. 5.59.
[50] Mart. 8.33.
[51] Mart. 4.46.
[52] Mart. 11.18.

but ended with a silver spoon lighter than a needle.[53] Sextus gave him a pound of silver the first year, but only half a pound of pepper the next.[54]

But small gifts for the giver could be substantial for the receiver. Patrons were expected to give their clients some money when they came to pay their respect, symbolically denoted as a hundred *quadrantes* by satirical poets. But such a 'trifle' could significantly improve the client's income.[55]

Truly substantial gifts were mainly limited to crisis situations. When Cicero left Italy in exile, Rabirius Postumus gave him gold.[56] More commonly, friends stepped in to pay debts. Thus, Cicero paid the debts of his son's friend L. Tullius Montanus because "it pertains to our duty" (*pertinet ad nostrum officium*).[57] Caesar would have paid the debts of Marc Antony,[58] C. Scribonius Curio,[59] and L. Aemilius Paullus.[60] Marc Antony offered money to young Q. Cicero in 44 with which to pay his debts.[61]

Sometimes patrons made exceptionally large donations to enable the receivers to enhance or maintain their social rank.[62] Pliny contributed 50,000 sesterces to the dowry of Quintilianus's daughter.[63] Calvina received 100,000 sesterces.[64] He gave 40,000 sesterces to Metilius Crispus on the occasion of his promotion to centurion,[65] and 300,000 sesterces to Romatius Firmus to provide him with the *census equester*.[66]

Cicero's letters of recommendation provide a fascinating catalogue of favors done to friends and protégés. Most letters introduce businessmen, young politicians, or senators with private interests to provincial governors. Cicero wrote an elaborate letter of recommendation to the governor of Asia on behalf of the businessman Cluvius from Puteoli who managed the investments of Pompey

[53] Mart. 8.71.
[54] Mart. 10.57.
[55] Verboven 2002, pp. 95-99.
[56] Cic., *Rab. Post.* 47
[57] Cic., *Ad Att.* 12.52.1.
[58] Cic., *Phil.* 2.4; Plut., *Pomp.* 58.1; Shatzman 1975, pp. 297-304.
[59] Plut., *Pomp.* 58.1; Vell. Pat. 2.48.3-4; Lucan. 1.269; 4.819-820; App., *Civ.* 2.26; Dio 40.60.2; Shatzman 1975, pp. 396.
[60] Plut., *Caes.* 29.3; *Pomp.* 58.1; Suet., *Iul.* 29.1; App., *Civ.* 2.26; Dio 40.63.2; Shatzman 1975, pp. 289-290.
[61] Cic., *Ad Att.* 15.21.1. See also *Ad Att.* 13.42.1; 14.14.1; 19.3; 15.19.2; 21.1; 16.5.2.
[62] Apuleius prided himself on having provided dowries for the daughters of some of his friends and teachers: Apul., *Apol.* 23.2.
[63] Plin., *Ep.* 6.32.
[64] Plin., *Ep.* 2.4.
[65] Plin., *Ep.* 6.25.3.
[66] Plin., *Ep.* 1.19.

and needed the governor's help against five cities who owed him money.[67] Cluvius also helped Cicero to invest money.[68] When he died, he left a large part of his inheritance to Cicero and to Caesar. Cicero's share was worth well over a million sesterces. The third – and probably main heir, was a businessman called T. Hordeonius who no doubt took over Cluvius's network and business.[69]

Similar arrangements were behind the fortunes of other wealthy businessmen as Atticus's adoptive father Q. Caecilus, C. Rabirius Postumus, P. Sittius, T. Pinnius or C. Vestorius. While these *affairistes* needed political connections to operate, politicians depended on their business expertise to invest cash and manage their debt claims.

Gift-exchange was closely related to the unequal distribution of entitlements in the Roman world, both qualitatively – as in the case of the businessmen who offered expertise and networks in exchange for political backing – and quantitatively – as in the case of protégés and clients.

Yet, gift-exchange alone was rarely a determining factor in allocating resources or entitlements. Under the Republic, elections were the mechanism by which power was conferred upon politicians who had been preselected on the basis of qualifications regarding minimum property and morals. Since the late second century BCE rhetoric and programs concerning issues as land distributions, debt relief or food supply played an increasing role. The part of gift-exchange relations was to build temporary alliances allowing candidates to optimize their chances on the volatile political market.[70] Military success came to the fore with the civil wars. When things stabilized again under Augustus, hereditary monopolies and religion took over.

Gift-exchange offered access to minor positions and furthered one's career, but the exercise of power was not based on gift-exchange. Although benefactions to citizens and soldiers boosted the popularity of consuls and generals, their authority did not rely on them.

Gift-exchange certainly provided an important economic strategy. It procured resources otherwise available only within closed family groups, like credit or information. But production and distribution were not determined by gift-exchange. The mobilization of labor was primarily determined by kinship, slavery and market exchange. Products were sold for cash or on credit. Roman markets may have been imperfect, fragmented and predominantly local; they were markets nonetheless.

[67] Cic., *Ad Fam.* 13.56.
[68] Cic., *Ad Att.* 6.2.3.
[69] See Andreau 1983.
[70] Exemplified in the *Commentariolum Petitionis* written by Quintus Cicero for his brother.

Institutionally, the role of gift-exchange was primarily that of facilitating interaction. In the absence of bureaucratic procedures, gift-exchange relations gave access to centers of decision making and to the assignment of minor offices and resources. In economic life, gift-exchange fulfilled the role later played by impersonal organizations and institutions as bills of exchange, stock markets, public debt or published price lists.

Tensions often arose.[71] A good example is the allocation of public contracts. The magistrates responsible were supposed to adjudicate tax contracts to the highest bidder, and contracts for public works to the lowest bidder. In reality contracts were routinely assigned to 'friends'.

One of Cicero's witnesses against Verres, Q. Tadius, testified that he had given money to Verres in exchange for lucrative contracts. Tadius was a relative of Verres's mother and a close friend of his father.[72] The sensitivity of some officials to the needs of *publicani* is clear also in the case of P. Valerius, a local tax-farmer in Cilicia who went bankrupt under Cicero's governorship. Valerius's sureties (*praedes*) consequently risked being sued. At least two of them, M. Anneius and Q. Paconius Lepta, were *amici* of Cicero on whose staff they served as legate and prefect. By manipulating the provincial accounts Cicero managed to release them from their obligations.[73] Cato the Elder's censorship became famous for the straightforwardness with which the eccentric conservative ignored bribes and influence. The case was exceptional enough to be noted by his biographers.[74] It is interesting to see here how gift-exchange touched with bribery and market relations.

c. The 'emics' of gift-exchange

To the Roman mind, *beneficia, gratia* and *fides*, and their close connection with *existimatio*, served as a template to make sense of social practice. The template was applied even when it was recognized that the logic underlying a social act had little to do with gift-exchange or that the social agents were motivated by self-interest rather than kindness or a sense of obligation.

While sincerity was expected in the ideology of *gratia*, insincerity was not a valid excuse not to reciprocate. Hence, Martial, Horace and Pliny describe gifts

[71] As Paul Veyne put it: Roman aristocrats "étaient sans cesse tiraillés entre ce qu'ils devaient à l'Etat et ce qu'ils devaient à leurs 'amis', entre leur devoir de citoyen et leurs devoirs interindividuels" (Veyne 1976, p. 386). For a similar view see also Brunt 1986.

[72] Cic., *Verr.* 2.1.128.

[73] Cic., *Ad Att.* 5.21.14; *Ad Fam.* 5.20.3-4. The case is obscure. See Shackleton Bailey 1977, vol. 1, pp. 467-468.

[74] Plut., *Cat. Mai.* 19; Liv. 39.44.7.

as baits on an angler's hook.[75] Martial excused himself to Quintianus because he sent merely a poem on the *Saturnalia*, but only small gifts were truly disinterested: He who gives a lot, expects a lot in return.[76] Publilius Syrus' *Sententiae* are deliberately ambiguous: "(Only) bad or stupid people think that *beneficia* are given"[77].

Testamentary habits provide a good example of how the gift-exchange template served to express, judge and influence social action. *Gratia* and *fides* obliged testators to mention their friends in their wills. According to Seneca it was the ultimate proof that *gratia* was disinterested and sprang from virtue, rather than from a desire to pursue one's own interest.[78] To be left out of a friend's will was shameful, either for the testator (if the omission was unwarranted) or for the heir or legatee (if the omission was justified). When there were no natural heirs, *amici* stood to inherit substantially.

The practice gave scope for flatterers and villains to lure wealthy childless testators into inscribing them in their wills. The practice loomed large in the mind of Roman authors. Literature abounds with accusations of "inheritance hunting" (*captatio*); a moral crime that was almost by definition impossible to prove because a *captator* behaved exactly as a true friend would. When the businessman Q. Caecilius died, he left his fortune almost entirely to his favorite nephew Atticus. His powerful friend and protector L. Lucullus, to whom he owed his wealth, received nothing. The funeral procession was attacked and Caecilius' corpse dragged through the streets, according to Valerius Maximus, because the people were indignant about the testator's lack of gratitude.[79] Cicero, however, praised Caecilius' choice of his nephew Atticus as duteous.[80]

Like patronage in 1960 rural Italy, gift-exchange in Roman culture took a mythical dimension. Nowhere else is this more clear than in public munificence or euergetism. Euergetism was elaborately analyzed by Paul Veyne, who eloquently captured its ambiguities but refused to explain it in terms of gift-*exchange*. According to Veyne, public donations served to express the social distance between notables and common citizens. They confirmed the self-

[75] Mart. 5.18.7-10; Hor., *Ep.* 1.7.73; *Serm.* 2.5.25; Plin., *Ep.* 9.30.

[76] Mart. 5.18; 59; 10.87.

[77] Publ. Syr., *Sent.* B37 (ed. Meyer): *Beneficia donari aut mali aut stulti putant.* See also *Sent.* B5 (ed. Meyer): *Beneficium accipere libertatem est uendere*: "To accept a kindness (*beneficium*) is to sell your liberty".

[78] Sen., *Ben.* 4.22.1.

[79] In fact, the man had been a notorious usurer and his disrespect towards Lucullus may have had nothing to do with the events that took place. Nevertheless, the fact that Valerius Maximus (7.8.5) was able to propose this explanation as credible testifies to the strength of Caecilius's moral obligation to leave a substantial share to his benefactor.

[80] Cicero, *Ad Att.* 3.20.1; Nep., *Att.* 5.1-2.

identity of notables as an elite group, but their 'regime' did not depend on it, nor was there any return gift involved.[81]

Zuiderhoek, on the other hand, recently described euergetism as the "icing on the cake"; it neither made the cities much richer or their elites much poorer. At the same time, however, he does stress the gift-*exchange* dimension of euergetism[82] Regardless of the intentions of benefactors, by accepting benefactions citizens acknowledged their obligation to respect and honor them in return for the benefactions received, thereby strengthening the regime of the notables.

Clearly, Veyne's point of view is not totally off the mark. By acknowledging their obligation to respect and honor public benefactors, the citizens acknowledged the benefactors' social pre-eminence. Thus, euergetism signified rather than established the superior moral and social status of the benefactors. Public benefactions and *gratia* did not generate the authority that notables enjoyed. The symbolic capital held by the latter was effective regardless of gift exchange practices or obligations. But by signaling and legitimizing the notables' pre-eminence euergetism affirmed and thereby consolidated it. Euergetism may be seen as a form of symbolic violence. The recipients of the gift accepted a social order in which they were structurally disadvantaged. It implied a voluntary submission that goes far beyond gift-exchange obligations.

3. Conclusion

While from an etic perspective gift-exchange was an important ingredient of social relations, it was mainly so because it was intertwined with formal and informal institutions based on other principles. From an 'emic' perspective it was ascribed to institutional arrangements that were patently not based on reciprocity.

Epicureans claimed that self-interest was the basis of friendship. Cicero objected: If *amicitia* is based on advantage, then why foster it when this advantage disappears? The Epicurean's answer was: "So that I would not incur ill will when I stop to support a friend".[83] In other words: for reputation's sake. But why would gift-exchange continue to be central in determining people's respectability if self-interest was so visibly its driving force?

Roman civic culture acknowledged extensive basic rights to resources (based for instance on citizenship). Its institutional fabric, however, distributed enti-

[81] Veyne 1976; see the critique of Andreau – Schmitt – Schnapp 1978 and of Garnsey 1991. See also the contribution by Sabine Colpaert elsewhere in this volume.

[82] Zuiderhoek 2006. See also Zuiderhoek 2009. Note, however, that inscriptions are not always a faithful representation of reality. The language of euergetism could easily be used to cover up other motives, see van Nijf 2000, p. 26 ("myth of euergetism").

[83] Cic., *Fin.* 2.79: *Ne in odium ueniam, si amicum destitero tueri.*

tlements and capabilities very unevenly without adequate impersonal mechanisms for resources to change hands. Civic institutions created entitlements to public goods, such as protection, enforcement of property rights, salaried positions etc., yet the bureaucratic apparatus and state organization was unable to allocate and guarantee these entitlements effectively. Thus for instance property rights were guaranteed in Roman law, but no effective police force or justice existed to guarantee them.

Markets existed, allowing agents to exchange resources to increase their capabilities, but information and enforcement costs were high. There were no impersonal debt instruments or stock markets. Gift-exchange relations provided dependable information and allowed building complex organizations.

Although to some extent gift-exchange allowed resources to circulate, it primarily served as a stabilizer for non-reciprocity based institutional arrangements. Prime among these were property, prestige and dominance based capabilities that greatly favored small segments of the population. In this way, gift-exchange was a core element in a system of symbolic violence. It provided a powerful support for social and political institutions that were structurally unequal, disadvantageous to the majority of the people and deeply opposed to the principles of reciprocal altruism underlying gift exchange, yet that at the same time relied on the instincts for strong reciprocity and tit-for-tat exchange to uphold social norms.

Bibliography

Andreau, Jean: *A propos de la vie financière à Pouzzoles; Cluvius et Vestorius*, in: *Les 'Bourgeoisies' municipales italiennes aux IIe et Ier siècles av. J.-C.*, Paris – Naples 1983, pp. 9-20.

Andreau, Jean – Pauline Schmitt – Alain Schnapp: *Paul Veyne et l'évergétisme*, in: *AnnESC* 23 (1978), pp. 307-325.

Barrett, Louise – S. Peter Henzi: *Monkeys, Markets and Minds: Biological Markets and Primate Sociality*, in: *Cooperation in primates and humans. Mechanisms and evolution*, ed. by Peter M. Kappeler – Carel P. van Schaik, Berlin 2006, pp. 209-232.

Benveniste, Emile: *Don et échange dans le vocabulaire indo-européen*, in: *Année sociologique* s. 3, 2 (1948-1949), pp. 7-20.

Bourdieu, Pierre: *Esquisse d'une théorie de la pratique: précédé de trois études d'ethnologie kabyle*, Paris 2000^{2}.

Bowles, Samuel – Herbert Gintis: *A Cooperative Species: Human Reciprocity and Its Evolution*, Princeton 2011.

Brunt, Peter A.: *Amicitia in the Late Roman Republic*, in: *PCPhS* 11 (1965), pp. 1-20 = Peter A. Brunt: *The Fall of the Roman Republic and Related Essays*, Oxford 1988, pp. 352-381.

Brunt, Peter A.: *Cicero's officium in the Civil War*, in: *JRS* 76 (1986), pp. 12-32.

Cotton, Hannah M.: *The Role of Cicero's Letters of Recommendation: 'iustitia' versus 'gratia'?*, in: *Hermes* 114 (1986), pp. 443-460.

Dixon, Suzanne: *A Lousy Ingrate: Honour and Patronage in the American Mafia and Ancient Rome*, in: *International Journal of Moral and Social Studies* 8 (1993), pp. 61-72.

Fehr, Ernest – Urs Fischbacher: *The Nature of Human Altruism*, in: *Nature* 425 (23 October 2003), pp. 785 – 791.

Ferguson, Yale H.: *Chiefdoms to City-States: the Greek Experience*, in: *Chiefdoms: Power, Economy and Ideology*, ed. by Timothy K. Earle, Cambridge – New York 1991, pp. 169–192.

Finley, Moses I.: *The World of Odysseus*, London 1977^{2}.

Freyburger, Gérard: *Fides. Étude sémantique et religieuse depuis les origines jusqu'à l'époque augustéenne*, Paris 1986.

Gallant, Thomas W.: *Risk and Survival in Ancient Greece*, Cambridge 1991.

Garnsey, Peter: *The Generosity of Veyne*, in: *JRS* 81 (1991), pp. 164-168.

Gill, Christopher – Norman Postlewaith – Richard Seaford (ed. by), *Reciprocity in Ancient Greece*, Oxford 1998.

Gilman, Antonio: *Trajectories towards Social Complexity in the Later Prehistory of the Mediterranean*, in: *Chiefdoms: Power, Economy and Ideology*, ed. by Timothy K. Earle, Cambridge – New York 1991, pp. 146-168.

Gintis, Herbert: *Strong Reciprocity and Human Sociality*, in: *Journal of Theoretical Biology* 206 (2000), pp. 169–179.

Gintis, Herbert: *The Hitchhiker's Guide to Altruism: Gene-culture Co-evolution and the Internalization of Norms*, in: *Journal of Theoretical Biology* 220 (2003), pp. 407–418.

Gintis, Herbert – Samuel Bowles – Robert Boyd – Ernst Fehr (ed. by): *Moral Sentiments and Material Interests: the Foundations of Cooperation in Economic Life,* Cambridge (MA) 2005.

Gintis, Herbert – Joseph Henrich – Samuel Bowles – Robert Boyd – Ernst Fehr: *Strong Reciprocity and the Roots of Human Morality*, in: *Social Justice Research* 21 (2008), pp. 241–253.

Gouldner, Alvin W.: *The Norm of Reciprocity. A Preliminary Statement*, in: *Friends, Followers and Factions: A Reader in Political Clientelism*, ed. by Steffen W. Schmidt – Laura Guasti – Carl H. Landé – James C. Scott, Berkeley 1977, pp. 28-42.

Gowdy, John: *Hunter-Gatherers and the Mythology of the Market*, in: *The Cambridge Encyclopedia of Hunters and Gatherers*, ed. by Richard B. Lee – Richard Daly, Cambridge 1999, pp. 391-398.

Graeber, David: *Debt: The First 5,000 Years*, New York 2011.

Hands, Arthur R.: *Charities and Social Aid in Greece and Rome*, London 1968.

Henrich, Joseph – Robert Boyd – Samuel Bowles – Colin Camerer – Ernst Fehr – Herbert Gintis (ed. by): *Foundations of Human Sociality: Economic Experiments and Ethnographic Evidence from Fifteen Small-scale Societies*, Oxford – New York 2004.

Herman, Gabriel: *Ritualised Friendship and the Greek City*, Cambridge 1987.

Herman, Gabriel: *Morality and Behaviour in Democratic Athens: A Social History*, Cambridge 2006.

Humphrey, Caroline – Stephen Hugh-Jones: *Barter, Exchange and Value*, in: *Barter, Exchange and Value. An Anthropological Approach*, ed. by Caroline Humphrey – Stephen Hugh-Jones, Cambridge 1992, pp. 1-20.

Imbert, Jean: *De la sociologie au droit: la 'fides' Romaine*, in: *Droits de l'antiquité et sociologie juridique. Mélanges Henri Lévy-Bruhl*, Paris 1959, pp. 407-415.

Ingham, Geoffrey: *Money is a Social Relation*, in: *Review of Social Economy* 54 (1996), pp. 507-529.

Kim, Henry S.: *Archaic Coinage as Evidence for the Use of Money*, in: *Money and Its Uses in the Ancient Greek World*, ed. by Andrew Meadows – Kirsty Shipton, Oxford 2001, pp. 7-22.

Kim, Henry S.: *Small Change and the Moneyed Economy*, in: *Money, Labour and Land. Approaches to the Economies of Ancient Greece*, ed. by Paul Cartledge – Edward E. Cohen, London – New York 2002, pp. 44-51.

Lendon, John Edward: *Empire of honour. The Art of Government in the Roman World*, Oxford 1997.

Le Rider, Georges: *La naissance de la monnaie: pratiques monétaires de l'Orient ancien*, Paris 2001.

Mathew, Sarah – Robert Boyd: *Punishment Sustains Large-scale Cooperation in Prestate Warfare*, in: *Proceedings of the National Academy of Sciences* 108 (2011), pp. 11375–11380.

Michel, Jacques-Henri: *Gratuité en droit romain*, Bruxelles 1962.

Millet, Paul: *Lending and Borrowing in Ancient Athens*, Cambridge 1991.

Noë, Ronald: *Digging for the Roots of Trading*, in: *Cooperation in Primates and Humans. Mechanisms and Evoluation*, ed. by Peter M. Kappeler – Carel P. van Schaik, Berlin 2006, pp. 233-261.

North, Douglass C.: *Understanding the Process of Economic Change*, Princeton 2005.

North, Douglass C. – John Joseph Wallis – Barry R. Weingast: *Violence and Social Orders: A Conceptual Framework for Interpreting Recorded Human History*, Cambridge – New York 2009.

Plourde, Aimée M.: *Human Power and Prestige Systems*, in: *Mind the Gap. Tracing the Origins of Human Universals*, ed. by Peter M. Kappeler – Joan Silk, Berlin – Heidelberg 2010, pp. 139-152.

Polanyi, Karl: *The Economy as Instituted Process*, in: *Trade and Market in the Early Empires. Economies in History and Theory*, ed. by Karl Polanyi –Carl M. Arensberg – Harry W. Pearson, New York – London 1957, pp. 243–270.

Price, Michael E.: *The Resurrection of Group Selection as a Theory of Human Cooperation*, in: *Social Justice Research* 21 (2008), pp. 228–240.

Sahlins, Marshall D.: *Stone Age Economics*, Hawthorne 1972.

Saller, Richard P.: *Personal Patronage under the Early Empire*, Cambridge 1982.

Schaps, David M.: *The Invention of Coinage and the Monetization of Ancient Greece*, Ann Arbor 2004.

Schwartz, Seth: *Were the Jews a Mediterranean Society? Reciprocity and Solidarity in Ancient Judaism*, Princeton – Oxford 2010.

Seaford, Richard: *Money and the Early Greek Mind*, Cambridge 2004.

Shackleton Bailey, David R.: *Cicero: Epistulae ad Familiares*, Cambridge 1977.

Shatzman, Israel: *Senatorial Wealth and Roman Politics*, Brussels 1975.

Silk, Joan – Robert Boyd: *From Grooming to Giving Blood: The Origins of Human Altruism*, in: *Mind the Gap. Tracing the Origins of Human Universals*, ed. by Peter M. Kappeler – Joan Silk, Berlin – Heidelberg 2010, pp. 223-244.

Silverman, Sydel F.: *Patronage as Myth*, in: *Patrons and Clients in Mediterranean Societies*, ed. by Ernest Gellner – John Waterbury, London 1977, pp. 7-19.

Tandy, David W.: *Warriors into Traders: the Power of the Market in Early Greece*, Berkeley – Los Angeles 1997.

Trivers, Robert: *Reciprocal Altruism: 30 Years Later*, in: *Cooperation in Primates and Humans. Mechanisms and Evolution*, ed. by Peter Kappeler – Carel P. van Schaik, Berlin – Heidelberg 2006, pp. 67-84.

Van Nijf, Onno: *Inscriptions and Civic Memory in the Roman East*, in: *The Afterlife of Inscriptions: Reusing, Rediscovering, Reinventing and Revitalizing Ancient Inscriptions*, ed. by Alison E. Cooley, London 2000, pp. 21–36.

Verboven, Koenraad: *The Economy of Friends. Economic Aspects of amicitia and Patronage in the Late Republic*, Brussel 2002.

Verboven, Koenraad: *Demise and Fall of the Augustan Monetary System*, in: *Crisis and the Roman Empire*, ed. by Olivier Hekster – Gerda de Kleijn – Daniëlle Slootjes, Leiden – Boston 2007, pp. 245-257.

Verboven, Koenraad: *Currency, Bullion and Accounts. Monetary Modes in the Roman World*, in: *RBN* 155 (2009), pp. 91-121.

Veyne, Paul: *Le pain et le cirque. Sociologie historique d'un pluralisme politique*, Paris 1976.

Zuiderhoek, Arjan: *The Icing on the Cake: Benefactors, Economics and Public Building in Roman Asia Minor*, in: *Patterns in the Economy of Roman Asia Minor*, ed. by Stephen Mitchell – Constantina Katsari, Swansea 2006, pp. 167-186

Zuiderhoek, Arjan: *The Politics of Munificence in the Roman Empire: Citizens, Elites, and Benefactors in Asia Minor*, Cambridge – New York 2009.

Section two

Gift and Society

Lucia Cecchet

Gift-giving to the Poor in the Greek World

1. Giving to the poor in the pagan world

Gift-giving in the ancient world has been studied as a mode of reciprocal relation: the act of giving requires an equal return from the recipient. This is the principle that makes gift-giving a way of building mutual relationships of different types (political alliances, economic contacts, mutual assistance in case of need).[1] If this premise is correct, a problem arises in the event that the recipient is unable to return an equivalent gift. This breaks the first and most fundamental rule of reciprocity, and provokes either the breakup of the relationship between the giver and the recipient, with consequent hostility or, alternatively, it places the recipient in the position of debtor. A recipient who fails to reciprocate is expected to make amends by offering a service to the donor. The gift, in this case, is not to be returned in kind, but in a different and less straightforward manner. It is apparent that this scenario applies to the case in which a significant difference exists in terms of social and economic standing between the donor and the recipient. This dynamic of exchange is best described as the building of a relationship of dependence, of which patronage in the ancient world provides an example.

Nonetheless, relations of reciprocity between individuals of different social standing did not always lead to the formation of client-patron relationships in the ancient world. In the Greek sources of the archaic and classical periods we find some attestations of gift-giving addressing individuals from whom no return was expected in terms of goods-exchange, and from whom services were not always claimed as a reward. I refer to the case of giving to the poor and the destitute.[2]

[1] The literature on gift-giving and reciprocity in the ancient world is vast. With regard to ancient Greece, I limit myself here to two fundamental works: von Reden 1995 and Gill – Postlethwaite – Seaford 1998.

[2] We should bear in mind that the Greek word πένης (poor) has a very broad meaning. This term applied to all those who worked for their living, including individuals who were probably well above the subsistence line. There is a clear tendency in the literary record of the classical period to treat the category of the πένητες as if it was internally homogeneous, although it is clear the word applies to a wide variety of economic and social conditions. The only distinction that is clearly made in ancient sources is that between πένης and πτωχός, the latter being the destitute (see Aristophanes' definition in *Plut.* 550-554). In the cases presented in this paper, I do not use the word poor as referring exclusively to the destitute.

This represents a very particular type of gift-giving.[3] The gift is not always an object spontaneously offered by the donor, but often a desired object, for which the recipient advances an explicit request – usually food in the case of the destitute.

Scholars have often noted that giving to the poor in the pagan world was a sporadic and non-institutionalised practice, which had no prescriptive rationale either in the field of ethics or in that of philosophy and religion.[4] In 1939 Bolkestein raised a crucial question, i.e. which groups of people Greek society and ethics considered worthy of actions of solidarity and assistance. He listed the categories of recipients of social obligations as follows: parents, old people, friends, guests, fellow-citizens, victims of injustice, victims of misfortune, suppliants and, at least in the classical period, widows and orphans. The poor failed to make the list.[5] He noted that in Greek philosophical and ethical thought we do not find any suggestion that values such as ἔλεος and πραότης (pity) should be directed towards the poor. Good deeds and willingness to help were addressed to fellow-citizens and, in general, towards the state, but never specifically towards the poor.[6]

Nonetheless, the literary record shows that giving food, clothes and shelter to beggars and vagabonds was regarded as moral social behaviour as early as the archaic period. For example, Nausicaa explains to Odysseus that her gift to him of clothes and food is appreciated by Zeus, protector of foreigners and beggars.[7] The swineherd Eumaeus hosts the beggar Odysseus in his hut,[8] and Athena encourages him to beg for food at the banquet in Ithaca, saying that the good ones among the suitors will give him bread.[9] In one of Euripides' tragedies, Helena cries when she learns that her servant has refused bread to a vagabond.[10]

[3] The practice of giving to the poor has been largely studied with regard to charity in Jewish and Christian cultures (for a recent bibliography, see Finn 2006 and Gardner 2013), but far less attention has been paid to the evidence for this practice in the pagan world.

[4] Within studies on poverty in the early Roman Empire, Parkin 2006, pp. 60-61, has argued that begging was ineffective in classical antiquity because almsgiving was not sanctioned by any morality. Cf. Meggitt 1998, p.166.

[5] Bolkestein 1939, pp. 95-115.

[6] Bolkestein 1939, pp. 114 and 200. Bolkestein made the important point – which was widely accepted in later studies – that Christian charity and almsgiving did not stem from pagan practices (cf. Parkin 2006). For the religious motivations of Christian almsgiving, see the evidence collected by Finn 2006, pp. 176-220.

[7] *Od.* 6.208-209: πρὸς γὰρ Διός εἰσιν ἅπαντες / ξεῖνοί τε πτωχοί τε, δόσις δ'ὀλίγη τε φίλη τε.

[8] *Od.* 14.45-54.

[9] *Od.* 17. 336-355.

[10] Eur., *Hel.* 789-792.

All this can be explained by the fact that the suppliant was sacred according to Greek *ethos* and religion,[11] and a beggar asking for food is in fact a particular type of suppliant. Giving to the one who asked was regarded as a just action; the central point is that it was never considered an action free from the obligation to reciprocate. Hands, in *Charities and Social Aid in Greece and Rome*, highlighted that in the Greek and Roman pre-Christian culture a return was also expected from the poor.[12] His study, however, focused only on return in terms of services – a type of return leading to client-patron relationships. I will argue in this paper that other kinds of rewards were also valued. The mode in which the principles of reciprocity were enforced in giving to the poor is not immediately apparent. The nature of the reward is a question that deserves our attention because it sheds light both on the purpose of giving and on the mode of relation that the act of giving establishes.

2. Giving to the beggar: the case of the *Odyssey* and *Works and Days*

As I noted above, the given object is not always a gift in the conventional sense; sometimes the recipient makes an explicit request for it. Odysseus, disguised as a beggar, makes frequent requests for food and shelter. In *Odyssey* 17 he enters the palace of Ithaca and approaches each of the suitors, who have gathered at the banquet, begging for bread with his hand stretched out.[13] Not only is the action of giving not spontaneous here, even the position of Odysseus as a recipient must be legitimated: he is required by Antinous to fight against a rival, Iros, who begs permanently at Ithaca.[14] The winner will be awarded the possibility of partaking in the banquets, and no other beggar will be allowed to receive food at court.[15]

Aristocratic banquets at Ithaca are described as an occasion on which giving food to the poor takes place on a regular basis, for Antinous refers to the fact that many beggars gather at court.[16] This is interesting in the light of the fact that food sharing on a reciprocal mode is attested since the archaic period in the form of the *eranos*, originally a meal to which every diner was required to contribute.[17] Yet the banquet at Ithaca is the tragic reverse of an *eranos*: it is in fact an

[11] Gould 1973. For the body-language associated with the act of begging by the suppliant, see in particular p. 94.
[12] Hands 1968, p. 30.
[13] *Od.* 17.365-368.
[14] *Od.* 18.1-2: πτωχὸς πανδήμιος, ὃς κατὰ ἄστυ / πτωχεύεσκ' Ἰθάκης.
[15] *Od.* 18.43-49: αἰεὶ αὖθ' ἡμῖν μεταδαίσεται, οὐδέ τιν' ἄλλον / πτωχὸν ἔσω μίσγεσθαι ἐάσομεν αἰτήσοντα.
[16] *Od.* 17.345.
[17] The method of contribution seems to have varied: Pindarus (*Ol.* 1.39) attests that the

abuse of the hospitality of the absent host, Odysseus. While themselves breaching the code of reciprocity, the suitors claim from the beggar a reward for their generosity. He will have to start running small errands at the palace, just as his predecessor Iros used to do in exchange for his daily bread.[18]

One might think that this dynamic reflects the perverse world of the suitors in which generosity finds no place, but it might also be that in the society described in the *Odyssey* giving to the destitute followed certain rules. Beggars should 'earn' their daily bread by performing basic duties, as this can integrate them in the community and show them how to escape extreme need.

Similarly, giving to the beggar represents a form of reassurance for the donor: should she ever become poor, she will be helped in the same way by the rich. Significantly, Odysseus tells the banqueters that in the past he was also a rich man, who lived in a wealthy house and used to give hospitality to foreigners.[19] His words serve the function of a *memento* to the banqueters: wealth is not a lasting condition and anyone, regardless of their background, can be reduced to poverty through their own fault or unhappy chance.

Together with this 'insurance for the future', however, the banqueters' giving provides them with a more immediate kind of reward. Their action is a way to enforce and make visible their position in the social hierarchy:[20] they are aristocrats claiming the throne of Odysseus. Giving food to the beggars gathered at court is how the donors show that they have a superior status, decisive power, and surplus of means. Exhibition of prestige and display of wealth through the action of giving are widely practised in order to affirm social status in the society described in the Homeric poems.[21] This is one of the cases in which the asym-

participants were required to return hospitality by providing a dinner or guests were required to bring a gift to the host. In classical Athens the *eranos* in the form of a shared meal continued to exist (Aristoph., *Fr.* 408 Kock; Arist., *Eth. Nic.* 1123a) but in the sources of the fourth century BCE it is mostly referred to as a friendly loan raised among several contributors with no interest rate, aimed at providing financial capital for a business (Hyp., *Ath.* 7-11, about a perfume shop), or at ransoming a person from slavery (Dem. 18.31; 53.8; 59.31). The *eranos* credit was based on reciprocity: see Demosthenes' metaphor (57.101 and 184-5): "whatever you lend to other people they should make a similar loan (*eranos*) to you on another occasion" (transl. D. M. MacDowell; for comment, see MacDowell 1990, p. 323).

18 On Iros running small errands, see *Od.* 18.3-4: οὕνεκ' ἀπαγγέλλεσκε κιών, ὅτε πού τις ἀνώγοι. One of the etymologies proposed for the name Iros in antiquity is the name Iris, the messenger of the gods, and referred to the errands fulfilled by the beggar in Ithaca. This etymology has, however, been rejected by Pagani 2005, pp. 193-209.

19 *Od.* 19.70-77.

20 Kloft 1988, p. 86. On gift-giving as a mode to enforce power relations in archaic Greek society, see Domingo Gygax 2013, pp. 47-48.

21 On the display of wealth through gifts in the Homeric society, see Donlan 1980, p. 4:

metrical nature of the relation is more apparent, as it includes the two extreme poles of the social ladder: the aristocrat and the beggar.

When the difference in social standing between the donor and the recipient is smaller, the purpose of giving and the nature of the return change significantly. In the rural village of Ascra described by Hesiod in *Works and Days,* no display of wealth or political prestige or affirmation of hierarchy is evident among the peasants.[22] The protagonists are farmers in an agrarian community in which there is no space for generosity without exchange of goods. The dynamics of giving and taking among the peasants follow the basic rule of reciprocity in terms of exchange of goods and favours.[23] This is splendidly illustrated by Hesiod in a verse that has often been cited by commentators for its proverbial character: "Give to one who gives, but do not give to one who does not give".[24] The basic principle of reciprocity is strictly enforced, to the point that gift-exchange is an action calculated in terms of quantity and quality. The poet advises his brother Perses:

> "Take fair measure from your neighbour and pay him back fairly with the same measure, or better, if you can; so that if you are in need afterward, you may find him sure".[25]

Any excess in giving is aimed at a good return in future. The life of the Ascran farmer, as described by the poet, is that of hard work under the constant threat of poverty and hunger.[26] It is apparent that this reality leaves no hope to those who cannot return goods or favours. The destitute remain outside the

"The possession of great wealth was a conspicuous sign of success – visible proof of prowess and leadership. It was also the means by which prestige and rank were enhanced, since it enabled the holder to give valuable gifts to guest-friends (*xeinoi*) and to reward followers, thereby insuring and increasing loyalty and dependency"; cf. also Donlan 1981, pp. 137-175; on the object as 'status symbol' of the archaic elites, see Duplouy 2006, pp. 174-183. On the various functions of the gift in Homeric society, see von Reden 1995, pp.18-76.

22 I do not refer here to Hesiodean society as a whole – which includes the aristocratic world of the *dorophagoi basileis* (the "gift-eating kings") of Thespiai – but simply to the social structure and the internal dynamics of the village of Ascra.

23 Specifically, they follow the model of generalised reciprocity, which is typical of kinship and friendship relations according to Sahlins's 1972 classification. On generalized, balanced and negative reciprocity, see in particular pp. 185-276.

24 Hes., *Erg.* 354; transl. G. W. Most. On the proverbial character of the verse, see Lamberton 1988, *ad loc.*

25 Hes., *Erg.* 349-351: εὖ δ' ἀποδοῦναι, / αὐτῷ τῷ μέτρῳ, καὶ λώιον αἴ κε δύνηαι, / ὡς ἂν χρηίζων καὶ ἐς ὕστερον ἄρκιον εὕρῃς; transl. G. W. Most.

26 Hes., *Erg.* 299-302.

dynamics which regulate the life of the community.[27] For this reason, Hesiod warns his brother Perses that if he asks for food from his neighbour, he will be given it only once or twice, and the third time he will be sent away.[28]

Begging for food in Hesiod's Ascra could not be accepted as an established practice, because giving with no hope of return in kind was perceived as a high risk for the donor. Giving to the destitute on a regular basis can be practised in a context in which at least a good number of individuals are above the level of subsistence, but is clearly more problematic if the members of the community face a constant risk to their survival.[29] The banqueters at Ithaca have both the material possibility of giving and the strong motivation to make visible the superiority of their position; neither of these conditions applies to the Ascran farmer.

3. Cancellation of debts in the archaic poleis: a form of gift-giving?

In the Greek *poleis* of the archaic period forms of economic support provided by the rich to the poor are described by sources in the context of commonly agreed actions directed from the upper towards the lower strata of the citizen population.

Some examples of these practices are attested by Aristotle. One of these concerns the internal policy adopted in Tarentum. As often in *Politics*, the historical context and the chronology of the events are not clearly defined. All we know from Aristotle is that the inhabitants of Tarentum made property communal for use by the needy.[30] Evidently, in Tarentum a coordinated action of gift-giving was carried out by one part of the citizen population towards the other. The interesting fact is that there is a well-defined perception of the reciprocal nature of the exchange: the rich give because they know that they will get something back. The return is neither an object nor a service; rather it is the preservation of the political stability of the *polis*.

[27] For a discussion of the models of peasant society in modern anthropology and their application to Hesiod's Ascra, see Edwards 2004, pp. 80-126. Although many of the points he makes are correct, I do not agree with his conclusion that Ascra was not a peasant society, and that the village was politically independent from Thespiai. On reciprocity in Hesiod's Ascra, see also Schmitz 2004, pp. 26-101.

[28] Hes., *Erg.* 401.

[29] On strategies for coping with risk and responses to famine in the ancient world, see Garnsey 1988 and Gallant 1991. Specifically on reciprocity as a way to cope with survival risk, see Gallant 1991, pp. 143-169.

[30] Arist., *Pol.* 6.1320b: καλῶς δ᾽ ἔχει μιμεῖσθαι καὶ τὰ Ταραντίνων. ἐκεῖνοι γὰρ κοινὰ ποιοῦντες τὰ κτήματα τοῖς ἀπόροις ἐπὶ τὴν χρῆσιν εὔνουν παρασκευάζουσι τὸ πλῆθος. See Fuks 1979-80, p. 179; Newman 1902, pp. 536-537.

Alexander Fuks, in an article devoted to the exploration of practices of sharing between the rich and the poor in the Greek poleis,[31] commented on this passage of Aristotle that this type of solution to – and prevention of – social conflict was explicitly theorised in Greek political thought first by Democritus and then by Plato.[32] Democritus argued that

> "when the wealthy decide to lend to the poor, to help them and to benefit them, by so doing it is at last possible to express pity, to cease being isolated, to become friends, to defend each other, to live in harmony as citizens…"[33]

Plato, in *Laws*, highlights the necessity for a group of men who possess abundance of land and have debtors in the city to give some of their property to the poor from time to time by remitting their debts and distributing land.[34] These actions of public giving are advocated as necessary to the well-being of the whole city. Both donors and recipients have something to gain. The interpretative model of gift-giving is very helpful in explaining these relations, but requires that we abandon both the notion of the gift as something freely chosen by the donor and the idea of a return in terms of goods or services. The gift symbolises the relation of reciprocity, which underlies political stability. The preservation of this balance is the expected return.

From the fourth century BCE onward, sources, probably influenced by the observation of later events, tended to label key episodes in the archaic history of some *poleis* in terms of land redistribution and cancellation of debts.[35] This is not the place to discuss the thorny question of the reliability of their accounts;[36] what interests us is that these political measures were described in terms that recall reciprocal exchange and mutual benefit between donors and recipients. Lycurgus' alleged redistribution of land in seventh-century BCE Laconia was dictated, as sources attest, by the necessity to address the extreme disparity of

[31] Fuks 1979-80, pp. 172-189.

[32] Fuks 1979-80, pp. 172-174. Fuks also quotes a fragment of Archytas (*Fr.* 3 DK) in which the tyrant deals with equality achieved through reckoning (*logismos*) and he advocates the necessity for the rich to give to the poor.

[33] Democr., *Fr.* 255 DK: ὅταν οἱ δυνάμενοι τοῖς μὴ ἔχουσι καὶ προτελεῖν τολμέωσι καὶ ὑπουργεῖν καὶ χαρίζεσθαι, ἐν τούτωι ἤδη καὶ τὸ οἰκτίρειν ἔνεστι καὶ μὴ ἐρήμους εἶναι καὶ τὸ ἑταίρους γίγνεσθαι, καὶ τὸ ἀμύνειν ἀλλήλοισι καὶ τοὺς πολιήτας ὁμονόους εἶναι…; transl. A. Fuks.

[34] Plat., *Leg.*736c-e.

[35] This is the case, for example, in the interpretations of the Solonian crisis by 4th-century BCE sources (see Rosivach 1992, pp. 153-157), and also Plutarch's narrative of the crisis in Lycurgus' Sparta (see nn. 37-38 below).

[36] See n. 39 for the case of archaic Sparta and n. 53 for that of archaic Megara.

wealth among the Spartans.[37] According to Plutarch, Lycurgus managed to persuade the rich to let their land be reallocated,[38] and this act of giving is described as the foundation of the Spartan constitution.[39]

A public action of a different kind was how Solon put an end to civil strife in Attica in the early sixth century BCE. He did not redistribute land, as some had hoped.[40] The *seisachtheia* (the shaking-off of burdens or, as interpreted in later sources, debt relief) apparently consisted in the cancellation of the obligations of the peasants to give in kind to the landowners.[41] The reason behind this obligation has been the subject of much discussion, the main hypotheses being that the *hektemoroi* were a class of serfs, or debtors who defaulted on their debts, or peasants obliged to work for the wealthy after being unlawfully driven off communal land.[42] What we do know is that the imposition of giving led to impoverishment and loss of liberty in relation to some of the peasant population: some of the Athenian *penichroi* (poor) were sold abroad as slaves.[43] Conse-

[37] Plut., *Lyc.* 8.1-2. Land redistribution in Laconia in the archaic period is attested by a fragment of Tyrtaeus quoted by Aristotle (*Fr.* 1 West *apud* Arist., *Pol.* 1306b). References to economic inequalities and social conflicts in Sparta are also attested by Herodotus (1.65-68) and Thucydides (1.18.1), yet neither mentions redistribution of land.

[38] Plut., *Lyc.* 8.2: συνέπεισε τὴν χώραν ἅπασαν εἰς μέσον θέντας ἐξ ἀρχῆς ἀναδάσασθαι.

[39] Apart from the fragment of Tyrtaeus mentioned above (see n. 37), we do not have further evidence from the archaic age attesting to land redistribution in Laconia. It is widely believed that the sources on the history of Sparta ascribe to the archaic period a crisis which in fact happened much later, as the references in Herodotus and Thucydides suggest (see n. 37). This crisis reached its peak in the mid-3rd century BCE when an attempt to redistribute land was made by King Agis IV. For fundamental work on Sparta, see Hodkinson 1983, pp. 239-281; Hodkinson 1993, pp. 146-176; Hodkinson – Powell 1999; Hodkinson 2000; Hodkinson – Powell 2002; Hodkinson 2006, pp. 111-162.

[40] In *Fr.* 34 West a reference is made to those disappointed that Solon did not redistribute the land. Plutarch refers to a secret promise made by Solon to the poor that he would carry out redistribution (Plut., *Sol.* 14.1) and also to his eventual decision not to do so (*Sol.* 15.6). This might, however, be a late tradition. An association between debt cancellation and land redistribution is often made by sources from the 4th century onwards; see *supra*, n. 35.

[41] Arist., *Ath. Pol.* 2.2-3; Plut., *Sol.* 15.3-4.

[42] For a discussion of different interpretations of the question of the *hektemoroi*, see Cassola 1964, pp. 25-67. He argued in favour of the view that the land which the *hektemoroi* worked was originally communal land, unlawfully disposed of by the wealthy. For a presentation of the different views on the question, see also Rhodes 1981, pp. 89-96. For recent work on Solon and the 6th-century BCE crisis in Attica, see Block – Lardinois 2006, esp. the contributions by Bintliff (pp. 321-333), Forsdyke (pp. 334-350), and Ober (pp. 441-460).

[43] See Sol., *Fr.* 4.23-25 West *apud* Dem. 19.255.

quently, social conflict emerged in Attica.[44] Solon's *seisachtheia* put an end to the distorted system of giving and taking, and eventually led to a resolution of the crisis.[45] His verses on *eunomia* (good government) were still sung at aristocratic banquets two centuries later[46] and the general relief granted by his reforms was universally acknowledged in classical Athens.

The dynamic of giving and receiving in Lycurgus' Sparta and Solon's Athens must be contextualised within actions of public reform involving the whole community. Yet again, the action of giving – redistribution of land at Sparta, cancellation of 'debts' at Athens – was a necessity for both donors and recipients in the context of violent disruptions of civic order. It is apparent that neither Lycurgus nor Solon acted as donors; rather, they are portrayed as mediators between the givers (the wealthy landowners) and the recipients (the poor, e.g. landless Spartans and Athenian peasants).

In Aelian's *Varia Historia*,[47] we read that in Corinth and in Mytilene (when exactly we cannot say)[48] some of the rich remitted the debts of the poor. By so doing, Aelian says, they did not gain money, but life itself, because those creditors who did not cancel the debts were killed by the debtors.[49] The debts owed by the lower to the upper strata of the citizen community rendered peaceful co-habitation impossible. The interesting aspect is that as described by Aelian debt cancellation is a reciprocal action: the debtors had their obligation remitted; the creditors had their lives saved.

One further example of what was at stake if the collective and reciprocal bond between the social parts of the *polis* was broken is provided by a famous episode in the archaic history of Megara. The event is narrated by Plutarch in his response to the question: what is the *palintokia*?[50] At some point in the sixth century BCE after the end of the tyranny, Megara experienced a popular rebellion. According to Plutarch, the poor entered the houses of the rich, asking

[44] Plut., *Sol.* 13.2-3.

[45] Plut., *Sol.* 14.2-3 says that Solon's intervention was regarded both by the wealthy and by the poor as the only viable solution to the crisis, and that they were both convinced they would benefit from the end of the conflict.

[46] A sceptical view of the authenticity of Solon's verses was expressed by Lardinois in Block – Lardinois 2006, pp. 15-35. For arguments in favour of the authenticity of Solon's laws, see Rhodes in Block – Lardinois 2006, pp. 248-260.

[47] Aelian., *VH* 14.24.

[48] According to von Pöhlmann (1925^3, vol. 1, p. 334) Aelian uses here a 4th-century BCE source, but the events to which he refers might be earlier.

[49] Fuks 1979-80, pp. 183-184; von Pöhlmann (1925^3, vol. 1, p. 334) commented that social order breaks down when the character of urgency and the entity of the request ("die Not, die Dringlichkeit und die Größe des Bedarfs") violate the basic rule on which economic relations are based, namely exchange of goods of equivalent value.

[50] Plut., *Quaest. Gr.* 18.

to be entertained and given food. Eventually, they decided by decree to take back the interests they had paid on their debts and this was what they called *palintokia*.

Plutarch's source is likely Aristotle's *Constitution of the Megarians*,[51] but its loss makes it impossible for us to assess the reliability of his account, and the only extant fragments of Megarian local historians are of mythological content.[52] Whether or not this story is a fourth-century BCE elaboration of historical events,[53] the dynamics of the events described here are of particular interest. The poor claimed gifts and the action of giving was regarded as an obligation of the rich, to the point that their failure in respecting it was punished with violence.

Forsdyke interpreted this episode as the degeneration of a customary ritual of inversion.[54] These rituals, which are attested both in the Greek and in the Roman worlds, entailed a reversion of roles similar to that which happens in carnival (so, for example, the poor would sit at a rich man's banquet, while the landlord served at table).[55] Thus, the normal direction of the action of giving (from the rich to the poor) is inverted, presenting as the stronger player the party which until then had received and therefore was perceived as the weaker.[56] What makes this episode special, according to Forsdyke, is the fact that at some point in the sixth century BCE the ritual in Megara turned to violence.

This interpretation, however, ignores one fundamental problem: does this episode mark the degeneration of an established ritual or did this historical event give birth to the ritual (by which the memory of the event was preserved)? It seems more probable that Plutarch (or his sources) merged two distinct elements: on the one hand, the characteristics of the ritual of inversion in historical times (e.g. the poor entering the houses of the rich and claiming gifts); on the other, the violent episode that had inspired the ritual, the exact characteristics and dynamics of which cannot be reconstructed. Plutarch may well be describing here the

[51] Halliday 1928, pp. 99-100; Figueira 1985, p. 113; Okin 1985, p. 11.

[52] Figueira 1985 argued that the Megarians did not write at all about the political history of Megara, but I agree with Okin (1985, p. 29) that this is unlikely. It is more probable that a selection was made at a later stage from the material of the local histories of Megara. See also Forsdyke 2005, p. 77, n.15.

[53] See the recent interpretation by Forsdyke (2005, p. 76), who points out Plutarch's anachronistic use of the words "democracy" and "demagogues" when referring to archaic Megara.

[54] Forsdyke 2005, pp. 73-92.

[55] Forsdyke 2005 draws on a large variety of examples both from the ancient world and from the Middle and Modern Ages. Among the rituals of inversion in the ancient world she mentions the Festival of Kronos in Attica (Accius, *Ann.* 2-7 Warmington); the Saturnalia-like festivals in Greece (Ath. 14.639); and the Feast of the Swallow (*FGH* 526 F 1). For examples from Modern Europe, see Forsdyke 2005, p. 80 with notes.

[56] Inversion was also highlighted by Millett 1989, p. 22.

initial episode of violence that gave origin to the ritual in Megara, and he attributes to this event the characteristics of the ritual, i.e. the poor entering the houses of the rich and asking for food. What is interesting is that the preservation of the memory of this episode celebrated the 'social contract' between the upper and the lower strata of Megarian society, and reminded the Megarian elites of the consequences they would incur if ever they failed to honour it.

4. Between civic duty and generosity: private and public giving in democratic Athens

In our best-known example of Greek *polis*, Athens, cancellation of debts as a public measure is never attested during the classical period. Despite the fact that gift-giving to the poor is rarely mentioned in the sources for the history of classical Athens, we know of some significant cases: the most famous is that of the aristocrat and general Cimon. Aristotle says that

> "...he supplied maintenance to a number of the members of his deme; for anyone of the Laciadae who liked could come to his house every day and have a moderate supply, and also all his farms were unfenced, to enable anyone who liked to avail himself of the harvest".[57]

Cimon seems to have practised gift-giving on a regular basis: Theopompus says that

> "...he always took around with him two or three youths who had some small change and ordered them to make a contribution whenever someone approached and asked him; [...] whenever he saw one of the citizens ill-clothed, he would order one of the youths who accompanied him to change clothes with him".[58]

To our question about the nature of the return on Cimon's giving, Theopompus himself says: "from all these things, he won his reputation and was first

[57] Arist., *Ath. Pol.* 27.3: ...ἔπειτα τῶν δημοτῶν ἔτρεφε πολλούς. ἐξῆν γὰρ τῷ βουλομένῳ Λακιαδῶν, καθ' ἑκάστην τὴν ἡμέραν ἐλθόντι παρ' αὐτὸν ἔχειν τὰ μέτρια. ἔτι δὲ τὰ χωρία πάντα ἄφρακτα ἦν, ὅπως ἐξῇ τῷ βουλομένῳ τῆς ὀπώρας ἀπολαύειν; transl. H. Rackham. Specifically on aid to the poor in classical Athens, see Christ 2012, pp.17-26. The evidence collected by Christ, however, largely concerns cases of assistance by the *polis*, such as the public pay given to war orphans and widows. On claims of private charity in Attic oratory, see Christ 2012, p. 21, n. 40.

[58] *FGH* 115 F 89: ...περιήγετο μὲν ἀεὶ νεανίσκους δύ' ἢ τρεῖς ἔχοντας κέρματα τούτοις τε διδόναι προσέταττεν, ὁπότε τις προσέλθοι αὐτοῦ δεόμενος [...] ὁπότε τῶν πολιτῶν τινα ἴδοι κακῶς ἠμφιεσμένον, κελεύειν αὐτῶι μεταμφιέννυσθαι τῶν νεανίσκων τινα τῶν συνακολουθούντων αὐτῶι; transl. P. Millett. Cf. Plut., *Cim*. 10.2-3.

of the citizens" (ἐκ δὴ τούτων ἁπάντων ηὐδοκίμει καὶ πρῶτος ἦν τῶν πολιτῶν).[59] The distribution of gifts in the case of Cimon was not only a public display of welfare and prestige: it had a well-defined political purpose, for in democratic Athens even the poorest citizens had the right to vote and to elect generals. Cimon's generosity had a return in terms of political support,[60] to the point that it is not by chance that he was elected *strategos* ten times – and perhaps more – between 477 and 461 BCE.[61]

Millett notably argued that democratic ideology weakened the relation of dependence of poor citizens from rich patrons by centralising the redistribution of income through public pay. In his view, Cimon's behaviour bears testimony to an early phase of democracy in which remnants of the old aristocratic practice of politics were still present.[62] These remnants disappeared in the second half of the fifth and fourth centuries BCE, because social aid towards citizens in need was provided by the democratic institutions.[63] It is interesting to note that in the *Constitution of the Athenians*, Aristotle describes Pericles' decision to introduce public pay as a way of contrasting the gifts that Cimon distributed among citizens.[64] This means, quite clearly, that Aristotle did regard one of the most important features of democracy – public pay – as something that fulfilled the function of a gift. But he also says that Pericles gave to the multitude "what was their own" (διδόναι τοῖς πολλοῖς τὰ αὑτῶν).[65] Public pay was thus a gift that the *polis* owed to the citizens. The recipients of this 'public gift' were not only – and not specifically – the poor, but the whole citizen community, though it is clear

[59] *Ibid.*; transl. P. Millett.

[60] By so doing Cimon did not gain economic capital (return of goods) but social capital (a network of supporters). On social capital, see Bourdieu 1980. On the concept of social capital in relation to liturgy and public giving at Athens, see Degand 2011, pp. 95-106; cf. also the paper by T. Blank in this volume.

[61] Hignett 1952 (p. 191 with n. 4) argued that Cimon probably held the *strategia* without a break from 477 to 461 BCE.

[62] Millett 1989, pp. 24-25. According to Isocrates (*Areopag.* 32-36) the relations between rich and poor in 4th-century Athens had changed compared with the good old days. This change was in the mode of giving. The rich were no longer making loans to the poor at favourable rates. Millett has convincingly read this passage as a case of "crypto-oligarchic ideology" (1989, p. 26), namely a nostalgic reference to the decline of patron-client relations in the mature age of Athenian democracy. Isocrates does not speak here of gifts, but of loans. Yet in this context the difference is subtle: a gift in expectation of a return is not radically different from a loan, as we noted before about the nature of the return in giving to the poor.

[63] Millett (1991, p. 77) also points to types of mutual assistance between citizens, such as loans of the *eranos* kind, which, he suggests, were granted also to the very poor and slaves.

[64] Arist., *Ath. Pol.* 27.4; see Rhodes 1981, pp. 338-340.

[65] *Ibid.*

that the purpose of public pay was to encourage the political participation of those for which a three-obol pay-packet would be of significant help.[66]

Nonetheless, gift-giving to the poor as a way of establishing private relationships of dependence is attested in Athens after Cimon. As Millett himself pointed out, the figures of the *kolax*, the adulator, and the *parasitos*, the parasite, are stock characters in the comedies of the fifth and fourth centuries BCE; for example, we find them in Eupolis' *Flatterers* (dated to 421 BCE).[67] The recurring characteristic of these figures is their attachment to a rich citizen and their presence at banquets where they perform – unofficially of course – the role of jester. In return, they receive food, and in some cases even money. These forms of gift-giving between non-equals, which led to quasi patron-client relations, were long-lasting phenomena that democracy did not manage to sweep away completely.[68]

Public donations were made in the classical period in the form of liturgies, yet in this institution the *discrimen* between generosity and obligation is blurry. Liturgies were made to satisfy the needs of the *polis* in many aspects of common life, from military defence (*trierarchia*) to religious festivals.[69] They were compulsory for the wealthy, and specific procedures existed for their establishment, though rich citizens often offered to undertake them on a voluntary basis.[70] Attempts to evade liturgies are also attested,[71] and we know that legal procedures such as the *antidosis* were deployed to show up such evasion.[72]

[66] Three obols were paid to jurors in the late 5th century BCE. Jury pay was introduced by Pericles around the mid-5th century BCE (Arist., *Pol.* 1274a; *Ath. Pol.* 27.4), probably in the region of one or two obols. It was then raised to three obols by Cleon (Aristoph., *Eq.* 51; 797-800; Schol. Aristoph., *Vesp.* 88, 300; Schol. Aristoph., *Av.* 1541). In the early 4th century BCE the three-obol stipend was given to members of the Assembly (Arist., *Ath. Pol.* 41.3; Aristoph., *Eccl.* 180-188). Scholars have long debated whether or not three obols could effectively support life in the 4th century BCE; see Markle 1985, pp. 265-297, Todd 1990, pp. 146-173. On the standard Athenian wages, see Loomis 1998, pp. 232-239.

[67] Eupol., *Kol. Fr.* 159 Kock. For the figure of the *kolax* and of the parasite in Athenian comedy, see Duncan 2006, pp. 102-119.

[68] For further evidence on the survival of patron-client relations in classical Athens, see Millett 1989, pp. 33-37; cf. Zelnick-Abramovitz 2000, pp. 65-80.

[69] Festival liturgies included, apart from the Choregia and the Hestiasis, the Architheoria, Arrhephoria, Hippotrophia, Kanephoria, Euandria, Euoplia, and Eutaxia (for relevant sources see Oehler 1925). Liturgy was imposed on those citizens whose income was at least three talents (Is. 3.80, Dem. 38.64; see Davies 1981, p. 28 for liturgical census) with the exception of widows and female heirs (Dem. 14.16). Archons were exempted from trierarchy during their office (Dem. 20.28). Liturgies were imposed also on metics (Dem. 29.18), and on those who had been granted Athenian citizenship and met the wealth requirements (Dem. 20.40).

[70] Evidence for compulsion is treated in Christ 2006, pp. 188-190. The demands were limited by law to no more than one festive liturgy within two years (Dem. 20.8, Is. 7.38)

The institution of liturgies suggested reciprocal support between the upper and the lower strata of the citizen community. Their character of obligation, however, makes the concept of giving problematic. A strong tension seems to have existed between the public democratic discourse, aimed at promoting liturgies as a duty of the wealthy towards the *polis*, and the individual rhetoric of giving, aimed at stressing personal generosity.[73] The public and private forensic speeches of the fourth century offer substantial evidence of the fact that, notwithstanding the compulsory character of liturgies, a 'rhetoric of generosity' often accompanied their performance.[74]

In some cases, this rhetoric assumes the traits of aggressive arrogance. The rich Athenian Meidias is described by Demosthenes as boasting excessively about his donations.[75] He is presented as a negative model of a rich citizen, one who has often tried to escape his duty of public giving. The logic that moves Meidias' self-perception as a liturgist is made clear by his words, as cited by Demosthenes: he claims with arrogance the public respect of his fellow-citizens, reminding them on every occasion that he is both a performer of liturgies and one of those who pay the *eisphora* (property tax) in advance.[76] Meidias, it seems,

and no more than one liturgy at the same time (Dem. 20.19; 21.155; 50.9). On the appointment of liturgists, see Arist., *Ath. Pol.* 56.3; 57.1 and 61.1.

[71] On liturgy avoidance, see Christ 1990, pp. 147-169; on concealment of property, see Gabrielsen 1986, pp. 99-114; Ferrucci 2005, pp. 159-162; Christ 2006, pp. 191-194.

[72] In this procedure, any citizen could challenge another to exchange property. According to Dem. 42.1 the *antidosis* was introduced by Solon, but in the light of what we now know this is an unlikely story and probably reflects the attempt to legitimate the procedure. On the functioning of the *antidosis*, see Gabrielsen 1987, pp. 7-38; Christ 1990, pp. 160-168. Christ (1990, p. 163; cf. 2006, p. 198) notes that sources treat *antidosis* as a routine procedure.

[73] For example, in *C. Leocr.* 139-140, Lycurgus refers to those who advertise as acts of generosity the public services that they have only performed in order to prove their wealth and not to benefit the city.

[74] For a collection of the relevant evidence, see Christ 2006, pp. 201-2. For the 'rhetoric of reciprocity', see also Millett in Gill – Postlethwaite – Seaford 1998, pp. 227-253, and the paper by T. Blank in this volume.

[75] Dem. 21.153-154 with commentary by MacDowell 1990. Specifically on the figure of Meidias, see Ober 1994, p. 94.

[76] Dem. 21.153. The *eisphora* was a direct tax on wealth, which was exacted under special circumstances by assembly decree mostly for military purposes. It was imposed on citizens of the liturgical census – those liable to pay liturgies (the minimum threshold was a three-talent worth property, according to Davies 1971, pp. xxiii-xxiv and 1981, p. 28). The older piece of literary evidence for this tax is provided by Thucydides (3.19.1), who notes that an *eisphora* was imposed in 428/7 BCE in the sum of 200 talents. Epigraphic evidence is earlier: the so-called Callias decree (*IG* 1^3.52) alludes to an *eisphora* in 434/3 BCE.

belonged to the very rich,[77] and he never missed a chance to highlight his position as a donor of the highest rank. But Demosthenes reminds his fellow citizens that Meidias treats them in an unacceptable manner. The orator highlights the character of obligation of public donations and the occasions on which Meidias tried to avoid them.[78]

One could argue that Demosthenes was making a strong point here against the perception of liturgy as a gift, but his position should rather make us ponder the nature of public gifts in Athenian democracy. The just donor is not simply the one who gives; he is the one who gives while knowing that his action is rightful and beneficial to the whole community.[79] Generosity and socio-political justice were closely bound.

5. Giving to the poor and euergetism in the Hellenistic period

Things gradually changed in the Hellenistic period.[80] For example, in a *polis* of Asia Minor in the second century BCE, it would have been impossible to criticise the pride of a rich citizen acting as a *euergetes*, a public benefactor, and no public orator could have argued that such donors fulfilled their duty. From the mid-fourth century BCE, with the diffusion of the practice of the *epidoseis*,[81] and later on with the euergetic donations which became a typical feature of civic life in the Hellenistic *poleis*, public gifts were increasingly celebrated as acts of spontaneous generosity,[82] despite the fact that we have evidence for explicit

[77] According to Philochorus (*FGH* 328 F 41) the system of collection of the *eisphora* was reformed in 378/7 BCE: the ca. 1,200 *eisphora*-payers were grouped into 100 taxation-units, the *symmoriae*, each comprising ca. 10 to 15 members. The richest among these were required to pay the full amount in advance and to collect subsequently the individual quotas from their fellow *eisphora*-payers.

[78] Dem. 21.165 (public donations are a civic duty, see the examples of Niceratus, Euctemon, Euthydemus); 21.166-168 (Meidias evades liturgies); 21.185 (Meidias treats other citizens as beggars).

[79] On the relation between liberty and civic obligation in democratic Athens, see Liddel 2007.

[80] On the development from the liturgies of the classical age to the euergetic donations of the Hellenistic period, see Veyne 1976, pp. 186-228. For an argument against the interpretation of euergetism as a sign of the decline of the polis, see Brélaz 2009, pp. 37-56. On the origins of euergetism, see Domingo Gygax 2006, pp. 269-295; on euergetism and gift exchange, see Domingo Gygax 2003, pp. 181-200; 2009, esp. pp. 172-175, and 2013, pp. 50-53.

[81] First attested in Dem. 21.161.

[82] The two fundamental studies on Hellenistic euergetism are those of Veyne 1976 and Gauthier 1985. Veyne's main point was that in the Hellenistic age the values of civic solidarity, as manifested in the classical *poleis*, came to an end, favouring the emergence

requests being made by the *polis* and pressure being exerted on wealthy citizens.[83]

In the famous honorific decree for Protogenes of Olbia,[84] issued in the late-third or early-second century BCE at Olbia on the Black Sea, we find both a reference to the request for a donation made by the demos in the assembly and an explanation of the rationale of Protogenes' decision to pay off the debts of his fellow citizens:

> "when (the people) asked that [the debtors] should be freed from their debts / he freed everyone from all debts and did not [charge] any (interest), believing it more [glorious] for himself to enjoy [the] goodwill [of all]".[85]

The *euergetai* secured their reward in terms of gratitude and collective appreciation by giving public visibility to their generous actions: monuments and inscriptions were displayed with the aim of preserving the memory of the donations for centuries to come. We assist, therefore, in the development of a complex rhetoric of generosity and gratitude, which is well attested by honorific decrees.

Acts of solidarity and help to the poor are sporadically attested in terms of private giving by citizen to citizen in the Hellenistic period. In a third-century description of central Greece by Heraclides Creticus or Pseudo-Dicaearchus,[86] the author says that the inhabitants of Oropus give what they have to their needy fellow citizens and to foreigners, and allow them to take freely, being men who "respect justice, good faith and hospitality".[87] Giving in Oropus seems to be

of the *euergetēs*, who was either a member of the citizen elites or a foreigner. In either case, his donations were never presented as public duties, unlike the liturgies in classical Athens. By contrast, Gauthier argued that the evidence points to continuity between the 4th-century practices of euergetism and those until the end of the 3rd century BCE (what he terms "haute époque hellénistique", "Early Hellenistic Age"). It is only in the course of the 2nd century ("basse époque hellénistique") that the euergetism becomes a "système de gouvernement" of a minority of wealthy citizens (1985, pp. 66-75). For a comparison of these two approaches, see Domingo Gygax 1994, pp.119-134.

[83] The *polis* could prompt wealthy citizens to act as benefactors by grating them honours before the actual donations were made, so that they would feel obliged to donate; on this practice, see Domingo Gygax 2009, pp. 163-191.

[84] *Syll.*[3] 495; *SEG* 49.1041.

[85] *Syll.*[3] 495.185-187 (side B); transl. M. M. Austin: ἀξιώσαντος δὲ ἄφεσιμ ποιήσασ|[θαι τοῖς χρ]ήσταις ἀφῆκε πᾶσι πάντα καὶ οὐδένα |[ἐπράξατο, ενδοξ]ότερον αὐτῶι νομίσας εἶναι| [τὸ τὴν πάντων αὐτῶι] ὑπάρχειν εὔνοιαν. The last five lines of side B cannot be fully restored, but it is probable that they contained the second part of the comparison.

[86] Heracl. Cret. 1.9 Pfister (= Müller *FHG* II 255). See Walbank 1979, p. 72; Austin 2006, pp. 198-201.

[87] Transl. M. M. Austin.

limited to private and well-established relations between citizens. The case of Hellenistic Rhodes is different: Strabo, describing the *eunomia* (good government) of the city in his own day, says that, although the *polis* was not a democracy, the Rhodians cared to preserve good relations with the poor, and for this reason they provided them with food:

> "the wealthy support those in need according to the old tradition, and they have liturgies through which the poor are provided with food".[88]

This suggests that two practices of giving existed in Rhodes at least as late as the first century BCE: a customary practice between rich and poor based on private relations, which is described as an ancient tradition, and an institutional channel for giving, namely public liturgies.[89]

The epigraphic record describes cases in which public donations were specifically directed to the poor, in the form of food, dowries for the daughters of the poor and burials of poor citizens. An honorary decree from Priene, issued shortly after 129 BCE, describes several benefactions of Moschion, a wealthy citizen of Priene. During a major grain shortage, Moschion sold grain to his fellow-citizens at a reduced price "so that the entire demos might be saved along with their wives and children".[90]

An inscription from the Carian city of Iasos of the year 196 BCE describes the euergetic donation of Queen Laodice III to the city. The stele contains the letter of Laodice III to the citizens of Iasos and the text of the decree awarding honours to the Queen and to her husband Antiochus III.[91] In the letter Laodice promises to provide grain for ten years to the city and that the proceedings from the sale would be used to grant dowries to the daughters of poor citizens.[92] Similarly, we read in Diodorus Siculus that the Macedonian Queen Phila, wife of Demetrius, at some point after 306 BCE arranged marriages for poor girls at her own expense.[93]

[88] Strab. 14.2.5; transl. M. M. Austin. See also Veyne 1976, p. 222.

[89] Migeotte highlighted the original character of liturgies in Rhodes as specifically aimed at the poor, whereas traditional euergetism in the Hellenistic and imperial age was normally aimed at the whole citizen community. He argued that "loin d'être une mesure philanthropique ou charitable, l'institution rhodienne reflétait donc une sorte de pacte social, dans lequel riches et moins riches trouvaient leur advantage" (Migeotte 1989, p. 521).

[90] *I. Priene* 108.72-73; transl. P. Thonemann. The several benefactions of Moschion are mentioned in the decree in lines 41-50; 57-60; 68-73; 82-87; 97-99.

[91] *I. Iasos* 4.1-32 (letter of Laodice III); 33-110 (honorary decree for Laodice III and Antiochus III).

[92] *I. Iasos* 4.16-25; see the revision of the text and comment by Nafissi 2001, pp. 101-146.

[93] Diod. Sic. 19.59.4. See Pomeroy 1984, pp. 15-16; Carney 2000, p. 169; Ramsey 2011,

In both the above cases the donor was a queen. The political discourse of the Hellenistic monarchy tended to see gifts as a sign of the virtue and generosity of the monarch. In Iasos a ritual was introduced to commemorate the generosity of Laodice III and, at the same time, to highlight the importance of her gift for the life of the whole community.[94]

The *euergetes* could also be a wealthy citizen from a neighbouring *polis*. A very interesting case is described for the imperial age: in a fragment from an honorary inscription found in the Lycian *polis* of Xanthos and dating to the second half of the second century CE, we find a list of the gifts offered by Opramoas, a very wealthy citizen of Rhodiapolis, to the citizens of Xanthos.[95] The list is introduced by the formula δωρεὰς ἔδωκεν "he gave as gifts". Some of the gifts are explicitly aimed at the poor: as well as paying for the children of all the citizens of Xanthos (τὰ δὲ τέκνα πάντα τῶν πολιτῶν παιδεύει τε καὶ τρέφει), Opramoas also paid for the burials of poor citizens, the dowries of girls from poor families and the living costs of the needy (δίδωσιν δὲ καὶ κηδευτικὸν τοῖς βιώσασιν, ἐκδίδωσιν δὲ καὶ τὰς πενιχρὰς παρθένους, τρέφει δὲ καὶ τοὺς πενομένους).[96]

Indeed, this is a rather exceptional case of euergetism, as no parallel is known to the generosity of Opramoas, whose donations were made in several *poleis* of the Lycian *koinon* according to the inscriptions in his mausoleum in Rhodiapolis.[97] Yet it would be wrong to dismiss this case as an exception to the rule or simply as testimony to a later phase of euergetism. Although we should take into account that, as late as the mid-second century CE, both Roman imperial administration and the diffusion of Christian religion played a role in shaping the practice of public benefactions in the Greek *poleis* of Asia Minor, it is also true that Opramoas' donations might well have been rooted in earlier forms of euergetism, of which Phila's and Laodice III's benefactions provide significant examples.

In other cases the citizen community in its entirety was involved in public giving. Public subscriptions could be undertaken by a large number of citizens as urgent measures to cope with severe hardships in the city. From the Thessalian

pp. 510-527.

[94] *I. Iasos* 4.33-110. On the ritual in honor of Laodice III and Antiochus III in Iasos, see Nafissi 2001. Domingo Gygax (2013, p. 52) made the important point that when the donation was made by a monarch the honours awarded to the benefactor "served to mask what was in fact the main component of the countergift: submission".

[95] Balland 1981, n. 67 (pp.185-186). Cf. Balland 1981, n. 66 (pp. 173-174). For the dating of the two fragments after the year 152 CE, see Balland 1981, p. 174.

[96] Balland 1981, n. 67.24-25 (children's education), 30 (burials), 31 (dowries), 32 (feeding the poor).

[97] The 32 decrees and 38 letters from the mausoleum of Opramoas in Rhodiapolis have been collected, translated and commented on by Kokkinia 2000.

city of Crannon during the mid-second century BCE we have a decree attesting to public giving by the whole community in order to relieve the *polis* of its debts.[98] A request is made by the assembly for all the citizens of Crannon to make a contribution; the word "gift" (δουρρὰν) is explicitly deployed in the text of the inscription.[99] The donations were not imposed as an obligation, and the sum was freely chosen by the donors according to their means. The circumstances appear to be exceptional: the *polis* was heavily indebted as a consequence of the prolonged wars, which can be identified in all probability with the conflict between Rome and Antiochus III (192-188 BCE) and between Rome and Perseus (171-168 BCE). A solution for the crisis is proposed in the assembly: the community (*koinon*) decides that all the citizens should come to the help of the city, each according to his private means.[100] The contributors are invited to declare the amount of their donation:

> "Those who wish should declare to the city in the assembly the sum each wishes to contribute as a gift (δουρρὰν) for the aforementioned debts".[101]

Remembrance is granted by a specific provision: those who have made a donation are inscribed on the stele. The decree orders that the list of the contributors, which has not survived, must report the sum each person has offered and be located in the most distinguished place on the acropolis.[102]

Though in this case the public donation was intended to help the whole *polis* and not specifically the poor, it is clear that larger contributions were expected from the wealthy and to a much lesser extent, if at all, from the lower strata of the citizenry. The poor citizens of Crannon would have been constantly reminded by the stone inscription of the generosity, and a sense of civic duty of their richer fellows.

[98] Béquignon 1935, n.1; Moretti 1967, vol. II, n. 99; Migeotte 1992, n. 34. For a recent English translation, see Austin 2006, pp. 227-228. On public subscriptions in the Greek cities during the Hellenistic period, see Chaniotis 2013, pp. 89-106 and Ellis-Evans 2013, pp. 107-121.

[99] l. 22: δουρρὰν (Moretti 1967; Migeotte 1992); δούρραντα (Béquignon 1935).

[100] ll. 15-20.

[101] ll. 20-23.: καὶ ἐπαγγέλλασθαι | τᾶ πόλι τὸς δευμένος παρ' ἐκκλεισσίαι, | ἕκαστον καττό κε βέλλειτει δουρρὰν τᾶ | {τα} πόλι ἐν τὰ διασαφειμένα δάνεια. I reproduce here and in the following the translation by M. M. Austin

[102] l. 40: ἐν ἀ|[κροπόλει ἐν τοῦ ἐπιφ]ανεσστάτου τόπου (Béquignon 1935, Moretti 1967, Migeotte 1992). Regarding the reward for the donors, Austin (2006, p. 228, n. 4) notes that "the city has nothing to offer except gratitude". Yet this is in fact the usual reward for *epidoseis*. Public gratitude at Crannon was sanctioned by the erection of a stele bearing the names of the benefactors.

The cases mentioned above suggest that giving to the poor was practised in the Greek *poleis* during the Hellenistic period in the form of public benefactions. The fact that the names of the donors were inscribed on stone and, in some cases, the benefaction was celebrated through the foundation of rituals, shows that these acts of social aid were officially recognised as fundamental to the well-being of the entire citizen community.

6. Conclusion

Although it is true that help to the poor was not sanctioned by Greek religion, and that Greek gods, unlike the Jewish and Christian God, did not reward the donor, the evidence so far points to the fact that the action of giving from the upper towards the lower strata of the citizen population was performed both at the private and at the public level in the archaic, classical and Hellenistic *poleis*.

The main point is that the act of giving was aimed at a return on the gift during one's lifetime, the nature of which has been explored in this paper. The assumptions underlying this act were two: first, on the level of private giving, the person who was asked to give might one day have to receive. Reciprocity was a form of insurance. Second, even if a return in the form of goods could not be expected, other kinds of rewards, such as services, social control, and presser-vation of political stability, were valued.

Common acts of public giving were aimed at preventing turmoil and at preserving social order in the *polis*: from the archaic to the Hellenistic period public giving implemented the principle of social cohesion. Reciprocal advan-tage between the parties involved remained the *conditio sine qua non*.

Bibliography

Austin, Michel M.: *The Hellenistic World from Alexander to the Roman Conquest: A Selection of Ancient Sources in Translation*, Cambridge 2006.

Balland, André: *Fouilles de Xanthos VII. Inscriptions d'époque impérial du Létôon*, Paris 1981.

Béquignon, Yves: *Études Thessaliennes VII*, in: *BCH* 59 (1935), pp. 36-77.

Block, Josine H. – André P. M. H. Lardinois (ed. by): *Solon of Athens: New Historical and Philological Approaches*, Leiden 2006.

Bolkestein, Hendrik: *Wohltätigkeit und Armenpflege im vorchristlichen Altertum*, Utrecht 1939.

Bourdieu, Pierre: *Le capital social. Notes provisoires*, in: *Actes de la recherche en sciences sociales* 31 (1980), pp. 2-3.

Brélaz, Cédric: *Les bienfaiteurs, «sauveurs» et «fossoyeurs» de la cité hellénistique?: une approche historiographique de l'évergétisme*, in: *L'huile et l'argent. Gymnasiarchie et évérgetisme dans la Grèce hellénistique*, ed. by Olivier Curty, Paris 2009, pp. 37-56.

Carney, Elizabeth Donnelly: *Women and monarchy in Macedonia*, Norman 2000.

Cassola, Filippo: *Solone, la terra e gli ectemori*, in: *PdP* 19 (1964), pp. 25-67.

Chaniotis, Angelos: *Public Subscriptions and Loans as Social Capital in the Hellenistic City: Reciprocity, Performance, Commemoration*, in: *Epigraphical Approaches to the Postclassical Polis. Fourth Century BC to Second Century AD*, ed. by Paraskevi Martzavou – Nikolaos Papazarkadas, Oxford 2013, pp. 89-106.

Christ, Matthew R.: *Liturgy Avoidance and Antidosis in Classical Athens*, in: *TAPhA* 120 (1990), pp. 147-169.

Christ, Matthew R.: *The Bad Citizen in Classical Athens*, Cambridge 2006.

Christ, Matthew R.: *The Limits of Altruism in Democratic Athens*, Cambridge 2012.

Davies, John Kenyon: *Athenian Propertied Families. 600-300 B.C.*, Oxford 1971.

Davies, John Kenyon: *Wealth and the Power of Wealth in Classical Athens*, Salem 1981.

Degand, Martin: *L'Antiquité à l'épreuve des sciences sociales. Les liturgies athéniennes*, in: *AC* 80 (2011), pp. 95-106.

Domingo Gygax, Marc: *Evergetismo e historia: Paul Veyne y Philippe Gauthier comparados*, in: *Prometheus* 20 (1994), pp. 119-134.

Domingo Gygax, Marc: *Euergetismus und Gabentausch*, in: *Métis* 1 (2003), pp. 181-200.

Domingo Gygax, Marc: *Les origines de l'évergétisme: échanges et identités sociales dans la cité grecque*, in: *Métis* 4 (2006), pp. 269-295.

Domingo Gygax, Marc: *Proleptic Honours in Greek Euergetism*, in: *Chiron* 39 (2009), pp. 163-191.

Domingo Gygax, Marc: *Gift-Giving and Power Relationships in Greek Social Praxis and Public Discourse*, in: *The Gift in Antiquity*, ed. by Michael Satlow, Malden – Oxford 2013, pp. 45-60.

Donlan Walter F.: *The Aristocratic Ideal in Ancient Greece. Attitudes of Superiority from Homer to the End of the Fifth Century B.C.*, Lawrence 1980 = Walter F. Donlan: *The Aristocratic Ideal and Selected Papers*, Wauconda 1999, pp. 1-222.

Donlan, Walter F.: *Reciprocities in Homer*, in: *CW* 75 (1981), pp. 137-75.

Duncan, Anne: *Performance and Identity in the Classical World*, Cambridge 2006.

Duplouy, Alain: *Le prestige des élites. Recherches sur les modes de reconnaissance sociale en Grèce entre les Xᵉ et Vᵉ siècles avant J.-C.*, Paris 2006.

Edwards, Anthony T.: *Hesiod's Ascra*, Berkeley 2004.

Ellis-Evans, Aneurin: *The Ideology of Public Subscriptions*, in: *Epigraphical Approaches to the Postclassical Polis. Fourth Century BC to Second Century AD*, ed. by Paraskevi Martzavou – Nikolaos Papazarkadas, Oxford 2013, pp. 107-121.

Ferrucci, Stefano: *La ricchezza nascosta: osservazioni su ἀφανής e φανερὰ οὐσία*, in: *MedAnt* 8 (2005), pp. 145-169.

Figueira, Thomas J.: *The Theognidea and Megarian Society*, in: *Theognis of Megara: Poetry and the Polis*, ed. by T. J. Figueira – Gregory Nagy, Baltimore 1985, pp. 112-158.

Finn, Richard D.: *Almsgiving in the Later Roman Empire: Christian Promotion and Practice, 313-450*, Oxford 2006.

Forsdyke, Sara: *Revelry and Riot in Archaic Megara: Democratic Disorder or Ritual Reversal?*, in: *JHS* 125 (2005), pp. 73-92.

Fuks, Alexander: *Τοῖς ἀπορουμένοις κοινωνεῖν: The Sharing of Property by the Rich with the Poor in Greek Theory and Practice*, in: *SCI* 5 (1979-1980), pp. 46-63 = Alexander Fuks: *Social Conflict in Ancient Greece*, Leiden 1984, pp. 172-189.

Gabrielsen, Vincent: *Φανερά and ἀφανὴς οὐσία in Classical Athens*, in: *C&M* 37 (1986), pp. 99-114.
Gabrielsen, Vincent: *The Antidosis Procedure in Classical Athens*, in: *C&M* 38 (1987), pp. 7-38.
Gallant, Thomas W.: *Risk and Survival in Ancient Greece: Reconstructing the Rural Domestic Economy*, Cambridge 1991.
Gardner, Gregg E.: *Charity Wounds: Gifts to the Poor in Early Rabbinic Judaism*, in: *The Gift in Antiquity*, ed. by Michael Satlow, Malden – Oxford 2013, pp. 173-188.
Garnsey, Peter: *Famine and Food Supply in the Graeco-Roman World: Responses to Risk and Crisis*, Cambridge 1988.
Gauthier, Philippe: *Les cités grecques et leurs bienfaiteurs (IVe-Ier siècle avant J.C.). Contribution à l'histoire des institutions*, Paris 1985.
Gill, Christopher – Norman Postlewaith – Richard Seaford (ed. by), *Reciprocity in Ancient Greece,* Oxford 1998.
Gould, John: *Hiketeia*, in: *JHS* 93 (1973), pp. 74-103.
Halliday, William R.: *The Greek Questions of Plutarch*, Oxford 1928.
Hands, Arthur R.: *Charities and Social Aid in Greece and Rome*, Ithaca 1968.
Hignett, Charles: *A History of the Athenian Constitution to the End of the Fifth Century B.C.*, Oxford 1952.
Hodkinson, Stephen: *Social Order and the Conflict of Values in Classical Sparta*, in: *Chiron* 13 (1983), pp. 239-81.
Hodkinson, Stephen: *Warfare, Wealth and the Crisis of Spartiate Society*, in: *War and Society in the Greek World*, ed. by John Rich – Graham Shipley, London 1993, pp. 146-176.
Hodkinson, Stephen: *Property and Wealth in Classical Sparta*, London – Swansea 2000.
Hodkinson, Stephen: *Was Classical Sparta a Military Society?*, in: *Sparta and War*, ed. by Stephen Hodkinson – Anton Powell, Swansea 2006, pp. 111-162.
Hodkinson, Stephen – Anton Powell (ed. by): *Sparta: New Perspectives*, London 1999.
Hodkinson, Stephen – Anton Powell (ed. by): *Sparta Beyond the Mirage*, Swansea 2002.
Kloft, Hans: *Gedanken zum Ptochos*, in: *Soziale Randgruppen und Außenseiter im Altertum*, ed. by Ingomar Weiler, Graz 1988, pp. 81-106.
Kokkinia, Christina: *Die Opramoas-Inschrift von Rhodiapolis: Euergetismus und soziale Elite in Lykien*, Bonn 2000.
Lamberton, Robert: *Hesiod*, New Haven – London 1988.
Liddel, Peter P.: *Civic Obligation and Individual Liberty in Ancient Athens*, Oxford 2007.
Loomis William T.: *Wages, Welfare Costs and Inflation in Classical Athens*, Ann Arbor 1998.
MacDowell, Douglas M.: *Demosthenes: Against Meidias (Oration 21)*, Oxford 1990.
Markle, Minor M.: *Jury Pay and Assembly Pay at Athens*, in: *Crux. Essays Presented to G.E.M. De Ste Croix on His 75th Birthday*, ed. by Paul A. Cartledge – David Harvey, Exeter 1985, pp. 265-297.
Meggitt, Justin J.: *Paul, Poverty and Survival*, Edinburgh 1998.
Migeotte, Léopold: *Démocratie et entretien du peuple à Rhodes*, in: *REG* 102 (1989), pp. 515-528.
Migeotte, Léopold: *Les souscriptions publiques dans le cités grecques*, Genève 1992.
Millett, Paul: *The Avoidance of Patron-Clients Relations in Classical Athens*, in: *Patronage in Ancient Society*, ed. by Andrew Wallace-Hadrill, London 1989, pp. 15-47.

Millett, Paul: *Lending and Borrowing in Ancient Athens*, Cambridge 1991.

Moretti, Luigi: *Iscrizioni storiche ellenistiche, vol. 1: Attica, Peloponneso, Beozia*, Firenze 1967.

Nafissi, Massimo: *L' iscrizione di Laodice (I.Iasos 4). Revisione del testo e nuove osservazioni*, in: *PdP* 56 (2001), pp. 101-146.

Newman, William L.: *The Politics of Aristotle. Vol. 4: Essay on Constitutions, Books 6-8, Text and Notes*, Oxford 1902.

Ober, Josiah: *Power and Oratory in Democratic Athens: Demosthenes 21, Against Meidias*, in: *Persuasion: Greek Rhetoric in Action*, ed. by Ian Worthington, London 1994, pp. 85-108.

Oehler, Johann: *Leiturgie*, in: *RE* XII/2, Stuttgart 1925, coll. 1871-1879.

Okin, Louis A.: *Theognis and the Sources for the History of Archaic Megara*, in: *Theognis of Megara: Poetry and the Polis*, ed. by T. J. Figueira – Gregory Nagy, Baltimore 1985, pp. 9-21.

Pagani, Lara: *Due etimologie di nomi omerici in Asclepiade di Mirlea (Astyanax e Arnaios)*, in: *Eikasmos* 16 (2005), pp. 193-209.

Parkin, Anneliese: *You Do Him No Service: An Exploration of Pagan Almsgiving*, in: *Poverty in the Roman World*, ed. by Margaret Atkins – Robin Osborne, Cambridge 2006, pp. 60-82.

Pomeroy, Sarah B.: *Women in Hellenistic Egypt: from Alexander to Cleopatra*, New York 1984.

Ramsey, Gillian: *The Queen and the City: Royal Female Intervention and Patronage in Hellenistic Civic Communities*, in: *Gender & History* 23 (2011), pp. 510-527.

Rhodes, Peter J.: *A Commentary on the Aristotelian Athenaion Politeia*, Oxford 1981.

Rosivach, Vincent J.: *Redistribution of Land in Solon, Fragment 34 West*, in: *JHS* 112 (1992), pp. 153-157.

Sahlins, Marshall D.: *Stone Age Economics*, Hawthorne 1972.

Schmitz, Winfried: *Nachbarschaft und Dorfgemeinschaft im archaischen und klassischen Griechenland*, Berlin 2004.

Todd, Stephen: *Lady Chatterley's Lover and the Attic Orators: The Social Composition of the Athenian Jury*, in: *JHS* 110 (1990), pp. 146-173.

Veyne, Paul: *Le pain et le cirque. Sociologie historique d'un pluralisme politique*, Paris 1976.

von Pöhlmann, Robert: *Geschichte der sozialen Frage und des Sozialismus in der antiken Welt*, München 1925³; Repr. Darmstadt 1984.

von Reden, Sitta: *Exchange in Ancient Greece*, London 1995.

Walbank, Frank W.: *A Historical Commentary on Polybius, 3: Commentary on Books 19-40*, Oxford 1979.

Zelnick-Abramovitz, Rachel: *Did Patronage Exist in Classical Athens?*, in: *AC* 69 (2000), pp. 65-80.

SABIEN COLPAERT

Euergetism and the Gift

1. Introduction

> "*Panem et Circenses*: pourquoi le don à la collectivité, le mécénat envers la cité, occupe-t-il une si grande place dans la vie antique... Ces dons d'un individu à la collectivité sont ce qu'on appelle l'évergétisme".[1]

In the first sentence of his seminal work on euergetism, Veyne places the word "gift" right at the centre of euergetism.[2] The gift, as a practice or phenomenon not confined to Greco-Roman society, has been studied in and throughout various cultures and periods. Referring to euergetism as a form of gift-giving implies that the theory and principles of the gift and gift exchange have to at least be taken into consideration when studying euergetism.

In this contribution an outline will be given on how the study of the concept of euergetism has evolved. In parallel, an evaluation will be made of how the theory of gift exchange and its principles have influenced the approach and added to our understanding of euergetism. The limits of the gift-exchange model for analysing epigraphic sources will be discussed briefly. Turning to Dio Chrysostom's 46th speech, other mechanisms underlying euergetism will be pointed out.

As an overarching term, euergetism can refer a wide variety of traditions, periods, regions and actors throughout Antiquity. Our historical focus will be on euergetism by the elite in the Greek cities of Asia Minor during the Hellenistic and Roman period, excluding the euergetic initiatives of Hellenistic kings and emperors as well as of their officials.

[1] Veyne 1976, p. 9. Euergetism is frequently introduced using the word "giving". E.g. *OCD*[3], *s.v.* euergetism: "phenomenon of voluntary gift-giving"; Zuiderhoek 2009, p. 1: "the boom in elite public giving".

[2] Euergetism in this contribution refers to the interaction between wealthy individual members of the elite using their means, connections and/or talents to provide the community or a city (or part thereof) with services or amenities (e.g. buildings, festivals, distributions, embassies), and the community acknowledging the contributions and officially awarding honours as crowns, statues, proclamations and so on. A few among many definitions or descriptions: Domingo Gygax 1994, p. 119; Rogers 1993, p. 188; van Nijf 2000, p. 23; Domingo Gygax 2003, pp. 182-183; Zuiderhoek 2009, p. 9 on civic euergetism.

2. The origin of euergetism as a concept and research topic

The ancient Greeks and Romans were very familiar with the reality of euergetism, but never seem to have conceptualised it, or not in the same way as modern research does.[3] A similar conceptual blind spot can be observed within the study of ancient history itself: until the publication of Veyne's *Le Pain et le Cirque* in 1976, benefactors and benefactions were duly observed and taken into consideration but never studied as a research topic in their own right.[4] It was Veyne who elaborated the neologism "euergetism" into a concept and made us look upon the ancient world through euergetic eyes.[5] With an approach that is sociological as well as historical, and with invariants as points of reference, he first and foremost argues what euergetism was not: redistribution, potlatch, class struggle, taxation, and de-politicisation to name but a few. Rather, Veyne emphasises the importance of "distance sociale",[6] and the psychological factors that made the elite contribute.[7] He further states that the being in place of a "régime des notables" was a prerequisite for the development of euergetism in the Greek cities.[8] Euergetism intertwined with a regime of notables made its appearance roughly around the beginning of the Hellenistic period and remained part of the Greco-Roman society until the end of the fourth century CE.[9]

In 1985 Gauthier studied the phenomenon of benefactors[10] from a very different methodological angle in *Les cités grecques et leurs bienfaiteurs*.[11]

[3] Veyne 1976, pp. 20-21. Veyne points to the Greek notion of φιλοτιμία but describes it as too large and emphasising the reasons for euergetism. Similar reasoning by Zuiderhoek 2009, p. 6. On the importance of conceptualisation, Veyne 1978, pp. 141-143.

[4] Brélaz 2009, p. 40. Brélaz offers a lucid outline of the historiography of euergetism in non- and conceptualised form for the Greek city of the Hellenistic period throughout his contri-bution. To mention one expert on the non-conceptualised theme: Robert 1969, e.g. when describing the casus of Theophanes of Mytilene and referring to "le système des évergètes" (p. 42).

[5] The neologism euergetism was first used by Boulanger 1923, p. 25, in his work on Aelius Aristides and again by Marrou 1948, pp. 160-161, 405.

[6] See the remark by Garnsey 1991, p. 167: "The significance of this term is that it fills the void created by the elimination of any explanation in terms of power. That V. will not have".

[7] For more thorough reviews of *Le pain et le cirque*: Andreau – Schmitt – Schnapp 1978; Garnsey 1991; Domingo Gygax 1994. For a sociological review: Stinchcombe 1980.

[8] Veyne 1969, p. 789; Veyne 1976, pp. 236 and 263.

[9] Veyne 1976, p. 184. For the decline of euergetism in Asia Minor in the 3rd century CE and the need for further research, see Zuiderhoek 2009, pp. 154-159. For the changes honorific inscriptions for benefactors underwent in late Antiquity, see Roueché 1997, pp. 353-368. See also the article by Lellia Cracco Ruggini in this volume.

[10] Brélaz 2009, p. 39, remarks that Gauthier uses the concept euergetism as well as the technical term "euergetes" sparingly, but instead prefers "bienfaiteurs".

Intended to be a contribution on institutional history, his research examines the way Greek cities rewarded their benefactors. On the basis of a thorough analysis of the epigraphic sources, Gauthier reconstructs the evolution these honours underwent throughout the Hellenistic period.

As to civic euergetism in the cities of Asia Minor during the Imperial period, the recent research of Arjan Zuiderhoek can be added. In *The politics of munificence in the Roman Empire* Zuiderhoek provides an explanation, not so much for the existence, but for the proliferation of euergetism during the first two centuries of the Empire against the background of the growing disparities in wealth and in power within the cities.[12]

3. Euergetism is giving

When it comes to the gift and gift exchange, the interpretation and understanding of Mauss and those of Veyne are essentially different, as Silber has demonstrated comparing the work of both authors: Mauss analysed and defined the gift, in his fundamental study *Essai sur le don*, as a universal practice, the nature and the principles of which reveal themselves to be similar and homogeneous over different practices, societies and periods.[13] The unifying principle lies in the elements of giving, receiving and giving in return. Veyne sets out to define the historical uniqueness of euergetism as a form of gift.[14] For Veyne, “il n’existe pas de modèle général au niveau du vécu”: the gift as having constant and defined characteristics, as the accumulation of prestige or entailing a return, is but an illusion.[15] Referring to Mauss, he argues that the *Essai sur le don* does not provide a theory of the gift, nor a model that is universally

[11] See Domingo Gygax 1994, pp. 119-134 for a detailed comparison of the methods and analyses by Veyne and Gauthier.

[12] Zuiderhoek 2009, p. 12 for a summary of his approach. See also Rogers 1991a for the foundation of Vibius Salutaris; Kokkinia 2000 for the case study of Opramoas of Rhodiapolis; Quaß 1993 for an extensive inventory of euergetic initiatives by the elite, without intending to analyse the concept euergetism in its own right. In fact, Quaß does not use the concept throughout his study.

[13] Mauss 1923-1924. See Silber 2004, pp. 191-195. Silber terms Mauss’s interpretation as “a- ou trans-historique” (p. 191). Mauss was not the first to study the gift. See Wagner-Hasel 2003, especially pp. 143-159 for an elucidating outline of pre-Maussian theory of the gift and gift exchange and the influence on Mauss; see also Wagner-Hasel’s paper in this volume.

[14] Silber 2004, pp. 195-199.

[15] Veyne 1969, pp. 788-789. Veyne’s arguments and opinion on the gift and gift exchange as a model are here perhaps more emphatically expressed than in *Le pain et le cirque*.

applicable.[16] Veyne seems primarily opposed to a comparative approach of euergetism, resulting in the study of similar practices over different societies.[17]

In his conception of the gift in relation to euergetism, Veyne observes a rather strict and particular distinction between gift and exchange. He defines a gift as *what* is given and the *fact* that it is given. Through the act of giving one does not intend to acquire commodities but in fact renounces material goods in order to solidify personal relationships. Originally an episode in a given relationship, the gift also becomes a symbol confirming that relationship.[18] Exchange, however, implies material satisfaction on both sides.[19] This notion of the gift is seen to be consistent with further statements on euergetism throughout Veyne's study. On the one hand, euergetism was a disinterested practice, not expecting a return as it had no function in assigning power or wealth to the elite; the regime of notables would have functioned without euergetism.[20] On the other hand, through giving the elite put its social distance on display.[21] Giving was experienced as a pleasure and therefore a tendency of the elite, even when there was social pressure or obligation involved.[22]

In their review of Veyne's *Le pain et le cirque*, Andreau, Schmitt and Schnapp explicitly comment on the fact that Veyne neglected the elements of expecting as well as receiving a return in his analysis of euergetism as gift behaviour, including those returns that were immaterial and of a political nature.[23] The focus on the disinterested giver in Veyne's conception of euergetism as gift seems to provide an explanation for this absence. This one-sidedness consequently makes the role of the receiving and returning party rather incidental. A passage in Veyne is, in this regard, striking:

> "Spontanéité multipliée par la contrainte, l'évergétisme, qu'il soit ostentation gratuite ou paiement symbolique *ob honorem*, a toujours deux caractères: il est civique, il va au bénéfice de la cité ou de l'ensemble des citoyens, et il est le fait d'une classe, celle des notables, qui donne parce qu'elle se sent supérieure au

[16] Veyne 1969, p. 793.
[17] Veyne 1969, p. 787.
[18] Veyne 1976, pp. 81-89, with the telling subtitle "Don ou échange, mais pas les deux" (p. 82). See also Silber 2004, p. 198. Veyne's interpretation of the gift bears close resemblance to that of the modern legal concept of making a gift: see Wagner-Hasel 2003, pp. 150-152 on the revision of the gift in the German civil code.
[19] Veyne 1976, pp. 82-83.
[20] Veyne 1976, p. 311.
[21] Veyne 1976, p. 334.
[22] Veyne 1976, p. 234.
[23] Andreau – Schmitt – Schnapp 1978, p. 317. See also p. 320: "Si la philosophie, l'économie et la science politique sont souvent invoquées à l'appui de ses démonstrations l'anthropologie est niée ou ignorée."

corps du peuple; cela est essentiel: l'évergétisme est l'expression d'une supériorité politique; la cité est divisée en deux camps, ceux qui reçoivent et ceux qui donnent".[24]

Notwithstanding this one-sided interpretation of euergetism with emphasis on the elite as active partner, Veyne paints a quite lively picture of how benefactors were honoured.[25] The honours are described as "un des grands faits politiques" of both the Hellenistic and Roman period as they assent the affiliation to the "order"[26] of the elite and signal the superiority of that order.[27] Indicative as they are in terms of social distance and superiority, Veyne does not consider these honours as a return or an element of reciprocity. In the end, "loin d'expliquer l'évergétisme, le goût des honneurs s'explique par l'évergétisme".[28] In the context of euergetism *ob honorem*, the perspective changes somewhat: euergetism is to be considered a symbolic compensation ("pourboire") by the elite for the privilege of government and power.[29]

4. Honours for benefactors

Gauthier introduces his research as concerning

"l'*attitude* des communautés envers leurs bienfaiteurs, plutôt que le *rôle* joué par ceux-ci dans la cité".[30]

Analysing the *de facto* reciprocal element in a euergetic exchange does not mean that Gauthier applies a – Maussian or other – gift model. In the end Gauthier did not intend to study euergetism but the evolution of honours for benefactors from an institutional perspective. Nevertheless Gauthier's con-

[24] Veyne 1976, p. 236. The image of a divided society between haves and have-nots resurfaces several times, e.g. on pp. 269 and 278.

[25] Veyne 1976, pp. 269-280. Emphasising the role of the elite itself in awarding and composing these honours, attention is even turned to the non-elite citizens involved. Veyne indicates that the honours require a study in their own right (p. 270).

[26] Andreau – Schmitt – Schnapp 1978, pp. 314-315 remarking on Veyne's use of "ordre" and "classe".

[27] Veyne 1976, pp. 269 and 279.

[28] Veyne 1976, p. 280.

[29] Veyne 1976, pp. 258 and 265-266. See also p. 324 for the notion of benefactors as already been rewarded by social distance. As a mechanism, it resembles what Domingo Gygax 2003, p. 191, terms "informal reciprocity" in Athens during the 4th century BCE: for their privileged position, rich citizens were required to give a return towards the community by means of benefactions.

[30] Gauthier 1985, p. 3 (emphasis by Gauthier).

clusions had a considerable impact on our understanding of euergetism. While Veyne had placed both a "régime des notables" and euergetism at the beginning of the Hellenistic period,[31] Gauthier argues, based on a thorough analysis of the epigraphic source material, that such conception of euergetism as "système de gouvernement" related to a "régime des notables" can only be discerned from the late Hellenistic period onwards; around that time "les grands évergètes", whose honorific status signals their influential and powerful position, become apparent in the honorific epigraphy.[32] This is important, as euergetism has been and still is regarded as indicative of the position of the elite and as conducive to the process of oligarchisation in the Greco-Roman city.[33] Changes in the interpretation and evaluation of euergetism generate a considerable impact on how the society in the *polis* is perceived. In itself this is an indication of the degree to which euergetism was interwoven in the fabric of the *polis*.[34]

5. Euergetism is giving for a return

The analysis of the reciprocal element honour has led to a chronological refinement of euergetism in the Hellenistic period. The introduction of an exchange dimension and reciprocity has in addition led to further insights into the functioning of and motivations behind euergetism. Veyne's unilateral view of euergetism as disinterested gift giving has been criticised by scholars who stress the importance of reciprocity and the return by the community in the form of honours.[35] The reciprocal principle – and by extension the theory of gift exchange – is very much the corner-stone of Domingo Gygax's interpretation of

[31] Veyne 1976, e.g. pp. 210-215. Similar continuity in Quaß 1993, especially pp. 347-348. But see already Robert 1960, p. 325, for the specificity of the late Hellenistic period.

[32] Gauthier 1985, pp. 66-75; 1993, p. 223; 2005, p. 2. For an opposite view, one of continuity regarding the position of notables in the Greek cities during the entire Hellenistic period: Habicht 1995, pp. 87-92. According to Gruen 1987, p. 230, followed by Rogers 1991b, p. 98, Gauthier based his observation about the change to a "système de gouvernement" on rather sparse evidence. For a recent in-depth and detailed analysis of the late Hellenistic period in terms of continuing political activity of citizens in relation to the power of the elite, see the contributions in Fröhlich – Müller 2005.

[33] Brélaz 2009, pp. 43-49 for a critical analysis of the relation euergetism – decline of democracy in the Hellenistic period.

[34] Veyne 1976, p. 22 for the expression "fait social total". According to Silber 2004, p. 196, this is an instance where Veyne stays close to Mauss. Wagner-Hasel 2003, pp. 156 and 160, remarks that the notion "total social phenomenon" of Mauss in turn was not a novelty but had been preceded in Jhering's study of hospitality in Antiquity.

[35] van Nijf 1997, pp. 116-117; Domingo Gygax 2003, pp. 182-183; 2006, p. 271-272; Zuiderhoek 2007, p. 203; 2009, p. 113.

euergetism as a relationship of reciprocity.[36] He points to the similarities between gift exchange in the Archaic period and euergetism, and tries to bridge the chronological gap between both practices, exploring the origins of euergetism.[37] In his analyses of the functioning of euergetism, he outlines the complexity of euergetic exchange, discerning informal and institutional levels of reciprocity.[38]

Despite being symbolic and non-material, honours mattered as they reflected and conferred status and prestige upon the benefactors. Van Nijf indicates that the presence of honorific monuments, and the considerable political deliberation they represent, underwrote the superiority of the elite.[39] Zuiderhoek links the interest of the elite when giving with the legitimation of their political position and power.[40] From this perspective the honours decreed by the community were of seminal importance, as they expressed the consent of the community in this legitimation process. In this "highly politicised form of exchange", both the elite and non-elite acted on shared values and beliefs regarding legitimacy of power and social hierarchisation.[41] When considering the "uneasy coexistence in sociological discourse" on contemporary gift-giving between explanations in terms of 'moral cement' on the one hand and acquiring and exercising power on the other, Zuiderhoek's interpretation of euergetism can be seen as bringing these opposed views closer together. Social bonds between elite and non-elite were solidified while at the same time the superiority of the elite and the oligarchic nature of society was accepted and confirmed.[42]

The bestowal of honours by the community was not a mere immaterial, trivial formality following a euergetic initiative. The process entailed the drafting of an honorific decree by the institutions and the putting up of an inscription

[36] E.g. Domingo Gygax 2009, p. 172.

[37] Domingo Gygax 2003 and 2006. Domingo Gygax argues that euergetism as defined by Veyne was not "le produit direct" of the Hellenistic polis (2006, p. 294), but has roots in earlier reciprocal traditions and exchanges between cities and foreigners, athletes or aristocrats. For proleptic honours, elucidating the historical relationship between gift exchange and euergetism: Domingo Gygax 2009.

[38] For the informal/non-institutional and institutional levels of reciprocity: Domingo Gygax 2003, pp. 189-191; 2006, pp. 274 and 294; 2009, p. 185.

[39] van Nijf 1997, pp. 116-119, terming the interaction between benefactors and the community as symbolic exchange.

[40] Zuiderhoek 2007, pp. 203-204; 2009, pp. 113-115 and 149-150.

[41] Zuiderhoek 2009, pp. 119-122. Euergetism is conceived as a system of symbolic exchange, but enhanced by applying the Beetham–model on political legitimacy in order to explain the link between symbols and legitimacy. For more in depth exploration of the model's elements of shared beliefs and consent in the Imperial Greek city, see pp. 122-133.

[42] For both interpretations on contemporary gift giving: Osteen 2002, p. 17. See also Zuiderhoek 2009, p. 116, on the paradox of ancient munificence.

testifying to the euergetic nature of an individual, but could equally result in acclamations, the official proclamation of the benefactor's name during festivals or other large gatherings, the ceremonial crowning of statues, the permanent presence in symbolic and important public places and/or the sending of letters to the Roman authorities.[43] Deciding on and acting out honours was the community at work, keeping their part of the euergetic bargain. The benefactors' need for these honours/legitimation gave the *demos* (the people) some political leverage in their relation with the elite.[44]

6. Euergetism is receiving to return

It was Rogers who brought to attention the involvement of the *demos*, as well as of the *boule* (the council), in creating and shaping the foundation of Salutaris at the beginning of the second century CE in Ephesos.[45] This foundation comprised a yearly lottery and distribution of money at the time of the mysteries of Artemis and the donation of type-statues and images to be carried in a procession through Ephesos on regular occasions throughout the year.[46] Rogers underlines the preliminary negotiations with the *boule* and the participation of the *demos* in the creation of the foundation, as well as in prominently disclosing the documents and procedures in public. Given the role of civic institutions and the community in perpetuating the foundation, discussion on an organisational level, prior to accepting the foundation, was indispensable. The foundation would in the end be a "self-representation of the demos", putting on display the civic order and hierarchy of Ephesos by means of rituals.[47] Turning his attention to the foundation of Demosthenes in Oinoanda around 125 CE,[48] and applying what he terms a "democratic" model of euergetism, Rogers explains the difference in outlook of the foundation between the first promise in 124 CE and the proposal including a second promise about a year later as a result of consultation, discussion and negotiations with the *boule* and the *demos*.[49] The involvement of the community led to the incorporation of the Imperial cult as well

[43] Veyne 1976, pp. 271-278; Zuiderhoek 2009, pp. 7 and 123-129.

[44] Zuiderhoek 2007, pp. 203-204 and 211; 2009, p. 106. See also van Nijf 1997, p. 117 on the "nervous"-ness of benefactors before the decision of the assembly.

[45] *I.Ephesos* Ia.27; Greek text and English translation in Rogers 1991a, pp. 152-185.

[46] Rogers 1991a, pp. 83 and 86, estimates that the procession set out at least once every two weeks and comprised 260 participants, of which 250 ephebes, within the city walls.

[47] Rogers 1991a, especially pp. 24-30. Rogers points out also that the inscription testifies to a "visible and self-conscious elite in Ephesos" (p. 23).

[48] *SEG* 38.1462; for a detailed publication, translation and extensive commentary of the foundation documents, see Wörrle 1988.

[49] Rogers 1991b, pp. 93-95.

as the participation of surrounding villages. Here the community can be inferred at work in the euergetic process on another level. Not restricted to returning honours after a contribution had been accomplished, the participation of the community could influence the final shape and content of a euergetic initiative and in the end be essential to its realisation.

Since the work of Rogers, the notions of involvement and influence have replaced the idea of a passive, receiving or merely honouring community of citizens, including the role played by the *demos*.[50] This involvement surpasses a strictly euergetic framework and can be situated in a larger socio-political context.[51] The political culture of the Greco-Roman *polis* bears witness to a dominant role of the elite, based on their wealth and social rank, in an outspoken oligarchic society, to the continuity and alterations of democratic institutions in the *poleis*, as well as to on-going popular political activity and participation.[52] Euergetism can also thus contribute to a better understanding of socio-political life as it testifies to the functioning of civic institutions,[53] while at the same time it pertains to the political participation of the *demos* as well as to the politicisation of elements outside traditional politics.[54]

On the *philotimia*-model of euergetism Rogers comments:

> "Scholars who have employed this model have usually under-emphasized the extent to which, as Mauss pointed out long ago, the city, or group of beneficiaries

[50] E.g. van Nijf 1997, p. 159; Zuiderhoek 2007, especially pp. 203 and 205-206; 2009, p. 106.

[51] Zuiderhoek 2008a, pp. 421-422 with solid arguments for euergetism as "useful proxy for political life in a wider sense".

[52] Zuiderhoek 2008a for the Imperial Greek city, especially pp. 419-425; recent and comprehensive outline on the post-classical city in general and with focus on political culture and style in van Nijf – Alston 2011; for Aphrodisias, see Chaniotis 2005. See also Ma 2000b, especially pp. 121-122, remarking on the traditional scholarly focus on elite behaviour as opposed to aspects such as the political role of the demos and negotiation; Salmeri 2000, pp. 69-74; Heller 2009 for the issue of Romanisation of institutions and elite in the Greek cities during the imperial period. See also Pleket's critique on applying the left wing stereotype of popular behaviour. Protest by the *demos* is not to be seen as an emancipatory movement, but rather as venting "dissatisfaction, primarily with the malfunctioning of the benefactors rather than with the political system as such" (Pleket 1998, pp. 211-212; quote on p. 212). On the unfortunate dichotomy "oligarchic" and "democratic" when discussing Greek civic politics, see Zuiderhoek 2008a, p. 418.

[53] See Brélaz 2009, p. 45 for euergetism as indication for institutional functionality and vitality in the Hellenistic period.

[54] Indications on euergetic initiatives as festivals providing "para-political" occasions for popular expression (and partially explaining the ambiguity towards munificence as reflected in the title of the article): Zuiderhoek 2008a, pp. 207-210 and 213; processions, banquets and festivals as examples: van Nijf – Alston 2011, pp. 11-13.

> in such exchanges could impose obligations and values upon benefactors both through demands for certain kinds of services and amenities, as well as the act of receiving them."[55]

In this context, the 'receiving' element of Mauss' theory is explicitly named. When applying the Maussian principles of gift exchange on civic euergetism, and taking into consideration that the euergetic exchange took place between a member of the elite and the community as represented in the civic institutions,[56] receiving turns out to be a conscious and determinant phase. The underlying thought is that the community, through its civic institutions and procedures, not only 'received' when it deemed the contribution acceptable but also, when necessary and/or possible, tried to render it so. Zuiderhoek argues convincingly that the negotiation process was essential to make euergetism in general 'work', accommodating the expectations and goals of the parties involved in the exchange.[57] Of course not every gift would have been debated and negotiated in the same way: contributing a column for a collective building project would have entailed far less – if any – debate compared to a foundation as that of Salutaris. Once the contribution was approved and accepted by the community, formal reciprocity came into play: the community was held to acknowledge the euergetic nature of the giver by awarding the appropriate honours.

7. The importance of negotiating when giving and receiving

Not or not enough negotiating could indeed have consequences.[58] This becomes apparent when taking a closer look at the legally binding stipulations in foundation decrees. When the city is said to be responsible for the execution of a foundation, this responsibility and inherent risks had to be evaluated and

[55] Rogers 1993, p. 189. The *philotimia* model is characterised by the assumption that the benefactor "not only initiated the exchange but also determined the objects of the exchange and their symbolic value". Rogers adds that the models – he refers furthermore to a collective benefits and institutional model – are aimed at bringing out common assumptions made when studying gift giving, rather than referring to characteristics in euergetism itself. See Rogers 1991b, p. 94, n. 10 with specific reference to the application of the *philotimia* model by Wörrle.

[56] Zuiderhoek 2009, p. 117, rightfully remarks that the institutionalised context of the *polis* is a crucial factor to the interpretation of euergetism.

[57] Zuiderhoek 2009, pp. 105-107; 2008a, p. 421, n.8 for references to decrees mentioning negotiations.

[58] Eck 1997, pp. 328-329, referring to the example of the costs donated buildings could generate for the community, either for their finishing or upkeeping.

accepted by the city.[59] By comparing the documents regarding a foundation in Kerkyra, containing both the proposal and the ultimate decree, Harter-Uibopuu demonstrates that Kerkyra succeeded in negotiating and obtaining an adaptation to its advantage. Contrary to the original proposal, the city is in the decree no longer liable to repay the foundation capital in case of certain violations. The decree puts the liability with the individual(s) who actually acted against the stipulations and are held to pay a fine to the donors or their heirs. The *polis* was to keep the capital.[60] Sharing the same values and ideals did not automatically mean agreeing on how they should be acted out.

While the community could influence what they received, benefactors were not without influence themselves when receiving awarded honours. Van Nijf terms the honorific monuments and inscriptions as the social or political capital, upon which the benefactor could claim his or her prestige and status. As a political resource and a visual representation of that capital, these honours were duly deliberated, evaluated and approved by the community, fellow elite members and non-elite citizens alike.[61] It would then, of course, help to have sympathetic supporters, proposing or endorsing the desired honours.[62] Taking the cost for a statue upon oneself could provide an opportunity to influence the execution and make sure that one's statue stood out in a subtle way.[63] It might even have been a preliminary condition for being awarded a statue.[64] Obviously there was very little chance that the negotiations themselves would end up being mentioned on stone.

To summarise: by taking the theory of gift exchange and its principles into consideration and approaching euergetism as a form of exchange, the importance and the role of honours are highlighted, leading in turn to study the relationship between euergetism and the legitimation of power of the elite. It encourages situating and studying euergetism in the context of the system of 'honour'.[65] As a

[59] Harter-Uibopuu 2011, p. 124.

[60] *IG* 9/1^2, 4, 798. The foundation is dated in the 2nd century BCE. For a more detailed analysis see Harter-Uibopuu 2011, pp. 131-134.

[61] van Nijf 1997, pp. 113-116 and 118; 2000, p. 27. Van Nijf refers both to formal rules and informal conventions.

[62] For factions inside the *boule*, see Pleket 1998, pp. 206-207.

[63] van Nijf 2000, p. 26, for the involvement of the honoured elite member (or his/her relatives) in setting up honorific monuments.

[64] Eck 1997, p. 317. See also Dio Chrys., *Or.* 31.9: either the community or the honoured person could pay the cost for the monument.

[65] For the importance and working of honour as system, ideology and rhetoric in relation to government in the Roman Empire, see Lendon 1997. For benefactions as form of honour relation, see especially pp. 84-89. Lendon does not use the concept euergetism to refer to public benefactions and stresses that the understanding of honour is crucial for gaining insight into the phenomenon of benefactions (p. 89).

model of interaction and mode of operation, gift exchange has sharpened the awareness of the role and involvement of the community throughout the entire process. Euergetism reveals itself as a complex interactive process, during which stages of giving, negotiating, receiving and returning could overlap and influence, even shape, each other.

8. The limits of gift exchange for studying euergetism

What we know about euergetism is chiefly learned through honorific decrees or inscriptions.[66] These documents not only record a successful euergetic outcome but are, as an honorific element, the result of this process at the same time. Moreover, honorific inscriptions stand for a considerable part of the epigraphic corpora in general. Both the abundance and nature of the source material have had and still have a considerable impact on the way we evaluate and explain euergetism. This becomes obvious when looking at the economic and financial explanations that have been formulated for euergetism.

The overwhelming amount of epigraphic evidence regarding benefactors in combination with a notion of the city as unable to supply and manage the necessary funds to meet the expenses *polis* life required, has led to the impression that Greek cities, both in Hellenistic and Imperial times, were dependent on wealthy individuals who took over because the civic institutions failed.[67] In more recent studies, the pessimistic view on city finances and the economic explanatory model for euergetism were thoroughly discussed and revised. Although hardly ever mentioned in epigraphic sources, the financial possibilities and administration of Greek cities were definitely different from modern practice, but certainly not lacking or failing. And contrary to earlier and widespread opinions, cities could fall back on diversified, flexible and non-negligible revenues.[68] The elite could and indeed did contribute when cities

[66] The statues, monuments and locations in relation to inscriptions and their mutual interaction are in no way trivial when interpreting the conveyed message: Eck 1999, especially pp. 68-70. In relation to euergetism van Nijf 1997, pp. 117-120; 2000, p. 27. For our purpose however, the message runs along the same honorific line as the inscriptions.

[67] For a summary of this economic explanation with references: Brélaz 2009, pp. 38 and 49-50 for the Hellenistic period; Schwarz 2001, pp. 11-12 and 39; Zuiderhoek 2009, pp. 23 and 41-42 for the Imperial period. See also Zuiderhoek 2007, p. 212, n.54.

[68] Migeotte 1997, p. 193; Schwarz 2001, pp. 24-25 and 435 for the lack of information on city finances in epigraphy. Zuiderhoek 2009, pp. 37-49 with an instructive summary of Schwarz 2001 (review of Schwarz by Migeotte 2004). Brélaz has built a similar case for the Hellenistic period: Brélaz 2009, pp. 50-54, with references to the research of Migeotte. For euergetism put into perspective in the context of public building: Halfmann

encountered difficulties,[69] but euergetism is no longer to be explained as simply being rooted in chronic financial distress or incapacity of the cities. The quantity of honorific inscriptions in combination with the lack of source material on city finances has led to an, at first sight, logical yet premature explanation.

From a qualitative and modern perspective, honorific inscriptions are not unproblematic because elements not contributing to the honorific discourse were banned.[70] It hardly comes as a surprise that the indications for negotiations and involvement of the community are included in documents relating to foundations. Besides testifying to the benefactor's benevolence, these documents can describe in more detail statutes on the use, organisation and management of the foundation and can contain implicit information on the process leading to the final version of the foundation. Honorific inscriptions accompanying honorific statues are in general far less detailed, resulting in a vague and standardised honorific discourse. The entire process was often re-duced to the final result, signalling in retrospect the gift but above all the virtuous-ness of the benefactor as well as the acknowledgement of the community. In the end, the reason of existence for these inscriptions was to be honorific, not to record and pass on extensive and objective reports on euergetism.[71] This makes the affinity with gift exchange stand out, as the elements of giving and returning are highlighted. The honorific bias of the sources poses nevertheless constraints on the extent to which the model of gift exchange can contribute to understanding and explaining the social reality of euergetism in all its diversity.

9. Dio Chrysostom and euergetism in a non-honorific context

In what has become his 46th speech, Dio Chrysostom addresses the assembly of his hometown Prusa in the aftermath of a confrontation with an angry crowd.[72] As the price of grain had increased, a crowd had set out to Dio and at least one other unknown person to express their anger and demand solutions. In the following assembly, the grain problem was put on the agenda. Throughout his speech the orator is found defending himself by emphasising his reputation and innocence, as well as criticising the brutal, citizen unworthy behaviour of the

2001, p. 4. See already the remarks of Eck 1997, pp. 307-315, in relation to euergetism.

[69] Migeotte 1996, p. 89; 1997, p. 193.

[70] Eck 1997, p. 331.

[71] As John Ma points out, there is little or no use in deploring that we are confronted with "a smoke-screen hiding historical fact". The euergetic discourse is an historical fact in its own right: see Ma 2000a, pp. 193-194.

[72] The speech is considered to be the first given in Prusa and dating to the reign of Vespasian, before Dio Chrysostom's exile: Salmeri 2000, pp. 63-64.

crowd.[73] Jones' appreciation that

> "the speech has a double purpose, to calm the mob and at the same time to rescue Dio from election to the liturgy"

is quite on the mark.[74] The speech describes primarily a conflict between Dio and the community of Prusa and is rather contradictory to the idea of euergetism. When shifting the attention away from a euergetic outcome and moving the focus beyond the actual elements of exchange, euergetism as a larger dynamic appears less inconsistent with the conflict between Dio and Prusa.

How serious the grain situation or crisis at Prusa actually was, however, is difficult to evaluate.[75] The price of grain had risen enough to make the people in Prusa experience it as unjust or unacceptable and take up action. This situation perfectly illustrates the working of a moral economy in Prusa towards the end of the first century CE. Erdkamp has convincingly demonstrated that the concept of a moral economy, developed by Thompson in the context of the eighteenth century grain riots in England, can successfully be applied to study the urban food markets and food riots in Antiquity.[76] Both the elite and non-elite polis members agreed on the morals governing the food supply and the appropriate behaviour of the elite / landowners. When these morals were not respected or obligations shunned, protests would follow. The responsibility for solving the situation rested in the end with the elite.[77] In this respect it is not very surprising that Dio, as member of the elite, found an angry crowd (almost) on his doorstep.

Dio's attitude comes across as ambivalent. On the one hand he underwrites the morals and obligations governing the food market in Prusa. His statement that he is blameless because he had not hoarded grain and as a result had not driven up the price, implies that there were other who actually did and that their behaviour, provoking the difficulties, was wrong and a rightful cause for anger.[78]

[73] Dio Chrys., *Or.* 46.2; 4; 6; 7; 11; 12 for references to violent, highly inappropriate behaviour of the crowd. Dio Chrys., *Or.* 46.2-5 for the reputation, benefactions and virtues of his forefathers and *Or.* 46.6-8 for his own merits and character.

[74] Jones 1978, p. 22.

[75] Dio Chrys., *Or.* 46.8 refers to ἀπορία, a situation of difficulties or shortage. In 46.10 he states that the price of grain had indeed gone up, but would in other cities still be considered normal. This remark was apparently met with loud protest.

[76] Erdkamp 2002; allowing the criticism of Bohstedt on Thompson's concept, p. 95; for Dio Chrysostom's case, p. 105.

[77] Erdkamp 2002, pp. 107-115.

[78] Not only those having produced the most grain (Dio Chrys., *Or.* 46.8), and so the elite, hoarded. Kokkinia 2008, pp. 144-146, points to the storing of grain beyond the usual need by small farmers when a bad harvest announced itself, resulting in the price of grain going up.

The same reasoning goes for contributing money:[79] he seems to suggest that others were far more obvious targets and less entitled to unwillingness, seen the scale of their activities in the money-lending business.[80] At the end of his speech Dio offers a solution: appointing a person to manage or oversee the market, to be selected from the citizens who had not yet taken on a liturgy.[81] Dio implicitly states that people hoarding grain and profiting to a point where it goes against the welfare and interest of the community, are indeed responsible;[82] that wealthy citizens and thus the elite should contribute, starting with the most affluent; that the elite, as providers of liturgists with means, should step in. On the other hand, Dio disputes being under any obligation to contribute himself: he has not hoarded grain, is not an affluent moneylender and he has already performed most outstandingly the heaviest liturgies.[83] The crowd was barking up the wrong tree in the elite forest.

What started out as a crisis and conflict induced by the principles of moral economy had evolved into a euergetism prone interaction.[84] Giving, either as a private citizen or when performing a liturgy, for the provision of affordable and sufficient grain in times of shortage is a familiar, although not very frequent, euergetic topic.[85] And so Polykritos was honoured around 275 BCE for lending money and bringing his own grain on the market in a time of shortage.[86] Another

[79] Probably to a grain fund: Erdkamp 2005, p. 278.

[80] Dio Chrys., *Or.* 46.8. Whether or not Dio paraphrases accusations that were aimed at him personally and if so, justified, is of secondary importance here. Possibly it was a rhetorical trick, trying to shift the attention from him, merely being rich and elite, to those who could be held directly responsible for the shortage. For the orator the crowd's anger resulted from envy because he recently had bought land and built a portico. According to Jones 1978, pp. 20 and 24, Dio as a wealthy man was charged of being glad to spend for himself but not for the community.

[81] Dio Chrys., *Or.* 46.14. In case no such candidates were available, the assembly could appoint whomever they wanted. No mention is made of a communal grain fund or civic magistrates. For the regular presence and organisation of such funds, see Erdkamp 2008, especially pp. 109-114; Zuiderhoek 2008b, pp. 162-173.

[82] Erdkamp 2002, p. 109; pp. 114-115 for the moral obligation to respect the benefit of the community and not just aim for profit.

[83] Dio Chrys., *Or.* 46.8; 6 for the liturgies in the past. As a result Dio was not a priori unwilling, but a priori excused. Only when no rich citizen without prior liturgy could be found, Dio would be back in the picture as a candidate for contributing.

[84] For the emic and etic perspective, see the contribution by Koenraad Verboven in this volume.

[85] Erdkamp 2008, p. 117. Euergetism in Asia Minor was not frequently targeted at the urban food supply, see Zuiderhoek 2008b, p. 172; 2009, p. 76.

[86] *I.Erythrai* 28.25-29. The honorary decree lists all accomplishments and benefactions by Polykritos for the city.

example is Atalante in Termessos in the second century CE.[87] Dire straits as a food shortage provided the elite with an opportunity to display their goodwill and zeal towards the community in an effective, albeit rather fleeting and limited, way.[88] Contrary to the widespread and ceaselessly repeated image of the ever benevolent and zealous *euergetes*, despite the opportunity to prove himself solicitous for the welfare of his follow citizens,[89] or to rival with his peers for the gratitude of his fellow citizens, not to mention his implicit agreeing on an euergetic styled solution, Dio did not come forward.

If we suppose for a moment that, after being encouraged or pressured,[90] Dio – or for that matter another member of the elite – did contribute, most likely he would have been praised and honoured as a benefactor not unlike Polykritos some 350 years earlier in Erythrai. In fact, the circumstances of Polykritos' intervention seem not so much different than those in Prusa: the inscription links the shortage in Erythrai with people no longer providing the market with grain.[91]

Zuiderhoek pointed at the parallel between the working of the moral economy and that of euergetism as systems: both are based on accepted reciprocal obligations between the elite and non-elite. As long as the elite lived up to its euergetic obligation, disparities of wealth and power would not become a bone of contention.[92] In the cases of Dio and Polykritos the actual processes of the moral economy and euergetism seem to merge into one continuous dynamic. The role and involvement of the community in Prusa are far more outspoken and of a different nature, due to the urgency of the situation and because it was described in a non-honorific text.[93] Upon the rather pressing demand to respect moral obligations and act, the elite, or at least some of its more willing members, would change their behaviour from making profit at the expense of the community towards "using their wealth in a socially responsible way".[94] The

[87] *TAM* 3, 1, 4 and 62; van Nijf 2000, pp. 21-23.

[88] Erdkamp 2002, p. 96, rightfully points out that "the ancient elite never had the economic capacity to ward off shortages".

[89] Zuiderhoek 2008b, pp. 172-177 for the meaning, symbolic and other, of food within euergetism and the image of the benefactor as benevolent parent.

[90] Erdkamp 2008, p. 117 describes the "targeted violence" as "a very persuasive argument" for contributing.

[91] Logically, but no doubt unintentionally, this seems to indicate that Polykritos was as much part of the cause as of the solution: Kokkinia 2008, p. 147.

[92] Zuiderhoek 2009, pp. 69-70.

[93] A crowd would not present itself on a wealthy man's doorstep with stone and fire to press for a Salutaris-styled procession, but pressure and constraint in more tempered and different forms were by no means absent in other less vital euergetic situations: see Kleijwegt 1994, for constraint on the elite, especially to undertake offices. See also Veyne 1976, pp. 234-236.

[94] Borrowing Gordon's definition, "euergetism is the socially responsible use of wealth":

nature of the situation itself changes from an overt conflict and crisis, opposing non-elite and elite, into an example of civic harmony and elite virtuousness. This change is reminiscent of the possibility, suggested by von Reden, to consider both *eisphora* and *leitourgia* as ritual conversions transforming money or wealth from a private context into means for the *polis*.[95] In the case of Dio and related to the specific context of a grain shortage and the working of a moral economy, euergetism can be conceived as functioning in a similar way, by transforming grain and/or money from a negative, profit-driven, individual sphere into a benefical, social and communal one.

Compared to the more usual exclusively honorific narrative, the non-honorific speech of Dio provides us with a very different outlook on euergetism. As a result the principles of gift exchange are less explicitly present, although certainly not absent. Throughout Dio Chrysostom's speech, indications are found for the operating of a moral economy and euergetism within a continuous dynamic. When reformulating the events from this perspective, the idea of conversion between transactional orders seems to provide more insight into euergetism. In other euergetic contexts, and as a result of the nature of the initiative as well as of the source, elements pertaining to moral economy or transactional orders will be less obvious or not traceable at all. However they should not *a priori* be dismissed or ignored.

10. Conclusions

The introduction and application of gift-exchange principles, be it intentionally or *de facto*, have decidedly generated an impact on the study of euergetism. This is all the more important as the way we understand and interpret euergetism carries with it consequences for our view on other aspects of ancient society at large.

At the same time as being conceptualised, euergetism was approached and defined as a disinterested gift, with focus on the giver and thus the elite. The detailed analysis of the *de facto* reciprocal element has resulted into a revision of the chronology of euergetism as a "système de gouvernement" in relation to the regime of notables. The element of reciprocity has brought the function and

Gordon 1990, p. 231.

[95] von Reden 1995, pp. 96-97, referring to Parry and Bloch, who describe how in various non-Western societies money or goods can be converted by means of rituals or symbolic operations from the transactional order characterised by commerce, short-term transactions with strangers and competition into another transactional order involving long term goals and social order: Bloch – Parry 1989, pp. 23-30. They stress (p. 29) not suggesting universality or uniformity.

meaning of immaterial honours to attention, leading to the interpretation of euergetism as relationship of reciprocity and as a symbolic exchange. The role and involvement of the community was not restricted to the decision and bestowal of honours as reciprocating party. In the civic institutions, euergetic projects could be discussed, evaluated, negotiated and accepted by the community. As a form of symbolic exchange and with emphasis on honours as form of consent, the role of euergetism in the legitimation of power and the oligarchisation within the Greek cities of the Imperial period has further been elucidated and defined.

Greco-Roman society was very eager to display and propagate a by and large euergetic self-image. In this image the conveyed information is all in all narrowed down to the outcome of the euergetic process. This honorific version is on a formal level easily aligned with elements of gift exchange. But as the example of Dio Chrysostom demonstrates, euergetism was not exclusively honorific and is not to be restricted to a gift exchange dimension. Other mechanisms and principles can equally contribute to the analysis and understanding of euergetism as a complex and prominent social phenomenon in the Greek *polis*.

Bibliography

Andreau, Jean – Pauline Schmitt – Alain Schnapp: *Paul Veyne et l'évergétisme*, in: *AnnESC* 33 (1978), pp. 307-325.

Bloch, Maurice – Jonathan P. Parry: *Introduction: Money and the Morality of Exchange*, in: *Money and the Morality of Exchange*, ed. by Jonathan P. Parry – Maurice Bloch, Cambridge 1989, pp. 1-33.

Boulanger, André: *Aelius Aristide et la sophistique dans la province d'Asie au IIe siècle avant notre ère*, Paris 1923.

Brélaz, Cédric: *Les bienfaiteurs, «sauveurs» et «fossoyeurs» de la cité hellénistique?: une approche historiographique de l'évergétisme*, in: *L'huile et l'argent. Gymnasiarchie et évérgetisme dans la Grèce hellénistique*, ed. by Olivier Curty, Paris 2009, pp. 37-56.

Chaniotis, Angelos: *Macht und Volk in den kaiserzeitlichen Inschriften von Aphrodisias*, in: *Popolo e potere nel mondo antico*, ed. by Gianpaolo Urso, Pisa 2005, pp. 47-61.

Domingo Gygax, Marc: *Evergetismo e historia: Paul Veyne y Philippe Gauthier comparados*, in: *Prometheus* 20 (1994), pp. 119-134.

Domingo Gygax, Marc: *Euergetismus und Gabentausch*, in: *Métis* 1 (2003), pp. 181-200.

Domingo Gygax, Marc: *Les origines de l'évergétisme: échanges et identités sociales dans la cité grecque*, in: *Métis* 4 (2006), pp. 269-295.

Domingo Gygax, Marc: *Proleptic Honours in Greek Euergetism*, in: *Chiron* 39 (2009), pp. 163-191.

Eck, Werner: *Der Euergetismus im Funktionszusammenhang der kaiserzeitliche Städte*, in: *Actes du Xe Congrès Internationale d'Epigraphie grecque et latine*, ed. by Michel Christol, Paris 1997, pp. 305-331.

Eck, Werner: *Öffentlichkeit, Monument und Inschrift,* In: *Atti del XI Congresso*

Internazionale di Epigrafia greca e latina, ed. by Silvio Panciera, Roma 1999, pp. 55-76.
Erdkamp, Paul: *A Starving Mob has no Respect. Urban Markets and Food Riots in the Roman World 100 BC – 400 AD*, in: *The Transformations of Economic Life under the Roman Empire*, ed. by Lukas de Blois – John Rich, Amsterdam 2002, pp. 93-115.
Erdkamp, Paul: *The Grain Market in the Roman Empire*, Cambridge 2005.
Erdkamp, Paul: *Grain Funds and Market Intervention in the Roman World*, in: *Feeding the Ancient Greek City*, ed. by Richard Alston – Onno M. van Nijf, Leuven 2008, pp. 109-125.
Fröhlich, Pierre – Christel Müller, ed. by: *Citoyenneté et participation à la basse époque hellénistique*, Genève 2005.
Garnsey, Peter: *The Generosity of Veyne*, in: *JRS* 81 (1991), pp. 164-168.
Gauthier, Philippe: *Les cités grecques et leurs bienfaiteurs (IVe-Ier siècle avant J.C.). Contribution à l'histoire des institutions*, Paris 1985.
Gauthier, Philippe: *Les cités hellénistiques*, in: *The Ancient Greek City State*, ed. by Mogens Herman Hansen, København 1993, pp. 211-231.
Gauthier, Philippe: *Introduction*, in: *Citoyenneté et participation à la basse époque hellénistique*, ed. by Pierre Fröhlich – Christel Müller, Genève 2005, pp. 1-6.
Gordon, Richard: *The Veil of Power: Emperors, Sacrificers and Benefactors*, in: *Pagan Priests. Religion and Power in the Ancient World*, ed. by Mary Beard – John North, London 1990, pp. 199-231.
Gruen, Erich S.: *Philippe Gauthier. Les cités grecques et leurs bienfaiteurs*, in: *JHS* 107 (1987), p. 230.
Habicht, Christian: *Ist ein 'Honoratiorenregime' das Kennzeichen der Stadt im späteren Hellenismus?*, in: *Stadtbild und Bürgerbild im Hellenismus*, ed. by Michael Wörrle – Paul Zanker, München 1995, pp. 87-92.
Halfmann, Helmut: *Städtebau und Bauherren in römischen Kleinasiens. Ein Vergleich zwischen Ephesos und Pergamon*, Tübingen 2001.
Harter-Uibopuu, Kaja: *Money for the Polis. Public Administration of Private Donations in Hellenistic Greece*, in: *Political Culture in the Greek City after the Classical Age*, ed. by Onno M. van Nijf – Richard Alston, Leuven 2011, pp. 119-139.
Heller, Anna: *La cite grecque d'époque imperial: vers une société d'ordres?*, in: *AnnHSS* 64 (2009), pp. 341-373.
Jones, Christopher P.: *The Roman World of Dio Chrysostom*, Cambridge 1978.
Kleijwegt, Marc: *Voluntarily, but under Pressure: Voluntarity and Constraint in Greek Municipal Politics*, in: *Mnemosyne* 47 (1994), pp. 64-78.
Kokkinia, Christina: *Die Opramoas-Inschrift von Rhodiapolis: Euergetismus und soziale Elite in Lykien*, Bonn 2000.
Kokkinia, Christina: *Grain for Cibyra. Veranius Philagros and the 'Great Conspiracy'*, in: *Feeding the Ancient Greek City*, ed. by Richard Alston – Onno M. van Nijf, Leuven 2008, pp. 143-158.
Lendon, Jon E.: *The Empire of Honour. The Art of Government in the Roman World*, Oxford 1997.
Ma, John: *Antiochos III and the Cities of Western Asia Minor*, Oxford 2000a.
Ma, John: *Public Speech and Community in the Euboicus*, in: *Dio Chrysostom. Politics, Letters and Philosophy*, ed. by Simon Swain, Oxford 2000b, pp. 108-124.
Marrou, Henri Irenée: *Histoire de l'éducation dans l'Antiquité*, Paris 1948.

Mauss, Marcel: *Essai sur le don. Forme et raison de l'échange dans les sociétés archaïques*, in: *L'Année sociologique* n.s. 1 (1923-1924), pp. 30-186.

Migeotte, Léopold: *Les finances des cités grecques au-delà du primitivisme et du modernisme*, in: *Energeia: Studies on Ancient History and Epigraphy Presented to H.W. Pleket*, ed. by Johan H. M. Strubbe – Rolf A. Tybout – Hendrik S. Versnel, Amsterdam 1996, pp. 79-96.

Migeotte, Léopold: *L'évergétisme des citoyens aux périodes classique et hellénistique*, in: *Actes du Xe Congrès Internationale d'Epigraphie grecque et latine*, ed. by Michel Christol, Paris 1997, pp. 183-196.

Migeotte, Léopold: *Schwarz: Soll oder Haben*, in: *Gnomon*, 76 (2004) pp. 341-345.

Osteen, Mark: *Introduction. Questions of the Gift*, in: *The Question of the Gift. Essays across Disciplines*, ed. by Mark Osteen, London – New York 2002, pp. 1-41.

Pleket, Henri W.: *Political Culture and Political Practice in the Cities of Asia Minor in the Roman Empire*, in: *Politische Theorie und Praxis im Altertum*, ed. by Wolfgang Schuller, Darmstadt 1998, pp. 204-216.

Quaß, Friedemann: *Die Honoratiorenschicht in den Städten des griechischen Ostens. Untersuchungen zur politischen und sozialen Entwicklung in hellenistischer und römischer Zeit,* Stuttgart 1993.

Robert, Louis: *Recherches épigrahiques VII. Décret de la confédération Lycienne à Corinthe*, in: *REA* 62 (1960), pp. 324-342.

Robert, Louis: *Theophane de Mytilène à Constantinople*, in: *CRAI* 113 (1969), pp. 42-64.

Rogers, Guy M.: *The Sacred Identity of Ephesos: Foundation Myths of a Roman City,* London 1991a.

Rogers, Guy M.: *Demosthenes of Oenoanda and Models of Euergetism*, in: *JRS* 81 (1991b), pp. 91-100.

Rogers, Guy M.: *The Gift and Society in Roman Asia: Orthodoxies and Heresies*, in: *SCI* 12 (1993), pp. 188-199.

Roueché, Charlotte: *Benefactors in the Late Roman Period: the Eastern Empire*, in: *Actes du Xe Congrès Internationale d'Epigraphie grecque et latine*, ed. by Michel Christol, Paris 1997, pp. 353-368

Salmeri, Giovanni: *Dio, Rome and the Civic Life of Asia Minor*, in: *Dio Chrysostom. Politics, letters and philosophy*, ed. by Simon Swain, Oxford 2000, pp. 53-92.

Schwarz, Hertha: *Soll oder haben? Die Finanzwirtschaft kleinasiatischen Städte in der römischen Kaiserzeit am Beispiel von Bithynien, Lykien und Ephesos (29 v. Chr. – 284 n. Chr.)*, Bonn 2001.

Silber, Ileana F.: *Entre Marcel Mauss et Paul Veyne: pour une sociologie historique comparée du don*, in: *Sociologie et sociétés* 36 (2004), pp. 189-205.

Stinchcombe, Arthur L.: *Book review Le pain et le cirque*, in: *American Journal of Sociology,* 86 (1980), pp. 650-654.

van Nijf, Onno M.: *The Civic World of Professional Organisations in the Roman East*, Amsterdam 1997.

van Nijf, Onno M.: *Inscriptions and Civic Memory in the Roman East*, in: *The Afterlife of Inscriptions: Reusing, Rediscovering, Reinventing and Revitalizing Ancient Inscriptions,* ed. by Alison E. Cooley, Dorset 2000, pp. 21-36.

van Nijf, Onno M. – Richard Alston: *Introduction and Preview*, in: *Political Culture in the Greek City after the Classical Age*, ed. by Onno M. Van Nijf – Richard Alston, Leuven 2011, pp. 1-26.

Veyne, Paul: *Panem et circenses: l'évergétisme devant les sciences humaines,* in: *AnnESC* 14 (1969), pp. 785-825.

Veyne, Paul: *Le pain et le cirque. Sociologie historique d'un pluralisme politique*, Paris 1976; repr. Paris 1995.

Veyne, Paul: *Comment on écrit l'histoire, suivi de Foucault révolutionne l'histoire*, Paris 1978.

von Reden, Sitta: *Exchange in Ancient Greece*, London 1995.

Wagner-Hasel, Beate: *Egoistic Exchange and Altruistic Gift. On the Roots of Marcel Mauss's Theory of the Gift*, in: *Negotiating the Gift. Pre-modern Figurations of Exchange*, ed. by Gadi Algazi – Valentin Groebner – Bernhard Jussen, Göttingen 2003, pp. 141-171.

Wörrle, Michael: *Stadt und Fest: Studien zu einer agonistischen Stiftung aus Oinoanda*, München 1988.

Zuiderhoek, Arjan: *The Ambiguity of Munificence*, in: *Historia* 56 (2007), pp. 196-213.

Zuiderhoek, Arjan: *On the Political Sociology of the Imperial Greek City*, in: *GRBS* 48 (2008a), pp. 417-445.

Zuiderhoek, Arjan: *Feeding the Citizens: Municipal Grain Funds and Civic Benefactors in the Roman East*, in: *Feeding the Ancient Greek City*, ed. by Richard Alston – Onno M. van Nijf, Leuven 2008b, pp. 159-180.

Zuiderhoek, Arjan: *The Politics of Munificence in the Roman Empire: Citizens, Elites and Benefactors in Asia Minor*, Cambridge 2009.

LELLIA CRACCO RUGGINI

From Pagan to Christian Euergetism

With this contribution I propose to delineate the passage from the pagan to the Christian euergetism during the period from the third to the sixth century. It was by no means a rapid or unequivocal phenomenon, varying in duration and manner according to the place of occurrence.

In many ways the public liberalities of the Christians represented the continuation of those of the pagans; but they also introduced several innovations in conformity with their own thought. I would like to show how the euergetism in public works of the Christians (both of the clergy and the laity), manifested in the construction of churches, monasteries, hostels and hospitals – but also of 'lay' public buildings such as arcades, baths, bridges, workshops and so on – was substantially the continuation of the pagan monumental euergetism (which tended to prefer the construction of walls, amphitheatres, temples and public basilicas),[1] while maintaining the same consequence of an amalgamation among differing cultures and social strata. However, the Christian objectives, at least in theory, excluded any dimension that was not exclusively charitable.

But it was, above all, the emperors of the fourth and fifth centuries and, after them, barbarian kings such as the Goth Theodoric, who claimed to be the successors of the Christian emperors in the West that went on with 'lay' munificence for entirely political purposes that aimed to gain a broad consent among the subjects. The private liberalities, on the other hand, were increasingly oriented towards spectacles, at times accompanied by the public distribution of money. Their purpose was no longer to secure a career within the municipalities, but rather at the centre in direct subordination to the highest level of political power. They represent, at least until the Gothic-Byzantine war in Italy, a transformation and a progressive weakening of civic spirit that, up to a certain point, had sustained the monumental euergetism. They are not the result of an already existing economic crisis, as some often still maintain.[2]

Financial imbalances had always been present in the Roman cities, inasmuch as they derived not from an imprudent management of the resources available,

[1] Krause 1987; Cracco Ruggini 1989, p. 247 with note 124 (ancient sources and further bibliography there). On the specific Christian connotations of the concept of charity, especially from Cyprian of Carthage onwards and from a theological point of view, see Canetti in this volume.

[2] For a more general consideration of some of these ideas, see references in Cracco Ruggini 1989, pp. 240-255.

but rather from the structural characteristics of civic administration themselves. In fact, the cities did not possess the means to carry out their expenditure as theoretically autonomous *res publicae.* The normal income in their balance sheets was made up of rents from municipal property – mostly land, from indirect taxes for the use of the aqueduct and of the public baths, from any harbour dues, from *summae honorariae*, from foundations, legacies or bequests – generally, however, these were linked to well-defined uses. But a direct municipal taxation did not exist. It was considered to be a sign of subordination incompatible with the traditional characteristics of the city – except in the most exceptional cases which were subject to the approval of the emperor.[3] Thus for any extraordinary expenditure reliance had to be made exclusively on the spontaneous intervention of the wealthy classes or of the emperor – through his intermediaries. The largely haphazard nature of this integrative mechanism, therefore, did not allow the cities to implement any real financial policy. More and more often this mechanism is accompanied by a growth in imperial liberalities: and the increasing number of the cities in the first two centuries of the empire also brought with it a proportional fractioning of innumerable urban territories, with the consequent contraction of their profits.[4]

In any case, regardless of the extent to which euergetism was founded on this apparently fragile equilibrium with structural imbalances, local patriotism eventually transformed this civic munificence into a veritable way of life, an expression of that *amor civicus* extolled in numerous inscriptions.[5] It was clear that the financing of public works, of games or spectacles, the distributions of money and food on the occasion of the games themselves, or – at times – when supplies were insufficient, public sacrifices offered by the traditional elites and followed by banquets, the alimentary foundations for poor youths intended to strengthen military conscription were invariably based on a political ideology; and, in due course, it was also at a political level that the fruits were later gathered, consolidating individual powers that had already been acquired or enabling ambitious *nouveaux riches* to gain access to the municipal magistracies by demonstrating their generosity over a period of one or two generations. Thus the largesse of the local worthies was destined to the people not because they were needy – a concept which later formed the basis of Christian charity – but

[3] See, for example, the letter of Antoninus Pius which authorises a Macedonian city to exact one denarius from every free citizen: Oliver 1958; Corbier 1985; Corbier 1988, pp. 265 and 273 with note 6.

[4] Strabo and Helianus, during the reign of Augustus, talk of 474 cities in all the empire, while in the 3rd century they seem to have almost tripled (around 1200): Cracco Ruggini 1989, p. 241 with note 102 and Lepelley 1999.

[5] Giardina 1988a.

because they constituted a political group that voted, acclaimed and sustained its own benefactors in every circumstance. Thus their support was directly proportional to their wealth and not to their indigence. And the system functioned for as long as the results were guaranteed and continued to arouse interest.

The quantity of the epigraphic evidence for euergetism is endless;[6] and the frequency in these centuries with which the municipal magistrates boast of having carried out public building *ob honorem* – that is, maintaining the promises made to the people before the election – serves only to confirm the political motivation of such an abundance of liberalities.[7] And the distribution of riches was to continue for many centuries, nourished by a particular blend of civic ethic and religious motivations, but especially by the love of the prestige that derived from it (*philotimía*, even posthumous). "Piety towards the gods and generosity towards men" is the definition of the liberality of public benefactors given in a Greek inscription at the beginning of the fourth century CE found near Stratonicea in Caria.[8] "This is wealth, this is power" (*hoc est habere, hoc est posse*) proclaimed the people of an African town whose exultation is recorded in a mosaic in the villa of Smirat in Tunisia. The mosaic represents a hunting scene (*venatio*) offered by the notable, Magerius, between 235 and 250 CE at a cost of 4000 *denarii*; the *munerarius*, acclaimed by the people as an hero, is said to have paid 1000 *denarii* instead of 500 for each of the four tigers killed by the *bestiarii*. Greek horoscopes also associated ambition, power and munificence.[9]

The *philotimia* thrived on competition, at times dilapidating entire fortunes for the love of popularity (*euphemia*). And as early as the first decades of the second century CE Philostratus, in the *Life of Apollonius* – where the protagonist-philosopher is presented as a semi-divine benefactor of the cities he visits – had understood the importance of this motivation, attributing to Apollonius of Tyana the recipe for good municipal government in these terms:

> "in order for a city to be governed in the best possible way by its inhabitants there must be a blend of general concord and particular interest".[10]

In fact, the patronage of an urban community served to unify an unequal society

[6] See especially the abundant documentation gathered by Duncan-Jones 1982^2; see also Veyne 1976, on which especially Andreau – Schmitt – Schnapp 1978; Cracco Ruggini 1989, p. 241 with n. 106. On the euergetism consisting in animal sacrifices see particularly Rives 2012.

[7] Garnsey 1974, p. 232; Jacques 1981; Jacques 1984, p. 722; Gros 1985.

[8] Deschamps – Cousin 1888, pp. 101-104, nr. 22, lines 9-12.

[9] *AE* 1967, 549; see also Neugebauer – Van Hoesen 1959, p. 97; Beschausch 1966; Galsterer 1982, p. 94; Johnston 1985; Beschausch 1987; Metcalf 1993.

[10] Philostr., *V. Apoll.* 4.8; see Garnsey 1970, pp. 103-152.

but at the same time also insisted on the social differences that separated benefactors from those who benefited. Thus the former Roman juridical principle of the law being equal for everyone had, over time, been transformed into a legislation that discriminated between *honestiores* and *humiliores*. In the period between the Antonini and the Severi such a transformation also manifested itself at a municipal level, exacting different fines from the decurions and from the *populus*.

But competitiveness of *philotimia* usually functions when the number of possible competitors is large and open, as Peter Brown observed some years ago.[11] Therefore the euergetic spirit weakened progressively as the city elites became more restricted and closed, and the gulf between the few extremely rich and the many poor became wider. Among the poor there were now even some of the decurions: already at the end of the first century CE both the *tabula Malacitana* and Pliny the Younger seem to refer to notables at times in difficulty with the expenditure deriving from their municipal responsibilities (*inviti*).[12]

However, it would be a mistake to interpret this reversal of tendency as proof of a generalised impoverishment, as one still frequently reads even today in a large part of modern historiography. Imperial intervention in urban life undoubtedly played a decisive part in it. The growing importance of the patronage of the Prince bore with it a transforming effect on urban life[13] – although it was generally solicited by the municipal powers themselves as being politically opportune and economically advantageous. It mainly took the form of tax remissions[14] but, above all, of liberality with regard to public monuments inasmuch as this was the most enduring manifestation of the presence of the supreme power everywhere within the empire in accordance with the Roman model of town planning.[15] Private euergetism at first followed not dissimilar models even for *vici*. But when, at a certain moment, the emperor became "the sole source of the people's happiness" and of public ceremonial (as proclaimed

[11] Brown 1978, pp. 27-53.

[12] On the *lex* of the *municipium* of Malaga in the age of Domitian see *FIRA*, I, 208-219, n. 24 = *ILS* 6089; Liebenam 1900, p. 209; Jacques 1984, pp. 383-285.

[13] Veyne 1976, pp. 638-642.

[14] A sign of 'moderation' according to a *speculum principis* such as the *Institutio Traiani*, between the 4th and 5th centuries: Carrié 1975; Cracco Ruggini 1985, p. 235; Cracco Ruggini 1989, p. 213 with n. 116; on the *Institutio Traiani* see Callu 1984.

[15] '*Villes-vitrine*', that is the monumental transcription of the social, cultural, religious and ideological functions that the city was considered a permanent expression, especially until the end of the 3rd century CE; the advantages that city life theoretically offered everyone were paved streets, squares, thermal baths, aqueducts, walls with towers and monumental gates without any defensive function and so forth: especially *Geschichte der Wasserversorgung* 1988; Cracco Ruggini 1989, pp. 223-224 and 244-246.

by an inscription in Cyprus in honour of Maximian Herculius in the age of the Tetrarchy),[16] not only imposing his personal approbation – through the governors – of the construction of public buildings, but also not even allowing whoever had paid for or carried out the construction to confer his own name on it,[17] the disaffection towards the state progressively increased and local patriotism more and more often took different routes, directing its ambitions and wealth elsewhere.

From an age of equilibrium one gradually passes to an 'age of ambition', from benevolent patronage to the exercise of power. And this happened when paganism still held sway, over the period from the end of the second century to the first decades of the third.[18] It was now the imperial approbation that counted most.[19] This is already evident in the episodes such as that of Alexander of Abonoteichos at the time of Marcus Aurelius, in which the *charismata* of the healer were accompanied by special imperial concessions for the city of his birth – or else in cases such as those testified to by several inscriptions in Asia Minor in which, among services to the community, one finds that of having undertaken at his own expense the transport of supplies to the imperial troops during a

[16] *AE* 1972, 667. This sort of monopoly of patronage and consensus possessed by the emperor undoubtedly served to regulate a number of local expenditures and the more contested rivalries for political prestige among the municipal elites, but even when the imperial benevolence (*indulgentia*) appeared to intervene in person, arousing the gratitude expressed in numerous urban inscriptions, in reality such interventions deducted the sum from the tributes to be paid locally to the governor of the province. Thus they constituted a partial reduction of the sums due locally, while nevertheless reinforcing the cliché of the Prince as the protector of the city. We should also reflect on the fact that often those in power had no interest in improving urban life, being more concerned to safeguard the rural areas as they were sources of *annona*, for example in Sicily, in Egypt or the Gallic Picardy. Great wealth both public and private, in fact, appertains mainly to the country for the entire Roman age, while the city simply manages to get by, degraded and depressed, without any significant increments that were not in one way or another linked with supplies: Cracco Ruggini 1982-1983; Gabba 1986; more optimistically Wilson 1988; on other regions Cracco Ruggini 1989, pp. 249-250.

[17] *D* 50.10.13; *CTh.* 15.1.31; further sources and bibliography in Cracco Ruggini 1989, p. 248, n. 126.

[18] See n. 11.

[19] See also the laws that, during the second half of the 4th century and the first half of the 5th, regulated city expenditure for walls and public buildings allotting a quarter or a third of the municipal income, to substitute the ever more reduced private liberalities. By now these expenditures were largely withdrawn from local control and in various ways entrusted to agents of the *res privata* (that is, the administrators of the imperial property): for instance *CTh.* 15.1.18 (374 CE), 32 and 33 (395 CE), 41 (401 CE), 49 (412 CE). See Camodeca 1979.

Persian expedition, possibly that of Severus Alexander or of Gordian III. Thus services to the citizens and those to the empire are mingled without distinction. And even when, at times, private individuals spontaneously undertook public works and the restoration of urban monuments, they seem to have done so especially when visits by the emperor were imminent, or, in any case, as homage to the reigning *Augustus*. Later, the Christian bishops at times inherited this custom for the very reason that they were assimilated to high-ranking imperial officials.[20]

As already stated, what mostly concerned the notables of the provinces had by now become an imperial career. Therefore, while conserving their political aims, in fact they increasingly turned away from their own cities, concentrating above all on grandiose spectacles that were offered in Rome, Milan, Constantinople or in other more or less temporary residences of the court and of the government offices, when high posts or magistracies were conferred. At the same time, the greatest expenditure on the part of these wealthy notables was now directed not so much towards the construction of public buildings, but rather towards that of their own private residences, often suburban or in the country, that rivalled the imperial palaces both in their extent and in the sumptuousness of the materials used and the representations – behaviour that formerly would have been considered an unbecoming sign of vainglory, of *tryphé*. One need only recall the villa of *Philosophiana*/Piazza Armerina.[21]

Certain Christian proprietors continued in their turn to concern themselves with urban euergesis but now, at its centre, there was the Church. This was the case, for example, with the alms, donations and constructions at Hippo Regius and at Thagaste at the time of Augustin by Melania and Pinianus, the extremely rich Roman senatorial couple who had fled to Africa after the devastations of Alaric in Italy; or at Antioch a few years earlier at the time of John Chrysostom, who refused the traditional values. He dreamed of re-creating the city as an agglomerate of Christian families intent on managing their lives solely in accordance with their own austere virtues, and not with the exigencies of the entire urban community – which he reproved for exercising charity itself with a mentality that remained pagan, still obsequious to social discrimination. He

[20] Cracco Ruggini 1989, pp. 251-252 (examples there).

[21] See for instance *CTh.* 1.16.9 (364 CE, from Aquileia) to the governor of *Lucania et Bruttorum*, Marius Artemius. As far as Piazza Armerina is concerned (a senatorial residence rivalling the imperial palaces), it was for this very reason that the 4th-century *villa* was thought for a long while to be imperial; the bibliography on Piazza Armerina is endless: see for example Carandini – Ricci – de Vos 1982, especially pp. 393-403; Garraffo 1988.

presented himself as the ambassador of a different city – the ambassador of the poor.[22]

The polemic of the Christians, especially from Tertullian onwards, concentrated particularly on the entertainment aspects of euergetism. Their links with the old pagan mentality were deplored. They were, at the same time, the only cohesive social force that competed with the Christian ceremonies within urban life.[23] In 386 CE the future bishop of Ippona, Augustin, in his *Contra Academicos*, describes the case of Romanian – a very rich landowner of *Thagaste,* former protector of his family, who, thanks to spectacles and hunts in the amphitheatre staged at his expense with great munificence, had gained immense popularity together with honours, both municipal (the city patronage) and provincial (the African priesthood). However, also pagans such as the sophist Libanius in Antioch and the philosopher Themistius in Constantinople testified to the survival of the city ideals during the fourth century; and sometimes they deplored the vanity of those who squandered immense sums to stage spectacles in the theatre and the hippodrome, seeking the tumultuous applause of the people.[24]

The continued existence – at least to a certain degree – of also a monumental euergetism is shown above all by archaeological remains and by inscriptions. As far as Italy is concerned, still at the time of Theodoric the fact that in the *Variae* by Cassiodorus the space dedicated to architecture, to mechanical engineering and to games is not only conspicuous but resembles that shown by the most grandiose ceremonials and merits attention at the highest levels, seems to indicate that the Goth king (just as the emperors who had preceded him) had entirely taken over from private individuals in the matter of public liberalities of a 'lay' nature, deliberately creating a clear sign of continuity.[25]

Thus euergetism had not ceased, but it had undoubtedly changed its nature. It was to continue "as long as cities exist" (*dum urbes erunt*) as a high imperial official, the African Sextus Aurelius Victor, wrote in the middle of the fourth century, still convinced that urban life was a synonym of eternity. As is well-known, in fact, the provinces of *Africa* continued for a long time to be a 'museum' of the city institutions – though they were changed in their substance –

[22] Ioh. Chris., *De vana gloria* (SC 188, pp. 76-79); *De eleem.* 1 and 6 (PG 51, coll. 261, 269-270). See Brown 1988, pp. 305-322. It seems very probable that this also happened in the case of the *balnea* that Thagaste had constructed on the advice of Melania Jr. and of the *vir spectabilis* Oronzio, celebrated by an epigram of the *Anthologia Latina*: Lepelley 1975, pp. 13-39; Lepelley 1979, vol. I, pp. 298-303; Cecconi 1988; Giardina 1988b; Cracco Ruggini 1989, pp. 252-255 (examples there, together with their sources).

[23] Dagron 2011; more generally Lugaresi 2008.

[24] Them., *Or.* 2.27 a-b. See Rivolta 1985.

[25] Cracco Ruggini 2008, pp. 31 and 46-47, note 25; see also Fauvinet-Ranson 2006.

and of a surviving civic spirit.[26] But by now a time was approaching in which the inhabitants of the Roman-barbarian kingdoms in the West were to cease any participation in liberalities in favour of the urban communities, just as their sovereigns were doing. In fact, it was no longer necessary in a fragmented, non-affluent, not open and uncompetitive society.

Bibliography

Andreau, Jean – Pauline Schmitt – Alain Schnapp: *Paul Veyne et l'évergétisme*, in: *AnnESC* 23 (1978), pp. 307-325.

Beschausch, Azedine: *La mosaïque de la chasse à l'amphithéatre, découverte à Smirat*, in: *CRAI* (1966), pp. 134-157.

Beschausch, Azedine: *À propos de la mosaïque de Smirat*, in: *L'Africa romana. Atti del IV Convegno di Studio (Sassari, 12-14 dicembre 1986)*, ed. by Attilio Mastino, Sassari 1987, vol. II, pp. 677-680.

Brown, Peter: *The Making of Late Antiquity*, Cambridge (MA) – London 1978.

Brown, Peter: *The Body and Society. Men, Women and Sexual Renunciation in Early Christianity*, New York 1988.

Callu, Jean-Pierre: *Manus inermis. Le phénomène bureaucratique et l'Histoire Auguste*, in: *NAC* 13 (1984), pp. 229-248.

Camodeca, Giuseppe: *Curatores rei publicae I*, in: *ZPE* 35 (1979), pp. 225-236.

Carandini, Andrea – Andreina Ricci – Mariette de Vos: *Filosofiana, la villa di Piazza Armerina. Immagine di un aristocratico romano al tempo di Costantino*, Palermo 1982.

Carrié, Jean-Marie: *Les distributions alimentaires dans les cites de l'empire romain tardif*, in: *MEFRA* 87 (1975), pp. 995-1101.

Cecconi, Giovanni Alberto: *Un evergete mancato: Piniano a Ippona*, in: *Athenaeum* 66 (1988), pp. 371-389.

Corbier, Mireille: *Fiscalité et dépenses locales*, in: *L'origine des richesses depensées dans la ville antique*, ed. by Philippe Leveau, Aix-en-Provence 1985, pp. 219-232.

Corbier, Mireille: *L'impôt dans l'empire romain: résistences et refus (Ier-IIIe siècles)*, in: *Forms of Control and Subordination in Antiquity*, ed. by Tōru Yuge – Masaoki Doi, Tōkyō 1988, pp. 259-274.

Cracco Ruggini, Lellia: *Sicilia, III/IV secolo: il volto della non-città*, in: *Kokalos* 28-29 (1982-1983), pp. 477-515.

Cracco Ruggini, Lellia: *L'annona di Roma nell'età imperiale*, in: *Misurare la terra: centuriazione e coloni nel mondo romano. Città, agrcoltura, commercio: materiali da Roma e suburbio*, Modena 1985, 224-236.

Cracco Ruggini, Lellia: *La città imperiale*, in: *Storia di Roma* IV (*Caratteri e morfologie*), ed. by Emilio Gabba – Aldo Schiavone, Torino 1989, pp. 201-266.

Cracco Ruggini, Lellia: *Cassiodorus and the Practical Sciences*, in: *Vivarium in Context*, Vicenza 2008, pp. 23-53.

[26] Aur. Vict. 33.29. See Cracco Ruggini 1989, pp. 211-212; 255.

Dagron, Gilbert: *L'hippodrome à Constantinople. Jeux, peuple et politique*, Paris 2011.

Deschamps, Gaston – Georges Cousin: *Inscriptions du temple de Zeus Panamaros: le prêtre Sempronius Clemens*, in: *BCH* 12 (1888), pp. 82-104.

Duncan-Jones, Richard: *The Economy of the Roman Empire. Quantitative Studies*, Cambridge 1982².

Fauvinet-Ranson, Valérie: *Decor civitatis, decor Italiae. Monuments, travaux publics et spectacles au VIᵉ siècle d'après les "Variae" de Cassiodore*, Bari 2006.

Gabba, Emilio, *La Sicilia romana*, in: *L'impero romano e le strutture economiche e sociali delle province*, ed. by Michael H. Crawford, Como 1986, pp. 71-85.

Galsterer, Halmut: *Stadt und Territorium*, in: *Stadt und Herrschaft. Römische Kaiserzeit und hohes Mittelalter*, ed. by Friedrich Vittinghoff, München 1982, pp. 75-106.

Garnsey, Peter: *Social Status and Legal Privilege in the Roman Empire*, Oxford 1970.

Garnsey, Peter: *Aspects of the Decline of the Urban Aristocracy in the Empire*, in: *ANRW* 2.1 (1974), pp. 229-252.

Garraffo, Salvatore (ed. by): *La villa romana del Casale di Piazza Armerina*, Palermo 1988.

Geschichte der Wasserversorgung III: *Die Wasserversorgung antiker Städte: Mensch und Wasser, Mitteleuropa, Thermen, Bau/Materialen, Hygiene*, Mainz 1988.

Giardina, Andrea: *Amor civicus. Formule e immagini dell'evergetismo romano nella tradizione epigrafica*, in: *La terza età dell'epigrafia*, ed. by Angela Donati, Faenza 1988a, pp. 67-87.

Giardina, Andrea: *Carità eversiva: le donazioni di Melania la Giovane e gli equilibri della società tardoromana*, in: *StudStor* 19 (1988b), pp. 127-142.

Gros, Pierre: *Modèle urbain et gaspillage des resources dans les programmes édilitaires des villes de Bithynie au début du IIᵉ siècle après J.-C.*, in: *L'origine des richesses dépensées dans la ville antique*, ed. by Philippe Leveau, Aix-en-Provence 1985, pp. 69-86.

Jacques, François: *Volontariat et competition dans les carrières municipales durant le Haut-Empire*, in: *Ktema* 6 (1981), pp. 261-270.

Jacques, François: *Le privilège de la liberté politique imperiale et autonomie municipale dans les cités de l'Occident romain (161-244)*, Roma 1984.

Johnston, David: *Munificence and "municipia": Bequests to Towns in Classical World*, in: *JRS* 75 (1985), pp. 105-112.

Krause, Jens-Uwe: *Spätantike Patronatsformen im Westen des Römischen Reiches*, München 1987.

Lepelley, Claude: *Saint Augustin et la cité romano-africaine*, in: *Jean Chrysostome et Augustin*, ed. by Charles Kannengiesser, Paris 1975, pp. 13-39.

Lepelley, Claude: *Les cités de l'Afrique romaine au Bas-Empire*, Paris 1979.

Lepelley, Claude: *Témoignages épigraphiques sur le contrôle des finances municipales par les gouverneurs à partir du règne de Dioclétien*, in: *Il capitolo delle entrate nelle finanze municipali in Occidente ed in Oriente*, Roma 1999, pp. 235-247.

Liebenam, Wilhelm: *Städteverwaltung im römischen Kaiserreiche*, Leipzig 1900.

Lugaresi, Leonardo: *Il teatro di Dio. Il problema degli spettacoli nel cristianesimo antico (II-V secolo)*, Brescia 2008.

Metcalf, William E.: *Whose Libertas? Propaganda and Audience in Early Roman Empire*, in: *RIN* 95 (1993), pp. 337-346.

Neugebauer, Otto – Henry B. Van Hoesen: *Greek Horoscopes*, Philadelphia 1959.
Oliver, James H.: *A New Letter of Antoninus Pius*, in: *AJP* 79 (1958), pp. 52-60.
Rives, James B.: *Between Orthopraxy and Orthodoxy: Constantine and Animal Sacrifice*, in: *Costantino prima e dopo Costantino. Constantine Before and After Constantine*, ed. by Giorgio Bonamente – Noel Lenski – Rita Lizzi Testa, Bari 2012, pp. 153-163.
Rivolta, Paola: *Miti letterari e programmi politici nelle orazioni giulianee di Libanio*, in: *Clio* 21 (1985), pp. 525-546.
Veyne, Paul: *Le pain et le cirque. Sociologie historique d'un pluralisme politique*, Paris 1976.
Wilson, Roger J. A.: *Towns of Sicily During the Roman Empire*, in: *ANRW* 2.11/1 (1988), pp. 90-106.

ANDREAS M. FLECKNER

The *Peculium*: A Legal Device for Donations to *personae alieno iuri subiectae*?

1. Introduction

Gift-giving and the question of whether there was some sort of 'gift economy' in the ancient world have received considerable attention among scholars from disciplines such as sociology, anthropology, and economics.[1] Legal historians, though, have only infrequently added to the discussion, and likewise the law of donations has so far been largely ignored in the 'gift economy' discourse. To some degree, this indifference is justified, because gift-giving is the prime exemplar of human interactions shaped by social rather than legal norms. However, non-commercial exchange is embedded not only in social, political, and economic but also in legal relationships. Moreover, legal sources from antiquity often include, aside from their principles and rules, important information about social circumstances that are not documented elsewhere. It is therefore never a wise move to disregard the vast amount of legal sources, especially those that build upon cases from the real world. At the same time, legal historians who are interested in the law of donations would be well advised to follow the gift-giving discussion in neighboring academic fields, and to consider those findings in their own research.

This chapter aims to show how both sides could profit from more collaboration by drawing the readers' attention to an institution of Roman law that so far has rarely been mentioned in works on ancient social history[2] – and even less in the context of gift-giving – but offers interesting insights in both regards: the *peculium*.[3] Part 2 introduces the *peculium* as a mechanism by which sons, slaves, and other *personae alieno iuri subiectae* could hold assets. Part 3 reveals

[1] For many valuable comments and suggestions, I am grateful to Alfons Bürge, who has been following and stimulating my research on the *peculium* for many years, as well as to Marietta Auer, András Földi, Egbert Koops, Thilo Kuntz, Sebastian Lohsse, John MacLeod, and several participants of the conference that gave rise to this volume. The usual disclaimers apply. Some sections are based on Fleckner 2010, especially pp. 217-237; 253-260; 292; 299-325; 335; 420-441; 495.

[2] See, for instance, the scattered references to the *peculium* by Rostovtzeff 1957[2], vol. II, p. 580 n. 23 and p. 624 n. 51 as well as by Alföldy 2011[4], pp. 190 nn. 405; 191; 299.

[3] The main monographs on the *peculium* (all written by lawyers) are von Mandry 1876; Micolier 1932; Buti 1976; Brinkhof 1978; Żeber 1981; Di Porto 1984; Fleckner 2010.

a puzzle that emerges from the sources: is the *peculium* a special legal device for donations to *personae alieno iuri subiectae*, or rather a vehicle for business investments by the persons who exert authority over the *peculium* holders? Part 4 describes how the *peculium* of sons became more independent over time, a transformation that reflects the broader social changes in the Roman Empire. Part 5 concludes with an outlook and an agenda for further research.

One note on the limits of this chapter: while it would be tempting to preface the analysis of the *peculium* with an overview of the Roman law of donations and its social implications, this chapter will, for several reasons, refrain from taking this path. First of all, the Roman law of donations is a topic too broad to cover and too complicated to follow in a brief book chapter. Second, there are many excellent overviews to which this chapter could hardly add anything new.[4] Last but not least, another chapter in this volume discusses a special feature of the Roman law of donations, and thereby allows readers to get an illustrative impression of the legal framework for gifts.[5]

2. The *peculium*: a chance for *personae alieno iuri subiectae* to hold assets

The *peculium* is an estate dedicated to sons, slaves, and other *personae alieno iuri subiectae* that is to some extent separated from the property of the person whose authority they are subject to (a *persona sui iuris*: typically the *pater familias*, the head of the family, for sons, and the *dominus*, the master, for slaves).[6] For *personae alieno iuri subiectae*, the *peculium* was a chance to hold and acquire assets on their own. This may not sound like an important privilege to the modern observer, let alone a great 'gift', but in ancient Rome it was both of those things for persons who otherwise lacked any autonomy in financial matters.

To understand the *peculium*'s far-reaching implications, it is indispensable briefly to run through the basic contract and property rules (a.), as well as the basic *peculium* rules (b.). This will give all readers, irrespective of their background, a common starting point for further deliberations, and it will also reveal the main reasons why the *peculium* may deserve more attention in the context of gift-giving (c.).

[4] Kaser 1971², pp. 601-604; Kaser 1975², pp. 394-400; Zimmermann 1990, pp. 477-507; Kaser – Knütel 2008¹⁹, pp. 259-262.

[5] García Morcillo (in this volume).

[6] For the convenience of the reader, it is assumed in all remaining parts of the chapter that the *peculium* holder is either a son or a slave.

a. Basic contract and property rules

There are four basic contract and property rules that are important to keep in mind for anyone intending to study the *peculium*:

1. Sons, slaves, and other *personae alieno iuri subiectae* have no power of agency; if they enter into a contract with a third party of their own accord, the person who exerts authority over them is not bound.[7]
2. *Personae alieno iuri subiectae* have no legal capacity to hold property.[8]
3. Whatever they 'acquire' becomes – with a few exceptions – immediately the property of the person whose authority they are subject to.[9]
4. *Personae sui iuris* cannot hold a *peculium*, but instead have *bona*, a general property; for *personae alieno iuri subiectae* it is the opposite.[10]

b. Basic *peculium* rules

The *peculium* is a set of items that sons, slaves, and other *personae alieno iuri subiectae* hold on their own. Quintus Aelius Tubero, an early Roman jurist of the first century BCE, highlights this feature when he defines the *peculium* as what a slave, with his master's permission (*domini permissu*), keeps separate (*separatum*) from the master's property.[11] For Aelius Marcianus, a jurist of the third century CE, the *peculium* is similar to a human being (*peculium simile esse homini*), a term apparently coined by Papirius Fronto in the late second century CE: like a human being, the *peculium* is born (*nascitur*), grows (*crescit*), decreases (*decrescit*), and eventually dies (*moritur*).[12]

[7] For the general principle, see (as to slaves) Gai. (8 ad ed. prov.), *D* 50.17.133: *melior condicio nostra per servos fieri potest, deterior fieri non potest.* In addition, see, e. g. Papin. (3 resp.), *D* 16.1.27.1 and *Inst.* 4.6.10.

[8] Gai., *Inst.* 2.87: *ipse enim, qui in potestate nostra est, nihil suum habere potest* ≈ Gai. (2 inst.), *D* 41.1.10.1, as well as in many other sources, e. g. Gai., *Inst.* 2.96; Ulp. (27 ad ed.), *D* 50.16.182; *Inst.* 2.12.pr.

[9] The most famous expression of this principle is Gai. (2 inst.), *D* 41.1.10.pr.: *adquiruntur nobis non solum per nosmet ipsos, sed etiam per eos quos in potestate habemus* ≈ Gai., *Inst.* 2.86 ≈ Gai., *Epit.* 2.1.7 ≈ *Inst.* 2.9.pr.

[10] Succinctly for slaves Ulp. (27 ad ed.), *D* 50.16.182: *pater familias liber "peculium" non potest habere, quemadmodum nec servus "bona".*

[11] As indirectly reported by Ulp. (29 ad ed.), *D* 15.1.5.4: *peculium autem Tubero quidem sic definit, ut Celsus libro sexto digestorum refert, quod servus domini permissu separatum a rationibus dominicis habet, deducto inde si quid domino debetur.*

[12] Marcian. (5 reg.), *D* 15.1.40.pr.: *peculium nascitur crescit decrescit moritur, et ideo eleganter Papirius Fronto dicebat peculium simile esse homini.*

With these general characterizations of the past in mind: which of the *peculium*'s main features should a modern observer be aware of in the context of gift-giving?

1. All items belonging to the *peculium* remain (or, in the case of acquisitions, immediately become) the property of the person who exerts authority over the *peculium* holder; in other words, the grant of a *peculium* has no effect on the aforementioned rule that *personae alieno iuri subiectae* lack the legal capacity to hold property.[13] But, unlike under basic property rules, the *peculium* holder is, in general, free to sell the items that belong to the *peculium* without specific permission.[14] This power (*libera administratio peculii*) is the key feature of the *peculium*: a *peculium* holder may, with regard to his *peculium*, act and behave as if he were the owner of the items belonging to the *peculium*. On a side note: *personae alieno iuri subiectae* may not, without specific permission,[15] give away *peculium* items for free, because, to paraphrase the classical Roman jurist Ulpian (of the early third century CE), a son is not empowered to manage the *peculium* and then waste it.[16] Put differently, *peculium* holders are denied full freedom of disposition, one of the core elements of ownership. In a society in which gift-giving is critical for establishing and maintaining contacts, such a limitation is of course a great disadvantage. Yet, this interesting aspect of gift-giving has to be left to other studies, because the present chapter focuses on the *peculium* as a possible legal device for donations *to* (not *by*) *personae alieno iuri subiectae*.
2. Persons vested with a *peculium* still lack powers of agency in a modern sense. However, if they enter into contracts with third parties or create other liabilities that are related to the *peculium*, their creditors are given specific legal actions – the *actio de peculio*,[17] the *actio de in rem verso*,[18] and the *actio tributoria*[19] – to sue the father or master who exerts authority over the *peculium* holder.

[13] *Inst.* 2.12.pr.: *iure civili omnium qui in potestate parentum sunt peculia perinde in bonis parentum computantur, acsi servorum peculia in bonis dominorum numerantur* (n. 90).

[14] See, e. g., Paul. (60 [62?] ad ed.), *D* 15.1.46: *qui peculii administrationem concedit, videtur permittere generaliter, quod et specialiter permissurus est.*

[15] For more information, see n. 81 and accompanying text.

[16] Ulp. (44 ad Sab.), *D* 39.5.7.pr.: *filius familias donare non potest, neque si liberam peculii administrationem habeat: non enim ad hoc ei conceditur libera peculii administratio, ut perdat.* See also, e. g., Iulian. (27 dig.), *D* 39.6.15.

[17] Gai., *Inst.* 4.69; 72a; 73; 74; 74a; *D* 15.1: *de peculio*; *D* 15.2: *quando de peculio actio annalis est*; *Inst.* 4.7.pr.; 4.7.4; 4b; 4c; 5; 5a; 6.

[18] Gai., *Inst.* 4.72a; *D* 15.3: *de in rem verso*; *Inst.* 4.7.4; 4a; 4b; 5; 5a; 6; 8.

[19] Gai., *Inst.* 4.72; 74a; *D* 14.4: *de tributoria actione*; *Inst.* 4.7.3.

3. The *peculium* creditors may seize any item of the father's or master's property, but his liability is – in general[20] – limited to the value of the items that currently form the *peculium* (*peculio tenus*, *quatenus in peculio sit*, etc.).[21]
4. Most important for this chapter: the position that *personae alieno iuri subiectae* obtain with their *peculium* is unstable. The person whose authority they are subject to can reclaim any *peculium* item or even dissolve the entire *peculium* at any time and for any reason.[22] Consequently, if the *peculium* holder dies, under classical Roman law all items revert back to his father or master.[23] For this very reason a number of Roman emperors stepped in, enacted various constitutions that allowed sons to dispose of their *peculium* items by will, and thereby created, supported by an emerging legal doctrine, two variations of the standard *peculium*: the *peculium castrense* and the *peculium quasi castrense*.[24]

All taken together, persons vested with a *peculium* to some degree and in some respects acquired autonomy in financial matters or, to put it more colorfully, a status with features similar (though not identical) to that of *personae sui iuris*.[25]

[20] For the details, see Fleckner 2010, pp. 301-310 (with a diagram on p. 304).

[21] See, e. g., *Inst.* 4.6.10: *actiones autem de peculio ideo adversus patrem dominumve comparavit praetor, quia licet ex contractu filiorum servorumve ipso iure non teneantur, aequum tamen esset peculio tenus... condemnari eos*; *Inst.* 4.6.36: *nam si non minus in peculio sit, quam persequimur, in solidum pater dominusve condemnatur: si vero minus inveniatur, eatenus condemnat iudex, quatenus in peculio sit*; *Inst.* 4.7.4: *id eatenus praestare debeat, quatenus peculium patitur.*

[22] Succinctly (for slaves) Paul. (4 ad Sab.), *D* 15.1.8: *contra autem simul atque noluit* [sc. *dominus*], *peculium servi desinit peculium esse*; see also, e. g., Pomp. (7 ad Sab.), *D* 15.1.4.pr.; Ulp. (29 ad ed.), *D* 15.3.1.1; Ulp. (29 ad ed.), *D* 15.3.5.3. The exceptions to this general rule are irrelevant in this chapter's context.

[23] This is one of the main reasons for title *D* 15.2: *quando de peculio actio annalis est.* The motivation of the *praetor* is reproduced in Ulp. (29 ad ed.), *D* 15.2.1.pr.: *praetor ait: post mortem eius qui in alterius potestate fuerit, posteave quam is emancipatus manumissus alienatusve fuerit, dumtaxat de peculio et si quid dolo malo eius in cuius potestate est factum erit, quo minus peculii esset, in anno, quo primum de ea re experiundi potestas erit, iudicium dabo.* See also Ulp. (29 ad ed.), *D* 15.2.1.3: *cum morte vel alienatione extinguitur peculium*; Pomp. (4 ad Q. Muc.), *D* 15.2.3: *desiit morte servi vel manumissione esse peculium*; Ulp. (29 ad ed.), *D* 15.3.1.1: *morte servi exstinctum est peculium.*

[24] For more details on this transformation, see Part 4 of this chapter.

[25] Paul. (4 ad Plaut.), *D* 15.1.47.6: *quia quasi patrimonium liberi hominis peculium servi intellegitur, ubicumque esset. Inst.* 4.6.10: *peculio..., quod veluti patrimonium est filiorum filiarumque, item servorum.*

c. Conclusion: gift-giving and the *peculium*'s basic legal framework

With these general rules in mind, it is obvious why the *peculium* may be of interest in the context of gift-giving: sons, slaves, and other *personae alieno iuri subiectae* can only hold assets if the person whose authority they are subject to decides to either give them certain items for their *peculium*, or let them keep what they have received from elsewhere. All that sons and slaves possess is, at least in a broader sense, a 'gift' by their father or master. In view of the important role that sons and slaves played in Roman society, the grant of a *peculium* as a special kind of 'gift giving' is a phenomenon that deserves more attention: in general and specifically by those that are sympathetic to the idea of a 'gift economy'.

3. The puzzle: a legal device for donations or for business ventures?

The *peculium*'s basic legal regime, as outlined in the previous part, is well documented in the sources and common knowledge among legal historians. Surprisingly, though, the *peculium*'s role in Roman society has remained largely obscure. Lawyers often ignore or avoid inquiries of this type,[26] and scholars from other fields have not fully discovered the *peculium* so far.[27] But this very question – the *peculium*'s social function – results in a puzzle that directly links the *peculium* with the topic of the present volume.

The puzzle starts with the evidence that has come down to us: there are not many institutions of Roman law that legal sources discuss more frequently than the *peculium*; the *Digest* alone refers over one thousand times to the *peculium*,[28] supplemented by many provisions elsewhere.[29] Equally remarkable is that other sources hardly mention the term: in the whole work of Cicero, for instance, the word *peculium* appears no more than three times,[30] in Suetonius' *De vita*

[26] On the *peculium*'s social function, see, most importantly, Bürge 2010, pp. 369-391; see also, in a different context, Fleckner 2010, pp. 229-237.

[27] For two typical examples, see the references in n. 2; for exceptions, see some of the works in n. 49 and 54 as well as, for instance, Saller 1994, pp. 119, 123-125, 129, 218-221 and Aubert 2013, pp. 192-206.

[28] The principal titles are *D* 14.4: *de tributoria actione*; *D* 15.1: *de peculio*; *D* 15.2: *quando de peculio actio annalis est*; *D* 15.3: *de in rem verso*.

[29] Gai., *Inst.* 3.56; 58; 4.69; 72; 72a; 73; 74; 74a; *CTh.* 2.32: *de peculio*; *Inst.* 2.20.17; 20; 3.7.4; 4.6.8; 10; 36; 4.7.pr.; 3; 4; 4a; 4b; 4c; 5; 5a; 6; 8; *CJ* 4.26: *quod cum eo qui in aliena est potestate negotium gestum esse dicitur, vel de peculio seu quod iussu aut de in rem verso*.

[30] Cic., *Verr.* 2.1.93: *peculia omnium vicariique retinentur* and Cic., *Verr.* 2.3.86: *nihil omnino peculi* as well as (allegorically) Cic., *Par. Stoic.*, 5.39: *cupiditate peculii*.

Caesarum only twice,[31] in Pliny the Elder's *Naturalis historia* or Juvenal's *Saturae* but once.[32] Even the number of passages that, without using the expression, still seem to deal with circumstances that would constitute a *peculium* from a legal standpoint is amazingly low.[33] This stark contrast to the legal sources is puzzling. The only noteworthy exception is Plautus, who refers to the *peculium* in nine out of twenty-one comedies.[34] Plautus, however, precedes the works of the classical Roman jurists by some centuries. Papyri,[35] inscriptions,[36] and archeological record[37] give a mixed picture, but confirm that the term *peculium* is nowhere as prominent as in the legal sources.[38] Against this background, it is not surprising that legal historians dominate the discussion and that there are so few studies of the *peculium* by other scholars such as sociologists, anthropologists, or economists.

From the basic rules outlined in part 2 of this chapter, two distinct facets of the *peculium* become discernible: for those who are subject to another's authority, the receipt of a *peculium* gives some degree of financial independence and autonomy; in this light, the *peculium* could be understood as a legal device for donations to *personae alieno iuri subiectae* (a.). For those who exert authority, the grant of a *peculium* offers the prospect of participating indirectly, and therefore at lower risk, in business ventures that the recipient may conduct; the *peculium* could then be seen as an instrument for investments in business enterprises (b.). However, a closer examination of both explanations shows that

[31] Suet., *Tib.* 15.2: *ulla aliter quam ut peculio referret accepta*, as well as *Tib.* 50.1: *peculio concesso a patre*.

[32] Plin., *NH* 34.15: *ex peculio Sp. Cassi*; Iuv. 3.189: *cultis augere peculia servis*.

[33] See, for instance (in chronological order), Cic., *Rosc. Am.* 44; Diod. Sic. 37.5.3; Plin., *NH* 33.145; Mart. 2.68; Plut., *Cato mai.* 21.7; Suet., *Otho* 5.2. The two best examples among these are probably Cic., *Rosc. Am.* 44 (see text accompanying n. 41) and Plut., *Cato mai.* 21.7 (reproduced in n. 42, describing how Cato entered into commercial transactions with his slaves).

[34] Plaut., *Asin.* 277; 498; *Bacch.* 465; *Capt.* 1028; *Cas.* 199; 258; *Merc.* 96; *Most.* 253; 863; 875; *Pseud.* 1188; *Stich.* 751; *Trin.* 434 (all cited according to Lindsay's edition). Not included in this list are references to *peculiaris* and similar derivatives. Żeber 1981, p. 13, states that "[t]he word *peculium* and thus the institution itself occurs in thirteen of the twenty-one of his plays", but in fact not all of the references given by Żeber 1981, p. 20 n. 2, include the term *peculium*.

[35] Taubenschlag 1955^2, pp. 87-91.

[36] Eck – Heinrichs 1993, especially nn. 39; 151; 246; 310; 343; 363.

[37] Schumacher 2001, especially pp. 163-180.

[38] Unlike for the legal and literary sources, the current state of research makes it impossible to get an exhaustive account of the *peculium*'s usage and occurrence elsewhere.

neither succeeds in adequately deciphering the *peculium*'s social function and that additional research is necessary to unravel the mystery (c.).

a. *Peculium*-granting as gift-giving

The notion of 'giving' is intrinsically tied to the emergence and rise of the *peculium*. *Pecus* means either cattle (with the genitive *pecoris*) or a single animal (with the genitive *pecudis*).[39] The etymology and the later usage of the term indicate that, in the beginning, the *peculium* typically consisted of cattle that were left to sons or slaves to allow them some sort of independent breeding or other business.[40] This practice seems to have remained a common occurrence for many centuries. Even as late as the beginning of the first century BCE, Cicero describes (though without explicit reference to the *peculium*) how a son in his father's lifetime (*patre vivo*) managed estates on his own; Cicero calls this a tradition (*consuetudo*), a sign of affection (*benevolentia*), and an honor (*honor*).[41] Over time, the field of application evidently grew and fathers or masters became used to granting their sons and slaves *peculia*, or to letting them keep items that they had received from other persons. In case of the sons, the *peculium* helped them gain experience in financial matters and gave them a chance to demonstrate their skills before they took over the family estates. For the slaves, the *peculium* opened a path to freedom if they made enough money to ransom themselves.[42] In the writings of the classical jurist Ulpian, the *peculium* has already departed from its material origins; it has become an abstract estate.[43]

[39] For etymological overviews see, most importantly, *ThLL* 1991, *s. v. peculium*, as well as von Uxkull-Gyllenband 1937, col. 13; Kaser 1975^2, p. 64 n. 38; Żeber 1981, pp. 9-10; Lohsse 2013, pp. 5121-5122. For more details, see Gnoli 1978, pp. 204-218 and Amirante 1983, pp. 1-15.

[40] Varro, *RR* 1.2.17: *servis peculium, quibus domini dant ut pascant*; Fest., *s. v. peculium* (290.34-35 Lindsay): *peculium servorum* ‹ex› *pecore item dictum est, ut* [ex] *pecunia patrum familiae*; Paul. Diac. ex Fest., *s. v. peculium* (291.3-4 Lindsay): *peculium servorum a pecore dictum, sicut et pecunia nobilium*; in addition see, e. g., Plin., *NH* 33.43: *signatum est nota pecudum, unde et pecunia appellata*.

[41] Cic., *Rosc. Am.* 43-44.

[42] Interesting in this context (*peculium*?) Plut., *Cato mai.* 21.7: ἐδίδου [sc. Κάτων] δὲ καὶ τῶν οἰκετῶν τοῖς βουλομένοις ἀργύριον· οἱ δ' ἐωνοῦντο παῖδας, εἶτα τούτους ἀσκήσαντες καὶ διδάξαντες ἀναλώμασι τοῦ Κάτωνος μετ' ἐνιαυτὸν ἀπεδίδοντο. πολλοὺς δὲ καὶ κατεῖχεν ὁ Κάτων, ὅσην ὁ πλείστην διδοὺς ἐωνείτο τιμὴν ὑπολογιζόμενος. On the significance of Plutarch's account, see also the note at the end of n. 33.

[43] Ulp. (29 ad ed.), *D* 15.1.5.3: *peculium dictum est quasi pusilla pecunia sive patrimonium pusillum*. For the details, see (directly following) Ulp. (29 ad ed.), *D* 15.1.5.4; Cels. (6 dig.), *D* 15.1.6; Ulp. (29 ad ed.), *D* 15.1.7.pr.

But why this plethora of *peculium* rules, why the countless provisions with specifics, particulars, details? The *Digest* alone, as already mentioned, refers to the *peculium* more than one thousand times. While the sheer number of rules may be just a consequence of the fact that the *peculium* touches many areas of ancient life, and thus of Roman law, this circumstance cannot account for the staggering sophistication of the *peculium* regime (which is so complex that modern observers, even teachers of Roman law, again and again misunderstand it).[44] Even fundamental aspects such as the liability of the person who exerts authority over the *peculium* holder (under the three actions related to the *peculium*) or the separation of assets (from other assets of the father or master and within the *peculium*) require graphical representations to become fully comprehensible.[45] And some examples in the sources are almost impenetrable on first reading.[46]

Last but not least: why is the *peculium* – or at least the phenomenon in practice that the term denotes – not better documented elsewhere? Countless sources have survived that illustrate how common gifts and donations were in Roman society, both between *personae sui iuris* as well as from them to their sons and slaves (especially *mortis causa*). What makes adding items to *peculia* or leaving items with the sons and slaves for their *peculia* so different that many sources have remained silent about it?

b. *Peculium*-granting as venture-funding

There has always been a second explanation for the *peculium*'s rise: masters may have employed the *peculium* as a vehicle to invest indirectly in larger

[44] For references, see Fleckner 2010, p. 304 n. 24 and Fleckner 2011, pp. 684-685 and 687.

[45] See Fleckner 2010 with two diagrams on the father's or master's liability (p. 303), and on the separation of assets (p. 423). For the difficulties in determining the *peculium*'s content and value, see most recently Aubert 2013, pp. 192-206.

[46] Such as (quoted in its entirety to illustrate the complexity) Ulp. (29 ad ed.), *D* 15.1.17: *si servus meus ordinarius vicarios habeat, id quod vicarii mihi debent an deducam ex peculio servi ordinarii? et prima illa quaestio est, an haec peculia in peculio servi ordinarii computentur. et Proculus et Atilicinus existimant, sicut ipsi vicarii sunt in peculio, ita etiam peculia eorum: et id quidem, quod mihi dominus eorum, id est ordinarius servus debet, etiam ex peculio eorum detrahetur: id vero quod ipsi vicarii debent, dumtaxat ex ipsorum peculio: sed et si quid non mihi, sed ordinario servo debent, deducetur de peculio eorum quasi conservo debitum: id vero, quod ipsis debet ordinarius servus, non deducetur de peculio ordinarii servi, quia peculium eorum in peculio ipsius est (et ita Servius respondit), sed peculium eorum augebitur, ut opinor, quemadmodum si dominus servo suo debeat.*

business ventures. After this notion had more or less been buried in German works of the nineteenth century for a long time,[47] some Italian scholars rediscovered it three decades ago and developed it into a complex system of indirect business funding.[48] This time the idea was met with great enthusiasm, prompting researchers from all over the world and from various perspectives (law, history, economics) to add to the discussion.[49]

What is the basis of this explanation? Think, as a starting point, of a master who was mulling over launching a substantial business venture, but was afraid of the risk resulting from it. Instead of running the business on his own, he could transfer the funds and assets to one of his slaves and thereby limit his risk, in general, to the current value of the *peculium*, basically without forgoing any of the business' chances. In that way, the master could set up a business enterprise with a sort of limited liability. Now, if several masters pooled their funds and vested a common slave with the capital, they could mitigate some of the structural disadvantages of the *societas*,[50] the institution for joint trading and other common purposes under Roman law.[51] Unlike gift-giving, teaming up and indirectly investing in larger business ventures would indeed be sophisticated enough to justify the *peculium*'s complex legal regime.

However, contrary to widespread imagination, the sources that have come down to us do not support the assumption that the *peculium* was indeed used to fund larger enterprises. There is, to the best of common knowledge, not a single literary source, no papyrus, no inscription that provides evidence for a larger business enterprise that rests upon the *peculium* of a common slave; even the legal sources which, as mentioned before, exhaustively discuss all constellations that one could think of, rarely refer to joint enterprises and do not touch upon larger common business ventures based on *peculia* at all.[52] Against this back-

[47] Dietzel 1859, pp. 1-18; Roesler 1860, pp. 51-64; Bekker 1861, pp. 499-567.

[48] Di Porto 1984; Serrao 1989; Petrucci 1991; Di Porto 1992, pp. 231-260; Di Porto 1997, pp. 413-452; Petrucci 2002; Cerami 2007-2008, pp. 92-99; Pesaresi 2008; Cerami – Petrucci 2010[3].

[49] Aubert 1994; Földi 1996, pp. 179-211; Hansmann – Kraakman – Squire 2006, pp. 1358-1360; Lazo 2009, pp. 141-158; Abatino – Dari-Mattiacci – Perotti 2011, pp. 365-389. In addition, see the references in n. 54.

[50] Fleckner 2010, pp. 239-496, discussing four structural features: separation of ownership from control; protection of the capital providers' private assets; protection of the capital association's common assets; and transferability of the capital providers' share in the association. The advantages of the *peculium* compared to the *societas* relate to the first, second and fourth feature (for the third feature, see n. 65).

[51] The main monographs on the *societas* (all written by lawyers) are del Chiaro 1928; Poggi 1930-1934; Wieacker 1936; Arnò 1938; Szlechter 1947; Arangio-Ruiz 1950; Bona 1973; Hernando Lera 1992; Santucci 1997; Meissel 2004; Fleckner 2010.

[52] Fleckner 2010, pp. 229-237; to this section should be added a discussion of Serrao

ground, the idea of the *peculium* as a vehicle for investments in larger businesses is, as already noted elsewhere, an anachronistic thought experiment,[53] confusing the modern doctrine with the ancient reality.[54]

c. Conclusion: gift-giving and *peculium* functions

Despite spirited debates in recent decades, the role of the *peculium* in Roman society remains puzzling, because neither of the two possible explanations is compelling.

The first explanation, the *peculium* as an instrument for donations to *personae alieno iuri subiectae*, is well supported by legal sources and occasionally confirmed in other places. There is no doubt that it was indeed very common for fathers and masters to make gifts to their sons and slaves or to let them keep items that they had acquired from elsewhere. However, the purpose of gift-giving alone fails to explain why the legal regime became so complex. If the main function of the *peculium* was merely to allow *personae alieno iuri subiectae* to receive presents and hold them on their own, would this have led to cases that warrant the masses of highly sophisticated rules that the Roman jurists developed for the *peculium*?

The second explanation, the *peculium* as an instrument for funding larger business ventures, would give good reasons for the complexity of the legal regime. Yet, while some *peculium* provisions are well-suited for business enterprises, others are not. In any case, and this is the main objection to this way of reasoning, there is no evidence to corroborate this idea because no sources have come down to us that give proof of larger common business ventures that rest upon *peculia*. Of course, *absence of evidence is not evidence of absence*, but with so many sources on the relationship between masters and slaves that have survived, it is highly unlikely that, by some coincidence, all sources would have been destroyed that relate to larger business enterprises that masters had set up through their slaves' *peculia*.

With both explanations unpersuasive, are there any additional ideas that may help come closer to unraveling the mystery? A renowned scholar of Roman law has recently put forward a third hypothesis: the *peculium* as a mechanism to

1989, especially pp. 33-35 (inscriptions) and pp. 49-61 (*tabulae Pompeianae*).

[53] Fleckner 2010, p. 235 ("anachronistisches Gedankenspiel").

[54] Bürge 2010, p. 384 ("errore di confondere la costruzione dogmatica moderna con la realtà antica"). For further criticism, see Bürge 1988, pp. 856-865; Montanari 1990, pp. 5-6 n. 7; Talamanca 1990, pp. 814-815 n. 8; Labruna 1994, p. 129; Andreau 1999, p. 26 n. 56; pp. 68-70; Bürge 1999, pp. 197-200; Andreau 2004, pp. 114 and 123-125; Meissel 2004, pp. 65 and 155-156; Grotkamp 2005, p. 142; Chiusi 2007, pp. 1032-1035.

compensate for the slaves' lack of capacity to participate in litigation.[55] Viewed in this light, the *peculium*'s function is less, if at all, to further the grantor's interests than to allow *personae alieno iuri subiectae* to establish legal relations and to protect the creditors that originate from such interactions. This new explanation, a first fruit of a larger research project, promises to revolutionize our understanding of the *peculium*, and it is hoped that a more comprehensive account by the same author will follow soon.[56]

In general, any further deliberations would profit greatly from a closer examination of material outside the legal sources and from the input by scholars of other disciplines than legal history. While some of the legal sources without doubt refer to real cases, especially in the Codes of Theodosius and Justinian, and therefore allow direct insights into the *peculium*'s role in practice, others, in particular the fragments from the legal literature that form the *Digest*, may be standard cases that were passed from generation to generation irrespective of their relevance in daily life. Put differently, despite the vast number of legal sources that deal with the *peculium*, their analysis alone will not suffice to understand the *peculium*'s role in ancient society. This is especially true for any attempt to verify the first explanation, the *peculium* as a legal device for donations to *personae alieno iuri subiectae*, because gift-giving is, as mentioned at the outset of this chapter, the prime exemplar of human interactions which often follow social rather than legal norms.

Ultimately, it is probably not too far-fetched to assume that only a combination of several factors may satisfactorily explain the picture that the sources draw. The reason is that, unlike today, when legal institutions are often regulated by a single piece of legislation drafted with a clear intention in mind, the legal framework for the *peculium* was, as is typical for Roman law, a bouquet of provisions resulting from different periods and by distinct authors.[57] It would be no surprise, then, if the heterogeneous collection of sources that have come down to us revealed more than one function or role of the *peculium* in ancient society. After all, seven centuries passed between Plautus' frequent references to the *peculium* (second century BCE), the work of the classical jurists (first-second century CE), and the compilation of their fragments in the *Digest* (sixth century CE). Over this period, Roman society was subject to many earth-shattering transformations, Roman law experienced major modifications, and it is highly

[55] Bürge 2010, pp. 369-391, in a nutshell on p. 381 ("un gruppo di fonti ci permette di verificare la nostra ipotesi secondo la quale a Roma il *peculium* era legato alla realtà degli schiavi viventi e agenti in maniera indipendente, e marcava sul piano del diritto il modo in cui veniva compensata la capacità processuale mancante – in particolare la legittimazione passiva").

[56] As indicated by Bürge 2010, p. 369 n. 1.

[57] Similar to the legal framework for *societates*, see Fleckner 2010, pp. 607-610.

plausible that the *peculium*'s predominant function or functions in society may have varied as well. The following sections will give a few examples of such changes and thereby support the view that the *peculium*'s role in Roman society was more versatile than any single explanation could account for.

4. The transformation: social change and increasing financial independence of sons

Under general *peculium* and property rules, all items in the *peculium* belong to the father's or master's property despite the *peculium*'s existence.[58] From a strictly legal standpoint, the person who exerts authority over the *peculium* holder could regain *any* of the *peculium* items at *any* time for *any* reason.[59] A father could even take away his son's *peculium* with various estates and slaves from one moment to the next.[60] This instability remains a fundamental objection both against the explanation of the *peculium* as a legal device for donations (since gifts are typically irretrievable) as well as against its interpretation as an instrument for investments in larger business enterprises (since it thwarts the idea of committing capital and personnel in the long term).[61] It is true that, in practice, the *peculium* may have been a more stable institution because of social restrictions on reclaiming *peculium* items. However, this assumption is only plausible for the *peculia* of sons,[62] not so much for the *peculia* of slaves,[63] especially if they were established with a clear intention to fund business enterprises for the master's benefit. In any case, there are other threats to the *peculium*'s stability that are completely independent from the father's or master's good intentions. First, if the *peculium* holder dies, all *peculium* items revert back to the father or master because he is still their owner.[64] Second, if the father or master defaults on a debt, his creditors will have the power to seize all his assets, including the *peculium* items, again because they are still part of his property.[65]

[58] Out of the sources presented in part 2 of this chapter, see especially *Inst.* 2.12.pr. (nn. 13 and 90) as well as Gai., *Inst.* 2.87 (n. 8) and Ulp. (27 ad ed.), *D* 50.16.182 (n. 10).

[59] Succinctly (for slaves) Paul. (4 ad Sab.), *D* 15.1.8: *contra autem simul atque noluit* [sc. *dominus*], *peculium servi desinit peculium esse*; for further references, see n. 22.

[60] Explicitly recognized as early as by von Mandry 1876, p. 170.

[61] On the *peculium*'s instability, see Bürge 1988, p. 860; Bürge 1999, p. 199; Bürge 2010, p. 385; Fleckner 2010, pp. 227-228, 236 and 424.

[62] von Jhering 1854, pp. 215-216 n. 324 (kept in later editions of the work); Kaser 1938, p. 85; Kaser 1971^2, pp. 64 n. 37, 287 and 344; Saller 1994, pp. 124-125.

[63] Kaser 1971^2, p. 114 n. 14; less restrictive Kaser 1938, p. 85 and, for items received from third parties, Buchwitz 2012, p. 229.

[64] For references, see n. 23.

[65] Fleckner 2010, pp. 420-441. The issue is highly controversial, yet the sources that have

Against this background, it becomes understandable why the traditional legal regime was amended several times to increase the *peculium*'s independence from the father's influence and fortune. One of these amendments led to a general protection of the son's *peculium* against confiscations of the father's property (a.); other measures gradually strengthened the financial independence of sons who were in military and civil service (b.). None of these changes, though, extends to the *peculia* of slaves; this casts further doubt on the suggestion that the *peculium* was employed as an instrument for investments in larger business ventures (c.).

a. General protection against confiscations of the father's property

In the context of the protection of minors, the Digest features a long fragment by Ulpian that includes, *inter alia*, the following segment:

> *nec eo movemur, quasi intersit filii peculium habere: magis enim patris quam filii interest, licet aliquo casu ad filium peculium spectet: ut puta si patris eius bona a fisco propter debitum occupata sunt: nam peculium ei ex constitutione Claudii separatur.*[66]

In this passage, Ulpian brings up an exception to the general rule that all *peculium* items belong to the father's property: according to a constitution of the emperor Claudius (41-54 CE), the son's *peculium* will be separated from his father's property if the latter is confiscated by state authorities.[67] Claudius' constitution would not have been necessary if the *peculium* had already been protected against claims by the father's creditors (including state authorities) under the traditional regime. It is rather surprising that this fragment, although it provides evidence, by virtue of an *argumentum e contrario*, for the *peculium*'s instability under general rules and therefore questions the *peculium*'s suitability to fund larger business ventures, has received so little attention in the *peculium* literature, especially by those who support the view that larger business ventures were set up through *peculia* of common slaves.[68]

come down to us (such as Ulp. [11 ad ed.], *D* 4.4.3.4, see n. 66 and accompanying text) allow no other conclusion but that the *peculium* items were *not* protected against the claims of the father's or master's creditors.

[66] Ulp. (11 ad ed.), *D* 4.4.3.4.

[67] On this fragment, see from the last decades (though mostly with a different focus) Brinkhof 1978, pp. 175-176; Wacke 1991, p. 61; Ankum 1993, pp. 1-25; Wacke 1994, p. 494; Longo 2003, pp. 102-103 and 298-301; Wacke 2006, p. 313; Musumeci 2007, pp. 3733-3735.

[68] For the fragment's implications in this context, see Fleckner 2010, pp. 228; 236; 423;

For this chapter, the fragment is illuminating in two regards. The first interesting aspect is Ulpian's remark that he will maintain his opinion despite the son's interest in having a *peculium* (*intersit filii peculium habere*) because, as Ulpian states, the *peculium* is more in the father's than in the son's interest (*magis enim patris quam filii interest*).[69] It seems that this notion is so obvious to the ancient reader that Ulpian can allude to it without any elaboration on the reasons why, if at all, the father has an interest in the *peculium*. This fact, of course, challenges the *peculium*'s characterization as an instrument for gift-giving: while many donations please both the grantor as well as the grantee, one would probably not go so far as to state as a general rule that donations are more in the giver's than in the recipient's interest. In other words, Ulpian's remark indicates that granting *peculia* was, even for classical Roman jurists, not analogous to making presents, but rather an institution from which the fathers (and perhaps also the masters) tended to benefit more than the sons (or the slaves).

It is not the praetor or jurists like Ulpian who break with the traditional regime, but an emperor such as Claudius. This is the second interesting aspect in this fragment, and it is telling in many ways. First, it is one proof among others that the *peculium* developed from a subdivision of the father's or master's property into an estate of *personae alieno iuri subiectae*, not *vice versa*. Second, the general protection of the son's *peculium* against confiscations of the father's property was not a fruit of Roman jurisprudence, not of their comprehensive scientific analysis of the law and their sophisticated legal doctrine, but a political decision by an emperor, most likely due to popular demand. Third, the fact that it protects the *peculia* of sons rather than those of slaves against state authorities is an indication that investing in larger business ventures was not the *peculium*'s main field of application. For if it had been important, Roman businessmen would have pressed for protection against confiscations of their co-masters' properties, and emperors such as Claudius would probably have reacted in a similar way. After all, an emperor who pleases weak sons would not have failed to please their strong fathers.

b. Specific provisions for sons in military and civil service

The etymology of the term *peculium* and the *peculium*'s usage in the sources indicate that the *peculium* evolved from cattle and other items that fathers or masters left to *personae alieno iuri subiectae* for independent breeding and, more generally, for business activities on their own.[70] This traditional arrangement is

425-426; 428 and 436-437.

[69] Ulp. (11 ad ed.), *D* 4.4.3.4.

[70] See Part 3a for references.

referred to simply as *peculium* in the classical sources, and it has been the subject of this chapter so far. It is interesting to note, from the perspective of social change, that in later periods two variations from the long-established *peculium* arose that led to a division of the *peculium* into three distinct phenomena: the standard *peculium* (later called *peculium paganum* or still merely *peculium*), the military *peculium* (*peculium castrense*), and the quasi-military *peculium* (*peculium quasi castrense*).[71]

What distinguishes the new *peculium* forms from the traditional *peculium*? The *peculium castrense* originates, as its name reveals (*castrensis* is an adjective to *castrum*: fort, camp), from the sons' military service.[72] The *peculium quasi castrense* is an extension to sons employed in state administration.[73] At least under its basic definition, the *peculium castrense* covers all items that a son receives on the occasion of or in connection with his military service, ranging from farewell presents at the commencement of duties to acquisitions as a soldier.[74] With respect to the items belonging to the *peculium castrense*, sons became capable of acting as owners, despite their unaltered status as *personae alieno iuri subiectae*.[75] The main legal consequence of this capacity, and probably the key rationale for its emergence, was that sons could dispose of their *peculium castrense* items by will.[76] Making provisions for the case of death may

[71] *CJ* 3.28.37.1 (531 CE): *in castrensibus etenim peculiis introducta est et alia subdivisio et peculii triplex invenitur causa. vel enim paganum est peculium vel castrense vel quod medietatem inter utrumque obtinet, quod quasi castrense nuncupatur*. All three *peculium* forms are also mentioned by Ulp. (44 ad Sab.), *D* 39.5.7.6.

[72] The most important sources are *D* 49.17: *de castrensi peculio*, as well as *CJ* 12.30: *de castrensi omnium palatinorum peculio*, and *CJ* 12.36: *de castrensi peculio militum et praefectianorum*. The main works on the *peculium castrense* are Fitting 1871; La Rosa 1953; Lehmann 1982, pp. 183-284.

[73] *CTh*. 6.36; *CJ* 12.30: *de castrensi omnium palatinorum peculio*. In addition to the works mentioned in n. 72, see Mastrangelo 2005, pp. 261-308.

[74] The best (though incomplete) definition is given by Macer (2 de re milit.), *D* 49.17.11: *castrense peculium est, quod a parentibus vel cognatis in militia agenti donatum est vel quod ipse filius familias in militia adquisiit, quod, nisi militaret, adquisiturus non fuisset. nam quod erat et sine militia adquisiturus, id peculium eius castrense non est*. See also, e. g., *PS* 3.4.3: *castrense enim peculium est quod in castris adquiritur vel quod proficiscenti ad militiam datur*.

[75] Gai. (1 ad ed. prov.), *D* 5.1.4: *lis nulla nobis esse potest cum eo quem in potestate habemus, nisi ex castrensi peculio*; Ulp. (64 ad ed.), *D* 14.6.2: *filii familias in castrensi peculio vice patrum familiarum fungantur*; *Inst*. 2.12.pr.: *sed scilicet proprium eius esse id quod in castris adquisierit, quamquam iure civili omnium qui in potestate parentum sunt peculia perinde in bonis parentum computantur, acsi servorum peculia in bonis dominorum numerantur*.

[76] Succinctly *Inst*. 2.12.pr.: *militibus qui in potestate parentum sunt, quibus de eo quod in castris adquisierint permissum est ex constitutionibus principum testamentum facere*.

not look like an important legal right for sons who are still subject to their father's authority, but it is of course important if they put their life at risk in the army while their own families are left without proper funds at home. The *peculium castrense* offers a remedy for this delicate situation: if a son dies, items belonging to his *peculium castrense* do not automatically revert back to his father (as normal *peculium* assets would), but get distributed according to his will instead. On a side note (again because this is interesting in the context of gift-giving, but outside the scope of this chapter): while *personae alieno iuri subiectae* are generally not empowered to donate *peculium* items,[77] sons may do so with respect to their *peculium castrense*.[78]

How did the special provisions for the *peculium castrense* and the *peculium quasi castrense* emerge? They are the result of a long process, to be seen in two broader contexts: first the transformation from compulsory military service to a professional army, and second – which is related to the former – the trend toward more financial autonomy and independence for sons from their fathers. The *peculium castrense* is one of the most influential legal devices in both regards.[79]

Under the traditional regime, a son was, as just noted, generally not authorized to make gifts out of his *peculium*, neither *inter vivos* nor *mortis causa*.[80] While it is true that his father could grant special permission for such donations,[81] a son could not, even with explicit consent by his father, dispose of *peculium* items by will.[82] The first emperor who broke with this tradition and allowed sons to make a will disposing of items in the *peculium castrense*, was most certainly Augustus (27 BCE-14 CE).[83] His direct successors seem not to

[77] See the references in n. 16; for exceptions, see n. 81 and accompanying text.

[78] Ulp. (44 ad Sab.), *D* 39.5.7.6: *haec omnia locum habebunt in paganis: ceterum qui habent castrense peculium vel quasi castrense, in ea condicione sunt, ut donare et mortis causa et non mortis causa possint, cum testamenti factionem habeant*. See also, e. g., Ulp. (33 ad Sab.), *D* 24.1.32.8 and Iulian. (27 dig.), *D* 39.6.15.

[79] For details on the rise of the *peculium castrense*, see Fitting 1871, pp. 3-23; 92-148 and 340-387; La Rosa 1953, pp. 223-235; Lehmann 1982, pp. 265-277.

[80] See nn. 16 and 77 and accompanying text.

[81] Marcian. (9 inst.), *D* 39.6.25.1: *filius familias, qui non potest facere testamentum nec voluntate patris, tamen mortis causa donare patre permittente potest*.

[82] Gai. (17 ad ed. prov.), *D* 28.1.6.pr.: *qui in potestate parentis est, testamenti faciendi ius non habet. adeo ut, quamvis pater ei permittat, nihilo magis tamen iure testari possit* (≈ *Inst.* 2.12.pr.); Marcian. (9 inst.), *D* 39.6.25.1: *non potest facere testamentum nec voluntate patris* (n. 81).

[83] Ulp., *Epit.* 20.10: *sed divus Augustus [Marcus] constituit, ut filius familiae miles de eo peculio quod in castris adquisivit testamentum facere possit*; *Inst.* 2.12.pr.: *exceptis... militibus qui in potestate parentum sunt, quibus de eo quod in castris adquisierint permissum est ex constitutionibus principum testamentum facere. Quod quidem initio tantum militantibus datum est tam ex auctoritate divi Augusti quam Nervae nec non*

have maintained this innovation. Instead, it took eleven decades before Nerva (96-98)[84] and Trajan (98-117)[85] renewed Augustus' provision.[86] Immediately thereafter, though, Hadrian (117-138) dramatically increased the *peculium castrense*'s weight: thus far, the *peculium castrense* had been limited to sons currently in military service, now Hadrian extended it to those that had retired from the army, turning the *peculium castrense* from a temporary into a lifetime privilege.[87] In addition, Hadrian let sons manumit slaves out of the *peculium castrense*, a right that brought more benefits in Roman society than modern observers may appreciate.[88]

Roman jurisprudence had hitherto been rather uninterested in the *peculium castrense*. Hadrian's measures, however, prompted the jurists to mull over the *peculium castrense*'s legal character and to increasingly interpret it as an estate almost entirely separated from the father's reach and property.[89] Whereas the main impulses for the rise of the *peculium castrense* originate from the emperors, the development of the *peculium castrense* from a collection of various privileges into a coherent institution of partial legal capacity is the product of legal analysis rather than political decisions.[90]

optimi imperatoris Traiani. In the Digest (though without references to Augustus), see especially (in chronological order) Iulian. (27 dig.), *D* 39.6.15; Ulp. (33 ad Sab.), *D* 24.1.32.8; Ulp. (45 ad ed.), *D* 29.1.11.pr.; Ulp. (44 ad Sab.), *D* 39.5.7.6 (n. 78).

84 *Inst.* 2.12.pr.: *ex auctoritate... Nervae* (n. 83).

85 *Inst.* 2.12.pr.: *ex auctoritate... optimi imperatoris Traiani* (n. 83).

86 Probably at the same time, i.e., around the turn of the century (100 CE), Juvenal (provided that he is the author of this satire) confirms that the rule is (again) in force: Iuv. 16.51-52: *solis praeterea testandi militibus ius vivo patre datur.*

87 *Inst.* 2.12.pr.: *postea vero subscriptione divi Hadriani etiam dimissis militia, id est veteranis, concessum est.*

88 Mod. (6 reg.), *D* 37.14.8.pr.: *servum a filio familias milite manumissum divus Hadrianus rescripsit militem libertum suum facere, non patris*; Ulp. (41 ad ed.), *D* 38.2.3.8: *si quis filius familias servum de castrensi peculio manumiserit, ex constitutione divi Hadriani patronus est admittique poterit ad contra tabulas bonorum possessionem ut patronus*; Marcian. (1 inst.), *D* 38.2.22: *si filius familias miles manumittat, secundum Iuliani quidem sententiam, quam libro vicensimo septimo digestorum probat, patris libertum faciet: sed quamdiu, inquit, vivit, praefertur filius in bona eius patri. sed divus Hadrianus Flavio Apro rescripsit suum libertum eum facere, non patris*; Tryph. (18 disp.), *D* 49.17.19.3: *denique filium posse manumittere talis* [sc. *castrensis*] *peculii servum Hadrianus constituit.*

89 This gradual change becomes visible in the works of Papinian, Paulus, and Ulpian (all of the early 3rd century CE). See, for instance, Papin. (9 resp.), *D* 40.5.23.2; Papin. (35 quaest.), *D* 49.17.15.3; Papin. (35 quaest.), *D* 49.17.15.4. Paul. (11 quaest.), *D* 35.2.18. pr. Ulp. (11 ad ed.), *D* 4.4.3.10; Ulp. (64 ad ed.), *D* 14.6.2; Ulp. (67 ad ed.), *D* 49.17.2. More controversial is the interpretation of Tryph. (18 disp.), *D* 49.17.19.3.

90 The result of this discrete transformation is succinctly summed up in *Inst.* 2.12.pr.: *sed*

Later, Emperor Constantine (306-337) extended the *peculium castrense*'s personal scope to certain state officials and thereby created what would later become known as the *peculium quasi castrense*.[91] Justinian (527-565) strengthened the character of these two *peculia* as separate estates: he explicitly forbade fathers to reclaim items from the *peculium castrense*,[92] further extended the scope of the *peculium quasi castrense*,[93] and – as a result of his general reform of intestate succession[94] – prevented *peculium* items from reverting back to the father if the son dies without a will.[95]

What motivated the emperors to expand the scope of these variations from the standard *peculium*? It was probably a combination of several factors. To begin with, there are a number of reasons for according a greater degree of separation from the father's assets to items received on the occasion of or in connection with military service. First, the sons were typically out of their fathers' reach during their military service, making them *de facto* more independent from their fathers. Second, while farewell presents may have constituted a major part of the *peculium castrense* at the commencement of duties, they probably lost significance over time compared to acquisitions by the sons as a soldier; if the *peculium castrense* consisted mainly of items gained through the sons' own efforts, this gave good reason to develop the *de facto* independence toward more *de jure* autonomy.[96] However, these inherent reasons alone cannot

scilicet proprium eius esse id quod in castris adquisierit, quamquam iure civili omnium qui in potestate parentum sunt peculia perinde in bonis parentum computantur, acsi servorum peculia in bonis dominorum numerantur.

[91] See, in particular, *CJ* 12.30.1.pr. (Constantine, 326 CE): *omnes palatinos, quos edicti nostri iam dudum certa privilegia superfundunt, rem, si quam, dum in palatio nostro morantur, vel si parsimonia propria quaesierint vel donis nostris fuerint consecuti, ut castrense peculium habere praecipimus. quid enim tam ex castris est, quam quod nobis consciis ac prope sub conspectibus nostris adquiritur?*

[92] *Inst.* 2.12.pr.: *ex hoc intellegere possumus, quod in castris adquisierit miles, qui in potestate patris est, neque ipsum patrem adimere posse neque patris creditores id vendere vel aliter inquietare.*

[93] See, in particular, *CJ* 6.61.7.1 (Justinian, 530 CE) and *Nov. Iust.* 123.19 (Justinian, 546 CE). See also (mostly or even entirely a summary of the *status quo ante*) *CJ* 3.28.37.1 (531 CE).

[94] *Nov. Iust.* 118 (543 CE): *constitutio quae iura adgnatorum tollit et successiones ab intestato definit.*

[95] For the former regime, see (in chronological order) Pomp. (2 sen. cons.), *D* 38.17.10.pr.; Tryph. (18 disp.), *D* 49.17.19.3; Papin. (27 quaest.), *D* 49.17.14.pr.; Paul. (11 quaest.), *D* 35.2.18.pr.; Ulp. (14 ad ed.), *D* 49.17.1; Ulp. (67 ad ed.), *D* 49.17.2. Already with an important restriction (*nullis liberis vel fratribus superstitibus*) *Inst.* 2.12.pr.: *si vero intestati decesserint nullis liberis vel fratribus superstitibus, ad parentes eorum iure communi pertinebit.*

[96] An indication for this rationale (if it is not merely irony) is Iuv. 16.52-54: *nam quae*

fully explain the increasing independence of the *peculium castrense*. After all, there were probably many other sons whose *peculia* were mainly the result of their own work, for instance sons engaged in commerce, and neither the emperors nor the jurists stepped in to make them more independent from their fathers.[97] The privileges related to the *peculium castrense* only become explicable in the broader context of the benefits that soldiers enjoyed in legal relations: as one of the many means to make the military service more attractive, and specifically to compensate for the soldiers' inexperience in legal affairs.[98] The growing privileges associated with the *peculium castrense* probably also reflect the political weight that the army gained over time and exploited to receive more favorable treatment.

Is there anything we can infer from the *peculium castrense* and the *peculium quasi castrense* to better understand the standard *peculium*'s role in ancient society? First, many of the special provisions confirm, through an *argumentum e contrario*, the standard *peculium*'s limited independence from the person who exerts authority over the *peculium* holder, a fact that questions both the *peculium*'s character as a gift and its suitability to fund larger businesses. Another important *argumentum e contrario* can be derived from the provision that items belonging to the *peculium castrense* are protected against claims by the father's creditors.[99] This is a clear indication that the standard *peculium* lacks such shielding, an important detail that the proponents of the *peculium*'s employment for investments in larger businesses have overlooked so far.[100] Last but not least, neither the *peculium castrense* nor the *peculium quasi castrense* could have served as a basis for common business ventures because they were not open to slaves. This is again an indication that the *peculium*'s main field of application was outside the funding of larger business enterprises.

sunt parta labore militiae placuit non esse in corpore census, omne tenet cuius regimen pater (whether this satire is really by Juvenal or not does not matter in this context).

[97] For an exception, see *Inst.* 2.9.1: *quod autem ex alia causa sibi filius familias adquisivit, huius usum fructum quidem patri adquiret, dominium autem apud eum remaneat, ne, quod ei suis laboribus* [!] *vel prospera fortuna accessit, hoc in alium perveniens luctuosum ei procedat.*

[98] As generally noted by *CJ* 6.30.22.pr. (Justinian, 531 CE): *arma etenim magis quam iura scire milites sacratissimus legislator existimavit.* In the context of the *peculium castrense*, see *Inst.* 2.11.pr.: *supra dicta diligens observatio in ordinandis testamentis militibus propter nimiam imperitiam constitutionibus principalibus remissa est.*

[99] *Inst.* 2.12.pr.: *quod in castris adquisierit miles... neque patris creditores id vendere vel aliter inquietare* (n. 92).

[100] For the details, see Fleckner 2010, pp. 430-437.

c. Conclusion: gift-giving and more autonomy of *peculia*

Two aspects of the trend toward more autonomy of *peculia* deserve greater attention, both for studies of the *peculium*'s social function and, more specifically, for the question of whether the *peculium* served as a legal device for donations to *personae alieno iuri subiectae*. First, all changes outlined in the foregoing sections are limited to the *peculia* of sons; none of the new rules applies to the *peculia* of slaves. Second, the increasing autonomy of certain *peculia* is almost exclusively the result of specific measures by various Roman emperors; none of the major changes is the product of Roman jurisprudence.

Both observations improve our understanding of the *peculium*'s role in Roman society. If there had been an economic demand for larger business ventures based on the *peculia* of common slaves, the Roman jurists (who had close ties to the circles that would possibly have invested in such ventures) as well as the Roman emperors (who would not have ignored such circles' wishes over a period of many centuries) would likely have removed the main legal hurdles for larger *peculia* businesses. Yet, no constitution has come down to us through which a Roman emperor stepped in, eliminated any of those barriers, and thereby made the legal regime more favorable. It is true that Roman jurisprudence came up with a rule to separate items that are dedicated to a certain branch office from other assets (a *peculium* in the form of the *merx peculiaris*).[101] However, only two fragments have survived that touch upon this rule, and their scope is limited to the creditors of the slave business; whether the slave businesses were made more stable by protecting them against interference by the masters and by the masters' creditors, is not dealt with in these two fragments – again a detail that is often overlooked by those that believe in larger business enterprises based on *peculia*.[102] In contrast, as mentioned earlier, the *peculium castrense* turned into an estate almost entirely separate from the father's property and influence. Consequently, Maecianus – one of the more conservative jurists (second century CE)[103] – wrote not of the *peculia* of slaves engaged in business, but only of the *peculium castrense* that it was separated from the father's property (*hoc peculium a patris bonis separetur*).[104] That Roman law developed more autonomy for certain *peculia* of sons, but not for the *peculia* of common slaves (where asset separation would have been among the key prerequisites to fund larger business enterprises), is a clear indication that at least in the mind of the public, the *peculium* was intended primarily for sons rather than slaves.

[101] Ulp. (29 ad ed.), *D* 14.4.5.15-16.
[102] Fleckner 2010, pp. 437-441.
[103] Compared to Papinian, Paulus, and Ulpian (n. 89).
[104] Maec. (1 fideic.), *D* 49.17.18.4.

What does this mean for the *peculium*'s possible role as a legal device for donations to *personae alieno iuri subiectae*? The answer is ambivalent: the more independent the *peculia* were, the closer they came to a 'true' gift. When the father has no right to reclaim *peculium* items, when his creditors may not seize them, and when the son is allowed to dispose of them by will, then all additions to his *peculium*, such as the farewell presents at the commencement of duties, get close to gifts that were given to *personae sui iuris*. Yet, and this is the second part of the answer that conflicts with the first part, such donations were probably not the main factor that drove the development of the new *peculia* forms. The fact that those *peculia* increasingly consisted of items acquired through the sons' own efforts is likely to have been more significant. Put differently, while the *peculium castrense* and the *peculium quasi castrense* functioned well as legal devices for donations to *personae alieno iuri subiectae*, this was only a by-product.

5. Outlook: gift-giving, *peculium* functions, and further research

Following this excursion into an institution that the 'gift economy' discourse has hitherto left unexplored: what can be learned from the *peculium* for the broader area of gift-giving in ancient Rome? The direct implications are relatively insignificant: as mentioned in two side notes, sons, slaves, and other *personae alieno iuri subiectae* were, as a general rule, not empowered to give away their *peculium* assets for free; sons, however, could donate items that belonged to their *peculium castrense*.[105] Considering the sons' and slaves' importance in Roman society, these side notes may deserve more attention by those examining the idea of a 'gift economy'. The focus of this chapter, though, was not on donations *by* sons, slaves, and other *personae alieno iuri subiectae*, but rather on the question of whether and to what extent the *peculium* could be explained as a legal device for donations *to* such persons.

From the legal sources, the focal point of scholarship so far, the *peculium*'s role in Roman society and, as a sub-item, in a possible 'gift economy' remains obscure. To begin with, the relations between persons who exert authority and those that are subject to it do not follow the traditional pattern. When a father or master leaves items to his son or slave, this transfer can constitute any or all of the following: an investment because he hopes that the son or slave will increase the value of the *peculium*; a form of exchange or trade because he expects some

[105] Donations by *personae alieno iuri subiectae* are briefly dealt with in the outline of the basic *peculium* rules (nn. 15-16 and accompanying text) as well as in the context of the increasing independence of sons in military and civil service (nn. 77-78, 81 and accompanying text).

kind of consideration in return; a stimulus for sons to show that they are prepared to take over the family business, or an incentive for slaves to work harder and make enough money to ransom themselves; a gift to recognize services that the father or master has already received; subsistence money to support the son's or slave's living; alms to please the gods; or a signal for peers that will deduce the father's or master's prosperity, *inter alia*, from his sons' and slaves' possessions. The question of whether the *peculium* fits into the notion of 'gift economy' is even more complex: if the *peculium* is employed as a legal device for donations to *personae alieno iuri subiectae*, the grantor's motivation will, as just outlined, often lie outside economic reasoning. Where masters use the *peculium* to participate indirectly in larger business ventures of their slaves, there is no doubt about their economic reasoning, but it will be difficult to discern the notion of giving in their behavior: after all, if they are mainly driven by financial motives, it is not too far-fetched to assume that they will dissolve the *peculium* or reclaim some of its items whenever they need the money for other purposes or become aware of better investment opportunities. In the latter case, the money left to the slave is neither a 'gift' nor a 'loan' but rather 'equity'. Whatever the underlying motivation for granting a *peculium* or adding to an already existing *peculium* is, it seems that *giving* for *economic reasons* was not a typical motive for persons who exert authority over the *peculium* holder, let alone the *peculium*'s main function in ancient Rome. But the *peculium* may serve as a good test case to study the various reasons that grantors may have had to make and to exchange gifts.

Donations to *personae alieno iuri subiectae* help explain the rise of the *peculium*, but the present chapter has shown that it is doubtful that the *peculium* specifically emerged as a legal device for such gifts. Is there any other rationale that could adequately explain the picture that the sources draw of the *peculium*? To date, no such reason has come up. Instead, it seems that the *peculium* was driven by a bundle of motives that varied over time and, possibly, in different places, ranging from an institution mainly in the master's interest to a vehicle for more financial autonomy of sons. However, these are all provisional assumptions because, despite prominent calls for more research,[106] there is still much to be explored.

Almost everything we know about the *peculium* today is of legal origin, while other sources only rarely, if at all, mention the term. What is the reason for this discrepancy? The most obvious answer may be that the word *peculium* was a *terminus technicus* that did not leave the legal sphere. If this is true, then the discrepancy is merely a terminological incongruity and it should not pose any

[106] Kaser 1971², pp. 287 n. 47 and 344 n. 26, as well as Finley 1985², p. 221. For the question of who is the main beneficiary of the *peculium*, the grantor or the grantee, see Wacke 1994, p. 494 n. 77 and Wacke 2006, p. 313.

problems to find non-legal sources that deal with phenomena that a Roman jurist would have called a *peculium*. However, to date only a few such instances have been brought to light, much less than the prominence of the *peculium* in the legal sources would suggest.[107] It is probably the greatest desideratum for further research, especially by scholars of the classics, to find more examples or to confirm, through a process of elimination, that the phenomenon is less prominent outside the legal sources. If more sources come up, this will greatly advance our understanding of the *peculium*'s possible role in a 'gift economy' and, more generally, of its function in ancient Rome. If it turns out that there is little additional evidence outside the legal sources, this may call the prior scholarship into question. Was the *peculium* in daily practice perhaps less important than previously thought? An overdeveloped legal institution that Roman jurists loved to discuss for the sake of its complexity – regardless of its relevance in the real world?

Bibliography

Abatino, Barbara – Giuseppe Dari-Mattiacci – Enrico Perotti: *Depersonalization of Business in Ancient Rome*, in: *Oxford Journal of Legal Studies* 31 (2011), pp. 365-389.

Alföldy, Géza: *Römische Sozialgeschichte*, Stuttgart 2011^4.

Amirante, Luigi: *Lavoro di giuristi sul peculio – Le definizioni da Q. Mucio a Ulpiano*, in: *Studi in onore di Cesare Sanfilippo*, vol. III, Milano 1983, pp. 1-15.

Andreau, Jean: *Banking and Business in the Roman World*, Cambridge 1999.

Andreau, Jean: *Les esclaves "hommes d'affaires" et la gestion des ateliers et commerces*, in: *Mentalités et choix économiques des Romains*, ed. by Jean Andreau – Jérôme France – Sylvie Pittia, Paris 2004, pp. 111-126.

Ankum, Johan Albert: *La position juridique du "filius familias" mineur en droit romain classique*, in: *Mélanges Felix Wubbe*, Fribourg 1993, pp. 1-25.

Arangio-Ruiz, Vincenzo: *La società in diritto romano*, Napoli 1950.

Arnò, Carlo: *Il contratto di società*, Torino 1938.

Aubert, Jean-Jacques: *Business Managers in Ancient Rome. A Social and Economic Study of Institores (200 B.C. – A.D. 250)*, Leiden – New York – Köln 1994.

Aubert, Jean-Jacques: *Dumtaxat de peculio: What's in a Peculium, or Establishing the Extent of the Principal's Liability*, in: *New Frontiers: Law and Society in the Roman World*, ed. by Paul J. du Plessis, Edinburgh 2013, pp. 192-206.

Bekker, Ernst Immanuel: *Zweckvermögen, insbesondere Peculium, Handelsvermögen und Actiengesellschaften*, in: *ZHR* 4 (1861), pp. 499-567.

Bona, Ferdinando: *Studi sulla società consensuale in diritto romano*, Milano 1973.

Brinkhof, Jacobus: *Een studie over het peculium in het klassieke Romeinse recht*, Meppel 1978.

[107] See n. 33 (with references to Cicero, Diodorus Siculus, Pliny the Elder, Martial, Plutarch, and Suetonius).

Buchwitz, Wolfram: *Servus alienus heres. Die Erbeinsetzung fremder Sklaven im klassischen römischen Recht*, Wien – Köln – Weimar 2012.

Bürge, Alfons: *Review of Andrea Di Porto, Impresa collettiva e schiavo "manager" in Roma antica (II sec. a. C. – II sec. d. C.)*, in: *ZRGRA 105* (1988), pp. 856-865.

Bürge, Alfons: *Römisches Privatrecht. Rechtsdenken und gesellschaftliche Verankerung: Eine Einführung*, Darmstadt 1999.

Bürge, Alfons: *Lo schiavo (in)dipendente e il suo patrimonio*, in: *Homo, caput, persona – La costruzione giuridica dell'identità nell'esperienza romana,* ed. by Alessandro Corbino – Michel Humbert – Giovanni Negri, Pavia 2010, pp. 369-391.

Buti, Ignazio: *Studi sulla capacità patrimoniale dei "servi"*, Napoli 1976.

Cerami, Pietro: *Impresa e societas nei primi due secoli dell'impero*, in: *AUPA* 52 (2007-2008), pp. 75-132.

Cerami, Pietro – Aldo Petrucci: *Diritto commerciale romano – Profilo storico*, Torino 2010^3.

Chiusi, Tiziana J.: *Diritto commerciale romano? Alcune osservazioni critiche*, in: *Studii in onore di Luigi Labruna*, vol. II, Napoli 2007, pp. 1025-1041.

del Chiaro, Emile: *Le contrat de société en droit privé romain sous la République et au temps des jurisconsultes classiques*, Paris 1928.

Di Porto, Andrea: *Impresa collettiva e schiavo "manager" in Roma antica (II sec. a. C. – II sec. d. C.)*, Milano 1984.

Di Porto, Andrea: *Filius, servus e libertus, strumenti dell'imprenditore romano*, in: *Imprenditorialità e diritto nell'esperienza storica*, ed. by Matteo Marrone, Palermo 1992, pp. 231-260.

Di Porto, Andrea: *Il diritto commerciale romano: una "zona d'ombra" nella storiografia romanistica e nelle riflessioni storico-comparative dei commercialisti*, in: *Ricerche dedicate al professor Filippo Gallo*, vol. III, Napoli 1997, pp. 413-452.

Dietzel, Gustav: *Die Commanditen-Gesellschaft und die actio tributoria*, in: *ZHR* 2 (1859), pp. 1-18.

Eck, Werner – Johannes Heinrichs: *Sklaven und Freigelassene in der Gesellschaft der römischen Kaiserzeit*, Darmstadt 1993.

Finley, Moses I.: *The Ancient Economy*, London 1985^2.

Fitting, Hermann: *Das castrense peculium in seiner geschichtlichen Entwickelung und heutigen gemeinrechtlichen Geltung*, Halle 1871.

Fleckner, Andreas M.: *Antike Kapitalvereinigungen – Ein Beitrag zu den konzeptionellen und historischen Grundlagen der Aktiengesellschaft*, Köln – Weimar – Wien 2010.

Fleckner, Andreas M.: *Review of B. Stelzenberger, Kapitalmanagement und Kapitaltransfer im Westen des Römischen Reiches*, in: *ZRGRA* 128 (2011), pp. 677-695.

Földi, András: *Remarks on the legal structure of enterprises in Roman law*, in: *RIDA* 43 (1996), pp. 179-211.

Gnoli, Franco: *Di una recente ipotesi sui rapporti tra "pecus", "pecunia", "peculium"*, in: *SDHI* 44 (1978), pp. 204-218.

Grotkamp, Nadine: *Missbrauch und Gebrauch des peculium*, in: *MBAH* 24 (2005), pp. 125-145.

Hansmann, Henry – Reinier Kraakman – Richard Squire: *Law and the Rise of the Firm*, in: *Harvard Law Review* 119 (2006), pp. 1333-1403.

Hernando Lera, Julio: *El contrato de sociedad: la casuistica jurisprudencial clasica*, Madrid 1992.

Kaser, Max: *Der Inhalt der patria potestas*, in: *ZRGRA* 58 (1938), pp. 62-85.

Kaser, Max: *Das römische Privatrecht I: Das altrömische, das vorklassische und klassische Recht*, München 1971².

Kaser, Max: *Das römische Privatrecht II: Die nachklassischen Entwicklungen*, München 1975².

Kaser, Max – Rolf Knütel: *Römisches Privatrecht*, München 2008¹⁹.

La Rosa, Franca: *I peculii speciali in diritto romano*, Milano 1953.

Labruna, Luigi: *Il diritto mercantile dei romani e l'espansionismo*, in: *Le Strade del Potere. Maiestas populi romani, Imperium, Coercitio, Commercium*, ed. by Alessandro Corbino, Catania 1994, pp. 115-137.

Lazo, Patricio: *"Iussum" y "Nominatio" en las adquisiciones a través de dependientes*, in: *REHJ* 31 (2009), pp. 141-158.

Lehmann, Burkhard: *Das Eigenvermögen der römischen Soldaten unter väterlicher Gewalt*, in: *ANRW* 2.14 (1982), pp. 183-284.

Lohsse, Sebastian: *Peculium*, in: *The Encyclopedia of Ancient History*, ed. by Roger S. Bagnall – Kai Brodersen – Craige B. Champion – Andrew Erskine – Sabine R. Huebner, Chichester 2013, vol. 9, pp. 5121-5122.

Longo, Sara: *Filius familias se obligat? Il problema della capacità patrimoniale dei filii familias*, Milano 2003.

Mastrangelo, Luigi: *Il peculium quasi castrense. Privilegio dei palatini in età tardo antica*, in: *RIDA* 52 (2005), pp. 261-308.

Meissel, Franz-Stefan: *Societas. Struktur und Typenvielfalt des römischen Gesellschaftsvertrages*, Frankfurt 2004.

Micolier, Gabriel: *Pécule et Capacité Patrimoniale. Étude sur le pécule, dit profectice, depuis l'édit "de peculio" jusqu'à la fin de l'époque classique*, Lyon 1932.

Montanari, Massimo: *Impresa e responsabilità. Sviluppo storico e disciplina positiva*, Milano 1990.

Musumeci, Francesco: *Pregiudizio del minore e protezione edittale in età imperiale*, in: *Studii in onore di Luigi Labruna*, vol. VI, Napoli 2007, pp. 3715-3737.

Pesaresi, Roberto: *Ricerche sul peculium imprenditoriale*, Bari 2008.

Petrucci, Aldo: *Mensam exercere: studi sull'impresa finanziaria romana (II secolo a. C. – metà del III secolo d. C.)*, Napoli 1991.

Petrucci, Aldo: *Profili giuridici delle attività e dell'organizzazione delle banche romane*, Torino 2002.

Poggi, Agostino: *Il contratto di società in diritto romano classico*, Torino 1930-1934.

Roesler, Carl F. H.: *Die rechtliche Natur des Vermögens der Handelsgesellschaften nach römischem Rechte*, Erlangen 1860.

Rostovtzeff, Michael: *The Social and Economic History of the Roman Empire*, Oxford 1957².

Saller, Richard P.: *Patriarchy, Property and Death in the Roman Family*, Cambridge 1994.

Santucci, Gianni: *Il socio d'opera in diritto romano: conferimenti e responsabilità*, Padova 1997.

Schumacher, Leonhard: *Sklaverei in der Antike. Alltag und Schicksal der Unfreien*, München 2001.

Serrao, Feliciano: *Impresa e responsabilità a Roma nell'età commerciale. Forme giuridiche di un'economia-mondo*, Pisa 1989.

Szlechter, Émile: *Le contrat de société en Babylonie, en Grèce et à Rome. Étude de Droit comparé de l'Antiquité*, Paris 1947.

Talamanca, Mario: *Società (dir. rom.)*, in: *Enciclopedia del diritto*, vol. 42, Varese 1990, pp. 814-860.

Taubenschlag, Rafał: *The Law of Greco-Roman Egypt in the Light of the Papyri (332 B.C. – 640 A.D.)*, Warszawa 1955[2].

von Jhering, Rudolf: *Geist des römischen Rechts auf den verschiedenen Stufen seiner Entwicklung*, vol. 2.1, Leipzig 1854.

von Mandry, Gustav: *Das gemeine Familiengüterrecht mit Ausschluss des ehelichen Güterrechtes*, vol. II, Tübingen 1876.

von Uxkull-Gyllenband, Moritz A. W.: *Peculium*, in: *RE*, vol. 37, Stuttgart 1937, coll. 13-16.

Wacke, Andreas: *Peculium non ademptum videtur tacite donatum. Zum Schicksal des Sonderguts nach der Gewaltentlassung*, in: *Iura* 42 (1991), pp. 43-95.

Wacke, Andreas: *Die Notbedarfseinrede des enterbten Haussohns*, in: *SDHI* 60 (1994), pp. 469- 497.

Wacke, Andreas: *Die libera administratio peculii. Zur Verfügungsmacht von Hauskindern und Sklaven über ihr Sondergut*, in: *Sklaverei und Freilassung im römischen Recht*, ed. by Thomas Finkenauer, Berlin – Heidelberg – New York 2006, pp. 251-316.

Wieacker, Franz: *Societas: Hausgemeinschaft und Erwerbsgesellschaft. Untersuchungen zur Geschichte des römischen Gesellschaftsrechts 1*, Weimar 1936.

Żeber, Ireneusz: *A Study of the peculium of a Slave in Pre-Classical and Classical Roman Law*, Wrocław 1981.

Zimmermann, Reinhard: *The Law of Obligations. Roman Foundations of the Civilian Tradition*, Cape Town – Wetton – Johannesburg 1990.

MARTA GARCÍA MORCILLO

Limiting Generosity: Conditions and Restrictions on Roman Donations

1. Introduction

Can a gift under condition still be considered a gift? To what extent did legal rules of gift-giving match, contest or contradict the principle of altruism – but also of reciprocity and self-interest – that were commonly associated with acts of *liberalitas* in Roman literature? The present article will discuss the specific case of the *donatio* and the problems and challenges – moral, legal, social and economic – posed by it. After a short introduction, I will look at the conflicts between ideal purposes and practices of gift-giving in Roman literature, above all in the philosophical treaties by Cicero (*De Officiis*) and Seneca (*De Beneficiis*), but also at a few comparative empirical cases outlined by authors such as Martial and Pliny the Younger. A brief insight of Roman classical law with particular emphasis on the *donatio mortis causa* and the *donatio inter virum et uxorem* will follow. The third section will discuss the Romans' search for a manageable balance between free (unlimited) generosity and self-interest in gifts between individuals.

2. Gift-giving in Roman law: an outline

In order to frame the questions outlined above it is useful to look briefly at some basic definitions of this practice in the Digest. Under Roman law, only persons in full possession (*personae sui iuris*) could make gifts.[1] Donations could consist of money, estates and different sorts of objects, including non-material ones, such as the right to use someone's house,[2] or a pact with a debtor to delay the release of the payment of the debt.[3] Excluded from gifts were the income or *usufructus* of a property given itself as a gift, yet gifts could also involve the cultivation of another person's land, in which case the donee did not

[1] Ulp. (44 ad Sab.), *D* 39.5.7.pr. Note, for instance, the exceptions of sons in military and civil service and of the son-in-power who has been given a free administration of his *peculium* by the *pater familias* and who was specifically granted the faculty of making gifts. On the *peculium* see Fleckner in this volume.
[2] Papin. (29 quaest.), *D* 39.5.27.
[3] Pomp. (33 ad Sab.), *D* 39.5.9.pr. See also below.

have any right of retention of expenses incurred in the cultivation[4]. An important aspect to take into account is also that gifts needed to always be measurable in money, because this was the only way to put a limit to their size. A text by Gaius specifies in this regard that gifts could not be sized in respect to offspring, fruits, rent, or wages.[5] As we will see below, Gaius' reasoning addresses specifically the apparent contradiction of a gift being transformed into a marketable commodity. So how did this legal doctrine harmonise with the altruistic aims of gift-giving and the moral considerations attached to them?

The jurist Julian differentiates between *donationes* in the proper sense, which are those made for no other reason than to practice liberality (*liberalitas*) and generosity (*munificentia*), and conditional gifts made

> "with the intention that it should become the property of the recipient only after something else has happened", or "with the intention that it should immediately become the property of the recipient but that if something else does or does not happen, it should revert to himself".[6]

The *donatio mortis causa* was included in this category. As Ulpian states, it was indeed of great importance to define the *causa* of a donation and the *conditio* set upon it because a recovery (*repetitio*) of the gift by the donor was applicable in the second case.[7]

The clear setting of two categories of donations – with or without conditions – can be understood as a recognition that the conditional gift was not driven by pure generosity, but by a reciprocal relation of exchange. Should we then speak of reciprocity in this case, considering that the return of that something-to-be-done in exchange of the gift could not be avoided and had been fixed in advance? And to make things even more complicated, can we speak at all about reciprocity for cases in which the condition to fulfil is not in the same category as the thing given by the donor? The donation *sub condicione* was also clearly not a matter of exchange of favours or *a do ut des* issue. What was it then? An insight into casuistry will hopefully help us to better understand the flexibility, but also the complexities of this multifaceted phenomenon. Why did Romans set conditions and obligations to a praxis defined *per se* by the idea of gratuity?

[4] Iulian. (17 dig.), *D* 39.5.14.

[5] Gai. (3 de legat.), *D* 39.5.11: *Cum de modo donationis quaeritur, neque partus nomine neque fructuum neque pensionum neque mercedum ulla donatio facta esse videtur.*

[6] Iulian. (17 dig.), *D* 39.5.1; transl. A. Watson.

[7] Ulp. (76 ad ed.), *D* 39.5.3.

3. Framing gratuity and generosity in Roman society

The unconditional nature of the gift represents a well-known scholarly battleground in social sciences. One of the keystones of the debate is the principle of reciprocity understood as a relationship of exchange between donor and donee that unavoidably creates debts and obligations.[8] According to some views, reciprocity emerges as a consequence (and not as the aim) of a relationship of trust that is originally enabled by a sincere and true unconditional gift. Reciprocity thus grows first in the spirit of the receiver of the gift, not in that of the giver.[9]

Gift-giving in ancient Rome addressed essential questions both on the reception and acknowledgment of gratuity and reciprocity in social relationships and on the role of utilitarism in certain forms of gifts. The limits of generosity stay indeed at the centre of a prolific discussion on the role of euergetism and public benefactions in ancient Rome started by Paul Veyne's monumental work *Le pain et le cirque* (1976),[10] and it also emerges as a revealing factor of scholarly research on patronage and *amicitia*.[11] The Roman concept of gift-exchange linked *liberalitas* with *gratia*, which involved a moral obligation to reciprocate. The importance of this mechanism for the establishment and consolidation of symmetrical relations – between friends – and asymmetrical – between patrons and clients – issued not only political and social status, but also

[8] A short insight to this debate through three fundamental authors: while Mauss explains the gift as a triple obligation of giving, receiving and repaying (1923-1924, pp. 37-41), his pupil Lévi-Strauss refers to the concept of reciprocity following the model of mercantile relationships as the key that defines this phenomenon in modern societies (1950). Bourdieu describes the gift as an *illusio* between giver and receiver, who agree to play a game of exchanges that prevails over any act of generosity (1994; 1997).

[9] Gouldner 1973, pp. 260-299, states that gift-giving should be an act of beneficence (generosity) based on the idea of 'something for nothing', and thus not on the principle of reciprocity that brings the giver closer to the *homo oeconomicus*. In this regard, Caillé 2007[2], pp. 93-119, elaborates the apparently contradictory concept of "conditional unconditionality", which acknowledges that only a gift that is demonstrably unconditional and disinterested will, in the long term, generate advantages to both the giver and the receiver. This point of view is also followed by Chanial 2011, pp. 32-40 and 52-53, who insists on the difference between exchange and gift-giving, being the first conditional and instrumental ("to give in exchange of something") and the second one unconditional and personal ("to give to someone").

[10] Veyne 1976. On Veyne's influence in scholarship see Garnsey 1991, pp. 164-168; more recently Lomas – Cornell 2003; Zuiderhoek 2007, pp. 196-213; 2009.

[11] See White 1978, pp. 79-92; Rouland 1979; Saller 1982, Wallace-Hadrill 1989; Dixon 1993, pp. 451-464; Spisak 1998, pp. 243-255; Bowditch 2001; Verboven 2002 and 2011, pp. 404-421; Griffin 2003, pp. 92-113.

economic interests and business relationships, as Verboven has demonstrated.[12] The consolidation of this phenomenon was also capital for the creation of contractual relationships.[13] As shown in the present volume, the idea of gift-giving as an integral element of an embedded economy should not be understood as a simple contrast to the rational utilitarism often applied to modern societies. In addition to the achievement of symbolic capital in form of social advantages, prestige or status,[14] gift-exchange contributed to specific economic needs and aims, to the acquisition and transfer of wealth and to the achievement of profit. The attribution of a monetary value to gifts not only helped to solve conflicts of legitimate possession, but was also evidence of the metamorphosis of the thing given into a good that could enrich and impoverish.

In exploring the tensions, conflicts and compatibilities between self-interest and generosity in gift-giving, both moral and legal literature shared the same preoccupation for keeping the spirit of an honourable praxis, despite the utilitarian goals often attached to it. In the case of the *donatio,* rather than an example of the contradictions between philosophical-moral theory and praxis, the limitations and conditions imposed on this action should be regarded as a complementary, measured response to both.

Cicero's *De Officiis* and Seneca's *De Beneficiis* are our most important sources for the understanding of the moral considerations that framed gift-giving in Roman society. While Cicero's work addresses mainly the relationship between state and citizen, Seneca explores the interpersonal relationships between individuals in more depth. The importance of private property emerges in both authors as an essential principle of social cohesion.[15]

Following the model of Panaetius' moral treaty bearing the same title, Cicero's *De Officiis* was intended as a guide to marrying moral principles and economic interests,[16] a balance between duties (*officia*) and benefits (*beneficia*).[17] Written towards the end of 44 BCE, Cicero's *De Officiis* also discusses contemporary problems, such as the limits of generosity (*liberalitas*),[18] and the injustices provoked by those who harm others in their desire for magnificence and glory (*cupidi splendori et gloriae*). Specific examples of this

[12] Verboven 2002. On volume and scale as key factors to understanding the importance of these social bonds, see pp. 23-32.

[13] On the importance of *fides* and *gratia* in the creation of legal contracts, see Michel 1962. On *nexum* and *mancipatio* see Watson 1975, pp. 111-149.

[14] Bourdieu 1994, pp. 41-51.

[15] See in particular the last section of this present paper on *temperantia*.

[16] On Panaetius' influence in Cicero's *De officiis*, see Gärtner 1974; Lefèvre 2001. On the economic and ethical models in *De Officiis* see Lotito 1981, pp. 79-126; Narducci 1985, pp. 93-125.

[17] This model is discussed by Feuvrier-Prévolat 1985, pp. 257-290.

[18] See in particular Cic., *Off.* 1.42.

damaging practice are the cases of Sulla and Caesar, who transferred money from lawful owners to aliens.[19] *Liberalitas* should, in Cicero's mind, be driven by *cautio* because otherwise gifts and liberal acts can also be the consequence of the greed to plunder and mask the desire of the giver for glory and ostentation.[20]

While the political and economic competition of Late Republican *nobiles*, their resulting indebtedness, and the mobility of fortunes provide a strong momentum for Cicero's denunciation of the abuses of *liberalitas*,[21] the author also addresses the principles that should lead any act of generosity to the wider community, in addition to the relationship between giver and receiver. According to Cicero, *beneficentia* should match *dignitas*, which implies also that the *vir bonus* should be very cautious when choosing the person he wants to benefit, and he should conduct himself with the best of virtues: *modestia*, *temperantia* and *iustitia*.[22] Cicero is concerned about reciprocity and gratitude, noting that the *vir bonus* should always return a benefit given to him.[23] The *animus* of the giver is also considered by Cicero as the key that qualifies the nature of the favour, a spirit that should not be driven by rashness or sudden impulses (*multa temeritate quadam sine iudicio*), but should look instead at those that are most in need, starting by those to whom he has social bonds.[24] In addition to avoiding harming others, Cicero recommends that individual generosity should also take into account the limits of the individual's own resources.[25] This idea, as we will see below, marries altruism in social relationships with the essential role played by patrimony, its preservation and its enlargement in elite mentality.[26]

Seneca's *De beneficiis* is no doubt our most important source for the understanding of the ideological frame that explained and justified generosity in the form of benefits (as gifts or services) within the context of social relationships.[27] As Griffin has shown, we need to look at this work not only as a Stoic

[19] Cic., *Off.* 1.43.
[20] Cic., *Off.* 1.44.
[21] On the problem of debts that affected the *nobiles* in Cicero's times, see Royer 1967, pp. 191-240; Ioannatou 2006; Rollinger 2009. On the high mobility of properties in this period see Rawson 1976, pp. 85-102.
[22] Cic., *Off.* 1.45; 1.46. Cicero adds that *fortis animus et magnus* does not help in a man who is not perfect and not wise but too impetuous (*ferventior plerum*).
[23] Cic., *Off.* 1.47.
[24] Cic., *Off.* 1.49-50. On the application of these ideas in Cicero's relationships of clientelism and patronage see extensively Deniaux 1993; Verboven 2002.
[25] Cic., *Off.* 1.52.
[26] As Cicero himself admitted, the loss of patrimony due to political or economic reasons represented a sort of social death: *Quinct.* 49-50; *Rosc. Amer.* 21-23. The need to enlarge their own patrimony through diverse economic and financial activities was also a priority for upper class Romans, cf. Andreau 1999, pp. 9-29; Minaud 2005, pp. 106-109.
[27] On *De Beneficiis* see: Chaumartin 1985; Griffin 2003, pp. 92-113; Fear 2007, pp. 460-468; Engberg-Pedersen 2008, pp. 15-44; Li Causi 2009, pp. 227-252.

treaty that elevates *beneficia* as a philosophical – and almost unattainable – ideal, but as a proper social guide and a pattern of conduct to be followed by virtuous Romans in their relationships among equals.[28] *De beneficiis* also provides a valuable, complementary contribution to the complex and pragmatic juridical treatment of this phenomenon. The essential principle of Seneca's Stoic conception of *beneficium* is liberality, meaning the absolute lack of expectations by the donor, other than the gratitude of the receiver.[29] The clear statement *beneficium qui dat, vult excipi grate* defines a benefit as a pure act of altruism in opposition to *negotiatio*, in which a giver wishes for something to be given in exchange.[30] As for the beneficiary, he should receive in the same spirit (*animus*) in which the thing was given. A different attitude, according to Seneca, would mean the submission of the benefit to the worst of the conditions: the expectation of a reward or compensation.[31] Seneca clarifies that the clue to the benefit does not reside in the nature of what is given – material things or services; these are just marks (*signa*) of the real gift, which lies in the spirit (*animus*), in the will (*voluntas*) of the giver.[32] The spirit by itself should thus fulfil the giver, regardless how the thing is received.[33] Accordingly, no bonds or obligations should be imposed by the giver since a benefit is not a loan.[34] However, Seneca envisages a sort of reciprocity in the relationship between giver and receiver by

[28] Griffin 2003, pp. 92-113. Seneca describes himself his work as a *lex vitae*: *Ben.* 1.4.2.

[29] Seneca insists that the purpose of the benefit should be to service and give pleasure, Sen., *Ben.* 2.31.2.

[30] Sen., *Ben.* 2.31.2: *Non enim in vicem aliquid sibi reddi voluit; aut non fuit beneficium, sed negotiatio;* 2.31.3: *beneficium qui dat, vult exipi grate; habet, quod voluit, si bene acceptum est. Sed speravit emolumenti aliquid. Non fuit hoc beneficium, cuius proprium est nihil de reditu cogitare.*

[31] Sen., *Ben.* 2.31.4: *Quod accipiebam, eo animo accepi, quo dabatur: reddidi. Alioqui pessima optimae rei condicio est: ut gratus sim, ad fortunam mittor! Si illa invita respondere non possum, sufficit animus animo.*

[32] Sen., *Ben.* 1.5.1-2: *Debere enim se ait alius pecuniam, quam accepit, alius consulatum, alius sacerdotium, alius provinciam. Ista autem sunt meritorum signa, non merita. Non potest beneficium manu tangi; res animo geritur. Multum interest inter materiam beneficii et beneficium; itaque nec aurum nec argentum nec quicquam eorum, quae pro maximis accipiuntur, beneficium est, sed ipsa tribuentis voluntas.*

[33] Seneca provides in this passage a definition of benefit, Sen., *Ben.* 1.6.1-2: *Quid est ergo beneficium? Benevola actio tribuens gaudium capiensque tribuendo in id, quod facit, prona et sponte sua parata. Itaque non, quid fiat aut quid detur, refert, sed qua mente, quia beneficium non in eo, quod fit aut datur, consistit, sed in ipso dantis aut facientis animo. Magnum autem esse inter ista discrimen vel ex hoc intellegas licet, quod beneficium utique bonum est, id autem, quod fit aut datur, nec bonum nec malum est.*

[34] Sen., *Ben.* 4.40.5; 6.35-3-4. Cf. Griffin 2003, p. 99.

considering that the benefit is simply paid by gratitude, because gratitude and not the thing given is the equivalent of the giver's *animus*.[35]

Seneca's particular conception of reciprocity should, however, not be regarded as a simple exchange of *beneficia*. Giving, receiving and returning are for him benefits in their own right, and not part of an intentional chain of interests. They are united by a sort of invisible circle that he compares with the continuous and harmonious hand-dance of the three Graces, which is neither restricted nor properly tied.[36] This rather ethereal notion of *beneficia* contrasts with other passages of the work, in which gratitude appears in the form of an expectation and investment by the giver.[37] In two passages Seneca compares the giver of benefits with a farmer that has to be more careful in choosing the ground when he has experienced sterility after sowing (a metaphor for the ungrateful receiver of benefits).[38]

Assuming that Seneca faces unavoidable tensions and conflicts between the idealisation of elite social relationships and on-ground experience of those relationships, we can recognise in this work an effort to show the grateful receiver as an extra motivation for the giver, who should in any case assume gift-giving as a benefit by itself. The recommendation to select and discriminate benefits supplies a truly practical contour to Seneca's philosophical work that is specifically addressed to the *vir bonus*. And it is in this frame – as in Cicero's *De Officiis* – where we meet a plausible and adequate response to the limits of generosity. In this regard Seneca specifies what sort of benefits should be given and in what way.[39] The classification starts with what is considered necessary (*necessaria*), because without it we are not able to live (*sine quibus non possumus vivere*). Within this group, Seneca settles a second level of necessary benefits, which include *libertas*, *pudicitia* and *mens bona*, as well as the essential elements that shape the identity of the *pater familias* (e.g. children, wives and household gods).[40] The second category are useful *beneficia* (*utilia*), without which we should not live (*non debemus*), and it is composed of benefits such as

[35] Accordingly, goodwill should be repaid by goodwill, Sen., *Ben*. 2.35.1.

[36] Sen., *Ben*. 1.3.2-5. According to Griffin 2003, p. 97, this metaphoric digression tries to explain the horizontal relationships of *amicitia* as a link between equals.

[37] See in this regard Fear 2007, pp. 460-468. Saller 1982, p. 12, defends the idea of mutual benefits between giver and receiver in the practice of generosity. On Seneca's use of *creditum* to define *beneficia* and on the resort to economic concepts in *De Beneficiis*, see Li Causi 2009, pp. 232-246.

[38] Sen., *Ben*. 4.9.2 and 7.32. The passages are commented by Fear 2007, pp. 465-466, who compares them with the anecdote in 1.14.4, in which Seneca judges positively the benefits of the virtuous man with those generously given by a *meretrix* to her clients and argues that in both there is a will to maximise the return, in this case of *beneficia amabilia*.

[39] Sen., *Ben*. 1.11.

[40] Sen., *Ben*. 1.11.4.

money – yet not in excess (*pecunia non superfluens*) – and beyond what is reasonable, as well as public offices and the process that makes it possible to progress in the *cursus honorum*.[41] All benefits beyond these two categories are considered superfluous (*ex abundanti*), and thus require a careful and measurable choice by the giver.[42] The third, and last, category is constituted by things that are pleasurable (*iucunda*) – particularly those that endure (*mansura*) – and without which we are not willing to live (*sine quibus nolumus*). Seneca's preference for giving things that are endurable and as imperishable as possible is explained by the importance he gives to keeping alive the memory of the benefit by letting the object speak by itself, particularly to those who have been ungrateful.[43] The detailed discrimination and the setting of hierarchies of *beneficia* define Seneca's handling of this elusive and complex phenomenon; his aim is to supply clear patterns of conduct to social relationships and responses to the ambivalent *animus* of a gift-giver.

The need to discriminate and regulate *liberalitas*, and the preoccupations about the impact of generosity on the management of private resources expressed by Cicero and Seneca find valuable testimonial replica in authors such as Martial and Pliny the Younger. From different genres both authors report first-hand situations in which gift-giving not only appears as an indispensable instrument of social relationships, but as a practice that reinforces and challenges patrimonial wealth.

The list of epigrams dealing with gifts given, neglected, expected, negotiated and returned (or not) is so large that they represent a recurring theme in Martial's work.[44] As Spisak states, rather than mirroring Martial's preference for human sordidness, material interests and selfishness, gift-giving emerges in the poems as a normalised act inherent in social bonds such as those of friendship and patronage.[45] Gifts and gift-giving in Martial measure attitudes towards wealth and patrimony. Well-known are the so called 'gift-as-hooks' epigrams, which denounce abuses to institutions such as marriage and succession by will and

[41] Sen., *Ben*. 1.11.5.

[42] Sen., *Ben*. 1.11.5-6.

[43] Sen., *Ben*. 1.12.1. Seneca even shows his preference for wrought silver rather than coined silver (*libentius donabo argentum factum quam signatum*), for *signa* rather than *vestes* that are supposed to deteriorate rapidly. The reason for this is that some tend to keep gratitude only so long as the gifts are in use.

[44] This issue is extensively discussed by Spisak 1998, pp. 243-255; 2007, pp. 35-51.

[45] In Martial we often find the contrast between friends who expect to share their fortunes and to engage in a real sustainable reciprocity (5.42: *extra fortunam est quidquid donator. Quas dederis solas semper habebis opes*) and others who measure friendship through the weight and value of the gifts received (9.71; 10.29). Martial also deals with the problems of the obligation of giving and of the impossibility to please everyone (e.g. 9.55; 10.11).

dowry-hunters,[46] and by suitors of wealthy men or women.[47] On occasions, gifts and debts to friends go hand in hand and are part of *amicitia* bonds that characterise long-lasting relationships and make a complex network of obligations, favours and contra-favours from reciprocity.[48]

Pliny's attitudes towards gifts, as well as towards loans, sales and other sorts of transactions can be placed midway between moral concerns, social obligations and his own lucrative interests.[49] The need to justify his actions and to explain his aims, particularly in those cases where the perspective of profit shadows his own conduct, permit the reader to discern the differences and limits between what is rightful and what is not. For instance, the concern for his own reputation and the acknowledgement of social and legal rules play a relevant role in a gift arranged between Pliny and Ausidius Curianus. Curianus agreed to give him the equivalent of the share inherited by Pliny according to the will of Pomponia Galla, who was the mother of Curianus and who had disinherited him.[50] By accepting the deal, Pliny publicly renounced his share to the benefit of Curianus. The latter could in this way restore his reputation, while Pliny would get his money back through a donation that was conditioned by the agreement (*tacita conventione*).[51]

4. *Donatio* in Roman law: conditions and restrictions

As we have seen above, monetary estimations of gifts were aimed at resolving conflicts and avoiding irregularities and abuses and, as Seneca recognised, they were also morally acceptable if they were reasonable. The need to regulate gifts can be traced back to the *lex Publicia de cereis* (209 BCE) and the *lex Cincia de donis et muneribus* (204 BCE).

While the first, according to Macrobius, forbade gifts made with selfish purposes by clients (*per avaritiam a clientibus ambitiose munera*) during the

[46] Cf. Mart. 5.18: *imitantur hamos dona*. In this sense see also Mart. 6.62; 6.63; 8.27; 11.44; 11.55; 11.67; 11.86. Martial gives presents to someone who has promised to name him heir to a quarter of his estate, cf. 9.48. In 8.38, Martial explains the difference between real generosity and the selfish purposes of legacy hunters through the case of Melior, who persisted in honouring the memory of his friend after his death. On gifts as hooks see also 5.18 and Verboven's paper in this volume.

[47] See for instance Mart. 1.10.

[48] See Mart. 2.30; 2.41; 2.43 and 2.44. According to Martial both loans and gifts are expected from friends.

[49] On Pliny's thoughts and practices of *liberalitas* see Griffin 2007, pp. 469-474.

[50] Plin., *Ep*. 5.1.1-3.

[51] On Pliny's concerns about legal formalities regarding gifts see also Plin., *Ep*. 2.4.2; 7.18.2; 10.4.2. Cf. Sherwin-White 1966, pp. 312-313.

Saturnalia, other than the traditional, symbolic candles,[52] the extracts of the *lex Cincia* known to us reveal certain exceptions to a general prohibition of donations among individuals.[53] Among the prohibitions the law prevented advocates – whose services were supposed to be non-remunerated – from accepting gifts in payment for their professional activity. Although this prohibition was certainly taken into account at the end of the Republic, Cicero shows that remunerations were regularly accepted despite legal restrictions.[54] Later legislations tried to regulate this situation by imposing a legal limit to the remuneration of advocates.[55] The *lex Cincia* also established an exception to the prohibition of gift-giving to certain *personae*, including relatives up to a certain degree, which allowed, for instance, gifts between husband and wife.[56] As we will see, this *exceptio* regarding the *donatio inter virum et uxorem* was revoked between the end of the Republic and the Augustan age, when this practice had already become a source of patrimonial conflicts. The *lex Cincia* further permitted gifts not exceeding a certain amount. The specific figure is, however, not known to us. This restriction reflected the liberal character of the law, but also the concerns regarding the splitting of patrimonial goods, anticipating the criticism towards excessive gifts formulated by Cicero in *De officiis*.[57] The sensibility of the law towards the malpractice of gifts in connection with the increasing mobility of patrimonial fortunes in Rome since the Middle Republic would explain why it stipulated the possibility of the revocability or *replicatio* of the gift by the donor, which made the *donatio* imperfect in juridical terms.

A *donatio* was considered as an *actio donationis causa* that implied a free patrimonial attribution, thus a voluntary transfer of a property in benefit of a particular person.[58] Accordingly, the action should not impose obligations on the

[52] Macrob., *Sat.* 1.7.33. Macrobius explains this old custom in *Sat.* 1.7.31-32.

[53] On the *lex Cincia* see Casavola 1960 and Recoder de Casso 2005.

[54] In *Mur.* 8, Cicero refers to the generous rewards he has received for his services as advocate: *nam cum praemia mihi tanta pro hac industria sint*. A letter written by Cicero to Atticus in 60 BCE, *Ep. Att.* 1.20.6, shows that the Arpinate accepted a gift of a book, after being sure that the *lex Cincia* would allow it. Later sources report the famous anecdote of the orator Hortensius, who was accused by Cicero of accepting a silver sphynx from Verres for his services at court: Plut., *Cic.* 11, Plin., *NH* 34.18, Quint., *Inst. Or.* 6.3.98.

[55] A letter by Pliny the Younger reports a polemic edict under Claudius that prosecuted clients who paid sums superior to 10.000 for legal assistance: Plin., *Ep.* 5.9. See also Tac., *Ann.* 11.6; Ulp. (8 de omn. trib.), *D* 50.13.1.10-11. Cf. Crook 1995, pp. 129-131; Verboven 2002, pp. 76-77. A passage by Martial confirms the common practice of remunerating the patron at court: Mart. 1.98.

[56] Paul. (71 ad ed.), *Fr. Vat.* 298-311; cf. *Fontes Iuris Romani Antiqui*, vol. I^7, n. 5.

[57] Cic., *Off.* 1.44; 2.54: *multi enim patrimonia effunderunt inconsulte largiendo*. As noted by Biondi 1961, p. 28 and Verboven 2002, pp. 77-78.

[58] Both expressions appear as synonyms in a further passage by Ulp. (50 ad ed.), *D* 2.15.1.

donee, although it could include conditional or modal restrictions, as seen above.[59] The contrary of *liberalitas* was *negotium*. This point is made clear by a commentary to the *lex Iulia et Papia* by Paul, who explicitly opposes *liberalitas* to *negotia* in the case of the troubling *donatio mortis causa*.[60] However, this did not prevent the jurists from allowing actions that combined both business transactions and gifts.[61] These sorts of pseudo-donations were still acknowledged as *donationes* because what defined them was the *animus donandi*, meaning here not the altruistic spirit of the donor, but rather the will to accomplish the gift through an agreement.[62] The *donatio* was thus not a typical act or legal instrument – as a contrast to the testament – but a *causa* of juridical acts, which also made possible the revocability until its execution. Although donations could be accomplished through unilateral instruments (e.g. *delegatio*), bilateral agreements, such as *mancipatio*, *stipulatio*, *traditio*, *pactum*, *in iure cessio* etc., are more commonly attested. Especially prevalent was the *mancipatio*. Originally conceived as a formal act of acquisition of *res mancipi*, this procedure gradually became an act of conveyance for different purposes, including the *donatio*. The agreement was originally performed through the weighting of a piece of bronze on a balance (*per aes et libram*), which was later substituted by the symbolic payment of a piece of coin to the donor.[63] Mauss drew attention towards this ritual in order to show that early Roman law bore the traces of a 'primitive' gift-exchange economy.[64] Yet, beyond this image of archaism, the continuity of the symbolic ritual of the *mancipatio* during the Principate reveals the need to resort to this bilateral performance to formalise the transfer of the property in *causae* – such as the *donatio* – that were not proper juridical acts and were considered imperfect due to their revocability.[65] The performance and its

[59] As Biondi explains (1961, p. 31), the possibility of *revocatio* of the thing was not conceived as an obligation imposed to the *donatio* but a circumstance admitted by the *actio donationis*.

[60] Paul. (6 ad l. Iul. et Pap.), *D* 39.6.35.3.

[61] This is explicitly stated in a passage by Ulpian (71 ad ed.), *D* 39.5.18.pr.: *Aristo ait, cum mixtum sit negotium cum donatione, obligationem non contrahi eo casu, quo donatio est, et ita et Pomponius eum existimare refert.*

[62] According to Biondi 1961, pp. 35-36 both *animus donandi* and *liberalitas* were inalienable elements of the *donatio*. Michel 1962, pp. 237-240; 293 clarifies that the validity of the juridical act depended upon the objective declared will of the donor (*animus donandi*) independently from his subjective aims (e.g. *liberalitas*).

[63] The ritual *per aes et libram* was linked with the ancient institution of *nexum* and is recorded in the literary sources, e.g. Varr., *LL* 7.105. On the creation and evolution of the *mancipatio* from sale to conveyance as a consequence of the consolidation of private property in Rome, see Watson 1968, pp. 16-20; Diósdi 1970, pp. 62-74.

[64] Mauss 1923-1924, pp. 47-53.

[65] This circumstance was later reformed in a law by Constantine in the year 323 CE (*CTh.* 8.12.4) that created the so called *donatio perfecta*: an irrevocable gift that left the *lex*

meaning is best described by Gaius in his *Institutiones*, in which *mancipatio* is defined as an *imaginaria venditio*.[66] The act of gift-giving is thus frequently referred to as *mancipatio donationis causa nummo uno*.[67] The formal ritual of the *mancipatio* was necessary to validate the act and to foster and protect the *animus donandi*. The handing over of a coin symbolised also the acquisition of the gift by the donee. If a gift could formally change hands against a sesterce, how should we understand that the same gift might be also subjected to a 'real' monetary estimation? This apparent contradiction can be explained if we consider that the gift given (e.g. an estate) turned into a possession of the donee and it was under this new form – which is separated from the act of donation – that the thing could be regulated and limited according to its economic estimation.

Assuming that classical Roman law considered donation as an imperfect, revocable act of *liberalitas*, and that it was precisely the gratuity of this act, which remained as an inalienable principle of this practice, how did Roman legislators struggle with the challenges of conditional gifts? The regulations of conditions are extensively discussed in cases regarding wills and legacies that are grouped in *Digest* 35.1. Despite the protection of the testator's will by law, any *condicio* imposed to a donee should not be impossible to fulfil.[68] In a commentary to a rescript of Antoninus Pius, Valens states that legates should consider the latest *condicio* settled (*in legatis novissimam*), while gifts should be expected to have the lightest one (*in libertatibus levissimam conditionem spectandam esse*).[69] Julian differentiates between two sorts of conditions: those

Cincia without effect. The law by Constantine also allowed that a simple promise to give could be used as a consensual contract in gifts with a value of less than 500 *solidi*. Higher sums required still a formal agreement. Cf. Biondi 1961, p. 25

[66] The performance included an oral formula by the taker of the *mancipatio*, who confirmed the 'purchase' (*mihi emptus*) according to Quiritary right, the presence of witnesses and the use of bronze scales, Gai., *Inst.* 1.119. The *mancipatio* might involve *servi* to free persons, *animalia* and *praedia*: Gai., *Inst.* 1.121. The use of bronze pieces that were originally weighted is traced back by Gaius to the Twelve Tables: Gai., *Inst.* 1.122.

[67] Funerary inscriptions attest to this ritual in donations of *loca*, *monumenta* and *ollae*. For examples from Rome see Caldelli – Crea – Ricci 2004, pp. 312-324. The use of an imaginary sale was thus necessary to secure the full transfer of ownership in cases involving properties under *ius Italicum,* see Ulp., *Fr.* 19.6 Bäcking. The gift of provincial land did not require *mancipatio*, Gai., *Inst.* 1.120; *Fr. Vat.* 259; 293; 313. On a possible donation under *ius Italicum* in Hispania Tarraconensis see Plin., *Ep.* 10.4.3. Cf. Biondi 1961, p. 25.

[68] See for instance Ulp. (6 ad Sab.), *D* 35.1.3: *Optinuit impossibiles condiciones testamento adscriptas pro nullis habendas*; Ulp. (5 disp.), *D* 35.1.19: *In condicionibus primum locum voluntas defuncti optinet eaque regit condiciones.*

[69] Val. (1 fideic.), *D* 35.1.87. Gaius specifies that if the *libertas* is made by

of fact that depended on something happening at certain point, and those established by law, which were required to be satisfied by the heir.[70] Paul divides the latter between those that depend on something that needs to be given (*ut quid detur*), and on something that needs to be done (*ut quid fiat*).[71] In case of unfulfillment, an *usucapio* could be applied against the donee. Roman jurists also regulated more complex situations, such as the case of a gift accomplished through an intermediary,[72] a circumstance that might mask the remission of a debt by the donor to a creditor. A passage by Gaius clearly states that anything owed needed to be deducted first – also in the case of hypothecated land given as a gift.[73] In addition, Julian discussed the remission of debts through indirect donations of money agreed bilaterally by stipulation, a practice that could be equalled to a *delegatio*.[74] The main preoccupation shown by the jurists in the Digest was thus to prevent any responsibility transferred to the donee regarding possible debts carried by the donor and illegal appropriations by intermediaries.[75]

a. *Donatio mortis causa*

The *donatio mortis causa* was one of the most common forms of gift *sub condicione*.[76] Marcian's definition of this special sort of conditional gift explains its aims and essence:

fideicommissum, again the later condition should prevail, Gai. (1 fideic.), *D* 35.1.90.

[70] Iulian. (31 dig.), *D* 35.1.21: *Multum interest, condicio facti an iuris esset: nam huiusmodi condiciones 'si navis ex Asia venerit' 'si Titius consul factus 'erit', quamvis impletae* essent, *impedient heredem circa adeundam hereditatem, quamdiu ignoraret eas impletas esse: quae vero ex iure venient, in his nihil amplius exigendum, quam ut impletae sint.* A temporal condition is exemplified by Julian through the hypothetical case of "Titius who gives me money on the condition that the money becomes mine when Seius is elected consulship. When this happens the money will be mine, even if the donor dies in between", Iulian. (60 dig.), *D* 39.5.2.5; transl. A. Watson. A similar case would be the *donatio* of a slave under the condition of being released after five years, Ulp. (71 ad ed.), *D* 39.5.18.1.

[71] Paul. (7 ad l. Iul. et Pap.), *D* 35.1.60. Maecian distinguishes between temporal conditions happening during the testator's life, those expected after his death and those regarding a specific or indefinite period, Maec. (2 fideic.), *D* 35.1.91.

[72] Pomp. (17 ad Sab.), *D* 39.5.4.

[73] Gai. (3 de l. ad ed. p.), *D* 39.5.11.

[74] Iulian. (60 dig.), *D* 39.5.2.2. The action described is that A releases the debt of B by making a gift to the creditor C equivalent to the debt (see also 39.5.21). A failed gift to C would thus make A responsible according to the *stipulatio* agreement (see also 39.5.33).

[75] Iavol. (6 ep.), *D* 39.5.25.

[76] On the legal coverage of this practice see Amelotti 1953; Rüger 2011. On the *donatio mortis causa* in wills see Champlin 1991.

> "A gift *mortis causa* occurs when one wishes to have the property oneself rather than let the donee have it but even more wishes the donee to have it in preference to one's heir".[77]

A *donatio mortis causa* was generally arranged in case of imminent danger (robbery, dangerous travelling, etc.), illness, old age, or just upon reflection of own death.[78] The self-interested purpose of the *donatio mortis causa* was reinforced by the possibility of revoking the act at any time and of reclaiming the thing if the donor did not die or if he just changed his mind.[79] The hypothetical character, the conflicts with testamentary legacies, the vagueness of the *animus donandi*, and the lack of *liberalitas* questioned this practice as a proper donation.[80]

Again one of the main worries expressed by legal authors was the possibility of using the mechanism of the donation to pay debts through intermediaries. As happened with legacies, a gift *mortis causa* was invalid in the case of an insolvent donor. A further preoccupation might have concerned the possibility that a *donatio mortis causa* would replace, in certain circumstances, a will, particularly on account of the 5% inheritance tax that was charged to the heirs.[81] Gaius' *Institutes* refer to a monetary limitation of one thousand asses to be accepted from legacies and *donationes mortis causa* in the *lex Furia testamentaria* (second century BCE). Gaius also notices an easy way to avoid this prohibition for those who wanting to legate or donate: e.g. in an estate of five thousand asses, the donor could simply leave it to five different people, and by doing so dissipate the entire property.[82]

The *donatio mortis causa* presents some parallels with certain forms of Roman endowments that were aimed at preserving the interest of the donor or testator.[83] This was the case of sepulchral donations of money (e.g. to *collegia*, *municipia* etc.) made under the condition that the anniversary (*dies natalis*) of

[77] Marc. (9 inst.), *D* 39.6.1.pr.: *Mortis causa donatio est, cum quis habere se vult quam eum cui donat magisque eum cui donat quam heredem suum*; transl. A. Watson.

[78] Ulp. (32 ad Sab.), *D* 39.6.2.

[79] Paul. (6 ad l. Iul. et Pap.), *D* 39.6.35.3.

[80] An exception is the anecdote of a donor who wanted to help his uncle – who was also his debtor – in order to avoid that the latter be obligated to pay the indebted sum to his heirs in the case of the death of the former, Marcell. (l. s. resp.), *D* 39.6.28.

[81] On the *vicesima hereditatium* introduced by Augustus see Dio 55.25.1-6; Plin., *Pan*. 37-39. Cf. Günther 2005.

[82] Gai., *Inst*. 4.225.

[83] Alf. (5 dig.), *D* 35.1.27. According to Andreau 1977, pp. 157-209, two types of foundations can be distinguished: "*reflexes*" and "*non-reflexes*". While in the first the benefit of the endowment reverted to the founder himself, in the second there was a benefit towards individuals, communities and institutions.

the deceased be celebrated every year, or that flowers be set on his tomb, or that a banquet be organised in his memory.[84]

All in all, in the *donatio mortis causa* altruism seemed to be relegated to a secondary aim behind the self-interest of the giver.

b. *Donatio inter virum et uxorem*

The *donatio inter virum et uxorem* was a matter of major interest and concern for Roman legislators.[85] Its restrictive regulation in classical Roman law is linked with a reform of the *lex Cincia* possibly dated to the end of the Republic or to the Augustan age.[86] While gifts between men and women were perfectly valid before marriage, and also compatible with the dowry, this practice became quite restrictive once they became spouses.[87] Ulpian makes it clear: inter-marital gifts should be avoided, and the reason for this is

> "to prevent people from impoverishing themselves through mutual affection by means of gifts which are not reasonable (*non temperantes*), but beyond their means (*profusa*)".[88]

Ulpian insists on the problem of damaging affection by bringing to light an imperial decree of the Severans that rooted the prohibition in the belief attributed to the *maiores* that marriage based on love alone could affect the reputation (*fama*) of the spouses. The measure tried to prevent a generous partner from becoming poorer (*melior in paupertatem incideret*) and the less generous one from becoming richer (*deterior ditior fieret*).[89]

The main reason to avoid gifts between wife and husband was the need to protect the patrimony of the family transmitted preferably through the paternal

[84] See for instance *CIL* 11.132 = *ILS* 7235 = *AE* 1979.140 (Ravenna); *CIL* 14.246 (Ostia); *CIL* 6.1872 (Roma); *AE* 1987.198-199 (Ostia). On this and other cases of endowments in *collegia* see Tran 2006, pp. 174-203; Liu 2008, pp. 231-256.

[85] Accordingly, it is assigned a full title (24.1) in the Digest. On legal literature see Misera 1974; Gade 2001.

[86] While Watson 1968, pp. 229-232, attributes to Augustus the reform that restricted gifts among spouses, Gardner 1986, pp. 71-78, and Treggiari 1991, p. 370, defend an earlier date in connection to a law by Q. Mucius Scaevola: Pomp. (5 ad Q. Muc.), *D* 24.1.51.

[87] On gifts to the concubine, Papin. (12 resp.), *D* 39.5.31.

[88] Ulp. (32 ad Sab.), *D* 24.1.1: *Moribus apud nos receptum est, ne inter virum et uxorem donationes valeret. Hoc autem receptum est, ne mutuo amore invicem spoliarentur donationibus non temperantes, sed profusa erga se facilitate*; transl. A. Watson.

[89] Ulp. (32 ad Sab.), *D* 24.1.3; transl. A. Watson. On marital affection see Ulp. (33 ad Sab.), *D* 24.1.32.13.

line.[90] This was obviously very important in view of a hypothetical divorce.[91] Indeed, divorce represented the real menace to the Roman patrimonial system since being married was considered a temporary situation, and this was also reflected in the function of the dowry as a sort of loan to be returned to the wife in case of divorce.[92] This preoccupation was already evident in the Voconian Law of 169 BCE, which forbade members of the first census class to declare women as heirs and limited gifts and legacies that exceeded testamentary dispositions.[93] The status of wives and daughters at the end of the Republic and at the beginnings of the Principate in relationship to family property changed notably on account of the numerous cases of female fortunes attested.[94] The regulation of the *donatio inter virum et uxorem* and the interest of the jurists in detailing specific circumstances were principally aimed at avoiding the enrichment of the spouses (generally of the wife) at the expense of marriage.[95] This was included in a decree by Hadrian and commented by Ulpian, according to which if a woman buys properties (*praedia*) thanks to the gift given by her husband, an estimate should be made of the extent to which the woman was enriched.[96] The jurists also prevented transfers of landed property arranged between spouses with the appearance of undervalued sales.[97] The same principle was contemplated for the *locatio viliore pretio*,[98] for the *societas donationis*

[90] As Treggiari 1991, p. 379, states: "there was a clear link between *matrimonium* and *patrimonium* (the estate, strictly that of a *paterfamilias*)".
[91] As Treggiari 1991, p. 365, notes, wife and husband generally had separate property, if we exclude the dowry and wives that were *in manu*. The tendency was however towards the sharing of marital property, favouring always the husband's rights over it.
[92] On the function of the dowry and its economic importance see Saller 1994, pp. 204-224; Gardner 1998, pp. 85-93 and 234-236.
[93] On the Voconian Law see *FIRA* III, n. 70; cf. Gardner 1986, pp. 170-178; Treggiari 1991, p. 366.
[94] Treggiari 1991, p. 370.
[95] Several passages in the chapter insist in fact that gifts should be avoided if they enrich the wife by making the husband poorer, e.g. Ulp. (32 ad Sab.), *D* 24.1.17.pr; Clem. (5 ad l. Iul. et Pap.), *D* 24.1.25; Pomp. (14 ad Sab.), *D* 24.1.31. See also Biondi 1961, p. 40.
[96] Ulp. (31 ad Sab.), *D* 24.1.7.3.
[97] See for instance Ulp. (33 ad Sab.), *D* 24.1.32. In general terms, gifts masked as sales were treated according to the regulation of donations, which contemplated the *usucapio* of the thing after its deliverance, cf. Herm. (2 iuris ep.), *D* 41.6.6; Ulp. (32 ad Sab.), *D* 24.1.5.5; Pomp. (14 ad Sab.), *D* 24.1.31.4; Afr. (4 quaest.), *D* 16.1.17.pr; Ulp. (7 disp.), *D* 18.1.38; Pomp. (14 ad Sab.), *D* 24.1.31.3-6; Ulp. (33 ad Sab.), *D* 24.1.32.24-26; Ulp. (32 ad Sab.), *D* 24.1.5.5; Ulp. (31 ad Sab.), *D* 24.1.7.6; Ulp. (7 disp.), *D* 18.1.38; Afr. (4 quaest.), *D* 16.1.17.pr. Cf. Biondi 1961, p. 41; Treggiari 1991, p. 368.
[98] Ulp. (31 ad Sab.), *D* 24.3.7.8; Paul. (36 ad ed.), *D* 24.3.25.4; Papin. (10 quaest.), *D* 24.1.52.pr.

causa,[99] for gifts to the spouse through intermediaries,[100] and for any other form of *negotium mixtum cum donatione*. Other forms of enrichment restricted by law involved complex considerations, such as gifts of raw material that could increase their value (and price) through manufacturing.[101] This was the case with a plot given by the husband to the wife on which she built an *insula*. This property could be claimed back by the husband after he compensated his wife.[102]

Gifts of money (even considerable) among spouses were permitted or not according to their purpose and always pending whether it made the wife richer.[103] Aims such as the rebuilding of a burned house, the holding of banquets, the purchase of perfumes, of slaves to be manumitted, of votive objects, of the oil used in a temple, of a burial place or the spending of a husband's gift in *sportulae pro cognato* were considered valid.[104] Although the donation of funerary *loca* between spouses is also epigraphically attested,[105] the general tendency in funerary donations seems to have been the explicit omission of familiar relationships and other social filiations (e.g. *amicitia* and patronage), which could mirror legal restrictions upon these practices.[106] According to the Digest, donations between spouses were permitted *mortis*, *divortii* or *exilii causa*,[107] and during special occasions, such as the Matronalia.[108]

As regards to gifts that are consumed, Ulpian states that *unguenta* and other perishable things should be allowed in inter-marital gifts,[109] as well as gifts of money spent in things used for living, but that were not considered to enrich the wife or to provoke extra costs.[110] This argument contrasts with Seneca's passage seen above in which he declares his preference for gifts that last and are not

[99] Ulp. (33 ad Sab.), *D* 24.1.32.24.

[100] Ulp. (32 ad Sab.), *D* 24.1.3.13; Ulp. (32 ad Sab.), *D* 24.1.5.4; Paul. (5 quaest.), *D* 23.4.28.

[101] The jurists mention, for instance, the case of wool turned into clothes, Ulp. (32 ad Sab.), *D* 24.1.21.pr.; Pomp. (14 ad Sab.), *D* 24.1.31.pr.-1.

[102] Pomp. (14 ad Sab.), *D* 24.1.31.2.

[103] Ulp. (32 ad Sab.), *D* 24.1.21.pr.

[104] Ulp. (31 ad ed.), *D* 24.1.7.8-9; Paul. (71 ad ed.), *D* 24.1.14; Ulp. (43 ad Sab.), *D* 24.1.34; Ulp. (32 ad Sab.), *D* 24.1.17.

[105] As shown in an inscription from Rome dated to the 1st century CE, CIL 6.14573: *C. Iulius Praetutinianus coniugi locum donavit*.

[106] Caldelli – Crea – Ricci 2004, pp. 312-324, esp. 324. Here Ricci analyses 174 inscriptions attesting to *donationes* connected with *iura sepulcrorum*, and suggests a link between the omissions and the legal restrictions on *donationes*.

[107] Nerv. (l. resp.), *D* 39.6.43; Paul. (l. s. reg.), *D* 24.1.43. On these cases see Treggiari 1991, pp. 368-369.

[108] Pomp. (14 ad Sab.), *D* 24.1.31.8.

[109] Ulp. (31 ad Sab.), *D* 24.1.7.1.

[110] Pomp. (14 ad Sab.), *D* 24.1.31.9; Paul. (7 ad Sab.), *D* 24.1.28.pr; Cels. (1 dig.), *D* 24.1.47.

perishable (e.g. plate rather than coined money).[111] Although both cases illustrate gift-giving within two different social institutions – matrimony and friendship – both share a preoccupation with the enrichment of the donee through an inappropriate – illegal or immoral – use of a gift.

In general terms, the juridical regulations of the *donatio inter virum et uxorem* tended to favour the position of the husband-donor, who was in any case protected by the right to revoke the gift, but also entitled to reclaim it in the case of divorce or of the wife's death.[112] A provincial edict by Antoninus Pius extended the permitted *donationes honoris causa* because they helped the ascension of the husband on the census and his candidacy for the Senate or for the equestrian order, and facilitated the holding of *ludi*.[113] Pius' edict was the response to a practice that was quite common among Romans. An example of instrumental gifts *honoris causa* between relatives is provided by Pliny, who, in a letter to the emperor Trajan, discusses the case of a member of the provincial elite who aspired to achieve the rank of a senator thanks to the generous gift of his own mother.[114]

5. *Liberalitas cum temperantia*?

The restrictions and exceptions upon intermarital gifts reveal a serious concern of Roman jurists towards the dispersion of patrimonial goods provoked by an institution that was meant to provide continuity and security and not to break the natural succession line of the *paterfamilias*. Did these limitations and prohibitions question or contradict the principle of *liberalitas* inherent to gift-giving as expressed by Cicero and Seneca? Is the gap between legal casuistry, praxis and the ideals of social conduct by the elite really so big? In my view, the aforementioned quoted passage by Ulpian introducing the donation *inter virum et uxorem* (24.1.1) provides an interesting meeting point worthy of detailed exploration.

In associating love with *donationes non temperantes sed profusae*, Ulpian identifies the roots of the problem, which does not reside in fraudulent activities caused by selfishness and material interests, but in the uncontrollable emotions of marital love that can end up damaging the patrimony. Put in a different way, *temperantia* is opposed to the irrational impulses that menace the ultimate pur-

[111] Sen., *Ben*. 1.12.

[112] For examples, see Cels. (9 dig.), *D* 24.1.48; Papin. (11 resp.), *D* 20.1.1.4; Iavol. (13 ep.), *D* 24.1.50.pr.

[113] Gai (1 ad ed. prov.), *D* 24.1.42.

[114] Plin., *Ep*. 10.4. Romanus, who was a protégé of Pliny, had received four million sesterces as a gift (*liberalitas*) from his own mother in addition to the inheritance of his father, cf. Sherwin-White 1966, pp. 563-564.

pose of matrimony, the preservation of patrimony. Ulpian's use of *temperantia* takes us inexorably back to Cicero and to Seneca and, more broadly, to the reception of Platonic-Stoic virtues in Rome. Plautus' and Terence's adaptations of New Greek comedy resort to *temperantia*, *modestia* and *continentia* as common translations of the polyvalent Greek term *sophrosyne*.[115] In this context, *temperantia* appears mostly associated with matters of love.[116] In Plautus' *Mercator*, we are told the story of the young Charinus, who has won a reputation of being intemperate, immodest, and an unjustified waster (*intemperantem, non modestum, iniurium trahere*),[117] to the point that his father accuses him of taking loans and dilapidating his patrimony (*sua rem*) because of his foolish love for *meretrices*.[118] The link between irrational love and the wasting of the own patrimony as opposed to *sophrosyne* finds eloquent precedents in the speeches of Demostenes and Aeschines.[119] The multifaceted notion of *sophrosyne* as self-control that is developed in Plato's ethical and political works,[120] also became a model for the administration of both public and private affairs, of the state and the household.[121] Cicero's efforts to adapt the Platonic virtues to Roman qualities crystallises in *De inventione*, in which the author defines *sophrosyne* as *temperantia*, which along with *continentia*, *clementia* and *modestia* compose his version of the four cardinal virtues.[122] They emerge also as qualities to be expected from military rulers and from those who are in charge of public resources and offices.[123]

[115] On the reception of *sophrosyne* in Roman comedy, see North 1966, pp. 258-263. On *sophrosyne* in Aristophanes and the Greek comedy see Rademaker 2005, pp. 225-233.

[116] See, for instance, Plaut., *Epid.* 111: *in amore temperes*; Ter., *Haut.* 580: *hominis frugi et temperantis*.

[117] Plaut., *Merc.* 51-58.

[118] Plaut., *Merc.* 44-47.

[119] Both Aeschines and Demostenes define the *sophron* citizen as someone who is moderated in expenses and who does now waste money following passions and pleasures. See for instance Aeschines's first speech against Timarchus, in which prostitution is equaled with the wasting of money, 1.28-31. See also Dem. 38.26, on the need of *sophronyne* to preserve the own patrimony. For these and other instances, see Rademaker 2005, pp. 235-243.

[120] E.g. in *Gorg.* 507a and *Rep.* 431c-d.

[121] See Plat., *Charm.* 171e; Lys. 21.16-19.

[122] Cic., *Inv.* 2.164: *temperantia est rationis in libidinem atque in alios non rector impetus animi firma et moderata dominatio*. Cicero adapts here the Platonic virtues and equates *temperantia* with the Greek s*ophrosyne*. Also in other combinations, *Cat.* 25; *Mur.* 60. The term appears here as opposed to *voluptas*, *luxuria* and *libido*, Cic., *Nat. deor.* 3.38; *Cat.* 25; 41; cf. Scheidle 1993, pp. 30-31.

[123] On *modestia* and *temperantia* as Cicero's qualities in his office as governor of Cilicia, Cic., *Ep. Att.* 6.2.4; and of those expected from his brother Quintus in Asia, *Ep. Q. fr.* 1.1.8-9; also applied to his friend Atticus' virtues, *Ep. Att.* 1.9.22. See also *Phil.* 13.10.

But it is in *De Officiis* that the author – probably inspired by Panaetius – finds in the idea of temperate *liberalitas* both a model of virtue compatible with *mos maiorum* and a response to specific contemporary problems such as the excessive and impetuous expenditures that exhausted private fortunes and menaced public resources.[124] Cicero sees here restraint (*temperantia*) and modesty (*modestia*) as antidotes against the agitations of the spirit (*perturbationes animi*) and the immoderate passions,[125] that transgress reason and due measure.[126] His call for reason, restraint and modesty is not only addressed to those extravagant (*prodigi*) men who practise public distributions, hold banquets and gladiatorial games, but also to the liberal (*liberales*) ones, who help friends and family in need and assist them in acquiring and enlarging their property (*in re quaerenda vel augenda*).[127] Cicero admits his preference for services (*opera*) rather than for money (*pecunia*), not only because the former mirror the virtues of the honourable man and the latter simply comes from a safe (*ex arca*), but also because gifts of money from a private patrimony (*ex re familiari*) exhaust the very source of *benignitas*.[128] Although Cicero admits that sometimes it is good to give money, this should be done with diligence and moderation, for many have wasted their patrimony by rash gifts of money (*multi enim patrimonia effuderunt, inconsulte largiendo*) and ended up being in need themselves.[129] The orator's solution is to allow only a restrictive *benignitas* in the use of *res familiaris*, and to set a limit of expenditures according to the capacity of the individual's own resources.[130] This moderated attitude Cicero applies not only to gifts, but also to other transactions, such as buying, selling and leasing. A productive liberal attitude can thus only be acceptable if personal wealth is managed with rational care and with no suspicion of meanness or avarice. *Liberalitas* without exhausting one's own patrimony is, accordingly, *pecuniae fructus maximus*.[131]

Temperantia appears as a *virtus militaris* in *De imperio Cn. Pompei* (40-42).

[124] Cic., *Off.* 1.42-52. And above.

[125] Cic., *Off.* 1.93.

[126] Cic., *Off.* 1.102-103.

[127] Cic., *Off.* 2.55-56.

[128] Cic., *Off.* 2.52.

[129] Cic., *Off.* 2.54.

[130] Cic., *Off.* 2.55: *Quam ob rem nec ita claudenda res est familiaris, ut eam benignitas aperire non possit, nec ita reseranda, ut pateat omnibus; modus adhibeatur isque referatur ad facultates*. See also *Off.* 2.58.

[131] Cic., *Off.* 2.64: *Conveniet autem cum in dando munificum esse, tum in exigendo non acerbum in omnique re contrahenda, vendundo emendo, conducendo locando, vicinitatibus et confiniis aequum, facilem, multa multis de suo iure cedentem, a litibus vero, quantum liceat et nescio an paulo plus etiam, quam liceat, abhorrentem. Est enim non modo liberale paulum non numquam de suo iure decedere, sed interdum etiam fructuosum. Habenda autem ratio est rei familiaris, quam quidem dilabi sinere*

Although Cicero's specific interest for *temperantia* found no equivalent treatment – both in depth and in breadth – in later authors, the consolidation of self-restraint and moderation as virtues attached to rulers, magistrates and in general to the *vir bonus* took roots during the early Principate.[132] Seneca's categorisation of benefits in *De Beneficiis* and his recommendation not to expend money on gifts beyond what is reasonable resorts also to the need to use resources with moderation and temperance.[133] As is Cicero, Seneca is also interested in *temperantia* as a philosophical virtue. In his moral letters, he elevates self-control as the perfect virtue that, along with *prudentia*, *moderatio*, *parsimonia*, *constantia*, should constrain our passions and desires.[134] Seneca recognises these virtues as models for what he considers as *decorum*, *iustum* and *legitimum*.[135]

In Trajan's *Panegyric*, Pliny the Younger defends self-restraint and moderation as essential qualities in the management of public resources.[136] The same idea is expressed in his correspondence in relation to private affairs. In a letter written to his relative Calvina, a woman who had inherited her father's debts, Pliny reminds the woman – and the reader – about his generous contribution of 100.000 sesterces to her dowry and about other grants made by him to her father. As a demonstration of his good feelings towards Calvina and in order to preserve the reputation and honour of her father, Pliny announces that he will make her a gift of money equal to the amount owed to him, which will cancel the debt.[137] The self-praising tone of the letter continues with an affirmation that such an onerous *donatio* will not greatly harm his modest and limited resources and incomes, which are the source of his *liberalitas*, because

flagitiosum est, sed ita, ut inliberalitatis avaritiaeque absit suspicio. Posse enim liberalitate uti non spoliantem se patrimonio nimirum est pecuniae fructus maximus.

[132] During the Roman Principate, *temperantia* was also attributed to rulers, Tac., *Ann.* 2.72-73; *Hist.* 2.90.2; Plin., *Pan.* 2.7; and to honourable men, e.g. *CIL* 11.6035. On *modestia*, *moderatio* and *temperantia* in Roman literature see the philological study by Scheidle 1993, in particular pp. 29-38 and 69-93.

[133] Sen., *Ben.* 1.4.2; 2.34.4.

[134] Sen., *Ep.* 85.2; 85.14; 88.29; *V. beat.* 10.3.

[135] Sen., *Ep.* 66.8-9.

[136] In *Pan.* 41.1-2 Pliny underlines that Trajan's generous gifts never impoverished the public treasure.

[137] Plin., *Ep.* 2.4.1-2: *Si pluribus pater tuus vel uni cuilibet alii quam mihi debuisset, fuisset fortasse dubitandum, an adires hereditatem etiam viro gravem. Cum vero ego ductus affinitatis officio, dimissis omnibus qui non dico molestiores sed diligentiores erant, creditor solus exstiterim, cumque vivente eo nubenti tibi in dotem centum milia contulerim, praeter eam summam quam pater tuus quasi de meo dixit - erat enim solvenda de meo -, magnum habes facilitatis meae pignus, cuius fiducia debes famam defuncti pudoremque suscipere. Ad quod te ne verbis magis quam rebus horter, quidquid mihi pater tuus debuit, acceptum tibi fieri iubebo.*

they are managed with self-restraint (*temperanda*) and without excessive flow (*ne nimia profussione*).[138] Pliny insists on the exception he is making for Calvina, by underlining that although on this occasion the figure surpasses his usual expenses he will manage to balance his accounts.[139] Beyond Pliny's patronising tone and very subjective underestimation of his own vast patrimonial wealth,[140] this letter demonstrates to what extent moral concerns about conducting oneself with self-restraint when making use of private fortunes for gifts represented a real consideration for members of the Roman elite.

Far from being anecdotic, Ulpian's appeal to *temperantia* in gifts among spouses mirrors a moral pattern already settled in Roman society and shows once more the sensibility of Roman jurists towards patrimonial ideology and the frequent problems and situations that menaced and challenged it.

6. Conclusion

The theme of damaging love illustrated in Plautus' *Mercator* and addressed also by Ulpian leads us back to the debate about gifts led by passions. The idea of the material costs of love and of love that threatens fortunes also plays a relevant part in Martial's *Epigrams*.[141] The problem materializes above all when *res familiaris* is confronted with marriage. Inter-marital love emerges, in this context, as a real menace towards patrimony and its preservation and the response of the Roman jurists in this and in other forms of gift-giving clarifies without nuances that any form of honourable virtue, including *liberalitas*, should be first submitted to a patrimonial ideology that settles rules but also virtues (e.g. *temperantia*, *moderatio* etc.). In this regard, when Ulpian differentiates honourable from dishonourable gifts, the former devoted to friends and relatives and the latter to prostitutes, he makes clear that both were equally valid on grounds of affection (*affectionis gratia*);[142] which contrasts with the jurist's own criticism of marital love in the already quoted passage on *temperantia*. We now know why. It is obvious that jurists were particularly interested in the resolution of practical problems rather than in the construction of abstractions and morals,

[138] Plin., *Ep.* 2.4.3: *Nec est quod verearis ne sit mihi onerosa ista donatio. Sunt quidem omnino nobis modicae facultates, dignitas sumptuosa, reditus propter condicionem agellorum nescio minor an incertior; sed quod cessat ex reditu, frugalitate suppletur, ex qua velut fonte liberalitas nostra decurrit.*

[139] Plin., *Ep.* 2.4.4: *Quae tamen ita temperanda est, ne nimia profusione inarescat; sed temperanda in aliis, in te vero facile ei ratio constabit, etiamsi modum excesserit.*

[140] See Sherwin-White 1966, pp. 149-150, on Pliny's immense fortune, patrimony, savings and resources.

[141] Mart. 11.27; 11.55; 12.13.

[142] Ulp. (32 ad Sab.), *D* 39.5.5.

and that what Ulpian unveils here was indeed a practical problem that had to do with the aims of gifts and the need to regulate them. Yet we cannot deny that jurists like Ulpian and others reflected also specific moral, social and philosophical concerns such as those formulated by Cicero and Seneca. Even if the concept of *animus donandi* did not perfectly match the altruistic spirit drawn by social and philosophical ideology, the will of the donor was the essential element that defined and formalised a praxis that despite its common use did not find a definitive shape until the age of Constantine. The voluntary character of the *donatio* and its revocability favoured the position of the donor, which explains why legal sources dedicated remarkable attention to a phenomenon such as the *donatio mortis causa*.

As we have seen across this paper, both literary and legal sources met with similar preoccupations regarding the spending of excessive sums of money, the transfer of real estate, and above all the menace of the dissemination and division of *res mancipi* and *familiaris*. The need to regulate and balance economic outgoings on account of the limitation of private resources was a conditional factor of public and private *beneficentia* and *liberalitas*. *Temperantia* and *moderatio* were received as appropriate responses to the excesses of gift-giving and other monetary expenditures. The appeal to *temperantia* in Roman literature thus mirrors a certain awareness of the finitude of economic resources and of the potential conflicts and problems attached to their redistribution according to irrational criteria that challenged individual fortunes and traditional institutions. The search for a middle way between individual and collective interests, between unconditional generosity and the care of resources as factors to be considered in the construction of social relationships through gift-giving finds – not by chance – echoes in recent sociological approaches to Mauss and to Aristotelian ethics.[143] A temperate habitus that relegates damaging passions and prioritises a reasonable circulation of material goods appears according to some contemporary views as a valid alternative to the apparent utilitarianism of social relationships and gift-giving in modern capitalistic societies.[144] Despite the logical economic and social differences, the regulation of *donationes* encountered similar concerns by setting conditions and limitations that made this practice legally viable while it also protected a fundamental instrument of power in Roman society. We may conclude that patrimonial ideology set the real limits of generosity in ancient Rome.

[143] Following Maus, Caillé 2007², pp. 100-101, resorts to the Nicomachean Ethics (6.13) and to the idea of linking virtue with reason to find a proper measure of gifts.
[144] See Caillé 2007², pp. 93-120; Fistetti 2011, pp. 100-103.

Bibliography

Amelotti, Mario: *La 'donatio mortis causa' in diritto romano*, Milano 1953.

Andreau, Jean: *Fondations privées et rapports sociaux en Italie romaine*, in: *Ktema* 2 (1977), pp. 157-209.

Andreau, Jean: *Banking and Business in the Roman World*, Cambridge 1999.

Biondi, Biondo: *Le donazioni*, Torino 1961.

Bourdieu, Pierre: *Raisons pratiques. Sur la théorie de l'action*, Paris 1994; Engl. Transl.: *Practical Reason: On the Theory of Action*, Stanford 1998.

Bourdieu, Pierre: *Méditations pascaliennes*, Paris 1997.

Bowditch, Phebe Lowell: *Horace and the gift Economy of Patronage*, Berkeley 2001.

Caillé, Alain: *Anthropologie du don*, Paris 2007².

Caldelli, Maria Letizia – Simona Crea – Cecilia Ricci, *Iura sepulcrorum a Roma: consuntivi tematici ragionati. A-B: Donare, emere, vendere, ius habere, possidere, concedere, similia. Donazione e compravendita, diritto sul sepolcro e diritti di sepoltura*, in: *Libitina e dintorni. Libitina e i luci sepolcrali. Le leges libitinariae campane. Iura sepulcrorum: vecchie e nuove iscrizioni*, Roma 2004, pp. 312-324.

Casavola, Franco: *Lex Cincia. Contributo alla storia delle origini della donazione romana*, Napoli 1960.

Chanial, Philippe: *Homo donator. Il dono come grammatica delle relazioni sociali*, in: *Homo Donator. Come nasce il legame sociale*, ed. by Philippe Chanial – Francesco Fistetti, Genova 2011, pp. 7-67.

Champlin, Edward: *Final Judgements. Duty and Emotion in Roman Wills 200 B.C. – A.D. 250*, Berkeley 1991.

Chaumartin, François-Régis: *Le De beneficiis de Sénèque, sa signification philosophique, politique et sociale*, Paris 1985.

Crook, John A.: *Legal Advocacy in the Roman World*, London 1995.

Deniaux, Élizabeth: *Clientèles et Pouvoir à l'époque de Cicéron*, Roma 1993.

Diósdi, György: *Ownership in Ancient and Preclassical Roman Law*, Budapest 1970.

Dixon, Suzanne: *The Meaning of Gift and Debt in the Roman elite*, in: *ECM* 37 (1993), pp. 451-464.

Engberg-Pedersen, Troels: *Gift-Giving and Friendship: Seneca and Paul in Romans 1-8 on the Logic of God's Χάρις and Its Human Response*, in: *HThR* 101 (2008), pp. 15-44.

Fear, Trevor: *Of Aristocrats and Courtesans: Seneca, De Beneficiis 1.14*, in: *Hermes* 135 (2007), pp. 460-468.

Feuvrier-Prévolat, Claire: *"Donner et Recevoir": Remarques sur les pratiques d'échanges dans le De Officiis de Cicéron*, in: *DHA* 11 (1985), pp. 257-290.

Fistetti, Francesco: *Homo donator: un paradigma metadisciplinare per le scienze sociali*, in: Philippe Chanial – Francesco Fistetti, *Homo donator. Come nasce il legame sociale*, Genova 2011, pp. 69-102.

Gade, Gunther Dietrich: *Donationes inter virum et uxorem*, Berlin 2001.

Gardner, Jane F.: *Women in Roman Law and Society*, London 1986.

Gardner, Jane F.: *Family and Familia in Roman Law and Life*, Oxford 1998.

Gärtner, Hans Armin: *Cicero und Panaitios. Beobachtungen zu Ciceros de officiis*, Heidelberg 1974.

Garnsey, Peter: *The Generosity of Veyne*, in: *JRS* 81 (1991), pp. 164-168.

Gouldner, Alvin Ward: *For Sociology. Renewal and Critique in Sociology Today*, London 1973.

Griffin, Miriam: *De Beneficiis and Roman Society*, in: *JRS* 93 (2003), pp. 92-113.

Griffin, Miriam: *The younger Pliny's Debt to Moral Philosophy*, in: *HSPh* 103 (2007), pp. 451-481.

Günther, Sven: *Die Einführung der römischen Erbschaftssteuer (vicesima hereditatium)*, in: *MBAH* 24 (2005), pp. 1-30.

Ioannatou, Marina: *Affaires d'argent dans la correspondance de Cicéron: l'aristocratie sénatoriale face à ses dettes*, Paris 2006.

Lefèvre, Eckard: *Panaitios' und Ciceros' Pflichtenlehre: vom philosophischen Traktat zum politischen Lehrbuch*, Stuttgart 2001.

Lévi-Strauss, Claude: *Introduction to the Work of Marcel Mauss*, in Marcel Mauss, *Sociologie et anthropologie*, Paris 1950, pp. ix-li.

Li Causi, Pietro: *Fra creditum e beneficium. La pratica difficile del 'dono' nel De Beneficiis di Seneca*, in: *Quaderni del ramo d'oro online* 2 (2009), pp. 226-252 [http://www.qro.unisi.it/frontend/node/55; last access 4 sept. 2013].

Liu, Jinyu: *The Economy of Endownments: the Case of the Roman collegia*, in: *Pistoi dia tèn technèn. Bankers, Loans and Archives in the Ancient World. Studies in honour of Raymond Bogaert*, ed. by Koenraad Verboven – Katelijn Vandorpe – Véronique Chankowski, Leuven 2008, pp. 231-256.

Lomas, Kathryn – Tim Cornell (ed. by), *'Bread and Circuses'. Evergetism and Municipal Patronage in Roman Italy*, London – New York 2003.

Lotito, Gianfranco: *Modelli etici e base economica nelle opere filosofiche di Cicerone*, in: *Società romana e produzione schiavistica III: Modelli etici, diritto e trasformazioni sociali*, ed. by Andrea Giardina – Aldo Schiavone, Roma 1981, pp. 79-126.

Mauss, Marcel: *Essai sur le don. Forme et raison de l'échange dans les sociétés archaïques*, in: *L'Année sociologique* n.s. 1 (1923-1924), pp. 30-186; Engl. Transl.: *The Gift. Forms and Functions of Exchange in Archaic Societies*, London 1974.

Michel, Jacques-Henri: *Gratuité en droit romain*, Brussels 1962.

Minaud, Gérard: *La comptabilité à Rome. Essai d'histoire économique sur la pensée comptable commerciale et privée dans le monde antique romain*, Lausanne 2005.

Misera, Karlheinz: *Der Bereicherungsgedanke bei der Schenkung unter Ehegatten*, Cologne and Vienna 1974.

Narducci, Emanuele: *Valori aristocratici e mentalità acquisitiva nel pensiero di Cicerone*, in: *Index* 13 (1985), pp. 93-125.

North, Helen F.: *Sophrosyne. Self-Knowledge and Self-Restraint in Greek Literature*, Ithaca – New York 1966.

Rademaker, Adriaan: *Sophrosyne and the Rhetoric of Self-Restraint. Polysemy and Persuasive Use of an Ancient Greek Value Term*, Leiden – Boston 2005.

Rawson, Elizabeth: *The Ciceronian Aristocracy and Its Properties*, in: *Studies in Roman Property*, ed. by Moses I. Finley, Cambridge 1976, pp. 85-102.

Recoder de Casso, Emilio: *La ley Cincia en sus circunstancias históricas*, Madrid 2005.

Rollinger, Christian: *Solvendi sunt nummi. Die Schuldenkultur der späten römischen Republik im Spiegel der Schriften Ciceros*, Berlin 2009.

Rouland, Norbert: *Pouvoir politique et dépendance personnelle dans l'Antiquité romaine*, Bruxelles 1979.

Royer, Jean-Pierre: *Le problème des dettes à la fin de la République romaine*, in: *RD* 45 (1967), pp. 191-240.

Rüger, David: *Die donatio mortis causa im klassischen römischen Recht*, Berlin 2011.

Saller, Richard P.: *Personal Patronage under the Early Empire*, Cambridge 1982.

Saller, Richard P.: *Patriarchy, Property and Death in the Roman Family*, Cambridge 1994.

Scheidle, Kurt: *Modus optimum. Die Bedeutung des 'rechten Maßes' in der römischen Literatur (Republik – frühe Kaiserzeit)*, Frankfurt 1993.

Sherwin-White, Adrian N.: *The Letters of Pliny: A Historical and Social Commentary*, Oxford 1966.

Spisak, Arthur L.: *Gift-giving in Martial*, in: *Toto Notus in Orbe. Perspektiven der Martial Interpretation*, ed. by Farouk Grewing, Stuttgart 1998, pp. 243-255.

Spisak, Arthur L.: *Martial. A Social Guide*, London 2007.

Tran, Nicolas: *Les membres des associations romaines. Le rang social des collegiati en Italie et en Gaules sous le Haut-Empire*, Rome 2006.

Treggiari, Susan: *Roman Marriage. Iusti coniuges from the Time of Cicero to the Time of Ulpian*, Oxford 1991.

Verboven, Koenraad: *The Economy of Friends. Economic Aspects of amicitia and Patronage in the Late Republic*, Bruxelles 2002.

Verboven, Koenraad: *Friendship among the Romans*, in: *Social Relations in the Roman World*, ed. by Michael Peachin, Oxford 2011, pp. 404-421.

Veyne, Paul: *Le pain et le cirque. Sociologie historique d'un pluralisme politique*, Paris 1976.

Wallace-Hadrill, Andrew (ed. by): *Patronage in Ancient Society*, London 1989.

Watson, Alan: *The Law of Property in the Later Roman Republic*, Oxford 1968; Repr. 1984.

White, Peter: *Amicitia and the Profession of Poetry*, in: *JRS* 68 (1978), pp. 74-92.

Zuiderhoek, Arjan: *The Ambiguity of Munificence*, in: *Historia* 56 (2007), pp. 196-213.

Zuiderhoek, Arjan: *The Politics of Munificence in the Roman Empire: Citizens, Elites and Benefactors in Asia Minor*, Cambridge 2009.

Section three

Gifts to the Gods, Gifts to the Priests

MAJA GORI

Metal Hoards as Ritual Gifts: Circulation, Collection and Alienation of Bronze Artefacts in Late Bronze Age Europe

1. Introduction

Approaching gift giving in prehistoric societies presupposes an inquiry based on the relation between social practises and their material outcomes.[1] Proceeding backward from the material outcomes of a social performance to the reconstruct-tion of the performance itself assumes the analysis of things as products of the *chaîne opératoire*, and their entanglements in different cultural webs. As remembered by Gosselain:

> "objects may acquire a wide range of meanings during their manufacture and use, as they pass through the hands of various individuals, embedded in different social strategies and networks. [...] This concept may be extended easily to *chaîne opératoires* or production sequences".[2]

Chaîne opératoire is intended as not only the technological processes that stand behind the manufacture of single objects, but also economic and social elements of the production, distribution, consumption, discard, reuse and final abandonment of a specific material object. Technology studies help us capture the meanings and the variations of the intricate socio-political, economic and cultural networks that were built and abandoned and can be traced through their material expression.[3] One train of thought in material culture studies concedes to objects a 'life' and multiple careers entangled in cultural webs, which reaffirm a culture's ability to translate things into signs.[4] Yet H. Hahn considers this complementary to the semiotic approach, an acknowledgment to the existence of an infinitely expandable universe of needs, motives and desires, and argues that the

[1] I am grateful to David Fontijn and Arianna Bruno for reviewing the manuscript. Thanks to their comments and remarks this paper's quality was substantially improved. Certainly all the mistakes remain my responsibility.
[2] Gosselain 2000, p.189.
[3] Brysbaert 2011, pp. 1-3.
[4] This approach is exemplified by the work of Arjun Appadurai, Alfred Gell, Richard Davis and Nicholas Thomas. See also Hodder 2012.

isolation of the individual and the individual's need to find a distinct place in the society are basic drivers in both concepts.[5]

Since Kopytoff's seminal article on *The cultural biography of things*,[6] the biographical perspective has become salient and approaching objects' 'social life' in uncommercialized societies has led to consider their high cultural categorization of the exchange value. Lately, Hahn and Weiss dealt with the biography of things as material objects when they travel. This approach is related to the idea that things follow specific pathways, which may be routes and destinations that have little in common with those of people, institutions or traditions. In many cases, things that are perceived as originating elsewhere play a specific role, and to them might be assigned a superior value on account of their foreign provenience.[7]

This paper argues that the metal objects buried in Late Bronze Age hoards were intentionally put out of circulation and left in a dead end as a ritual and performative act of gift giving. The subtraction of a great quantity of wealth – tangible and symbolic – was performed through codified practices that involved different segments of the society i.e. different actors.[8] In hoarding practices the display of status, wealth and power can be regarded as the expressions of elites' ambitions to exhibit and institutionalise their political power.[9]

2. Late Bronze Age metallurgy and hoarding practices

Hoard is an umbrella term, which involves the collection of entire or fragmented artefacts either for ritual or not-ritual purposes, as well as for permanent or temporary safekeeping and deposition. Metal hoards can be found in wet and dry lands and their composition represents either a simultaneous act or a collection of artefacts over an extended period of time.[10]

During the entire Bronze Age, the deposition of metal in hoards is documented in a wide area that covers Europe and extends to Eurasia. In the Early Bronze Age, metal hoards are frequently formed by objects often belonging to one artefact's category – axes, torques, rings, halberds, etc. – and generally buried entirely intact. At the transition from the Early to the Middle Bronze Age,

[5] Hahn 2012, p. 7.
[6] Kopytoff 1986, pp. 64-91.
[7] Hahn – Weiss 2013.
[8] See Carlà – Gori in this volume.
[9] Due to limited space here, it is not possible to deal exhaustively with hoard burial locations, which however represent a fundamental aspect of hoarding practices. For the most recent contribution on this topic refer to Hansen – Neumann –Vachta 2012 and in particular to the contributions of Fontijn and Hansen – Neumann –Vachta.
[10] Bruno 2012.

a radical change in the organisation of metal circulation is indicated by the intensification of depositional activity and the appearance of hoards formed by scraps. This phenomenon is recorded with major intensity in Central Europe.

C. Pare interpreted this change as the widespread use of weighed metal, mainly in form of fragmented bronze, as a means of payment.[11] An increasing number of studies proved that scraps and entire bronze artefacts retained a pre-ponderal value, although ponderal series were never identified with certainty.[12]

Hoarding particularly flourished in the Late Bronze Age, when the number of metal depositions – in form of hoard or single objects – spectacularly increased. Although different metallurgical circles are quite well recognised and defined on the basis of objects' typological frequency and geographic distribution – i.e. the Carpathian circle, the Atlantic area, the Alpine region, etc. – R. Peroni and G. L. Carancini[13] defined the Late Bronze Age metallurgical production in Europe as "metallurgical *koiné*" on the basis of metallurgy's great technological and typological homogeneity, which contrasts with the myriad of different 'archaeological cultures' that characterized the European Bronze Age.[14] However, bronze swords, spearheads, sickles, daggers, axes, etc. were recovered in different archaeological contexts, often very far one from another, and they frequently show a remarkable typological affinity, if not a real formal and technical standardisation.[15] In a few cases, it is even possible to recognise the provenience from a single mould of more metal artefacts.

Interregional goods exchange occurred within a complex set of non-economic as well as economic relations, which also channelled raw materials and labour between societies. Exchange, reciprocity and bargain entail, as by-product, the diffusion of ideas and techniques, embedded in the exchanged objects and spread through direct contact between agents.[16] Adoption and replication of new technologies are driven by cultural choices, and the relation

[11] On this topic see Pare 1999, pp. 510-514, which speaks for this period of "weighted currency economy". According to Pare 2000, p. 29, the first evidence of the system of bronze exchange based on hoarded scrap metal occurred in the Bühl-Ackenback horizon at the transition from the Early to the Middle Bronze Age (16th century BCE), and was then adopted over most of the European Metallurgical Province.

[12] On the use of fragmented sickles as premonetary artefacts see Primas 1986 and Sommerfeld 1994.

[13] Peroni – Carancini 1997, pp. 595–601.

[14] Peroni and Carancini have interpreted Late Bronze Age hoards as a transcultural phenomenon characterised by craftsmen's and finished product's great mobility. In their interpretation, the "metallurgical koiné" (*koiné metallurgica*) reflected the increasingly high demand for prestige goods of the élites, which shared a common system of values and ideologies.

[15] Huth 2000, pp. 177-193.

[16] Humphrey – Hugh-Jones 1992.

between social identity and techniques impacts the dynamics of shaping and replicating technological traditions.[17] The spread of a new technology implies a "technological domestication" and a "translation" that consents the recipient society to integrate the new expertise and its social and cultural meaning into its social fabric, triggering off a series of social and economic changes.[18] At craft level the acquisition of certain technological skills involves more intensive forms of social interaction, as is the case of metallurgy. During the Bronze Age metalworking assumes an important role in spreading and reproducing social systems.

Late Bronze Age[19] metal hoards can be regarded as particularly suitable to approach the analysis of 'gift giving' in prehistoric Europe since they represent an archaeological source in which the interaction between wealth, performance and status can be well recognized.[20]

Central Europe		
	Relative chronology	Absolute Chronology BCE
'Urnfield Cultures'	Ha B2–B3	1050-750
	Ha B1	1100-1000
	Ha A1–A2	1250-1050
	Br D	1400-1200
	Br B–C	1500-1300

In the Late Bronze Age, high standardisation characterizes a number of passages of the *chaîne opératoire* which stands behind hoarding, i.e. the modalities through which metal objects were collected, assembled, processed and finally buried. It is reasonable to argue that the standardisation in the material outcomes of behaviour presumes the standardisation of the behaviour itself. In

[17] Gosselain 2000, pp. 187-217.
[18] Chapman 2002, pp. 77-78.
[19] This follows Reinecke's traditional relative chronology system, as Late Bronze Age are intended the phases from Br C to Ha B3, which in calendar years roughly correspond to the lapse of time comprised between 1500 and 750 BCE (refer to the table in this page). See Sørensen – Rebay 2008 on the construction of "urnfield" as a chronological and cultural concept.
[20] In the European Late Bronze Age the coexistence of wealth, performance and status can be recognized in several contexts – one for all in burials – but metal hoards entail in their composition also an explicit economic value that is difficult to recognise in other archaeological evidences.

other words, underneath the replication of hoarding practices stand codified social rules and behaviours which were shared by prehistoric communities at super-regional level.[21]

3. 'Ritual' and 'profane' metal hoards

Hoards can be classified and defined according to several parameters, like the number of objects that form the hoard, their typological classification, their conservation state and the place where they were buried, but the most controversies arose around their functional classification.

Varying and conflicting interpretations were given to hoards and hoarding practices by different research traditions,[22] insomuch that D. Fontijn argues that the 125 years old 'ritual/profane' distinction in scientific literature represents an epistemological rather than an empirical problem.[23] The common feature bringing together 'profane' hoards was their interpretation as tradesmen's or craftsmen's' 'temporary safe boxes'. In 'profane' hoards metal was supposed to be recoverable for trade or reuse and buried to protect it from looting and robberies. Thus, metal burial was traditionally interpreted as the consequence of political instability caused by the emergence and the affirmation of the warrior elites.[24] Recent scholarly work on this topic regards as very implausible that during some phases of the Bronze Age the position of stored or hidden objects should have been forgotten, while in others they were recalled with so much accuracy that little metalwork survives.[25]

Bronze hoards were perceived as the material manifestation of the long-distance bronze trade, which was one of the most salient characteristics of European late prehistory. From the early twentieth century onwards, archae-ologists have been mapping Bronze Age metalwork trade routes on the basis of distribution maps of hoard finds. This interpretation of hoard-like merchant's treasures was supported by the presence of objects entirely new or half-finished,

[21] Maraszek 2000, pp. 209-224.
[22] Bradley 1990, pp. 15-17
[23] Fontijn 2002, pp. 13-22.
[24] Von Brunn 1968, p. 232 cited in Fontijn 2002.
[25] Bradley 2005, pp. 146-147; Needham 2001, pp. 275-298. According to Fontijn 2000, p. 14, "Reinecke's *Katastrophentheorie* fit[s] neatly within the cultural-historical emphasis on migrations as explanation for changes in material culture [in fashion at the time] and presupposes a quite disastrous scenario, where entire communities hide their valuables, and never come back in the region. We may expect that such fundamental changes would leave traces in other aspects of the archaeological record as well (settlements, graves). The theory becomes less attractive when the hoards in question all come from inaccessible locations, from where it would be impossible to retrieve them."

generally of the same type, originated from different "metallurgical circles", whose co-presence was explained as the result of long-distance commerce.[26]

Different study traditions put major or minor emphasis on some aspects of the hoards phenomenon rather than another, but in general the studies connected to rituality prevailed in Northern Europe, while in Western Europe the emphasis on the functional aspects was predominant. For example, in her study on Danish social and religious organization, J. Levy drafted the general criteria to identify and distinguish between 'ritual' and 'non-ritual' hoards in the wake of a long established study tradition.[27] Ritual hoards are the ones buried in places where they cannot be recovered, they are usually composed by particular objects, often in association with other elements that can be interpreted as the material remains of ritual practices – like animal bones, rests of fire, etc. – and are typically buried out of settlements. On the other hand, non-ritual hoards are characterized by being buried in places where they can be easily retrieved or in settlements, and are composed predominantly by functional objects like axes or sickles or by metal scraps or ingots. Non-ritual hoards are in turn classified into three sub-groups: personal hoards,[28] craftsmen's hoards[29] and merchants' hoards.[30] R. Bradley criticized several aspects of Levy's classification system, arguing that her interpretation was influenced by a too intuitive approach, which penalized less attractive findings.[31] In his review of the Dutch Voorhout hoard, D. Fontijn

[26] Fontijn 2008, pp. 9-10.

[27] Levy 1982.

[28] 'Personal hoards' are composed by an ensemble of metal objects stored together that can be still utilized after the recovery, like complete military panoply or different types of ingots. 'Personal hoards' would thus, according to Levy, represent a treasure that belonged to a single person or group.

[29] 'Craftsmen's hoards', defined also as industrial hoards, are composed by scrap metal objects to be founded again and re-casted. 'Craftsmen hoards' are interpreted by Levy as storage places belonged to the smith's workshops.

[30] 'Merchants' hoards' are composed by non-refined objects, freshly made pieces stored together to await the finishing and the distribution to the customers. This type of hoards, which appear only in a developed stage of the Urnfield period, would have belonged to the metallurgists themselves or to a person with the function of intermediary between the producer and the consumer.

[31] Bradley 2005, p. 146. One of the most important criticisms that Bradley made of Levy's classification is that her interpretation was strongly influenced by the archaeological record available from Denmark, where peat bogs create an anaerobic ambient ideal for preserving intact organic archaeological remains. The widespread use of sophisticated excavation techniques combined with the scientific analysis of organic and inorganic remains in their provenance contexts can completely turn over an interpretation that was given by only considering the metal objects. The opposition between 'ritual' and 'non ritual' hoards can be easily emphasized when it involves the presence of unique and outstanding items like the Trundholm sun chariot, buried in a peat bog in Denmark, or the

criticized the intuitive and self-explanatory approach used to explain the function of hoards categorized as 'profane'. Voorhout hoard is considered as an almost paradigmatic example of a trader's stock, but this interpretation rests mainly on the basis of suggestions derived from a collection of (similar) axes, which evokes a notion of serial production and mass commodity exchange but never sustained with arguments.[32]

Little attention was given in the past to the exact find spots and contexts, disregarding a huge amount of important data connected to hoarding practices. Thanks to the research undertaken in the last twenty years focusing on the contextual evidence, the interpretation of metal depositions as votive offering to a supernatural power replaced the interpretation of hoards as 'craftsmen's' or 'merchants'' stocks.[33]

4. Scrap hoards and ritual performance

The overwhelming majority of Late Bronze Age metal depositions is composed by fragmented objects. As their definition assumes, scrap hoards are composed by metal objects, often in considerable quantity, and reduced into pieces. The analysis of some of the *chaîne opératoire*'s steps that stand behind the production of metal scraps has proved helpful for interpreting scrapping as ritual practice. L. Nebelsick made striking observations on the hoard of Crévic, in north-eastern France, which can be considered a significative example of a Early Urnfield scrap hoard.[34] In Crévic there is an unusually high proportion of unfinished and miscast artefacts which were analyzed by L. Nebelsick focusing the attention onto the damage to the artefacts. An axe blade was almost cut away by a massive blow, and one of the spearheads, which still presents visible traces of casting, was bent, pressed against a surface and then had its head broken. Complex and elaborated damages are recognizable also on the other objects that form the hoard.[35] The breaking points seem not to be casual, but intentionally chosen. Some scraps are twisted or bended, operations that cost time and effort and imply a precise choice of the parts of the artefacts to be processed and good knowledge of the objects' anatomy. Bronze is hard to work with and does not

metal hoard containing the Nebra sky disc which was found in northern Germany. On the other hand, for the less attractive hoards composed just by scraps the relation to cult practice results less intuitive and entails stronger explanation efforts, especially when they were accidentally recovered and excavated without paying much attention to their provenience context, as happened in most of the cases.

[32] Fontijn 2008, pp. 5-17.

[33] Hansen 2012, p. 7.

[34] Nebelsick 2000, p.160.

[35] Nebelsick 2000, p. 160 and Fig. 11.1.

break easily. Bronze objects were very likely reduced to scraps by people who had at least some metallurgical knowledge. The treatment to which they were subjected speaks in favour of an intentional defunctionalisation of metal objects and transformation of their meaning and status trough "uncontrolled rage, euphoric frenzy and ecstatic violence".[36] The presence of unfinished and miscast artefacts suggests the practice of casting objects expressly for these scrapping ceremonies where 'ritual violence' was used. Voluntary destruction was recorded also in several other Late Bronze Age hoards in Atlantic Europe.[37]

A similar 'violent behaviour' is frequently recorded also in hoards belonging to different metallurgical circles. The hoard of Koprivnica (Croatia), for example, belongs to the so-called Danube-Carpathian metallurgical circle and presents similar characteristics. Koprivnica is composed of forty-seven bronze scraps. Signs of ritual violence are particularly evident on a bronze ring which was intentionally twisted and bent to hold together a fragmentary razor, a small fragment of a socketed axe and a twisted wire.[38]

There are several studies that deal with the fractures of metal objects, in particular with the s.c. *Waffenbruch*,[39] which demonstrate that the pattern of the objects buried in hoards followed a deliberately chosen canonical selection.[40] Lately, the relation between scraps and entire weapons was analysed by A. Čivilytė in her study on weapons' depositions in north-central Europe.[41] Comparing different types of damaged bronze weapons – swords, daggers, axes, spearheads – which were found in different contexts, A. Čivilytė demonstrates that there are certain deposition trends that can be observed. The breaks operated on the weapons before their deposition in hoards followed different rules in respect to the weapons deposed in the graves. Swords, for example, were unlikely buried entire in graves, but they were often buried entire in a hoard and particular parts of the scrapped sword were more likely to enter in the hoard than others.[42]

J. Brück argues that fire and fragmentation were media of transformation for the human self,[43] and that technological operations from the raw material to the

[36] Nebelsick 2000, p. 163.
[37] For the treatment of bronze sword before deposition see Quilliec 2008.
[38] Vinski-Gasparini 1973; Clados 1997, pp. 174-176.
[39] See for example Maraszek 1998, p. 94; 2000, pp. 209-224.
[40] Hansen 1994; Sommerfeld 1994. On this topic for the Early Bronze Age see also Needham 1988.
[41] Čivilytė 2009, pp. 125-145.
[42] For hoards composed of different categories of artefacts and their relation to graves during Neolithic and Copper Age in south-eastern Europe see Chapman 2000, pp. 112-131.
[43] Brück 2006, pp. 306-307.

finished product were highly ritualised.[44] Technologies such as metallurgy and potting

> "acted as metaphors for the production of the self. Similarly, they may have provided people with the resources to understand and conceptualize the formation and dissolution of social relations".[45]

Furthermore, metalworking should definitely not be regarded as an everyday activity either for the production of finished object or for the reduction of the objects to scraps.[46] Metallurgy in ethnographic examples is often documented in association with cult practices, and metalworking is considered an activity that entails strong ritual significance.[47] In a recent study that draws close parallels between African ethnographic societies and ancient Greece, S. Blakely demonstrates the close relation that exists between metallurgy and ritual and political powers.[48]

5. Display of scraps as display of gifts

Considering the impressive amount of metal scraps that form some hoards, it can be argued that, in certain cases, metal objects were originally held by a larger segment of the society and that they were not the original property only of a single chief or enlarged family. Those data point to the capacity of one or more individuals – elite members? Priests-metallurgists? – to subtract from the society a certain quantity of wealth[49] and destine it to the hoarding ritual.

Furthermore, it is very unlikely to recompose the metal scraps that form Late Bronze Age hoards into a single object, i.e. each metal scrap comes from a different item. Together, these data suggest that the participation to the hoarding practice probably involved a large segment of the society or more communities. L. Nebelsick[50] suggests that the fragmented material could have been divided into a divine and human share. Following this idea, it can be proposed that a fragment of a sickle's or an axe's blade, for example, could have become part of

[44] Brück 2001, p. 157.
[45] Brück 2006, p. 306.
[46] Barndon 2004 and Haaland 2004 cited in Bradley 2005, pp. 150.
[47] Bradley 2005, pp. 163-164.
[48] Blakely 2006, pp. 166-179.
[49] As Bartelheim and Stäuble (2009, p. 2) pointed out, "in recent years, research in many parts of Europe has increasingly showed that there was a lot more to the Bronze Age economy than simply manufacturing bronze or producing food to ensure subsistence and to exchange for metals". See also Hänsel 1995.
[50] Nebelsick 2000, pp. 169-170.

the hoard while the remaining part of the object remained in the hands of the original owner as a symbolic token that certified the participation to the hoarding ceremony. I see no impediment in the subsequent recycling of these 'tokens' to produce new metal objects. Once executed, the duty as gift-to-gods through the assignment of one of its parts – which represented the "substitute object for humans"[51] in the hoarding ceremony – the 'token', i.e. what remained of the object, could have returned into the mundane sphere, be reintegrated in its role of commodity and be re-casted to produce new metal items.

Also, in several large scrap hoards a co-presence of objects that belong to different chronological horizons[52] can be observed.[53] Older objects usually represent a minimal percentage of the total objects that form Late Bronze Age hoards.[54] It can be suggested that the presence of older artefacts in hoards reflects 'gift giving' practices as well. Following A. B. Weiner's theory on gift paradox, older objects in hoards can be interpreted as the "inalienable possessions" which are ideally kept by their owners from one generation to the next within the closed context of family, descent group or dynasty. These things are imbued with the intrinsic identities of their owners and embodied the ancestor's histories.[55] The transmission of inalienable possessions representing the ancestors promotes authority.[56] M. Rowland argues that:

> "in contexts where objects are destroyed or taken out of circulation through burial or some other form of intentional symbolism, such objects become a memory in their absence, and therefore the essence of what has to be remembered. The opportunities for manipulating the possibilities of repetition are therefore abolished in an act of sacrifice or destruction that severs connection with its original status".[57]

From archaeological record it is not possible to infer with certainty if metal hoards were assembled by collecting objects originally exchanged as gifts

[51] Godelier 1999, pp. 121-138.

[52] Especially in large hoards, it is frequent to find few objects which belong to a chronological horizon which is ca. 50-100 calendar years preceding in respect to the one to whom belong most of the objects.

[53] The dating of metal objects, when the provenience context is unknown or when it is not possible to undertake scientific analysis to establish their absolute chronology, is usually undertaken on typological basis and through comparison with other objects that come from contexts – graves, settlements, etc. – dated with radiocarbon or other scientific methods. Metal objects can be dated quite well on the basis of formal attributes.

[54] In Slovenia, for example, the hoards of Jurka Vas, Hočko Pohorje and Čermožiše. See Teržan 1996 and Gori 2003.

[55] Weiner 1992, pp. 6-8.

[56] Weiner 1992, pp. 105-106.

[57] Rowlands 1993, p. 146.

between community members or between different communities, but – at least in some cases – it can be very plausible.

The hoard of Le Petit Villatte[58] (France) is composed by four 'panoplies', which, like the other objects that form the hoard, are reduced to scraps. Stylistic analysis combined with difference in patina colour of the metals that compose Le Petit Villatte suggest that the 'panoplies' came from three distinct European regions. In P. Y. Milcent's interpretation, each of the exotic assemblages that form a part of the Le Petit Villatte hoard consists in the panoplies of two 'couples' (a warrior and a woman). The local metalworking cannot be assigned to any particular individual and is mainly formed by scraps.[59] The presence of personal warfare equipments originating from different geographic areas suggests that Le Petit Villatte hoard was the material outcome of a gift giving ceremony between élites belonging to different 'metallurgical circles'. The rank value of each class of goods varies inversely with the frequency of its use, and the quality differences between goods are markers of the rank of events, as well as rank of persons. Luxuries and exotica tend to serve essentially for low-frequency events that are highly esteemed.[60] C. A. Gregory pointed out that what a gift to god accomplishes is the "*alienation of the inalienable*", given that a gift is an inalienable thing.[61] In this perspective, Le Petit Villatte can be interpreted as the final passage of a chain of gifts, where the hoarding performance (gifts to god) represents the final stage of a series of reciprocity (gifts to men). It is tempting to establish a parallel between Le Petit Villatte panoplies and the weapons exchanged between Hector and Ajax to demonstrate to everybody their temporary friendship and their equal courage.[62]

An important aspect that needs to be underlined is the weapons' function as prestigious objects. According to metallurgical analysis it seems that several weapons which entered the archaeological record in hoards or as grave goods had the primary function of status displayer, and belonged to the sphere of luxury and representation, and that they were not used directly in combat.[63] Material transfer through gift plays an important role as a specific procedure in

[58] Milcent 1998, pp. 55-69. Le Petit Villatte dates to the ninth century BCE (Ha B2-B3).
[59] However, Milcent points out that among local bronzes it is possible to identify several homogeneous sub-sets, like a batch of ten entire bracelets of type Ballingen or eight bracelets of type Homburg (Milcent 1998, pp. 63-64).
[60] Douglas and Isherwood 1996, p. 83.
[61] Gregory 1980, p. 645 (original emphasis).
[62] On 'gift-giving' in the Homeric poems see Bertelli in this volume.
[63] Swords, spears and daggers (Čivilytė 2009). A completely opposite opinion is presented by Mödlinger 2011. For use-wear analysis and the background surrounding the real quantity of swords in circulation during the Bronze Age see Molloy 2011.

communicative rituals where the quality of the owner is articulated through the possession of the object.[64]

Considering these aspects together through a diachronic perspective that embraces the entire Urnfield period, it is clear that hoarding phenomenon needs to be regarded as a complex combination of different cultural and social practices culminating in a gift to gods where metal objects are permanently removed from the economy and left in a dead end.[65]

6. 'Merchants' hoards': ingots as ritual gift

From the Middle Urnfield Period, hoards diminish progressively in number. During the Late Urnfield Period, in addition to tools and weapons, hoards are also composed by jewellery, metal vessels, horse gears, armours, helmets, fibulae, metal ingots, etc. During the Late Urnfield period, excepting scrap hoards, appear hoards composed by unfinished objects which entered the archaeological record without having been used before and without showing signs of ritual violence.

The hoard of Kanalski Vrh I (Slovenia), for example, was buried on the top of a hill in a hollow between two rocks, 50 cm below the present surface, probably in a vessel.[66] The ingots had been placed at the bottom of the vessel and the other objects were placed above them. A second hoard composed only by ingots (Kanalski Vrh II) was buried on the same hill, approximately two kilometres from the first hoard. The hoard of Kanalski Vrh I is composed by wheel-shaped pendants, rings, elaborated necklaces, small phalerae, winged axes and many other decorative elements, with a few of them broken like the pendant with double bird protome.[67] The pendants have casting and moulding traces, and in most of them no accuracy in manufacture is present: the suspension-eye and the decorative rays are missing, and even after an accurate finishing process, they would not reach the quality of other pendants belonging to the same type.

[64] Mauss 1923-24; Godelier 1999; se also Rowlands 1993, in particular pp. 147-149, where he argues that "sacrifice and the production of memory are intertwined in the New Ireland material. This technique of gift production through mnemonics allows its imagery to be spread over an expanding region and to serve as a means for the creation and the apprehension of new forms of ranking".

[65] For religious aspects between the Late Bronze Age and the Early Iron Age in Europe refer to Schauer 1996.

[66] Žbona-Trkman – Bavdek 1996, pp. 31-71.

[67] Žbona-Trkman – Bavdek 1996, p. 65. One comparable pendant was found in a grave from Grünwald, Bayern. From the Terramare area in north-western Italy come several antler pins close to the bronze pendants. The double bird protome or *barca solare* has an explicit cultural meaning in all Europe.

Most of the pendants seem to have been casted in the same mould. Just like the pendants, also the three winged-axes are also freshly casted: the wings were not folded and the blade not sharpened. In the same hoards many ingots' fragments are also present; one of them has an 'ear of wheat-like' decoration.[68] Like the other unfinished metal objects found in contemporary hoards, the artefacts in 'mint' condition that compose the first hoard of Kanalski Vrh can be interpreted as ingots. The wheel-motives represented on the pendants of Kanalski Vrh I have a very wide chronological and geographical diffusion, and a strong symbolic value,[69] and their direct typological ancestors can be considered the central European pins-head, typical of the Middle Bronze Age tumuli culture.[70] During the Late Urnfield Period, wheel-shaped pendants and wheel-shaped pin-heads became increasingly popular and entered the archaeological record as grave goods or formed hoards together with other objects of high symbolic value, such as the hoard of Coste del Marano, Italy. In Coste del Marano wheel-shaped pendants and wheel-shaped pin-heads were buried together with other prestige artefacts like an axe-shaped pendant and two drinking cups with the handle shaped as bull protome.[71]

The 'mint' condition axes of Kanalski Vrh I may have been expressly produced in the form of ingots to be discharged during hoarding performance.[72] The same status of non-usable objects can be recognised in the axes buried in other contemporary hoards.[73] Following P. Turk, it can be argued that also the wheel-shaped pendants held the status of non-usable objects, i.e. ingots, in which symbolic and material values merged together.[74] The use of metal with a clear economic, i.e. quantitative value (ingots) as a gift to the gods reflects also changes occurring on the economic level in Late Urnfield societies. In their 'social life'[75] as gifts to the gods, the ingots buried in hoarding ceremonies retained

[68] Žbona-Trkman – Bavdek 1996, p. 66.

[69] They are often present in funerary contexts. See, for example, Colonna 2006, p. 304.

[70] De Angelis – Francozzi – Gori 2007, pp. 117-120.

[71] Peroni 1961.

[72] Rowlands 1993, p. 149: "Malangan sculptures are by no means unique as collections of objects made for destruction. Potlatch ceremonials of the North West Coast served equally to construct memory and bestow fame through the destruction of objects. More recently, Richard Bradley (1990) has argued for the same model for Bronze Age metalwork deposits in Europe. And when compared with the work of Kristian Kristiansen (1978) on consumption and circulation of metalwork, we would appear to have elements of both Malangan and Kula type memory systems functioning in the European Bronze Age".

[73] For the Balkan region see Gori 2006, pp. 208-212 on the axes from Torovicë in Albania.

[74] Turk 2001, pp. 249-271.

[75] Appadurai 1986.

together their symbolic, qualitative and quantitative values, while when the same objects circulated in the mundane economic distribution networks they restrained mainly their quantitative value.

7. Conclusion

The analysis of the *chaîne opératoire*'s steps that stand behind the metal artefacts forming the so-called 'mundane' or 'profane' hoards clearly speaks in favour of their interpretation as ritual rather than functional depositions. In all cases, hoarding performance entails an everlasting alienation of prestige goods – in form of scraped or entire metal objects or casted and rough metal ingots – which can be interpreted as a 'gift to gods'.[76] In scrap hoards metal objects undergo a process of ritual defunctionalisation which radically transforms their status and meaning.[77] Hoarding performance seems to have been complex and articulated as it involved different segments of the society with different statuses (metal holders, metal producers, etc.).

In 'merchants' hoards' the transformation process appears to be less marked, and the buried objects retained, at least partially, their previous status and meaning. Metal items were probably purchased directly from the metallurgists in the form of ingots and mint-fresh objects and given to the gods as such. As it can be observed in Kanalski Vrh I, ritual violence is absent[78] and the hoarding performance seems to be simplified in respect to the one observed in the scrap hoards.

In both cases, the ritual and the mundane-economic sphere of hoarding are not to be detached and merge together trough the life-path of the objects, which – entire and fragmented – pass through different stages that define their transitory value and meaning. Differences in the hoard's composition and the objects' state of conservation are not expressions of the hoard's functional variation. Rather, they mirror the changes in social structure occurred during the Late Urnfield period.

Late Bronze Age hoards represent an alienation of metal from a natural person (the individual, the community) to a non-natural person (god). Gifts to the gods cannot be returned and these are the only gifts that increase personal

[76] Mauss 1923-24, pp. 12-16.
[77] Appadurai 1986, pp. 3-63.
[78] Fragmentation and ritual violence are widely recorded also in late Urnfield period hoards, for example in Škocjan-Mušja Jama (Slovenia), if we want to remain in the Carpathian basin's fringes (see Turk 2012, fig. 3 p. 134), or in Rimessone, Italy (Toune 2009). The change observed regards mainly the composition of the hoard, with the introduction of new types of objects, cast ingots and bronze cakes during the last phases of the Late Bronze Age. For example, for the distribution of ingots known as *doppelaxtförmige Barren* see Turk 1995, pp. 49-52.

prestige over a long period, when the relation of the giver to a god is manifestly a vehicle for the expression of relations between humans.[79] In other words, ritual gifts are not given with the aim of trying to gain a tangible counter-gift by the gods, but to establish a prominent position in the community. Such conspicuous consumption at the end of the Bronze Age needs to be understood in its social and political milieu.

At the beginning of the Urnfield Period, cemeteries present typical features: the predominant, if not exclusive, body treatment is incineration in a urn; the graves are gathered in clusters and grave goods are generally absent or composed by pottery and rare metal objects. In the Carpathian Basin, between Sava and Drava Rivers, the cemeteries contemporary to the 'first' and 'second hoard phases'[80] hold just a few metal objects, mainly personal jewellery. The 'austerity' of these graves contrasts greatly with the wealth exhibition observed in contemporary hoards. Exhibition of power through wealth display was not made in the occasion of death, where apparent 'equality' was showed through the paucity of grave goods and standardisation of the burials. The wide distribution of metal deposits (hoards and single finds) in the region suggests that they could have supplemented and substituted for the burials of one segment of the society.

R. Bradley argues that any form of bronze deposition had, as a prime purpose, the overt destruction of property as a demonstration of extraordinary surplus and ability to dispose of it to ritual ends: the destruction of wealth in prehistoric societies was one very striking way of achieving and maintaining rank, deposition being not about economic but about competitive consumption.[81] According to K. Randsborg, a "period of greatest economic stress would see the greatest competition", and local elites would find it harder to maintain and pass their prominent position from one generation to another.[82] K. Kristiansen argues through evidence of warfare that during the Urnfield period the rise of a new warrior aristocracy in Central Europe, along the Danube to the Rhine, can be seen. The way to increase political power would be via warfare and not via production, as can be seen in the organisation of people and resources, the size and nature of political control. In K. Kristiansen's perspective, hoards are interpreted as signs of changes in the use of wealth which presumed changes in social and economic strategies, where the 'economy' of bronze exchange determines the rate of deposition.[83] The 'Berlin school' emphasizes the cultual aspect of hoarding practices.[84] This interpretation is based on the composition of Late

[79] Gregory 1980, pp. 644-646.

[80] As defined by Vinski-Gasparini 1973.

[81] Bradley 1982; 1984, 105; 1988.

[82] Randsborg 1974, pp. 38-61; 1995.

[83] Kristiansen 1998. On this topic see also Needham 2001.

[84] Hänsel 1997, pp. 11-22.

Bronze Age German hoards, which reflects a deliberately chosen canonical selection from the then current bronze artefact spectrum. Some of the bronze objects in use during the Urnfield Period never entered the archaeological record in a hoard,[85] and axes and sickles – two of the most popular bronze items in central Europe – may have been connected with rituals as butchering and harvesting tools. The presence of bronze ingots has been connected to the offering of value in form of an aniconic gift offered to the gods.

An increased emphasis on wealth consumption in funerary contexts can be observed in the Late Urnfield period, when ritual practices expressed through metal hoarding were partially absorbed in funerary ceremonies.[86] In this perspective it can be argued that during the Early Urnfield period local elites were not able to maintain and pass their prominent position from one generation to another, and inter-clan rivalry motivated the alienation of metal in form of hoards as gift to gods. On the contrary, in the Late Urnfield period, as can be inferred by metals distribution pattern in graves, the social status becomes inheritable and social stability increased. Through this diachronic perspective, the difference between Early and Late Urnfield hoards has to be interpreted in an economic and sociological rather than in a functional perspective. The introduction of different types of objects and different ritual performances corresponds to different modes in which wealth was displayed and consumed, alike directed to achieve and maintain status.

As C. A. Gregory observed in his study on modern Papua, where a gift-to-men was replaced by a gifts-to-god system, it is the ranking achieved by alienation that is important, not the mode of alienation itself.[87] Following P. Bourdieu's habitus theory, it can be argued that Late Bronze Age hoarding performances can be regarded as the transfiguration of economic acts into symbolic acts, where the gift ceases to be a material object to become a symbol suited to creating a social link.[88]

Bibliography

Appadurai, Arjun: *Introduction: Commodities and the Politics of Value*, in: *The Social Life of Things: Commodities in Cultural Perspective*, ed. by Arjun Appadurai, Cambridge 1986, pp. 3-63.

Bartelheim, Martin – Harald Stäuble (ed. by): *Die Wirtschaftlichen Grundlagen der Bronzezeit Europas*, Rahden 2009.

Bourdieu, Pierre: *Practical Reason*, Stanford 1998.

[85] Hänsel 1997, pp. 13-14.
[86] Bradley 1990.
[87] Gregory 1980.
[88] Bourdieu 1998, p. 104.

Blakely, Sandra: *Myth, Ritual, and Metallurgy in Ancient Greece and Recent Africa*, Cambridge 2006.

Bradley, Richard: *The Destruction of Wealth in Later Prehistory*, in *Man* (N.S.), 17 (1982), pp. 108-122.

Bradley, Richard: *The Social Foundation of Prehistoric Britain: Themes and Variations in the Archaeology of Power*, London 1984.

Bradley, Richard: *Hoarding, Recycling and the Consumption of Prehistoric Metalwork: Technological Change in Western Europe*, in: *World Archaeology*, 20 (1988), pp. 249-260.

Bradley, Richard: *The Passage of Arms. An archaeological analysis of prehistoric hoards and votive deposit*, Cambridge 1990.

Bradley, Richard: *Ritual and Domestic Life in Prehistoric Europe*, New York 2005.

Brysbaert, Ann (ed. by): *Tracing Prehistoric Social Networks through Technology. A Diachronic Perspective on the Aegean*, New York 2011.

Brück, Joanna: *Body Metaphors and Technologies of Transformation in the English Middle and Late Bronze Age*, in: Joanna Brück, *Bronze Age Landscapes: Tradition and Transformation*, Oxford 2001, pp. 149-160.

Brück, Joanna: *Fragmentation, Personhood and the Social Construction of Technology in Middle and Late Bronze Age Britain*, in: *Cambridge Archaeological Journal*, 16 (2006), pp. 297-315.

Bruno, Arianna: *Spears in Context: Typology, Life-Cycles and Social Meanings in Bronze Age Italy*, PhD thesis – Manchester 2012.

Chapman, John: *Fragmentation in Archaeology. People, Places and Broken Objects in the Prehistory of South Eastern Europe*, New York 2000.

Chapman, John: *Domesticating the Exotic: the Context of Cucuteni-Tripolye Exchange with Steppe and Forest-steppe Communities*, in: *Ancient Interactions: East and West in Eurasia*, ed. by Katherine V. Boyle – Colin Renfrew – Marsha A. Levine, Cambridge 2002, pp. 77-78.

Čivilytė, Agne: *Wahl der Waffen. Studien zur Deutung der bronzezeitlichen Waffendeponierungen im nördlichen Mitteleuropa*, Bonn 2009.

Clados, Christiane: *Pustakovec*, in: *Gaben an die Götter. Schatze der Bronzezeit Europas*. ed. by Alix Hänsel – Bernhard Hänsel, Berlin 1997, pp. 174-176.

Colonna, Cecilia: *Necropoli dell'ultima età del bronzo nell'area padana. Per una loro cronologia relativa*, Lucca 2006.

De Angelis, Sara – Giorgia Francozzi – Maja Gori: *I pendagli della media e tarda età del Bronzo nell'Italia centro-settentrionale: stile e simbologia*, in: *Annali Università di Ferrara* N. S. 2007, pp. 117-120.

Douglas, Mary – Baron Isherwood: *The World of Goods. Towards an Anthropology of Consumption*, London 1996.

Fontijn, David: *Sacrificial Landscapes. Cultural Biographies of Person, Objects and Natural Places in the Bronze Age of Southern Netherlands, c. 2300-600 BC*, in: *Analecta Praehistorica Leidensia* 33/34 (2002).

Fontijn, David: *"Traders' Hoards". Reviewing the Relationship Between Trade and Permanent Deposition: the Case of the Dutch Voorhout Hoard*, in: *Hoards from the Neolithic to the Metal Ages. Technical and Codified Practices* ed. by Caroline Hamon – Bénédicte Quilliec, Oxford 2008, pp. 5-17.

Godelier, Maurice: *L'énigme du don*, Paris 1996 Engl. Transl.: *The enigma of the gift*, Chicago 1999.

Gori, Maja: *I Ripostigli Sloveni dell'età dei Campi di Urne, cronologia e analisi funzionale della composizione*, Tesi di Laurea, Roma 2003.

Gori, Maja: *Nuovi dati relativi alla circolazione di bronzi tra le due sponde dell'Adriatico meridionale nell'età del Bronzo finale: il ripostiglio di Torovicë (Albania)*, in *Studi in onore di Renato Peroni*, Firenze 2006, pp. 208-212.

Gosselain, Olivier P.: *Materializing Identities: An African perspective*, in: *Journal of Archaeological Method and Theory*, 7 (2000), pp. 187-217.

Gregory, Chris A.: *Gift to Men and Gift to God: Gift Exchange and Capital Accumulation in Contemporary Papua*, in: *Man* (N.S.), 15 (1980), pp. 626-652.

Hahn, Hans P.: *Words and Things: Reflection on People's Interaction with the Material World*, in: *Materiality and Social Practice. Transformative Capacities of Intercultural Encounters*, ed. by Joseph Maran – Philipp Stockhammer, Oxford 2012, pp. 4-12.

Hahn, Hans P. – Hadas Weiss (ed. by): *Mobility, Meaning & Transformation of Things. Shifting Contexts of Material Culture through Time and Space*, Oxford 2013.

Hänsel, Bernhard (ed. by): *Handel, Tausch und Verkehr im Bronze- und Früheisenzeitlichen Südosteuropa*, München 1995.

Hänsel, Bernhard: *Gaben an die Götter. Schatze der Bronzezeit Europas. Eine Einführung*, in: *Gaben an die Götter. Schatze der Bronzezeit Europas*, ed. by Alix Hänsel – Bernhard Hänsel, Berlin 1997, pp. 13-22.

Hansen, Svend: *Studien zu den Metalldeponierung während der älteren Urnenfelderzeit zwischen Rhonetal und Karpathenbecken*, Bonn 1994.

Hansen, Svend – Daniel Neumann – Tilmann Vachta (ed. by): *Hort und Raum. Aktuelle Forschungen zu Bronzezeitlichen Deponierungen in Mitteleuropa*, Berlin 2012.

Hansen, Svend: *Vorwort der Herausgeber*, in: *Die Kupfer- und Bronzedepots der frühen und mittleren Bronzezeit in Rumänien*, ed. by Tudor Soroceanu, Cluj-Napoca 2012, p. 7.

Hodder, Ian: *Entangled. An Archaeology of the Relationship between Humans and Things*, Chichester 2012.

Humphrey, Caroline – Stephen Hugh-Jones: *Barter, Exchange and Value. An Anthropological Approach*, Cambridge 1992.

Huth, Christoph: *Metal Circulation, Communication and Traditions of Craftsmanship in Late Bronze Age and Early Iron Age Europe*, in: *Metals Make the World Go Round. The Supply and Circulation of Metals in Bronze Age Europe*, ed. by Christopher F.E. Pare, Oxford 2000 pp.177-193.

Kopytoff, Igor: *The Cultural Biography of Things: Commodization as Process*, in: *The Social Life of Things: Commodities in Cultural Perspective*, ed. by Arjun Appadurai, Cambridge 1986, pp. 64-91.

Kristiansen, Kristian: *Europe Before History*, Cambridge 1998.

Levy, Janet E.: *Social and Religious Organization in Bronze Age Denmark. An Analysis of Ritual Hoard Finds*, Oxford 1982.

Maraszek, Regine: *Spätbronzezeitliche Hortfunde entlang der Oder*, Bonn 1998.

Maraszek, Regine: *Late Bronze Age Axe Hoards in Western and Northern Europe*, in: *Metals Make the World go Round. The Supply and Circulation of Metals in Bronze Age Europe*, ed. by Christopher F.E. Pare, Oxford 2000, pp. 209-224.

Mauss, Marcel: *Essai sur le don. Forme et raison de l'échange dans les sociétés archaïques*, in: *L'Année sociologique* n.s. 1 (1923-1924), pp. 30-186; Engl. Transl.: *The Gift. Forms and Functions of Exchange in Archaic Societies*, London 1974.

Milcent, Pierre-Yves : *Le Petit-Villatte à Neuvy sur-Barangeon (Cher): lecture d'un dépôt complexe*, in : *L'atelier du bronzier en Europe du XXe au VIIe siècle avant notre ère 3. Production, circulation et consommation du bronze*, ed. by Claude Mordant, Paris 1998, pp. 55-69.

Mödlinger, Marianne: *Ritual Object or Powerful Weapon – The Usage of Central Europe Bronze Age Swords*, in: *Bronze Age Warfare: Manufacture and Use of Weaponry*, ed. by Marion Uckelmann – Marianne Mödlinger, Oxford 2011, pp. 153-166.

Molloy, Barry: *Use-wear Analysis and Use-patterns of Bronze Age Swords*, in: *Bronze Age Warfare: Manufacture and Use of Weaponry*, ed. by Marion Uckelmann – Marianne Mödlinger, Oxford 2011, pp. 67-84.

Nebelsick, Louis: *Rent Asunder: Ritual Violence in Late Bronze Age Hoards*, in: *Metals Make the World go Round. The Supply and Circulation of Metals in Bronze Age Europe*, ed. by Christopher F.E. Pare, Oxford 2000, pp. 160-175.

Needham, Stuart P.: *Selective Deposition in the British Early Bronze Age*, in: *World Archaeology*, 20 (1988), pp. 229-248.

Needham, Stuart P.: *When Expediency Broaches Ritual Intention: the Flow of Metal between Systemic and Buried Domains*, in: *The Journal of the Royal Anthropological Institute*, 7 (2001), pp. 275-298.

Pare, Christopher F.E.: *Weights and Weighing in Bronze Age Central Europe*, in: *Eliten in der Bronzezeit. Ergebnisse zweier Kolloquien in Mainz und Athen*, Mainz 1999, pp. 421-514.

Pare, Christopher F.E.: *Bronze and the Bronze Age*, in: *Metals Make the World go Round. The Supply and Circulation of Metals in Bronze Age Europe*, ed. by Christopher, F.E. Pare, Oxford 2000, pp. 1-38.

Peroni, Renato: *Italia, Ripostigli dell'età dei metalli.* 1: I.3. *Ripostigli del massiccio della Tolfa*. 2: I.4-5. *Ripostigli del Grossetano*, in: *Inventaria Archaeologica*, Firenze 1961.

Peroni, Renato – Gianluigi Carancini: *La koinè metallurgica*, in: *Le Terramare la più antica civiltà padana*, ed. by Maria Bernabò Brea – Andrea Cardarelli – Mauro Cremaschi, Modena 1997, pp. 595-601.

Primas, Margarita: *Die Sicheln in Mitteleuropa I (Österreich, Schweiz, Süddeutschland)*, Münich 1986.

Quilliec, Bénédicte: *Use, Wear and Damage: Treatment of Bronze Swords Before Deposition*, in: *Hoards from the Neolithic to the Metal Ages. Technical and Codified Practices*, ed. by Caroline Hamon – Bénédict Quilliec, Oxford 2008, pp. 67-78.

Randsborg, Klavs: *Social Stratification in Early Bronze Age Denmark: a Study in the Regulation of Cultural Systems*, in: *Prähistorische Zeitschrift* 49 (1974), pp. 38-61.

Randsborg, Klavs: *Hjortspring. Warfare and Sacrifice in Early Europe*, Aarhus 1995.

Rowlands, Michael: *The Role of Memory in the Transmission of Culture*, in: *World Archaeology*, 25 (1993), pp. 141-151.

Schauer, Peter (ed. by): *Archäologische Forschungen zum Kulturgeschenken in der jüngeren Bronzezeit und frühen Eisenzeit Alteuropas*, Regensburg 1996.

Sommerfeld, Christoph: *Gerätegeld Sichel. Studien zur monetären Struktur bronzezeitlicher Horte im nördlichen Mitteleuropa*, Berlin 1994.

Sørensen, Marie Louise – Katharina Christina Rebay: *The Impact of 19th Century Ideas on the Construction of 'Urnfield' as a Chronological and Cultural Concept*, in: *Construire le temps. Histoire et méthodes des chronologies et calendriers des derniers millénaires avant notre ère en Europe occidentale*, ed. by Anne Lehoërff, Bibracte 2008, pp. 57-67.

Teržan, Biba (ed. by): *Depojske in posamezne kovinske najdbe bakrene in bronaste dobe na Slovenskem II,* Ljubljana 1996.

Toune, Bastien : *Fragmentation et objets "manipulés" dans le dépôt de Rimessone (Latium). Pour une autre approche des dépôts de la fin de l'âge du bronze en Italie centrale*, in: *Du Matériel au Spirituel: Réalités archéologiques et historiques des «dépôts» de la Préhistoire à nos jour*, ed. by Sandrine Bonnardin – Caroline Hamon– Michel Lauwers – Bénédicte Quilliec, Antibes 2009 pp. 195-201.

Turk, Peter: *Das Depot eines Bronzegießers aus Slowenien – Opfer oder Materiallager?*, in: *Handel, Tausch und Verkehr im Bronze- und Früheisenzeitlichen Südosteuropa*, ed. by Bernhard Hänsel, München 1995, pp. 49-52.

Turk, Peter: *The Weight of Objects in Late Bronze Age Hoards in Slovenia and Possibilities for Determining Weight Standards*, in: *Arheološki Vestnik* 52 (2001), pp. 249-271.

Turk, Peter: *Die Waffenfunde aus der Mušja jama/Fliegenhöle bei Škocjan, Slowenien*, in: *Waffen für die Götter. Krieger, Trophäen, Heiligtümer*, ed. by Wolfgang Meighörner, Innsbruck 2012, pp. 134-137.

Vinski-Gasparini, Ksenia: *Kultura polja sa žarama u Sjevernoj Hrvatskoj. Die Urnenfelderkultur in Nordkroatien*, Zadar 1973.

Weiner, Annette B. : *Inalienable Possessions. The Paradox of Keeping-While-Giving.* Berkeley – Los Angeles – Oxford 1992.

Žbona-Trkman, Beatriče – Alma Bavdek: *Depojski najdbi s Kanalskega Vrha*, in: *Depojske in Posamezne Kovinske najdbe bakrene in bronaste dobe na slovenskem II*, ed. by Biba Teržan, Ljubljana 1996, pp. 31-71.

IRENE BERTI

Value for Money: Pleasing the Gods and Impressing Mortals in the Archaic and Early Classical Age.

1. Introduction

Reciprocity between gods and men was a basic premise of Greek religion.[1] Almost the whole of Greek cultic practice was founded on the belief or hope that the gods reacted to what mortals did: that they punished injustice and crime and that they helped in difficult times. When people were poor, ill, or threatened by a danger they prayed to a god and promised a reward; when their hope had been fulfilled, the danger averted, or their efforts crowned by success, they provided a gift for the god in return. These gifts were monuments of gratitude and expression of a well-functioning relationship between god and human. As Robert Parker illustrated in his seminal article on reciprocity,[2] the language of *charis* was central to the logic of gift and counter-gift, which was so typical of Greek religion. Mortals gave gifts or made sacrifices, which were *charienta* or *kecharismena* to the gods, and requested a return which was itself *chariessa*. The primary meaning of *charis* is charm, delight, or that which causes it. The ideas of reciprocity and repayment are not associated with *chari*-words in a direct semantic way, but rather in the function, expressed by *charis*, of bridging the divide between men and mortals through an exchange of kindnesses: one gift or act provided with power to please (*charis*) will summon another, which will in turn evoke yet another. But a *charis*, even when given in return for a *charis*, is not a mere recompense; it is more essentially the expression of a social relation.[3]

[1] This article developed from my research on materiality and the presence of Athenian inscriptions in the CRC 933 "Material Text Cultures" at Heidelberg. I wish to thank Lucia Cecchet and Enrica Culasso, who both improved this paper with valuable suggestions and precious criticisms, and James Thorne for his help with the English. Errors and omissions are solely mine.

[2] Parker 1998, pp. 105-125.

[3] On *charis* in the exchange with the gods, see also also Versnel 1981, pp. 42-64 (with a slightly different interpretation) and now Patera 2012, pp. 53-97: she notices that the relation of reciprocity with the gods is not a contract, because at least the gods are not compelled to repay the human beings. The exchange of 'pleasant things' between humans and gods should not be confused with a market trade, because the main point in this relation is neither to exchange goods with equivalent value, nor to exchange goods through the intermediation of a settled value (like money). Parker 1998, pp. 121-125,

Fundamental elements of the communication between men and gods were prayer, votive gift and sacrifice. They all played almost the same function – to establish a relationship – and could appear together: a loud spoken prayer usually accompanied a sacrifice and probably also the dedication of a gift; sometimes the prayer was included in the dedication and inscribed on the object itself.[4] Reciprocity can be observed in particular in the mechanism of gift giving and sacrifice, which provides materiality to this relationship. Votive dedication and sacrifice were both gifts for the gods.[5] Whereas a sacrifice went to the god in the form of smoke, or was partly eaten by the participants and/or the priests, a dedication survived as a physical object in the sanctuary and became, in a certain way, not only a possession of the gods, but also, especially if it was a valuable object, a part of the temple treasure. In addition, because of their visibility, dedications were a good medium to commemorate and communicate (for instance marriage, athletic victories, or military achievements). They were thus a very special kind of gift, because the giver benefited from them as well as the recipient.

The Athenian Acropolis has provided hundreds of dedicated objects in the form of marble or bronze statues, vases, small figurines, votive plaques and votive basins (made out of stone or bronze), as well as small altars and pillars.[6] Beside all these dedications which have survived, we should consider the great number – probably the majority – which have not come to us because they were made of less durable materials like textiles, wood and ceramic (vases, *pinakes*, small figurines) or because they were melted down in the periodical *kathairesis*. The latter, usually very expensive objects made of precious metals, are known only from their mention in the inventories of the treasuries keeping the record of all destroyed dedications. Besides these, one should not forget the bloody and bloodless sacrifices offered to the gods in form of *thysia*, holocaust or *theoxenia*.

The aim of this paper is to illustrate some of the mechanisms of dedication to the gods, the forms of social and religious communication implied with it, and how they interacted with the economic aspects of making a dedication in a public sanctuary. I will concentrate my analysis on the finds from the archaic and

describes the relation between god and humans as an asymmetric reciprocity.

4 Parker in *ThesCRA*, vol. 1, p. 270, diminishes the role of the prayer during the dedication, stating that generally, one dedicated an object just by "setting it up" (ἀνατίθημι). On prayer and religious mentality see Versnel 1981, pp. 1-64.

5 For a good overview both of the definitions and of the different types of sacrifice and dedications, see *ThesCRA*, vol. 1, pp. 59-134 and 269-318.

6 A still very valuable collection of inscribed dedications from the Athenian Acropolis is to be found in *DAA*. For a new approach and a revision of the chronology of the single dedicated statues, see Keesling 2003b. Votive reliefs and plaques (with and without inscriptions) are collected by Schulze 2004 and Comella 2002 (including also non-Athenian material). For an overview of the vases founded in the Acropolis excavation, see Graef – Langlotz 1925-1933. For the bronze finds, see de Ridder 1896.

classical Athenian Acropolis in a case study focusing especially on inscribed objects (bronze and marble offerings, as well as ceramic votives) and sacrificial calendars.

2. The object and the dedication: the role of the inscription

The most common word in ancient Greek for "votive offering" is *anathema*, and the most frequently used verb for "setting up a votive offering in a sanctuary" is *anatithenai*. This terminology suggests that offerings were preferably placed at a certain height from the ground.[7] The archaeological remains show that they were often nailed on a wall or supported by a pedestal. Among the supports of dedications from the Athenian Acropolis, we find small pillars with rectangular or hexagonal cross-sections, fluted or unfluted columns. A particular type of pillar, already occurring during the archaic period, became extremely popular during the classical period as a support for votive statues. It has a rectangular cross-section, and tapers slightly from the bottom to the top, where there is a sort of rectangular capital.[8] These pillars could support different kinds of objects: marble or bronze reliefs, statues (again in bronze or in stone), tripods, and vases.

Free-standing statues were not unusual among the dedications on the Acropolis during the late archaic and early classical periods. Unlike many votive statues of the archaic period, which bear the inscription on the leg or on the peplos,[9] in the Athenian dedications from the Acropolis the inscription does not usually run on the statue itself, but on the supporting base, pillar or capital.

Painted votive plaques were usually made of wood or ceramic, rarely in metal. They could be hung in many different places in the sacred precinct: close to the altar, on cult images, and on the temple walls.[10] Votive reliefs made out of stone were put on a pillar just like the free-standing *anathemata*.

Although not every votive object needed to be furnished with an inscription, many of the surviving offerings do, providing help to understand the reason for the dedication and the social status of the dedicator.

Votive ceramic *pinakes* usually just have a very simple dedication formula like ἱερὸν τοῦ θεοῦ; ὁ δεῖνα τῷ θεῷ; ὁ δεῖνα μ' ἀνέθηκε τῷ θεῷ, but sometimes

7 van Straten 1992, p. 248. See also Day 2010, p. 6, n. 17 (insisting on the ritual implication of the terminology) and Patera 2012, pp. 18-21 (on both the real and the symbolic meaning of *anathema*).

8 van Straten 1992, pp. 248-249. The dedication is here usually written on the capital.

9 See for instance Nikandre's *kore* from Delos (NM 1; *ID* 2), Mantiklos' bronze statuette from Thebes (Boston MFA 03.997; *CEG* 326) or Isches's giant kouros from Samos (Samos, *Arch. Mus.* 645; *IG* 12.6.2.560).

10 Schulze 2004, p. 7.

they also disclose the name of the potter.[11] Schulze suggests that the presence of the inscription increased the prestige of the object, especially during the Archaic age, when writing was still not very common; the presence or not of a dedicatory inscription would in this case make a difference in value and price of the single *pinax*.[12] But with the increase in the level of literacy as early as the sixth century BCE the importance of the inscription as an element adding prestige had surely diminished significantly. The frequent presence, however, of the names of the potter and painter probably reveals the intention of commercial publicity, and the highly developed market for these objects at the end of the archaic age. The *pinakes* are all Athenian products, which could easily be bought at the agora and dedicated on the Acropolis.[13]

Free-standing statues, marble basins or shields and marble reliefs also usually had a dedicatory inscription. The extant inscribed bases from the Acropolis attest an obsessive interest in the recording of personal names,[14] thus reminding us of the second important function of these objects: as a medium of display of prestige.

Like the dedicated objects, dedicatory inscriptions could also be very diverse:[15] they could be very short, just recording the possession of the god (τοῦ θεοῦ; τοῦ θεοῦ εἰμι), or recording just the name of the dedicator and the name of the god (ὁ δεῖνα τῷ θεῷ), thus underlining the relation between the two names, the dedicator and the recipient. The most extended type of dedicatory inscription, recording the dedication in a narrative style, pointed out the dedicator's wish to preserve the memory of the act of dedication, as a ritual communication with the divine. In this case the inscription did not just aim to record the god's ownership, but also to preserve the memory of the interaction between a named dedicator and a named god by means of a ritual offering.[16] Dedicatory inscriptions of the 'narrative type' could take the form of an epigram. In this case they represented an additional – poetical – gift for the gods. The epigram was one of the pleasing things that gods, like mortals, seemed to particularly appreciate.[17]

We do not know much about the ceremony of dedicating an object – if there was a ceremony at all. Day recalls the close conceptual association of dedication and sacrifice, suggesting that the ritual during which a dedication was given

[11] Schulze 2004, p. 46.
[12] Schulze 2004, p. 46.
[13] Schulze 2004, p. 47. *Contra*, see Viviers, 1992, pp. 42-43, who thinks that the signature of the artist is an element increasing the social prestige of the object, implying the social recognition of the artist and implicitly increasing the social prestige of the clients that buy and dedicate the signed objects (see also p. 50).
[14] Keesling 2003a, pp. 41-54, and in particular p. 42.
[15] Lazzarini 1976, pp. 47-354 is a still very useful collection of dedicatory formulas.
[16] Day 2010, pp. 6-7.
[17] Day 2010, p. 7.

typically included sacrifice, accompanied by prayers and libations, followed by the dedication of the durable gift.[18] Stressing the functional connection between sacrifice, dedication and preservation of the memory, Day especially highlights the commemorative and celebratory role of the votive dedications.

In the iconographic sources the act of offering a dedication is rarely depicted,[19] and even less frequent is the representation of sacrifice and the offering of durable gifts together.[20] But if we cannot exclude that small objects could be dedicated during an animal sacrifice, then we should not generalize and conclude that every dedication was accompanied by a sacrifice. The opposite, I think, could be true: because sacrifice was an ephemeral thing, we can easily understand that people wanted to keep memory of it with a *pinax* representing the sacrifice itself or a related subject.[21] Literary and epigraphical sources point out that small dedications were usually placed by the givers themselves as close as possible to the divinity, usually without intervention of the priests – who only intervened later, to arrange and organize the objects.[22] This suggests that the ceremony, if there was one, was very simple.[23]

Did visitors to a sanctuary read inscriptions and in which circumstances? Large outdoor dedications frequently stood nearby or were oriented towards altars, or they could be set on the sacred way. This means that they were usually put in a place where they could be seen.[24] The high position (on a pedestal,

[18] Day 2010, p. 5.

[19] Acr. 577 (Dickins 1912, pp. 117-118), a man seated on a chair hands and offering to a standing Athena; van Straten 1992, p. 264 (*Münzen und Medaillen* 40, Basel 1969, n. 95), a man and a youth carry ritual vessels (or votives?) and a branch with a hanging *pinax*. In opposition, representations of sacrifice are a favorite subject both on *pinakes* and marble reliefs, especially in the classic period: see Comella 2002, pp. 18-19 and van Straten 1995, pp. 57-100.

[20] See for instance van Straten 1995, p. 196 (V 16), Fig. 18: a man carrying a panathenaic amphora and leading a goat.

[21] See for instance Herond., *Mim.* 4.19-20, where Kokkale after the sacrifice of a cock is urged to put her *pinax* to the right of Hygiaia's statue. On memory of sacrifice see van Straten 1995, pp. 159-160.

[22] *Il.* 6.303; Aesch., *Sept.* 277-278; Eur., *Hipp.* 73-74; Herond., *Mim.* 4.19-20; Paus. 9.19.5. This is also clearly stated by the many Hellenistic sacred laws that forbade hanging votives in a particular part of the sanctuary (maybe already too full!), or to set up dedications in places where they prevent the passage. See for instance *LSS* 107, 10-18; *LSS* 123, 1-4. See also Patera 2012, pp. 109-113.

[23] I see no need to suppose a complex ceremony for every private dedication, but I suppose that the dedication of a big monument was a performance which could only with difficulty take place unnoticed and one can surely imagine at least a prayer or a libation accompanying the action.

[24] Day 2010, p. 10.

column or pillar) helped the monument to communicate to the viewer/reader, by putting the inscription at eye-level.

Contrary to scholars who hold that inscriptions were rarely read,[25] Day presents evidence of archaic literacy and shows that great effort was put into the visual display of the texts in order to attract the attention of viewers and guide them to correct reading. This is evident in the case of Telesinos' epigram, oriented for the convenience of the readers who were seeking the best view of the – now lost – bronze statuette.[26] Especially among inscriptions on stone, the letters are relatively large and regularly shaped and, to enhance legibility and attract attention, they were usually filled with bright paint.[27] The text could accompany or draw the viewer all the way around an object that was interesting from different points of view. Long lines could be written on round supports, as in the case of the *kore* dedicated by Aischines around 500 BCE:[28] the first short lines written on the supporting capital are oriented to the front of the *kore* which stood on it, but the third extends to the right. One could read the first lines whilst enjoying the frontal view of the statue and then, following the inscription, have a look at the *kore*'s left profile. Visual reception went together and interacted with the reading approach.

Although visitors were of course free to ignore inscriptions and many probably did, some will have stopped and read, at least the first lines. Especially in case of epigrams, partial reading could be less rare then we may think, because ancient readers could easily supplement hard to read parts from their knowledge of poetry or other inscriptions. As Day pointed out, the appearance of similar language in inscribed hexameters from different places suggests that epigrams were constructed out of a widespread poetic formulary with which poetically competent readers would be familiar. Epigrams, like the one of Telesinos, were written by someone who knew traditional poetic speech. And any reader imbued with the same literary *paideia* would be used to the inscription's vocabulary,

[25] See for instance W. V. Harris 1989, W. V. Harris 1996, p. 73 and recently Bing 2002, pp. 39-66.

[26] *IG* 1^3.728: Φαρθένε ἐν ἀκροπόλει Τελεσῖνος / ἄγαλμ' ἀνέθεκεν Κέτ(τ)ιος, *h*ôι χαίροσα διδοίες / ἄλ(λ)ο ἀναθε̂ναι. The inscription is aligned with the front of the plinth: the viewer looking frontally at the striding goddess could easily read the text by leaning the head slightly to the right. See Day 2010, pp. 1-4; 14-15 and 17 (with fig. 1.1 and 1.2, p. 2). For the typology of the statue see Keesling 1995, pp. 223-241 and Keesling 2003b, pp. 81-84. On the expedients to facilitate reading, see also Keesling 2003a, pp. 42-44.

[27] See for example *IG* 1^3.610 (= *DAA* 211, red); *IG* 1^3.611 (= *DAA* 215, red); *IG* 1^3.699 (= *DAA* 217, red and blue); *IG* 1^3.770 and 770 bis (= *DAA* 230, red and blue); *IG* 1^3.710 (= *DAA* 231, red).

[28] Day 2010, pp. 48-50 (with fig. 4.1-2, p. 52; *IG* 1^3.631: Αἰσχίνες ἀνέθεκεν / Ἀθεναίαι τόδ' ἄγαλμα / εὐχσάμενος δεκάτεν παιδὶ Διὸς μεγάλο).

syntax and religious rhetoric.[29] Many inscriptions show the same cluster of ideas, turning around the theme of *charis* and reciprocity. These recurring motifs, and the formulaic structure that underline them, were familiar to the ancient reader, who could easily imagine, by simply reading some key words, what the inscription was about.[30]

The 'pleasing gifts' (*agalmata*) displayed in a sacred place increased the prestige of the god, showed the importance of the sanctuary and stimulated the emulation of the worshipers. Famous shrines with all their dedicated objects were a kind of 'tourist attraction': people coming to visit the sanctuary during great festivals or on more private occasions, in order to pray or sacrifice, took the chance to have a look around and admire the splendour of the setting and all the beautiful works of art displayed.[31] Thus the sanctuary benefited from the presence of 'pleasing gifts' even when they did not have an intrinsic value.

3. How expensive was it to buy a gift for the goddess?

From a human point of view, the act of making a votive offering was, first of all, an economic transaction, implying that somebody bought an object and offered it to the gods, transforming personal property into the property of the recipient gods. In order to understand the economics of dedication, we need to consider not only how much a dedication cost, but also how much money the dedicators had to spend and why they decided to invest their money in a dedication.[32]

We do not know much about prices of *anathemata* during the archaic and classical periods. We can of course imagine that a free-standing marble statue was generally more expensive then a ceramic plaque. But even in this case, it was not only the material or the dimensions that determined the price, but surely

[29] Day 2010, pp. 40 and 42 shows very convincingly that apparently difficult archaic inscriptions like the Mantiklos epigram (*CEG* 326) could be easily read and understood by a public that was used to hear epic poetry with Homeric echoes and to read formulaic inscriptions.

[30] On *charis* in Telesinos' epigram, see Parker 1998, pp. 110-111. For other Athenian inscriptions (metric and non) centered on the theme of reciprocity or using the *charis* terminology see for instance: *IG* 1^3.634 (restored); 711; 776; 791; 872; 887.

[31] Bacch., *Od.* 3.17-19; Eur., *Ion* 82-183; Herond., *Mim.* 4, especially 20-25a. Hdt. 1.51-52 described in great detail and with evident admiration the precious objects dedicated by Croesos at Delphi and at the Amphiareion in Oropos. See also van Straten 1981, p. 75 and Day 2010, pp. 27-29; 67-73. Even if our testimonies concern mainly the classical and late classical periods, we can also imagine that during the archaic age people reacted to dedications in a sanctuary in the same way.

[32] For a good overview of the subject, see Keesling 1995, pp. 395-407.

also the quality of the work. So, even though we can infer, from the 'materiality' of ceramic relief and marble or bronze statue, that ceramic *pinakes* were conceived as more 'everyday' dedications, we still notice a great difference in quality from *pinax* to *pinax*, so that we can be sure that they also had different prices.

The majority of motifs displayed on archaic and early classical *pinake*s from the Athenian Acropolis are mythological scenes, images of the divinity and scenes of everyday life. Athena is usually represented as *promachos* or *polias*. Other mythological scenes like the labours of Herakles or the myth of Theseus can be easily interpreted as mythical projection of aristocratic values such as courage, *andreia* and sporting competition, allowing some conclusions on the social status of the dedicator and sometimes on the occasion of the dedication. The same system of values seems to be implicit also in the reliefs representing the goddess on a chariot and, more generally, images of horses and horsemen. War scenes and warriors quite explicitly evoke the values of the manly aristocratic *arete* in opposition to the world of craftsmanship or female work.[33] But the choice of the represented scenes does not always allow us to recognize the motivation or the status of the dedicator. Clearly, one could simply offer to Athena a particular image because one thought it was appropriated to her cult. In this case the image would reflect much more the divine personality and her cult than the ideal and moral world of the dedicator, let alone his motivation. The fact that the dedicatory inscriptions are usually short and stereotyped – as is typical for this kind of votives – does not help us to understand the needs and demands of the dedicators.

Although *pinakes* seem to be a more ephemeral dedication than a life-size statue, it would be a mistake to consider them as an expression of the lower classes in contrast to more impressive *anathemata*. *Pinakes* were surely also dedicated by wealthy people and members of the city elite, as demonstrated by some decorations which show clearly aristocratic subjects.[34] These small dedications, conceived just for the need of the dedicator, could not compete in ostentation with marble and bronze statues, and seem to be less conditioned by the rules of self-display and competition for personal prestige and visibility. Nevertheless they are a good medium of communication with the gods, giving visibility to the act of dedication and preserving memory of it.[35] In addition to that, the possibility to put a *pinax* inside the temple and very close to the cult

[33] Schulze 2004, p. 49. On the display of aristocratic *arête* in general see Duplouy 2006 (with bibliography) and, especially for the funerary context, Marchiandi 2008 and 2012, pp. 221-236 (particularly pp. 230-233).
[34] Schulze 2004, p. 50.
[35] Schulze 2004, p. 50.

statue – seeking thereby a more intimate contact with the divine – could be reason enough for choosing this type of votive instead of a monumental one.

On the other side, not every free-standing statue was of good quality and not all statues were equally expensive. Variations in size, type, function and material of the statues made in the sixth and fifth centuries BCE point to a considerable variation in prices. Bronze, for instance, had a substantial intrinsic value; moreover, as we know from the expense-accounts of the fifth-century cult statues of the Athenian Hephaisteion, the production process of bronze artifacts was particularly expensive, as it needed a great variety of non-reusable materials.[36] In contrast, marble from the state owned quarries on Pentelikon and Hymettos appears from Athenian building accounts not to have any cost as material, at least when it was used for public projects.[37] On the other hand, there is no evidence for the sale of Attic marble to private individuals in the fifth century.[38] However, quarrying and transport costs were always considerable even for a short distance, and they surely affected the cost of the final product. Marble from Paros and Naxos, still very used in private dedications at the end of the sixth century, was very expensive.[39]

Inscriptions are again a very helpful resource in trying to understand who dedicated what and why. But the cases in which we know the profession of the dedicators are unfortunately very few and even in these lucky cases, we know too little about salaries and wages to understand who could really afford what, how frequently, and what impact this practice had on the household economy. Nevertheless, some observations can be made.

While most of the dedicators chose to reveal only their names, some dedicators from the lowest classes did also record their profession – perhaps because of their pride in making, as simple workers, a dedication that had nothing rival to the aristocratic ones.[40] Amongst others, we have fullers, a tanner and a washerwoman.[41]

[36] *IG* 1^3.472; see also Keesling 1995, pp. 396 and 398.
[37] See for instance *IG* 1^3.436, 23-24 (building accounts of the Parthenon).
[38] Burford 1965, p. 29, stated that quarry-stone did not have a price in itself; labour and transport made up the costs. At least for the fifth century BCE, one cannot talk with certainty of a commercial exploitation of quarries. For a different interpretation of the fifth-century sources and for some later evidences of private contracts to exploit quarries, see Marginesu 2010, p. 119.
[39] Keesling 1995, p. 397. Scanty information about prices of marble and bronze statues can be found in the literary sources: see for instance Diog. Laert. 4.45 and 6.35. Nevertheless, these pieces of information are very difficult to interpret, because they refer to very different historical contexts and ages. See also Keesling 1995, pp. 400-401.
[40] Keesling 2003b, pp. 69-71.
[41] *IG* 1^3.554; 616; 905; 646; 794.

In the absence of an inscription, it is not always safe to try to deduce the profession and the social status of the dedicator from the image or the object dedicated, because they do not always have a direct relation to the social background or to the crafts of their dedicators. In some cases, a repertoire of images could of course signal a connection to a particular social identity. A classic case are the images of riders, which almost certainly point to a dedicator from the knights class.[42] But the cases in which this mechanism works without doubt are very few. An isolated horse with horseman could just as well be an image referring to the myths attached to the relevant god, or to the epithets of the cult. A baker woman, for instance, could dedicate a shield to Athena because of Athena's warrior characteristics.[43] Nor is it possible, from the materials we have, to argue that rich people always made expensive dedications while poor people always small and cheap ones, because often the quality and the cost of the votive depended not (or not only) on the economic resources of the dedicator but on the occasion of the dedication, even though obviously a monumental dedication was a better medium than a poor one in terms of impact on contemporaries. But even in this case, a rich person would not always make a rich offering: he would differentiate between one occasion and another and also probably between god and god.[44] We know, for instance, of a *tamias*, surely a member of the *pentakosiomedimnoi*, who offered 'just' a simple altar in *poros* stone, and of the treasurers of Athena, who made a collective dedication of a small bronze tablet, probably to commemorate their office as superintendents of the bronze dedications.[45]

On the other hand, we have positive evidence that sometimes people in humble professions could make big and expensive dedications.[46] We can easily envision the fisherman saving money for a whole year to make a beautiful offering for Athena as a reward for having rescued him in a dangerous situation

[42] Especially oversized bronze statues of horses and horsemen, as well as bronze tripods – a typical offering of athletes – point to members of the aristocracy, sometimes to very wealthy members of it. See Keesling 2003b, pp. 89-91; for bronze offerings and the aristocracy see also Marchiandi 2012, pp. 221-236.

[43] *IG* 1^3.546.

[44] See also Keesling 1995, pp. 395-408.

[45] *IG* 1^3.590 (= *DAA* 330); *IG* 1^3.510; see also Keesling 1995, pp. 305-306; 320-321 and 328.

[46] See for instance Simon the fuller (*DAA* 49 = *IG* 1^3.616), the base for a marble *kore* statue; Polyxenos, the son of Mneson the fuller (*DAA* 342 = *IG* 1^3.905), a *perirrhanterion*; Polykles the fuller (*IG* 1^3.554), a bronze vase; Smikros, the tanner (*DAA* 58 = *IG* 1^3.646), a *kore* statue; a carpenter (*tekton*), whose name has been lost (*DAA* 196), the base for a marble horse statue; Smikythe the washerwoman (*DAA* 380 = *IG* 1^3.794), a marble basin; Phrygia the baker (*IG* 1^3.546), a bronze shield. For a detailed analysis of these evidences, see Keesling 2003b, pp. 69-71.

or after a particularly good catch.[47] A different case are the dedications by potters and vase painters, because, even if they are surely not members of the elite, they could be very wealthy in the fifth century and at least some of them could afford to make an expensive dedication. Keesling identifies seven Athenian potters or vase painters who dedicated statues on the Acropolis.[48] Also in this case, the occasion, rather than their financial resources determined the quality and the size of the dedication. And even if the desire for self-display and the competitive ethos were good enough reasons to make particularly big offerings, dedications on the Athenian Acropolis seem to have been more generated by occasions (and surely also by fashions and personal taste), than by social status alone.[49] Moreover, the ability to afford a monumental dedication carries with it economic implications that do not inevitably reflect social status: so, if agonistic victory is a typically aristocratic occasion, then the craftsmen could have had important reasons of their own (a good deal, an unexpected profit) and financial means to make an extraordinary gift to Athena.[50] Imposing votive statues can thus be a proof of wealth, but not always necessarily of aristocracy.

Holloway tries to find a connection between the formulas of dedication, the dedicated object, and the social status of the dedicators.[51] Contesting the interpretation that sees in the *kore* the counterpart of the male *kouros* and therefore an expression of the aristocratic ethic, he relates the offer of *korai* to the Athenian business class. The inscriptions associated with the dedication of these statues underlines the relation with key concepts like wealth and success by using the terminology of *aparche* and *dekate* that evoke the world of labor and of profit. These words seem to appear particularly often in the few inscriptions that mention the profession of the dedicator, and very seldom in inscriptions that can be connected without any doubt to the aristocratic world.[52]

[47] *IG* 1^3.828 (= *DAA* 229): the dedicatory inscription states that Naulochos dedicated a *kore*, not preserved; see also from Eleusis *IG* 1^3.994, a stone altar dedicated by Autandros and Mys to Poseidon, to celebrate catching a swordfish.

[48] Keesling 2003b, p. 73. For some caution in the identification of potters, see also Keesling 2005, pp. 415-421.

[49] An interesting case is the dedication, known only from the literary sources, of a certain Anthemios, who dedicated a statue (or a relief) of himself with a horse to celebrate his elevation from the census of the *thetai* to the one of the *hippeis* (*Ath. Pol.* 7.4). In this case public display, social status and occasion coincide. I am grateful to Lucia Cecchet, who brought this passage to my attention.

[50] Keesling 2003b, p. 75; E. M. Harris 2002, pp. 67-99 identifies already in the fifth century a "middle class" of artisans and merchants with good liquidity.

[51] Holloway 1992, pp. 267-274.

[52] *Contra* Keesling 2003b, pp. 91-93, who sees no connection between the social status of the dedicators and the dedicated objects.

In the category of marble votive reliefs it is also easy to observe differences in dimensions and quality, what surely meant different prices: if the big, 'metopal' ones can be compared for quality, prestige and price to the free-standing statues,[53] the smaller and standard ones are probably closer to the ceramic *pinakes*. An attempt to define the costs of the marble votive reliefs can be done by comparing this class of materials with the Attic marble decree stelae (with and without relief), whose prices are well attested for the fourth and third century BCE. From the publication formulas of the Attic decrees we know that they could cost between 10 and 60 dr., but the majority were around 20-30 dr. Van Straten comes to the conclusion that a simple votive relief – with little depth and a short inscription – could be bought in the fourth century for 10 dr.[54] Nevertheless caution is required in the interpretation of such prices, because they refer to publicly commissioned inscriptions that were probably, as usual for state commissioned jobs, contracted out.[55] Thus, there could be a considerable difference between the price for the private individual and the price, established in an auction, for the city. Moreover, there is reason to think that the amounts mentioned are just the highest authorized costs, not the real price.[56]

In addition to that, almost all the known prices for inscribed marble stelae are from the fourth century on. The only evidence for the fifth century is a long opistographic (height *ca.* 98 cm) stele, apparently without relief, whose total cost of 62 dr. was intended to cover "working, engraving and erecting the stele".[57] The price of 10 dr., suggested by van Straten, for a votive relief seems undoubtedly too low for the fifth century – especially considering that a sacrificial sheep cost around 15 dr.[58] Prices starting from 20-30 dr. seem more appropriate.

The building accounts from the Athenian Erechtheion (409-406 BCE) mention that the sculptors of the frieze (height 0,58-0,65 m.) are paid on average *ca.* 60 dr. per adult male figure.[59] Examples with these dimensions are not rare – although admittedly many are bigger – amongst the archaic free-standing votive

[53] See for instance the relief of the potter Acr. 1332 and the fragments with representation of mythical episodes Acr. 120, NM 43; Comella 2002, pp. 16-18.
[54] van Straten 1974, p. 187.
[55] Clinton 1996, p. 746. That contracts for inscribing a stele were put out to bid is suggested by the usual fifth-century formula οἱ πολεταὶ ἀπομισθοσάντον κατὰ τὸν νόμον.
[56] On prices of inscribed steles see Berti (forthcoming).
[57] *IG* 1^3.386, accounts of the Eleusinian *epistatai*. The indication of the single item costs and the fact that the amount is not rounded off seem to point out that in this case the effective cost (without bidding?) of the job has been written down and not just the maximum authorized.
[58] Lambert 2002, pp. 363-364 and 393 (*Fr*. 3, 60-76), and *infra*, n. 95 with related text.
[59] *IG* 1^3.159; 161; 169; 175; 178; 476. See also Randall 1953, pp. 199-210. Some caution is required in using this evidence: it is of course impossible to state if this would also be the price for the public.

statues. Considering that they usually were set up on a support bearing an inscription, we must add at least 20-40 dr. to the 60 mentioned in the Erechtheum building accounts – depending on whether the support was a fluted column or just a simple pillar. We can thus calculate the probable total cost of such a gift at approximately 80 to 100 dr.

Summing up, I would like to suggest a hypothesis on possible prices for votives: a free-standing statue of modest dimensions could have cost between 80 and 100 dr.; a modest marble votive relief with a short dedicatory inscription around 20-30 dr.; a marble shield without figurative representation, probably less. Ceramic *pinakes* – at least the small and the mass produced ones - were also probably in the same price category under 20 dr.

On the other side, we have some evidence about wages and salaries, at least from the fifth century BCE onwards.[60] We know, for instance, that a simple worker on a building site was paid 1 dr. per day at the end of the fifth century,[61] while around 329/8 a skilled one could earn up to 2½ dr. per day.[62] Hoplites and sailors around 430 BCE were paid 1-2 dr. per day.[63] Priestly emoluments could be as little as 3 ob. per day in the same period, while the priestess of Athena Nike was paid 50 dr. per year.[64] If we consider that surely a part of this earned money entered the domestic economy and was used for the everyday needs, in order to save 100 dr., would take from 200 days (putting aside about ½ dr. per day) to 50 days (putting aside 2 dr. per day), which was not impossible, even for a simple worker. This means, that in one year, he could have made one or even two expensive dedications, like a less-than-life-size free-standing statue. But in order to know to what extent votive offerings affected the 'family budget' it is not enough to compare the hypothetical prices of the single votives with the evidence about wages and salaries, because we do not know how people (and especially people from the lower social classes) lived, to what extent these wages were their only support, or if they had other incomes. The lifestyle of the ancient Athenians and their domestic economy was probably quite different from the consumption oriented society we are used to. It is reasonable to suggest that in the archaic and early classical age the role of self-sufficiency in the domestic economy was still very important. We know for sure that grain was bought on the market and that its price increased considerably during period of *stasis* or war.[65]

[60] On the subject, see Loomis 1998.

[61] Building accounts of the Erechtheion: *IG* 1³.475.54-57; 66-67; 69; 71; 255-256 etc.; *IG* 1³.476.35-38; 124-134.

[62] Eleusis, *IG* 2².1672.26-28; 110-111; 177-178.

[63] Thuc. 3.17.4.

[64] *IG* 1³.250 A 28, B. 32; *IG* 1³.35.10. See also, for a good overview about salaries, Loomis 1998, pp. 261-312.

[65] See von Reden 2010, pp. 199-200, and generally on prices pp. 125-155. See for the fourth century Dem. 42.20; 50.6; 56.9.

But clothes for the members of the family were probably woven at home by the women, vegetables and eggs for the everyday meals were probably available from the courtyard without needing to be bought, and citizens from the countryside demes probably had some fields or at least a vegetable garden, even if they were not really landowners. We should thus not be misled by low salaries, because they were probably not the only income.[66] Comparing the evidence of classical Athens with that of other pre-modern societies, Ober concludes that daily wages were substantially above the subsistence level and allowed a decent middling standard: a large middling population therefore had, at the end of the fifth century, some surplus consumption capacity.[67] After surveying the evidence of the salaries and of the possible costs of sculptural works, Keesling arrives at the conclusion that the one drachma per day earned by the workmen of the Erechtheion in the fifth century was enough to buy a marble dedication without sculpture (for instance a marble basin), a small object in bronze, a votive relief or perhaps even a small marble statue; a life-size bronze statue was, however, not affordable.[68] Monumental dedications were, therefore, if not exactly an everyday purchase, not beyond the reach of common people and cannot be interpreted as the exclusive expression of the religious needs of the elite.

One should also keep in mind that such big, impressive and beautiful dedicated objects, destined to be placed outside, and to be seen and read, were surely very important in terms of the personal prestige of the dedicators and of the sanctuary in which they were displayed, but they did not need to be necessarily the most expensive ones in terms of economics. We know from the temple inventories that smaller objects in precious metals like silver, gold and bronze, together with vessels and other ritual equipments, were kept in the interior of the temples.[69] The evidence for the donation of such metal objects to sanctuaries in the sixth and fifth centuries BCE suggests that these gifts, especially those made of gold and silver, were more expensive than most of the statuary dedicated in the open air. In addition, they were probably very prestigious because – at least when they were inscribed with the dedicator's name –

[66] It is also possible, that some skilled workers were doing more than one job at the same time: this seems to be the case of the metic Manis in the Erechtheion's account, who undertook nearly every type of work with wood, gluing cymatia, making coffer lids and carving ceiling rosettes (*IG* 1^3.476.8-12; 35-28; 114-115): all these 'extra' works were paid on the basis of piece or job. Generally on subsistence economy, see also von Reden 2010, pp. 133-134.

[67] Ober 2010, pp. 262-265.

[68] Keesling 1995, p. 401; but admittedly the great majority of bronze statuettes found on the Acropolis is quite small (under 30 cm).

[69] *IG* 1^3.4, attesting the duties of the *tamiai* of the Hekatompedon in making the list of the bronze vessels kept inside the temple and stating the necessity of an inspection ("opening for viewing", ll. 19-20) twice a month, is good evidence for the value of these objects.

they allowed the dedicator to associate his or her gift directly with the cult rituals, both in a symbolic (for instance by donating miniature reproductions of cult vessels) and in a practical way (when the objects were meant to be used).[70] Further, they were usually put inside the temple, thus compensating for the fact that they were not visible to everybody by their proximity to the god.

Other factors, such as the frequency of the donations, must be taken into consideration. Many of the dedications from the Athenian Acropolis refer to the fulfillment of a vow. The worshipper here typically promised to make an offering on the condition that some benefit requested of the gods was received. When the gods benefited the worshipper, he/she had to fulfill the vow.[71] But the reasons for a dedication were numerous and the inscriptions recording the act of offering also record different, more 'routine' actions: for instance as *aparche* (first fruits), or as a *dekate* (from the tithe). These dedications, in which the prayer for a favor is not explicitly formulated, even if it may be implied, are the development of a bond with the god and show the 'daily', continuous character of these gift-giving relationships. With a *dekate* or an *aparche*, one confirmed the participation in an ongoing exchange of favors, that did not rule out asking or praying for a very concrete favor in a very concrete situation, but it was not limited to this. The regularity of this relationship between men and gods seems to be another important element that could not be replaced by a rich 'once in a lifetime' dedication.[72] A certain Onesimos dedicated on the Athenian Acropolis, probably at short intervals, no fewer than seven marble basins as *aparchai* to Athena.[73] The importance of the intrinsic worth of the dedicated object must therefore be evaluated within the context, being only one of many factors.

Were the dedicated objects an inalienable possession of the gods, or were they a possession of the sanctuary, that could be used and invested? Although this is a central question – especially with regard to donations in precious materials – to understand the economy of a sanctuary, it is a difficult one to

[70] Keesling 1995, pp. 406-407.

[71] See also Keesling 2003b, pp. 4-5.

[72] Patera 2012, pp. 76-77. The philosophic reflection about sacrifice and dedication points to the same direction: that one has to offer according to his means and that it is not the material value of the object that makes it valuable in the eye of the gods, but the intention of the dedication (see for instance Hes., *Op.* 336-337; Plat., *Leg.* 955e; Xen., *Mem.* 1.3.3; 4.3.17; Aristot., *Nic. Eth.* 1163b and *Eud. Eth.* 1243b; Isoc., *Nik.* 20). On this subject, which cannot be examined here, see Meijer 1981, pp. 232-259; Aubriot-Sévin 1992; Bruit-Zaidman 2001.

[73] *IG* 1^3.926-932 (= *DAA* 349-353). The same Onesimos seems to have dedicated, on another occasion, also a base supporting probably four bronze statuettes (*IG* 1^3.699 = *DAA* 217. See also Keesling 1995, pp. 409-410; 2003b, p. 73; 2005, pp. 401-403). Keesling 1995, pp. 408-413 identifies five more possible examples of multiple private dedications.

answer with certainty. We know for sure that precious gifts for the gods could be used in difficult time as a resource of the polis[74] and that old and broken metal *ex voto* could be melted down, in order to make space for new ones or to cast another votive.[75] In this latter case it was usual, at least from the fourth century on, to keep a record of the melted objects and of the dedicator's name on a stone stele.[76] Also, the later widespread practice of sanctuary loans seems to contradict the idea of the inalienability of the gods' possessions.[77] In this case the sanctuary functioned as a kind of bank, in which resources were stored in the form of non-monetized goods, in gold, silver, and other precious metals. Ampolo suggests that even in poleis with a developed monetary economy the 'anathematic' and the monetary system of accumulation in temple treasures actually coexisted until the Hellenistic period.[78] The sacred treasures constituted a sort of 'reserve-fund' that was stored normally in the temples but remained at the disposal of the city, in case of need.[79] Patera convincingly downplays the principle of inalienability, showing that the dedicated objects – at least the metal ones – were not removed from the market, but could be invested and reused by the sanctuary and by the polis, without apparently contradicting the fact that they were 'sacred' and thus, at least from the point of view of a modern observer, untouchable.[80] The system of the offerings thus participated in the economy of the sanctuary.

[74] See for instance, Thuc. 2.13.3-5: at the beginning of the Peloponnesian war Pericles reassures the Athenians about the finances of the Athenian state and explicitly mentions, beside the monetized resources coming from the tributes, the coined and uncoined resources from the temple treasures, the latter consisting of private and public offerings, as well as cult vessels; in Thuc. 6.46.3 the Egestaeans, seeking the Athenian alliance, show the Athenian ambassadors how rich their state is by showing them all the *anathemata, oinochoai* and *thymiateria* collected in the treasure of Aphrodite at Eryx; Ampolo 1989-1990, pp. 274-276; Patera 2012, p. 84.

[75] This practice is well attested for the Athenian Asklepieion (see Aleshire 1989, pp. 83 and 316).

[76] See for example, *IG* 2^2.839 (from the Athenian sanctuary of Heros Iatros, third century BCE).

[77] Patera 2012, p. 89. We must anyway consider, that the great majority of the evidences for this practice are from a later period. For an early example of sanctuary loans, see *IG* 1^3.248 (Rhamnous, 450-440 BCE).

[78] Ampolo 1989-1990, pp. 271-279.

[79] Ampolo 1989-1990, p. 272.

[80] Patera 2012, pp. 83-97, 250; *contra* Linders 1989-1990, pp. 281-285.

4. Sacrifice

While we tend to make a distinction between sacrifice and durable gifts for the gods, in Archaic and Classical Greece *thysiai* and *anathemata* fell into the same category of *ta hiera*. Offerings of food to the gods took different forms, ranging from bloodless gifts like barley cakes, fruits, and cheese to animal sacrifice.

In Greek cult practice the most significant and widespread ritual action is constituted by the non-destructive sacrifice (*thysia*), in which the gods receive an offering, usually of meat or other comestibles, followed by the consumption of the edible parts of the sacrifice by the participants.[81] Offering meat seems to have been an important element of the ritual in the archaic and classical period.[82] The meat offered to the gods could be a portion or a whole animal, it could be burnt, or offered in raw pieces placed on the altar or on a table near the altar. But it could also take the form of a cooked meal offered in an integrated ceremony – and mostly in combination with other food – in which the god was presented with a table and a *kline* and invited to have a banquet (*trapezomata* or *theoxenia*).[83]

Other forms of ritual, like holocausts – in which the victim was completely destroyed – or *sphagia* – rituals focusing on the slaughtering of the victim and the pouring out of blood – were also possible and even preferred on some special occasions. But this type of bloody sacrifice with a great waste of edible goods does not seem to have been the norm; on the contrary, there is reason to think that such rituals were practiced predominantly when misfortunes persuaded the worshiper that his relation with the gods was disturbed and therefore a 'powerful action' was needed to restore it, or on the occasion of other 'high-intensity rituals' like oaths and purification.[84]

In a divine banquet the mortals also seemed to take part, in one way or another: parts of the animals were given to the cult officers as a repayment[85] or they were sold, or consumed on the spot by the worshipers[86]. The gift for the

[81] *ThesCRA*, vol. 1, pp. 61-64; vol. 2, pp. 215-216.

[82] On the offering of meat, see Ekroth 2011, pp. 15-41. On sacrifice of barley, cakes, cheese and bread see Kearns 2011, pp. 89-103.

[83] See Ekroth 2011, pp. 16-17. On *thysiai* and *theoxeniai* see also *ThesCRA*, vol. 2, pp. 215-216 and 226-227.

[84] See Ekroth 2002, especially pp. 217-242; 270-276 and 325-330.

[85] *ThesCRA*, vol. 1, pp. 120-121 (on the animal parts attributed to the priests). See for example *LSCG* 12 A, 8-11 (450 B.C.): the priestess is paid 50 dr. per year and receives, additionally, the legs and the skin of the sacrificed animals; *LSS* 18 A, 33-35 (fifth century): the priestess has to receive a thigh and a side. See also Patera 2012, p. 118, note 124.

[86] *ThesCRA*, vol. 1, p. 122; see for instance *LSCG* 10 C 18-22 (before 460): distributions

gods thus also becomes a gift for the humans, or the opportunity for good business. This confirms that the offerings are part of the economic life of the sanctuary, in quite the same way as any other sanctuary properties.

An extremely fragmentary *lex sacra* of 510-480 from the Athenian Eleusinion records the offerings for the gods, introducing detailed regulations for the quantity each god had to receive.[87] Already in the first half of the fifth century we notice the tendency to insert into sacrificial calendars the prices for offerings and victims and – sometimes – of monetary fees to be paid to the priests. An early example is provided by the regulations for the Mysteries in the city Eleusinion (ca. 460 BCE).[88] Some years later (403, but probably recording and re-editing older texts) the so-called Calendar of Nikomachos already specifies the prices of each offering.[89]

Sacrificial calendars from the end of the fifth century onward show that the most expensive victims – adult cattle – cost between 40 and 90 drachmas in the fifth and fourth century.[90]

of raw meat; *LSCG* 13, 25-26 (421-420 BCE): the *metoikoi* have to receive the meat of the sacrificed cattle; *LSS* 38 A, 28-32 (from Delphi, around 425 BCE): the private individuals are allowed to take one third of the skin of the sacrificed public victims each. For the prescription οὐ φορά, stating that the meat has to be consumed on the spot, see for instance *LSCG* 18.

[87] *IG* 1^3.232.59-68: "[-- of barley? hal]f-sixths s[e]ven, of w[ine choes s]ix and a [h]alf chous [----a six]th, of ho[n]ey cu[ps ei]ght, of olive oil half-chou[s----a hal]f-fourth, of cheese [three] fourths, [of be]an[s--, of sesame white th]ree ch[oinikes], of bl[ack three choi]nike[s---t]wo".

[88] *IG* 1^3.6.5-20: "[---]obol[----]festiv[al organizers are to take ha]lf obol [per d]ay [from t]he iniate e[a]ch one]. The priest[es]s of Demeter is to take at the Lesser My[st]eries from [the in]itiate each one an obol and at [the G]rea[ter M]ysteries an o[bol from the initi]ate each one. A[ll the obo]ls are [to be] of the goddesses [except] for six hundred an[d thousand dr]achmae" (one should notice in any case that these are not prices for sacrificial victims but for services and for facilities, to be paid to the administrators of the sanctuary).

[89] For a new edition of the Nikomachos Calendar, with commentary, see now Lambert 2002, pp. 353-399. For prices, see for instance, Fr. 3, 1-15: "six chous of [wine] *price?*, one chous [of oil], *price?* half a chous of honey *price?*. Parts reserved for the priests *amount?* In the second last day of the month from the sacrifices listed per months (OR: from the funds for every month): to Athena a cloak of pure [wool] *price?* to Athena Ergane a sheep, [price 12 dr.], to Athena in front of the temple a sheep, [12 dr.], total…".

[90] *NGSL* 1 (Sacrificial calendar of Thorikos); *IG* 1^3.375; *LSCG* 20 B (but *LSS* 10, adult cattle: 25 dr.). See also Keesling 1995, p. 406; van Straten 1987, pp. 164-167; *ThesCRA*, vol. 1, p. 101. Caution is required in the analysis of sacrificial calendars, because they usually list the public offerings and only seldom the private ones. Also, they usually refer to a later period than the one considered in this paper.

The high costs of these animals explain the fact that they are not very common as an offering: van Straten calculates the percentage of adult cattle offered at around 3,5% of all sacrificial animals mentioned in sacrificial calendars, while the great majority of animals offered are sheep (around 58%),[91] which usually cost between 10 and 15 drachmae per animal.[92]

The iconographic material is an important documentary source for the study of ancient Greek sacrifices, although the images seldom precisely reveal details like size, age and sex of the victim; nonetheless it is usually possible to recognize the species of the animals.[93] In the Attic red-figure vases – representing mostly mythological scenes or public festivals – the majority of the animals represented are cattle, followed by sheep and pigs. If we look at the private votive reliefs, we find a different situation: the majority of sacrificial animals depicted are pigs (around 50%), followed by sheep and adult cattle. In the sacrificial calendars sheep are clearly predominant, in votive reliefs pigs, and in vase paintings cows and bulls.[94] In sacrificial calendars the price for adult sheep ranges from 10 to 17 dr., and for lambs from 4 to 7 dr. Adult pigs are more expensive than adult sheep, but young piglets are very cheap (3 to 3½ dr.).[95] Van Straten's analysis of the offerings in the sacred calendars shows that the sheep that were sacrificed were predominantly adults, while the majority of swine were young piglets. Probably the same pattern applies also to the votive reliefs and we can conclude that there too the majority of sacrificed sheep are adult, while the majority of sacrificed pigs are young.[96] This probably means that the majority of animals sacrificed by private individuals were not expensive.

Usually, the gods did not get the whole animal, but just part of it.[97] The parts of the animal destined for the gods were put on an offering table (*trapeza*) or on the altar. They could be burnt and sent to the gods in the form of smoke, but they could also just be left on the table, as a symbolic offering. What happened with the food offered to the gods when it was not burnt? Patera suggests convincingly, that that too ended in the hands of the cult ministers at the end of the cult action, thus implying that, at least in some cases, it is the act of offering that counts, and not the offer itself.[98] The same destiny was reserved to the small objects (statuettes, drinking vessels, incense, garlands and so on) that could be put on the offering tables together with the food. The objects could thus change their status

[91] van Straten 1987, pp. 164-165.
[92] *LSCG Suppl.* 10; 132; *LSCG* 18; 20.
[93] For a detailed study of images of animal sacrifices, see van Straten 1995.
[94] Van Straten 1987, pp. 164-167.
[95] *LSCG Suppl.* 10; 132; *LSCG* 18; 20.
[96] Van Straten 1987, p. 167.
[97] *TheSCRA* I, p. 119; *LSCG* 28; *LSAM* 24 A 33; 40, 5; 44, 6; 48, 17; 52 B 6; 63, 7. See Patera 2012, pp. 114-121.
[98] Patera 2012, pp. 116-119.

over time, depending on the function they had: once the properties of the gods (objects or food offerings) were not useful anymore in the cult action, they became property of the humans (of the sanctuary or of the priests) again, a fact that confirms the ambiguous character of the inalienability of divine property.[99]

Comparing this evidence with the great *anathemata* and the durable dedications, we can conclude that the sacrifices offered by private individuals were usually quite cheap. Whilst also people of a less wealthy condition sometimes made the effort to invest a considerable sum of money for an expensive *anathema*, which would be durable and seen by many visitors and worshipers, rarely would a private individual of any financial means have paid for a sacrifice more costly than a sheep. Onerous performances, in which the meat was redistributed or sold to the participants, seem to have been a prerogative of the *polis*, reserved for great festivals. When individuals particularly wanted to honor the gods they usually did not offer a meal that would dissolve in smoke, but a statue – perhaps even with a written dedication – or a precious object, thus transforming their own money into a property of the gods, whilst receiving prestige and visibility as a reward. It may be interesting to note that the ritual performance implied by a sacrifice seems, in the archaic period, to have been considered generally as 'less visible' and therefore less durable in the memory than the dedication of a solid object, although the sacrifice of many animals and the distribution of meat would have surely made a positive impression both upon the gods and upon the fellow-citizens.[100] Although for later periods we have testimony of impressive sacrifices as a medium of commemoration – for instance, legacies to organize sacrifice in memory of the dead – this possibility of making a durable impression by means of non-durable offerings does not seem to have existed in the archaic period.

5. Conclusion

The economy of gifts to the gods is a very complex one, made up of many different circumstances and motivations. Some of them are of a commercial nature (purchase and production of a votive, transformation of wealth into illiquid forms dedicated to the gods, accumulation of value and investment of resources by the sanctuary, sale or distribution of meat during cult actions). Some

[99] On the presentation of food offerings to the gods, see Patera 2012, pp. 113-121.

[100] Examples of impressive sacrifices performed by private individuals are to be found in the literary sources, but they usually refer to mythical figures, as in the famous episode of Croesus offering three thousand of each kind of animal fit for sacrifice to Apollo (Hdt. 1.50). See also: *Il.* 6.93-94; *Od.* 4.352; 477-478; 582; 11.132-133; 13.250; Soph., *Trach.* 760-761.

others, on the contrary, are not, like the celebratory and commemorative function of the gifts and the prestige they produced for the dedicators.

The gifts for the gods could be ephemeral (like sacrifice, with or without consumption of the edible goods), or durable (statues, reliefs, vases and cult vessels, precious objects). Some of the durable gifts were able to be transformed into capital and reinvested (as in case of valuables used in case of necessity, or melted to make a new dedication), some immobilize the money spent in the purchase and could not be reused (as in the case of a marble statue). Archaeological evidence shows that gifts could sometimes be given anonymously, but that they often record the name of the dedicator, and sometimes also the occasion and/or the profession of the dedicator, contributing in this way more effectively to the prestige and to the social visibility of the giver. A wealthy offering is therefore not automatically and not necessarily a prestigious one; the relevance of a dedication is made up by qualities including beauty, visibility, and presence (or not) of an inscription and its potential to associate the dedicator with the cult. In the relation to the gods other factors have also to be taken in consideration: the intentions and the purity of the dedicator, as well as the continuity and regularity of the offerings. Beside daily gifts (offerings of flowers, cakes, small animals and *pinakes*) there are '*una tantum* gifts' (sculptures, precious objects, expensive animals like cattle). The ephemeral and the long lasting offerings interlink when the worshiper offers a relief representing a sacrifice or a ceramic reproduction of perishable offerings like cakes and animals. The oral aspects of the ritual should not be forgotten: almost certainly dedications were accompanied by prayers, which could be silent or spoken aloud; in the latter case they were not only intended for the gods, but surely also for the other worshipers.

The god was only one of the actors in this complex network of exchanges. He returned (or not!) the gifts and the favors he received from the dedicators and responded to the relation in terms of reciprocity. The participation of the god in the exchange system is not to be interpreted as a mere trade. As Parker pointed out, the concept of *charis*, that distinguished the relation with the god, is the key to understand the exchange of gifts between human and gods: it is an exchange of favors, a voluntary – even if socially prescribed – relationship of friendship. The exchange between men and gods never took place automatically, the price was never the point and the value of the exchanged goods could not be calculated in relation one to another.[101]

The other – all human – actors of this complex social network were much more subject to the rules of trade: the dedicators who purchased their gifts in the shops close to the sanctuary, the marble or metal workers and the potters producing and selling the objects to be dedicated, the occasional visitors of the sanctuary and the participants in the rituals, who admired the gifts for the gods,

[101] Parker 1998, pp. 118-119.

read the name of the potters and marble workers and became the target of their advertisement, the participant to the rituals sharing the consumption of the food offerings, were all elements of an economic network.

The sanctuary, by way of the cult officers, managed and supervised the gifts, investing in prestige and visibility (especially in case of monumental dedications, with or without an inscription). The gifts without an intrinsic value also therefore produced a surplus in terms of prestige, encouraging the emulation of the other worshipers and the competition in making the most beautiful gifts. In addition to that, the cult officers were sometimes paid with parts of the sacrificial animals or were allowed to sell parts of the sacrificed victims and thus make a profit from the offering.

One last question should be mentioned: how much did piety cost for the average Athenian? We have seen that even monumental dedications were probably not unaffordable, but the frequency of the occasions on which dedications and sacrifices were usually made could, I think, have made piety a quite expensive habit. The use of the *dekate/aparche* terminology suggests that, even if we do not know how often, the worshipper felt himself bound regularly to renew the relationship of reciprocity with the gods. Also the criticism of the philosophers against excessively expensive dedications can be interpreted as a symptom of a tendency to extravagance and a confirmation that out of piety some people spent a lot.[102]

If the bronze, silver and golden goods could be melted down and re-used, making up (in coined or un-coined form) liquidity for the sanctuary, the votive marble statues withdrew the wealth from the circulation, giving a return only in terms of prestige. This 'dedicatory habit' was very typical of the archaic and early classical age, but already around the end of the fifth centuries was going to be downsized, and we find more precious small objects but less monumental sculpture. Sculpture does not disappear from the gifts to the gods, but the type of the votive relief becomes predominant and replaces the *kouroi* and *korai* of the archaic age. The typical votives of the fourth century are the ones attested by the Athenian Asklepieion: beside anatomical *ex-votos*, we find silver and bronze vessels, *pinakes*, small plaques and coins.[103] The changing of the votive praxis is an index of a change both in society – the transformation of the aristocratic *ethos* – and in the economical praxis – with a growing monetary economy in which circulation of commodities is more important than transformation of capital into illiquid forms. This process seems to reflect a change in the mentality, implying

[102] See for instance Plat., *Rep.* 364b-365a; Xen., *Mem.* 1.3. 3 (and supra, n. 70).The fact that reciprocity could be misunderstood and interpreted as a commercial relationship, in which the rich can buy, bringing more expensive offerings, more favor than the poor, is implicit in the polemic against rich *anathemata*. See Parker 1998, pp. 118-119.

[103] Linders 1987, pp. 118-121; Keesling 2003b, pp. 61-62.

less 'public display' of private wealth in the form of monumental offerings and a more extensive use of money surplus for rentable investments and private needs.[104]

Bibliography

Aleshire, Sara B.: *The Athenian Asklepieion. The People, Their Dedications, and the Inventories*, Amsterdam 1989.

Ampolo, Carmine: *Tra economia, religione e politica: tesori e offerte nei santuari Greci*, in: *Anathema. Regime delle offerte e vita dei santuari nel Mediterraneo antico*, ed. by Gilda Bartoloni – Giovanni Colonna – Cristiano Grottanelli, Roma 1989-1990, pp. 271-279.

Aubriot-Sévin, Danièle: *Prière et conceptions religieuses en Grèce ancienne jusqu'à la fin du Ve siècle av. J.-C.*, Lyon 1992.

Berti, Irene: *Costi di produzione e meccanismi di pubblicazione delle iscrizioni attiche* (forthcoming)

Bing, Peter: *The Un-read Muse? Inscribed Epigrams and Its Readers in Antiquity*, in: *Hellenistic Epigrams*, ed. by Annette Harder – Remco F. Regtuit – Gerry C. Wakker, Leuven 2002, pp. 39-66.

Bruit-Zaidman, Louise: *Le commerce de dieux. Eusebeia, essai sur la piété en Grèce ancienne*, Paris 2001.

Burford, Alison M.: *The Economics of Greek Temple Building*, in: *PCPhS* 191 (1965), pp. 21-34.

Clinton, Kevin: *Review of Carol L. Lawton, Attic Document Reliefs*, in: *BMCRev* 96.9.21 (1996) [http://bmcr.brynmawr.edu/1996/96.09.21.html; last access 4 Sept. 2013].

Comella, Annamaria: *I rilievi votivi greci di periodo arcaico e classico. Diffusione, ideologia, committenza*, Bari 2002.

Day, Joseph W.: *Archaic Greek Epigram and Dedication: Representation and Reperformance*, Cambridge 2010.

de Ridder, André H.: *Catalogue des bronzes trouvés sur l'Acropole d'Athènes*, Paris 1896.

Dickins, Guy: *Catalogues of the Acropolis Museum I: Archaic Sculpture*, Cambridge 1912.

Douplouy, Alain: *Le prestige des élites. Recherches sur les modes de reconnaissance sociale en Grèce entre les Xe et Ve siècles avant J.- C.*, Paris 2006.

Ekroth, Gunnel: *The Sacrificial Rituals of Greek Hero-Cults in the Archaic to the Early Hellenistic Periods*, Liège 2002.

Ekroth, Gunnel: *Meat for the Gods*, in: *Nourrir les dieux? Sacrifice et représentation du divin*, ed. by Vinciane Pirenne-Delforge – Francesca Prescendi, Liège 2011, pp. 15-41.

Graef, Botho – Ernst Langlotz: *Die antiken Vasen von der Akropolis zu Athen*, Berlin 1925-1933.

[104] On wealth, economic surplus and market in the classical and early Hellenistic periods, see E. M. Harris 2002, pp. 67-99 and Ober 2010, pp. 241-286.

Harris, Edward M.: *Workshop, Marketplace and Household. The Nature of Technical Specialization in Classical Athens and Its Influence on Economy and Society*, in: *Money, Labour and Land. Approaches to the economies of ancient Greece*, ed. by Paul Cartledge – Edward E. Cohen – Lin Foxhall, London – New York 2002, 67-99.

Harris, William V.: *Ancient Literacy*, Cambridge (MA) 1989.

Harris, William V.: *Writing and Literacy in the Archaic Greek City*, in: *ΕΝΕΡΓΕΙΑ: Studies on Ancient History and Epigraphy Presented to H.W. Pleket*, ed. by Johan H. M. Strubbe – Rolf Albert Tybout – Hendrik S. Versnel, Amsterdam 1996, pp. 57-77.

Holloway, Ross R.: *Why korai?*, in: *OJA* 11 (1992), pp. 267-274.

Kearns, Emily: *Ὁ λιβανωτὸς εὐσεβές καὶ τὸ πόπανον: the Rationale of Cakes and Bloodless Offerings in Greek Sacrifice*, in: *Nourrir les dieux? Sacrifice et représentation du divin*, ed. by Vinciane Pirenne-Delforge – Francesca Prescendi, Liège 2011, pp. 89-103.

Keesling, Catherine M.: *Monumental Private Votive Dedications on the Athenian Acropolis, ca. 600-400 B.C.*, Ann Arbor 1995.

Keesling, Catherine M.: *Rereading the Acropolis Dedications*, in: *Lettered Attica. A Day of Attic Epigraphy*, ed. by David Jordan – John Traill, Toronto 2003a, pp. 41-54.

Keesling, Catherine M.: *The Votive Statues of the Athenian Acropolis*, Cambridge 2003b.

Keesling, Catherine M.: *Patrons of Athenian Votive Monuments of the Archaic and Classical Periods*, in: *Hesperia* 74 (2005), pp. 395-426.

Lambert, Stephen: *The Sacrificial Calendar of Athens*, in: *ABSA* 97 (2002), pp. 353-399.

Lazzarini, Maria Letizia: *Le formule delle dediche votive nella Grecia arcaica*, in: *Memorie dell'Accademia Nazionale dei Lincei* 19 (1976), pp. 47-354.

Linders, Tullia: *The Melting Down of Discarded Metal Offerings in Greek Sanctuaries*, in: *Anathema. Regime delle offerte e vita dei santuari nel Mediterraneo antico*, ed. by Gilda Bartoloni – Giovanni Colonna – Cristiano Grottanelli, Roma 1989-1990, pp. 281-285.

Linders, Tullia: *Gods, Gifts and Society*, in: *Gifts to the Gods*, ed. by Tullia Linders – Gullog C. Nordquist, Uppsala 1987, pp. 118-121.

Loomis, William T.: *Wages, Welfare Costs and Inflation in Classical Athens*, Ann Arbor 1998.

Marchiandi, Daniela: *Le necropoli ateniesi del V secolo tra tradizione arcaica e tendenza all'omologazione*, in: *Atene e la Magna Grecia dall'età arcaica all'Ellenismo*, Taranto 2008, pp. 105-136.

Marchiandi, Daniela: *Le consuetudini funerarie dell'élite ateniese: i lebeti bronzei di Myrina (Lemnos)*, in: *Gli Ateniesi fuori dall'Attica: modi d'intervento e di controllo del territorio*, ed. by Enrica Culasso Gastaldi – Daniela Marchiandi, Roma 2012, pp. 221-236.

Marginesu, Giovanni: *Gli epistati dell'Acropoli. Edilizia sacra nella città di Pericle, 447/6 – 433/2 a.C.*, Atene – Paestum 2010.

Meijer, Pieter A.: *Philosophers, Intellectuals and Religion in Hellas*, in: *Faith, Hope and Worship, Aspects of Religious Mentality in the Ancient World*, ed. by Hendrik S. Versnel, Leiden 1981, pp. 216-263.

Ober, Josiah: *Wealthy Hellas*, in: *TAPhA* 140 (2010), pp. 241-286.

Parker, Robert: *Pleasing Thights: Reciprocity in Greek Religion*, in: *Reciprocity in Ancient Greece*, ed. by Cristopher Gill – Norman Postlethwaite – Richard Seaford, Oxford 1998, pp. 105-125.

Patera, Ioanna: *Offrir en Grèce ancienne. Gestes et contextes*, Stuttgart 2012.
Randall, Richard H. jr., *The Erechtheum Workmen*, in: *AJA* 57 (1953), pp. 199-210.
Schulze, Barbara: *Die Votivtafeln der archaischen und klassischen Zeit von der Athener Akropolis*, Möhnesee 2004.
van Straten, Folkert T.: *Did the Greeks Kneel before Their Gods?*, in: *BABesch* 49 (1974), pp. 159-189.
van Starten, Folkert T.: *Gifts for the Gods*, in: *Faith, Hope and Worship, Aspects of Religious Mentality in the Ancient World*, ed. by Hendrik S. Versnel, Leiden 1981, pp. 65-151.
van Straten, Folkert T.: *Greek Sacrificial Representations: Livestock Prices and Religious Mentality*, in: *Gifts to the Gods*, ed. by Tullia Linders – Gullog C. Nordquist, Uppsala 1987, pp. 164-167.
van Straten, Folkert T.: *Votives and Votaries in Greek Sanctuary*, in: *Le sanctuaire grec. Huit exposés suivis de discussions*, ed. by Albert Schachter – Jean Bingen, Genève 1992, pp. 247-290.
van Straten, Folkert T., *Hiera Kala. Images of Animal Sacrifice in Archaic and Classical Greece*, Leiden – New York – Köln 1995.
Versnel, Hendrik S.: *Religious Mentality in Ancient Prayer*, in: *Faith, Hope and Worship, Aspects of Religious Mentality in the Ancient World*, ed. by Hendrik S. Versnel, Leiden 1981, pp. 1-64.
Viviers, Didier: *Recherches sur les ateliers de sculpteurs et la cité d'Athènes à l'époque archaïque. Endoios, Philergos, Aristoklès*, Bruxelles 1992.
von Reden, Sitta: *Money in Classical Antiquity*, Cambridge 2010.

Michael L. Satlow

Markets and Tithes in Roman Palestine

1. Introduction

Like his uncle Emile Durkheim, Marcel Mauss was as engaged with the present as he was with the 'archaic' societies about which he wrote. A sporadically committed communitarian, Mauss's work on the gift had at least one eye on the present. He makes this explicit at the end of *The Gift*, when he writes:

> "One can also see how this concrete study can lead not only to a science of customs, to a partial social science but even to moral conclusions, or rather, to adopt once more the old word, 'civility', or 'civics', as it is called nowadays. Studies of this kind indeed allow us to perceive, measure, and weigh up the various aesthetic, moral, religious, and economic motivations, the diverse material and demographic factors, the sum total of which are the basis of society and constitute our common life..."[1]

Members of archaic society – who understood and structured their exchanges around the notion of the gift – stand in contrast to the icy rationality that governs modern transactions. We should look to the past, Mauss tells us, specifically to how ancient societies understood reciprocity as reinforcing group solidarity rather than as isolated, self-interested transactions in order to add some much needed civility to our economics.

Mauss needed the existence of a 'gift economy' to strengthen his critique of modern practices. Whether a true 'gift economy' actually existed is highly doubtful. Yet at the same time, Mauss provides a useful set of questions for thinking about economic questions. In contrast to the assumptions of classical economic theory, not all economic transactions deliver economic gains; 'gifts' might circulate within an economic framework even as they do other work.

In this paper, I want to focus on a specific case in the ancient world in which 'gifts' functioned within an economic framework. In Roman Palestine, between ca. 200-600 CE – well after the destruction of the temple in Jerusalem by the Romans in 70 CE – many Jews continued to bring religious offerings to the Jewish priests, or *kohanim* (singular: *kohen*). This system of offerings was, to at least some degree, institutionalized rather than spontaneous, and had a series of economic and social ramifications.

[1] Mauss 1923-1924, p. 83.

The argument of the paper is, I hope, rather straightforward. The Hebrew Bible outlines a complex 'system' (it is hardly coherent and organized enough to deserve that name) of offerings to the God of Israel. The rabbis of late antiquity appropriated this biblical heritage and developed from it both the norms for the continuation of such practices and an understanding of its means. Given the academic rather than practical flavor of many rabbinic discussions, and the relatively marginal place of the rabbis in their (non-rabbinic) communities, these rabbinic laws raise the question of whether and to what extent Jews actually did continue to bring offerings to the *kohanim*. I argue that the evidence suggests that the practice continued for a surprisingly long time. The final part of the paper will then explore the wider ramifications of such a system of offerings, the reasons that they might have continued, and the theoretical implications that this has for understanding the interplay of gift and economy in the ancient world.

2. Tithes: foundations

The Hebrew Bible presumes the existence of two clerical classes, both of which are inherited from father to son. The first, larger, class is that of the Levites, presumed to be the lineal descendants of Levi, one of the twelve sons of the patriarch Jacob. Moses and Aaron were both Levites. Aaron's descendants, though, gain a new status – that of priest, or *kohen*. Throughout the history of biblical Israel, the status and role of both of these classes was highly contested, although by the fifth century BCE they had more or less stabilized. The priests primarily administered the sacrificial system at the temple and the Levites assisted them in a variety of ways. The Levites had a position subordinate to the priests.[2]

The sacrifices were largely understood as 'gifts' to God. The 'gift', however, was not the entire animal; with rare exception animal sacrifices at the temple were not wholly consumed on the altar. Parts of the animal, along with the smell of the burning flesh, were the parts that God took; the priests, those who brought the animal, or some combination thereof, ate the remainder of the animal. Functionally, giving a gift to God meant giving a gift to the priests, and in some cases, the Levites as well. By accepting, sacrificing, and then eating the animal in the proper state of ritual purity, the priest played a critical role in reinforcing the ongoing reciprocal relationship between God and Israel, whether as a communal whole or the individual households of which it was constituted.[3]

Gifts to the priests, however, did not only take the form of what we normally call a sacrifice. The Hebrew Bible prescribes an elaborate system of gifts, which

[2] Blenkinsopp 1995, pp. 92-98.
[3] Hubert – Mauss 1899. There is a large literature on the 'meaning' of sacrifice in the Hebrew Bible. For an overview, see Janzen 2007.

are at times justified as really being gifts to God, and at other times as recompense to the priests, who did not receive an allotment of land after Israel subdued Canaan. The biblical account of these regular, prescribed gifts is not entirely consistent, but when seen as a whole they break down into seven discrete types:

1. The First Fruits: According to *Ezekiel* (44:30) and passages in *Exodus* (23:19; 34:26) the first fruits – presumably of all major crops (*Num*. 18:12 and *Deut*. 18:4 specifically mention oil, wine, and grain), although the exact amount is unspecified – goes to the priest. The Exodus passages specify that the gift is to be made at the "house of YHWH, your God". This is also part of the oath made in *Nehemiah* 10:36. According to the law in *Deuteronomy* 26:1-11, the first fruits are brought to the (single) temple and the owner consumes them; in *Numbers* 18:13 the priests consume them.
2. Heave Offerings (*Terumah*): Throughout the Bible, the term *terumah* often refers to gifts made to the priests. The term is most often used generally (e.g. *Num*. 5:9; *Deut*. 12:6), but in one case is applied specifically to the dough offering (*Num*. 15:19; see below). It is unclear to me if the Hebrew Bible specifies a specific obligation to give heave offerings beyond, for example, voluntary gifts or parts of sacrifices to the priests, but this is how later sources understand it.
3. Tithe: A tenth of each crop (here again, which crops and how such accounting is to be done are not specified in the Hebrew Bible) is to be set aside. These tithes generally are not given to the priests directly. The Hebrew Bible is inconsistent about the disposition of these tithes. According to *Numbers* 18:21-24 and *Nehemiah* 10:38 the tithes go to the Levites; *Numbers* 18:25-29 states that the Levites are to give 10% of the tithes that they receive to the priests. This is designated the *terumah*, the term, as noted above, that the Bible elsewhere uses also to refer either to the priestly portion of a sacrifice (*Lev*. 22:10-14) or more vaguely to gifts given to the priests (e.g., *Neh*. 10:38). *Deuteronomy* (14:28-29; 26:12-15), however, states that the tithe goes to the Levites only once every three years, and even then the Levite is expected to share it with the poor (but not the priest). For the other two years of the three-year cycle the owners consume the tithes themselves in the Temple (*Deut*. 14:22-23). *Leviticus* 27:32 also assigns a tithe of cattle, and *Leviticus* 27:30 implies that the tithes belong entirely to the priests, although owners can 'redeem' these goods by paying a 20% penalty.
4. Dough: The 'first' portion of the dough (or bread) was to be given to priests (*Num*. 15:17-21; *Neh*. 10:38; *Ezek*. 44:30).
5. First born animals: The first born of every animal was to be given to the priests. Animals that were fit for sacrifice were to be slaughtered and eaten by the priest and his family in a state of purity (*Num*. 18:17-18; *Neh*. 10:37; *Exod*. 22:29; 34:19; but *Deut*. 15:20 has the owner eat the consecrated animal in Jerusalem). For animals unfit for sacrifice due to species (e.g., horse, ass),

an assessment was to be made and the proper amount of money was to be given to the priests (*Num.* 18:15; with an additional 20% according to *Lev.* 27:27). According to *2 Chronicles* 31:6, in the time of Hezekiah the Israelites brought tithes of their livestock to the priests in Jerusalem, but it is not clear if a tithe on livestock was to be applied annually.

6. 'Profane' flesh: *Deuteronomy* 18:3 specifies that certain portions of a slaughtered sacrifice (*zevaḥ*) were to be given to the priest. This was later taken to mean that from any meat slaughtered for consumption a portion was to be given to the priest, although it is unclear if this is the original meaning of this verse.[4]
7. Wool: The first-shearing of the sheep belongs to the priest (*Deut.* 18:3).

There is, clearly, substantial ambiguity and even tension within the Bible itself, which as a whole remains unclear about exactly which produce gets assessed; how much it is assessed; whom the assessment belongs; and where it is to go or be eaten.[5]

Jewish literature from the Hellenistic and Roman period attempted to address some of these biblical ambiguities, while at the same time confusing matters further. Most sources – including Tobit, the Book of Jubilees, Philo, and Josephus – harmonize the differing tithe laws in the Bible (3, above) by assuming the existence of a "second tithe". They each understand the nature of this second tithe somewhat differently. According to the second-century BCE Book of Jubilees, the second tithe is actually a "tithe of tithes".[6] Tobit and Josephus assume not only that the second tithe is a full tithe taken after the first tithe is given to the Levites, but that the tithe that Deuteronomy commands be given to the poor every third year is yet an additional tithe – a third tithe.[7] In the book of Judith, there is yet more confusion: she claims that tithes – that is, the first tithe to be given according to the Bible to the Levites – is instead consecrated to the priests (*Judith* 11:13). The Dead Sea scrolls also interpret and otherwise adapt these biblical laws.[8]

These sources also predictably disagree about the origin of and reason for these gifts. Jubilees attributes the origin of the tithe to a dream that Levi had, and a subsequent gift to him from his father Jacob.[9] Philo too takes the tithes for

[4] Philo, *Spec. leg.* 1.147.

[5] According to *Deut.* 18.6-8, all the offerings are clearly made in Jerusalem, and should a Levite wish to receive his share he must travel there. This centralized understanding is not present in the other biblical texts.

[6] *Jubilees* 32.10.

[7] *Tobit* 1.6-8; Joseph., *AI.* 4.240-243.

[8] Cf. 11Q19 lx 6-11 (with a fragmentary parallel at 4Q524 6-10); 11Q20 xliii 2-17; 4Q270 2.ii.6-9.

[9] *Jubilees* 32.1-9.

granted, explaining that the first-fruits of all wine, wheat, barley, oil, and fruits be given to the priest,

> "so that the priests may not have merely bare necessaries, just keeping themselves alive in comparatively squalid conditions, but enjoy abundance of the luxuries of life and pass their days amid cheerful and unstinted comfort in the style which befits their position".[10]

The Jews, Philo says, are happy to keep the priests well appointed:

> "The cities pay under compulsion and [sic] reluctantly and groan under the burden... But our people pay gladly and cheerfully. They anticipate the demand, abridge the time limits and think that they are not giving but receiving".[11]

Following the Bible, Philo assigns the tithe to the Levites – as wages for their work in the temple – and insists that the Levites tithe this tithe for the priests.

According to our sources, this was not an academic discussion: Jews actually did deliver tithes prior to 70 CE. Josephus, for example, states that when in the Galilee at the very beginning of the war against Rome, his colleagues,

> "having amassed a large sum of money from the tithes which they accepted as their priestly due",[12]

almost returned home. Josephus, by contrast, claims that he declined the tithes brought to him in the Galilee, even though he was lawfully entitled to them.[13] Elsewhere he states that during the siege of Jerusalem, the high priests used to take the tithes due to them by force from the threshing floors, leaving other, poorer priests to starve.[14] The Gospels and Paul too assume the giving of tithes and first-fruits.[15]

These sources suggest that tithing in general was an established institution in Jerusalem and the Galilee by the mid-first century CE. The precise mechanisms of this institution are unclear to us, and perhaps they were also fluid in antiquity. There is no evidence that Jews outside of the land of Israel gave offerings to the priests and Levites, although it is certainly possible that they did in some locations.[16]

[10] Philo, *Spec. leg.* 1.134, transl. F. H. Colson.
[11] Philo, *Spec. leg.* 1.143-144, transl. F. H. Colson.
[12] Joseph., *Vit.* 63; cf. Mason 2001, p. 57, nn. 335-336.
[13] Joseph., *Vit.* 80.
[14] Joseph., *AJ* 20.181; 20.205-7.
[15] *Mt* 23.23; *Lc* 11.42; *Rom.* 11.16.
[16] The 'temple tax' was meant to support the operation of the Jerusalem temple and cannot be considered in this category. The evidence for its actual collection and payment outside of the land of Israel is, in any case, weak. See Schürer 1979^2, pp. 270-272. There

With the destruction of the temple in 70 CE one might have expected the institution of tithing to wither. Priests and Levites, after all, lost their physical institutional home and, without being able to offer sacrifices, much of their *raison d'être*. Yet, surprisingly, Jews in Roman Palestine continued to give gifts to priests and Levites. Before considering the evidence for this claim, I want first to consider how the rabbis dealt with these biblical prescriptions.

2. Tithes: the Rabbinic system

Rabbinic literature of late antiquity deals extensively with the gifts owed to the Levites and priests. The Mishnah, redacted in the early third century CE, devotes entire tractates to the topics of tithes (*Ma'asrot*), second tithes (*Ma'aser Sheni*), heave offerings (*Terumot*), first fruits (*Bikkorim*), and dough offerings (*Hallah*). Additional tractates are devoted to dealing with the case of tithed produce that has been mixed with non-tithed produce (*Kilayim*) as well as doubtfully tithed produce (*Demai*). These tractates flesh out the vague biblical laws, often specifying what, how much, and in what manner these gifts are to be given. Other rabbinic laws that deal with the same topics can be found in the Tosefta, which dates from around the same time as the Mishnah, and the Palestinian Talmud, which was redacted in the late fourth century CE. Given this large and complex body of law, I want here only to sketch in broad terms the requirements for each of these gift categories as understood by the rabbis:

1. Terumah: The recommended amount is 2,5% of produce by weight after the first fruits have been taken.[17] The heave offering is given to a priest; he or members of his household are to consume it.[18] Produce that has the status of heave offerings is not to be eaten by those outside of priestly households. Should a non-priest accidentally eat it, she or he would have to make restitution, with an additional 20% penalty.[19]
2. Tithes: Almost all cultivated produce (not just grains, oil, and wine) is subject to tithes.[20] The tithe is 10% of the crop and is payable to Levites. The Levites were expected to give 10% of this tithe to the priests. The tithe (but not the portion given to the priests) could be eaten by anyone in any ritual state.[21] It

was a Jewish temple in Leontopolis, but we know almost nothing about its actual operation.

[17] Mishnah *Terumot* 3.7; 4.3; 4.6.

[18] Mishnah *Terumot* 2.4; 8.1.

[19] Mishnah *Terumot* 6.1.

[20] Mishnah *Ma'asrot* 1.1.

[21] Mishnah *Bikkorim* 2.1.

was thus free to circulate on the market. All cattle, sheep, and goats are also tithed, with the actual animals to be given chosen randomly.[22]

3. First Fruits: First fruits are in part treated like heave offerings (*terumah*); only priests and members of their household can eat it.[23] Unlike heave offerings, though, first fruits are treated as property, and can be used to purchase certain goods and pay debts.[24] Because the rabbis required that the first fruits be brought to Jerusalem, unlike the *terumah* and tithes, the rules governing them were not applicable when the Jerusalem temple was not standing.[25]
4. First-born Animals: The first-born (or in the case of an unclean animal, an equivalent clean one) of all (quadruped) animals are given to the priests. Priests can sell them under certain conditions.[26] Blemished firstlings must be redeemed (with the price of redemption going to the priest), but the deconsecrated firstling cannot be sold in the market.[27] First-born humans need to be redeemed with a gift of five *selas*, in Tyrian coinage (the standard of the Jerusalem temple) to the priests.[28]
5. Second Tithe: This is a 10% tithe on the produce left after the taking of first fruits, *terumah*, and the first tithe. It – either the produce itself or produce bought with its monetary equivalent – is to be consumed by the owner in Jerusalem. On the third and sixth years of the seven-year sabbatical cycle it is to be given to the poor.
6. Dough: Dough offerings have the status of *terumah*; they are to be eaten by the priest in a condition of ritual purity.[29] The dough offering is usually 4,17%; for those making bread for sale in the market (e.g., bakers) it is half that rate, 2,09%.[30]
7. Flesh: From all (quadruped) animals slaughtered for meat, parts of the animal must be given to the priests; this is an obligation that is applicable inside and outside the land of Israel, when the temple is standing and when not.[31]
8. Wool: The first shearing of sheep must be given to the priests. As in the case of flesh, this gift is applicable in all times and places.[32] There must be enough wool given to make a small garment and it should be bleached and not dyed.[33]

[22] Mishnah *Bekorot* 9.1; 9.7.
[23] Mishnah *Bikkorim* 2.1; 3.12.
[24] Mishnah *Bikkorim*. 3.12.
[25] Mishnah *Bikkorim*. 2.3.
[26] Mishnah *Ma'aser Sheni* 1.2.
[27] Mishnah *Bekorot* 5.1.
[28] Mishnah *Bekorot* 8.3; 8.7.
[29] Mishnah *Hallah* 1.9; 4.8.
[30] Mishnah *Hallah* 2.7.
[31] Mishnah *Hullin* 10.1.
[32] Mishnah *Hullin* 11.1.
[33] Mishnah *Hullin* 11.2.

Like the Bible, the rabbis impose a heavy obligation on the landowner; the rabbis require no such offerings from craftsmen, tradesmen, and merchants. It is also important to keep in mind that these offerings are in addition to taxes due to Rome and the requirements to support the poor (both discussed below). The rabbis, however, had no power to actually enforce these laws, and it is almost certain that most Jews in the Galilee at this time would not have been familiar with or cared very much about rabbinic law as such.[34] Without the power of compulsion from either rabbis or priests, would landowners actually have given these gifts?

3. Evidence for continued tithe giving

Surprisingly, at least some Jews in Roman Palestine did continue to give gifts to God through the priest throughout late antiquity. The evidence is more suggestive than definitive, but it converges from different directions. Rabbinic laws, stories, cases, and exhortations (each of which constitute a distinct kind of evidence) all assume the continuation of the practice. Other evidence that comes from outside of rabbinic literature – including liturgical poetry and an inscription – buttress the impression given by this literature. While none of these sources can conclusively prove the extent of the practice, taken together they suggest that it was at least not uncommon.

a. Rabbinic Law. Rabbinic law is largely prescriptive rather than descriptive, and thus is an extremely slippery source for the recovery of actual practices. Some of the legal details relating to tithing, though, seem to assume a concrete social reality in which they were given. The Mishnah, for example, specifies the case of separating heave-offerings when the priest is immediately on hand.[35] Another mishnah deals with the case of a priest who comes to a farm to collect his first-born animal before it is weaned and thus eligible to be given to him.[36] Rabbinic texts assume the existence of the *ḥavurah*, a group defined by its adherence to tithing practices.[37] A talmudic tradition talks of how people "today" deliberately attempt to evade tithes by finding loopholes; the story assumes that "today" tithes should be given.[38] In a discussion of whether the obligation to tithe falls on the shipper of produce or its recipient, the law is determined with the assumption that most people do tithe before they ship.[39] A priest is allowed to sell a field with the stipulation (presumably what we would call a covenant) that

[34] Cohen 1999; Schwartz 2001, pp. 103-28; Miller 2006.
[35] Mishnah *Terumot* 2.4.
[36] Mishnah *Bekorot* 4.1.
[37] Mishnah *Demai* 2.2-3. Cf. Cohen 1999, pp. 956-959.
[38] Babylonian Talmud *Berakhot* 35b.
[39] Palestinian Talmud *Ma'asrot* 5.1; 51c.

he should receive the tithes (not the *terumah*) from the field.[40] There are also extensive rabbinic laws on the use of oil that had originally been given to priests as *terumah*, perhaps suggesting the continued practice of giving gifts of oil to the priests.[41] In one extensive passage, the Palestinian Talmud takes the giving of tithes for granted, debating only about whether rabbis are entitled to receive them.[42] All of these laws seem to preserve details relating to the continuation of the practice of giving tithes from the second through fourth centuries CE.

b. Rabbinic Stories. Many rabbinic stories involve the giving of tithes and other priestly gifts. For our purposes whether or not these stories report actual historical incidents is far less important than the fact that they take for granted the practice, assuming that their readers will as well. One story, for example, illustrates a general principle about how to tithe one's own produce if it was located in a distant place:

> "One whose produce is far from him must designate the tithe verbally. Once Rabban Gamaliel and the elders were travelling by boat [at the time when his produce needed to be tithed]. Rabban Gamaliel said: "The tithe I will measure out is given Joshua, and its place [i.e., the land on which the tithe rests] is rented to him. The other tithe [i.e., second tithe] that I will measure out is given to Akiva ben Joseph, who will distribute it to the poor, and its place is rented to him". Rabbi Joshua said: "The tithe that I will measure out is given to Elazar ben Azariah, and its place is rented to him". And they received the rent money [of the places where the tithes were located] from each other".[43]

The story is fanciful: four rabbis traveling together find a legally acceptable way to transfer their tithes even when stuck on a boat. Rabban Gamaliel transfers the first tithe to Joshua, a Levite, and the second tithe to Akiva, who is portrayed as a distributer of charity to the poor. Rabban Gamaliel is a priest and hence need not give *terumah*. Joshua, though, does need to give *terumah* from the tithe that he just received, and so transfers that produce to a priest, Elazar ben Azariah. One need not accept the veracity of the story to see that the story only makes sense against the assumption that these practices were alive and comprehensible to its audience.

Many other rabbinic stories similarly take for granted the continued giving of priestly and levitical gifts. Another story set in the first two centuries CE, has Rabbi Tarfon asserting his right to collect his heave-offerings.[44] A Babylonian tradition assumes that a tithe on animals continued after the destruction of the

[40] Palestinian Talmud *Demai* 6.3; 25c.
[41] Mishnah *Terumot* 11.10; Palestinian Talmud *Terumot* 11.7; 48a-b.
[42] Palestinian Talmud *Ma'aser Sheni* 5.5; 56b-c.
[43] Mishnah *Ma'aser Sheni* 5.9.
[44] Tosefta *Hagiga* 3.33. Cf. Tosefta *Ketubot* 5.1.

temple.[45] There are several rabbinic reports of rabbis in the late third century CE exacting the "second tithe" and even bringing it to Jerusalem.[46] A series of stories in the Palestinian Talmud tell of rabbis redeeming their second tithes; in one, a rabbi in Rome observed merchants redeem at the lower, Roman, market rate the second tithe of dates imported from Israel.[47] These stories would make little sense to an audience unfamiliar with the practice.

c. Rabbinic Cases. Rabbinic literature contains many 'case reports'. These are usually pithy accounts of legal cases that came before rabbis along with how they ruled. Rabbinic cases, which differ in form and rhetorical force from stories, are often taken by modern scholars as reflecting actual events.[48]

Many of these cases deal with issues of tithing. In one, a rabbi's tithed produce being mixed with untithed produce resulted in a question to a colleague.[49] A similar case, this time involving *terumah* (which can only be eaten by a priest) mixed with regular food came before Rabbi Akiva.[50] Those of the house of "Bar Ashtor", who lived in a place where there were no Jews, asked a rabbi if they were required to separate tithes on the work of their gentile tenants; ultimately R. Aimi said no.[51] One relatively late report records a woman forgetting to separate *terumah* before Shabbat.[52] A woman consulted a rabbi about the status of the plants produced from seeds of *terumah* produce that had been dropped.[53] A man asked a rabbi about the permissibility of cooking with oil that was originally given as *terumah*.[54] These case reports, and many others, accept the giving of *terumah* and tithes as normal practices.[55]

It is also possible, but by no means certain, that the many rabbinic cases that relate to purity – together with the many stepped pools that were located in Jewish settlements in Roman Palestine that may have been used for ritual purification – indirectly testify to the continuation of tithing. According to rabbinic law, after the destruction of the temple ritual purity was most directly related to sexual activities and the eating of tithes. The bulk of the cases and the location of

45 Babylonian Talmud *Shabbat* 54b.
46 See the sources and discussion in Büchler 1912, pp. 16-17.
47 Palestinian Talmud *Ma'aser Sheni* 4.1; 54d.
48 Cf. Hezser 1993.
49 Tosefta *Demai* 5.22. Cf. Palestinian Talmud *Demai* 5.9; 24d.
50 Mishnah *Terumot* 4.13
51 Palestinian Talmud *Demai* 6.1; 25b.
52 Palestinian Talmud *Demai* 7.1; 26a.
53 Palestinian Talmud *Ma'aser Sheni* 5.7; 52b.
54 Palestinian Talmud *Pesahim* 7.3; 34b.
55 Tosefta *Terumot* 1.15; Tosefta *Terumot* 2.13; Tosefta *Demai* 4.13; Tosefta *Ma'aser Sheni* 5.9; Tosefta *Ma'aser Sheni* 3.18; Tosefta *Shevi'it* 5.2; Palestinian Talmud *Ma'aser Sheni* 4.5; 55b-c; Palestinian Talmud *Terumot* 5.8; 43d. According to Hayim Lapin, cases involving tithes increase among later rabbis (Lapin 2012).

the pools (often by agricultural establishments) might suggest a connection to priestly gifts.[56]

d. Rabbinic Exhortations. Many rabbinic dicta urge the continued giving of tithes and *terumah* and discourage their neglect. One relatively late story, for example, tells of a man who would faithfully tithe his field and prosper. Upon his death, his son began to reduce the amount that he tithed and found that his field produced proportionally less.[57] God, according to another source, causes earthquakes when Israel does not properly tithe.[58] Rabbinic law expected women to be careful about serving only tithed produce; negligence in this area allowed a man to divorce his wife without returning her dowry.[59]

A few rabbinic traditions comment directly on the prevalence of tithing, but these sources are difficult to evaluate. According to one rabbi, most people set aside their dough offerings in their house.[60] How does he know? Similarly but conversely, a Talmudic passage interrupts a legal account to assert that in actual public practice people were not setting aside their *terumah*.[61] Elsewhere, though, Rabbi Eleazar said in the name of Rabbi Hoshaya that there is a legal presumption that Jews properly gave the *terumah*.[62] These differing assessments are not surprising, as they are formed not on the basis of survey data but vague impressions and rhetorical need. Nevertheless, it seems safe to assert on the basis of these sources that priestly gifts and tithes were being given through late antiquity, even if we cannot ascertain the full extent.

e. Liturgical Poetry. Jewish liturgical poems from late antiquity, *piyyutim*, do not quite provide independent evidence for the continued practice of tithing. The shadowy authors of these poems appear to have been familiar with many rabbinic traditions. At the same time, however, their *Sitz im Leben* as public performances in the synagogue make them a valuable source for considering what the authors felt would be understandable to their audience.

It is thus not insignificant that the *piyyutim* testify to both the prominence of the public reading of the passage in Deuteronomy 14 dealing with tithes during holiday services in the synagogue and the continuation of the practice of tithing itself.[63] The institution of this passage as a regular part of the holiday lectionary appears to date from late antiquity. This fact, along with the treatment of the tithes in the *piyyutim* as a living practice, suggests not only the continuity of the

[56] According to Cohen, 27,6% of the tannaitic cases concern purities (Cohen 1999, p. 968). On the 'stepped pools', see Amit – Adler 2010; Miller 2010.

[57] *Pesikta d'Rav Kahana* 10.1. The story is related in the name of Rabbi Levi.

[58] Palestinian Talmud *Berakot* 9.2; 13c.

[59] Mishnah *Ketubot* 7.6; Palestinian Talmud *Ketubot* 7.6; 31b.

[60] Palestinian Talmud *Orlah* 2.1; 61d.

[61] Palestinian Talmud *Ma'aser Sheni* 5.3; 56b.

[62] Palestinian Talmud *Peah* 8.2; 20d.

[63] Fleisher 1967; Hollender 2007.

practice, but perhaps even its growing interest to and strength within the communities in which these poems circulated.

f. Inscription. A single, but extensive and important, inscription has a status similar to that of the *piyyutim*: it shows a clear connection to rabbinic circles although its public display in a synagogue might speak to a wider audience. The inscription was found on a mosaic floor of a synagogue in Rechov, about 5 km southwest of Beit She'an in the Jordan Valley. An enormous inscription of 29 lines in Hebrew that dates probably to the fifth century CE, its contents are largely paralleled in rabbinic literature.[64] The inscription details both the kinds of produce subject to the Jewish agricultural laws – i.e., the laws of the sabbatical year (*shevi'it*) and all other years the tithes – and the geographical limits to which these laws apply. That is, only produce from the "Land of Israel" is subject to these laws, so the inscription (and the rabbinic parallels) detail which cities and areas actually 'count' as part of the Land of Israel. Some cities within the borders of what might otherwise be considered 'Israel', such as Beit She'an itself, are not subject to these laws because they were thought to be gentile habitations.

Like the *piyyutim*, this inscription would seem to testify to the continued practice of tithing in late antique Roman Palestine. This was a didactic or reference text, not a decoration or an intellectual exercise. A comparison with its rabbinic parallels further sharpens its function. In contrast to the parallels in extant rabbinic texts, this inscription arranges the geographical locations so that Beit She'an and locations near it are first. This appears to be a text that was meant to be consulted for practical guidance.

Seen together, these sources strongly suggest that Jews continued to tithe into late antiquity.[65] These Jews lived for the most part, perhaps entirely, in Palestine. We do not know what percent of the Jewish population would have given any priestly or levitical gifts, and for those who did, we do not know to what extent they would have followed rabbinic guidelines (or, conversely, whether rabbinic guidelines emerged from common practice). It would be interesting to compare these prescriptions and practices with those of neighbors, especially Christians, who developed a rich vocabulary and set of practices for supporting clergy. That comparison, however, is beyond the scope of this paper.[66]

[64] The text of the inscription, with a brief commentary, can be found in Naveh 1978, pp. 79-85 (no. 49). Treatments of the inscription are Sussman 1973-74; Sussman 1974-75; Sussman 1981. The rabbinic parallels to the inscription are Tosefta *Shevi'it* 4.8-11; *Sifre Deuteronomy* 51; Palestinian Talmud *Demai* 2.1; 22d; Palestinian Talmud *Shevi'it* 6.1; 36c.

[65] *Pace* Schwartz 2001, pp. 128-161. Schwartz does not explicitly address tithes here, but they are relevant to assessing how "Jewish" Jews remained after the destruction of the temple.

[66] Cf. Caner 2013.

What if a significant number of Jews, though, did remit such gifts in a way that conformed to some degree to the rabbinic guidelines? From an economic perspective, how might that actually 'look' for the landholders, the recipients of the gifts, and the economy as a whole? This is obviously a speculative exercise, but one that reveals the practical ramifications of a truly embedded economy.

4. Economic ramifications I: landholders

This part of the paper adopts a more quantitative approach. Despite our uncertainty about many aspects of the economy of the Roman world, specifically at the level of local regions, some very rough assumptions and 'back of the envelope' calculations at least begin to help us to grasp the practical implications of tithing.

Just to make things a little more concrete, I take for my example the region of Sepphoris, in northern Israel. We know from literary references and archaeological excavations that Sepphoris was a major regional political and economic hub from the first through the seventh centuries CE.[67] In the Byzantine period, the city encompassed about 30 hectares (1 hectare=10 dunams=2,47 acres). Magen Broshi suggests that the maximum population density of cities in Byzantine Palestine was 400 people/hectare.[68] We would thus arrive at a maximum population for Sepphoris of about 12000.

Rabbinic sources identify a typical field as containing enough land to allow for the sowing of "20 *bet se'ahs*" of grain, which works out to 3,13 hectares.[69] Archaeological surveys do not, at the moment, provide any data about average farm sizes in Roman Palestine, and even if they did, it is likely that individuals owned more than one, non-contiguous plot. By way of comparison, in Mandate Palestine family "Fellah" farms were on average about 7-10 hectares, so the rabbinic estimate might be low.[70] In the region of Sepphoris, it is thought that animal husbandry was practiced at a relatively low intensity.[71] Moreover, some of this land would undoubtedly have been devoted to growing legumes and other vegetables. So for the purpose of calculations regarding cereals – which undoubtedly served as the staple crop – I will use low and high estimates of 3 and 7 hectares for the average farm.

We are equally uncertain about grain yields. Today, developed countries routinely have yields of more than 5000 kg cereal/hectare/year, whereas less developed countries (primarily in Africa) have yields of under 1000 kg cereal (or

[67] See the essays in Martin Nagy 1996.

[68] Broshi 1979, p. 5.

[69] Ben-David 1974, p. 135.

[70] Elazari-Volcani 1930, p. 54. Some scholars argue that the landholding patterns in Palestine remained more or less stable over this period of time.

[71] Safrai 1994, p. 171.

cereal equivalent)/hectare/year.[72] In Mandate Palestine, wheat yields ranged from around 300-760 kg/hectare/year.[73] The yields tend to cluster in the higher end of this range, so for calculations I will assume an average yield of 600 kg cereal/hectare/year.[74]

This means that using the 'small' average farm size (3 hectares) we would have an annual yield of 1800 kg cereal. A large (7 hectares) would produce 4200 kg cereal in a year. This would be the gross amount, before deductions.

Twenty five percent of the crop would be set aside for planting for the next year.[75] We have little hard data on the amount given to Rome as tax. While recent scholarship has suggested that in the fourth century 10% of cereal crops were given to Rome, I will use the more conservative number of 20% for the sake of these calculations.[76] From the remainder, the farmer gives the various tithes.

For the sake of simplicity, I will not factor in a few other deductions. The rabbis call for a regimen of separate gifts to the poor (e.g., leaving corners of the fields and gleanings), which in any case were not substantial.[77] As noted above, the rabbis also think that there is no longer a need to bring first fruits.[78] Finally, I am not including the "second tithe", which although attested in rabbinic literature is to be consumed by the landowner; it cannot be classified as a priestly or levitical gift.

The tithing deductions would begin, according to the rabbis, at the 2,5% given to the priests as *terumah*, an amount computed only on grain designated for consumption. 10% would now be computed from the remainder as the first tithe. The results of these calculations can be seen in the scheme:

[72] http://www.nationmaster.com/graph/agr_cer_yie_kg_per_hec-cereal-yield-kg-per-hectare (last access 26 Aug. 2013).

[73] Elazari-Volcani 1930, pp. 41-42.

[74] Scholars have suggested that grain yields in Roman Palestine were two to three times this amount. Cf. Felix 1963, pp. 160-169; Safrai 1994, p. 110. I am using conservative estimates.

[75] Ben-David 1974, p. 135.

[76] On Roman taxation of agricultural produce, see Hopkins 1980; Bagnall 1985; Hopkins 1995-1996, pp. 200-201 (arguing for a rate of taxation at 10% or less).

[77] Cf. Hamel 1990; Gardner 2009.

[78] However, the mosaics of several Palestinian synagogues do portray the giving of first-fruits, perhaps indicating that this was more widely practiced than the rabbis suggest. Cf. Weiss 2005, pp. 101-104.

	Amount (%)	Amount for 3/7 hectare farm (kg)	Balance for 3/7 hectare farm (kg)
Total product	/	/	1800/4200
Set aside for next year's crop	25%	450/1050	1350/3150
Taxes to Rome	20%	360/840	990/2310
Terumah	2,5%	34/79	956/2231
First Tithe	10%	96/223	860/2008

So when taxes, grain for replanting, *terumah*, and tithes are subtracted from the annual produce of our two hypothetically typical farms, there remains between 860 and 2008 kg of cereal.

Magen Broshi suggests that in antiquity, per capita annual cereal consumption was around 200-250 kg.[79] Hence, a farm of 3 hectares could be expected to support one family of four. Without remitting the *terumah* and tithes, the family might barely be able to support an additional member. At the upper end of the scale (i.e., a farm of 7 hectares), however, there may well have been surplus. A family of five living somewhat above subsistence could generate a surplus of 500 kg/cereal each year. Sepphoris, with its maximum population of 12000 (the majority of whom were not primarily engaged in agriculture) would require some 2,4 million kg of cereals annually, so this surplus would have found a ready market.[80]

These numbers clearly are not telling the whole story. They suggest an economy that worked, but hardly on more than subsistence level. Yet the archaeological excavations of Sepphoris suggest a relatively wealthy city. It is possible, probably likely, that at least some of the land that was factored into these equations was used for cash crops rather than cereals, especially olives. One hectare of olive trees could produce 130 liters of oil each year, even when the biennial production of olives is factored in. Olive oil might then be exported, with proceeds used to buy grain.[81]

Yet no matter how one adjusts the data, they sharpen our understanding of an important tension. On the one hand, these farms did not have much surplus; they had enough, but not enough to invest in ways that would easily allow them to increase their incomes. On the other hand, the actual *terumah* and tithe

[79] Broshi 2002, p. 123. Hopkins 1995-1996, p. 198, sees 250 kg/person as a minimum.

[80] To achieve this amount of surplus wheat, 33600 hectares are necessary (assuming the surpluses calculated for the 7 hectare farm). This is the equivalent of the land within a 15 km radius around a central point (e.g., Sepphoris). Some evidence suggests that Sepphoris could not supply its own grain, importing it instead from the Golan. Cf. Safrai 1994, p. 112.

[81] Safrai 1994, pp. 118-126.

payments, although painful, were theoretically possible. The numbers thus add plausibility to the evidence surveyed above that these Jews were still engaged in the practice of giving these gifts, even if they do not reveal whether these gifts would approach the amount prescribed by the rabbis.

The tithes would also have had a macroeconomic impact. Taking approximately 5% of the available cereal out of market circulation would have had an impact on prices in the marketplace, especially because the demand of essential foodstuffs is not elastic.[82] The poor would particularly feel the economic impact of these higher prices, although the *pe'ah* (an additional 'tax' of leftovers from the field that were supposed to be left for the poor), if actually practiced, would have allowed the very poor to subsist at near subsistence level.

5. Economic ramifications II: priests

According to modern demographic studies, approximately 3-5% of Jews are *kohanim*, or priests.[83] While we cannot say for sure that the same proportion existed in antiquity, we can again use this number for the sake of argument. If we take into account only the *terumah*, we can see immediately approximately 4% of the population would begin – before having done any actual work – with approximately 4% of the available food (this takes into account the fact that the shares that were put aside for next-year's sowing and given as taxes are not counted as 'available'). It is likely that at this time the much larger share that comprised the first-tithe was also given to priests rather than, or at least in addition to, Levites.[84] Simply to get a sense of what this means, if we assume the Jewish population of Sepphoris at 12000 (a high estimate, since Sepphoris was certainly not entirely Jewish), then of this population 480 would be priests. Now, if there were 4500 farms of seven hectares each in the Sepphoris region, we would arrive at a total *terumah* of 355500 kg cereal, or about 741 kg cereal per priest. If each priest maintained his own household, this was not quite enough to survive on, but it would be close.

The impact of these cereal gifts would have been significantly enhanced by the gifts of another 4% of privately prepared dough. This alone might have provided the bulk of the nutritional needs of the priests, and would have been in addition to the *terumah* of oil, pulses, and vegetables, along with some flesh of butchered animals. Combined with the *terumah* of grain and oil – and before a

[82] Markets and pricing add an additional level of complexity that is beyond the scope of this paper. See Rosenfeld – Menirav 2005, pp. 137-169.

[83] Bradman – Thomas – Goldstein 1999.

[84] There is significant debate and ambiguity within the sources on who received the tithe. Cf. Palestinian Talmud *Ma'aser Sheni* 5.9; 56d. Later rabbinic sources attempt to shift the recipients to scholars. See Ôppenhaimer 1977, pp. 45-46.

priest earned any actual income for himself – it is clear that priestly families would have enjoyed a significant economic advantage.

This economic advantage had social ramifications. One area where this would have been particularly felt was the marriage market. For non-priestly landowners, marriage into a priestly family would have offered one way to improve their family's lot. Since, however, there were few eligible priestly men and a dowry payment would have been expected, one would expect that priestly marriages by and large would have served to consolidate already wealthy families; only they could afford to provide a sufficient dowry. Indeed, rabbinic literature testifies to the tendency of priests to marry into other priestly families.[85]

This economic advantage also must be factored into the current discussions about the role of *kohanim* in Jewish society after the destruction of the Jerusalem temple. Scholars have increasingly argued that despite rabbinic protestations against the priesthood, Jewish priests maintained for themselves a prominent role. The economic aspect of this prominence has largely been ignored, but understanding the priests as by and large wealthy could help to explain it.[86]

We do not know if priests gravitated toward one profession. It is clear, though, that they would have had a major competitive edge as farmers. Much of what they produced would be surplus, and in addition it was not subject to what was close to a 25% effective tax (the *terumah* and the first tithe, on the produce left after putting aside grain and paying taxes to Rome) on their produce. Yet on the other hand, there was a brake to infinite priestly expansion: the more land cultivated by priests, the fewer gifts they received. Where was the equilibrium? Were the priests organized enough to respond effectively to this problem? Both of these questions could use further research.

6. Reasons for tithing

While the temple in Jerusalem stood, priests had a very clear function: they administered the public cult. The Jerusalem temple was not only the apparent *raison d'être* for the priests, but it was also an extraordinarily rich and powerful institutional base. With the destruction of the temple we might expect to find priestly authority to decline quickly.

Whatever their relative decline, if the findings of this paper are correct, priests in fact maintained a powerful economic position, at least in Roman Palestine. Why? What accounts for the continued remission of tithes from subsi-

[85] Satlow 2001, pp. 147-148.

[86] For a summary of the argument for continued priestly prominence, see Alexander 2009. Alexander does mention this economic aspect but does not emphasize it sufficiently.

stence farmers to an already wealthy oligarchy, especially when there appears to have been little or no compulsion?

The primary reason would have been the persistence of the religious *mentalité* that promoted the priests as the conduits – maybe even especially since the destruction of the temple – for gifts to the God of Israel. In almost all ancient Mediterranean religions, it was assumed that it was proper to offer gifts to the gods. This might be done through a votive at a local temple or through alms.[87] For many Jews, as for many contemporary Christians, it could be done through gifts to human authorities. Gifts to the *kohanim* were seen as recompense neither for their service in the cult nor for their lack of ancestral land, but as gifts to God. For some Jews, this might have been seen as a simple *do ut des* transaction. For many, I suspect, it would have been seen more simply as what one does to maintain a proper and healthy relationship with the divine.[88]

There may have been social and economic advantages to continuing this practice. Keeping the priests in a position of (at least economic) power could help to reduce the potential strife that accompanies a leadership vacuum. There may also be an economic benefit. Some communities that survive at a subsistence level invest resources in a small segment of the population with the expectation that that investment will pay off for the communal good. This privileged class, for example, might acquire education that will increase agricultural productivity and then share this knowledge: buy an ox that is then loaned to neighbors, or pay for municipal buildings used by many. Might priests have served this role? Here a comprehensive study of the epigraphic record for patterns of priestly giving might be informative.[89]

7. Conclusions

In her study on medieval Christian gift-giving, Ilana Silber distinguishes two types of gift-giving. The first, almsgiving, she claims more or less adheres to Parry's notion of the disinterested gift; it was given without expectation of material reciprocity.[90] The second, and more interesting form of gift-giving, were offerings made to monasteries. These gifts often did carry with them expectations of reciprocity and, more importantly, operated as a "total social fact",

[87] For an overview of dedicatory inscriptions and gifts, see Haensch 2007, pp. 180-185. On almsgiving as a religious act, see Satlow 2010; Caner 2013.

[88] For this approach, see Hubert – Mauss 1899; Gudme 2013.

[89] Out of twenty names found in the dedication inscriptions from the synagogue in Sepphoris, only three – and all in a single Aramaic inscription – are marked as priests. Cf. Weiss 2005, pp. 203-204.

[90] Silber 1995, pp. 213-214; Parry 1986.

"*simultaneously* expressing all sorts of dimensions of social life (religious, legal, moral, political, familial, economic, aesthetic, etc.)".[91]

In Silber's analysis, the truly distinguishing feature of the medieval monastery was the immobilization of wealth for the collective good.

Silber's analysis of giving to medieval Christian monasteries maps very well, if not exactly, onto the phenomenon of Jewish tithe giving in Roman Palestine. Jews gave to *kohanim* with some expectation of reciprocity, both material and immaterial. To ask merely whether they were 'interested' or 'disinterested', however, largely elides the larger contexts in which they played vital roles. I have highlighted here the significant economic ramifications of these gifts on landowners, priests, and the market alike. In so doing, I have also touched on the social and political dimensions of these gifts, as they had significant impact on marriage patterns and the maintenance of a political and religious class of leadership.

Mauss argued that the gift operates as a total social fact only in archaic societies, later to be replaced by laws and markets. As I hope to have demonstrated here, the reality in Roman Palestine was far more complex. This should not be particularly surprising; even in modern societies the gifts made to non-profit entities are significant and are embedded in a wider social context. When we forget this, however, we risk significantly distorting our understanding of the past.

Bibliography

Alexander, Philip S.: *What Happened to the Jewish Priesthood after 70?*, in: *A Wandering Galilean: Essays in Honour of Seán Freyne*, ed. by Zuleika Rodgers, Leiden 2009, pp. 5-33.

Amit, David – Yonatan Adler: *The Observance of Ritual Purity after 70 C.E.: A Reevaluation of the Evidence in Light of Recent Archaeological Discoveries*, in: *Follow the Wise. Studies in Jewish History and Culture in Honor of Lee I. Levine*, ed. by Zeev Weiss – Oded Irshai – Jodi Magness – Seth Schwarz, Winona Lake 2010, pp. 121-143.

Bagnall, Roger S.: *Agricultural Productivity and Taxation in Later Roman Egypt*, in: *TAPA* 115 (1985), pp. 289-308.

Ben-David, Arye: *Talmudische Ökonomie: Die Wirtschaft des jüdischen Palästina zur Zeit der Mischna und des Talmud*, Hildesheim 1974.

Blenkinsopp, Joseph: *Sage, Priest, Prophet: Religious and Intellectual Leadership in Ancient Israel*, Louisville 1995.

Bradman, Neil – Mark G. Thomas – David B. Goldstein: *The Genetic Origins of Old Testament Priests*, in: *Population Specific Polymorphisms*, ed. by Colin E. Renfrew, Cambridge 1999, pp. 31-44.

Broshi, Magen: *The Population of Western Palestine in the Roman-Byzantine Period*, in: *Bulletin of the American Schools of Oriental Research* 236 (1979), pp. 1-10.

[91] Silber 1995, p. 238 (original emphasis).

Broshi, Magen: *Bread, Wine, Walls and Scrolls*, Sheffield 2002.

Büchler, Anton: *The Economic Conditions of Judaea after the Destruction of the Second Temple*, London 1912.

Caner, Daniel F.: *Alms, Blessings, Offerings: The Repertoire of Christian Gifts in Early Byzantium*, in: *The Gift in Antiquity*, ed. by Michael Satlow, Malden – Oxford 2013, pp. 25-44.

Cohen, Shaye J. D.: *The Rabbi in Second-Century Jewish Society*, in: *The Cambridge History of Judaism, Volume 3: The Early Roman Period*, ed. by William Horbury – William D. Davies – John Sturdy, Cambridge 1999, pp. 922-990.

Elazari-Volcani, Isaac: *The Fellah's Farm*, Tel Aviv 1930.

Felix, Yehudah: *Agriculture in the Period of the Mishnah and Talmud*, Jerusalem – Tel Aviv 1963.

Fleisher, Ezra: *Parashat ‵asar ta`aser' u'kri'atah b'yamot hag lephi minhagot 'eretz-Israel*, in: *Tarbiz* 36 (1967), pp. 116-155.

Gardner, Gregg E.: *Giving to the Poor in Early Rabbinic Judaism*, PhD. Dissertation, Princeton 2009.

Gudme, Anne Katrine: *Barter Deal or Friend-Making Gift? A Reconsideration of the Conditional Vow in the Hebrew Bible*, in: *The Gift in Antiquity*, ed. by Michael Satlow, Malden – Oxford 2013, pp. 189-201.

Haensch, Rudolf: *Inscriptions as Sources of Knowledge for Religions and Cults in the Roman World of Imperial Times*, in: *A Companion to Roman Religion*, ed. by Jörg Rüpke, Malden 2007, pp. 176-187.

Hamel, Gildas H.: *Poverty and Charity in Roman Palestine, First Three Centuries CE*, Berkeley 1990.

Hezser, Catherine: *Form, Function, and Historical Significance of the Rabbinic Story in Yerushalmi Neziqin*, Tübingen 1993.

Hollender, Elisabeth: *Parashat ‵Asser Te`asser' in Piyyut and Piyyut Commentary*, in: *Jewish and Christian Liturgy and Worship: New Insights into its History and Interaction*, ed. by Albert Gerhards – Clemens Leonhard, Boston 2007, pp. 91-107.

Hopkins, Keith: *Taxes and Trade in the Roman Empire (200 B.C.-A.D. 400)*, in: *JRS* 70 (1980), pp. 101-125.

Hopkins, Keith: *Rome, Taxes, Rents, and Trade*, in: *Kodai* 6-7 (1995-1996), pp. 41-75 = in: *The Ancient Economy*, ed. by Walter Scheidel – Sitta von Reden, Edinburgh 2002, pp. 190-230.

Hubert, Henri – Marcel Mauss: *Essai sur la nature et la fonction du sacrifice*, in: *Année Sociologique* 2 (1899), pp. 29-138; Engl. Transl.: *Sacrifice: Its Nature and Functions*, Chicago 1964.

Janzen, David: *Priestly Sacrifice in the Hebrew Bible: A Summary of Recent Scholarship and a Narrative Reading*, in: *Religious Compass* 2 (2007), pp. 38-52.

Lapin, Hayim: *Rabbis as Romans: The Rabbinic Movement in Palestine, 100-400 CE*, New York 2012.

Martin Nagy, Rebecca (Ed.), *Sepphoris in Galilee: Crosscurrents of Culture*, Winona Lake 1996.

Mason, Steve (Ed.), *Flavius Josephus, Life of Josephus*, Leiden 2001.

Mauss, Marcel: *Essai sur le don. Forme et raison de l'échange dans les sociétés archaïques*, in: *L'Année sociologique* n.s. 1 (1923-1924), pp. 30-186. Engl. Transl.: *The*

Gift: The Form and Reason for Exchange in Archaic Societies, foreword by Mary Douglas, New York 1990.

Miller, Stuart S.: *Sages and Commoners in Late Antique 'Erez Israel: A Philological Inquiry into Local Traditions in Talmud Yerushalmi*, Tübingen 2006.

Miller, Stuart S.: *Stepped Pools, Stone Vessels, and Other Identity Markers of 'Complex Common Judaism'*, in: *Journal for the Study of Judaism in the Persian, Hellenistic and Roman Period* 41 (2010), pp. 214-43.

Naveh, Joseph: *On Stone and Mosaic: The Aramaic and Hebrew Inscriptions from Ancient Synagogues* (in Hebrew), Tel Aviv 1978.

Oppenhaimer, Aharon: *The 'Am Ha-Aretz: A Study of the Social History of the Jewish People in the Hellenistic-Roman Period*, Leiden 1977.

Parry, Jonathan: *The Gift, the Indian Gift and the 'Indian Gift'*, in: *Man* 21 (1986), pp. 453-473.

Rosenfeld, Ben Zion – Joseph Menirav: *Markets and Marketing in Roman Palestine*, Leiden 2005.

Safrai, Zeev: *The Economy of Roman Palestine*, London 1994.

Satlow, Michael L.: *Jewish Marriage in Antiquity*, Princeton 2001.

Satlow, Michael L.: *"Fruit and the Fruit of Fruit": Charity and Piety among Jews in Late Antique Palestine*, in: *Jewish Quarterly Review* 100 (2010), pp. 244-277.

Schürer, Emil: *The History of the Jewish People in the Age of Jesus Christ*, vol. 2, Edinburgh 1979[2].

Schwartz, Seth: *Imperialism and Jewish Society, 200 B.C.E. to 640 C.E.*, Princeton, 2001.

Silber, Ilana: *Gift-giving in the Great Traditions: The Case of Donations to Monasteries in the Medieval West*, in: *European Journal of Sociology* 36 (1995), pp. 209-243.

Sussman, Yaakov: *Ketuvat halachtit me'emek beit shean*, in: *Tarbiz* 43 (1973-74), pp. 88-158; 44 (1974-75), pp. 193-195.

Sussman, Yaakov: *The Inscription in the Synagogue in Rehob*, in: *Ancient Synagogues Revealed*, ed. by Lee I. Levine, Jerusalem 1981, pp. 146-151.

Weiss, Ze'ev: *The Sepphoris Synagogue: Deciphering an Ancient Message through its Archaeological and Socio-Historical Contexts*, Jerusalem 2005.

LUIGI CANETTI

Christian Gift and Gift Exchange from Late Antiquity to the Early Middle Ages

I feel the writings of Cyprian of Carthage are a good starting point to introduce an issue that involves history, theology, sociology and economic anthropology at the same time. It is not unreasonable to claim that Cyprian was the father of Catholic ecclesiology.[1] Above all, in his treatise *De opere et eleemosynis*, composed around 255 CE, he skilfully exploited all the metaphorical potential of the term *munus* to mark the difference between the specific Christian and pagan connotations of the concept, which were familiar to his audience as they were rooted in the social forms and political languages of the ancient city. The term *munus* indicates a gift bestowed by the mercy of God, which satisfies the common need for salvation through the incarnation of the Son and the redemption of sins through his death and resurrection. At least in the meaning given by St. Paul that Cyprian adopted, salvific exchange is based on the idea that the Son of God accepted death to offer mortals the gift of immortality.[2] I will observe in passing that it is precisely this asymmetrical notion of the salvific exchange that reveals the Christian rejection of sacrifice as the direct symmetrical exchange of benefits between man and the divinity.[3] Indeed, nothing can be returned to a creator that has given and continues to give freely to men all the things that they need: health, prosperity and salvation.[4] At a later point I will provide some examples of how, from Antiquity onwards, the

[1] Frend 1984, pp. 322-325; 351-357 ; 403-411.
[2] Cypr., *De op. et eleem.* 1.9-10.
[3] Canetti 2002, pp. 105-109.
[4] See, for example, *Ad Diogn.* 3.3-4; Clem. Al., *Quis dives salvetur* 27.5; Greg. M., *Reg. ep.* 11.56; and also Thom. Aq., *In IV Sententiarum*, dist. 46, qu. 1, art. 2, qu. la 2 ("*Deus autem donator bonorum omnium est, et in eum omnis peccator peccat; unde ipse potest plus conferre de bonis quam sit alicui debitum, et minus inferre de malis, vel etiam poenam totaliter relaxare; nec in hoc contra justitiam, sed praeter justitiam faceret*"). Hénaff 2002, pp. 319-351, pointed out that the Pauline and Patristic reflection on grace (*cháris*) as a unilateral and unconditional divine gift – namely the refusal of ceremonial gift – are indebted to Judaism (*hén*), Aristotelianism (*philía*) and Stoicism (*beneficium*). At the same time, he rightly stressed that Christianity was able to create a much more powerful symbolic device: "un Dieu unique qui enveloppe tous les êtres humaines d'une affection inconditionnelle sans distinction de status, de sex ou de nation, qui se fait l'un d'eux, meurt pour eux et leur ouvre son royaume. Aucune école philosophique n'était en mesure de rivaliser avec un tel récit et un tel symbolisme (et c'est bein ce qui désolait Nietzsche)" (p. 349).

mentality and practice of Christians never became completely detached from traditional notions and practices of sacrificial exchange. At the same time, we must never forget that many aspects regarding the new spiritual meaning of sacrifice (namely the refusal of blood sacrifice) provided common ground between Christian theologians and Platonic philosophers in the Imperial Age (Origen and Porphiry).[5] Although Eusebius of Caesarea, an Origenian, wrote a polemic against the 'magician' Apollonius of Tyana,[6] at the time an apprentice philosopher at the temple of Aegae, he valued the latter's teaching when he tried to convince rich donors in Cilicia that Asclepius's healing work was not conditioned by the profusion of goods offered as vows by the devout.[7] Eusebius then showed that he was familiar with Apollonius's lost work on sacrifice,[8] to which Porphyry seems to have referred in his treatise on abstinence.[9]

However, let us now return to Cyprian. He used the word *munus* in the common sense of public office, a usage rooted in the notion of the donatives given by a magistrate in order to fulfill his office honourably. These included the ritual practice of subsidising circus games and performances, which were also defined as *munera* by way of metonymy.[10] This traditional usage allowed Cyprian to devise a truly effective apologue to convince the rich Christians of Carthage to show their generosity towards the poor.[11] It is Satan himself who takes centre stage in the dramatic *ludus* imagined by the preacher, a combination of theatre and legal action. The accuser invites Christ to show him Christian donors who are as generous in their donations to the poor as rich pagans were in financing theatrical contests and gladiator fights – all demonstrations of *pompa diaboli*, to use Tertullian's words,[12] or events and instruments of the most characteristic manifestations of idolatrous worship.

The title of Cyprian's treatise speaks volumes in itself: *opus* (along with its derivative *operatio* and the verb *operari*, which appear repeatedly during the course of the work) refers, above all, to the salvific acts of God and their associated benefits:[13] it is through Christ that the gift of the salvation of sinful

[5] Even those who defended and practised blood sacrifice, like Iamblichus and the emperor Julian, now attributed a new meaning and function rooted in Neo-Platonic theurgy and therefore oriented more towards the transformation of individual identity (the purification of the philosopher's soul) than towards the traditional preservation of collective identity. On this issue, see Chuvin 2004^2, pp. 237-240; Stroumsa 2005, pp. 14; 59-61; 76; 86; De Vita 2011, pp. 230-238; Rives 2013.

[6] Eus., *C. Hier.* 12.

[7] Philostr., *V. Apoll.* 1.10-11.

[8] Eus., *Praep. Ev.* 4.11-13; *Dem. Ev.* 3.3.11.

[9] Porph., *De abstin.* 2.34; see Canetti 2013, p. 439.

[10] Veyne 1976, pp. 82; 350; 357; 394; 661.

[11] Cypr., *De op. et eleem.* 22; see Lugaresi 2008, pp. 446-447.

[12] For example, Tert., *De spect.* 12; 24; see Lugaresi 2008, pp. 395-396 and 417-418.

[13] "For Cyprian, *operatio* was the secret of the 'vigor' of the Church. It showed that the

humanity is implemented and redeemed at the cost of the incarnation and sacrificial death of the Son of God. Works of charity, above all alms, are perhaps the most important means that God offered man to redeem himself from sins committed after baptism, which threaten the attainment of eternal life. This is perhaps the most distinctive expression of Christian *charis* ('charity'), the 'gift of grace' modelled on the divine grace which God gave by presenting himself in human form.[14] The absolute or socially unconditioned gratuitousness of the act of giving even to those who cannot reciprocate recalls, and to some extent repeats, the benefits connected to God's gratuitous act of participating in the human condition through Christ and offering man the means and signs to sanctify himself, thereby regain the resemblance to the creator obfuscated by sin. The wisdom literature of Judaism already saw alms to the poor in the following way:

> "He that hath pity upon the poor lendeth unto the Lord; and that which he hath given will he pay him again".[15]

The oldest known rule of a Christian community, dating from the late first century, exhorted people to "give by means of thy hands a redemption for thy sins" without any hesitation or regret, in the knowledge that "thou shouldest know who is the fair recompenser of the reward".[16]

We shall see how the whole issue was grounded in the divine basis of the act in question: Christ is the main cause but also the real recipient of the benefaction.[17] Therefore, even in the form of alms, charity definitely had a social and economic effect, albeit one directed at a neighbour, who was thought to reflect the face of God incarnate.[18] It is no coincidence that from the fourth century onwards the Christian notion of image and the justification of the worship of images, which came to the fore again in the eighth century following the defeat of the iconoclastic movement, were based precisely on the theological concept of divine economy and faith in the incarnation of the *persona* (image and substance) of the Son.[19]

Spirit of God was at work in the community" (Brown 2012, p. 42).

[14] Moussy 1966, pp. 445-473; Hénaff 2002, pp. 348-351; Rossi Monti 2008, pp. 3-12.

[15] *Prov.* 19.17; but already in *Tob.* 4.5-11; see Peterman 1997, pp. 24-25 and 37-38.

[16] *Didaché* 4.6-7.

[17] "Dans le premiers siècles du christianisme, les échanges des hommes avec Dieu sont posés en terme d'*imitatio*, et non de réciprocité" (Magnani 2009, p. 1023, which refers to Cypr., *De op. et eleem.* 25).

[18] According to Sotinel 2006, in Late Antiquity the economic impact of Christian gift was quite limited in all its forms. See Finn 2006 for a systematic analysis of almsgiving in the Christian Empire between Constantine and Theodosius II.

[19] An essential work on this topic is still Ladner 1953.

If the Christian gift expresses and constantly reactivates God's salvific act and his *clementia* (St. Paul's concept of *philanthropía*),[20] then all Christians, not only the destitute, are in need of charity. In the same way, every person is required to give alms, such as the widow in the Gospel who makes an offering on the basis of what she can afford.[21] This is one of the paradigms of this singular theological economy, which established an exchange system within the emerging Christian society,[22] and was frequently exploited by hagiographers and preachers from the early centuries onwards.[23] It is precisely because the charity gift was grounded in the divine economy that it offered Christians the opportunity to partly redeem their sins, helping to increase the celestial treasure.[24] The "treasure in heaven" from the Gospels[25] soon became the salvific capital introduced and managed by the divine banker, the *dokimos trapezites*, the proven assayer, or the reliable money-changer (in Latin: *probabilis trapezita* or *bonus nummularius*)[26] – a metaphor that the Church Fathers from Clement of Alexandria to Ambrose and John Cassian applied to every true believer as a follower of Christ.[27] Christ was considered to be the heavenly merchant, the main driving force behind this holy commerce fuelled by the virtues and merits of his perfect imitators, the saints, who were initially all the baptized, but soon became only the most perfect among them, namely martyrs and ascetics.

I shall return shortly to the importance of the cult of saints and their relics in the crucial phase of the pastoral and territorial grounding of the new salvific economy.[28] However, it is appropriate to recall briefly the legal and political implications of this theological basis of the notion of gift and benefit within Christianity. Cyprian almost always associated *opera misericordiae* with *opera iustitiae* (*iustitiae et misericordiae opera* or *eleemosynis atque operationibus*

[20] *Tit.* 3.4-5; on the different output of the Greek word *philanthropía* in pagan and Christian Latin writers, a useful work is still Pétré 1948, pp. 201-202.

[21] *Mc* 12.41-44; see also Cypr., *De op. et eleem.* 15.10.

[22] See Carrié 2006 regarding the structural originality of the Christian economic language, in which economics became the main metaphorical resource for soteriological discourse; there are also some remarks in Canetti 2012, pp. 30-31.

[23] See, for example, Greg. Tur., *Glor. mart.* 96.

[24] According to Augustine, through gifts to saints, namely those who carry out the ministry of preaching and teaching in Christian communities, *exigua portio fructuum terrenorum fit pretium regni caelorum. Seminantur spiritalia et metuntur carnalia. [...] Item seminantur carnalia et metuntur spiritalia. [...] O commercia veneranda sanctorum!* (Aug., *Serm.* 350/E = *Erfurt* 3.2-3); see Brown 2012, pp. 355-356.

[25] *Mc* 10.21; *Mt* 6.20; 19.21.

[26] On this *logion* and its sources, see Pesce 2004, pp. 687-688.

[27] See, for example, Clem. Alex., *Strom.* 1.28.177.1-2; II.4.15.4; Ambr., *Exp. in Luc.* I.2; Ioh. Cass., *Conl.* 1.20; 2.9; cf. Bogaert 1973; Todeschini 1992, p. 192; Todeschini 2002, p. 27.

[28] On this topic refer to the more specific contribution of Filippo Carlà in this volume.

iustis).[29] However, unlike Ambrose more then a century later and in a completely different context, he did not evoke a form of distributive justice that in some way reduced social inequality or even restored the common use of goods, originally established by God but then violated by the covetousness of the rich.[30] On the other hand, in St. Paul's opinion the remission of sins through works of justice and mercy (including charity) did not pay off our debt to divine justice, a debt which only the grace of baptism could compensate for. The *iustitia* underlying *opera misericordiae* was therefore valid as it expressed and reactivated the benefits of divine *clementia* (St. Paul's *philanthropia*), which manifested itself through the commandment of alms. In this way, when Cyprian exhorted Christians to obey a precept derived from the clemency of the Lord, he exceeded and at the same time avoided contradicting St. Paul's rejection of justification through works. There was therefore no justice in Christian society or in its supernatural foundation without the grace of mercy and charity.[31] This structural connection between *caritas* as a divine gift and the practice of authentic *iustitia* contained deep-rooted demystification of all idolatrous claims of earthly *nomos* and its Christian representatives (Byzantine autocracy and papal hierocracy) – a concept frequently found in the works of Augustine. It is an issue which came to have enormous repercussions on the development of political-legal thinking at least until the seventeenth century. This characteristic oscillation between the guarantee of redemption as a countergift resulting from good works and the opportunity to make deferred use of the salvific benefits supplied by virtue of the wealth of merits managed by the *ecclesia* (the mystical and sacramental body of Christ) embodies all the complexity of the Christian doctrine of grace, which gave rise to the development of polemics ranging from Pelagius and Augustine through Erasmus and Luther to Pascal and the Jansenists.[32] The two anthropological extremes of the notion of gift delimit the boundaries of two branches of ecclesiology: on one hand a perfect saintly community (the monastic ideal of renouncing the world and possession of material goods, with all the paradoxes that this led to) and on the other hand a community that lived and operated in the world and resigned itself to accepting both good seeds and tares without expecting to experience heavenly Jerusalem on Earth.[33]

The well-known paradox in contemporary thinking on the gift, first identified by Marcel Mauss, can be foreseen in the Christian claim that charity is given

[29] Cypr., *De op. et eleem.* 1.23-24; 2.9; 23.44-45.

[30] On Ambrose's economic thought, useful remarks can be found in Salamito 2006, pp. 35-36 and more recently in Brown 2012, pp. 131-134, 142-147. There was suspicion among some Homoeans in the court of Valentinian II and Justina that Ambrose had only helped the poor to gain their support and increase his tyrannical power. On this matter see Lizzi Testa 2012, p. 397.

[31] Guerreau-Jalabert 2000, pp. 29-38.

[32] On this, see Lettieri 1999.

[33] *Mt* 13.36-43.

gratuitously.[34] In principle, the *iusta operatio* of charity does not require an immediate countergift, as the latter is both experienced through its identification with life itself as a divine gift and deferred to the afterlife with salvation as its eschatological redemption. Although eternal reward certainly remains the biggest restriction to the Christian practice of a legitimate earthly economy, believers always experience and implement the imperatives of their faith in a community dimension, whether it be elitist or extended. They are entitled to expect certain earthly countergifts – acting as incentives and guarantees of the final victory over death – by virtue of daily compliance with the bond of faith that links them to God through baptism. This bond was definitely based on the sanctifying grace (*charis*) of the sacrament of Christian initiation and was secured by the moral precepts soon ratified by canonical law.[35] However, compliance with these norms of faith suggests that they expected countergifts: not only the pardoning of sins through confession, but also the *charismata* (authentic divine gifts) that Jesus indicated to his disciples, namely healing from disease and liberation from the power of demons. The disciples and perfect believers were occasionally able to carry out these charisms, which were the main virtues of thaumaturgic saints from the fourth century onwards along with prophecy. These saints became the biggest guarantors and best donors of physical and spiritual health both during life and especially after death – factors which were deemed to be a highly important surety of salvation. It is no coincidence that from the end of the fourth century onwards the relics of saints were increasingly frequently called *pignora sanctorum*.[36] With the promise of the resurrection of the body as well as the regeneration of the soul, conversion and the healing of bodies offered Christians a down payment for the future restoration of the ontological fullness that had been compromised by the fall into sin and mortality.[37]

Christians adopted an approach similar to pagans by expecting their God and saints to grant them more worldly forms of recompense such as material prosperity, political approval, social acclaim and prestige. These expectations are naturally more evident in historical, hagiographical and apologetic texts that attempt to accommodate them than in normative and doctrinal sources, which if anything tend to censor them. While it is true in theory that a believer (literally a creditor of faith) can never expect to receive income – an immediate countergift

[34] See, for example, Hénaff 2002, pp. 319-321; 350-351. The fruitfulness of Mauss's thinking on the paradoxes of the gift (Mauss 1923-1924) is attested to by the works of Godelier 1996 (with critical remarks by Hénaff 2002, pp. 201-203); Caillé 2000; Godbout 2000; Anspach 2002; Godbout 2007; Salsano 2008; a useful review is provided by Carosso 2011.

[35] For the early modern revival of these issues, see the interesting book by Clavero Salvador 1991, but also take into account the critical remarks by Hénaff 2002, pp. 369-378.

[36] On these developments see Canetti 2002, pp. 105-138.

[37] *2Cor.* 1.22; *Eph.* 1.14.

to the benefit he has bestowed through charity – from God, in practice the theological apparatus of alms needs to mobilize both old and new social networks, and therefore also hierarchies of prestige and function in order to be effective. Charity not only expresses, but also produces and increases a benefactor's status and reputation (*euergetes* in the ancient sense), and inevitably the more Christian communities started to integrate themselves into the surrounding society – to the point where bishops, who belonged to the ruling class, took on public roles within the state structure – the more notions of gifts and models of munificent behaviour tended to revisit and integrate the ancient apparatus of gift and reciprocity founded more on an antagonistic criterion than on St. Paul's principle of *charis*.[38] This explains Ambrose's exhortation to rich believers in Milan, who were loath to donate part of their possessions to the church as ransom for prisoners of war in the Balkans. Ambrose wanted to fuse holy vessels and furnishings as they were the treasure of the poor; among other things this led to the disappearance of the names of donors etched on silverware, a custom which enabled notables to perpetuate a traditional form of *euergesia* as an instrument of propaganda in the interest of family prestige and public approval.[39] In the same period, Jerome criticizes avarice, *radix omnium malorum* (*1Tim.* 6.10), but is even more critical of the duplicity – namely the persistence of the ancient ritual ostentation of worldly magnificence – of those who "give alms when playing the trumpet". A Roman noblewoman (perhaps Faltonia Proba) in the Basilica of St. Peter, preceded by eunuchs, distributed a coin to every poor person to look pious. When an old woman came forward to ask for a second coin, the noblewoman punched her in the face, paying blood money for such a great crime as Jerome glosses with bitter sarcasm.[40]

Here we can see the roots of the development of a practice that was destined to become extremely popular in the following centuries, but which was already well documented in Late Antiquity – for example, in the votive mosaics in the Basilica of Aquileia.[41] I am naturally referring to gifts to saints, the bestowal of generous offerings to God through his churches and earthly lieutenants. Indeed, saints became to all effects the owners (*domini*) of these churches and the heavenly administrators of the movable and immovable property capitalized inside them (liturgical furnishings, books and the buildings of worship themselves, with the enormous number of landed properties that started to accumulate from the sixth century onwards).[42] The technical instrument of this singular form

[38] The slippage was well observed by Brown 2002, pp. 77-78; and also in Brown 2012, pp. 62-68.

[39] Ambr., *De off.* 2.28.136-141; regarding this passage I accept the interpretation in Brown 1992, pp. 95-96. See also the contribution by Lellia Cracco Ruggini in this volume.

[40] Hier., *Ep.* 22.32; see Brown 2012, p. 267.

[41] Caillet 1993 remains the standard reference work on this topic.

[42] See, for example, Marazzi 1998; Rosenwein 1989; Rosenwein 1999. The legal status of the saints as owners for all purposes of ecclesiastical goods corresponds to the ambiguous

of taking possession of holy space and consecrating the goods connected to it (*res ecclesiae*) consisted of the presence of relics of saints transferred and buried inside altars.[43] In this form of a compromise between the Christian concept and traditional practice, the apparatus of gift did not only include the riches offered, deposited and managed by churches, but also fully expressed its power in creating the social tie at the very heart of the close community relationship between believers and saints, a relationship which was embodied most meaningfully in miracles.[44]

At this point, we should remember that, at least in the Latin West, the complexity of the cultural background of the gift increased as a result of the contribution made by barbarian societies.[45] Grave goods, holy furnishings, chronicles, poems, laws, sermons and hagiographies offer us models of societies founded on antagonistic reciprocity, such as the system of feud and revenge,[46] matrimonial exchanges,[47] the distribution of spoils of war,[48] the splendour of the endowment of private churches and monasteries,[49] and in general all those forms of accumulation, ostentation and dissipation of riches that attracted the attention of Marcel Mauss for their resemblance to Amerindian cultures that practiced *potlatch* and in which the sumptuous gift was accorded a prominent position.[50]

Gifts to saints immediately take on two main meanings. The first of these integrates the ancient aristocratic and later barbaric practice of making a sumptuous gift to the city and invisible powers, but also seems to continue the ancient practice of community charity by transforming earthly wealth into

status of ecclesiastical property. Giving gifts to saints prevented the risk of a bishop's goods being inherited by his family rather than the church after his death.

[43] Refer to Angenendt 1994, pp. 167-175; Snoek 1995, pp. 175-202; Yasin 2009, pp. 151-157; Canetti 2012, pp. 58-59, 76-77.

[44] The writings of Paulinus of Nola as a paradigm of this metaphorical association between *munus* and miracle are analyzed in Canetti 2002, pp. 110-112.

[45] For an extensive review of the sources Jobert 1977 is still useful; the question has now been revisited by Davies – Fouracre 2010.

[46] On this topic see Barthélémy – Bougard – Le Jean 2006; particular attention to the barbarian cultures of Central and Eastern Europe and the Scandinavian world is devoted by Modzelewski 2004, pp. 122-156. On the structural relationship between cerimonial gift and ritual revenge in segmentary societies see Hénaff 2002, pp. 283-288.

[47] A starting point is still the two volumes *Il Matrimonio*; more recently, and in connection with specific issues involved in familial assets and heritage, see Bougard – Feller – Le Jan 2002; Buhrer-Thierry 2010.

[48] Two classic books on this topic are still Duby 1973 and Cardini 1997[2]. A much less epic and conflictual interpretation is offered by Pohl 1992; on war, trade and gift-system in the Early Middle Ages see also Le Jean 2003, pp. 281-283.

[49] The literature on this subject is nothing short of immense; an original overview is offered by Baschet 2006[3], pp. 230-242; further bibliography in Canetti 2009, pp. 275-276.

[50] For a critical review on Mauss's concept of *potlach* see Hénaff 2002, pp. 158-161 and 182-185.

merits, namely the *opera beneficentiae* which augment heavenly treasure.[51] The church bestowed the spiritual benefits of this treasure through its monopoly on sacramental signs and the power to forgive sins.[52] Although it naturally managed, increased and fully exploited all the resources and powers that the *patrimonia* of saints enabled it to accumulate on an ongoing basis, the latter always ran the risk of being dispersed and fragmented as a result of the extent of its *dominium* and the attraction that these goods and powers exerted on aristocratic society.[53]

The second meaning of gifts to saints is strictly votive. In the eyes of the powerful – clergymen and laymen, men generally committed to warlike violence and subject to worldly temptation – building a church or monastery, furnishing it richly and providing it with profitable land and bequeathing it part of the family estate was an ideal means to guarantee salvation in the afterlife, and, at the same time, flaunt the signs of their status in typically aristocratic ways. Grave goods are an example of this overlapping between signs of status – apparently without any particular religious connotation but sometimes maybe rooted in the archaic practice of offering sacrifices and gifts in honour of the dead – and *donum pro anima*: ecclesiastical preaching and discipline was able to domesticate such practices, widespread among both the pagan aristocracy and noble converts (laymen and clergymen), from the eighth century onwards. This was precisely the time when the Church was asserting itself more and more clearly as the manager of rituals of remembrance and the promoter of the memory of the dead. While the use of sumptuous grave goods decreased, it was not due to the conversion of barbarians to Christianity, but to the ecclesiastical promotion of new strategies for the commemoration of the dead and the new ritual forms of manifestation of status. Goods were no longer buried: some were exhibited during the funeral, broken up and distributed to the poor in memory of the deceased and for the salvation of his soul, while others (especially land holdings) were given permanently to ecclesiastical institutions to celebrate the memory of the donor.[54] According to the *Vita* of bishop Eligius of Noyon (d. 661), rewritten in the eighth century, after his funeral he appeared in a dream to a courtier of Bathildis to admonish the Queen to give her precious jewels and ornaments (*insignia auri gemmarumque ornamenta*) to honour Christ and as alms for the poor. The Queen, however, decided to lay down her most precious jewels on the buried saint's head.[55]

[51] La Rocca 2004; Magnani 2010.

[52] Magnani 2002, pp. 311-314; Magnani 2009, pp. 1032-1034.

[53] On these topics, the case study of the ritual of *Laudatio Parentum* examined by White 1988 is enlightening.

[54] See the relevant summary of the issue provided by Barbiera 2012, pp. 209-210. Fundamental studies on this subject are those by Cristina La Rocca; see, for example, La Rocca 2004; see also the case study in La Rocca – Provero 2000.

[55] *V. Elig.* 2.41 (*MGH SRM*, IV, pp. 724-725 Krusch); see Barbiera 2012, pp. 21-22.

There was an even more archaic form through which the antagonistic dynamics of the apparatus of ceremonial gift were presented at the very heart of the relationship between a sanctuary, the titular patron saint of its assets and the believers devoted to him (who by no coincidence were also defined as *alumni* or even *servi* in medieval Latin), namely people tied to him by a holy pact that could only be broken under certain conditions, such as an oath. This applied to all those who literally devoted themselves to the saint in forms ranging from *oblati* – namely children offered as gifts and surety of salvation – to those who promised to serve the saint in his house for long periods or even for the rest of their lives.[56] They did this by giving part of themselves either in proprietary or symbolic form as a guarantee of or in exchange for a miracle, or received grace, in the form of votive offerings (*ex voto*).[57] It is no coincidence that hagiographic sources from the age of Augustine onwards associate miracles with the semantic field of gift and grace: Paulinus, Bishop of Nola, the great scholar and *alumnus* of Felix the martyr, defines miracles as munificent gifts that saints bestow on their devotees through their mortal remains:[58] water, oil, dust and soil that have been in contact with the living saint or his relics become his material "blessing" (*eulogia*), capable of transmitting the complete grace of miracle.[59]

This process of integration between the Christian economy of charity and the social dynamics of reciprocity can be seen at work from the fifth-sixth century onwards, but emerges to a greater extent from sources of feudal society from the ninth to the twelfth centuries. One of its most characteristic implications is the violent practice of the power of saints, who manifested their legitimate demand to see that the promises of their devotees or the duties of defaulting believers were fulfilled through revenge and physical punishment, sometimes resulting in the death of the ungrateful.[60] In a similar way to previous practice with pagan

[56] This institute was already foreseen in sixth-century Italy by the compiler of the *Regula Benedicti* (59.1-2); for the structural relationship between personal dedition and votive gifts to saints refer to Sigal 1985, pp. 107-115; on the history of this institute in the central and late Middle Ages see de Miramon 1999.
[57] Many episodes can be found in the miracle collections of Gregory of Tours; see, for example, *Glor. mart.* 96; *Virt. S. Iul.* 31; *Vit. Patr.*, 2. Also the gift of a simple everyday object always implies the commitment of the whole person offering his very life; on this topic refer to Sigal 1985, pp. 86-107, and especially Charuty 1992. For a theory of a structural relationship between the votive gift (especially in anatomical form) and human sacrifice (a relationship which is implicit in the practice of *mensuratio*, namely the weighing of the donor in correspondence to the gift in wax or precious metal) see the discussion in Canetti 2012, pp. 308-312; 347-348; 395-398.
[58] See note 44 above.
[59] Cf. Caner 2006; for the divine grace associated with sanctified oil see Canetti 2012, pp. 115-201. The practice of gift and countergift in early Byzantine miracle collections was examined by Déroche 2006. Some examples of *eulogiai* collections in 6th century Gaul and Rome are discussed in the article by F. Carlà in this volume.
[60] There are many examples in Barthélemy 1999, pp. 99-113; 130-137; 321-329; see also

gods, it was seen as advisable to show oneself to be munificent towards saints, even without a potential miracle. Saints sometimes appeared to believers in dreams, urging them to donate their most valuable possessions to acknowledge and honour divine authority with a profusion of *ornamenta ecclesiae*.[61] However, they appeared most frequently to usurpers in dreams and visions, threatening them and inflicting the most terrible punishments to make them return their ill-gotten gains.[62] These ways of interpreting the world strike a chord with modern sensibility, but the historian sees them as perfectly suited to the needs and operational logic of cultures that knew how to make the best use of language and ritual acts in the everyday management of their relationship with the invisible world.

It is now time to draw a conclusion: the paradoxical results of Christian gift-giving – the development of buildings as monuments and the growth of church assets; the sacrificial interpretation of liturgy and the sacraments – seem to be consistent with the paradoxes of charity and grace. It is true that church assets were always justified with a theological meaning, as the economic dimension and ornamental splendour were only the material foundation and visible sign of the form of holy commerce activated by divine glory and mercy, and to which man responded through charity as surety of salvation. However, when canonical law assimilated the material assets of churches with *res sacrae* in the Gregorian age (eleventh century), it gave rise to a further paradox, which heralded the beginning of economic modernity. From that moment on, church assets and revenue could no longer be separated from the sacramental dignity of the clergymen who administered them on behalf of their proprietors, namely Christ and his poor. At the same time though, this statute of the secular clergy was redefined in accordance with the monastic model on the basis of the hegemonic social class of *pauperes Christi*, a sacerdotal hierarchy of celibate men, whose individual chastity and poverty was seen as the best guarantee of optimal management of *res ecclesiae,* which had been removed, it was said, from the wrongful ownership of the laity.[63] In this way, *libertas ecclesiae*, a watchword of reformers, became the recovery of revenue and assets that had come into the private possession and usufruct of kings, emperors, bishops, abbots and noble families, and which now had to be managed in accordance with rational criteria, namely as interest-bearing public assets. It was followers of the *alter Christus,* Francis of Assisi, with their even more radical, although not anticlerical,

Canetti 2012, pp. 240-243.

[61] An extraordinary sequence of episodes of this kind can be found at the beginning of the 11th century in Bernardus Andeg., *Mirac. S. Fidis* 1.16-19 (ed. L. Robertini, Spoleto 1994, pp. 116-120). For an earlier age (8th century) see, for example, *V. Elig.* 2.39 (*MGH SRM*, IV, p. 724 Krusch).

[62] See again Bernardus Andeg., *Mirac. S. Fidis* 1.25, pp. 127-128 Robertini; this episode has been examined in relation to the rite of incubation dream by Canetti 2010, pp. 37-38.

[63] These developments are examined in Canetti 2012, pp. 243-277.

conception of *paupertas Christi*, who developed new theological strategies to justify the main instrument of the new economic and commercial development, namely financial credit. The latter became the new secularised form of faith and investment in future remuneration and could no longer be measured in terms of the ancient sureties of salvation in the afterlife (gifts of charity, saintly bodies and church treasure), but exclusively through money and its new credit-based surrogates.[64]

Bibliography

Angenendt, Arnold: *Heilige und Reliquien. Die Geschichte ihres Kultes vom frühen Christentum bis zur Gegenwart*, München 1997² (repr. Hamburg 2007).

Anspach, Mark R.: *À charge de revanche. Figures élémentaires de la réciprocité*, Paris 2002.

Barbiera, Irene: *Memorie sepolte. Tombe e identità nell'alto medioevo (secoli V-VIII)*, Roma 2012.

Barthélemy, Dominique: *L'an mil et la paix de Dieu. La France chrétienne et féodale. 980-1060*, Paris 1999.

Barthélémy, Dominique – François Bougard – Régine Le Jean (ed. by), *La Vengeance, 400-1200,* Rome 2006.

Baschet, Jérôme: *La civilisation féodal. De l'an mil à la colonisation de l'Amerique*, Paris 2006³.

Bogaert, Raymond: *Changeurs et banquiers chez les Pères de l'Église*, in: *AncSoc* 4 (1973), pp. 239-270.

Bougard, François – Laurent Feller – Régine Le Jan (ed. by), *Dots et douaires dans le haut Moyen Âge,* Roma 2002.

Brown, Peter: *Power and Persuasion in Late Antiquity. Towards a Christian Empire*, Madison – London 1992.

Brown, Peter: *Poverty and Leadership in the Later Roman Empire*, Hanover – London 2002.

Brown, Peter: *Through the Eye of a Needle. Wealth, the Fall of Rome, and the Making of Christianity in the West, 350-550 AD*, Princeton – Oxford 2012.

Buhrer-Thierry, Geneviève: *Fratelli e sorelle. Solidarietà familiari e spartizione del patrimonio nell'alto medioevo*, in: *Genesis* 9 (2010), pp. 55-66.

Caillé, Alain: *Anthropologie du don. Le tiers paradigme*, Paris 2000.

Caillet, Jean-Pierre: *L'évergétisme monumental chrétien en Italie et à ses marges d'après l'épigraphie des pavements de mosaïque (IVᵉ-VIIᵉ s.)*, Roma 1993.

Caner, Daniel F.: *Towards a Miraculous Economy: Christian Gift and Material Blessings in Late Antiquity*, in: *JECS* 14 (2006), pp. 329-377.

Canetti, Luigi: *Frammenti di eternità. Corpi e reliquie tra Antichità e Medioevo*, Roma 2002.

Canetti, Luigi: *Trésors et décor des églises au Moyen Âge. Pour une approche sémiologique des «ornamenta ecclesiae»*, in: *Du matériel au spirituel. Réalités*

[64] On these topics refer to the seminal works by Giacomo Todeschini (especially Todeschini 2002).

archéologiques et historiques des «dépots» de la prehistoire a nos jours, ed. by Sandrine Bonnardin – Caroline Hamon – Michel Lauwers – Bénédicte Quilliec, Antibes 2009, pp. 273-282.

Canetti, Luigi: *Sogno e terapia nel Medioevo latino*, in: *Terapie e guarigioni*, ed. by Agostino Paravicini Bagliani, Firenze 2010, pp. 25-54.

Canetti, Luigi: *Impronte di gloria. Effigie e ornamento nell'Europa cristiana*, Roma 2012.

Canetti, Luigi: *Rituali e mitologie del fuoco. Pagani e cristiani nella tarda antichità*, in: *Il fuoco nell'alto Medioevo*, Spoleto 2013, pp. 435-493.

Cardini, Franco: *Alle radici della cavalleria medievale*, Milano 1997[2].

Carosso, Marinella: *Le relazioni del dono. Chiavi di lettura recenti di un classico dell'antropologia*, in *Benefattori e beneficati. La relazione asimmetrica nel* de beneficiis *di Seneca*, ed. by Giusto Picone – Lucia Beltrami – Licinia Ricottilli, Palermo 2011, pp. 47-95.

Carrié, Jean-Michel: *Pratique et idéologie chrétiennes de l'économie (IVe-VIe siècles)*, in: *AntTard* 14 (2006), pp. 17-26.

Charuty, Giordana: *Le vœu de vivre. Corps morcelés, corps sans âme dans les pèlerinages portugais*, in: *Terrain* 18 (1992), pp. 46-60.

Chuvin, Pierre: *Chronique des derniers païens. La disparition du paganisme dans l'Empire romain, du règne de Constantin à celui de Justinien*, Paris 2004[2].

Clavero Salvador, Bartolomé: *Antidora. Antropología católica de la economía moderna*, Milano 1991.

de Miramon, Charles: *Les "donnés" au Moyen Âge. Une forme de vie religieuse laïque (v. 1180 – v. 1500)*, Paris 1999.

Déroche, Vincent: *Vraiment anargyres? Don et contredon dans les recueils de miracles protobyzantins*, in: *Pèlerinages et lieux saints dans l'Antiquité et le Moyen Âge. Mélanges offerts à Pierre Maraval*, ed. by Béatrice Caseau – Jean-Claude Cheynet – Vincent Déroche, Paris 2006, pp. 153-158.

De Vita, Maria Carmen: *Giuliano imperatore filosofo neoplatonico*, Milano 2011.

Duby, Georges: *Guerriers et paysans (VIIe-XIIe siècle): premier essor de l'économie européenne*, Paris 1973.

Finn, Richard D.: *Almsgiving in the Later Roman Empire: Christian Promotion and Practice, 313-450*, Oxford 2006.

Frend, William H. C.: *The Rise of Christianity*, Philadelphia 1984.

Godbout, Jacques T.: *L'esprit du don*, Paris 2000[2].

Godbout, Jacques T.: *Ce que circule entre nous. Donner, recevoi, rendre*, Paris 2007.

Godelier, Maurice: *L'énigme du don*, Paris 1996.

Guerreau-Jalabert, Anita: *Caritas y don en la sociedad medieval occidental*, in: *Hispania* 60 (2000), pp. 27-62.

Hénaff, Marcel: *Le prix de la vérité. Le don, l'argent, la philosophie*, Paris 2002.

Il matrimonio nella società altomedievale, Spoleto 1977.

Jobert, Philippe: *La notion de donation. Convergences: 630-750*, Paris 1977.

Ladner, Gerhart B.: *The Concept of Image in the Greek Fathers and the Byzantine Iconoclastic Controversy*, in: *DOP* 7 (1953), pp. 1-34.

La Rocca, Cristina: *Tesori terrestri, tesori celesti*, in: *Tesori. Forme di accumulazione della ricchezza nell'alto medioevo (secoli V-XI)*, ed. by Sauro Gelichi – Cristina La Rocca, Roma 2004, pp. 123-141.

La Rocca, Cristina – Luigi Provero, *The Dead and Their Gifts. The Will of Eberhard, Count of Friuli, and His Wife Gisela, Daughter of Louis the Pious*, in: *Rituals of Power,* ed. by Frans Theuws – Janet L. Nelson, Leiden – Boston – Köln 2000, pp. 225-280.

Le Jean, Régine: *La société du haut Moyen Âge. VIe-IXe siècle*, Paris 2003.

Lettieri, Gaetano: *Il metodo della grazia. Pascal e l'ermeneutica giansenista di Agostino*, Bologna 1999.

Lizzi Testa, Rita: *"Hi sunt thesauri ecclesiae". La ricchezza della povertà nell'Occidente latino*, in: *Les réseaux familiaux. Antiquité tardive et Moyen Âge. In memoriam A. Laiou et É. Patlagean*, ed. by Béatrice Caseau, Paris 2012, pp. 393-413.

Lugaresi, Leonardo: *Il teatro di Dio. Il problema degli spettacoli nel cristianesimo antico (II-V secolo)*, Brescia 2008.

Magnani, Eliana: *Le don au Moyen Âge: pratique sociale et représentations. Perspectives de recherche*, in: *Révue du M.A.U.S.S.* 19 (2002), pp. 309-322.

Magnani, Eliana: *Du don aux églises au don pour le salut de l'âme en Occident (IVe-XIe siècle): le paradigme eucharistique*, in: *Pratiques de l'eucharistie dans les Églises d'Orient et d'Occident (Antiquité et Moyen Âge)*, ed. by Nicole Bériou – Béatrice Caseau – Dominique Rigaux, Paris 2009, vol. II, pp. 1021-1042.

Magnani, Eliana: *«Un trésor dans le ciel». De la pastorale de l'aumône aux trésors spirituels (IVe-IXe siècle)*, in *Le trésor au Moyen Age. Discours, pratiques et objets*, ed. by Lucas Burkart – Philippe Cordez – Pierre Alain Mariaux – Yann Potin, Firenze 2010, pp. 51-68.

Marazzi, Federico: *I patrimonia Sanctae Romanae Ecclesiae nel Lazio, secoli IV-X: struttura amministrativa e prassi gestionale*, Roma 1998.

Mauss, Marcel: *Essai sur le don. Forme et raison de l'échange dans les sociétés archaïques*, in: *L'Année sociologique* n.s. 1 (1923-1924), pp. 30-186.

Modzelewski, Karol: *Barbarzyńska Europa*, Warszawa 2004; It. Transl. *L'Europa dei Barbari. Le culture tribali di fronte alla cultura romano-cristiana*, Torino 2008.

Moussy, Claude: *Gratia et sa famille*, Paris 1966.

Pesce, Mauro (ed. by): *Le parole dimenticate di Gesù*, Milano 2004.

Peterman, Glen W.: *Paul's Gift from Philippi. Conventions of Gift Exchange and Christian Giving*, Cambridge 1997.

Pétré, Hélène: *Caritas. Étude sur le vocabulaire latin de la charité chrétienne*, Louvain 1948.

Pohl, Walter: *Konfliktverlauf und Konfliktbewältigung: Römer und Barbaren im frühen Mittelalter*, in: *FMS* 26 (1992), pp. 165-207.

Rives, James B.: *Between Orthopraxy and Orthodoxy: Constantine and Animal Sacrifice*, in: *Costantino prima e copo Costantino / Constantine before and after Constantine*, ed. by Giorgio Bonamente – Noel Lenski – Rita Lizzi Testa, Bari 2013, pp. 153-163.

Rosenwein, Barbara H.: *To be the Neighbor of Saint Peter: the Social Meaning of Cluny's Property, 909-1049*, Ithaca 1989.

Rosenwein, Barbara H.: *Negotiating Space: Power, Restraint and Privileges of Immunity in Early Medieval Europe*, Manchester 1999.

Rossi Monti, Martino: *Il cielo in terra. La grazia fra teologia ed estetica*, Torino 2008.

Salamito, Jean-Marie: *Christianisme antique et économie: raison et modalités d'une rencontre historique*, in: *AntTard* 14 (2006), pp. 27-37.

Salsano, Alfredo: *Il dono nel mondo dell'utile*, Torino 2008.

Sigal, Pierre-André: *L'homme et le miracle dans la France médiévale (XI*^{e}*-XII*^{e} *siècle)*, Paris 1985.

Snoek, Godefridus J. C.: *Medieval Piety from Relics to the Eucharist. A Process of Mutual Interaction*, Leiden – New York – Köln 1995.

Sotinel, Claire: *Le don chrétien et ses retombées sur l'économie dans l'Antiquité tardive*, in: *AntTard* 14 (2006), pp. 105-116.

Stroumsa, Guy G.: *La fin du sacrifice. Les mutations religieuses de l'antiquité tardive*, Paris 2005; Engl. Transl. *The End of Sacrifice. Religious Transformations in Late Antiquity*, Chicago – London 2009.

The Languages of Gift in the Early Middle Ages, ed. by Wendy Davies – Paul Fouracre, Cambridge 2010.

Todeschini, Giacomo: *"Quantum valet?" Alle origini di un'economia della povertà*, in: *BISIME* 98 (1992), pp. 173-234.

Todeschini, Giacomo: *I mercanti e il tempio. La società cristiana e il circolo vizioso della ricchezza fra Medioevo ed Età Moderna*, Bologna 2002.

Veyne, Paul: *Le pain et le cirque. Sociologie historique d'un pluralisme politique*, Paris 1976; Repr. 1995.

White, Stephen D.: *Custom, Kinship, and Gifts to Saints: the Laudatio Parentum in Western France (1050-1150)*, London 1988.

Yasin, Ann Marie: *Saints and Church Spaces in the Late Antique Mediterranean. Architecture, Cult, and Community*, Cambridge 2009.

Section four

The Object Gift

LUCA PEYRONEL

Between Archaic Market and Gift Exchange: The Role of Silver in the Embedded Economies of the Ancient Near East during the Bronze Age

1. Introduction

> "(Copper says): Silver, you are forgotten in the soil inside the house. A scared mouse in a silent house […] – Silver, the palace is not your station! An obscure place, a grave, such is your station. Silver, banquets are not your assigned task – fasting is your assigned task. Silver, The task of making divine statues is not likely to fall within your capabilities. Why do you keep attacking me like a dog? You snake, get back in the darkest part of the house and lie down in your grave!".[1]

Among the so-called Mesopotamian Debate Poems, the one between silver and copper is only partially preserved.[2] Both metals display specific 'values' and have distinct roles presented as conflicting in nature. In this text this ideological opposition is, however, a kind of rhetoric fiction, used to emphasize their complementary spheres of use.[3] Silver is described with its primary function of wealth accumulation: "forgotten in the soil inside the house", in a place which is like a grave. From the half of the third millennium BCE onwards,[4] silver bullion were exactly in the same condition: sealed in jars and hidden below the floors. Silver is said to be without practical use, its 'life' is related only to its weight, in order to establish the value of other materials, a standard of equivalence. But we know that at the beginning of the third millennium BCE copper also had the same 'pre-monetary' function of silver. During the Early Dynastic IIIB (ca. 2500-2350 BCE) copper disappeared as a standard of reference, while silver

[1] The debate between Silver and Copper, Segment D, 38-46; translation from the Electronic Text Corpus of Sumerian Literature [http://etcsl.orinst.ox.ac.uk/section5/tr536.htm; last access 3rd Mar. 2014].
[2] For this reason here we cannot follow the overall development of the dispute; however, the intention of showing the importance of these metals, which were considered materials characterizing cultural life and urban society, is nevertheless clear.
[3] Vanstiphout 1990; 1992; see also Reinink – Vanstiphout 1991.
[4] Peyronel 2010.

became the only metal that fulfilled the functions of medium of exchange and payment, reserve of wealth and standard of equivalence.[5]

In this contribution, some reflections on the role of silver in the Near East during the Bronze Age will be presented in a reversed diachronic perspective with the attempt to specifically describe the sphere of use of this metal at the intersection of gift and commercial exchange systems.

In order to verify changes and developments in the use of silver, the following questions can be pointed out: What kind of archaeological and epigraphic insight do we have on silver exchange? Can this insight be used to shed light on silver circulation modalities? Were only silver precious objects that were exchanged as gifts or raw silver (ingots, rings, scrap metal) also circulated in the reciprocity networks?

2. International exchanges in the Near East during the Late Bronze Age

I will start by debating the Late Bronze Age (ca. 1600-1200 BCE), which is the most recent period analyzed in this paper, when written sources of different types, i.e. international diplomatic correspondence, administrative texts, political official documents, allow a deeper analysis in respect to the earlier periods.

A great amount of information on the system of diplomatic relations between 'great kings' – Egypt, Khatti, Mittani, Babylonia, Assyria, Alashiya – and unbalanced political relations between major kingdoms and vassal political entities – especially those located in the Levant such as Amurru, Ugarit, Qadesh, Byblos, Qatna, Amqi – comes from the Amarna letters, mostly dated to the Eighteenth Dynasty rulers Amenophi III and Amenophi IV/Akhenaten.[6] More than three hundred epistolary documents constitute the extraordinary archive discovered at Tell el-Amarna/Akhetaten; they are written in Akkadian on cuneiform tablets sent by independent states and vassal kingdoms to the Egyptian court. The 'diplomatic' correspondence dealing with inter-state relations was the result of intensive contacts of the courts, generating shared procedures of political interactions. The socio-economic development of the urban society, the regional political composition based on hierarchical relationships between states and vassal kingdoms, and the ideology of power shared by the elites of various political entities are the main features which shaped a common cultural system, a language and an operative model of international gift

[5] Milano 2003; Pomponio 2003.

[6] Moran 1992; Liverani 1998; 1999; see also Cohen – Westbrook 2000. Other sources (political treaties, annals, and administrative records), especially from Ugarit and Hattusha, offer important additional evidences: Singer 1999; Beckman 1999; Edel 1994.

exchanges during the Late Bronze Age.[7] The core of this system was certainly the ideology of prestige, with the necessity of demonstrating the social position through precious materials, valuable items and exotica. Regional and inter-regional exchanges[8] were embedded in and supported by diplomatic relations, in which the exchange of goods represented only a part of a wider and multiform web of relations. These relations were dynamic and varied, both in substance and ideological representations, combining ceremonial, redistributive and mercantile levels.[9]

We might carefully distinguish the operative procedures from their representation, taking into account the strong ideology which underlies the international relationships and the differences in the codes used in the written documents, i.e. if they were addressed to domestic or foreign audiences. Indeed, the same transaction can be described in completely different ways: as a gift, when mentioned in the letter sent to a peer, or as a 'tribute' in a celebratory presentation for domestic audience.[10]

First of all, considering the operative schemes, the social position of the parties and the typology of goods, we notice in the exchange system a dividing line between the prestige sphere (in relation to the objects but also to the subjects involved in the exchange) and the commercial one, which is related to primary products, most common goods and objects of everyday use and consumption. The highest level in the exchange system is that of ceremonial gift exchange. The gifts are usually objects in precious metals, ivory, furniture, clothes of high quality, or exotic and precious raw materials – mainly gold (from Egypt) and lapis lazuli (channeled from Middle Asia by the Kassites of Mesopotamia).[11]

[7] Zaccagnini 1973; 1987; Liverani 1990; 1994; Zaccagnini 1995; 2000; Liverani 2003; 2008.

[8] Besides circulation of goods, circulation of persons certainly allowed the strengthening of the overall system of political relations, and favored the development of a cultural *koiné*. Especially inter-dynastic marriages characterized the international policy of the period, representing the highest level of exchange of persons (Pintore 1978; Zaccagnini 1985; Meier 2000; Roth 2002, esp. pp. 85-132). Written documents inform on the dowry calculation and wedding gifts, showing the strong intersection with the exchange system and at the same time the reciprocity of the model, in which women enter in the hierarchical scheme of prestige goods, representing its apex. On movements of specialized personnel in the framework of diplomatic relations during the Late Bronze Age see Zaccagnini 1983b, pp. 250-256; on foreign craftsmen in Anatolia see Bonatz 2002.

[9] For a detailed analysis on the intersections of economic models and the circulation of persons, objects and information during the Late Bronze Age see Zaccagnini 1979.

[10] On this duality see especially Liverani 1979; 1990, pp. 205-210; 1994, pp. 183-217.

[11] Zaccagnini 1973, pp. 170-179; Cochavi-Rainey 1999; Feldman 2006, pp. 115-127. Similar range of materials and objects occur in the long-distance trade of the Middle Assyrian empire: Faist 2001.

Generally speaking, values and equivalences that are explicitly mentioned in the administrative documentation were rarely used at the ceremonial level of diplomatic correspondence, in which bargaining was not considered as an acceptable practice.[12] However, the two spheres are not always so firmly characterized, although the ideological representation hides the economic motives that stand behind the principles of reciprocity, acting through gifts and counter-gifts when the relationship is between peers. In fact, sometimes also ordinary raw materials and goods – raw base-metals, metal tools, wood, food – entered in the chain of greeting gifts, but in these cases the commercial nature of the relationship is more evident.[13]

The process is dissimulated by specific procedures in which the primary attention is directed to underline the equality of the referents, the envoy of the gift without interest and the lack of importance of the economic value of the gift received, and the lack of condition in the acceptance as natural consequences of brotherhood and friendship among kings.[14] However, in several cases, the rules of the etiquette are not observed and it seems that the desire of economic gain superseded that of prestige, as testified by frequent 'diplomatic' excuses, negotiations and complaints.[15]

If we look at the role of silver and gold we can observe differences reflecting the function of the two precious metals in the overall system.

Gold is, in fact, the prestige material and the gift par excellence for the ancient Near Eastern political entities during the Late Bronze Age, with a strong symbolic and ideological connotation.[16] Mittani, Assyria, Babylonia and Hatti

[12] Zaccagnini 1973, pp. 117-124.

[13] E.g. see the correspondence between the king of Alashiya (Cyprus) and the pharaoh Amenophi IV/Akhenaten (letters EA 33-39) shows that a great quantity of copper ingots were dispatched by the king of Alashiyah (Cyprus) to Egypt in order to obtain gold, ivory, linen textiles and other precious raw materials: Liverani 1999, pp. 414-421.

[14] Brotherhood (*ahhutum*), friendship (*atterūtu*), good relationships (*amātu banītu*) were underlined by the habit of exchanging greetings (*šulmus*) and (greeting-) gifts (*šulmānu*). According to the rules of the etiquette, gifts cannot be asked for, must be given, accepted and appreciated, and, finally, might be reciprocated: Zaccagnini 1973, pp. 95-117, with a detailed analysis of this ceremoniality and personalization of political relations; 1987.

[15] The prolonged negotiations in the Amarna letters (the model of 'endless quarrel') can be considered at the same time a way to keeping alive diplomatic relations through the dynamics of gift-giving and a system to obtain materials and goods lacking at homeland (with an ideal yearly rhythm of exchange). Bargaining can be dissimulated also adopting peculiar procedures, such as the practice of sending a 'provocative gift', consisting of precious materials (elephant tusks from Cyprus, lapis lazuli from Egypt, gold and ebony from Babylonia and Mittani) to kingdoms that were exporters of that commodity: see Liverani 1972, pp. 299-304; 1994, pp. 233-244; Zaccagnini 2000, pp. 145-149.

[16] Edzard 1960; see also Nicholson – Shaw 2000, pp. 161-164 on the Egyptian and Nubian sources. For the provenance of gold in Mesopotamia during the previous periods

obtained it from Egypt in form of precious objects, but probably also in form of gold-dust or small ingots and rings.[17]

It is interesting to note that the systematic refusal of the pharaoh Amenophi III to betroth an Egyptian princess to the Near Eastern 'great king' Kadashman-Enlil interrupted the reciprocal scheme of relations between peers, causing a shift on the 'commercial' aspects of the negotiation, in which gold, the material having the widest range of 'prestige' connotations (not only in economic terms), was requested to replace the desired bride.[18]

The extreme attention of the Near Eastern kings to check the quality and purity of the Egyptian gold (often with claims if incongruence emerged in relation to what they expected to receive) also reveals the interference of the commercial exchange system in the reciprocity of gift and counter-gift chain. However, the rules of the etiquette were maintained through different tricks: fault was addressed to the negligence of an Egyptian functionary, the request for more gold linked to specific needs, or explained by stressing the great abundance of the precious metal in Egypt.[19]

On the contrary, silver is considered belonging to the sphere of subsistence/ commodity. In fact, the rules of the etiquette excluded the circulation of silver/ currency at the level of gift exchanges in a way that is quite similar to the reluctance to give money as a gift in the contemporary society.

In the list of gifts between parties of equal political role, silver is exchanged only in the form of manufactured items, while its circulation in form of ingots or weighted pieces of metal is not attested.[20] Moreover, the economic value of a gift usually seems not to have been expressed through the indication of its value in silver, which would basically be its 'price', as it is known from unbalanced exchanges between Hatti or Egypt and their vassals, and especially from administrative documentation related to commercial transactions.[21] However, again, we can see the influence of the economic/commercial component in this ceremonial system of gift-giving: a series of qualifications of the different types

with a detailed discussion of the textual information see Reiter 1997, pp. 1-74.

[17] Zaccagnini 1973, pp. 172-173. E.g. Tushratta of Mittani asks Amenophi III for "much gold that has not been worked" (Amarna letter EA 20:72).

[18] See e.g. Liverani 1999, pp. 333-334 and 343-351 for the requests of the Kassite king Kadashman-Enlil to Amenophi III (Amarna letter EA 4).

[19] Zaccagnini 1973, pp. 66-69, with references to the Amarna letters.

[20] Liverani 1972, pp. 307-312; Zaccagnini 1973, p. 173.

[21] Zaccagnini 1973, pp. 80-83, 119-123. There are some exceptions confirming the rule. In a letter to the pharaoh (probably Amenophi III) sent by the king of Alashyia, the value of a quantity of precious wood in silver is explicitly stated and the king of Alashiya asks for the dispatch of "silver in a great amount" from Egypt: here silver is used as a standard of reference and as a mean of payment: Liverani 1999, pp. 27-29, 43-44; Kassianidou 2009.

of objects – quantity, typology, degree of quality, weight – are specified by the donor in order to implicitly allow the determination of the 'value' (in silver) of the goods sent.[22]

In the exchanges between the great kingdoms, silver as precious raw metal is excluded from the ceremonial level, or it appears only if the procedure has an implicit commercial significance, as can be seen e.g. in the letters sent by the king of Alashiya to the Egyptian court,[23] which involve materials of consumption. If the exchanges are between referents of different rank (e.g. a 'great' king and a vassal king, a king and a functionary, etc.), silver can be used with its economic function, but in many cases mixed forms are attested, in which gifts are added to silver (representing the means of 'payment'), in order to give prestige to the commercial exchange, in an evident situation of economic and extra-economic interactions.[24]

Written sources strongly attest the circulation of silver and gold vessels as gifts or tributes.[25] These bowls had standard shapes and weight (usually one mina or its fractional values).[26] Decoration, quality of the metal, and shape were precisely indicated and were considered parameters enhancing the value of the piece, defined first of all by its weight.[27] These vessels cannot be absolutely considered a kind of money, they are prestige goods, highlighting the rank of the owner and intended to increase his wealth.

In comparison with the frequent mentions in the texts, we have few archaeological evidences of these objects, mostly from the Levant and Cyprus, which can be compared with the precious vessels listed among the greeting gifts and dowry in the Amarna letters, although they come from cultic and elite tombs and not from palatial buildings.[28]

[22] Liverani 1972, pp. 308-309; Zaccagnini 1973, pp. 78-89.

[23] Kassianidou 2009.

[24] Liverani 1972, pp. 309-312, with references to the written sources.

[25] Zaccagnini 1979; 1991.

[26] Two main weight systems can be recognized in the Near East during the Bronze Age: the sexagesimal Mesopotamian system with a shekel of c. 8,4g, a mina of c. 500g (= 60 shekels), and a talent of c. 30kg (= 60 minas); and a more articulated metrological system in the Western regions (Anatolia and the Levant). The latter used the mina and the talent as common values: the talent (c. 28kg) consisted of 60 minas of c. 470g; in its turn the western mina was reckoned at 50 Levantine/Ugaritic shekels of 9,4g (coastal Syria and Palestine), or at 40 Anatolian/Hittite shekels of 11,7g (Anatolia), or at 60 Syrian/Karkemish shekels of c. 7,8g (Inner Syria). Moreover, the so-called Ugaritic shekel, was equivalent to the Egyptian *dbn* of the New Kingdom: Parise 1970-1971; Ascalone – Peyronel 2006, pp. 23-49, with updated bibliography; see also Chambon 2011, pp. 28-38, 80-99.

[27] Zaccagnini 1979.

[28] The practice of dedicating precious metal vessels as votive offerings to the deities (that

Two outstanding gold vessels from Ugarit were found on the acropolis near the Baal temple:[29] a hemispheric bowl with a mass of 179g, equal to 20 Levantine shekels, is chased on the outer face with a central rosette at the base and three concentric figurative registers with caprids and schematic plants, bulls and lions alternated with voluted palmettes, combats between animals, griffin sphinxes, and hunting scenes. The other bowl, weighing 218g (30 'Syrian' shekels of 7,5g), is a patera with straight sides showing an inner decoration in relief with four ibexes arranged in a frieze around the base and a wide register in which a hunting scene is depicted. A one-handled silver bowl discovered in a tomb at Enkomi is worked with golden inlayed sheets and shows a decoration of bucrania, lotus flower and rosettes delimited by semicircles, and has a precise parallel in a bowl found at Dendra in Greece.[30] Another interesting finding from Cyprus is a plain silver bowl from Hala Sultan Tekke, bearing a short cuneiform Ugaritic inscription below the rim ("Akkuya, son of Yiptahad(d)u made this bowl").[31] Silver jugs/pitchers with zoomorphic handles and silver decorated bowls – coming from two hoards containing precious metal wine sets found at Tell Basta, ancient Bubastis – show a decoration mixing Egyptian and Levantine themes.[32] Finally, a plain biconical gold chalice weighing half a western mina or 25 Levantine shekels of 9,4g, has been found in the Uluburun shipwreck: it has

means to the temples) is well attested in the written sources of the Late Bronze Age: Zaccagnini 1991, pp. 375-376. M. Feldman (2006) has proposed that a selected group of precious objects (ivories, metal vessels, pieces of furniture, faience objects) can be ascribed to an artistic *koiné* according to their iconographies, decoration and style, which exhibit a 'visual hybridity' related to a shared 'international' taste during the Late Bronze Age. The exchange of luxury objects as gifts supporting diplomatic relations revealed by the Amarna letters certainly had an important role in the circulation and re-elaboration of artistic motives in the Near East, although Feldman's re-definition of the 'international style' as a distinctive form of pictorial hybridity linked to non-narrative and non-ideological iconographies is not convincing. Weak points in Feldman's analysis are also the marginal consideration of the trade network and exchange mechanisms in Eastern Mediterranean, or the assumption that prestige artifacts displaying hybridity are not embedded in their socio-cultural contexts; see Harmansah 2008

[29] Feldman 2006, pp. 51-53, figs. 34-35, pls. 7-8; Yon 2006, pp. 164-165, nos. 56-57; Aruz – Benzel – Evans 2008, pp. 239-243, nos. 146-147.

[30] Courtois – Lagarce – Lagarce 1986, pp. 100-107; Kassianidou 2009, pp. 51-52, fig. 6.5. A plain silver cup from Tomb 92 at Vapheio has been also considered as a Mycenaean import, showing the wide web of eastern Mediterranean interconnections during the Late Bronze Age: see Matthäus 1985, pp. 185-186.

[31] Åström – Masson 1982; Kassianidou 2009, pp. 50-51, fig. 6.3.

[32] Feldman 2006, pp. 38-41; Lilyquist 2012. The Basta hoards can be probably dated between the 13th and 12th century BCE. The content suggests an identification as silversmith or merchant hoards, since also scrap silver, bar-ingots (with inscriptions) and rings are included in both assemblages.

no precise comparison though its general shape roughly resembles alabaster or faience vessels from Egypt and the Levant and can be interpreted as a prestige gift to be presented at the unknown final destination of the ship.[33]

Summing up, considering both archaeological and written sources, it can be argued that during the Late Bronze Age the circulation of silver by weight in the ceremonial exchange system seems to be very limited, and the economic/monetary function of the metal quite prevalent, since silver can be given as gift only when manufactured in prestige objects.

Was this ideological representation of silver exchange already attested in previous periods?

3. At the beginning of the archaic state: the case of the kingdom of Ebla (Early Bronze Age)

The earliest and most detailed information on exchange of silver and precious silver objects is dated to the twenty-fourth century BCE and comes from Ebla, where the cuneiform texts of the royal archives clearly show the intersection of the gift system with the circulation of silver as a mean of payment in a redistributive pattern.[34]

The administrative documents clearly attest to a domestic and a foreign circuit of exchange of precious objects and textiles. However, the texts recorded the deliveries through a 'neutral' terminology: e.g. "he/they gave"; "he/she has received".[35] The term "gift", *níg-ba*, is used only for textiles given to gods or is attested (rarely) in relation with special and particularly relevant occasions.

Goods given to members of the royal family, the family of the vizier and to officials and members of the administration consisted mainly of clothes delivered on a regular annual basis, but gold and silver objects and jewels allotments are also attested. These were marks of rank as well as precious goods for display. The circulation of such metal goods seems to be related to a redistributive model embedded in ceremonial practices and it was helped by the

[33] Aruz – Benzel – Evans 2008, pp. 353-355, no. 219. The Uluburun cargo probably represents a 'royal' venture (probably from Syria or Cyprus) dispatching a wide range of wealthy materials and objects together with tons of copper and tin ingots, which epitomize the intersection between trade and exchange of elite artefacts during the Late Bronze Age; the final destination of the cargo is debated, although it is probable that the venture was directed towards the Aegean: Yalçin – Pulak – Slotta 2005; Pulak 2008.

[34] Archi 1985a; Milano 1991; Maiocchi 2010; Archi 2011; see also Archi 2003; Biga 2003; Matthiae 2005.

[35] Archi 2011, p. 30.

fact that they were goods of standard weights. Four main types of metal objects can be recognized:[36]

1. The gold and silver plates or disks (DIB) with masses ranging from 10 shekels (ca. 78g) up to 1 mina (ca. 470g). Items weighing 16 and 20 shekels are the most attested ones, suggesting that specific needs linked to their modes of circulation/exchange imposed a highly standardized manufacture.[37]
2. Several types of daggers (*gír*) decorated with silver or gold, with a predominance of the so-called Martu dagger, with recurrent weights ranging from 20 to 60 shekels.
3. Silver and gold bracelets (*gú-li-lum*), again with standardized weights (especially 10, 20 and 30 shekels).[38]
4. Silver pendants (*bu-di*) delivered only to women and usually given in pairs weighing 20 shekels.

These objects were also offered as gifts on particular occasions, e.g. marriages, the birth of a son and funerals, and they have been recorded by the central administration.[39] Furthermore, a peculiar gift-chain is attested by some texts dealing with internal distribution of precious metal artifacts, especially daggers, which are listed in decreasing order of value.[40]

Ebla maintained political relations with a small number of kingdoms and city-states of equal importance (i.e. Mari, Nagar, Kish) and used precious gifts (mainly represented by the same objects cited before) to strengthen socio-political ties. It is interesting to note that also silver by weight is included among the exchanged goods.[41]

On the contrary, gifts for vassals and kingdoms under Ebla's control follow a different circuit: annual deliveries of textiles were regularly sent in change of silver or other metals, often listed as ingots (*NI-gi-tum*). This system can,

[36] Maiocchi 2010; see also Pasquali 2005, pp. 15-35 and 137-139.

[37] See esp. Maiocchi 2010, pp. 16-18. The exact meaning of the term DIB is debated and it is a matter of speculation linking it to any type of precious items discovered at Ebla. However, recently Maiocchi has proposed that a golden disk found in Building P4 (Matthiae – Pinnock – Scandone Matthiae 1995, p. 331 no. 125) could be considered as what is called DIB in the texts.

[38] Mander 1995; Pasquali 2005, pp. 137-139.

[39] Archi 2002.

[40] According to the interpretation of the texts, this peculiar gift-chain envisages that the first person receives the most valuable object, and then he delivers a less valuable one to the next individual. The people involved in this gift giving practice belong to the elites of the royal court and Pomponio (1998) has suggested that this movement of artifacts is linked to gifts given when an individual was 'promoted' to a higher status. See also Maiocchi 2010, pp. 7-12.

[41] On the political and commercial relations between Ebla and Mari see Archi 1985b; for an updated overview on the Eblaite international policy see Biga 2008.

therefore, be interpreted as a redistribution practice between unbalanced political entities, although the goods flow was not unidirectional and it implied ceremonial and ideological elements.

Silver vessels are rarely present among precious goods exchanged within the kingdom, while ceremonial weapons, ornaments, and plaques made of the same material represented the traditional mean of wealth accumulation. Vessel circulation is rather linked to the foreign ceremonial and gift exchange sphere and several different types of metal vessels intended for this purpose (or with a revetment of precious metals) are attested.[42]

It is interesting to note that all these materials and objects were recorded by the local administration with indications of the weights (or 'value') in silver, whatever the reasons and the mechanics of the exchanges (gift, tribute, commercial exchange) had been. This shows, on the one hand, the trend towards a standardized manufacture of some kind of items, and, on the other hand, the influence of the record-keeping needs by the central administration to calculate the precious-metal circulation.

Unfortunately, no complete silver objects or ingots have been found in the Royal Palace. However, several fragments and sheets of gold, silver and inlays of semi-precious stones and a large amount of raw lapis lazuli – more than 43kg – were spared from the sack of the building by the Akkadian army, giving an idea of the impressive amount of precious materials originally stored in the treasury.[43]

Information on gift exchange and precious goods circulation in the Early Dynastic Mesopotamian archives is scarce, but the analysis of the e_2-MI_2 archive of Lagash has shown the existence of a system of reciprocal exchanges (internal and external to the city-state).[44] We can visualize the wide range of precious goods and objects from Early Dynastic II-III graveyards in Mesopotamia, and in particular from the extraordinary rich funerary assemblages of the Royal Cemetery of Ur. Vessels in gold, electrum, and silver, lapis lazuli and carnelian beads, inlays and composite statuettes, have been found together with stone vases and manufactured items imported from the East along the highland routes linking Mesopotamia with Central Asia and Indus Valley.[45] We cannot directly

[42] Milano 1991, pp. 356-363; Pasquali 2005, pp. 39-47.

[43] Matthiae 2010, pp. 152-181; See Pinnock 2006 for the lapis lazuli.

[44] Prentice 2010, pp. 157-203. These exchanges are difficult to be precisely identified since the receiving and giving procedures are not registered in the same administrative document. However, Prentice demonstrates that a number of non-commercial exchanges occurred with places outside Lagash (Adab, Nippur, Urua and Dilmun), conducted in recurring events by people belonging to the highest social level. However, the same goods attested in the commercial exchange are received and given, including raw copper, tin-bronze, manufactured goods, agricultural products.

[45] Weber – Zettler 1998, esp. nos. 97-104 for precious metal vessels.

link these luxury objects with a system of gift exchange between Mesopotamian cities and foreign political entities, but later written sources (dating to the Neo-Sumerian period, c. 2100-2000 BCE) attest to contacts of diplomatic nature involving inter-dynastic marriages, envoys of messengers and gift-exchanges during the Ur III period.[46]

4. A composite economic world. The ambiguity of silver use during the Middle Bronze Age

Most of the information on gift exchanges during the Old Babylonian Period (ca. 2000-1600 BCE) comes from the Mari archives.[47] The correspondence of the town shed light on political relations based on a formal behavior, which can be compared with the later Amarna 'diplomacy'.[48]

Three main akkadian terms qualify 'gifts' in the Mari documents: *šûbultum*, *tâmartum*, and *qîštum*.[49] *Šûbultum* (lit. 'that which is sent') denotes gift-giving procedures between rulers or high-rank personages; its meaning probably corresponds to *šulmānu*, the typical term for a gift between partners of equal rank during the Late Bronze Age.[50] The gift given by the ambassadors is named *tâmartum*, and *qištum* as a rule is a 'gift' given to people placed in a lower hierarchical or socio-economic position.[51] It is possible to distinguish two coexistent circuits of gift-exchange between Mari and other political entities. Objects and products having ritual and symbolic values were donated on particular occasions: decorated thrones and 'royal' garments sealing political treaties, precious objects at the death of a king, and ceremonial weapons celebrating the military victory of an ally. On the contrary, textiles and GAL-vessels circulation was part of a system in which commercial nature was more explicit. Indeed, such gifts were delivered by messengers, which in turn received other silver vessels and rings in addition to provisions and textiles.[52]

A huge amount of data pertains to unbalanced and internal contacts, with the most attested term for 'gift' - *qištum* - denoting a 'gift'(/'reward') conveyed to a person of inferior rank.[53] In this case, the system is regulated by opposition between the 'lord' (*bēlum*) and the 'servant/slave' (*wardum*), or between the

[46] Sallaberger 1999, pp. 159-161; Potts 2002.
[47] Zaccagnini 1983a; Lerouxel 2002.
[48] Lerouxel 2002. On the political relations of Mari see Lafont 1992 and 2001.
[49] Lerouxel 2002, pp. 417-432.
[50] Lerouxel 2002, pp. 421-427. Goods entering in the palace as counter-gifts can be qualified as *šûrubtum*.
[51] Lafont 1992, p. 175; Lerouxel 2002, pp. 423-427.
[52] Kupper 1982, p. 165, Lerouxel 2002, pp. 456-457.
[53] Zaccagnini 1983a, pp. 194-196; Lerouxel 2002, pp. 429-432.

'father' and his 'son'.[54] Disparity of rank originates different patterns of exchange: the lord request performances of various kinds from those who are placed on an inferior level; the same prerogative compels the lord to act as a lord, making acts of generosity in favor of those who are of a lower rank. A marked degree of ambiguity can be observed: quite often merchants would have resorted to the ideology of reciprocity even during business debates and we find frequently the explicit mention of 'silver' value and 'price' of a good also in letters dealing with gift exchanges.

The evidence from the Mari archives seems to suggest that trade and economic needs influenced exchanges of gift. Silver entered in the gift mechanism in form of finished objects, but also its use to express 'value' and 'price' of the goods is present in the overall system. The growing importance of private trade and market at the beginning of the second millennium BCE is not a coincidence. The archives of the Old Assyrian merchants from Kanesh in Cappadocia, or those belonging to Ur seafaring traders in the Persian Gulf, demonstrate not only the use of silver as a means of payment but also 'prices' dependent upon supply and demand, risking profit and re-investment of 'capital'.[55]

Silver and gold vessels (GAL = *kâsum*), together with a new item, the ring or coil, represent, in this period, the two main types of objects used for wealth accumulation. Several types of precious metal vessels are attested to and it seems that there is not a marked degree of standardization by weight and shapes, but all the items are listed according to their quantity.[56] The precious bowls circulated as prestige and luxury objects considered as 'unique pieces', although the administration recorded carefully their weight/value in silver. A vessel of this kind might be the silver bowl found in the royal necropolis at Ebla (Hypogeum Q 78 C, the so-called "Tomb of the Lord of the Goats"), inscribed with the name of Immeya,[57] or the silver vessels from the enigmatic so-called Tôd treasure in Egypt.[58]

[54] Zaccagnini 1983a, pp. 211-213.

[55] Veenhof 1988; 1999; Michel 2005 (Old Assyrian trade network); for the Persian Gulf trade see Potts 1990, pp. 219-226. See also Peyronel 2008, pp. 91-134 and Lamberg-Karlovsky 2009.

[56] Zaccagnini 1979; Milano 1991, pp. 363-365. For the precious vessels attested in the Mari texts see now the detailed study of M. Guichard (2005).

[57] Archi – Matthiae 1979. A letter addressed to a personage named Immeya has been also found at Ebla making possible he was the same person buried in the princely tomb. On the vessel itself only the name is listed without any title.

[58] Pierrat-Bonnefois 2008; see also Menu 1994 for the archaeometric analysis of the silver. One hundred fifty-three precious metal vessels (most of them in silver) have been discovered in copper chests buried in the foundations of the temple at Tôd. Some of them are hammered plain bowls, but the majority are decorated by geometric motifs or

During the Ur III period (ca. 2100-2000 BCE) and the Old Babylonian period (ca. 2000-1600 BCE) there is also written evidence of manufacturing and deliveries of another kind of metal object called HAR/*šewirum*, which literally means 'ring'.[59] In particular, the Drehem Treasure Archive presents mainly lists with the phraseology "HAR received as gift".[60] A large number of silver rings have been recorded as precious artifacts given to high-ranking individuals and to the members of the crown. The circuit of distribution is linked to specific occasions or social events, such as marriages or births, celebrations of military victories or religious festivals. The rings are often given in pairs and their weight specified, ranging from one to ten shekels (from ca. 8,4 to 84g), whereas no specifications on a peculiar decoration are attested in the documentation. According to the epigraphic evidence it seems that the exchange of silver rings was a system allowing internal circulation of wealth, albeit strongly embedded into social and ideological spheres. Marvin Powell has rightly observed that these rings might have been related to coils and spirals found in the hoards (but also scattered in other contexts), and that they should have constituted a kind of pre-coinage money – thanks to an asserted value and to the possibility of fractioning.[61] The analysis of the Ur III metal texts shows in fact that HAR was manufactured according to standard weights, ranging from one to ten shekels, with an absolute predominance of five-shekel rings[62]. The rings were always weighted rather than counted, thus giving the possibility to check with precision the silver quantity.[63] These coils could have been a royal gift presented in the form of common raw silver: this could have been exchanged to obtain other goods or used for any other kind of payment as usual at that time. Several coils/rings found at Tell Asmar in the Diyala valley can be linked to this peculiar official and intersected circuit of gifts, although the specimens cannot be precisely dated.[64] They show clusters in relation to the shekel and its sub-multiples, with a peak between 7 and 9,5g. It must be noted, however, that there

schematic rosettes with *repoussé* work. Their shapes and decorations find no precise comparisons, although a general similarity with pottery shapes from the Aegean, Northern Levant and Anatolia has been suggested.

[59] Michalowski 1978; Milano 2003, pp. 40-43; Paoletti 2008, pp. 150-152.

[60] Paoletti 2008, pp. 129; 151.

[61] Powell 1978, see also 1996.

[62] Michalowski 1978, pp. 3-4; Powell 1978, pp. 212-219. Silver rings are attested also in the Mari administrative texts, with weights ranging from one to ten shekels: Kupper 1982, pp. 165-169; see also Arkhipov 2012, pp. 97-99.

[63] The procedure is well attested also in Egypt as testified by funerary wall-paintings from the Middle Kingdom: see e.g. Michailidou 2005, 17-18, fig. 5.

[64] Powell 1978, pp. 228-232, tab. 3; Peyronel 2010, pp. 933-934.

is no evidence of pieces of 5 shekels, the weight most attested in the Ur III texts.[65]

In the Near East, silver rings and coils are attested to also inside the so-called utilitarian hoards from the mid-third millennium BCE onwards.[66] These hoards attest three broad groups of silver items: finished objects, metal processed into more or less regular shapes, and scrap metal.[67] The distinction between these categories is not always easy as in the case of coils and rings. Sometimes they are very well-executed and could be related to the cited HAR known from texts, being at the same time ring-ingots and precious objects. In other cases they are simply circular lengths of rod, more or less thick, with the end beaten off or roughly cut.

These utilitarian hoards are usually discussed as a whole, leading to different interpretations ranging from bulk of silver as currency, stock-in-trade of merchants, deposits of silversmiths.[68] This often reflects the rigid opposition between modernist and primitivist scholars.[69] Instead, these findings might be analyzed as a typical archaeological material, without pre-conditioned models.[70] Bronze Age hoards (ca. 2500-1200 BCE) found in Mesopotamia and the Levant can be grouped according to their content into three categories: a) hoards with only silver items, in some cases with few gold pieces; b) hoards with silver items and other precious materials and objects; c) hoards with silver, precious mate-

[65] Peyronel 2010, p. 934. Refer to the graph fig. 12 that illustrates the results here described.

[66] A general distinction between utilitarian (non-ritual) hoards and ritual/votive deposits in Early Bronze Age Mesopotamia has been made by J. Bjorkman in her doctoral dissertation (1994), and it is also appropriate to refer to evidence from Cyprus during the Late Bronze Age (Knapp – Muhly – Muhly 1988). See also Bradley 1990 for prehistoric Europe and the chapter of M. Gori in this volume with an updated bibliography. Here collections of objects and scrap metal deliberately buried and hidden without an evident ritual or ceremonial function indicated by the context or typology of items are referred to as 'utilitarian hoards': cf. Peyronel 2010, p. 928, n. 13.

[67] Peyronel 2010; Thompson 2010.

[68] See e.g. Matthews 2003, where the Brak hoards are compared with hoards of different types.

[69] The debate on the interpretation of the ancient Mesopotamian economic structures is strongly influenced by the different evaluation of the degree of embeddedness of the economic activity into non-economic institutions: see Powell 1996 and 1999 for the formalist model and Renger 1995; 2003 for the neo-substantivist approach.

[70] For a discussion on the same problem in relation with the metal hoards from prehistoric Europe see the chapter by M. Gori in this volume, where a global approach in order to reconstruct the 'life-history' of the objects and the meaning(s) of the hoarding practice is correctly proposed, stressing the rituality of the hoarding performance and the change of functions that can be detected through the analysis of the material.

rials and handicraft or administrative economic tools.[71] Here, we take into account only hoards of the first type,[72] in which silver is attested by items which are functional to the accumulation of wealth, exchange and manufacture into objects (ingots, fractions of ingots, coils or rings, bars/rods and scrap metal); the objects are always contained in a ceramic vessel, sometimes sealed with clay or bitumen (without seal impression); the vessel containing silver is hidden under the floor of private houses;[73] intact ornaments are rare and if included in the hoards, they were reduced in pieces and therefore considered as such. Hoards containing only one type of silver item are not attested, indicating that a bar-ingot, a coil or a piece of broken ornament provided for the same function – i.e. accumulation of 'wealth'.[74] Neither objects nor bullion can be linked precisely to metrological units, although – especially rings and some ingots – have been probably manufactured with the intent of creating standard amounts of metal of comparable value.

These hoards are mainly related to private contexts, and it is noteworthy that in temples or palaces beside ritual/votive deposits of objects, utilitarian hoards are also attested but characterized by mixed types of materials and objects, often with some administrative devices included e.g. balance weights, clay seals, cuneiform tablets, indicating the direct control of the administration. The best evidence of the latter type is the so-called Ebabbar hoard, through which we have an extraordinary evidence for metrological operations probably realized by an official of the weights bureau of Ur. These operations are attested by balance sets and are recorded in short inscriptions on sealings, with a final recap indicated in a tablet, undoubtedly corresponding to the precious metal contents of the jar.[75]

5. Conclusion

At the end of this brief overview, what emerges both from epigraphic and archaeological data is that silver cannot be considered taking into account only

[71] Peyronel 2010, pp. 928-932, fig. 1.

[72] These hoards are attested in Syria and Mesopotamia during the Bronze Age at Khafaja and Chuera (Early Dynastic III), Tell Taya (Akkadian Period), Ebla (Old Syrian Period), el-Qitar, Munbaqat, Terqa (Middle Syrian Period): Peyronel 2010, fig. 1, A1-7.

[73] With the exception of silver bullion from a Middle Bronze grave discovered at Ebla.

[74] The same kind of silver hoards with silver pieces and scrap metal are widely attested during the 1st millennium BCE in the Near East (Thompson 2010). Hoards from Palestine dated to the seventh century BCE have been linked to a development towards a 'monetary' economy under Assyrian influence (Gitin – Golani 2001), without considering the earlier documentation, as rightly pointed out by Kletter (2003).

[75] Arnaud – Calvet – Huot 1979.

its economic aspect, which was linked to its use as currency and means of wealth accumulation. Its role related to gift exchange cannot be precisely defined, but there is no doubt that silver was offered as gift on specific occasions or given for specific rewards and that these exchange practices were strictly connected to ceremonial procedures and embedded in the social-political structure. This use of silver seems to be attested especially during Early (Ebla, Ur III) and Middle Bronze (Mari) Age within unbalanced gift-giving mechanism, which cannot, however, be explained as a simple redistributive system.

The ceremonial exchange of silver occurred mainly through standardized objects, i.e. vessels and rings, which retain together both symbolic and economic values. During the Late Bronze Age, only silver vessels seem to maintain this function, also in the international system of gifts between peers. But in this case the 'personality' of the object i.e. its peculiar decoration or shape, becomes the most important element determining its value, superseding its 'intrinsic' one. Archaeological data mainly consist of silver hoards linked to private contexts. These might be considered as bulks of precious materials to be used but not necessarily as the proof for the existence of a widely diffused market economy. Archaic market economy developed already during the third millennium BCE, side by side with the redistributive system of the public organizations and the circuit of ceremonial and gift exchange of prestige goods. Moreover, silver ring-money or silver by weight never had an exclusive economic function.

What was the economic value of silver in Bronze Age Mesopotamia cannot be correctly understood without taking into account the complex pattern of extra-economic elements which contributed to silver circulation, even when it simply passed by hand, in what we are attempted to define a 'payment'. After all, the metrological procedure of weighing silver on the balance, which was always necessary before coinage, never was a 'pure' economic operation for the Near Eastern people. In its ideological meaning it was proof of the correctness of the economic actions, established originally by Shamash, the sun-god, the god of justice, who created the exact measures and weights, fixed by the rulers through the official weights of the palace.[76]

Bibliography

Archi, Alfonso: *Circulation d'objets et métal précieux de poids standardisé à Ebla*, in: *Miscellanea Babylonica. Mélanges offerts à Maurice Birot*, ed. by Jean-Marie Durand – Jean-Robert Kupper, Paris 1985a, pp. 25-34.

Archi, Alfonso: *Les rapports politiques et économiques entre Ebla et Mari*, in: *Mari* 4 (1985b), pp. 63-84.

Archi, Alfonso: *Jewels for the Ladies of Ebla*, in: *ZA* 92 (2002), pp. 161-199.

[76] Ascalone – Peyronel 2001; Peyronel 2011, pp. 112-113.

Archi, Alfonso: *Commercio e politica. Deduzioni dagli archivi di Ebla (ca. 2400-2350 a.C.)*, in: *Mercanti e politica nel mondo antico*, ed. by Carlo Zaccagnini, Roma 2003, pp. 41-54.

Archi, Alfonso: *Gifts at Ebla*, in: *Studi italiani di metrologia ed economia del Vicino Oriente Antico*, ed. by Enrico Ascalone – Luca Peyronel, Roma 2011, pp. 43-56.

Archi, Alfonso – Paolo Matthiae: *Una coppa d'argento con iscrizione cuneiforme dalla "Tomba del Signore dei Capridi"*, in: *SEb* 1 (1979), pp. 191-193.

Arkhipov, Ilya: *Le vocabulaire de la métallurgie et la nomenclature des objets en métal dans le textes de Mari*, Paris 2012.

Arnaud, Daniel – Yves Calvet – Jean-Louis Huot: *Ilshu-Ibni-shu orfèvre de l'E.babbar de Larsa, la jarre L. 76-7 et son contenu*, in: *Syria* 56 (1979), pp. 1-64.

Aruz, Joan – Kim Benzel – Jean M. Evans (ed. by): *Beyond Babylon. Art, Trade, and Diplomacy in the Second Millennium B.C.*, New Haven-London 2008.

Ascalone, Enrico – Luca Peyronel: *Two Weights from Temple N at Tell Mardikh-Ebla, Syria. A Link between Metrology and Cultic Activities in the Second Millennium BC?*, in: *JCS* 53 (2001), pp. 1-12.

Ascalone, Enrico – Luca Peyronel: *Materiali e Studi Archeologici di Ebla VII. I pesi da bilancia del Bronzo Antico e del Bronzo Medio*, Roma 2006.

Åström, Paul – Emilia Masson: *A Silver Bowl with Canaanite Inscription from Hala Sultan Tekke*, in: *RDAC* (1982), pp. 72-76.

Beckman, Gary: *Hittite Diplomatic Texts*, Atlanta 1999.

Biga, Maria Giovanna: *Aspetti monetari e finanziari dell'area siro-palestinesi nel III e II millennio a.C.*, in: *Per una storia del denaro nel Vicino Oriente antico*, ed. by L. Camilli, Roma 2003, pp. 59-78.

Biga, Maria Giovanna: *Au-delà des frontières: guerre et diplomatie à Ébla*, in: *Or* 77 (2008), pp. 289-334.

Bjorkman, Judith K.: *Hoards and Deposits in Bronze Age Mesopotamia*, PhD thesis, University of Pennsylvania 1994.

Bonatz, Dominik: *Fremde "Kunstler" in Hattuša. Zur Rolle des Individuums beim Austausch materieller Kultur in der Spaten Bronzezeit*, in: *Brückenland Anatolien? Ursachen, Extensität und Modi des Kulturaustausches zwischen Anatolien und seinen Nachbarn*, ed. by Hartmut Blum – Betina Faist, Tübingen 2002, pp. 69-83.

Bradley Richard: *The Passage of Arms: An Archaeological Analysis of Prehistoric Hoards and Votive Deposits*, Cambridge 1990.

Chambon, Gregory: *Normes et pratiques: l'homme, la mesure et l'écriture en Méspotamie*, Berlin 2011.

Cochavi-Rainey, Zipora: *Royal Gifts in the Late Bronze Age, Fourteenth to Thirteenth Centuries B.C.E.: Selected Texts Recording Gifts to Royal Personages*, Bersheeba 1999.

Cohen, Raymond – Raymond Westbrook (ed. by): *Amarna Diplomacy: The Beginnings of International Relations*, Baltimore-London 2000.

Courtois, Jacques-Claude – Jacques Lagarce – Elisabeth Lagarce: *Enkomi et le Bronze Récent à Chypre*, Nicosia 1986

Edel, Elmar: *Die ägyptisch-hethitische Korrespondenz aus Boghazkoi in babylonischer und hethitischer Sprache*, Opladen 1994.

Edzard, Dietz O.: *Die Beziehungen Babyloniens und Ägyptens in der mitttelbabylonischer Zeit und das Gold*, in: *JESHO* 3 (1960), pp. 38-55.

Faist, Betina, *Der Fernhandel des assyrischen Reiches zwischen dem 14. und 11. Jh. v. Chr.*, Münster 2001.

Feldman, Marian, H.: *Diplomacy by Design: Luxury Arts and an "International Style" in the Ancient Near East, 1400-1200 BCE*, Chicago 2006.

Gitin, Seymour – Amir Golani: *The Tel Miqne-Ekron Silver Hoards: The Assyrian and Phoenician Connections*, in: *Hacksilber to Coinage: New Insights into the Monetary History of the Near East and Greece*, ed. by Miriam S. Balmuth, New York 2001, pp. 27-48.

Guichard, Michaël: *La vaisselle de luxe des rois de Mari – Matériaux pour le dictionnaire de babylonien de Paris. Tome II*, Paris 2005.

Harmansah, Ömür: *Review of M. Feldman, Diplomacy by Design*, in: *The Art Bulletin* 90 (2008), pp. 123-127.

Kassianidou, Vasiliki, *"May He Send Me Silver in Very Great Quantities" EA 35*, in: *Egypt and Cyprus in Antiquity*, ed. by Demetres Michaelides – Vasiliki Kassianidou – Robert Merrillees, Oxford 2009, pp. 48-57.

Kletter, Raz: *Iron Age Hoards of Precious Metals in Palestine - An 'Underground Economy'?*, in: *Levant* 35 (2003), pp. 139-152.

Knapp, Bernard – James D. Muhly – Polymnia Muhly: *To Hoard is Human. Late Bronze Age Metal Deposits in Cyprus and the Aegean*, in: *RDAC* 1988, pp. 233-262.

Kupper, Jean-Robert: *L'usage de l'argent à Mari*, in: *Zikir Šumim. Assyriological Studies Presented to F.R. Kraus on the Occasion of His Seventieth Birthday*, ed. by George van Driem – Theo J. H. Krispijn – Marten Stol – Klaas R. Veenhof, Leiden 1992, pp. 163-172.

Lafont, Bertrand: *Messagers et ambassadeurs dans les archives de Mari*, in: *La circulation des biens, des personnes et des idées dans le Proche-Orient ancien*, ed. by Dominique Charpin – Jean-Marie Durand, Paris 1992, pp. 167-183.

Lafont, Bertrand: *Relations internationales, alliances et diplomatie au temps des rois de Mari*, in: *Amurru* 2 (2001), pp. 213-328.

Lamberg-Karlovsky, Clifford C.: *Structure, Agency and Commerce in the Ancient Near East*, in: *Iranica Antiqua* 44 (2009), pp. 47-88.

Lerouxel, François: *Les échanges de présents entre souverains amorrites au XVIIIe siècle av. n. è. d'après les Archives royales de Mari*, in: *Florilegium Marianum VI. Recueil d'études à la mémoire d'André Parrot*, ed. by Dominique Charpin – Jean-Marie Durand, Paris 2002, pp. 413-463.

Lilyquist, Christine: *Treasures from Tell Basta: Goddesses, Officials, and Artists in an International Age*, in: *Metropolitan Museum Journal* 47 (2012), pp. 9-72.

Liverani, Mario: *Elementi 'irrazionali' nel commercio amarniano*, in: *OA* 11 (1972), pp. 297-317.

Liverani, Mario: *Dono, tributo, commercio: il ruolo dello scambio nella tarda età del Bronzo*, in: *AIIN* 26 (1979), pp. 9-28.

Liverani, Mario: *Prestige and Interest. International Relations in the Near East ca. 1600-1100 B.C.*, Padova 1990.

Liverani, Mario: *Guerra e diplomazia nell'Antico Oriente. 1600-1100 a.C.*, Roma-Bari 1994.

Liverani, Mario: *Le lettere di el-Amarna. 1. Le lettere dei 'Piccoli Re'*, Brescia 1998.

Liverani, Mario: *Le lettere di el-Amarna. 2. Le lettere dei 'Grandi Re'*, Brescia 1999.

Liverani, Mario: *The Influence of Political Institutions on Trade in the Ancient Near East (Late Bronze to Early Iron Age)*, in: *Mercanti e politica nel mondo antico*, ed. by Carlo Zaccagnini, Roma 2003, pp. 119-137.

Liverani, Mario: *The Late Bronze Age: Materials and Mechanisms of Trade and Cultural Exchange*, in: *Beyond Babylon. Art, Trade, and Diplomacy in the Second Millennium B.C.*, ed. by Joan Aruz – Kim Benzel – Jean M. Evans, New York 2008, pp. 161-169.

Maiocchi, Massimo: *Decorative Parts and Precious Artifacts at Ebla*, in: *JCS* 62 (2010), pp. 1-24.

Mander, Pietro: *The gú-li-lum (Bracelets) in the Economic Texts from Ebla*, in: *Oriens Antiqui Miscellanea* 2 (1995), pp. 41-87.

Matthäus, Hartmut: *Metallgefässe und Gefässuntersätze der Bronzezeit, der Geometrischen und Archaischen Period auf Cypern*, München 1985.

Matthews, Roger: *The HS3 Level 3 Hoard*, in: *Excavations at Tell Brak 4. Exploring an Upper Mesopotamian Regional Centre*, 1994-1996, ed. by Roger Matthews, Cambridge – London 2003, pp. 203-209.

Matthiae, Paolo: *Economia palatina a Ebla nell'età degli Archivi*, in: *L'economia palaziale e la nascita della moneta: dalla Mesopotamia all'Egeo*, Roma 2005, pp. 21-34.

Matthiae, Paolo: *Ebla. La città del trono. Archeologia e storia*, Milano 2010.

Matthiae, Paolo – Frances Pinnock – Gabriella Scandone Matthiae (ed. by): *Ebla. Alle origini della civiltà urbana. Trent'anni di scavi in Siria dell'Università di Roma La Sapienza*, Milano 1995.

Meier, Samuel A.: *Diplomacy and International Marriages*, in: *Amarna Diplomacy. The Beginnings of International Relations*, ed. by Raymond Cohen - Raymond Westbrook, Baltimore-London 2010, pp. 165-173.

Menu, Michel: *Analyse du trésor de Tôd*, in: *BSFE* 130 (1994), pp. 29-45.

Michailidou, Anna: *Weight and Value in Pre-Coinage Societies. An Introduction*, Athens 2005.

Michalowski, Piotr: *The Neo-Sumerian Silver Ring Texts*, in: *SMS* 2/3 (1978), pp. 43-58.

Michel, Cécile: *Le commerce privé des Assyriens en Anatolie: un modèle du commerce archaïque selon K. Polanyi*, in: *Autour de Polanyi. Vocabulaires, théories et modalités des échanges*, ed. by Philippe Clancier – Francis Joannès – Pierre Rouillard – Aline Tenu, Paris 2005, pp. 121-133.

Milano, Lucio: *Circolazione di recipienti d'oro e d'argento in Siria nell'Antico e Medio Bronzo*, in: *SdA* 5 (1991), pp. 353-368.

Milano, Lucio: *Sistemi finanziari e circolazione premonetaria in Mesopotamia e in Siria nel III millennio a.C.*, in: *Il regolamento degli scambi nell'antichità (III-I millennio a.C.)*, ed. by Lucio Milano – Nicola F. Parise, Roma-Bari 2003, pp. 3-58.

Moran, William L.: *The Amarna Letters*, Baltimore 1992.

Nicholson, Paul T. – Ian Shaw (ed. by.): *Ancient Egyptian Materials and Technology*, Cambridge 2000.

Paoletti, Paola: *Elusive Silver? Evidence for the Circulation of Silver in the Ur III State*, in: *Kaskal* 5 (2008), pp. 127-158.

Parise, Nicola, F.: *Per uno studio del sistema ponderale ugaritico*, in: *DdA* 4-5 (1970-71), pp. 3-36.

Pasquali, Jacopo: *Il lessico dell'artigianato nei testi di Ebla*, Firenze 2005.

Peyronel, Luca: *Storia e archeologia del commercio nell'Oriente antico*, Roma 2008.

Peyronel, Luca: *Ancient Near Eastern Economics: The Silver Question between Methodology and Archaeological Data*, in: *Proceedings of the 6th International Congress on the Archaeology of the Ancient Near East*, ed. by Paolo Matthiae – Frances Pinnock – Lorenzo Nigro – Nicolò Marchetti, Wiesbaden 2010, vol. 1, pp. 925-948.

Peyronel, Luca: *Mašqaltum kittum. Questioni di equilibrio: Bilance e sistemi di pesatura nell'Oriente antico*, in: *Studi italiani di metrologia ed economia del Vicino Oriente Antico*, ed. by Enrico Ascalone – Luca Peyronel, Roma 2011, pp. 105-161.

Pierrat-Bonnefois, Geneviev: *The Tôd Treasure*, in: *Beyond Babylon. Art, Trade, and Diplomacy in the Second Millennium B.C.*, ed. by Joan Aruz – Kim Benzel – Jean M. Evans, New Haven-London 2008, pp. 65-67.

Pinnock, Frances: *Raw Lapis Lazuli in the Royal Palace G of Ebla. New Evidence from the Annexes of the Throne-Room*, in: *Weights in Context. Bronze Age Weighing Systems of Eastern Mediterranean: Chronology, Typology*, Material, ed. by Maria Emanuela Alberti – Enrico Ascalone – Luca Peyronel, Rome 2006, pp. 347-357.

Pintore, Franco: *Il matrimonio interdinastico nel Vicino Oriente durante i secoli XV-XIII*, Roma 1978.

Pomponio, Francesco: *The Transfer of Decorative Objects and the Reading of the Sign DU in the Ebla Documentation*, in: *JNES* 57 (1998), pp. 29-39.

Pomponio, Francesco: *Aspetti monetari e finanziari dell'area mesopotamica*, in: *Per una storia del denaro nel Vicino Oriente antico*, Roma 2003, pp. 35-57.

Potts, Daniel T.: *The Arabian Gulf in Antiquity. Vol. I: From Prehistory to the Fall of the Achaemenid Empire*, Oxford 1990.

Potts, Daniel, T.: *Total Prestation in Marhashi-Ur Relations*, in: *Iranica Antiqua* 37 (2002), pp. 341-355.

Powell, Marvin A.: *A Contribution to the History of Money in Mesopotamia prior to the Invention of Coinage*, in: *Festschrift Lubor Matouš*, ed. by Blahoslav Hruška – Géza Komoroczy, Budapest 1978, pp. 211-243.

Powell, Marvin A.: *Money in Mesopotamia*, in: *JESHO* 39 (1996), pp. 224-242.

Powell, Marvin A.: *Wir müssen unsere Nische nutzen: Monies, Motives, and Methods in Babylonian Economics*, in: *Trade and Finance in Ancient Mesopotamia*, ed. by Jan Gerrit Dercksen, Leiden 1999, pp. 5-24.

Prentice, Rosemary: *The Exchange of Goods and Services in Pre-Sargonic Lagash*, Münster 2010.

Pulak, Cemal: *The Uluburun Shipwreck and Late Bronze Trade*, in: *Beyond Babylon. Art, Trade, and Diplomacy in the Second Millennium B.C.*, ed. by Joan Aruz – Kim Benzel – Jean M. Evans, New Haven-London 2008, pp. 289-310.

Reinink, Gerrit – Herman L.J. Vanstiphout (ed. by): *Dispute Poems and Dialogues in the Ancient and Medieval Near East*, Leuven 1991.

Reiter, Karin: *Metalle im Alten Orient unter besonderer Berücksichtigung altbabylonischer Quellen*, Münster 1997.

Renger, Johannes: *Subsistenzproduktion und redistributive Palastwirtschaft: Wo bleibt die Nische für das Geld? Grenzen und Möglichkeiten für die Verwendung von Geld im alten Mesopotamien*, in: *Rätsel Geld. Annäherungen aus ökonomischer, soziologischer und historischer Sicht*, ed. by Waltraud Schelkle – Manfred Nitsch, Marburg 1995, pp. 271-324.

Renger, Johannes: *Trade and Market in the Ancient Near East. Theoretical and Factual Implications*, in: *Mercanti e politica nel mondo antico*, ed. by Carlo Zaccagnini, Roma 2003, pp. 15-39.

Roth, Silke: *Gebieterin aller Länder. Die Rolle der königlichen Frauen in der fiktiven und realen Aussenpolitik des ägyptischen Neuen Reiches*, Freiburg 2002.

Sallaberger, Walther: *Ur III-Zeit*, in: *Mesopotamien. Akkade-Zeit und Ur III-Zeit*, ed. by Pascal Attinger – Marcus Wäfler, Freiburg 1999.

Singer, Itamar: *A Political History of Ugarit*, in: *Handbook of Ugaritic Studies*, ed. by Wilfred G.E. Watson – Nicolas Wyatt, Leiden 1999, pp. 604-733.

Thompson, Christine M.: *Sealed Silver in Iron Age Cisjordan and the 'Invention' of Coinage*, in: *OJA* 22 (2010), pp. 67-96.

Vanstiphout, Herman L. J.: *The Mesopotamian Debate Poems. A General Presentation (Part I)*, in: *Acta Sumerologica* 12 (1990), pp. 271-318.

Vanstiphout, Herman L. J.: *The Mesopotamian Debate Poems. A General Presentation. Part II. The Subject*, in: *Acta Sumerologica* 14 (1992), pp. 339-367.

Veenhof, Klaas, R.: *Prices and Trade: The Old Assyrian Evidence*, in: *Altorientalische Forschungen* 15 (1988), pp. 243-263.

Veenhof, Klaas, R.: *Silver and Credit in Old Assyrian Trade*, in: *Trade and Finance in Ancient Mesopotamia*, ed. by Jan Gerrit Dercksen, Leiden 1999, pp. 55-83.

Weber, Jill – Richard L. Zettler: *Metal Vessels*, in: *Treasures from the Royal Tombs of Ur*, ed. by Richard L. Zettler – Lee Horne, Philadelphia 1998, pp. 125-140.

Yalçın, Ünsal – Cemal Pulak – Rainer Slotta (ed. by), *Das Schiff von Uluburun. Welthandel vor 3000 Jahren*, Bochum 2005.

Yon, Marguerite: *The City of Ugarit at Tell Ras Shamra*, Winona Lake 2006.

Zaccagnini, Carlo: *Lo scambio dei doni nel Vicino Oriente durante i secoli XV-XIII*, Roma 1973.

Zaccagnini, Carlo: *Materiali per uno studio sulla 'moneta primitiva': le coppe d'oro e d'argento nel Vicino Oriente durante il II millennio*, in: *AIIN* 26 (1979), pp. 29-49.

Zaccagnini, Carlo: *On Gift Exchange in the Old Babylonian Period*, in: *Studi orientalistici in ricordo di Franco Pintore*, ed. by Onofrio Carruba – Mario Liverani – Carlo Zaccagnini, Pavia 1983a, pp. 190-253.

Zaccagnini, Carlo: *Patterns of Mobility among Ancient Near Eastern Craftsmen*, in: *JNES* 42 (1983b), pp. 245-264.

Zaccagnini, Carlo: *On Late Bronze Marriages*, in: *Studi in onore di Edda Bresciani*, ed. by Sandro F. Bondì – Sergio Pernigotti – Fabrizio Serra – Angelo Vivian, Pisa 1985, pp. 593-605.

Zaccagnini, Carlo: *Aspects of Ceremonial Exchange in the Near East during the Late Second Millennium BC*, in: *Centre and Periphery in the Ancient World*, ed. by Michael J. Rowlands – Mogen Larsen – Kristian Kristiansen, Cambridge 1987, pp. 57-65.

Zaccagnini, Carlo: *Ancora sulle coppe d'oro e d'argento del Vicino Oriente del Tardo Bronzo*, in: *SdA* 5 (1991), pp. 369-379.

Zaccagnini, Carlo: *Lo scambio dei beni nelle relazioni internazionali del Vicino Oriente durante il Tardo Bronzo: Istituzioni, ideologie, prassi*, in: *Les relations internationales*, ed. by Edmond Frézouls – Anne Jacquemin, Paris 1995, pp. 41-68.

Zaccagnini, Carlo: *The Interdependence of the Great Powers*, in: *Amarna Diplomacy. The Beginning of International Relations*, ed. by Raymond Cohen – Raymond Westbrook, Baltimore-London 2000, pp. 141-153.

THOMAS BLANK

Philosophy as *leitourgia:* Sophists, Fees, and the Civic Role of *paideia*

1. Introduction

In June 2011, the social media whistleblowers of WikiLeaks published an online clip in which a well-known series of TV credit-card commercials was parodied.[1] The original advertisements compare goods that are measurable by the medium of money (i.e. goods the credit card company claims to make affordable for its customers by its service) with those that are incommensurable and can therefore not be bought at all (social events, friendship, passion, etc.). In their simple message these spots present credit cards as key to acquiring everything that can be bought with money, whether cheap or (very) expensive. In the parody of these advertisements, WikiLeaks inverts the argument and presents itself as an organization that promotes goods that are not for sale or pricy, but priceless and of incomparable public benefit, such as democratic change and freedom.[2] The organization also claims that they, and their private donors, have not shunned personal risk or the private costs that arise from their efforts (such as running their servers, camouflage tactics, lawsuits, etc.). This message is personalized, in this spot, by the group's leading figure Julian Assange, who is shown under house arrest, unceasingly working for the good cause, thus depicted as personally shouldering all the burdens of Wikileaks' work: a strong, almost messianic picture. The gist is clear: WikiLeaks, under attack and harshly criticized by the political and economic establishment, presents itself as a publically useful organization suffering from unjust prosecution. The clip can be seen as part of a strategy of public vindication in a political environment hostile to WikiLeaks and its goals.

[1] The parody clip can be seen at http://wikileaks.org/Banking-Blockade.html (second video) [last access: 25th Nov. 2013]. I want to thank David C. Mirhady and Jake Clemens as well as the peer reviewers for their helpful and thorough comments on both content and, especially, the language of this paper. I alone am responsible for all remaining errors.
[2] At the climax of its narrative (in the form of a priamel: high costs, personal efforts, and risks undertaken by WikiLeaks and its supporters are emphasized with the simple statement: "Change as a result of your work: priceless"), the clip features pictures of protesting masses, probably in an Arabic country (Egypt?). This combination of picture and visual/spoken text implicitly yet strongly depicts WikiLeaks as the true originators of the so-called 'Arabic revolution'.

This paper is not focused on WikiLeaks and its quarrels with public authorities. Its focus is on the strategy of public vindication through pointing to one's own merits and benefactions while at the same time denigrating those who ignore the worth of these. The argument of being useful for the common good, of bearing private burdens and risks in order to secure social welfare, is one applied not only in WikiLeaks' plea for rehabilitation (and donations), but in many time periods and under differing circumstances. In Classical Greece this approach was famously used by some Athenian thinkers in the fourth century BCE at a moment and in a context of considerable influence for the development of the History of Ideas in Antiquity – and Western Modernity. In a similar way as in the WikiLeaks clip, philosophers and writers such as Plato, Isocrates, and Xenophon pointed to their own benefactions to state and society and to the burdens these imposed on themselves; in a similar way, this served a cause of proving wrong the hostile actions of state and community against philosophy. It is this line of arguments of Plato and his fellow philosophers that shall be at the centre of this paper.

Plato and his philosophic contemporaries depict themselves as benefactors to the polis and philosophy as their gift to society. Central to this self-portrait is the argument that they as philosophers did not take fees for their teaching,[3] an argument which they present in contrast to the so-called 'sophists' who are harshly criticized for their commercial profiteering and their sell-out of the

[3] Isocrates is often said to have taken exceptionally high fees (e.g. Teichmüller 1881, pp. 87-88 and 101; Burk 1923, pp. 48-49; Forbes 1942, p. 20; Eucken 1983, pp. 20-22; Lombard 1990, pp. 23 and 48-49; Too 2008, pp. 116-117). This assumption is mostly based on some statements in *Against the Sophists* (Isoc., *Or.* 13.3-5; see Böhme 2009, pp. 9-10; T. Blank 2014, pp. 40-42) and *Antidosis* (Isoc., *Or.* 15.40; 164; 174-175; 224-226) which are usually misinterpreted. In Isoc., *Or.* 15.40 (this section is the source for the later stories in [Plut.], *Vit. Dec. Or.* 837a; 838a; Philod. 2.178-179; *Hypoth. Isoc., Or.* 2) Isocrates reacts to the accusation of having taken a fee from Nicocles of Salamis for the teaching of law court speech. He reacts by stating that Nicocles, as a monarch in charge of all law courts, was not in need of any such education. It is simply not possible to deduce *e silentio* from this argument (as both Ancients and Moderns often have) that Isocrates thereby admits to taking fees in this or any other cases. Instead he refutes the accusation by challenging the whole idea of a king paying fees for an education of no use to him in his state (argument from probability, cf. *status coniecturalis*). Consequently, one should assume Isocrates is trying to suggest there were no fees involved at all in his interactions with the Cypriot tyrant (that is, if ever the two had any dealings with each other at all). In Isoc., *Or.* 15.164; 174-175; 224-226 Isocrates seems to admit openly to taking fees from foreigners who come to Athens to be educated by him (Too 2008, pp. 108-109). Yet the very point of his argument in these sections is exactly that the students from whom he charged fees were not Athenian citizens. As far as Athenians are concerned, Isocrates constantly joins Plato in the repudiation of fee-taking as immoral (see below). It is on this account that Isocrates is of importance for the topic of this paper.

incommensurable good of philosophic knowledge. It is this aspect of the debate that is relevant to the topic of this volume. The attempt to disauthorize the sophists' claims to teaching virtue by reproaching their practice of taking fees has often been commented upon, and during roughly the last decade theories of reciprocity and aristocratic gift-exchange have been influential in these interpretations. I will begin by giving a short overview over these discussions.

2. Recent views on the debate over teaching virtue for pay

That the sophists charged fees is one of the central elements of their characterization in both Ancient and Modern thought. Representative of this view is Aristotle's notorious definition of the *sophistês*:

> "[…] for the sophistic art consists in apparent and not real wisdom, and the sophist is one who makes money from apparent and not real wisdom […]".[4]

Likewise, contempt of money has long been an essential part in the description of the philosopher,[5] and it is common knowledge that fourth-century philosophers criticized the sophists on their practice of taking fees, a practice which they described as a dividing line between sophist and philosopher.[6]

[4] Arist., *Soph. El.* 165a: […] ἔστι γὰρ ἡ σοφιστικὴ φαινομένη σοφία οὖσα δ' οὔ, καὶ ὁ σοφιστὴς χρηματιστὴς ἀπὸ φαινομένης σοφίας ἀλλ' οὐ οὔσης […] (Transl. E. S. Forster); cf. the similar definitions in Arist., *Soph. El.* 171b; 175b; Plat., *Apol.* 19e-20a; *Prot.* 311e; 313c; 357e; *Gorg.* 519c-d; *Crat.* 391b; *Lach.* 186c; *Pol.* 493a; *Phaidr.* 266c; *Soph.* 224d; 231d; [Plat.], *Def.* 419c; Isoc., *Or.* 11.1-3; 13.3-5; Xen., *Mem.* 1.2.7; 1.6.11-14; *Cyn.* 13.8-9; Aeschin., *Or.* 1.117; 170-175. See Forbes 1942, p. 13; Hénaff 2002, pp. 49 and 122-123; Fredal 2008, pp. 154-155; Meister 2010, pp. 19-20; 41-43 and 132-135; Tell 2011, p. 13.

[5] E.g. Xen., *Apol.* 16; Diog. Laert. 8.8; Olympiod., *In Plat. Alc.* 1.119a. See Forbes 1942, p. 23; D. Blank 1985, p. 1; Corey 2002, p. 189; Hénaff 2002, pp. 49 and 77; Fredal 2008, pp. 154 and 165; Tell 2011, pp. 41 and 44-45.

[6] In this context, the term 'philosopher' does not imply a strict Platonic definition of philosophy, but rather denotes those intellectuals who adhere to the same or a similar line of argumentation in their dissociation from the sophists, among them especially Isocrates (who explicitly describes his own position as that of philosopher – Isoc., *Or.* 2.35; 3.1; 9.9; 13.11; 15.50; 181-186; 260; 266; 271 – as opposed to false philosophers and sophists – 13.1; 11; 14; 8.5; 10.6; 15.270-271; 285; cf. Kerferd 1981, pp. 131-138, Schiappa 1999, pp. 26 and 168-174) and Xenophon (who describes himself as a Socratic and takes a stance against sophistic teachers who misleadingly claimed to be philosophers, cf. Xen., *Mem.* 1.2.17-19; 4.2.23-24; *Cyn.* 13.5-6). Both also stress the taking of fees or acquisition of wealth among the more important motivations of sophistic teaching (Isoc., *Or.* 10.6; 11.1; 13.4-6; 11; Xen., *Mem.* 1.6.2-3; 11-14; *Symp.* 1.5; 4.1-2; 4.62; *Cyn.* 13.9).

The central sources for this philosophic criticism of sophistic profiteering were first collected in the 1940s by Clarence Forbes, and also later in a 1985 article by David Blank.[7] Blank's article was the first to focus on the philosophical aspects of the debate. Although he nowhere explicitly introduces theories of gift-exchange as a hermeneutical tool for understanding the debate, Blank nonetheless reveals central elements of the culture of the gift (offer, challenge, alliance)[8] among the ideals promoted by the philosophers in their anti-sophist invectives.[9]

According to Blank, fourth-century philosophers claimed that the establishment of the social bond of friendship (χάριν εἰδέναι)[10] should be recompense for the teacher's efforts in a process of educational exchange. The sophists were criticized because by introducing fees into this process they ignored aristocratic friendship as a crucial element of teaching virtue. Because of this difference between philosophers and sophists, only the former remained able to select their students freely by the measure of who was and who was not worthy of being taught.[11]

The idea of teaching as a gift has since been at the centre of most studies about the criticism against teaching virtue for pay. Certainly, the most comprehensive study in this respect is that undertaken by Marcel Hénaff in his 2002 book on the *Price of Truth*.[12] Hénaff regards Plato's critique of Hippias and other sophists as an attempt to denigrate the introduction of money and trade into the sphere of wisdom.[13] The main reason for Plato to do so was the view, implicit in

[7] Forbes 1942; D. Blank 1985 (list of *testimonia*: pp. 25-49). Forbes 1942, pp. 12-13, was first to state that the 'selling of wisdom' was among the central charges raised against the sophists by Plato and other Socratics. Philosophic criticism of sophistic money-taking had, of course, been included in earlier studies on Socratic philosophy and the sophists (e.g. Nestle 1942², pp. 259-262; later Kerferd 1981, pp. 25-29), but Forbes was the first to focus on the topic of payment for teaching and to collect the sources for it. His main interest lay in gathering information about the practice of fee-taking in Antiquity. His study is, therefore, rather positivistic and his attention for the theoretical or political background to its philosophic criticism rather limited. The study is, nonetheless, useful, as it does not focus exclusively on philosophical sources and even comprises some documentary material (like *papyri*) about the actual praxis of fee-taking in the Hellenistic World (Forbes 1942, pp. 29-57).

[8] Cf. the Introduction to this volume by Filippo Carlà and Maja Gori.

[9] Cf. Seaford 1998, pp. 3-5; Hénaff 2002, pp. 200-229; Fredal 2008, pp. 158-159.

[10] D. Blank 1985, p. 8. For *charis* and reciprocity see Millett 1998, pp. 231-232.

[11] D. Blank 1985, pp. 10-20; cf. e.g. Plat., *Apol.* 19d-e, *Prot.* 311b-d, *Euthyd.* 272a-b; 304b; Xen., *Mem.* 1.2.5-6; 6.5; 14. See also Corey 2002, pp. 196-203; Hénaff 2002, p. 48. Forbes 1942, p. 24 notes that only for rich men like Plato it was an easy position to demand the refusal of fees.

[12] Hénaff 2002, pp. 43-156.

[13] Hénaff 2002, pp. 65-81 on the depiction of the sophist as tradesman in Plato.

the sophistic practice of taking fees, that the worth of wisdom could be evaluated by the measure of money,[14] which rendered sophistic education a threat to traditional elite education. While the sophists made political education available to virtually everybody able to afford its monetary cost (including the *nouveaux riches* of Athens), the philosophers understood the relation between teacher and student as a relation of initiation into esoteric, almost sacral knowledge.[15] Pivotal to this process of philosophic education was the social bond between teacher and student, and the prestige entailed for the teacher – both resulting from a conceptualization of the educational process as a process of reciprocal care and benefaction.[16]

In similar terms, James Fredal has interpreted philosophic criticism of teaching for pay against the background of a supposed cultural turn in the Greek world, during which economic forms of exchange overtook gift-based forms of exchange without fully replacing them.[17] Building on Pierre Bourdieu's conception of the nature of gift-exchange, Fredal suggests that through the introduction of fees into the field of education, the sophists deliberately made visible the mechanisms of reciprocity at work in aristocratic education in order to delegitimize them.[18] This posed a severe threat to the social hierarchies and accumulation of symbolic capital involved therein; hence the opposition of Plato and other adherents to the traditional system.[19]

Very recently, Håkan Tell has challenged these interpretations on a number of their premises. Tell builds his interpretation on recent studies about the concept of sophistry and its depiction in Plato, namely studies by Edward

[14] Openly repudiated as a misleading assumption in Arist., *Eth. Eud.* 1243b, *Eth. Nic.* 1133b; 1164b. Cf. Hénaff 2002, pp. 160-162.

[15] Hénaff 2002, pp. 92-93; cf. Marrou 1948, pp. 67-68; Fredal 2008, p. 153 (Academy as *thiasos*). The alternative view in Corey 2002, pp. 195-196 is mistaken, insofar as Corey takes the recurrent notion of Socrates' being accessible for all citizens to mean that his education in *arête* also was. Yet that is not the case. The Platonic Socrates is willing to test all citizens whether they were apt for such an education, but would dismiss all that he would judge to be inept. Corey (pp. 197-198) states this himself, yet still regards the Socratic approach as more egalitarian than the 'sophistic' one. Socrates, however, simply selects his students by different criteria than the 'sophists', and his criteria are not less but more esoteric than the 'sophistic' criterion of monetary payment, because the decision whom to accept and whom to dismiss remains fully within his own judgment. The introduction of money into the transaction, if exclusively followed, deprives the teacher of exactly this capacity.

[16] Hénaff 2002, pp. 58-59; 88-90, as general rule of the ceremonial gift (pp. 219-224).

[17] Fredal 2008.

[18] Fredal 2008, pp. 156-160 and 165-167; cf. Bourdieu 1980, pp. 61; 100-111; 112-116.

[19] Fredal 2008, pp. 154-155.

Schiappa and Andrea Nightingale.[20] These scholars have argued that Plato's description of the sophists should be seen as an attempt at self-authorization by 'dissociation': in order to legitimize their own position as teachers, philosophers like Plato (and other Socratics) 'invented' an exclusive, positive tradition of wisdom and contrasted it with an 'other' that had to be 'invented' as well.[21] This 'other' was defined as a group separate from philosophy, though it originally belonged to the same tradition. It was negatively described by a number of disreputable qualities that rendered their claims to wisdom illegitimate. The 'other' was named "sophists" by way of (re)definition of terms such as *rhetorike*, *sophos*, *philosophos* and *sophistes*.[22] This interpretation poses a severe challenge to the idea that was dominant throughout the last century, that the sophists were a movement of intellectual innovators.[23] Rather, they came into being as a discern-

[20] Schiappa 1990; Nightingale 1995; Schiappa 1999; 2003[2]; Tell 2007; 2009; 2011. For possible objections against these interpretations cf. Hanson 2011.

[21] For the rhetorical concept of 'dissociation' see Perelman – Olbrechts-Tyteca 1958, pp. 255-257 ("Nous entendons par procédés de dissociation des techniques de rupture ayant pour but de dissocier, de séparer, de désolidariser, des éléments considérés comme formant un tout ou du moins un ensemble solidaire au sein d'un même système de pensée: la dissociation aura pour effet de modifier pareil système en modifiant certaines des notions qui en constituent des pièces maîtresses"), in detail pp. 550-609; cf. Schiappa 2003[2], pp. 3-6; Tell 2011, pp. 1-2. The idea that the 'sophists' were clearly discernible from other teachers of wisdom (Sages, poets, Presocratics, Socratics) can only be found in Socratic authors (and later authors influenced by them); cf. Nightingtale 1995, pp. 13-59; Tell 2011, pp. 82-84. On the protean meaning of terms such as *sophos* and *sophistes* before Plato see Tell 2011, pp. 21-37; different views about the development of these terms: Nestle 1942[2], pp. 249-250; Havelock 1983, p. 57; Fredal 2008, pp. 149; 151 and 155, and Meister 2010, pp. 15-18. Unlike Schiappa, Nightingale, and Tell, Meister links earlier instances of pejorative use of the term 'sophist' (such as Aisch., *Prom.* 944-952, Soph., *Fr.* 97, Eur., *Hippol.* 921-924) to the same group referred to as 'sophists' in Plato. This, in my opinion, disregards the fact that in Aristophanes, the only 5th century author who connects specific names with them, one of these names is that of Socrates himself (which forces Meister to talk of "Sokrates und die Sophisten" in respect of this piece, whereas Aristophanes clearly talks of 'Socrates *the* sophist' and of Socrates as teacher of 'sophists', cf. Aristoph., *Nub.* 360-361 and 1111; see Tell 2011, p. 26). Tell also points to Androtion (*FGH* 324 F 96) and Aeschin., *Or.* 1.173, who both call Socrates a 'sophist' in the fourth century still.

[22] Fredal 2008, pp. 151-155; Tell 2011, pp. 21-38.

[23] The idea of a 'sophistic enlightenment' has dominated views on the sophists throughout the twentieth century, cf. e.g. Nestle 1942[2], pp. 249-263; Jaeger 1947; Marrou 1948, pp. 77-78; Kerferd 1981, pp.18-29; Hénaff 2002, pp. 56-60 and 92; for a summary of this modern idea see Meister 2010, pp. 20-29 (with a clear focus on German scholarship). Fredal 2008, p. 148 notes the contentious status of the 'sophist movement' but doesn't decisively take sides in the debate. If anything, he seems to follow some parts of the 'dissociation' thesis, e.g. when he dismisses the idea the sophists were mainly concerned

ible group only by retrospective labelling and redefinition of the conditions for legitimate teaching.

Tell takes up this point. In his interpretation, teaching virtue for pay was one of the qualities ascribed to the so-called sophists in order to define and denigrate them at the same time and thus to dissociate them from the tradition they originally belonged to, namely the legacy of the Sages.[24] In this interpretation, our sources are not regarded as proof at all for the idea that the practice of taking fees was a sophistic innovation,[25] nor for the assumption that it was a practice exclusive to teachers whom Plato names "sophists".

Tell's arguments are convincing in many respects,[26] and they are especially important in stressing the rhetorical character of the ancient debate as that of invective. Yet he not only underestimates the theoretical background of that debate, namely the question of whether and how virtue could be taught at all, but he also neither poses nor answers the question why Plato and his contemporaries even felt the need to engage in such a 'dissociation' from parts of their own wisdom tradition. It is this question that I will try to answer at the end of this paper.[27]

with rhetoric (pp. 148-149), or when he acknowledges that the words *sophistês* and *philosophos* underwent redefinitions during the fourth century (p. 149).

[24] That the reproach of teaching for pay emerges as part of this process of dissociation can be seen in the fact that, before Plato, teaching for pay was not seen predominantly as problematic; it also did not apply exclusively to the sophists. Aristocratic teachers and poets, like Simonides and even Solon, were well known to have taken fees; cf. Isoc., *Or.* 15.235; 313 (yet see Tell 2011, p. 31); Cic., *De Orat.* 2.352-354; Quint., *Inst. Or.* 11.2.11-17; Phaedr. 4.22; 25. Cf. the close connection between sophistic fee taking and their negative depiction as listed by D. Blank 1985, p. 2; Corey 2002, p. 190; Tell 2011, p. 8; cf. also Hénaff 2002, pp. 49 and 68.

[25] Cf. Hénaff 2002, pp. 56-57.

[26] I do not agree with his interpretation of Isocrates' profession, however, as nothing more than the teaching of 'public speaking' (Tell 2011, pp. 31-37).

[27] Another question unresolved by Tell is whether there are any discernible reasons that, other than the taking of fees, might have influenced the 'philosophers' in choosing the objects of their anti-sophist invectives. While this question cannot be adequately addressed in this paper (for a recent panorama of the variety of topics addressed by different 'sophists' see Meister 2010), I might hint at the topic of possible moral implications of the respective sophist's teachings, that, at least for Plato and Isocrates, omitted all the epistemological prerequisites for successful education in virtue.

3. Sophistic commerce vs. philosophic altruism

What the Socratics criticize in the practice of sophistic teaching is that the hierarchy of private and public interest was inversed by their charging of fees.[28] Generally, the sophists are depicted as constantly trying to gain personal advantage both from their students and from the poleis they deal with when they are on diplomatic missions for their native cities. The philosophers, on the contrary, are presented as solely concerned with the welfare of those whom they are dealing with: students on the one hand, polis on the other. This can best be seen at the beginning of Plato's *Hippias Maior.* Hippias here explains that he did not often come to Athens because of his numerous civic duties, such as being an envoy of his polis Elis, which made him travel throughout Greece. Socrates reacts as follows:

> "That's what it is, Hippias, to be a truly wise and perfect man! For you are both in your private capacity able to earn much money from the young and to confer upon them still greater advantage than you receive, and in public affairs you are able to benefit your own state, as a man must who is to be not despised but held in high repute among the many. And yet, Hippias, what in the world is the reason why those men of old whose names are called great in respect to wisdom – Pittacus, and Bias, and the Milesian Thales with his followers, and also the later ones, down to Anaxagoras – are all, or most of them found to refrain from affairs of state?"[29]

What strikes Socrates about Hippias' explanation is that he, unlike Hippias himself, regards public duties as incompatible with the idea that Hippias also made an income by teaching during his journeys – something for which Hippias

[28] One of the ideas the Socratics seem to have in common is the subordination of private to public interest. Both spheres of interest are intertwined, insofar as it is assumed that one's own private interest is best served by securing the welfare of the community, e.g. Plat., *Pol.* 332c. Cf. Macé 2012a with collected sources in Macé 2012b; for the occurrence of the idea in Isocrates see Noël 2012; T. Blank 2014, pp. 620-621. Hénaff 2002, p. 55 partly acknowledges this, but bases some of his arguments on the mistaken assumption that *idia* and *koina* were regarded as strictly separate in Greek thinking (pp. 50-52 and 55).

[29] Plat., *Hipp. Mai.* 281b-c: τοιοῦτον μέντοι, ὦ Ἱππία, ἔστιν τὸ τῇ ἀληθείᾳ σοφόν τε καὶ τέλειον ἄνδρα εἶναι. σὺ γὰρ καὶ ἰδίᾳ ἱκανὸς εἶ παρὰ τῶν νέων πολλὰ χρήματα λαμβάνων ἔτι πλείω ὠφελεῖν ὧν λαμβάνεις, καὶ αὖ δημοσίᾳ τὴν σαυτοῦ πόλιν ἱκανὸς εὐεργετεῖν, ὥσπερ χρὴ τὸν μέλλοντα μὴ καταφρονήσεσθαι, ἀλλ' εὐδοκιμήσειν ἐν τοῖς πολλοῖς. ἀτάρ, ὦ Ἱππία, τί ποτε τὸ αἴτιον ὅτι οἱ παλαιοὶ ἐκεῖνοι, ὧν ὀνόματα μεγάλα λέγεται ἐπὶ σοφίᾳ, Πιττακοῦ τε καὶ Βίαντος καὶ τῶν ἀμφὶ τὸν Μιλήσιον Θαλῆν καὶ ἔτι τῶν ὕστερον μέχρι Ἀναξαγόρου, ὡς ἢ πάντες ἢ πολλοὶ αὐτῶν φαίνονται ἀπεχόμενοι τῶν πολιτικῶν πράξεων; (Transl. H. N. Fowler).

seems to have been famous.[30] Socrates depicts the ability to pursue both these ends successfully, private commerce and public action at the same time, as a truly astonishing talent. This thought is illustrated by the example of the Sages of old who did not take part in politics.[31]

Hippias suggests a conclusion from their example: the Sages, embodiments of *sophia* that they were, did not hold the same supreme *sophia* that is needed for what Hippias claims to be doing.[32] The irony underlying this argument is obvious. While Hippias regards the inability of the *sophoi* as proof that corroborates his claim to being supremely *sophos*, Socrates implies from that same fact that there is no such *sophia* that enables a person to be active in private commerce and public welfare at the same time.[33] At the end of this prefatory discussion it becomes clear not only that the Sages stayed away from politics, but that they also did not take fees. While sophists like Gorgias and Prodicus were using public offices as a means to create private income, none of the Sages of old had been known to have profited from their activity or to have engaged publicly at all.[34] This preliminary introduction to the dialogue ends in Socrates' highly ironic praise of Hippias:

> "That's a fine thing you say, Hippias, and strong testimony to your wisdom and that of the men of today and to their great superiority to the ancients. For the ancients, the fellows of Anaxagoras,[35] must have been very ignorant to judge from

[30] Cf. Plat., *Apol.* 19d-e. Hippias does not talk about his teaching profession in Plat., *Hipp. Mai.* 281-283, but he also does not protest at all against Socrates' introduction of this motif. Both Platonic speakers, therefore, presuppose that Hippias was well known as a travelling teacher who took fees for his services. On profiteering as motivation of travelling sophists (and sages) see Tell 2011, pp. 105-106.

[31] That the Sages were, in fact, known as politically active (see Tell 2011, pp. 29-31; 61-92) is of less interest here. What matters for us is that (in order to reproach sophistic mingling of politics and commerce) Plato claims they were not. For the activity of the 'sophists' in diplomatic missions cf. Meister 2010, p. 38.

[32] Plat., *Hipp. Mai.* 281c-d.

[33] Hénaff 2002, pp. 50-52. That this is what Socrates is trying to say becomes more obvious in Plat., *Hipp. Mai.* 282b-283b, when he turns the whole argument upside down, now asserting that the Sages did not take fees, but instead neglected their own interests. Indeed, the suggestion that the Sages were politically inactive proves to be nonsense when confronted with Plato's own confessions in other parts of his works and with our knowledge about the Sages from different sources such as Herodotus (cf. Forbes 1942, p. 23; Tell 2011, pp. 27-28 and 84-92). It therefore seems possible to regard the introduction of the Sages as politically inactive in Plat., *Hipp. Mai.* 281b-c as a joke Hippias is not able to understand.

[34] Plat., *Hipp. Mai.* 282b-d; D. Blank 1985, p. 16; Hénaff 2002, p. 52.

[35] I here depart from Fowler's free translation ("the earlier sophists of the school of Anaxagoras").

> what is said, according to your view; for they say that what happened to Anaxagoras was the opposite of what happens to you; for though much money was left him, he neglected it and lost it all so senseless was his wisdom. And they tell similar tales about others among the ancients. So this seems to me fine testimony that you adduce for the wisdom of the men of today as compared with the earlier men, and many people agree with me that the wise man must be wise for himself especially; and the test of this is who makes the most money".[36]

Hippias' 'insight', in fact, reveals how the wisdom of the sophists should be evaluated – yet it does not prove its quality but rather proves it to be non-existent. Conversely, it can be deduced from this ironical section both that the truly wise man must be wise for others – he even neglects wealth if it is bequeathed to him – and that he should not profit from his wisdom. It also follows that the performance of the wise man's wisdom should not be a political activity, but that he should withdraw from the political sphere and live as a private citizen (*apragmon*).[37] Moreover, among all activities under discussion here, teaching is the only one that the Sages are not denied. They are, therefore, described as privately teaching without pay for the good of others – the exact opposite of Hippias' self-description.

Who are the profiteers of this benefaction? On the one hand, of course, the students are immensely benefited. They get an education in virtue without any fees being charged for it.[38] This is the kind of benefaction in philosophic

[36] Plat., *Hipp. Mai.* 282e-283b: καλόν γε, ὦ Ἱππία, λέγεις καὶ μέγα τεκμήριον σοφίας τῆς τε σεαυτοῦ καὶ τῶν νῦν ἀνθρώπων πρὸς τοὺς ἀρχαίους, ὅσον διαφέρουσι. τῶν γὰρ προτέρων περὶ Ἀναξαγόρου λέγεται πολλὴ ἀμαθία κατὰ τὸν σὸν λόγον· τοὐναντίον γὰρ Ἀναξαγόρᾳ φασὶν συμβῆναι ἢ ὑμῖν· καταλειφθέντων γὰρ αὐτῷ πολλῶν χρημάτων καταμελῆσαι καὶ ἀπολέσαι πάντα· οὕτως αὐτὸν ἀνόητα σοφίζεσθαι. λέγουσι δὲ καὶ περὶ ἄλλων τῶν παλαιῶν ἕτερα τοιαῦτα. τοῦτο μὲν οὖν μοι δοκεῖς καλὸν τεκμήριον ἀποφαίνειν περῖ σοφίας τῶν νῦν πρὸς τοὺς προτέρους, καὶ πολλοῖς συνδοκεῖ ὅτι τὸν σοφὸν αὐτὸν αὑτῷ μάλιστα δεῖ σοφὸν εἶναι· τούτου δ' ὅρος ἐστὶν ἄρα, ὃς ἄν πλεῖστον ἀργύριον ἐργάσηται (Transl. H. N. Fowler). Cf. D. Blank 1985, p. 5.

[37] Positive statements about philosophic teaching free of monetary charge: e.g. Plat., *Euth.* 3d; *Apol.* 33a-b; *Ep.* 7.334b; cf. Seaford 1998, p. 8; Hénaff 2002, pp. 87-88. On Socrates' and Plato's *apragmonsyne* cf. Plat., *Apol.* 32b; 36b-c; *Ep.* 7.324b-325e; 330c-331d.

[38] In Plato's thought, virtue can, in fact, only be taught if no fees are involved. In *Meno*, for example, Socrates guides Anytus to overcome his wrong impression that teaching for pay was, in all fields, a sign of the competence of the teacher: they both come to the conclusion that this idea does not hold true in the case of teaching virtue, because, while the art of an education was the central justification for fee-taking, virtue could not possibly be taught as a *tekhne* (Plat., *Men.* 99e-100a; cf. Plat., *Gorg.* 519b-521a; see D. Blank 1985, p. 10). Only a teacher guided by divine inspiration (*theia moira*) was able to teach virtue (Plat., *Men.* 91a-c; Anytus' protest: Plat., *Men.* 91c; refutation of the idea of teaching virtue as a *tekhne*: Plat., *Men.* 95a-98c). It is obvious that the man guided by

teaching that has long been observed in the studies mentioned above. But there is another level at which a benefaction takes place, which has not been commented upon – the philosophers' benefaction towards the polis.

That teaching virtue is considered an activity of avail to the polis can be seen, for instance, in the *Gorgias*:

> "Socrates: Then this, it seems, is the reason why there is no disgrace in taking money for giving every other kind of advice, as about building or the rest of the arts.
> Callicles: It does seem so.
> So.: But about this business of finding the way to be as good as possible, and of managing one's own household or city for the best, it is recognized to be a disgrace if one is seen to decline to give advice except for a payment in cash, is it not?
> Ca.: Yes.
> So.: The reason evidently being that this is the only sort of service that makes the person so served desire to do one in return and hence it is felt to be a good sign when the service that one has done is repaid to one in kind; but when this is not so, the contrary is felt. Is the case as I say?
> Ca.: It is".[39]

theia moira is no one other than the true philosopher. Being the only one able to judge good from bad and justice from injustice infallibly, he alone is able to teach virtue (cf. Plat., *Pol.* 493a; see Forbes 1942, p. 13). On the impossibility of teaching virtue as a *tekhne* (and thus for pay) see also Plat., *Apol.* 20a-c; Isoc., *Or.* 13.3-4, 11-13. See Forbes 1942, pp.12-13 and 15; D. Blank 1985, p. 8; Hénaff 2002, p. 85. The point in Isocrates' criticism is not, as Forbes believes, that for a good as precious as virtue only very high fees were adequate, but that because of the incommensurability of virtue *no fee at all* could be high enough to pay for it. In Isocrates' view, in compensation for virtue fees no matter how high can only be ridiculously small and therefore inadequate. Teaching virtue for pay is a logical inconsistency in itself. Aristotle picks up this thread in his *Nicomachean Ethics* (1164a-1164b; cf. *Soph. El.* 165a; Forbes 1942, pp. 13 and 18-19; Tell 2011, p. 11). The argument that the sophists' claims about virtue as a result of their teaching mismatched their taking of fees can, therefore, be considered as an argument at the very core of the philosophers' criticism.

[39] Plat., *Gorg.* 520d-521a: ΣΩ· Διὰ ταῦτ' ἄρα, ὡς ἔοικε, τὰς μὲν ἄλλας συμβουλὰς συμβουλεύειν λαμβάνοντα ἀργύριον, οἷον οἰκοδημίας περὶ ἢ τῶν ἄλλων τεχνῶν οὐδὲν αἰσχρόν. ΚΑΛ· Ἔοικέ γε. ΣΩ· Περὶ δέ γε ταύτης τῆς πράξεως, ὅντιν' ἄν τις τρόπον ὡς βέλτιστος εἴη καὶ ἄριστα τὴν αὐτοῦ οἰκίαν διοικοῖ ἢ πόλιν, αἰσχρὸν νενόμισται μὴ φάναι συμβουλεύειν, ἐὰν μή τις αὐτῷ ἀργύριον διδῷ· ἦ γάρ; ΚΑΛ· Ναί. ΣΩ· Δῆλον γὰρ ὅτι τοῦτο αἴτιόν ἐστιν, ὅτι μόνη αὕτη τῶν εὐεργεσιῶν τὸν εὖ παθόντα ἐπιθυμεῖν ποιεῖ ἀντ' εὖ ποιεῖν, ὥστε καλὸν δοκεῖ τὸ σημεῖον εἶναι, εἰ εὖ ποιήσας ταύτην τὴν εὐεργεσίαν ἀντ' εὖ πείσεται· εἰ δὲ μή, οὔ. Ἔστι ταῦτα οὕτως ἔχοντα; ΚΑΛ· Ἔστιν (Transl. W. R. M. Lamb).

In crafts and any other field of technical knowledge (*tekhnai*), Socrates says, it is just to be a teacher for pay, but not so in the field of virtue and of improving state and household, in which it would be disgraceful to refuse giving advice unless there were a profit.

Interestingly, Socrates introduces an alternative reciprocity that was only at work in the field of virtue: imitation. The performance of virtue and counsel, he claims, instils in others a wish to imitate its performer (and thus virtue itself). The same process is described in the *Apology* as well, when Socrates explains that his followers were imitating his dialectical method of *exetasis*:

> "And in addition of these things, the young men who have the most leisure, the sons of the richest men, accompany me of their own accord, find pleasure in hearing people being examined, and often imitate me themselves, and then they undertake to examine others; and then, I fancy, they find a great plenty of people who think they know something, but know little or nothing. As a result, therefore, those who are being examined by them are angry with me, instead of being angry with themselves, and say that 'Socrates is a most abominable person and is corrupting the youth'".[40]

The students of the philosopher will imitate their teacher's virtue as well as his methods in performing this virtue. They will thus promulgate the virtue of their teacher among a greater number of other citizens. At a later point in the *Apology*, Socrates explicitly states that it is virtue, and the teaching of it, that creates welfare of any kind and not – as the sophists claim – payments (fees) that create virtue.

> "For I go about doing nothing else than urging you, young and old, not to care for your persons or your property more than for the perfection of your souls, or even so much; and I tell you that virtue does not come from money, but from virtue comes money and all other good things to man, both to the individual and to the state".[41]

[40] Plat., *Apol.* 23c-d: Πρὸς δὲ τούτοις οἱ νέοι μοι ἐπακολουθοῦντες, οἷς μάλιστα σχολὴ ἔστιν, οἱ τῶν πλουσιωτάτων, αὐτόματοι, χαίρουσιν ἀκούοντες ἐξεταζομένων τῶν ἀνθρώπων καὶ αὐτοὶ πολλάκις ἐμὲ μιμοῦνται· εἶτα ἐπιχειροῦσιν ἄλλους ἐξετάζειν· κἄπειτα, οἶμαι, εὑρίσκουσι πολλὴν ἀφθονίαν οἰομένων μὲν εἰδέναι τι ἀνθρώπων, εἰδότων δὲ ὀλίγα ἢ οὐδὲν. Ἐντεῦθεν οὖν οἱ ὑπ' αὐτῶν ἐξεταζόμενοι ἐμοὶ ὀργίζονται, ἀλλ' οὐχ αὐτοῖς, καὶ λέγουσιν ὡς Σωκράτης τίς ἐστι μιαρώτατος καὶ διαφθείρει τοὺς νέους. (Transl. W. R. M. Lamb); cf. 33a-c. See also Xen., *Mem.* 1.2.3.

[41] Plat., *Apol.* 30a-b: Οὐδὲν γὰρ ἄλλο πράττων περιέρχομαι ἢ πείθων ὑμῶν καὶ νεωτέρους καὶ πρεσβυτέρους μήτε σωμάτων ἐπιμελεῖσθαι μήτε χρημάτων πρότερον μηδὲ οὕτω σφόδρα ὡς τῆς ψυχῆς ὅπως ὣς ἀρίστη ἔσται, λέγων ὅτι οὐκ ἐκ χρημάτων ἀρετὴ γίγνεται, ἀλλ' ἐξ ἀρετῆς χρήματα καὶ τὰ ἄλλα ἀγαθὰ τοῖς ἀνθρώποις ἅπαντα καὶ ἰδίᾳ καὶ δημοσίᾳ (Transl. W. R. M. Lamb).

In this section, Socrates explicitly claims that through his midwifing of virtue he has been promoting welfare both private and public.[42]

Plato is not the only philosopher who by dissociating himself from sophistic profiteering presents himself as benefactor of individual and state at the same time. For Xenophon being a teacher of civic virtue, regardless of his absence from public office (*apragmosyne*), is equivalent to being a virtuous citizen.[43] Isocrates argues that way.[44] He states that the best 'fee' for the sophists is the moral development of his students into *kaloikagathoi*: these can themselves live as examples of virtue and thereby instil the desire to be virtuous – and of being educated by the same teacher – in further citizens. Causing the students to be good citizens is what best secures the social status (*eudoxia*) of the teacher.[45]

In the *Antidosis* Isocrates ridicules Gorgias, because, even though he had exacted the largest fees from his students, he had obviously lost most of his wealth through mismanagement.

[42] Cf. also Plat., *Apol.* 36c-d (see below n. 82).

[43] Xen., *Mem.* 1.6.13.

[44] Tell 2011, pp. 31-37 and 48-49 argues that Isocrates had a different conception of the term *sophistês* from Plato's. This is true, insofar as the term *sophistês* can have a rather neutral meaning in Isocrates' earlier works (Isoc., *Or.* 2.13; 13.14; 19; cf. T. Blank 2014, pp. 39-40); yet cf. the rather negative tone in Isoc., *Or.* 4.3; 82; 5.12; 29; 10.2; 9; 11.43; 15.268; 285, the unambiguous dissociation from 'sophists' in Isoc., *Or.* 12.5; 18; 15.2; 4; 148; 203, and the claim that the term "sophist" had been usurped by impostors in Isoc., *Or.* 15.215; 221; 235; in *Or.* 15.168; 197; 237, Isocrates reacts to his fictitious accusers' unfair attempt to count him among the 'sophists'. In Isoc., *Or.* 15.235 and 313 Isocrates points to the idea that in the days of Solon and the Sages (and down to the times of Anaxagoras, cf. Plat., *Hipp. Mai.* 281b-c), *sophistes* had a different (positive) meaning than in his own time. Indeed, in the same way as Plato (against the 'sophists'), Isocrates criticizes a very similar group of teachers. Also, when Isocrates calls his own profession *philosophia*, he is not just speaking of the art of public speaking (which he himself never performed), as is mostly assumed (e.g. Tell 2011, p. 33). Instead he frames his own profession as an education in virtue (Isoc., *Or.* 13.20-22). So, the analogies in his criticisms against teaching virtue for pay apply to the same type of teachers as Plato's critique, no matter how in both cases these teachers are called or who exactly is included in or excluded from the list (considering that the Presocratics belonged to the same wisdom tradition as the sophists before Plato (re)coined the term *sophistes*, I do not see how their inclusion in a list of profiteering teachers in Isoc., *Or.* 15.271 should be as 'shocking' as Tell 2011, pp. 32-33 believes). That is what is important for our discussion.

[45] Isoc., *Or.* 15.220: Οἶμαι γὰρ δήπου τοῦτό γε πάντας γιγνώσκειν, ὅτι σοφιστῇ μισθὸς κάλλιστός ἐστιν καὶ μέγιστος, ἢν τῶν μαθητῶν τινες καλοὶ κἀγαθοὶ καὶ φρόνιμοι γένωνται καὶ παρὰ τοῖς πολίταις εὐδοκιμοῦντες· οἱ μὲν γὰρ τοιοῦτοι πολλοὺς μετασχεῖν τῆς παιδείας εἰς ἐπιθυμίαν καθιστᾶσιν, οἱ δὲ πονηροὶ καὶ τοὺς πρότερον συνεῖναι διανοουμένους ἀποτρέπουσιν.

> "As a rule, you will find that none of the so-called sophists has gathered[46] much money. Some live their lives meagrely, others very modestly. The one who earned the most was Gorgias of Leontini. He spent time in Thessaly when the Thessalians were the most prosperous of the Greeks; he lived a long time and was concerned with making money. Since he had no fixed residence in any city, he had no public expenditure and did not have to pay taxes; moreover, he never married and had no children, and thus was untaxed even in respect to this unrelenting and costly liturgy.[47] Yet even with such an advantage in saving more than others, he left behind only a thousand staters".[48]

In Isocrates' depiction, Gorgias lived as the perfect parasite. He had neither family nor society to feel responsible for.[49] Instead, he lived among people with

[46] Too translates with "earned".
[47] I here depart from Too's translation ("not subject to this […] liturgy").
[48] Isoc., *Or.* 15.155-156: Ὅλως μὲν οὖν οὐδεὶς εὑρεθήσεται τῶν καλουμένων σοφιστῶν πολλὰ χρήματα συλλεξάμενος, ἀλλ' οἱ μὲν ἐν ὀλίγοις, οἱ δ' ἐν πάνυ μετρίοις τὸν βίον διαγαγόντες· ὁ δὲ πλεῖστα κτησάμενος, ὧν ἡμεῖς μνημονεύομεν, Γοργίας ὁ Λεοντῖνος, οὗτος διατρίψας μὲν περὶ Θετταλίαν, ὅτ' εὐδαιμονέστατοι τῶν Ἑλλήνων ἦσαν, πλεῖστον δὲ χρόνον καὶ βιοὺς καὶ περὶ τὸν χρηματισμὸν τοῦτον γενόμενος, (156) πόλιν δ' οὐδεμίαν καταπαγίως οἰκήσας οὐδὲ περὶ τὰ κοινὰ δαπανηθεὶς οὐδ' εἰσφορὰν εἰσενεγκεῖν ἀναγκασθείς, ἔτι δὲ πρὸς τούτοις οὔτε γυναῖκα γήμας οὔτε παῖδας ποιησάμενος, ἀλλ' ἀτελὴς γενόμενος καὶ ταύτης τῆς λειτουργίας τῆς ἐνδελεχεστάτης καὶ πολυτελεστάτης, τοσοῦτον προλαβὼν πρὸς τὸ πλείω κτήσασθαι τῶν ἄλλων, χιλίους μόνους στατῆρας κατέλιπεν (Transl. Y. L. Too).
[49] Gorgias' situation renders him free from all costs of maintenance of his private and public status. But his financial legacy proves that he is unable to treat his own affairs well. It is obvious that Isocrates is far from downplaying the income of Gorgias, as Tell 2011, p. 48 thinks he is. Instead, he intends to show that teachers who parasitically live from their students' money are incapable of keeping their income or wealth, but quickly gamble it away as a result of their inability to treat their own affairs well. Yet, to be a decent teacher he cannot teach what he cannot practice as a person. Corey 2002, p. 205 correctly states that the management of private and public affairs is one of the most common concepts behind the idea of 'political virtue' in Classical Greece. However, he wrongly deduces from this that the teaching of virtue was regarded as a teaching of a *tekhne*, for which it would be right to take fees. Obviously, Corey thinks of 'householding' in terms of modern economic thought and regards education in it as some sort of mathematical instruction. Yet this modern idea cannot be applied to Classical Greek thinking. In fact, *oikos*-management comprises economic aspects as well as social, religious, and military matters. The Classical Greek concept of virtue, in fact, is one of the topics that best demonstrate the embeddedness of social fields in Greek society. The un-technicality of the teaching of virtue, as Plato, Xenophon, Isocrates and Aristotle saw it, needs to be understood along these lines. It is a general ability of sound judgment and action, a capability to judge wrong from right in all possible situations and contexts; it is not just a business matter.

whom he was not socially related, and he lived from their incomes.[50] He is depicted as a burden to the *poleis* he lives in. Compare this with Isocrates' self-description in the surrounding chapters: in these, Isocrates reacts to a fictitious student's appeal that he should downplay his public and private achievements in order not to provoke envy and hatred among the many, who could judge him an anti-democrat on account of his absence from politics (*apragmosyne*)[51] and his wealth (conspicuously present in his over-performance of liturgies).[52] In reaction to this pessimistic view, Isocrates claims that envying liturgists was the strangest thing to do:

> "[…] I […] think, that those who are irritated by hearing me present myself to Athens as a liturgist who does what is ordered are the strangest and most difficult of all people. I do not need to enter my lot for public office, receive the benefits Athens gives to others, or, for that matter, defend and prosecute cases. I have organized my life not for the sake of wealth or out of arrogance, and I do not look down on those who do not live as I do myself. I loved peace and the quiet life (*apragmosynê*), and in particular I saw men who live this kind of life enjoying a good reputation both here and elsewhere. I thought that such a life was sweeter than the life of those who are always occupied and was, moreover, more suited to the activities in which I initially engaged".[53]

[50] Tell 2011, p. 45; cf. Fredal 2008, p. 155 (taking advantage of the students as a general argument in the denigration of the sophists).

[51] Isoc., *Or*. 15.144.

[52] Isoc., *Or*. 15.142-149, cf. 158. Isocrates' wealth is, as the student believes, presented too conspicuously by Isocrates' many liturgies. By his public generosity Isocrates could make the common citizens feel inferior and less worthy, so that the liturgies might instill hatred in them. What the student describes is nothing other than an interpretation of liturgies as conspicuous consumption (for the common good) that has the potential to establish social hierarchies. Yet in the student's opinion, the *demos*, adhering to egalitarian democratic ideals, will oppose any effort to be humbled by the generosity of a rich individual. Clearly, in the student's account, a struggle is taking place in Athens between egalitarian and hierarchical structures and ideologies; cf. also Too 2008, p. 235 n. 58 who points to the fact worth noting that the language of liturgy is applied to the description of Gorgias as well, who is said to have been free from all liturgical duties (even the maintenance of a family is described as a liturgy). Isocrates uses this as a contrast to the mention of his own liturgical activities in Isoc., *Or*. 15.145-146; 150-151; cf. 164-165.

[53] Isoc., *Or*. 15.150-151: Ἐγὼ δὲ [...] ἡγοῦμαι πάντων ἀνθρώπων ἀτοπωτάτους εἶναι καὶ σχετλιωτάτους, οἵτινες βάρεως ἂν ἀκούοιεν, εἰ λειτοργοῦντα μὲν ἐμαυτὸν τῇ πόλει παρέχω καὶ ποιοῦντα τὸ προσταττόμενον μηδὲν δέομαι μήτε κληροῦσθαι τῶν ἀρχῶν μήτε λαμβάνειν, ἃ τοῖς ἄλλοις ἡ πόλις δίδωσι, μήτ᾽ αὖ φεύγειν δίκας μήτε διώκειν. (151) Ταῦτα γὰρ συνεταξάμην οὐ διὰ πλοῦτον οὐ δι᾽ ὑπερηφανίαν οὐδὲ καταφρονῶν τῶν μὴ τὸν αὐτὸν τρόπον ἐμοὶ ζώντων, ἀλλὰ τὴν μὲν ἡσυχίαν καὶ τὴν ἀπραγμοσύνην ἀγαπῶν, μάλιστα δ᾽ ὁρῶν τοὺς τοιούτους καὶ παρ᾽ ὑμῖν καὶ παρὰ τοῖς ἄλλοις εὐδοκιμοῦντας,

Isocrates depicts his decision not to take part in the routines of Athenian democratic institutions as equivalent to the decision to define his place in society by (over)fulfilling his liturgical duties. He states that rather than being prosecuted at court (as the fictional framework of the *Antidosis* portrays him), and rather even than being given the usual material benefits the city provides its officials with, he should instead be praised by his fellow-citizens.[54] In the ideological struggle described by the student, Isocrates does not submit to the claim of (arithmetic) egalitarianism but promotes geometric equality, which assigns every citizen his political standing by the measure of his voluntary public achievements. The hierarchy proposed by Isocrates is a symbolic one. Praise and *eudoxia* are the recompense he claims for his private expenditures for the common good.

In contrast to Gorgias, Isocrates manages both private and public affairs well. He therefore concludes:

> [...] you [sc. will not] find that I have managed my public and personal affairs badly, since my living expenditures were less than I paid out for liturgies. Those who are thriftier in their personal lives than in their public expenditure rightly deserve praise.[55]

Important for our discussion is how Isocrates explains the source of his wealth. Here, we find an almost open confession that he actually was taking fees.[56] Yet he claims never to have accepted money from Athenian citizens, but only from foreigners.

> "[…] But I, who have never done any wrong, have kept away from sycophancy, and have instead benefited from foreigners, who think they have been treated well, find myself in this great peril, as if I had[57] done something terrible. Those

ἔπειτα τὸν βίον ἡδίω νομίσας εἶναι τοῦτον ἢ τὸν τῶν πολλὰ πραττόντων, ἔτι ταῖς διατριβαῖς ταῖς ἐμαῖς πρεπωδέστερον, αἷς ἐξ ἀρχῆς κατεστησάμην (Transl. Y. L. Too).

[54] This argument closely resembles the commonplace argument of 'public service' in court speeches that, as Paul Millet has argued, was meant to "win over the jury by parading the services [...] performed for the polis, regularly claiming to have carried out more than the bare minimum required by the law" (Millett 1998, p. 229).

[55] Isoc., *Or*. 15.158: [...] οὐθ' ἡμεῖς εὑρεθεῖμεν ἂν οὔτε τὰ περὶ τὴν πόλιν οὔτε τὰ περὶ ἡμᾶς αὐτοὺς κακῶς διῳκηκότες, ἀλλ' ἀπ' ἐλαττόνων ζῶντες, ὧν εἰς τὰς λειτουργίας ἀνηλώκαμεν. Καίτοι τοὺς εὐτελεστέρους ἐν τοῖς ἰδίοις ἢ τοῖς κοινοῖς ὄντας δίκαιόν ἐστι ἐπαινεῖν (Transl. Y. L. Too). Cf. the similar argument in Dem., 19.57-59; see Millett 1998, p. 237. This section is misunderstood by Corey 2002, p. 207, who cites it as an example of Isocrates' acceptance of *philargyria*. Corey mistakes greed (*philargyria*) with virtue-borne wealth.

[56] Isoc., *Or*. 15.161-165; 174-175.

[57] Too translates: "have".

> who have any sense should pray to the gods that most of our citizens could have this ability to take money from foreigners and with it make themselves useful to the city, as I have done".[58]

His public beneficence is limited to citizens of his polis. His teaching is in itself a benefit for the polis, because it provides the citizens with the intellectual means of being good citizens, and also with the means of educating others in being so. Thus, in Isocrates' self-defence, it becomes clearly visible that (at least for Isocrates) the decision between offering education as part of either an exchange of reciprocal gifts or a commercial exchange is a matter of social relation or distance.[59] The social bond between citizens of the same polis prevents him from commercially profiteering from his fellow-citizens. Instead he presents his teaching as a gift to them and to the polis as a whole. On the contrary, he gains the monetary wealth that enables him to do so from those to whom he is not socially related: foreigners.

Plato and Isocrates, in similar ways, present their teaching as distinct from (so-called) sophistic education.[60] While the main goal of sophistic teaching is the accumulation of wealth, the philosophers' intention is to benefit the polis. While Gorgias lived from the polis, Isocrates is living for it.

4. Individuals, the polis, and reciprocity

Here we should stop for a moment and ask if and how the motif of philosophy as beneficial can really be interpreted in terms of the process of gift-exchange. The mechanisms of gift-exchange are not exclusive to relations between individuals. Instead, actors in such an exchange can be definite groups, abstract collectives, and even the gods. What is especially important for the

[58] Isoc., *Or.* 15.164-165: [...] ἐγὼ δ' ὁς οὐδὲ περὶ ἕνα ποτ' ἐξήμαρτον, ἀλλὰ τῶν μὲν ἐνθένδε λημμάτων ἀπεσχόμην, παρὰ ξένων δὲ καὶ νομιζόντων εὖ πάσχειν ἐπορισμάμην τὰς ὠφελείας, ὡς δεινὰ ποιῶν εἰς τηλικουτονὶ καθέστηκα κίνδυνον. Καίτοι προσήκε τοὺς εὖ φρονοῦντας εὔχεσθαι τοῖς θεοῖς ὡς πλείστοις τῶν πολιτῶν παραγενέσθαι τὴν δύναμιν ταύτην, δι' ἣν ἔμελλον παρ' ἑτέρων λαμβάνοντες χρησίμους αὑτοὺς ὥσπερ ἐγὼ τῇ πόλει παρέξειν (Transl. Y. L. Too). Cf. Too 1995, pp. 109-111; Tell 2011, pp. 49-50 (with further references for this idea in Isocrates).

[59] For the role of social alliance and distance in theories of gift-exchange see the Introduction to this volume by Filippo Carlà and Maja Gori.

[60] Further similarities can be seen on other levels of the dissociation. Both Isocrates and Plato, for example, deny the seriousness of 'sophistic' teaching by describing it as children's games or joking (*paizein*, *paignia*, *paidie*), cf. Isoc., *Or.* 10.15; 11.8-9 (see T. Blank 2014, pp. 85-88; 91-93; 117-120; 152-154; Plat., *Soph.* 234a (see Hénaff 2002, pp. 79-80).

philosophers' rhetorical emphasis on the question of beneficence is that an exchange of gifts can take place between individuals and groups.[61] Recent studies on the subject of Classical and Hellenistic euergetism have shown that the idea of a unidirectional process in which gift-based exchange was subsequently replaced by the mechanisms of market and trade during the fifth century cannot be upheld, but that both forms of exchange coexisted, each of them of greater importance in some social fields and less in others.[62] With regard to the question of philosophic or 'sophistic' fee-taking, this perception is in full accord with Tell's notion that the practice of the travelling (and fee-taking) 'sophists' need not be regarded as distinct from the practice of older *sophoi*, namely the travelling Sages. Indeed, both were travelling throughout the Greek world, both were received by local citizens with whom they undertook relations of *xenia,* and both were involved in educational processes and displays of wisdom.[63] Yet the sophists are depicted as taking fees from foreign citizens with whom they were not related. On the contrary, the Sages are depicted as not taking fees, but only public honours (which, of course, could also be materially precious) from their *xenoi*, with whom they were socially related by the bond of *xenia.* In an analogous way, Isocrates does not deem it morally sound to take fees from his fellow-citizens, although he does not refrain from taking fees from strangers.

What most clearly separates the *sophoi* (i.e. 'sophists' and Sages) from Athenian philosophers in the post-Socratic era is that the latter's educational efforts, as can be seen in Isocrates, focus on their own polis. While the 'sophists' are shown to offer their service primarily to citizens of *poleis* other than their own (and in which they do not even reside), Plato and Isocrates stress that their education is intended to be useful for Athens and thus primarily for their fellow citizens. The social bond between philosophic teachers and their fellow-citizens is thereby rendered more important than dealings with citizens from other *poleis*. Philosophic education is depicted as a gift to the community to which the philosophers belong.

Marc Domingo Gygax has interpreted Hellenistic euergetism and public munificence in Classical *poleis* as forms of an exchange of benefits between

[61] Seaford 1998, p.1; Degand 2011, p. 97; cf. Domingo Gygax 2003, p. 172: "In the Greek world, euergetism implied essentially a relationship of reciprocity between a benefactor (εὐεργέτης) and the receiver of his/her benefaction (usually a polis)". Mauss 1923-1924, pp. 21-22 considered exchange between collectives even as the normal, primordial case of gift-exchange.

[62] Cf. Domingo Gygax 2003 and 2009. For the converse idea of a cultural turn in the modes of exchange see e.g. Seaford 1998, pp. 6 and 10-11; Hénaff 2002, pp. 115; 427-428; 482-483; Fredal 2008, pp. 155 and 166.

[63] Tell 2011, pp. 54-59 and 93-112.

polis and individual.[64] The reciprocal structure in the exchange of private expenditures for the community, on the one hand, and public honours (honorific statues and inscriptions, golden crowns, special seats in the theatre etc.) for individuals, on the other, helped secure the stability of the social bond between the polis and its distinguished rich citizens.[65] The polis directly benefitted from the wealth of its rich members. In return it publicly paid tribute to these expenditures by distribution of symbolic capital.[66] Ostentatious acknow-ledgement of the superiority of some in a supposedly (and formally) egalitarian society compensated for public expenditure of private wealth.[67]

Classical Athens with its egalitarian ideology even developed a system of formalized legal obligation[68] with regard to public munificence known as the system of *leitourgiai*. Even though it seems obvious that the legal obligation to liturgies gave them a character slightly different from the voluntariness of euergetism,[69] it seems reasonable to regard them along the lines of the rules of

[64] Domingo Gygax 2003, pp. 182-183; 2009; cf. Ober 1989, pp. 226-230; Millett 1998, pp. 243-251; Seaford 1998, p. 7. Mauss 1923-1924, p. 162 compared Athenian liturgies with public donations by modern societies' elites – a comparison that lacks precision in neglecting the legal character and mechanisms of public control in the liturgical system of Athens.

[65] Lys., 21.11; Aischin., *Or.* 3.236; Dem. 20.61; 151; Lyc. 1.139-140; see Domingo Gygax 2003, pp. 182-183; 188-190 and 199-200 and 2009, p. 174; Degand 2011, pp. 100-104; cf. Ober 1989, p. 226; Millett 1998, pp. 243-244; Seaford 1998, p. 5.

[66] Isoc., *Or.* 12.145; Millett 1998, p. 243; Domingo Gygax 2003, pp. 194-196 and 200; see also Lucia Cecchet's article in this volume. The legal mechanisms "to prevent corruption as well as provide a fair and equal system of participation" described by Taylor 2001 (p. 158) can be interpreted as means to secure the state's monopoly in giving and receiving gifts in a political context. Taylor (p. 160) rightly states that there were no clear-cut definitions separating gift-giving from political bribery. Indeed, how interpersonal gift-giving was evaluated may well have been a matter of perspective rather than definition.

[67] Cf. Thuc. 6.6.4; see Millett 1998, pp. 244-245. On hierarchical structures developing from gift-exchange see Mauss 1923-1924, pp. 170-171; on the conflicting ideologies of such hierarchies with democratic egalitarianism in Athens see Taylor 2001, pp. 164-166.

[68] In contrast to liturgies, there were no legal obligations to euergetism in Hellenistic times. Nonetheless, even euergetism was not fully voluntary. This can be seen in what Domingo Gygax 2009 (esp. pp. 165; 172-173; 187-188) calls "proleptic honours", i.e. public honours enacted by the polis before (!) any donations or other benefactions were conducted; such honours in advance were probably meant to secure future euergetic acts by symbolically indebting the potential benefactors (pp. 175-180). That reciprocal gift-giving can obtain a character of obligation was already perceived by Mauss 1923-1924, pp. 99-100.

[69] Domingo Gygax 2003, pp. 194-196. This also implies the existence of a sanctioning power which does not regularly occur in gift-exchange (cf. Seaford 1998, p. 2). But as far

the gift.[70] The legal coercion involved did not, for example, prevent the liturgists from entering an aristocratic competition of over-performance of these obligations. Additionally, many liturgists publicly boasted about their benefactions and, what is worth noting, they openly claimed recompense for their efforts by preferential treatment at court,[71] a phenomenon Paul Millett has called the "rhetoric of benefits".[72] Obviously, the legal character of liturgies coexisted with the idea that they were voluntary acts of beneficence.[73]

Against this background it seems reasonable to interpret the self-depiction of fourth-century philosophers as benefactors of the polis as an appeal to beneficial reciprocity along the lines of Millett's "rhetoric of benefits". That such appeals do exist on the level of the relation between teacher and student (i.e. claims for respect and deferential treatment towards the teacher), has been stated repeatedly in previous studies.[74] But, as we have already seen, the philosophers depict themselves as benefactors not only of their students but also of the *polis* as a whole. We should, in consequence, not be surprised to find appeals for recompense directed at the polis in their texts.

James Fredal has detected numerous such claims in the philosophic literature of the period. They refer to social status, not money, as recompense and occur most often in the very context of anti-sophist invective.[75] Xenophon's Socrates, for example, wonders why he was prosecuted by the state while other benefactors of the citizens were publicly praised.[76] In the *Symposium* he claims that

as taxes (*eisphora*) are concerned, the situation is not that of a private contract in which the sanctioning power is provided by a third party, an arbitrator such as a law court or a magistrate. Instead, the sanctioning power is embodied by one of the protagonists of the exchange: the state. If, however, not the polis in general but only its people (or even parts of the citizenry such as individuals, *demoi*, *phylai* etc.) are to be regarded as beneficiaries of liturgies, then the state can be seen as an arbitrator. See also Millett 1998, p. 243 and Degand 2011, p. 98 who stress the ambivalent characters of liturgies that were not always forced on the liturgists, but could also be voluntary or, if imposed by the *demos*, over-performed.

[70] This has been made clear by Millett 1998 and now especially by Degand 2011.

[71] Generally, the hope for recompense on the part of the donor does not preclude the rhetoric of euergetism; it does not even preclude genuine belief in the voluntariness of the donation (cf. Domingo Gygax 2009, p. 173). In a similar manner, legal obligation precludes neither the impression nor a conviction of public actions to be voluntary (cf. with similar observations on bribe-taking Taylor 2001, pp. 161-162).

[72] Millett 1998, cf. Domingo Gygax 2003, pp. 190-191 and 196; Fredal 2008, pp. 161 and 164-165 (on the rhetoric of "philosophic altruism"); Degand 2011, p. 98-100.

[73] Cf. Xen., *Mem.* 1.6.12-13, where Socrates reproaches the Athenians for wrongly attributing social status and political power to greedy demagogues instead of liturgists.

[74] D. Blank 1985; Hénaff 2002; Fredal 2008.

[75] Fredal 2008, pp. 164-165.

[76] Xen., *Apol.* 21.

teachers of useful citizens deserved a lot of recompense.[77] We have also seen that Isocrates claims he should be publicly praised rather than prosecuted at court because of his benefactions, which he explicitly parallels to liturgies (and even sides with his material liturgies) and, more often, euergetism.[78] In the *Panegyricus* he claims that intellectual benefactors should (at the very least) be honoured just as highly as Olympic victors.[79] He most probably adopted this idea from Plato, though originally it was formulated already by Xenophanes.[80] In Plato, it can be found in a famous section of the *Apology*[81] in which philosophic appeals to the polis are more obvious than in any other text: in his second speech, after being judged guilty by the jury, Socrates makes proposals for adequately measured punishment. He claims that, because punishment was recompense for one's actions, his penalty should equal to the worth of his deeds.[82] He then gives a description of these deeds and their impact on society, as he understands them: unlike the many, he had neglected his personal profit and household (*chrematismou te kai oikonomias*) as well as political influence (*strategion kai demegorion*) or activity among conspirators and factions (*synomosion kai staseon*); instead his efforts were directed at bringing about the greatest of benefactions (*euergetein ten megisten euergesian*) – that of caring most of all about the moral quality of self and state.[83] Socrates presents his activities as dedicated to the improvement of the morals of both citizens (actors in private affairs) and the polis (actor in political affairs). The recompense he claims for this is the following:

[77] Xen., *Symp.* 4.56-61 (notably phrased as πολὺν μισθὸν). This section is very ironic, as the payment of fees to the sophists by Socrates' young interlocutors is constantly ridiculed in this work (Xen., *Symp.* 1.5; 3.6; 3.10; 4.1-4; 4.14-15; 4.40; 4.62; 5.10).

[78] Isoc., *Or.* 15.158.

[79] Isoc., *Or.* 4.1-3.

[80] Xenophan., DK 21 B 2.

[81] Plat., *Apol.* 36b-e. This section was directly adapted in Isoc., *Or.* 4.1-3 (see above) and 15.95 (cf. Too 2008, p. 142) and indirectly in many others; it also occurs in Plato's *Seventh Letter* (Plat., *Ep.* 7.337c). Plato claims that the polis should take the risk of inaugurating a friendly reciprocity between philosophy and polis by being the first donor (cf. the idea of proleptic honours in Domingo Gygax 2009). By supplications and honours, the *aristoi*, able to guide the state by their virtue, should be reconciled with the polis. This is quite an obvious claim for symbolic capital, for symbolic hierarchies within an egalitarian state.

[82] Plat., *Apol.* 36b: [...] Εἶεν· ἐγὼ δὲ δὴ τίνος ὑμῖν ἀντιτιμήσομαι, ὦ ἄνδρες Ἀθηναίοι; ἢ δῆλον ὅτι τῆς ἀξίας; Socrates explicitly describes the process of judicial judgment and corresponding punishment as one of reciprocity by using the term *anti-timan*, i.e. "to honour in return (for one's actions)". Note also the etymological relation between *time* (τιμή, worth, honour) and *timoria* (τιμωρία, punishment).

[83] Plat., *Apol.* 36b-c.

> "What, then, does such a man as I deserve? Some good thing, men of Athens, if I must propose something truly in accordance with my deserts; and the good thing should be such as is fitting for me. Now what is fitting for a poor man who is your benefactor [sc. *euergetês*], and who needs leisure to exhort you? There is nothing, men of Athens, so fitting as that such a man be given his meals in the prytaneum. That is much more appropriate for me than for any of you who has won a race at the Olympic Games with a pair of horses or a four-in-hand. For he makes you seem to be happy, whereas I make you happy in reality; and he is not at all in need of sustenance, but I am needy. So if I must propose a penalty in accordance with my deserts, I propose maintenance in the prytaneum".[84]

This claim for recompense comprises all elements of the self-description of the philosopher as part of the polis. His actions are all aimed at the moral improvement of citizens and polis. This is what makes him a useful part of the polis, even though he is only able to perform this role as long as he is not involved in private or public office, but, free from an such occupation, lives in leisure (*schole*); finally, he is poor, which results from the very fact that his occupation is not an office for which he has taken any fees in return.[85] Socrates literally donates all his actions and their results (the morals of polis and citizens) to his polis, and he claims recompense. Following this line of thought, his claim for public dining at the Prytaneum appears a rather modest one on the material level, yet on a symbolic level it is not, if one considers the fact that this honour usually was only granted to war-orphans and Olympic victors.

Another, quite different, claim for recompense can be found at the end of Socrates' third speech in the *Apology*, when in his last public words he instructs the polis to be a judge of his own sons' conduct of life just the way he had been a judge of the city's conduct.[86] In this section, once again the idea becomes visible that imitation of the teacher is one of the actions of the student through which the spiritual liaison between teacher and student is made conspicuous. Interestingly, this time the 'student' intended to imitate his teacher is the polis as a whole. We can, therefore, assert that there is an analogy between the student-teacher and the polis-teacher relations. Socrates, the ideal Platonic philosopher, is benefactor to

[84] Plat., *Apol.* 36d-e: Τί οὖν εἰμι ἄξιος παθεῖν τοιοῦτος ὤν; Ἀγαθόν τι, ὦ ἄνδρες Ἀθηναῖοι, εἰ δεῖ γε κατὰ τὴν ἀξίαν τῇ ἀληθείᾳ τιμᾶσθαι· καὶ ταῦτά γε ἀγαθὸν τοιοῦτον ὅ τι ἂν πρέποι ἐμοί. Τί οὖν πρέπει ἀνδρὶ πένητι εὐεργέτῃ δεομένῳ ἄγειν σχολὴν ἐπὶ τῇ ὑμετέρᾳ παρακελεύσει; Οὐκ ἔσθ' ὅ τι, ὦ ἄνδρες Ἀθηναῖοι, πρέπει οὕτως ὡς τὸν τοιοῦτον ἄνδρα ἐν Πρυτανείῳ σιτεῖσθαι, πολύ γε μᾶλλον ἢ εἴ τις ὑμῶν ἵππῳ ἢ συνωρίδι ἢ ζεύγει νενίκησεν Ὀλυμπίασιν. Ὁ μὲν γὰρ ὑμᾶς ποιεῖ εὐδαίμονας δοκεῖν εἶναι, ἐγὼ δὲ εἶναι· καὶ ὁ μὲν τροφῆς οὐδὲν δεῖται, ἐγῶ δὲ δέομαι. Εἰ οὖν δεῖ με κατὰ τὸ δίκαιον τῆς ἀξίας τιμᾶσθαι, τούτου τιμῶμαι, ἐν Πρυτανείῳ σιτήσεως (Transl. W. R. M. Lamb).

[85] This last point is only implicit.

[86] Plat., *Apol.* 41e-42a.

both, and for that he claims recompense in the form of honour, prestige, acknowledgment, and imitation from both.

5. Conclusion: vindication by invective

In concluding this paper, I will delineate one possible explanation for this philosophic claim for recompense and integration. As Dean Hammer and Håkan Tell have argued, the world of the symposium and the Panhellenic games in archaic and early classical times provided Greek aristocrats with a platform for public representation and competition for symbolic capital, thus legitimizing their position of political superiority.[87] In this view, older traditions of wisdom seem to be fully integrated in a community in which aristocratic competition is not regarded as a danger to *isonomia*. At the end of the fifth century, as a result of two oligarchic regimes and of the civil war of 404-403 BCE, aristocracy and with it the aristocratic wisdom tradition had lost its position of legitimacy.[88] Antiphon as a supporter of the oligarchs of 411 BCE, Critias as head of the regime of 404 BCE, and finally Socrates as teacher of several oligarchs were all famous sophists[89] sentenced to death by democratic juries in the aftermath of civil strife.[90] Soon after the trial of Socrates, the idea emerged that the charge against the philosopher's alleged *asebeia* was only pretence, a substitute for the underlying charge of being the educator of the oligarchs.[91]

[87] Hammer 2004, esp. pp. 491-493; Tell 2011, pp. 93-146.

[88] The assumption that philosophic teaching was highly respected in Athens at this time (Hénaff 2002, p. 45) is fundamentally mistaken insofar as it rules out *a priori* politics as a background to the dissociation of philosophers and sophists.

[89] That Socrates could be regarded as a sophist has been shown in numerous studies, cf. e.g. Tell 2011, pp. 51 and 55-56. Even in the second half of the fourth century, it was still possible to regard Socrates as a sophist (Aischin., *Or.* 1.173; see D. Blank 1985, p. 20).

[90] Schiappa 1999, pp. 55-56 and 76. This interpretation of the sentence against Socrates seems possible if we consider that under the amnesty of 403 BCE only the Thirty themselves, but not their supporters, could be directly prosecuted for their activities during their regime (Andoc. 1.90-91). For Socrates, see Hansen 1995; Antiphon: Thuc. 8.68; see Fredal 2008, pp. 151-152. Interestingly, when Antiphon defends himself against this reproach in *P. Gr. Geneva* 264-267 F 1.1-25, it appears as if his taking of fees for speechwriting was used by the plaintiff as proof of his oligarchic (!) tendencies (in spite of Roussel 1925 I consider the fragments authentic, cf. Bleckmann 1998, pp. 377-378 n. 68). Obviously, this implies that the taking of fees from fellow-citizens could be regarded as something inappropriate within the social system of the citizenry, and could be interpreted as proof of political apostasy. For Critias see Xen., Mem. 1.2.12. Xenophon depicts Critias and Alcibiades as parasites trying to gain political profit from joining Socrates (Xen., *Mem.* 1.2.13-24).

[91] Plat., *Ep.* 7.324b-325e; 330c-331d.

There is little doubt that the teachers of aristocratic elites were in disrepute among many Athenians at the time when the debate about teaching virtue for pay arose.[92] This is also the context in which Plato, in the *Seventh Letter*, locates his decision to withdraw from politics and live as an *apragmon*. The reason for his political inactivity, as described here, is a disruption of social bonds – a schism between philosophy and polis.[93]

The philosophers present themselves as benefactors of the state in a situation, in which their profession has lost social credit, has lost symbolic capital within the polis. I want to suggest that their "rhetoric of benefit" should be seen as an effort to reconcile the city with a philosophic teaching that had become suspect for the very reason that it was performed privately and under the conditions of aristocratic reciprocity. By way of denigrating the sophists' profiteering and presenting philosophy as a benefaction not only to aristocratic students but just as well to the polis as a whole, Plato, Isocrates and others appeal to Athens to compensate these benefactions. One important motivation for the philosophic dissociation from the sophists can be seen in an attempt to regain the social capital that private elite education had formerly lost and to renew the social bond that had once integrated aristocracy within the polis.

On the other hand, the self-description of philosophers as *euergetai* and their claim for recompense quite obviously contains a severe reproach against the *polis* for mistreating philosophy by prosecuting it. This finally brings me back to the rhetoric of vindication in the WikiLeaks advertisement parody mentioned at the outset of this paper: both in the philosophic debate we have examined and in this spot, positive self-description serves as a means of rehabilitation and denigration at the same time. Both the fourth century philosophers and WikiLeaks claim that their own activities were distinct from commercial forms of exchange. Instead they depict themselves as benefactors to society who offered precious gifts of great usefulness to the community, whereas their opponents (whose role as enemies of philosophy/WikiLeaks is established by this very process of philosophic/WikiLeaks' self-depiction) are depicted as primarily interested in forms of commerce that are detrimental to the moral values of society. In both cases the strategy of vindication is similar: it is

[92] E.g. Isoc., *Or*. 5.29; 10.1; 11.1-3; 44-50; 12.5; 13.1-8; 15.168-170; cf. D. Blank 1985, p. 24; Tell 2011, pp. 34-35.

[93] Plat., *Ep*. 7.325d. His own *apragmosyne*, Plato explains, was a statement against bad political regimes (oligarchy of 404, democracy since 403), a statement he decided to make when he observed the selfishness of these regimes. This selfishness and the detriment it caused to the state he could observe most drastically in the bad treatment of philosophy, when Socrates was first threatened with death under the oligarchy, then sentenced to death under the reestablished democracy. For other examples for the political and social consequences of a suspension of reciprocal gift-giving between aristocratic elites and the polis see Cecchet in this volume.

invective by self-justification, and self-justification by invective. And, more than that, it is a challenge to the respective societies to stick to the rules of the gift.

Bibliography

Blank, David L.: *Socratics vs. Sophists on Payment for Teaching*, in: *ClAnt* 4 (1985), pp. 1-19.

Blank, Thomas: *Logos und Praxis. Sparta als politisches Exemplum in den Schriften des Isokrates*, Berlin 2014.

Bleckmann, Bruno: *Athens Weg in die Niederlage. Die letzten Jahre des Peloponnesischen Krieges*, Stuttgart – Lepizig 1998.

Böhme, Philipp: *Isokrates. Gegen die Sophisten. Ein Kommentar*, Berlin 2009.

Bourdieu, Pierre: *Le sens pratique*, Paris 1980; Engl. Transl. *The Logic of Practice*, Cambridge 1990.

Burk, August: *Die Pädagogik des Isokrates als Grundlegung des humanistischen Bildungsideals im Vergleich mit den zeitgenössischen und den modernen Theorien dargestellt*, Würzburg 1923.

Corey, David D.: *The Case Against Teaching Virtue for Pay. Socrates and the Sophists*, in: *History of Political Thought* 23 (2002), pp. 189-210.

Degand, Martin: *L'Antiquité à l'épreuve des sciences sociales. Les liturgies athéniennes*, in: *AC* 80 (2011), pp. 95-106.

Domingo Gygax, Marc: *Euergetismus und Gabentausch*, in: *Métis* 1 (2003), pp. 181-200.

Domingo Gygax, Marc: *Proleptic Honours in Greek Euergetism*, in: *Chiron* 39 (2009), pp. 163-191.

Eucken, Cristoph: *Isokrates. Seine Positionen in der Auseinandersetzung mit den zeitgenössischen Philosophen*, Berlin 1983.

Forbes, Clarence A.: *Teacher's Pay in Ancient Greece*, Lincoln 1942.

Fredal, James: *Why Shouldn't the Sophists Charge Fees?*, in: *RSQ* 38 (2008), pp. 148-170.

Hammer, Dean: *Ideology, the Symposium, and Archaic Politics*, in: *AJP* 125 (2004), pp. 479-512.

Hansen, Mogens Herman: *The Trial of Socrates: From the Athenian Point of View*, Copenhagen 1995.

Hanson Hans-Peder: *Review of Håkan Tell, Plato's Counterfeit Sophists*, in: *BMCRev* 2011.09.09 [http://bmcr.brynmawr.edu/2011/2011-09-09.html; last access 23/10/2013].

Havelock, Eric A.: *The Linguistic Task of the Presocratics*, in: *Language and Thought in Early Greek Philosophy*, ed. by Kevin Robb, La Salle 1983, pp. 7-82.

Hénaff, Marcel: *Le prix de la verité. Le don, l'argent, la philosophie*, Paris 2002; German transl.: *Der Preis der Wahrheit. Gabe, Geld und Philosophie*, Frankfurt 2009.

Jaeger, Werner: *Paideia. Die Formung des griechischen Menschen*, vol. 3, Berlin 1947.

Kerferd, George B.: *The Sophistic Movement*, Cambridge 1981.

Lombard, Jean: *Isocrate. Rhétorique et éducation*, Paris 1990.

Macé, Arnaud: *La genèse sensible de l'État comme forme du commun. Essai d'introduction générale*, in: *Choses privées et chose publique en Grèce ancienne. Genèse et structure d'un système de classification*, ed. by Arnaud Macé, Grenoble 2012, pp. 7-40.

Macé, Arnaud: *Platon (428/7-347/6)*, in: *Choses privées et chose publique en Grèce ancienne. Genèse et structure d'un système de classification*, ed. by Arnaud Macé, Grenoble 2012, pp. 429-462.

Marrou, Henri-Irénée: *Historie de l'éducation dans l'antiquité*, Paris 1948; Germ. Transl. *Geschichte der Erziehung im klassischen Altertum*, Freiburg 1957.

Mauss, Marcel: *Essai sur le don. Forme et raison de l'échange dans les sociétés archaïques*, in: *L'Année sociologique* n.s. 1 (1923-1924), pp. 30-196; Germ. Transl. *Die Gabe. Form und Funktion des Austauschs in archaischen Gesellschaften*, Frankfurt 1990.

Meister, Klaus: *Aller Dinge Maß ist der Mensch. Die Lehren der Sophisten*, München 2010.

Millett, Paul: *The Rhetoric of Reciprocity in Classical Athens*, in: *Reciprocity in Ancient Greece*, ed. by Christopher Gill – Norman Postlewaith – Richard Seaford, Oxford 1998, pp. 227-253.

Nestle, Wilhelm: *Vom Mythos zum Logos. Die Selbstentfaltung des griechischen Denkens von Homer bis auf die Sophistik und Sokrates*, Stuttgart 1942^{2}.

Nightingale, Andrea W.: *Genres in Dialoge. Plato and the Construct of Philosophy*, Cambridge – New York 1995.

Noël, Marie-Pierre: *Isocrate (436-338)*, in: *Choses privées et chose publique en Grèce ancienne. Genèse et structure d'un système de classification*, ed. by Arnaud Macé, Grenoble 2012, pp. 381-400.

Ober, Josiah: *Mass and Elite in Democratic Athens. Rhetoric, Ideology, and the Power of the People*, Princeton 1989.

Perelman, Chaïm – Lucie Olbrechts-Tyteca: *La nouvelle rhétorique. Traité de l'argumentation*, Paris 1958.

Roussel, Pierre: *La prétendue défense d'Antiphon*, in: *REA* 27 (1925), pp. 5-10.

Schiappa, Edward: *Did Plato Coin rhetorike?*, in: *AJPh* 111 (1990), pp. 457-470.

Schiappa, Edward: *The Beginnings of Rhetorical Theory in Classical Greece*, New Haven 1999.

Schiappa, Edward: *Protagoras and Logos. A Study in Greek Philosophy and Rhetoric*, Columbia 2003^{2}.

Seaford, Richard: *Introduction*, in: *Reciprocity in Ancient Greece*, ed. by Christopher Gill – Norman Postlewaith – Richard Seaford, Oxford 1998, pp. 1-11.

Taylor, Claire: *Bribery in Athenian Politics*, in: *G&R* 48 (2001), pp. 53-66 and 154-172.

Teichmüller, Gustav: *Literarische Fehden im vierten Jahrhundert v. Chr.*, vol. 1, Breslau 1881.

Tell, Håkan: *Sages at the Games. Intellectual Display and Dissemination of Wisdom in Ancient Greece*, in: *ClAnt* 26 (2007), pp. 249-275.

Tell, Håkan: *Wisdom For Sale? The Sophists and Money*, in: *ClPh* 104 (2009), pp. 13-33.

Tell, Håkan: *Plato's Counterfeit Sophists*, Cambridge 2011.

Too, Yun Lee: *The Rhetoric of Identity in Isocrates. Text, Power, Pedagogy*, Cambridge – New York 1995.

Too, Yun Lee: *A Commentary on Isocrates' Antidosis*, Oxford 2008.

FILIPPO CARLÀ

Exchange and the Saints: Gift-Giving and the Commerce of Relics

> "I appreciate these things, and they mean something to me, because *I remember* the occasion they were given on, and that it was from my mother, and *the relationship* we've had. And this is why I think that it's good to give gifts, because it does sort of *cement a relationship* and it gives you *something to remember* a person by. That's why I object to money. Money is kind of cold. It's spent usually on nothing in particular, and when it's gone the memory's gone".[1]

A central issue which needs to be considered when dealing with gift giving and its interactions with commercial exchange is the analysis of the objects exchanged – in other words, of the actual things given as a gift. There is indeed a general problem, in Antiquity as today, with accepting the fact that objects with a particular symbolic and/or sacred value can be intended as commodities and then eventually exchanged for money.[2] Since

> "considerable social effort was devoted to controlling these goods, yet the escape into wider social access did occur",[3]

money is often perceived as inappropriate to 'respect' the nature of the objects and express their real values.[4] Relics are such an object, and an analysis of the ways they were acquired and exchanged in Late Antiquity seems an interesting case study to analyse intersections and short circuits between gift giving, commercial exchange and other possible forms of transaction.

[1] Interview of Margaret Rose: Cheal 1988, p. 76.
[2] For a definition of commodities, see Kopytoff 1986, pp. 68-69: "a commodity is a thing that has use value and that can be exchanged in a discrete transaction for a counterpart, the very fact of exchange indicating that the counterpart has, in the immediate context, an equivalent value. [...] The exchange can be direct or it can be achieved indirectly by way of money, one of whose functions is as means of exchange". With "discrete transaction" Kopytoff means a transaction different from gift exchange, and aiming primarily only at obtaining the counterpart.
[3] Stark – Garraty 2010, p. 36, who define such goods "preciosities". See also Godelier's definition of "precious objects": Godelier 1996, pp. 222-226.
[4] On the problem of the definition of prices for such objects, see among others Kohl 2003, pp. 112-114 and 152-153, and also Osteen 2002, pp. 236-237, using an example from De Lillo's novel *Underworld*.

1. Sacred objects

At Smyrna Polycarp's martyrdom was consumed under Antoninus Pius, probably in 155 CE. The members of the local Christian community went immediately after the death of the Saint to pick up the remaining bones, "more valuable than precious stones, of more esteem than gold".[5] This expression shows clearly that relics, as objects, have a value which is not directly connected to the materials which compose them, is not so easy to calculate in monetary terms, and is mostly formed by their history and social and symbolic meaning. Relics are indeed 'sacred objects',[6] whose importance – and the capital they bear – is, for persons recognizing them as such,[7] not only economical,[8] and not even only specifically religious, but also social and political.[9]

[5] *Mart. Polyc.* 18.2.

[6] For a definition of 'sacred object', see Kohl 2003, pp. 10; 151-154. In the last years scholars of religion have underlined always more the role of materiality in the construction of beliefs, thus opening also new perspectives on sacred objects: see Lynch 2010, pp. 43-48.

[7] Hahn 2010, p. 291: "without some form of recognition, a relic is merely bone, dust, or scraps of cloth. An audience is essential. Its attention authenticates the relic". Reliquiaries, as Hahn shows in the article, are a part of the process of authentication. It is clear that for persons belonging to cultures not recognizing the sacred value of relics the process of their commoditization, which will be discussed in the course of this paper, is easier.

[8] The economic importance of relics is evident also in their role in increasing the amount of pilgrims and of general economic activity near the sanctuary, but also attracting offers and alms. This point is here not at stake; on it see Fichtenau 1952, pp. 75-76; Hermann-Mascard 1975, pp. 271-312; Hunt 1982, pp. 136-138; Buenacasa Pérez 2003.

[9] On the presence in the relics of different forms of capital see e.g. Boesch Gajano 1999, p. 259; Cutler 2001, p. 277; Canetti 2006, pp. 115 and 121-122; Guiance 2006, pp. 252-254; Stelladoro 2006, pp. 71-72. The creation of relics was a matter of sacral as of symbolic mentality, which cannot be separated and produce an embedded meaning of sacred value, legitimization of power, creation or consolidation of status. Apparently the pagans were well aware of this very early, if already in the story of Polycarp it is made clear that the "Others" wanted to let the relics disappear (e.g. *Mart. Polyc.* 17.1). The examples could be multiplied: in the *Martyrium Carpi, Papyli et Agatonicae* (47, Greek version) it is said that the Christians secretly stole the bones of the martyrs to keep them. See also e.g. Prudent., *Perist.* 5.389-392. Many *passiones* show the persecutors trying, after the death of the saint, to destroy their bodies: see e.g. *Mart. S. Vinc.* (BHL 8628-8631), 21-25. In the case of the martyrs of Lyon and Vienne the pagans carefully burned the bodies of the martyrs from Lyon sweeping then the ashes in the Rhone, but it is explicitly stated that this was done to avoid their burial and to offend Christian belief in resurrection, not in connection to an eventual cult of relics (Eus., *HE* 5.1.59-63). According to Rufinus, the pagans violated in the time of Julian John the Baptist's tomb, burning his relics and scattering his ashes (Ruf., *HE* 2.28. It could be marginally still remembered that nonetheless in Constantinople three heads of John the Baptist were

Relics are thus a perfect example of objects with a particular symbolic meaning,[10] which intervene in shaping social realities; they are products and producers at the same time of the social networks which incorporate them, since they can create connections and relations. Relics are thus, as all 'things', incarnations of 'social facts', objects which are produced by human relations, but at the same time actively cooperate in shaping them.[11] In Late Antiquity and in the Middle Ages relics were indeed perceived as active social actors, also thanks to the *dynamis* they were supposed to detain.[12] They were therefore no 'objects' in the passive sense attributed to the concept, in a way which was considered, before Latour's studies, typical of 'archaic societies' (so also in Mauss)[13], and which Pfister, in explicit connection to relics, called the *orendistisch* form of their cult,[14] and Turner would define a "liminar" understanding of symbols.[15]

known, a phenomenon already studied by Du Cange: Wortley 2004, 145-149). The idea that relics should be destroyed from pagan side is only the last demonstration of their character of particular objects, important as elements of cult but also, therefore, as identity markers. See also e.g. Greg. Tur., *Glor. Mart.* 34; 95. The centrality of the cult of the martyrs in the debate between pagans and Christians is clear also in Theodoret. Cyr., *Graec. Aff. Cur.* 8: see Brown 1976, pp. 177-178; Brown 1981, pp. 6-7. As it is well known, part of this debate is also the clear position of Eunapius about the cult of the relics, "bones and skulls of criminals who had been put to death for numerous crimes" (*Vit. Soph.* 472; transl. W. C. Wright). The Orthodox Christians will do, by the way, the same with potential Arian martyrs, such as George of Alexandria: Cracco Ruggini 1995, pp. 124-125.

[10] On the 'social construction' of the value of relics, see Geary 1986, pp. 174-181. This is an important part if the construction of value depends on the shared belief that the relics are really those of a Saint: thus we find already among the miracles of S. Martin the exposure of false relics, which had been till that moment honored by the local population: Sulp. Sev., *V. Mart.* 11 (see Fichtenau 1952, pp. 63-66; Hermann-Mascard 1975, p. 81). The Council of Carthage in 401 already took care of defining criteria to identify authentic relics: Dooley 1931, pp. 18-19 and 25-28; Hermann-Mascard 1975, pp. 77-79.

[11] On the objects as active protagonists of society, see, among others, Latour 1994, p. 606; Blandin 2002, in particular pp. 7-17; Gumbrecht 2004, pp. 78-90 (Late Antique culture, from this perspective, would be defined, according to Gumbrecht, as a "presence culture"). See now also Hodder's model of "entanglement": Hodder 2012, pp. 88-101. On 'sacred objects' as agents influencing human life and belief, see Lynch 2010, pp. 48-51. Specifically in relation to the relics, see e.g. Boesch Gajano 1999, p. 259.

[12] See, among others, Hermann-Mascard 1975, pp. 16-17; Boesch Gajano 1999, pp. 258-259; Stelladoro 2006, pp. 72-73; Wortley 2006a, 6-7; Angenendt 2007^2, pp. 155-158; Hartmann 2010, p. 591. See e.g. Greg. M., *Dial.* 4.6. According to Hunt 1981, pp. 179-180, relics are rather connected to "a species of devotion which hankered after physical objects and remains which could be seen to embody, for individual and community, the saint and his powers".

[13] Mauss 1923-1924, pp. 48-53, in reference to archaic Roman society.

[14] See Kohl 2003, pp. 52-53. John Chrysostom underlines e.g. that the blood of the saints

Since they are objects whose value is much higher than the material which composes them, it derives from their history and it is socially recognized,[16] relics not only share many characters with 'elite markers',[17] but also often assume the characters of Weiner's "inalienable possessions",[18] which are made such by

> "an immaterial aura of connection to other humans and to something greater than any individual human".[19]

And exactly as Weiner's inalienable possessions, they are made such by the possibility and indeed in the end the practice of their actual alienation,[20] which can happen in different forms and be regulated differently. An interesting example is provided by hagiographic literature: when Vigilius, bishop of Trento, was killed, the inhabitants of Brescia wanted his body back, and had to argue about it with the inhabitants of Trento. In the end, the Brescians got the body, and offered to the other party a silver vase as a gift;[21] this is not a price paid for the relic but a gift given for 'letting it go', to at least in part compensate the loss of an indeed alienated "inalienable possession".

The social meaning of the relic and the kind of social relationships it incorporated and shaped changed according to the owner of the relic itself.[22] On the one side there are forms of collective or better institutional ownership, i.e. relics which are owned by churches, by bishoprics, by the imperial house or

has a voice, even if it is heard not through the ears but through the conscience (*Hom. In Iuv. et Maxim.*: PG 50, 576). Marc Augé would identify in this, and in the general *dynamis* of the relics, a sign of their perception as "objet fétiche", which is coexisting and in tension with their perception as "objet symbole" (Augé 1988, p. 33).

[15] Bausinger 2011, pp. 28-29. Important in the development of this idea about relics was also the general conviction, widespread in Antiquity and in the Middle Ages, that the dead still could express personal wishes and intentions and be actively present in this world: Angenendt 2007², pp. 111-115.

[16] On the 'history' of individual objects and their re-functionalization see now the "second scale of sequencing of entanglements" proposed by Hodder 2012, p. 192.

[17] On "objet-signes" see Blandin 2002, pp. 94-98; see also pp. 250-251; Kohl 2003, pp. 130-132.

[18] Weiner 1992, pp. 6-8. In this sense can here be applied to relics and elite-markers what Godbout 2000², p. 241, says generally about gifts.

[19] Osteen 2002, p. 244.

[20] Weiner 1992, 146: "the alternative of hoarding one's shells in order to guard them from circulation so that they are truly inalienable defeats the very processes that constitute authority and renown". See also Thomas 1991, pp. 22-27 and 100.

[21] *Pass. Vigil.* 10.

[22] I will not enter here juridical problems such as defining who held the property of the relics: Constantine's letter of 324 (Eus., *VC* 2.40) seems in any case to recognize ownership of the graves of the martyrs to the church.

royal families.[23] Next to these, there are diffused forms of private possession.[24] It may be interesting to underline that this was not a novelty exclusively pertinent to Christian groups, since Lucian tells explicitly that, after the suicide of Peregrinus, he met many people who tried to reach the spot:

> "well, I turned back most of them by saying the deed had been done already, those to whom it was in itself highly desirable to see the actual spot, anyhow, and gather up some relics of the fire..."[25]

In both cases, in private as in public possessions, the relics always fulfill the three functions which Hartmann has recognized as typical of *Relikten*,[26] construction of identity, warranty of supernatural protection and legitimacy of a social/political position, but the forms of property lead to a radical differentiation in the form of value attributed to the relic and in their 'social power', according to the following scheme:

[23] On the distinction of 'communal' and 'individual' property see Hodder 2012, pp. 25-27. I will not deal here with the use of relics to legitimate political power, as e.g. in the constitution of the great treasure of relics in Constantinople, where such translations were often directed, not only because of the role of the Emperor, but also of the necessity to honor the imperial capital in spite of the substantial absence of local martyrs, killed in Byzantium during the persecutions (Delehaye 1933^2, pp. 232-237; Wortley 2006b, p. 209). On relics in Constantinople see Delehaye 1933^2, pp. 237-241; James 2001; Klein 2006, in particular pp. 79-88; Wortley 2006b, in particular pp. 214-220. On the possibility that situations like the one in Constantinople generally encouraged the practice of translating relics, see Kötting 1965, pp. 15-16.

[24] I differentiate 'individual' from 'group' mostly from the point of view of the character of property: also in the case of a group the decision to purchase or to sell can be taken by a single person, who is at the head of the community, such as a bishop, but the groups do not pose to its members the problem of death and heirloom, and substantially "tend to behave as if they were to live forever" (Douglas – Isherwood 1996^2, pp. 20-21). See also Kötting 1958, pp. 321-323. Differently from Kötting, I do not consider here as individual possessions cases of private persons who took bodies of martyrs dead in the persecution to bury them on their grounds (as it happened e.g. under Diocletian with Anastasius, buried by Asclepia on her property in Salona, as related by the *Acta Anastasii*; on the grave she built also a martyrium: see Klauser 1942, pp. 284-286), when this is connected to the impossibility of an official burial and to the will of providing a decent grave for the martyr: Cracco Ruggini 1995, pp. 125-126. Of course such burials on villa estates kept later an ambiguous statute between private and public: see on this topic Bowes 2008, pp. 135-146. On the definition of 'public' and 'private' in Late Antique religion, see Bowes 2008, pp. 8-15 ("private worship will be defined as the practice of ritual outside the space and/or supervision of the institutional church and/or its bishops").

[25] Luc., *Mort. Peregr.* 39.

[26] Hartmann 2010, p. 497.

	Private Ownership	*Group Ownership*
Construction of Identity	Family Relics	Patron Saints
Supernatural Protection	Amulets with Relics; Relics protecting the House	Curative Sanctuaries; Saints protecting from plague, etc.
Legitimacy of Social and Political Position	Heirlooms; Relics for Private Burial	Relics connected with exercise of Kingship, Bishopric, etc.

Some examples of functions of relics:
(a) Family Relics. Saint Macrina had a ring containing a piece of the True Cross – after her death her brother, Gregory of Nyssa, took it;[27] the relic had the added value of having already been possession of a a member of his family – and additionally of a sainted woman.
(b) Amulets with Relics. Hesperius, says Augustine, had received "from a friend" some soil from the Holy Land, which he kept above the bed to avoid being disturbed by evil spirits;[28] similar is the story of Theodoret of Cyrus, who slept with a bottle of oil of innumerable martyrs above the bed[29] and on the bed, under his head, and he also had a piece of cloth which belonged to Iacobus. The devil tells him one night that he would have already attacked him, had he not been protected by those.[30] Bishop Silvester of Chalon-sur-Saone had a bed of slender ropes; according to Gregory of Tours "my mother cut a small piece from this rope and hung it from the neck of a girl who was feverish with chills".[31] Saxer calls relics with this function "relique-talismans" and insists on their character of commodity.[32] In this he seems to misunderstand the function with the ownership: the commodization of the relics is due to the possibility of private possession rather than to the functions which, as is shown here, are the same also for 'public' and 'collective' relics.
(c) Relics protecting the House. According to Gregory of Tours, wax coming from the candles burning on S. Martin's grave and kept at home protected a house from fire but could also protect the fields if imposed on them. Gregory himself decided to put some on the highest tree he had in a vineyard.[33]

[27] Greg. Nyss., *V. Macr.* 30.
[28] Aug., *CD* 22.8. Hunt 1981, p. 177. On soil as relic see also Weidemann 1977, pp. 354-356; Donceel-Voûte 1995, p. 185 and especially Hartmann 2010, p. 633.
[29] This practice was very diffused: Antidiolus, e.g., slept with a flask with oil of S. Martin over the bed (*V. Patr. Jur.* 163); another example is in Greg. Tur., *Virt. Mart.* 2.32. See Weidemann 1977, pp. 359-361.
[30] Theodoret. Cyr., *Hist. Mon.* 21.16.
[31] Greg. Tur., *Glor. Conf.* 84 (transl. R. Van Dam). Many more similar examples are available in Gregory of Tours, e.g. *Glor. Conf.* 95. On Gregory of Tours and the many examples of relics and their cult he offers, see still Weidemann 1977.
[32] Saxer 1980, pp. 243-244. See also Angenendt 2007^2, pp. 158-159.
[33] Greg. Tur., *Virt. Mart.* 1.2; 1.34; *HF* 7.31. See Weidemann 1977, pp. 361-362.

(d) Heirlooms. Gregory of Tours inherited from his parents a golden medaillon containing relics;[34] the case of Macrina (a) also applies.
(e) Relics for Private Burials. Around the beginning of the fifth century Eusebia, a Macedonian diakonissa, had relics of the 40 martyrs, with which she wanted to be buried in a monastery of Macedonian monks, together with her friend, Caesarius' wife. The entire story came to light when Pulcheria found, after a dream, the relics.[35] According to Theodoret, Jacob "having collected from everywhere many prophets, and many apostles, and most of all martyrs, put them all in one box (*larnax*), wanting to live together with this saint people and to resurrect together with them".[36] These are therefore variants of the burials *ad sanctos*, which generally implied being buried next to the tomb of a martyr;[37] a variant which implies not only the private possession of relics but also a performance of a form of (more or less) conspicuous consumption, consisting in burying the relics with the body instead than leaving them as heirloom.
(f) Patron Saints. This is e.g. the function of Gervasius and Protasius in Milan or of Vitalis and Apollinaris in Ravenna.[38] See also, among others, the formulation offered by Maximus of Turin, when speaking of the city saints Octavius, Adventor and Solutor.[39]
(g) Curative Saints. This function of the saints can also be expressed in particular situations of need: Gregory of Tours tells that the inhabitants of Zaragoza, during a siege, brought the tunic of S. Vincent all around the city walls, thus removing the siege.[40] A formulation of this idea is also clearly expressed by John Chrysostomus in his homily on the Egyptian martyrs.[41]
(h) Relics connected to the Exercise of Power. E.g. Eulalia's tunic, held by the bishop of Merida, Masona, who refuses to bring it to king Leuvigild and claims having destroyed and drank it.[42]

Christian Fathers opposed the private possession of bodily relics (still now, in Church law a relic is not a private ownership but a possession, given in custody to a temporary guardian)[43] – a phenomenon assuming an evident relevance since

[34] Greg. Tur., *Virt. Mart.* 3.17; *Glor. Mart.* 10; 83. See also e.g. Greg. Tur., *Glor. Mart.* 75; *V. Arid.* 13 (where the object brought around the neck is called *crismarium*); 45; 56. Apparently Gregory attributed to this medaillon the fact that he was once avoided shipwreck: *HF* 8.14. *HF* 8.15 tells of a capsula on the neck of Vulfilaic containing dust from S. Martin's grave. For a later example concerning S. Wilfrid, see also Thacker 2000, p. 262.
[35] Sozom. 9.2.
[36] Theod. Cyr., *Hist. Rel.* (PG 82, 1449 a-c).
[37] Kötting 1965, pp. 26-27. The difference was not perceived by Delehaye 1933², pp. 134-135.
[38] See Heinzelmann 1979, pp. 31-35; Carlà 2010.
[39] Max. Taur., *Serm.* 12.
[40] Greg. Tur., *HF* 3.29. See Castellanos 1996, pp. 19-21 on the connection saint-city walls in Late Antique mentality.
[41] PL 50, 693-695.
[42] *V. Patr. Emer.* 5.6. See Castellanos 1996, pp. 12-14.
[43] 'Things', and particularly the ones bearing a 'special' value, need forms of regulation

the mid-fourth century,[44] which V. Saxer hypothetically connected to the end of the persecutions,[45] and which must be read in the broader context of the competition/interplay between forms of private and public cult and worship, which has been analyzed by K. Bowes.[46]

A reason for such opposition can be seen in Gregory of Tours, who refers to an impostor going around dragging a cross with cruets of holy oil and relics attracting attention and performing magical rites[47] – a possibility which he would not have had, would have it been forbidden to claim possession and property of (either real or false) relics. Another reason for this opposition may have been the problem of the distinction between personal belongings and the belongings of the Church, e.g. bishops who tried to pass to their heirs the goods they acquired while in charge.[48] This could be one of the reasons why the Council of Braga (675 CE) forbade the bishops to bring, on festive occasions, the relics of the martyrs around their necks.[49]

But the opposition to private possession or property is significant mostly because it implies automatically the necessity of subtracting the relics from normal exchange circuits as commerce – more specifically it implies forbidding the 'commoditization' of such objects[50] – while admitting a possible concurrence in their detaining by members of the community. Canon 36 of the Council of Laodicea (364 CE) forbids members of priesthood and of the clergy to produce relics, calling them "chains of the souls", and prescribes excommunication for

and disciplination, deriving from their insertion in subject-object-networks and from their particular temporalities, different from human ones: see Hodder 2012, pp. 86-87.

44 On the origins of the private cult of relics, and its eventual connection with previous practices, see Hartmann 2010, pp. 657-659.

45 Saxer 1980, p. 235. Saxer attributes in the evolution of the cult of martyrs and relics a big role to the Donatists; this point is here of no relevance. According to Heinzelmann 1979, p. 25, this opposition manifested itself together with the institutionalization of the Christian Church and the broader diffusion of the cult of relics, i.e. from the fourth century onwards.

46 Bowes 2008, in particular pp. 189-216. See also Brown 1981, pp. 31-34.

47 Greg. Tur., *HF* 9.6.

48 Greg. Tur., *HF* 8.39.

49 *Conc. Brag.* 5. See Castellanos 1996, pp. 14-15. See also Donceel-Voûte 1995, pp. 184-185, for the parallel, proposed in the text of the canon, between reliquary and Ark of the Covenant.

50 With commodization I mean the acquisition by these objects of an exchange value (in monetary or non monetary form, but as expression of quantity), which allows and regulates their transactions; of course the Marxian idea of the value of exchange as coagulation of working time does not apply. What applies is the fact that, as also in the case of Weiner's inalienable possessions, only the fact that the object can be exchanged attributes to it the exchange value. On commodities see Blandin 2002, pp. 127-128.

those who wear them.[51] Antonius, says Athanasius, opposed the Egyptian practice of keeping the bodies of holy men at home;[52] even if he did not disapprove of holding their clothes and belongings.[53]

This shows already the differentiation, introduced very early, between corporeal (or first class) relics and the objects which belonged to the saints (second class relics); third class relics are those which came into contact with the body of the saint after his death. The opposition of the church was to private possession of the first kind. Still, in the *Life of Severinus*, an example of this attitude can be found: someone says that he needs to meet Severinus to give him relics (of Gervasius and Protasius), which he has, and assures that he has the relics on himself not because of presumption (*temeraria praesumptione*) but of a pious necessity.[54] Later another man runs to the Saint to give him the relics of S. John the Baptist, which he previously owned privately, thus 'correcting' through the gift the existing situation.[55] In the Middle Ages, following S. Thomas, the majority of authors will admit the possibility of private possession of relics, but will still try to refrain this practice in the cases of the most important and most precious forms of relics, the 'notable' ones.[56]

Such opposition was in any case not successful in shaping the effective social practices. At the very beginning of the fourth century, Caecilian, who will become bishop of Carthage in 311 CE reprimanded, as an archdeacon, the rich woman Lucilla, who wanted to kiss the bone of a supposed martyr before taking the Eucharist.[57] The martyr was not a certified martyr, so we must suppose that

[51] See also, among others, Prudent., *Perist.* 6.130-141.

[52] Ath., *V. Ant.* 90. Wortley 2006a, in particular pp. 25-28, attributes to this Egyptian practice a central role in the birth and development of the veneration of relics. Angenendt 1992, p. 48, also suggests a possible influence of Egyptian traditions and practices (i.e. mummification), through monks, on the development of the tradition of the incorrupted bodies.

[53] Ath., *V. Ant.* 91.

[54] Eugipp., *V. Sev.* 9.2-3.

[55] Eugipp, *V. Sev.* 23.1.

[56] Boiron 2006, p. 19.

[57] Opt., *C. Don.* 1.16. It is in this sense not of central importance if the episode really happened at the turn of the third to the fourth century, as most of the scholars believe, or if it, as invention, rather expresses Optatus' disapproval of some contemporary practice in the 360s, as it has been recently proposed by Wiśniewski 2011. In any case such a practice should have been conceivable to be represented thus and I do not agree with the author when he claims that this description is not referring to a real practice but is only aimed at provoking disgust (a disgust based on the presupposition that at that time "holding separate body fragments was unacceptable", a position which, as it will be shown later, appears to be wrong). If Optatus may have exaggerated in portraying Lucilla as kissing the bone, the value of the passage to attest the private possession of the relics and individual forms of their cult is not to be disputed. Wiśniewski himself admits that the

the bone was not exposed in the church, and she must have taken it with her to the church.[58] In spite of this 'institutional' resistance relics were thus by the end of the fourth century a commodity, which could be owned, used and shown also by individual persons.

Gregory of Nyssa has himself nothing to say against private possession:[59] in his homily about St. Theodore he wrote that visitors to the shrines of the martyrs felt the need to take something with them, first wanting some soil, then relics.[60] Also meaningful is Paulin of Nola's description of what happened during the translation of relics of Timothy and Andrew:

> "This, then, was the means by which the faithful and zealous escorts of the relics were afforded a chance at the prompting of faith to break off some keepsakes from the holy bones as their deserved reward".[61]

The relics of the True Cross, says John Chrysostom, are looked for everywhere and by everyone, and both men and women like to have such pieces hanging from their necks.[62] In the fifth century, the *Miracula S. Stephani* report without any problem that some *servi Dei* owned relics of the Saint, which were sent to them from the Orient, without other people knowing it – this excludes any possible form of 'institutional possession'.[63]

The privately possessed relics do assume a different meaning and do represent a different form of capital than the relics owned by groups and institution. While the body of the patron saint in the main church of a town is a trace of the Christianization of the community, of the history of the city, a central element in the construction of a civic Christian identity,[64] the relic owned and brought around by the single individual is a means not of construction of a common identity but rather of underlining an individual separation, a personal

same practices in the time of Augustine were "no longer unanimously considered unacceptable".

[58] See also Dooley 1931, p. 26; Delehaye 1933^2, p. 60; Saxer 1980, pp. 232-234; Brenk 2003, p. 103. Greg. Tur., *Glor. Conf.* 38 speaks without problems of pilgrims bringing with them relics (clearly private) and deposing them on the altar during vigils.

[59] *CJ* 1.3.26 (459) is no prohibition of private property of relics, as Dooley 1931, p. 25, thought. Here it is not forbidden, that relics are kept at home; what is forbidden, is that they are shown in other public buildings than churches.

[60] Greg. Nyss., *Laud. Theod.* (PG 46.740a). See Hunt 1982, pp. 128-132; Wortley 2006a, p. 26.

[61] Paul. Nol., *Carm.* 19.353-359.

[62] Ioh. Chrys., *Contr. Iud. et Gent. Demonstr.* (PG 48.826).

[63] *Mir. S. Steph.* 1.1: *cum quodam loco vel die sermo supradictarum reliquiarum ab his servis Dei fieret, qui easdem sibimet de Orientis partibus missas nobis nescientibus haberent…*

[64] See e.g. Crom. Aq., *Serm.* 7.

distinction, of claiming for oneself a particular supernatural protection which distinguishes from the other members of the society.[65] Prudentius introduces so in the martyrium of S. Vincent many persons who

> "wet a linen garment with the drops of blood, to lay it up at home as a holy safeguard for their descendants".[66]

These objects thus assume not only the clear meaning of underlining the 'sacred' protection of the single persons (and their ancestors if such objects were an heirloom), they became also indicators of the social standing of the owner. The bishop Amator of Auxerre and his successor Germanus always had around their necks a *capsula* containing relics;[67] Gregory of Tours had inherited from his parents a golden medaillon containing relics.[68] These necklaces with relics were apparently only in ownership of persons of high status and of high wealth, since we know them only in connection with members of the aristocracy,[69] for whom they worked as a sort of status symbol.[70]

Already in the fourth century CE we know that, additionally, the houses of rich Christians had private oratories in which they kept and honored their own private relics.[71] Archaeologically the practice is revealed best through the chapel of a private house, found under the church of Ss. Giovanni e Paolo in Rome, "a

[65] It is a form of that "quest for the Ideal Companion" that Peter Brown has identified as central in the cult of the saints, and which is expressed e.g. by Ambrose (*De viduis* 9.54), when he presents the saints as relatives anyone is free to choose: Brown 1977, pp. 228-229; 240-242. See also Brown 1976, pp. 187-190.

[66] Prudent., *Perist.* 5.341-344. See also *Mart. S. Vinc.* (BHL 8628-8631), 20. There are many other examples: in the *Acta Cypriani* (4.2) the Christians put e.g. on the ground next to Cyprian, who is going to be killed, cloths of different kinds (*linteamina* and *manualia*), clearly to collect the blood; in Prudent., *Perist.* 10.841-845 the mother of a killed young christian boy uses her clothes to absorb his blood; in Prudent., *Perist.* 11.137-140 the Christians collect the pieces of S. Hippolytus and his blood.

[67] Steph. Afr., *V. Amat.* 25; Const. Lugd., *V. Germ.* 1.4, 3.15; Bed., *HEAngl.* 1.18. See Thacker 2000, pp. 262-263. *Capsula* can indicate also bigger reliquiaries (e.g. Greg. Tur., *VP* 15.1).

[68] See n. 34.

[69] On the social standing of Germanus: Const. Lugd., *V. Germ.* 1.1. Gregory of Tours was son of Florentius, son of Georgius; Gregory's mother was the granddaughter of the bishop Gregory of Langres: *PLRE* III A, *s.v. Georgius Florentius Gregorius* (Gregory of Tours), pp. 548-549.

[70] Hermann-Mascard 1975, p. 317. For archaeologically known examples see e.g. Leclerq 1948, pp. 2327-2328.

[71] On private church spaces, see now Bowes 2008, pp. 61-124, who claims that in elite homes the cult of relics took place in the first time and remarks how since the mid-fourth century CE Christian elite was controlling the circulation of relics (pp. 84-96).

household shrine, designed for the veneration of privately held relics"[72] with frescoes representing the martyrium of three unknown persons whose relics were kept in a reliquiary or in a cupboard where a niche is still visible.[73] Having relics, and staging their cult in this way, was therefore once more an important way of underlining the possession of a high social, but also of a high economical capital, materialized through the possibility of using a room of a house for this purpose.[74]

This use will go on among aristocratic families in the next centuries, as literary sources confirm. Gregory of Tours tells, for instance, of his oratorium, which he had built in the bishop's house at Tours already in the first year of his episcopate, with relics of Saturninus, Martin, Illidius and other saints.[75] Gregory refers also to an oratorium built by St. Senoch, who invited the bishop of Tours Euphronius to bless it and to bring relics to put inside the altar.[76] This practice was not only Western: Peter the Iberian, as a young man, hostage at the court of Theodosius II, and therefore living at the imperial palace in Constantinople,

> "possessed the bones of some holy martyrs [...]. These bones he placed with honor in a shrine in the bed-chamber where he was leading the ascetic life. [...] He completely decorated this house of prayer with his own hands".[77]

[72] Bowes 2008, p. 89.

[73] Brenk 1995, pp. 188-197; Crook 2000, pp. 44-48; Brenk 2003, pp. 98-105; Bowes 2008, pp. 88-92.

[74] Seeliger 2009, p. 364. Diefenbach 2007, pp. 379-390, interprets the chapel rather as place for the familiar conduction of an ascetic life and thinks that the cult there practiced – as in the other house oratoria – had a rather private nature and was not conceived "um im privaten Raum der *domus* den Besuchern und Klienten das gesellschaftliche Ansehen ihres Besitzers vor Augen zu führen". Even if it were so – and I am rather convinced that it was not, and that the possession of relics was meant, through this architectural frame, to be publicly shown in its physical exposition – what is relevant is not if persons were admitted inside the room, but the fact that in the society was spread the information that the owners of this house had a private oratorium, furnished with private relics; it was probably also known, from where they had such relics, a piece of information, as it will be shown, of great relevance in shaping the form of social capital the relics would represent and in determining the specific prestige connected with them. On the 'ambiguity' of the topography of the chapel, see also Bowes 2008, pp. 90-92.

[75] Greg. Tur., *Glor. Conf.* 20; *VP* 2.3. See Crook 2000, p. 49. Private appears to be also the oratory of the priest Aredius, where this kept a flask of oil from the tomb of S. Martin (*Glor. Conf.* 9). Hermann-Mascard 1975, p. 319 thought that these oratories would be later constructions; it seems rather, also because of the archaeological discoveries, that they were reserved to families of higher social status and bigger wealth.

[76] Greg. Tur., *VP* 15.1.

[77] *V. Petr. Iber.* 26-27 (transl. C. B. Horn – R. R. Phenix Jr.). The martyrs were from Persia, so we must presume that Peter took the relics from Iberia with him.

2. Transacting with relics

Owning a relic privately thus means having had the means of getting it, and this underlines once more – since

> "every exchange, as it embodies some coefficient of sociability, cannot be understood in its material terms apart from its social terms"[78]

– the specific social and economic position of the owner, his/her status and official recognition, with all the possible ensuing problems. Gregory relates, for instance, of a priest who after the insistence of a woman cut a piece of relic to give it to her; this was problematic – and led to the following miracle – not because of the act in itself (this form of private ownership was completely accepted by then), but because the particular woman was unworthy of it.[79]

Relics allow substantially four forms of passage of property: first is, of course, the *inventio* (1), finding them[80] – or being present to the martyrium or at the funeral of the Saint.[81] The 'desire' (in Simmelian terms) for relics, i.e. demand for them ("a socially regulated and generated impulse")[82] which is the origin of their value,[83] caused generally three phenomena:[84] the necessity of always 'finding' new bodies of saints, their division and the introduction of contact relics, which reveal the existence of a very high request in this sense in the fourth century,[85] shown clearly by literary sources in critical terms, which still underline a form of ecclesiastical opposition against these practices. According to the *Testament of the Forty Martyrs of Sebaste*, the soldiers asked to be buried all together in the village of Sarim, and that no one should steal for himself parts of their bodies.[86] The acts of S. Fructuosus have the same content, the faithful wanted relics of the martyr:

[78] Sahlins 1974, p. 183.
[79] Greg. Tur., *Glor. Mart.* 54.
[80] Michalowski 1981, pp. 400-401 insists correctly on the difference between *inventio* and *translatio*. Canetti 2006, p. 130, suggests the analogy between *inventio* and finding treasures.
[81] E.g. *Pass. S. Vigilii* 11: a merchant from Salona collects blood staining the street when the body of the martyr is brought into town.
[82] Appadurai 1986, pp. 29-33.
[83] Simmel 1900, pp. 32-35; Appadurai 1986, pp. 3-4.
[84] Kötting 1958, pp. 325-327; Boesch Gajano 1999, p. 262; Kohl 2003, pp. 50-51; Stelladoro 2006, pp. 74-75.
[85] Hunt 1981, pp. 174-175; Hunt 1982, pp. 135-136.
[86] *Test. XL Mart.* 3-4. Indeed many saints apparently were worried that their bodies could, after their death, be cut in pieces and distributed and asked not to do it, but it is not clear if this is in reference to private property: see e.g. Theod. Cyrr., *Hist. mon.* 3.18.

> "When the night fell, they hastened to the amphitheatre with wine in order to quench the smouldering bodies. This done, each one collected the ashes of the martyrs, so far as he could, and claimed them for his own".[87]

But the saint appeared immediately afterwards in dream to all those who took parts of his ashes to bring them back. In 446 the body of Hypatios was literally attacked by the mob, which wanted to take pieces of cloth, or hairs from the beard;[88] and with the fifth and the following centuries the examples only multiply.[89]

The Council of Cartage tried to regulate this phenomenon and denounce the excess of supposed relics revealed through dreams and visions, and many texts, still in the seventh century and later, report of 'wrong persons' who tried to find relics and incurred in God's wrath in the attempt, because the *inventio* was reserved to their better peers: the cantor Maurinus wanted to dig the body of S. Quentin, 'reserved' for S. Eligius. His hands stuck to the handle of the shovel, then they started to rot of worms and next day he died.[90]

In the cases of direct *inventio* the symbolic meaning of the relics is of course much less strong on the level of the definition of networks, but still very relevant in the constitution of groups and of family relations.[91] Increasing demand influences not only 'production' but also 'exchange', and the form of transition is of central importance in qualifying the object relic and the wealth, the status and performance of the relic holder, in influencing, modifying and determining the form of 'social capital' which will be embodied in the commodity itself.[92] Let us go back to S. Quentin: when Eligius found the body he "longed for relics and laid them aside for himself". He proceeded, immediately after the *inventio*, to pull out the teeth from the jaw, stating that miraculously this was still producing blood (which was of course quickly collected); then he extracted from the head and the arts the nails used to torture the saint and he cut the hair. He then proceeded to distribute these relics as gifts in many different places, and to offer through them comfort in sickness.[93]

[87] *Mart. Fruct.* 6; transl. H. Musurillo. Interesting is also a variant present in other manuscripts, which criticizes the choice of "dividing our bodies into parts", so that "many of you in the same city choose to keep them locked up in private resting-places".
[88] *V, Hypat.* 51.
[89] Germanus of Auxerre: Const. Lugd., *V. Germ.* 8.43. See Kaplan 1999, pp. 19-20.
[90] *V. Elig.* 2.6.
[91] Sbardella 2007, 121.
[92] Geary 1986, pp. 171-174. Central is of course the prerequisite that the relics do not lose their *dynamis* when physically moved, as expressed by Crom. Aq., *Serm.* 31.3. See also Carlà forthcoming.
[93] *V. Elig.* 2.6.

The second way of acquiring relics is indeed (2) a 'voluntary' exchange, the gift, or even the testamentary bequest.[94] This, which could be defined an 'expressive/symbolic gift',[95] is considered morally acceptable, because it does not 'contaminate' the sacred object with money, evaluates its history and in particular its previous possessor, with which a particular connection is expressed in clear way: this is what Godbout has called "valeur de lien", bonding-value, as opposed to use value and exchange value.[96] D. Cheal has also, by contextualizing gift in "moral economy", already underlined its function in the reproduction of social relations and had defined gifts as "tie-signs", which "contain evidence about the nature of the relationship between donor and recipient".[97]

In this sense such exchanges are a product of 'friendship' that has been perceived as central in the transaction of relics by Michalowski.[98] Relics can testify the familiar and personal connections: Macrina's ring with a fragment of the True Cross was thus left by her to her brother Gregory of Nyssa.[99] All this is valid for relics exchanged between 'groups',[100] for private possession and also for the passage from a collective to a private possession: when Cuthbert was exhumed his hair was cut, "which in manner of relics they might give to friends that asked of them".[101] They can also lose any cultic function and they can even lose any religious significance, to acquire an emotional, affective one.[102]

The bonding value can be in any moment destroyed, by its transformation in use value (consumption of the object) or in exchange value, when the object is

[94] Geary 1986, pp. 182-183. For a definition of 'gift', applicable more generally to what I defined "voluntary passage of property", see also Michalowski 1981, pp. 399-400. On testaments: Hermann-Mascard 1975, p. 320. The most famous example are the relics which passed from Gregory of Tours' father to his mother and then to Gregory himself: Greg. Tur., *Glor. Mart.* 83. See also Kohl 2003, pp. 60-62.

[95] Vandevelde 2000, p. 8.

[96] Godbout 2000^2, pp. 244-247. See also Bourdieu 1994, pp. 191-192.

[97] Cheal 1988, pp. 14-22. See also Camerer 1988, in particular p. 199, for an economic perspective on gifts as signals.

[98] Michalowski 1981, pp. 404-406; Geary 1986, p. 183; Sbardella 2007, p. 120.

[99] Greg. Nyss., *V. Macr.* 30.

[100] E.g. the relics of Gervasius and Protasius which Ambrose scattered all over Europe: Carlà 2010, pp. 206-209. Another good example are the relics sent by pope Vigilius in 538 to Profuturus of Braga, during the Priscillianist problem (Vigil., *Ep. ad Prof.*): Castellanos 1996, pp. 9-10. An analysis in this sense of Gregory the Great's gifts of relics has been proposed: Leyser 2000, pp. 299-302. In general on relics as constitutive elements of networks: Kötting 1958, pp. 331-332; Brown 1981, pp. 88-90; Geary 1984, pp. 167-168; Geary 1986, p. 183; Hunter 1999, pp. 420-421; Wirth 2005, pp. 328-329; Diefenbach 2007, pp. 363-365; Noga-Banai 2008, pp. 131-136.

[101] Bed., *HEAngl.* 4.30.

[102] Sbardella 2007, p. 122. On these gifts, with examples from contemporary time, see in general Sbardella 2007, pp. 120-125.

sold: economically speaking, the extended utility, which coincides in market exchange with substantive utility, is in reciprocal exchange formed also by the symbolic utility,[103] which is lost when the relic is 'passed' to the sphere of commercial exchange (3), the third form of transaction possible. This destruction implies a relevant loss from the symbolic perspective. A comparison between the second and third forms of acquisition appears particularly interesting in order to understand in which circumstances they were applied, how they were socially differentiated, and how they were practiced. The last possibility is (4) a 'violent' change in property, conquest or theft – which will become usual and 'institutionalized' in particular after the ninth century, but shows many traces also before.[104] The violent passage of property implies a different kind of action and the acquisition of a different kind of charismatic authority.[105]

Most usually, and in the socially most accepted form, relics are therefore given as a gift,[106] and the act of giving creates a bonding value. Gifts between persons having an official role, as between bishops or bishop and emperor, assumed a clear political and social meaning. Accepting a gift means recognizing the donor, establishing with him a bond, and showing with him a concordance in belief, opinion, intention, and belonging.[107] The basis of this is the possibility, intrinsic in the definition of objects as social facts, of an interaction on the distance:

> "En déhanchant l'interaction pour nous associer à des non-humains, nous pouvons durer au delà du temps présent, dans une autre matière que celle de nostre corps et interagir à distance, chose absolument impossible à un babouin ou à un chimpanzé".[108]

Famous is Paulinus' list of the relics he had in the church of S. Felix, with their provenances.[109] The importance of the dynamics of gift exchange when dealing with relics was indeed very clear to contemporaries: the Empress Eudocia founded in Theodoroupolis in Paphlagonia, when travelling in 439 CE

[103] Van de Klundert – Van de Ven 1999, pp. 6-7.
[104] S. Hilarion died e.g. in Cyprus, but his student Hesychius stole the body to bring it to Palestine (Sozom. 3.14.26; Hier., *V. Hil.* 32.6-7); the inhabitants of Tours stole Martin's body from Poitiers (Greg. Tur., *HF* 1.48).
[105] See Carlà forthcoming.
[106] Hahn 2010, pp. 295-296. On the meaning of gift in relation to relics and their cult, see also Canetti 2002, pp. 108-109. For Byzantine gifts of relics to the West in the Middle Ages, see Klein 2004b, pp. 288-293.
[107] Sbardella 2007, pp. 31 and 121.
[108] Latour 1994, pp. 603-604.
[109] Paul. Nol., *Carm.* 27.406-439. For a further example, see Ven. Fort., *Carm.* 1.2. But see also Ambrose's gifts of relics of Gervasius and Protasius: n. 100.

from Jerusalem to Constantinople after her trip to the Holy Land, a church of S. Stephen (whose body had been recovered only a few years before, in 425 CE, and had attracted a lot of attentions from all over the Empire), insisting on the fact that she, suffering after a foot injury,[110] donates to the new church exactly the foot of the Saint, which she had herself received as a gift.[111] So it is clearly stated that the relics changed hands in an 'honest' way, and that they are there to demonstrate the bonds tying the bishop of Jerusalem and the Imperial house, and this to the city of Theodoroupolis.

Gregory the Great sent in 591 CE, as a gift to the patriarch of Antiochia, S. Peter's keys[112] – sending the gift, and underlining, as he does, that Peter loved Antiochia – which he abandoned to move to Rome and to experience there his martyrium – implied underlining the superiority of Rome. Another example is the box full of relics (of Paul, Laurentius, Pancratius, Chrysantus and Daria and John and his brother), which Gregory of Tours received from Pope Pelagius II through a deacon, maybe Agiulf:[113] in this context these relics were again showing a communion and a networking with Rome in the very middle of the Schism of the Three Chapters.[114] When Justin II became Emperor, Queen Radegund, known as a relic collector, as the hagiographic tradition concerning her confirms,[115] used the opportunity to ask for relics. First of all she sent to Jerusalem for, but did not receive, a relic of the True Cross, which she then asked directly from Constantinople;[116] a move which had a political significance in trying to make her bonds to the imperial house stronger, and even more those of her 'patron' Sigebert, whom she begged for support for this embassy – Radegund would even have later Venantius Fortunatus write a poem of thanks, the *Vexilla Regis*, for Justin and Sophia.[117]

> "For political and religious reasons – on his side – Justin was ready to honour the catholic Franks, but he and Sophia seized the opportunity presented by Radegund to do so in a typical way – reinforcing devotion to relics and the cult of the holy

[110] Geront., *V. Mel.* 59.

[111] Doublet 1889, pp. 294-299. On the specific context and on Eudocia's interest for S. Stephan, see Clark 1982.

[112] Greg. M., *Reg. ep.* 1.25. On Peter's keys, see Fichtenau 1952, pp. 85-86.

[113] Greg. Tur., *Glor. Mart.* 82; *HF* 10.1. On Agiulf's trip, see Greg. Tur., *VP* 8.6. Gregory speaks in many occasions of deacons sent to Rome to take relics: *HF* 6.6.

[114] There are of course too many further examples to list them all: e.g. Aug., *Ep.* 212; Greg. M., *Reg. ep.* 6.50.

[115] Hahn 2006.

[116] Greg. Tur., *Glor. Mart.* 5; *HF* 9.40. See Klein 2004a, p. 77.

[117] Ven. Fort., *Carm.* 2.1-6 have all been composed in occasion of the arrival of the Cross. See Conway 1923, pp. 2-3; Cameron 1976, pp. 56-60.

cross, and using an artefact produced under imperial patronage to demonstrate imperial involvment"[118].

The relics arrived in a reliquiary (which is most probably not the one still preserved, a medieval replacement),[119] and their meaning was clear also to the aristocratic opposition: Maroveus, bishop of Poitiers, refused to receive them and rode away from the city; he was substituted by Euphronius of Tours.

Another well known case is the one of Theodolinda, Catholic queen of the Lombards, the first individual to create a steady connection to Rome through Gregory the Great, who sent her many relics. These were organized by the queen in a real collection in the Cathedral of Monza (to which they were donated), where they were displayed as a proof of Lombard majesty, piety and diplomatic relationships, also through the assemblage of *eulogiai* from Palestine (16 *ampullae* and one medaillon) and from Rome (28 *ampullae* sent by Gregory the Great containing oil collected at the tombs of different Roman saints and marked originally by papyrus strips, of which one is still extant; additionally a catalogue of the represented saints, originally 64, confirms that they were sent personally by Gregory to Theodolinda).[120]

The transaction of relics through gift giving attributes therefore to the object and its owner an entire range of possible social and political qualifications (also on a personal and emotional level), which are deeply connected to the kind of object and the position of the donor, but generally imply the recognition of a shared identity and its physical expression through the sacred object[121] – even if, as said, this could sometimes escape the religious level and remain significant only on the personal one. Exactly because of this reason, such gifts could also be required, as it happened in the case of Avitus of Vienne, who asked and obtained from Jerusalem a fragment of the True Cross,

[118] Cameron 1976, p. 67.

[119] Conway 1923 (presenting the object as the original reliquiary); Klein 2004a, pp. 178-180; Hahn 2006.

[120] Elsner 1997, in particular pp. 121-123. Similar collections were common in Europe, but were generally formed through progressive accumulation and not, as in the case of Monza, on the initiative of a single person: McCormick 2001, pp. 283-318, analyzes the collections of Sens and Chelles, insisting particularly on the geographical provenance of the relics as a marker of existing exchanges, a perspective which is only partially justifiable considering the possibilities of falsification but also of passage of the relics, in the form of gifts, from hand to hand, what therefore would exclude a direct provenance from the region where the saint lived and was eventually buried. The word *eulogia* has now been thoroughly analyzed by Caner 2013, pp. 26-28, who has demonstrated that it did not exclusively indicate this kind of objects; in this article the term will nevertheless be used only to indicate such flasks or different sorts of talismans connected to the cult of the Saints.

[121] Sbardella 2007, p. 121.

"gifts that are to be valued not in price (*pretium*), but in the rewards (*premium*) of salvation".[122]

At the same time, this form of gifts creates always an asymmetrical relation, implicit in the nature of the gift itself, as Sbardella has clearly emphasized: the debt which is created, as every time when a gift is given, is of a particular nature, and underlines a spiritual and hierarchical dependency, particularly evident when it is between communities.[123] This leads also to the development of a sort of forced gift (when the requirer is stronger), or to real struggles to define hierarchies of social as of political power. In 594 CE the Empress Constantina, wife of Maurice, wanted to receive the head or some other part of S. Paul for a new church in Constantinople dedicated to this saint. She asked thus Pope Gregory the Great to send it. Gregory denied with a very famous letter.[124] This letter will be better dealt with later, now it is important only to underline how Constantina tried to use her social weight as Empress to receive important relics from Rome, and how Gregory had to underline that he believed the idea had come from someone else (the patriarch, John the Faster) to make him appear disobedient to imperial orders. The gift and its denial are a central part in the negotiation of hierarchies and social relations.

3. Desire and demand

The possibility of a personal possession of relics, it has been said, implied the birth of a desire – a 'demand' – which had to be satisfied, for better or worse.[125] The worse could be theft,[126] or the other forms of 'violent' appropriation.[127] Already Hegeria tells us that the Wood of the True Cross in Jerusalem was kept under strict surveillance, because someone had previously bit a piece off – to have it for himself, of course.[128] Paulinus becomes even more exaggerated, since

[122] Avit., *Ep.* 84 (Migne)
[123] Sbardella 2007, p. 168.
[124] Greg. M., *Reg. ep.* 4.30.
[125] Hartmann 2010, pp. 633-634.
[126] Theft could have of course been practiced either for private possession or for a successive sale; the sources often do not say what should have happened with the relics, also because they generally refer of thefts which were miraculously avoided: e.g. Greg. Tur., *Glor. Mart.* 89.
[127] Some examples in Fichtenau 1952, pp. 77-78.
[128] *Peregr. Heg.* 37.2. Greg. Tur., *Glor. Conf.* 40 speaks of a tribune who prayed on the tomb of a martyr and then tried to strike it with a sword, clearly to take away some part, but was immediately and miraculously stiffened. Similar stories of people cutting splits from holy objects or stealing soil from holy places can be find in Bede: *HEAngl.* 3.2; 3.9; 3.17.

he explains how he wanted to detach a piece of ear from a living saint man. The reason, starting from the presupposition that it is pious and right to desire possession of relics, is the following:

> "If then it is a religious desire to visit those places, in which Christ entered and suffered and resurrected and from where he ascended, and it is a benediction to take and to have some soil from the same places or even a piece, at least similar to a straw, from the very wood of the Cross itself, think what bigger and fuller grace it would be to look at a living old man in testimony of divine Grace".[129]

This practice may have been more widespread than one could think: when the monk Iacobus was sick, but not dead yet, many people arrived from the neighbouring towns to take his body. The inhabitants had to defend his life with weapons and to simply bring away the still living monk.[130]

But apart from these 'excessive reactions', a demand creates generally an offer, and so the commerce of relics was quickly born, with all the problematic consequences depending on it.[131] Obtaining relics through purchase modified the form of capital and of social value of the relics themselves; in the case of private persons, in particular, while relics received as gifts implicitly insist on the bond with the donor, purchased ones are part of the performance of wealth and status, and the strongest element, as anthropologists have observed, is the pride for the possession of the object.[132]

As P. Geary showed for the Carolingian period "the popular desire for contact with holy men" increased the demand, which "outstripped the supply", thus generating a stronger relic trade in response.[133] The model seems applicable also to the fourth and fifth centuries: as Geary properly underlined, this kind of commerce was convenient for the merchants,[134] but also interesting for the

[129] Paul. Nol., *Ep.* 49.14.
[130] *Hist. Mon.* 21.9.
[131] Fichtenau 1952, p. 76; Buenacasa Pérez 2003, p. 133.
[132] Sbardella 2007, p. 177.
[133] Geary 1979, pp. 13-18; Geary 1990^2, pp. 37-38. See also Dooley 1931, p. 21; McCulloh 1980, p. 314. This phenomenon is recognized by Clark 2001, pp. 163-164, also for the late 4th century, and connected to the identity foundation of Christian communities.
[134] Geary 1979, p. 17: "For the merchants, relics were an excellent article of trade. They were small and easily transported, since even entire bodies of saints centuries old were nothing more than dust and a few bones which could be placed in a small cloth bag. As highly desirable luxury items, they brought an excellent price for very little capital investment. The risks were immaterial except for the danger of the wrath of the local populace at having their patron stolen if one bothered to steal genuine relics and the constant danger that the thief might himself lose the relics to another thief it he were not careful. Perhaps best of all, owing to lack of communication and information as well as to the peculiar nature of the items traded, the fact that the body of a particular saint had

bishops and the other persons involved, who could thus acquire – as it has been shown – objects which clearly enhanced their social capital. Commerce of relics was thus becoming widespread in the second half of the fourth century, and was getting widespread as a bottom-up issue,[135] also because the Church in the beginning was opposed to the commerce of relics, as it was opposed to the private ownership of them. Gaudentius of Brescia writes, between 398 and the first years of the fifth century, that after the execution of the Forty Martyrs of Sebaste,

> "when the ashes of the burned bodies, according to the orders of the persecutor, were thrown in the river, were not lacking devout hands, which either took away by stealing a part of the ashes or bought it for a price".[136]

Gaudentius is at least projecting back to the first quarter of the fourth century a practice that he knew and against which he was not critical – maybe also because in this case the purchase allowed to 'rescue' the relics at all.

This should not surprise since the two elements are deeply interconnected in the creation of a demand and the birth of the systems for its satisfaction. But there were other reasons for the ecclesiastical institutions to oppose the commerce of relics: a problem could be seen in the act of breaking down the bodies of the saints to proceed to their sale – or generally in the manumission of sacred objects. This point was quickly solved: that the relics go on having power even when they are cut into pieces is admitted in the second half of the fourth century by Gregory of Nazianzus,[137] and, in the West, by Victricius of Rouen and Paulinus of Nola:

> "yet the influence of an interred saint is not confined to the area where his whole body lies. Wherever there is part of a saint's body, there, too his power emerges. God takes a hand in offering proof of his blessed merits; the great power evinced

already been sold did not prevent one from selling it again to another customer at some future time". The same concept is repeated in Geary 1990², p. 52.

135 The idea that the commerce of relics was not really widespread till the 9th century, and that it did not involve persons of a high rank (so Hermann-Mascard 1975, pp. 341-342) must of course be abandoned: Geary 1990², p. 111, who argues for an enormous growth of the phenomenon since the final 8th century BCE.

136 Gaud. Brix., *Serm.* 17.34: *cum cineres exustorum corporum, mandato persecutoris, in fluvium jacerentur, non defuerunt religiosae manus, quae partem cineris vel furto eriperent, vel pretio compararent.*

137 Theodoret wrote that every single part of the body of the martyr has the same virtue and property of the whole body (*Graec. Aff. Cur.* 8: PG 83.1012 B-C), but a similar idea had already been expressed by Greg. Naz., *Or.* 4.69, who says that the drops of blood and "the small signs of martyrium" have the same power as entire bodies. See Delehaye 1933², pp. 62-63; Kaplan 1999, pp. 24-25.

> even in a particle of the saints' ashes proclaims the power of the bodies of apostles at the prompting of the World".[138]

Additionally, it could appear deeply problematic the fact that the discovery, translation and eventually sale of relics implied the opening of tombs and the manumission of corpses[139] – there is here no space to deal with this juridical problem, but it really does not seem to have been the real heart of the question, and quite quickly legislation allowed exceptions and special rules.[140]

It is therefore necessary to look further: a mention, and a condemnation, of relics commerce is to be found in Athanasius' *Festal Letter*, where this behavior is attributed to the Melitians:

> "Who can despise the heretics as much as they deserve? Who would not just like to run into them when they are insulting the bodies of the saints like false prophets? Who could endure unmoved the spectacle of the bodies of prophets and the bodies of martyrs thrown up and exhibited? This is not Christian behavior; Paul did not bequeath this to us; neither patriarchs nor prophets did this in the course of the ages. But it is the Melitians who have turned in this direction, to

[138] Victr. Rotom., *Laud. Sanct.* 9 (see Canetti 2006, pp. 123-124); Paul. Nol., *Carm.* 27.443-448 (transl. P. G. Walsh). Kötting 1965, pp. 23-24, dates around 350 the practice of dividing the bodies of the martyrs, even if admitting that it diffused probably earlier in the East. Crook 2000, pp. 20-22 also argues for a diffusion of the practice also in the West already in the 4th century. See also Hahn 2010, pp. 294-295. Angenendt 1992, pp. 39-40 and 2007², pp. 152-155, tried to demonstrate that this practice was unknown to the West still in the 6th (and till the 9th) century, using the argument that only 'redundant' parts (hair, nails, teeth and so on) were detached and distributed. This demonstration is not convincing, since most of the sources do not say exactly what part of the body has been separated, and Paulinus and Victricius, as shown, speak in general of the body. Additionally no ancient sources introduce in their reflection this distinction between 'essential' and 'redundant' parts. We must presume that such parts were only broken when because of particular symbolic and 'political' reasons it was necessary to keep in the community a still 'complete' body. Gregory the Great's famous argument, in the letter to Constantina (*Reg. ep.* 4.30), that it is not "Western use" to break down the bodies of the Saints must be understood as a discourse used by the pope to legitimate and 'universalize' his necessity of keeping in Rome the entire bodies, in particular of Peter and Paul, which were necessary as signs and markers of his power, and is indeed contradicted by a variant of the same episode, in which the request, rejected by Gregory, to receive corporeal parts of Paul, came from Franks: Garitte 1966, p. 408. As Canetti 2002, pp. 44-45, has underlined, it should be avoided to believe literally to the arguments used by Gregory in his letter, and it is necessary to understand whether Gregory was not reacting to an always more diffused practice that he still tried to contrast – exactly as in the case of the sale of relics.

[139] Mango 1990, pp. 51-53.

[140] See *infra*, n. 147.

> profit from it. It is being shrewd like Jeroboam who sold doves and changed money in the temple, as the Scripture says. There are no two ways about it: to those who were in error at that time and were driven out by whipping the Saviour said: "Do not make my Father's house a tradinghouse" These [Melitians] will doubtless hear Him saying to them: "Do not sell the bodies of my martyrs and do not make their fine confession a commodity to be traded, for the love of money", for they who commit such villainy will doubtless receive a commensurate punishment".[141]

It has been wondered if Athanasius' accusations are true,[142] but the accusation in itself shows that such a practice was existing and imaginable. Through such a sale, then, heretics and schismatic groups, as the Melitians, can come to possess holy relics of martyrs and saints. The problem is therefore connected to the fact that the relics, as such, should not be sold and should not receive a monetary evaluation, because the commoditization, destroying the "value de lien", implies a complete lack of control on the purchaser – which is not acceptable for a sacred object, whose quality as sacred must be preserved through transactions with persons who share the same beliefs.

In 386 CE, a law addressed to the praetorian prefect Cynegius forbids transfer-ring bodies, selling the relics of the martyrs and trafficking with them.[143] What is allowed is to build cult buildings on the relics of the martyrs – collective insti-tutional property and religious practice. It is perhaps interesting to underline that previous laws about violators of tombs insist on the fact that their aim were construction materials,[144] while in the second half of the fourth century the most precious objects to steal are the bodies, exactly because the commerce of relics had assumed a dimension which could interest and worry the lawgiver – the chronology is the same that can be reconstructed from other categories of sources.[145] The law of 386 CE will also appear in the Justinianic code slightly changed, or better simplified to a "no one should sell or commerce in the martyrs",[146] and a general analysis of the inclusions and modifications of older legislative texts in the Justinian code show without any doubt the radical change in interests which had intervened.[147]

[141] CSCO 151.44; quoted from Wortley 2006a, pp. 23-24.
[142] Wortley 2006a, pp. 23-25.
[143] *CTh.* 9.17.7.
[144] *CTh.* 9.17.1-4.
[145] Crook 2000, p. 23; Wortley 2006b, pp. 201-211.
[146] *CJ* 1.2.3: *Nemo martyres distrahat, nemo mercetur.*
[147] The title *de sepulchro violato*, *CJ* 9.19, contains a first law by Gordian (240), which forbade the sale of "things destined to religion" – it is of course a Christian interpretation that this law should fall under the title "the violation of tombs". *CTh.* 9.17.2 becomes *CJ* 9.19.3, much shorter and simplified: it is not clear anymore that the main problem in the original text were the stones. *CTh.* 9.17.3 disappears, while *CTh.* 9.17.4 is preserved. Of

As shown by Augustine, these rules were more or less observed, and around 400 CE Augustine also protests the existence of

> "many hypocrite persons wearing the habit; people who hang around the provinces and no one knows who sent them. They continuously move. Some of them commerce in the relics of the martyrs – if they are even martyrs",

sighs the bishop of Hippo Regius.[148] The already mentioned famous letter which Gregory the Great wrote to Constantina tells us that two years earlier monks from Greece were surprised in the night while unburying bodies from a cemetery. Asked why, they confessed that they would bring the bodies to Greece "as if they were relics of saints".[149] The doubt on the authenticity of the relics is a further confirmation of the level the demand – and therefore of presence on the market – of such commodities had reached.

The sale and the commerce of relics of first class, pieces of bodies of saints, were then indeed forbidden by the imperial law, while the commerce in relics of second and third class was allowed, and practiced. The existence itself of these further forms of relics, as it has been mentioned, has even been explained as a consequence of the extremely high demand for such objects.[150] But this was not enough and therefore there was, also in spite of ecclesiastical opposition, a widespread movement to an always broader practice of relics' exchange and commerce. Theoretically the relics have all the same properties – and different

Julian's law *CTh.* 9.17.5, the first to attack Christian practice, not only because it generally criticizes violation of tombs to find "ornaments" (which means building material but also bodies ashes), but also because it attacks the practice of celebrating funerals "through dense crowds of people and through the greatest throngs of bystanders" (on the connection of this law with previous texts about movement of bodies, especially in relation to the problem of *translationes* by day, see Laubry 2007, pp. 168-169), is kept only the first part. Cynegius' text, as said, is moved to *CJ* 1.2.3, but reappears also at *CJ* 3.44.14 (*de religiosis et sumptibus funerum*), which states "no one should move a human body to another place, without the permission of the Emperor" (on the general previous role of the Emperor in the movement of bodies, which was probably rare and connected to his role as *pontifex maximus*, see Laubry 2007, pp. 172-175). Another law, released by Diocletian and Maximian in 287 CE (*CJ* 3.44.10) allowed the translation of bodies which had not been given yet to their definitive eternal burial; it can be that this law was used sometimes to cover the moving of relics (and was maybe also used by Julian to justify the translation of S. Babylas out of the sanctuary of Daphne), but most of all its presence here makes evident, in addition to the entire transformation of the title 9.19, how the interest has changed, and the body – not the marble – is now at the center of the attention of the lawgivers when dealing with the violation of tombs.

[148] Aug., *Op. mon.* 28.36. See Buenacasa Pérez 2003, pp. 132-133.

[149] Greg. M., *Reg. ep.* 4.30.

[150] Heinzelmann 1979, p. 22.

sources tell, with different characters, the famous story of a cloth, left on the tomb of S. Peter, which bled when cut;[151] Gregory of Tours tells us that such cloths were afterwards heavier as before.[152] Sarcophaguses with holes to produce *eulogiai* are also known archaeologically.[153]

So-called third class relics are thus theologically relics exactly as the other ones, not less powerful, and are still today the most exchanged ones.[154] From similar objects Gregory the Great realized those *benedictiones* which he sent to his friends.[155] But if the religious component could be unchanged, it was not so on the social and economical level where the difference between the real bodies of the saints and the contact relics was neatly perceived.

The same distinction between 'primary', 'notable' relics and the other ones makes the first more desirable; if some of them are through the force of the law made inalienable or at least regulated in the possible forms of their transactions, their value becomes higher – and when sold, illegally, they had a completely different price. Dietrich Claude wrote that we miss sure indications that relics were among the objects of commerce, and that it is difficult to recognize if their transportation was caused by "devotion, passion of collection or even desire of gain". [156] Claude's terms are simply wrong because he presupposes an incompatibility between these three terms which does not exist. Economic rules reintroduced thus again that difference which was clearly perceived by the population, for which the tertiary relics were 'less interesting' or better 'less powerful' and which had been denied by the Church:

[151] Greg. M., *Reg. ep.* 4.30. See Garitte 1966, p. 408 (Latin translation of the episode, known through a Georgian source). Many other sources refer of miracles operated by or through contact relics.

[152] Greg. Tur., *Glor. Mart.* 27. See also Greg. Tur., *Virt. Mart.* 1.11. Bed., *HEAngl.* 3.3 also describes a tomb with holes to take dust, which can be then put in water and drank to heal illnesses. See Delehaye 1933², p. 118; McCulloh 1980, pp. 315-317; Crook 2000, p 26; Thacker 2000, p. 252.

[153] E.g. *Treasures of Heaven*, n. 4.

[154] See Sbardella 2002, pp. 247-249. The power of third class relics is already clear in the apocryphal Acts of Thomas (170). On the meaning of *brandeum*, which indicates only cloth, and not all contact relics, see McCulloh 1976, pp. 165-169. On the distinction of the three classes, see Dooley 1931, pp. 3-5; Hermann-Mascard 1975, pp. 41-49. See also, for an even more detailed classification, Kohl 2003, pp. 48-52. Canon Law distinguishes only among 'notable' relics (first class of particular significance) and 'non-notable' (all the others); of the first one private property is forbidden, but this will happen only in a much later moment: Hermann-Mascard 1975, pp. 327-328.

[155] E.g. Greg. M., *Reg. ep.* 1.29-30 (591); 3.33 (593); 7.23 refers of a key sent to Theoctista and shows clearly that also such objects can perform miracles.

[156] Claude 1985, p. 103.

> "l'offre devant faire face à la demand, ce sont également les ossements qui font l'objet principal du commerce des reliques",

as Donceel-Voûte wrote.[157]

What happens is therefore the spreading of a practice in a bottom-up movement,[158] symmetrical to that other diffusion of the practice of the theft of relics which, as G. Duby and P. Geary have shown,[159] is rather a top-down practice, since in the beginning the potentates, the aristocracies and the churches began to make use of dealers and thieves, and only later the practice was widespread to common people. Later indeed also 'institutions' would proceed to buy relics, as in the famous case of Liutprand buying the body of Augustine from the Saracens, which could still be justified with the necessity of getting the relic in Christian hands, as in the case of the 'ransom' of the Mandylion from the Arabs,[160] or in many other examples to be found in medieval chronicles.[161]

4. Money for the saints?

> "Il était acquis que les reliques étaient dotées d'une nature spirituelle qui leur conférait un statut juridique particulier interdisant certaines opérations",

writes Boiron.[162] Nonetheless, they were still sold and bought, under the pressure of a high demand. Even Marx, in the first book of the *Capital*, will cite the bones of the martyrs as example of the object which does not save itself from the logic of capitalism, and becomes purchasable – that extreme form of commodization in capitalism that he would call "fetishism",[163] in which money, being able to

[157] Donceel-Voûte 1995, pp. 186-188.

[158] The expression 'bottom-up' does not imply concepts such as 'popular devotion' or 'popular religiosity', which have been rightly abandoned, and of course I do not mean in any case to propose the existence of a double model of a population divided in 'elites' and 'people', as in the model of the democratization of culture (Brown 1981, pp. 12-22; Canetti 1999, p. 256; Carlà 2010, pp. 266-270; Hartmann 2010, p. 631). What is meant is rather the wide diffusion of a sensitivity, of an exigency, which economically is definable as 'demand' and which provokes a practical and then also an institutional answer.

[159] Geary 1990², p. 44.

[160] Cutler 2001, p. 252.

[161] Many examples are presented by Klein 2004b, pp. 306-312, who claims that after the Fourth Crusade in Byzantium "the distribution of relics can no longer be described in terms of either gift-giving or theft, but must rather be considered in terms of sale and purchase as an immediate result of the empire's dire economic situation" – but, as it has been shown, such dynamics were at work already much earlier.

[162] Boiron 2006, p. 26.

[163] On fetishism in Marx see Kohl 2003, pp. 91-98.

buy everything, becomes the object par excellence. But at stake here is not the general birth of wares, the overcoming of the use value in a 'mystical' meaning: the relic has in itself a symbolic value and is in itself of course characterized by a transcendent meaning, which is not connected with the general commoditization – according to Marx typical of capitalism.[164] To pinpoint is rather with "the entanglement of gift and commodity", as analyzed among others by Appadurai and Osteen,[165] the tension between the two categories and the actual continuous switching between them in the 'biography' of single objects, as made clear by Kopytoff.[166] In the end, the sale of relics is not the extreme form of capitalism, which does not rescue even the sacred objects from appearing on the market; on the contrary it is the most basilar form of presence in an object of particular values which make of it a fetish in the meaning of an object of desire – of demand.[167] Relics can thus become, when introduced in exchange circuits, what Appadurai defined as "commodities by diversion",

> "objects placed in a commodity state though originally specifically protected from it".[168]

At stake is substantially the general short circuit between sacred objects, gift giving and commercial exchange, which is not typical only of capitalist societies. *Premium* and *pretium* were maybe not so well separated as Avitus of Vienne would have wished, and as the example of Vigilius proposed in the beginning shows. This had been understood already by Silvestre in 1952, but he presumed, wrongly, that the distinction between gift (*donatio*) and sale (*venditio*) was then not so clearly and neatly drawn.[169] This is not the point; the point is the status of such particular objects, of which the sale is perceived as inappropriate but still is practiced because of a demand connected directly to the 'social capital' incorporated in the objects themselves.

[164] Complete commodification should consist in the abolishment of all forms of social relations, while in partial commodification social relations are still embedded in the community but partly driven out by the existence of markets: Van de Klundert – Van de Ven 1999, p. 12. See Appadurai 1986, pp. 7-9 on Marx and the existence of commodities also in pre-capitalistic societies.
[165] Appadurai 1986, pp. 11-13; Osteen 2002, p. 235.
[166] Kopytoff 1986, pp. 80-83.
[167] See Appadurai 1986, pp. 23-24; Thomas 1991, pp. 14-22 and 73-75; Godelier 1996, pp. 98-100.
[168] Appadurai 1986, p. 16.
[169] Silvestre 1952, p. 729. The mistake is therefore exactly the opposite of Marx's one: here is the pre-capitalistic society, which knew some sort of intermediate form between gift and commercial exchange, based on the expectance of a supernatural protection, the explanation of the commerce of relics.

In Antiquity as today it is problematic to accept the fact that objects with a particular symbolic and / or sacred value can be exchanged for money, which is perceived as 'cold' and inappropriate to express such values – i.e. the general unacceptance of exchange between objects to which different moral qualities are attributed.[170] This brought in some cultures to the construction of parallel currency systems for different kinds of commodities, organized hierarchically,[171] but the existence of a double system of reference is not extraneous to our own culture.[172] This is not the place to pose the question of why there should be this sort of perception – a problem faced by anthropologists, philosophers, economists, sociologists, etc.[173] It is here necessary to admit the existence of this problem and to recognize that the commerce of relics, with the characters which had been described, which developed already in the fourth-sixth centuries CE, is part of this broader context.

The problem is indeed still not solved, and the short circuit which surrounds a 'sacred' object, theoretically inalienable, but exchangeable, with a social capital which can be converted in an economic one, is still topical.[174] And the nature of inalienable objects can lead to forms of moral and juridical regulation of their transactions. Canon law still distinguishes, after S. Thomas, between notable relics, which must stay in the churches and are excluded from private possession, as it has been said, and non-notable relics, all the other ones.[175] Relics are inalienable, their sale is forbidden;[176] fabrication, sale, distribution or exposure to veneration of false relics is punished with excommunication.[177] From the ninth century Europe knew the great merchants of relics, made immortal by Chaucer and Boccaccio,[178] but the synod of Constance allowed bishops to excommunicate anyone who took profit out of relics.[179] Still later we find the two most famous

[170] Kopytoff 1986, pp. 73-74. Kopytoff describes the process of subtracting some objects or categories of objects from commodity exchange as "singularization".

[171] Kopytoff 1986, pp. 71-72; Douglas – Isherwood 1996^2, pp. 95-102; Godelier 1996, pp. 153-154.

[172] Godbout 2000^2, p. 18.

[173] Camerer 1999, pp. 197-198; Douglas – Isherwood 1996^2, pp. 36-38; Hénaff 2002, in particular pp. 24-40; Godbout 2000^2, e.g. pp. 230-234.

[174] Kopytoff 1986, pp. 76-77. Godelier 1996, pp. 288-289, connects this e.g. with today's problems concerning the sale of human bodies and their parts (organs, blood etc.).

[175] Canon 1281-1282. Dooley 1931, pp. 62-70; Boiron 2006, pp. 19-20.

[176] Hermann-Mascard 1975, p. 357; Boiron 2006, pp. 27-28. On the problematic relation between Church and money, see also Bourdieu 1994, pp. 202-211.

[177] Canon 1289; 2326. Dooley 1931, pp. 108-114; Boiron 2006, pp. 28-31.

[178] Boccaccio, *Decameron* 6.10.

[179] It has long been thought that canon 62 of the Lateran Council (1215) had forbidden the sale of relics (so still Angenendt 2007^2, p. 162); but already Silvestre 1952, pp. 723-728, showed that the canon is to be understood in another way, as prohibition to take the relics

examples of relic sale, in 1222, when Philip II Augustus of France bought from Baldwin I of Jerusalem a piece of the True Cross and in 1239, when Louis IX bought from Baldwin II the thorn crown, for 10000 gold coins. Or better: Baldwin gave as a gift the crown to Louis; Louis thankfully offered him a monetary gift; even Deusdona commerce proceeded in this way.[180] The short circuit creates a loophole where it is possible to intervene, and this happened already in Late Antiquity: when in 421 CE Pulcheria acquired for Constantinople S. Stephen's arm, she gave to the bishop of Jerusalem a huge amount of money and a monumental cross encrusted with gem, and the relic was qualified as a 'counter-gift'.[181]

Even today relics are claimed not to have a price, but they are actually exchanged against money – money which is meant as offer or as payment for the reliquary or for the job, and purchase is next to gift still the most practiced way to get relics.[182] Just a few examples: it is enough to play a little bit with *Google* to find the strict defensors of relics who founded the association "Apostolate for Holy Relics", claiming that they want to protect relics of the saints from purchase by irresponsible people and reintroduce their proper veneration.[183] Next to them, the "Society For All the Saints" from El Paso reminds us that it is forbidden to sell first and second class relics – but also that the prohibition falls if it helps rescuing the relic from "desecrating hands".[184] But people still want relics in their private possession: so it is possible to find the "Discount Catholic Store", where relics appear as a merchandise category immediately in the first menu – only 'allowed' Third Class relics.[185] Nonetheless other pages indeed do sell even corporeal relics without bigger problems, informing the clients that

> "All information is kept completely confidential. Your privacy and security is important to us. Thanks and Happy Shopping".[186]

It is not all; another page sells even primary relics, as an *ex ossibus* of Henry II.

out of reliquaries (see also Hermann-Mascard 1975, pp. 214-216 on the exposition of relics, and pp. 348-350, where she disagrees with Silvestre's reconstruction), even if he recognized how this rule *de facto* prohibited the "petty commerce" of relics. See also Dooley 1931, p. 29.

[180] Guiraud 1892, pp. 87-88; Hermann-Mascard 1975, pp. 350-352; Klein 2004b, p. 308.

[181] Theoph. 86.26-31 De Boor. For similar modern examples connected to surrogate motherhood, see Kopytoff 1986, pp. 85-86.

[182] Sbardella 2007, 171-172.

[183] http://www.apostolateforholyrelics.com/mission-statement.php (last access: 3rd August 2012).

[184] http://www.forallthesaints.info/index.htm (last access: 3rd Aug. 2012).

[185] http://www.discountcatholicstore.com/ (last access: 3rd Aug. 2012).

[186] http://www.griffithsprayerchaplets.com/ (last access: 3rd Aug. 2012).

But the disclaimer appearing at the top of the page intervenes in the loophole created by the short circuit between gift giving and commercial exchange: the relic itself is not on sale – it is given as a gift to the person who buys the reliquiary.[187]

That is the central point: on *Ebay*, like in Late Antiquity, objects with a particular social and symbolic value have to be protected and exchanged, alienated being unalienable, and in this intermingling of preservation and alienation the alternative, opposed and at the same time complementary forms of gift giving and commercial exchange show then as today their characters and their contradictions.

Bibliography

Angenendt, Arnold: *Der 'ganze' und 'unverweste' Leib – eine Leitidee der Reliquienverehrung bei Gregor von Tours und Beda Venerabilis*, in: *Aus Archiven und Bibliotheken. Festschrift für Raymund Kottje zum 65. Geburtstag*, ed. by Hubert Mordek, Frankfurt 1992, pp. 33-50.

Angenendt, Arnold: *Heilige und Reliquien. Die Geschichte ihres Kultes vom frühen Christentum bis zur Gegenwart*, München 2007^2.

Appadurai, Arjun: *Introduction: Commodities and the Politics of Value*, in: *The Social Life of Things: Commodities in Cultural Perspective*, ed. by Arjun Appadurai, Cambridge 1986, pp. 3-63.

Augé, Marc: *Le dieu objet*, Paris 1988.

Bausinger, Hermann: *Die Dinge der Macht*, in: *Die Macht der Dinge. Symbolische Kommunikation und kulturelles Handeln*, ed. by Andreas Hartmann – Peter Höher – Christiane Cantauw – Uwe Meiners – Silke Meyer, Münster 2011, pp. 27-34.

Blandin, Bernard: *La construction du social par les objets*, Paris 2002.

Boesch Gajano, Sofia: *Reliques et pouvoirs*, in: *Les reliques. Objets, cultes, symboles*, ed. by Edina Bozóky – Anne-Marie Hélvetius, Turnhout 1999, pp.255-269.

Boiron, Stéphane: *Définition et statut juridique des reliques dans le droit canonique classique*, in: *Reliques et sainteté dans l'espace médiéval*, ed. by Jean-Luc Deuffic, Saint-Denis 2006, pp. 19-31.

Bourdieu, Pierre: *Raisons pratiques. Sur la théorie de l'action*, Paris 1994.

Bowes, Kimberly D.: *Private Worship, Public Values, and Religious Change in Late Antiquity*, Cambridge 2008.

Brenk, Beat: *Microstoria sotto la Chiesa dei SS. Giovanni e Paolo: la cristianizzazione di una casa privata*, in: *RIA*, s. 3, 18 (1995), pp. 169-206.

Brenk, Beat: *Die Christianisierung der spätrömischen Welt. Stadt, Land, Haus, Kirche und Kloster in frühchristlicher Zeit*, Wiesbaden 2003.

[187] http://antiquariat-grundmann.de/Luxuspapier/Andachtsgraphik/Andachtsbildchen/Reliquien/reliquien.html (last access: 3rd Aug. 2012).

Brown, Peter: *Eastern and Western Christendom in Late Antiquity: A Parting of the Ways*, in: *The Orthodox Churches and the West*, ed. by Derek Baker, Oxford 1976, pp. 1-24 = Id.: *Society and the Holy in Late Antiquity*, Berkeley 1982, pp. 166-195.

Brown, Peter: *Relics and Social Status in the Age of Gregory of Tours*, Reading 1977 = Id.: *Society and the Holy in Late Antiquity*, Berkeley 1982, pp. 222-250.

Brown, Peter: *The Cult of the Saints. Its Rise and Function in Latin Christianity*, Chicago 1981.

Buenacasa Pérez, Carles: *La instrumentalización económica del culto a las reliquias: una importante fuente de ingresos para las iglesias tardoantiguas occidentales (ss. IV-VIII)*, in: *Santos, obispos y reliquias*, ed. by Luis A. García Moreno – María Elvira Gil Egea – Sebastián Rascón Marquez – Margarita Vallejo Girvés, Alcalá 2003, pp. 123-140.

Camerer, Colin: *Gifts as Economic Signals and Social Symbols*, in: *American Journal of Sociology* 94 (1988), *Supplement: Organizations and Institutions: Sociological and Economic Approaches to the Analysis of Social Structure*, pp. S180-S214.

Cameron, Averil: *The Early Religious Policies of Justin II*, in: *The Orthodox Churches and the West*, ed. by Derek Baker, Oxford 1976, pp. 51-67.

Caner, Daniel F.: *Alms, Blessings, Offerings: The Repertoire of Christian Gifts in Early Byzantium*, in: *The Gift in Antiquity*, ed. by Michael Satlow, Malden – Oxford 2013, pp. 25-44.

Canetti, Luigi: *Culto dei santi e dissezione dei morti tra Antichità e Medioevo*, in: *RSLR* 35 (1999), pp. 241-278.

Canetti, Luigi: *Frammenti di eternità. Corpi e reliquie tra Antichità e Medioevo*, Roma 2002.

Canetti, Luigi: *Verso un'archeologia delle collezioni. Reliquie e tesori tra Antichità e Medioevo*, in: *Sanctorum* 3 (2006), pp. 113-139.

Carlà, Filippo: *Milan, Ravenna, Rome: Some Reflections on the Cult of the Saints and on Civic Politics in Late Antique Italy*, in: *RSLR* 45 (2010), pp. 197-272.

Carlà, Filippo: *Gold and Gift in Gregory of Tours: The Social Importance of 'Élite Markers' in Merovingian Gaul*, in: *Just for Show? Displaying Wealth and Performing Status in the Ancient World*, ed. by Marta García Morcillo – Silke Knippschild, Cambridge, forthcoming.

Castellanos, Santiago M.: *Las reliquias de santos y su papel social: cohesion comunitaria y control episcopal en Hispania (ss. V-VII)*, in *Polis* 8 (1996), pp. 5-21.

Cheal, David: *The Gift Economy*, London-New York 1988.

Clark, Elizabeth A.: *Claims on the Bones of Saint Stephen: The Partisans of Melania and Eudocia*, in: *Church History* 51 (1982), pp. 141-156.

Clark, Gillian: *Translating Relics: Victricius of Rouen and Fourth-Century Debate*, in: *EME* 10 (2001), pp. 161-176.

Claude, Dietrich: *Der Handel im westlichen Mittelmeer während des Frühmittelalters*, Göttingen 1985.

Conway, Martin: *St. Radegund's Reliquiary at Poitiers*, in: *The Antiquaries Journal* 3 (1923), pp. 1-12.

Cracco Ruggini, Lellia: *Le morts qui voyagent: le repatriement, l'exil, la glorification*, in: *La mort au quotidien dans le monde romain*, ed. by François Hinard – Marie-Françoise Lambert, Paris 1995, pp. 117-134.

Crook, John: *The Architectural Setting of the Cult of Saints in the Early Christian West, c. 300-1200*, Oxford 2000.

Cutler, Anthony: *Gifts and Gift Exchange as Aspects of the Byzantine, Arab, and Related Economies*, in: *DOP* 55 (2001), pp. 247-278.

Delehaye, Hippolyte: *Les origines du culte des martyrs*, Bruxelles 1933².

Diefenbach, Steffen: *Römische Erinnerungsräume*, Berlin – New York 2007.

Donceel-Voûte, Pauline: *Le rôle des reliquaires dans les pèlerinages*, in: *Akten des XII. Internationalen Kongresses für christliche Archäologie*, Münster 1995, vol. 1, pp. 184-205.

Dooley, Eugene A.: *Church Law on Sacred Relics*, PhD Dissertation, Catholic University of America, Washington D.C., 1931.

Doublet, Georges: *Inscriptions de Paphlagonie*, in: *BCH* 13 (1889), pp. 293-319.

Douglas, Mary – Baron Isherwood: *The World of Goods. Towards an Anthropology of Consumption*, London – New York 1996².

Elsner, John: *Replicating Palestine and reversing the Reformation. Pilgrimage and Collecting at Bobbio, Monza and Walsingham*, in: *Journal of the History of Collections* 9 (1997), pp. 117-130.

Fichtenau, Heinrich: *Zum Reliquienwesen im früheren Mittelalter*, in: *Mitteilungen des Instituts für Österreichische Geschichtsforschung* 60 (1952), pp. 60-89.

Garitte, Gérard: *Histoires édifiantes géorgiennes*, in: *Byzantion* 36 (1966), pp. 396-423.

Geary, Patrick J.: *The Ninth-Century Relic Trade: A Response to Popular Piety?*, in: *Religion and the People, 800-1700*, ed. by James Obelkevich, Chapel Hill 1979, pp. 8-19.

Geary, Patrick J.: *The Saint and the Shrine: The Pilgrim's Goal in the Middle Ages*, in: *Wallfahrt kennt keine Grenzen*, ed. by Lenz Kriss-Rettenbeck – Gerda Möhler, Münich 1984, pp. 265-274 = Id.: *Living with the Dead in the Middle Ages*, Ithaca 1994, pp. 163-176.

Geary, Patrick J.: *Sacred Commodities: The Circulation of Medieval Relics*, in: *The Social Life of Things: Commodities in Cultural Perspective*, ed. by Arjun Appadurai, Cambridge 1986, pp. 169-191.

Geary, Patrick J.: *Furta Sacra. Thefts of Relics in the Central Middle Ages*, Princeton 1990².

Godbout, Jacques T.: *L'esprit du don*, Paris 2000².

Godelier, Maurice: *L'énigme du don*, Paris 1996.

Guiance, Ariel: *Santos, reliquias y milagros en la hagiografía visigoda*, in: *Reliques et sainteté dans l'espace médiéval*, ed. by Jean-Luc Deuffic, Saint-Denis 2006, pp. 245-260.

Guiraud, Jean: *Le commerce des reliques au commencement du IXe siècle*, in: *Mélanges G. B. De Rossi*, Paris 1892, pp. 73-95.

Gumbrecht, Hans Ulrich: *Production of Presence. What Meaning cannot convey*, Stanford 2004.

Hahn, Cynthia: *Collector and Saint: Queen Radegund and Devotion to the Relic of the True Cross*, in: *Word and Image: A Journal of Verbal/Visual Enquiry* 22 (2006), pp. 268-274.

Hahn, Cynthia: *What do Reliquiaries do for Relics?*, in: *Numen* 57 (2010), pp. 284-316.

Hartmann, Andreas: *Zwischen Relikt und Reliquie. Objektbezogene Erinnerungspraktiken in antiken Gesellschaften*, Berlin 2010.

Heinzelmann, Martin: *Translationsberichte und andere Quellen des Reliquienkultes*, Turnhout 1979.

Hénaff, Marcel: *Le prix de la verité. Le don, l'argent, la philosophie*, Paris 2002; German transl.: *Der Preis der Wahrheit. Gabe, Geld und Philosophie*, Frankfurt 2009.

Hermann-Mascard, Nicole: *Les reliques des saints. Formation coutumière d'un droit*, Paris 1975.

Hodder, Ian: *Entangled. An Archaeology of the Relations between Humans and Things*, Chichester 2012.

Hunt, Edward D.: *The Traffic in Relics: Some Late Roman Evidence*, in: *The Byzantine Saint*, ed. by Sergei Hackel, London 1981, pp. 171-180.

Hunt, Edward D.: *Holy Land Pilgrimage in the Later Roman Empire (AD 312-460)*, Oxford 1982.

Hunter, David G.: *Vigilantius of Calagurris and Victricius of Rouen: Ascetics, Relics and Clerics in Late Roman Gaul*, in: *JECS* 7 (1999), pp. 401-430.

James, Liz: *Bearing Gifts from the East: Imperial Relic Hunters abroad*, in: *Eastern Approaches to Byzantium*, ed. by Antony Eastmond, Aldershot 2001, pp. 119-131.

Kaplan, Michel: *De la dépouille à la relique: formation du culte des saints à Byzance du Ve au XIIe siècle*, in: *Les reliques. Objets, cultes, symboles*, ed. by Edina Bozóky – Anne-Marie Hélvetius, Turnhout 1999, pp. 19-38.

Klauser, Theodor: *Vom Heroon zur Märtyrerbasilika. Neue archäologische Balkanfunde und ihre Deutung* (1942) = Id.: *Gesammelte Arbeiten zur Liturgiegeschichte, Kirchengeschichte und christlichen Archäologie*, Münster 1974, pp. 275-291.

Klein, Holger A.: *Byzanz, der Westen und das 'wahre' Kreuz. Die Geschichte einer Reliquie und ihrer künstlerlischen Fassung in Byzanz und im Abendland*, Wiesbaden 2004a.

Klein, Holger A.: *Eastern Objects and Western Desires: Relics and Reliquiaries between Byzantium and the West*, in: *DOP* 58 (2004b), pp. 283-314.

Klein, Holger A.: *Sacred Relics and Imperial Ceremonies at the Great Palace of Constantinople*, in: *Visualisierungen von Herrschaft. Frühmittelalterliche Residenzen: Gestalt und Zeremoniell*, ed. by Franz Alto Bauer, Istanbul 2006, pp. 79-99.

Kohl, Karl-Heinz: *Die Macht der Dinge: Geschichte und Theorie sakraler Objekte*, München 2003.

Kopytoff, Igor: *The Cultural Biography of Things: Commoditization as Process*, in: *The Social Life of Things: Commodities in Cultural Perspective*, ed. by Arjun Appadurai, Cambridge 1986, pp. 64-91.

Kötting, Bernhard: *Reliquienverehrung, ihre Entstehung und ihre Formen*, in: *Trierer Theologische Zeitschrift* 67 (1958), pp. 321-334.

Kötting, Bernhard: *Der frühchristliche Reliquienkult und die Bestattung im Kirchengebäude*, Köln-Opladen 1965.

Latour, Bruno: *Une sociologie sans objet? Remarques sur l'interobjectivité*, in: *Sociologie du Travail* 4 (1994), pp. 587-607.

Laubry, Nicolas: *Le transfert des corps dans l'empire romaine: problèmes d'épigraphie, de religion et de droit romain*, in: *MEFRA* 119 (2007), pp. 149-188.

Leclerq, Henri: *Reliques et reliquiaires*, in: *Dictionnaire d'Archéologie Chrétienne et de Liturgie* 14/2 (1948), coll. 2294-2359.

Leyser, Conrad: *The Temptations of Cult: Roman Martyr Piety in the Age of Gregory the Great*, in: *EME* 9 (2000), pp. 289-307.

Lynch, Gordon: *Object Theory. Toward an Intersubjective, Mediated, and Dynamic Theory of Religion*, in: *Religion and Material Culture. The Matter of Belief*, ed. by David Morgan, London – New York 2010, pp. 40-54.

Mango, Cyril: *Constantine's Mausoleum and the Translation of Relics*, in: *ByzZ* 83 (1990), pp. 51-62.

Mauss, Marcel: *Essai sur le don. Forme et raison de l'échange dans les sociétés archaïques*, in: *L'Année sociologique* n.s. 1 (1923-1924), pp. 30-186. Engl. Transl.: *The Gift: The Form and Reason for Exchange in Archaic Societies*, foreword by Mary Douglas, New York 1990.

McCormick, Michael: *Origins of the European Economy. Communications and Commerce, A.D. 300-900*, Cambridge 2001.

McCulloh, John M.: *The Cult of Relics in the Letters and Dialogues of Pope Gregory the Great: A Lexicographical Study*, in: *Traditio* 32 (1976), pp. 145-184.

McCulloh, John M.: *From Antiquity to the Middle Ages: Continuity and Change in Papal Relic Policy from the 6th to the 8th Century*, in: *Pietas. Festschrift für Bernhard Kötting*, ed. by Ernst Dassmann – Karl Suso Frank , Münster 1980, pp. 313-324.

Michalowski, Roman: *Le don d'amitié dans la société carolinigienne et les translationes sanctorum*, in: *Hagiographies, culture set sociétés, IVe – XIIe siècles*, Paris 1981, pp. 399-416.

Noga-Banai, Galit: *The Trophies of the Martyrs. An Art Historical Study of Early Christian Silver Reliquiaries*, Oxford 2008.

Osteen, Mark: *Gift or Commodity?*, in: *The Question of the Gift. Essays across Disciplines*, ed. by Mark Osteen, London – New York 2002, pp. 229-247.

Sahlins, Marshall David: *Stone Age Economics*, London 1974.

Saxer, Victor: *Morts, martyrs, reliques en Afrique chrétienne aux premiers siècles*, Paris 1980.

Sbardella, Francesca: *Memoria e oblio attraverso corpi, resti, luoghi. Il caso delle reliquie di Françoise d'Amboise*, in: *Antropologia dello spazio. Luoghi e riti dei vivi e dei morti*, ed. by Adriana Destro, Bologna 2002, pp. 233-263.

Sbardella, Francesca: *Antropologia delle reliquie. Un caso storico*, Brescia 2007.

Seeliger, Hans Reinhard: *Das Geheimnis der Einfachheit. Bild und Rolle des Märtyrers in den Konflikten zwischen Christentum und römischer Staatsgewalt*, in: Die *Anfänge des Christentums*, ed. by Friedrich Wilhelm Graf – Klaus Wiegandt, Frankfurt 2009, pp. 339-372.

Silvestre, Hubert: *Commerce et vol de reliques au Moyen-Âge*, in: *RBPh* 30 (1952), pp. 721-739.

Simmel, Georg: *Philosophie des Geldes*, Leipzig 1900; Repr. Frankfurt 1989.

Stark, Barbara L. – Christopher P. Garraty: *Detecting Marketplace Exchange in Archaeology: A Methodological Review*, in: *Archaeological Approaches to Market Exchange in Ancient Societies*, ed. by Christopher P. Garraty – Barbara L. Stark, Boulder 2010, pp. 33-58.

Stelladoro, Maria: *Significato, ruolo, potere e culto delle reliquie*, in: *Reliques et sainteté dans l'espace médiéval*, ed. by Jean-Luc Deuffic, Saint-Denis 2006, pp. 65-87.

Thacker, Alan: *In Search of Saints: The English Church and the Cult of Roman Apostles and Martyrs in the Seventh and Eighth Centuries*, in: *Early Medieval Rome and the Christian West. Essays in Honour of Donald A. Bullough*, ed. by Julia M. H. Smith, Leiden – Boston – Köln 2000, pp. 247-277.

Thomas, Nicholas: *Entangled Objects. Exchange, Material Culture and Colonialism in the Pacific*, Cambridge (MA) 1991.

Treasures of Heaven. Saints, Relics, and Devotion in Medieval Europe, ed. by Martina Bagnoli – Holger A. Klein – Charles Griffith Mann – James Robinson, London 2010.

Van de Klundert, Theo – Jeroen van de Ven: *On the Viability of Gift Exchange in a Market Environment, Tilburg University – Center for Economic Research Discussion Paper 1999-113* (1999) [http://ideas.repec.org/p/dgr/kubcen/199913.html, last access 15th Aug. 2013].

Vandevelde, Antoon: *Towards a Conceptual Map of Gift Practices*, in: *Gifts and Interests*, ed. by Antoon Vandevelde, Leuven 2000, pp. 1-20.

Weidemann, Margarete: *Reliquie und Eulogie. Zur Begriffbestimmung geweihter Gegenstände in der fränkischen Kirchenlehre des 6. Jahrhunderts*, in: *Die Ausgrabungen in St. Ulrich und Afra in Augsburg 1961-1968*, ed. by Joachim Werner, München 1977, pp. 353-373.

Weiner, Annette B.: *Inalienable Possessions: the Paradox of Keeping-While-Giving*, Berkeley 1992.

Wirth, Jean: *Image et relique dans le christianisme occidental*, in: *Les objets de la mémoire. Pour une approche comparatiste des reliques et de leur culte*, ed. by Philippe Borgeaud – Youri Volokhine, Bern 2005, pp. 325-342.

Wiśniewski, Robert: *Lucilla and the Bone: Remarks on an Early Testimony to the Cult of Relics*, in: *JLA* 4 (2011), pp. 157-161.

Wortley, John: *Relics of the 'friends of Jesus' at Constantinople*, in: *Byzance et le reliques du Christ*, ed. by Jannic Durand – Bernard Flusin, Paris 2004, pp. 143-157.

Wortley, John: *The Origins of Christian Veneration of Body-Parts*, in: *RHR* 223 (2006a), pp. 5-28.

Wortley, John: *The Earliest Relic-Importations to Constantinople*, in: *Reliques et sainteté dans l'espace médiéval*, ed. by Jean-Luc Deuffic, Saint-Denis 2006b, pp. 207-225.

FSC
www.fsc.org
MIX
Papier | Fördert gute Waldnutzung
FSC® C083411

Kolibri 360 GmbH
Ferdinand-Jühlke-Straße 7
99095 Erfurt, Deutschland
produktsicherheit@kolibri360.de

Druck:
CPI Druckdienstleistungen GmbH
im Auftrag der
Kolibri 360 GmbH
Ferdinand-Jühlke-Str. 7
99095 Erfurt